Prior to the beginning of the Second World War, the Royal Hungarian Armed Forces – including the Air Force – prepared to engage the Little Entente forces; however, after a short skirmish prior to the war with the Slovaks, during the war their opponents became Soviet and American aviators. The Hungarian aces fought gallantly against such heavy odds and, after the war's end, the new Hungarian communist regime turned against them as well; this book is the unique story of the 38 Hungarian air aces of the Second World War. The overwhelming majority of related materials have been lost or destroyed, so the author has demonstrated truly Herculean efforts during his 25-year-long extensive research to write this monumental work. The book is based mostly on previously unpublished primary sources from Hungarian, German, Russian and American Archives, and also on the preserved documents of the aces and their families. The text is not limited to the highly detailed biographies of the 38 Hungarian aces; it also covers some important and related aspects such as air victory confirmation systems, air combat tactics and obtained awards. Besides this, the book contains more than 350 rare images – many of them are previously unpublished.

Csaba B. Stenge is a Hungarian archivist and military historian. He was born in Pécs in 1975, graduated with an MA from the faculty of History at the University of Pécs, and received his PhD (about the Royal Hungarian Air Force in World War II) from the same institution. He has worked at the Tatabánya City Archives since 2009, and became the director of the archives in 2011. His research focuses on the field of air warfare during World War II and the history of Hungarian armed forces in World War II. This work will be his tenth book (his fourth in English) and he has also published over 120 academic articles in four languages.

Forgotten Heroes

Aces of the Royal Hungarian Air Force in the Second World War

Csaba B. Stenge

Translated by Blanka Gálné Bíró and the author

Helion & Company

In loving memory of my Mother 1951-2019

Helion & Company Limited
Unit 8 Amherst Business Centre
Budbrooke Road
Warwick
CV34 5WE
England
Tel. 01926 499 619
Email: info@helion.co.uk
Website: www.helion.co.uk
Twitter: @helionbooks
Visit our blog http://blog.helion.co.uk/

Published by Helion & Company 2019. Reprinted in paperback 2022
Designed and typeset by Mach 3 Solutions Ltd (www.mach3solutions.co.uk)
Cover designed by Paul Hewitt, Battlefield Design (www.battlefield-design.co.uk)

Cover: *hadnagy* László Molnár achieves his 22nd confirmed aerial victory on 26 July 1944 in Austrian airspace, against one of the Lightnings of the 14th Fighter Group. (Graphics by Gyula Pozsgay, instructed by the author)

ISBN 978-1-804512-48-7

British Library Cataloguing-in-Publication Data.
A catalogue record for this book is available from the British Library.

Contents

Ace's Foreword[1]

I recommend this work to anyone who is interested, not in reading wartime 'tales', but in reading history, collected and recorded with meticulous precision, unbroken diligence, hard work, and utmost dedication.

Csaba Becze (from 2010 Csaba B. Stenge) has completed an enormous amount of research to get closer to his heroes. He searched for the dead and the living alike. He sacrificed his sweetest young years to to commemorate those who lived and died for God and the Homeland, and he daringly confirms that they were heroes.

Respect and heartfelt gratitude to him for this work.

Budapest, 20 May 2006
retired *hadnagy*, *vitéz* János Mátyás,
former *őrmester*, Royal Hungarian Air Force

1 It was a foreword for the first Hungarian edition.

Son of the Top Scoring Ace's Foreword

Dear Reader!
What could possibly have persuaded a young man, barely in his 20s, to turn his back on the sweet lures of young adulthood and to spend most of his time researching a period in Hungarian history that was even at the time handled by politicians with violent suppression, prohibition, and even persecution? Our author, heeding neither the benevolent warnings regarding the taboo he was approaching, nor the harsh neglect and reprisals he encountered, deliberately prepared himself to shed light on the most glorious period of our history of aviation in the Second World War – that is, the heroic struggle to regain and save our homeland.

He learned languages, and although his resources were scarce, he was adamant about traveling to distant countries where archives still retained some information regarding our airmen and their deeds. He met our airmen and their families who fled the country and went to the far corners of the world to avoid the communist terror, and these people have opened their hearts to him. At the same time, he acquired previously unknown documents and data from our former enemies and allies who still lived and were able to tell their stories first-hand.

Our author did his work in the very last moment. This way, from first-hand narratives and personal tales, from written and oral memories, he was able to reconstruct an era destroyed either by the storm of the world war or by the survivors themselves, fearing what the future may hold for them. The work of our author was so successful that his book literally became a sourcebook for other researchers, but it is not only for them – this work is also important for those who love and dare to 'dream big'; for older and younger generations alike, who look to the generation of their parents and grandparents with awe and watch their relentless resistance in a world crumbling around them.

This work is also important for the victims of communist repression, whose persistence in uniform for the love of their home country was seen as a sure sign of 'supporting Horthy and fascism' and who were killed or (in luckier cases) just harmed.

We should learn from this work. We should give due respect to the memory of these people. But we also need to thank the chronicler, who made this possible: thank you, Csaba.

Törökbálint, 19 April 2015
Dezső Szentgyörgyi, retired MALÉV-pilot

Preface

The achievements and biographies of our most accomplished aces in the Second World War are understandably topics of international interest, and it is not a coincidence that these topics have a considerably large international literature. (Our readers can also find relevant literary references in this work to the German, Soviet and American aces who fought alongside, or against, the Hungarian aces.) Nations are usually very proud of their pilots who accomplished exceptional things during the war, and there is considerable respect also for the opposing pilots; they are respected and subject of interest, and people would like to know more about their achievements. This is the case for the Hungarian pilots, whether in the United States or in Russia.

However, in Hungarian terms, the situation is not that promising, neither in terms of scientific literature nor in terms of respect. Of the primary sources regarding the Royal Hungarian Air Force, 99.8 percent were destroyed, predominantly at the end of the Second World War (in many aspects, the destruction of these primary sources is 100 percent). In the four and half decades between the occupation of the country by Soviet forces and the fall of Hungary's communist regime, it was not easy to research this topic because of harsh political reprisals – even if there had been a better chance of reconstructing or recovering many lost sources in the first few years after the war. (Pilots who are still living have suffered from politically backed attacks as late as the 2000s.) It is therefore not surprising that there is no historiographic precedence in this field, and that no prior researchers have tried to collect the available information and data relevant to the aces of the Royal Hungarian Air Force to compile their biography. Regarding the aerial victories (also referred as air victories or kills) specifically, a scientifically appropriate compilation has been created regarding the air victories of the Royal Hungarian Air Force air crews in the Second World War – naturally consisting of the accomplishments of the aces – namely, the work of Gyula Gaál in Australia (though his work was only based on those sources he was able to obtain, and for objective reasons many details were not included).[1]

I met the first Hungarian pilots referred to in this work in 1993, as a result of my very specific personal interest. My research has been ongoing for more than two and a half decades now, completely self-initiated and self-financed. At last, it started to take shape: in 2006, the first Hungarian edition of this work was published, and the second, revised and improved Hungarian

1 Gyula Gaál, 'Légi győzelmek: tízen felül', *Magyar Szárnyak Évkönyv*, 1998, pp. 50–61; Gyula Gaál, 'Légi győzelmek: tíz és kettő között', *Magyar Szárnyak Évkönyv*, 1999, pp. 16–34; Gyula Gaál, 'Légi győzelmek: egy és kettő', *Magyar Szárnyak Évkönyv*, 2000, pp. 25–38; Gyula Gaál, 'Légi győzelmek: a többiek', *Magyar Szárnyak Évkönyv*, 2001, pp. 56–65.

edition has been published 10 years after the first. The English edition is the updated version of the 2016 Hungarian edition.

This long project, which for me has become a life goal and a source of exceptional challenge, has involved meticulous research, down to the tiniest of details; this has been motivated by a number of factors.

Besides my exceptional interest in the topic, my respect for these warriors and my desire to know everything, it was also extremely important for me to pay an old debt: to make these heroes known, to help wider audiences understand their exceptional achievements and their ordeal after 1945 because of their commitment during the war, and to make their life and deeds known. It is not a coincidence that the title of the first edition was 'Forgotten heroes'.

Due to the destruction of the majority of relevant sources, I faced great difficulties during my research. Even collecting the names of those who can be considered as aces was a difficult task, and the compilation of biographies came after that. In the archives of *HM Hadtörténeti Intézet és Múzeum* (*HM HIM* – the Central Record Office of the Archives of the Military History Museum of Hungary), personal files are only kept for those who have served as commissioned officers, if they have any personal document files at all. The enlisted service personnel and reservists do not have any documentation retained at all; for the rest, we mainly have data for those who returned home after the war, but the majority of the aces did not do so. In many cases, the files only contain a personal registry sheet and a few short sentences; in even more cases, the registry sheet is also missing. Furthermore, even if the registry sheet is present, in many cases the data regarding birthdays, birthplaces, mothers' names, is not correct. These errors have been corrected in this work wherever possible on the basis of birth certificates of the Hungarian state civil regsitration, which are generally accepted as the most authentic. Therefore, in addition to these fragments found in the Hungarian and foreign archives, I relied heavily on documents preserved by the families themselves. Tracing the veterans scattered all over the world was, however, extremely difficult, and even when they were found, even when it was possible to trace the still-living veterans or their relatives, they were often not able to help. This was because, as so often happens, the families had nothing – in many cases, the survivors themselves destroyed any remaining documentation relating to their involvement in the Second World War at the beginning of the 1950s, when they were intensively persecuted and harassed. This was, for example, the case of the family of Lajos Tóth. In many cases, when these families fled or were forced to emigrate, they lost everything or left their possessions behind. Naturally, the passage of the years since the end of the war has also done its part in destroying documents; by the time the research began, in many cases the person concerned had already died before they could be contacted. Many primary sources in private hands have been lost in the two and half decades following the change in regime due to the passing of the veterans themselves, their widows or their brothers and sisters (many original documents used in creating this work have also been destroyed in the meantime following the death of their keepers). Some pilots also did not simply lack official documentation; there was no knowledge about their life and fate after the war – for example, nothing was known of Lajos Cseh, even within the close-knit community of long-range reconnaissance servicemen, or of Béla Lipcsey by the German fighters. It has also happened that former comrades had completely false information regarding the whereabouts or the fate of these veterans, which proved to be a dead end in terms of research, requiring further investigation to clear the obscured paths again. László Pál Szikora is a very good example of this – his former comrades seemed to think he had been shot down and killed in April 1961 during the Bay of Pigs Invasion as a mercenary pilot hired by the Central Intelligence Agency (CIA) – as is János Róza, whom his former comrades assumed had been shot dead on the western natural border during an attempted escape from behind the Iron Curtain at the end of the 1940s.

Naturally, because of the problems outlined above and because of the loss of sources, this material compiled will never be complete, but nor can we rely on or expect other significant material to be found that would significantly change our knowledge about the military careers of the people concerned. This is even more certain because my desire for completeness and perfection made me seek out almost all public and private collections, archives and sources during the course of researching this work. Apart from minor details regarding their personal lives, new information about the subjects of this work may only be collected regarding the details of their air victories. It should nevertheless be assumed that the data about the majority of air victories that is now missing will never be recovered.

The first edition of this work in 2006 brought about some positive developments in Hungarian society – for example, the existing war graves of pilots now receive considerably more attention and care than they did before – but there is plenty more to do. There is a grave which is still in a derelict, undeserving condition – the one of József Bejczy's – and there are even more debts to be paid to these soldiers. For example, Tibor Papp and Sándor Jásdi (Hautzinger) were both unlawfully demoted in rank after 1956, and their military rehabilitation and the restoration of their rank has not yet come about (despite efforts by the author).

For the completion of this work I have received help from a large number of people, without whose selfless help and support the work would have never been completed. Let the list of these people stand here, as I owe all of them the greatest gratitude.

The pilots who are introduced in this book: László Dániel, Mihály Karátsonyi, László Máthé, János Mátyás, György Michna, Endre Németh, Gyula Pintér, Béla Sűrű and Tibor Tobak.

In addition to them, the following Hungarian veterans: Miklós Cserny, István Csóka, Dr Jenő Farkas, Tamás Gersy, Tihamér Ghyczy, Sándor Horváth, László Lehoczky, Pál Nyemecz, János Péterdi A., János Pocskai, János Suttai Koppány, János Szentiványi, Gyula Szilaj Varga, Sándor Tanács, Emil Terray, Lajos Vargha and Tibor Varjas.

The following foreign veterans: Delore Athmann, Morris Barker, Tom Batey, Duane Bohnstedt, Sighart Dinkel, Arthur Fiedler, Robert Goebel, James Graham, Jack Lenox, George G. Loving, Vasily Pavlovich Mihalev and Robert G. Swinehart.

The relatives of the following Hungarian pilots/air crew mentioned in this work: Gellért Barsi, János Bánkuti, József Bejczy, Lajos Benkő, László Boldizsár, Lajos Buday, Lajos Cseh, István Fábián, Ervin Flóznik, Béla Füleky, Imre Harangi, Sándor Hautzinger, Frigyes Hefty, László Hemmert, Aladár Heppes, Gyula Horváth, Tibor Hóy, András Huszár, Pál Irányi, István Kálmán, Miklós Kenyeres, Ernő Kiss, Pál Kovács, Lajos Krascsenics, Mátyás Lőrincz, Ottó Lukács, Ferenc Málnássy, István Mocsáry, László Molnár, József Nagy, Ferenc Nyakas, Tibor Papp, János Róza, Tibor Sármási, Dezső Szentgyörgyi, Kálmán Szeverényi, Pál László Szikora, Pál Takáts, Lajos Tóth, György Ujszászy, László Varga and Károly Zajtai.

The relatives of the following American pilots/air crew members: Howard Baetjer, Louis Benne, Frank Bolek, Herbert B. Hatch, George E. Hochstetler, Charles Hoffman, Edward C. Jones, Valerian E. Klein, John C. Norris, Oscar Rau, John G. Schill, John J. Shepard and James C. Smyth.

The following Hungarian and foreign researchers and data providers: Christian Arzberger, Bernd Barbas, Nick Beale, Milan Benček, Christer Bergström, Mikhail Bikov, Don Brownlee,

Jack Cook, Elizabeth Cvitko, Boris Davidov, Gyula Gaál, Dmitri Khazanov, Gábor Horváth, Zoltán Jánkfalvi, Nikita Yegorov, Dmitri Karlenko, Robert Karstensen, Peter Kaššák, Kálmán Komjáthy, Tom Lowery, Károly Magó, Nándor Mohos, Carl Molesworth, Damon Notestone, Frank Olynyk, Jiří Plachý, György Punka, Kurt Rieder, Dr. Gergely Sallay, Matti Salonen, Dr. Éva Susa, Dr György Szabó, Dr. Norbert Számvéber, Péter Tarr, József Tomcsányi, Ferenc Tóth, Krisztián Tóth and Lawrence de Zeng.

The colleagues of the following institutions: *HM Hadtörténeti Intézet és Múzeum Fotóarchívuma, Hadtörténelmi Levéltára és Központi Irattára* (Photographic Archives, Military History Archives and Central Record Office of the Institute and Museum of Military History); *HM Személyzeti Osztálya* (Human Resource Department of the Ministry of Defense, Budapest); *Magyar Nemzeti Levéltár* (National Archives of Hungary); Bundesarchiv-Militärarchiv (Freiburg); the Air Force Historical Research Agency (Maxwell AFB); and Centralni Arhiv Ministerstvo Oboroni Rossijskij Federaciji (Podolsk).

I dedicate this work to the loving memory of my mother, who died suddenly while I was working on the final corrections of this English edition. She raised me up, taught me, guided me and inspired me to be a better person. She would deserve most of the acknowledgements related to this monumental work.

Last but not least, I would like to offer special thanks to the owner of Helion & Company Limited, Duncan Rogers, for making the English edition of this work possible.

15 February 2019
Tatabánya
The author

Introduction

During the course of researching this work, and while compiling the biographies that constitute the core of it, the author has followed the guidelines detailed below.

The author has indicated all airmen in question with the highest rank they achieved before the end of the war; furthermore, the author has listed all their titles and denominations of nobility awarded to him before the end of the war. For those who served after the end of the war, the author has also included their promotions in their biography, but has excluded introductions into the *Vitézi Rend* (the Hungarian Knightly Order of Vitéz). It is worth noting that Hungarian Statue IV of 1947 regarding the abolition of certain titles and ranks, a law still in force in the Republic of Hungary, has abolished the use of hereditary noble ranks and the vitéz title, also putting a ban on their use (albeit it is a lex imperfecta, a law without any sanction). In connection with the names, the author used the official name adopted by the person in question as a basis. In only one case did the official name differ slightly from the name in the original, official birth certificate: the author spelled the name of Béla Sűrű (who continued to live in Hungary) with long accents because of the contemporary trend of using them. Even though his name on the birth certificate is written 'Sürü', he always spelled his family name later on with long accents, as in Sűrű.

In addition, the author has listed the air victories of the airmen in a separate paragraph, first by confirmed kills (or at least those that could be considered confirmed), then by those that are unconfirmed, in parentheses. The author has also mentioned the successes he was able to find of the pilots against ground targets (here, and elsewhere, where no information has been found based

Without these men, the aces would not have been able to achieve their successes.
I. The selfless work of the ground crews, the mechanics, often carried out in extremely poor conditions on the frontline airfields, was of utmost importance for maintaining the serviceability of the air force units. This picture shows members of the ground mechanics crew of 102/1 Fighter Squadron, spending their break singing. Munkács (today Mukachevo, Ukraine), September 1944. (From the collection of László Máthé)

on reliable sources, the abbreviation *n.d.a.*, for 'no data available', is used.) Thereafter, the number of combat sorties completed by the airmen are listed, and the number of hours flown within the Royal Hungarian Air Force is recorded, to give the reader a clear picture of the airmen's level of experience. This is important because one of the major success factors in air combat was routine and substantial experience. For most of the airmen discussed in this work, the data on 'hours flown' also contains the number of hours flown within the *Horthy Miklós Nemzeti Repülő Alap* (*HMNRA*, the Miklós Horthy National Aviation Fund). This was not a military organization, but only a preparative course. In terms of hours flown, Hungary has been in a special situation. Until 1944, only a fraction of its full force was deployed on the Eastern Front, and the aircrews were replaced after serving a certain amount of time. Thus the majority of these aircraft crews and pilots – unlike their German counterparts – were not immediately deployed to front service after the completion of their training, but were able to continue working on their flying skills and gain more experience stationed at home. (In the case of German air crews, however, if the novices on the front survived the initial period when the losses were at their highest, they gained far more experience and achieved far larger numbers of aerial victories than those of Hungary, or indeed any other nation.) In the table, the known number of hours flown and the combat sorties are followed by the nickname or nicknames the airmen were given among their troops and their identification numbers. This data is followed by the combat decorations the pilots have received and a list of their air victories, with the most important known details attached; thereafter, the author has included a list of pilots the airmen flew, with the markings of the aircraft themselves, where known. After these details, the biography of the airmen is included. The author has tried to balance the data in terms of detailing the biographies of the most successful pilots as much as possible, with somewhat fewer details included regarding those pilots who did not have as many air victories. (In a work like this, which is based on extremely thin primary sources, it is very difficult to achieve a properly proportionate display; for example, a number of people are introduced here about whom almost nothing is preserved in the official sources.) The author has also written in detail about the unit commanders and the ones, who became aces against the Americans, who were considered to be toughter opponents; some more was also written about those who had either exceptional achievements or a longer-than-usual combat service. Of their fate and lives after the war, the author has described the military- and aviation-related events in their lives in more detail, and has also included a description of their discharge and the difficulties and persecution they had to endure. Of their personal lives the author has written as little as possible, because this is part of the private sphere of their life and, in general, is of less public interest.

The author has striven to indicate and (at the same time) to correct, if possible, the errors and misinformation published in earlier texts regarding the military careers and achievements of these individuals, including correcting dates and mistaken type identifications.

In certain cases, the author has also described events in detail where German and Hungarian pilots have claimed air victories at the same time in the same airspace. In other cases, when by comparing the sources from the different sides it seems certain that the Hungarian and not the German airman achieved a certain victory, the author has not discussed the German side of the narrative. In some cases where the actual situation can no longer be clarified, the author has avoided describing the shooting down of the aircraft in detail to prevent unnecessary debate.

In the case of the Messerschmitt Bf 109, the main aircraft type used by the Hungarian fighter pilots, the author has adhered to using the official German denomination, which remained 'Bf 109' until the end of the war – even though the type was called Me 109 in the majority of the Hungarian official papers (the manufacturing company, *Bayerische Flugzeugwerke AG*, was renamed *Messerschmitt AG* in 1938, but the older name was retained for the types that were developed earlier). The author has not specifically indicated the signs of foreign manufacture in the case of Hungarian-manufactured Bf 109 subtypes because this data is completely missing from the contemporary German and Hungarian military documents. In the case of Hungarian-manufactured Bf 109 subtypes, only the official factory documents of the *Magyar Waggon-és Gépgyár* – that is, the *MWG* (the Hungarian Wagon and Machine Factory) in Győr – feature the Ga sign, while for example in the case of the Hungarian manufactured Me 210 Ca–1 aircraft, the – *Ausland* sign featured in a number of military documents, mostly in capital letters in German documents.[1]

Without these men, the aces would not have been able to achieve their successes. II. The good wingman, who always followed and covered his element leader, was invaluable. This picture shows *szakaszvezető* László Varga, pilot of 5/2, then 102 and 102/1 Fighter Squadrons, who escorted the squadron's aces on a large number of missions. Varga completed 157 combat sorties, during which he achieved three confirmed victories, before he went missing on 11 December 1944 during a mission in the area of Vác. According to the author, he must have been the pilot of the Hungarian Messerschmitt that crashed and found at Telki. (From the author's collection)

As in Hungary the interest of the public has generally shifted toward fighter aircraft and their pilots (even though they were only a part of the whole air force), the author has not written solely about the fighter aces, but has included all the pilots of the Royal Hungarian Air Force who achieved at least five air victories to encourage the growth of public interest in the extraordinary achievements of the other branches of the air force – reconnaissance, bomber and ground-attack aircrews – where success was not measured by the number of aerial victories. The most substantial damage was inflicted on the Red Army by our bomber units, and the 'eyes' of the army command – the short- and long-range reconnaissance aircrews – were awarded significantly more decorations than our fighter pilots. This was not coincidence; they earned the decorations through their exceptional achievements.

At the same time, the author would like to underline (even as early as the introduction) that we could never emphasize enough the importance of the selfless service of the nameless soldiers of the ground crews, about whom no books have been written, but without whom the pilots would never have been able to achieve their successes.

1 For a detailed description of the manufacturing of Bf 109s in Győr, please see the *MNL Győr-Moson-Sopron Megye Győri Levéltára* (National Archives, Győr-Moson-Sopron County Archives, Győr), XI/15, Documents of the *MWG* in Győr. The exact location of the serial numbers of Bf 109s from Győr mentioned throughout this work is Box nr. 436, documents of the Air Group, aircraft numbers 1943.

The Hungarian Aces: Statistical Data

The term 'ace' is an honorary title referring to those pilots who have achieved at least five air victories, that is, shot down at least five enemy aircraft. The term was first used by the French in the First World War; the expression later gained international usage. Although almost all of the relevant contemporary documents have been lost during the course of the war (making it extremely difficult – in some cases impossible – to define exact individual achievements in Hungarian terms), based on the extensive research conducted by the author it is possible to state that altogether 38 persons can be deemed to be aces among the pilots of the Royal Hungarian Air Force in the Second World War. The majority of the 38 pilots (34 individuals) were fighter pilots, one of whom achieved his victories while serving in the *Luftwaffe*; of the remaining four, two were long-range reconnaissance pilots, one was a ground-attack pilot and one was a bomber pilot. The Hungarian aces of the Second World War achieved more than 370 air victories, almost 80 percent of them against Soviet, and over 20 percent of them against American opponents.

Besides an extensive knowledge in aircraft handling and flying, for the Hungarian aces, the extraordinary drive of motivation and commitment, bravery sometimes to the extent of recklessness and the difficult-to-grasp factor of luck all played a role in achieving these successes.

Two-thirds of the Royal Hungarian Air Force aces were officers; 25 of them were commissioned officers and four were in reserve. The others were non-commissioned officers, or enlisted pilots. The dominance of the officers in this regard is due to the fact that it was easier to achieve air victories when flying in a leader position than when flying as a non-commissioned officer or enlisted men, who mostly performed wingman duties. The other reason was that there were

The most dangerous opponent of the Hungarian fighters during 1944–45 was the American P-51D Mustang fighter aircraft. The Mustang in the picture belonged to Brigadier General Yantis H. Taylor, commander of 15th AAF's 306th Fighter Wing during the autumn of 1944. On the vertical stabilizer of the aircraft, the markings of all four Mustang Fighter Groups under his command can be seen: 31st FG: striped; 52nd FG: yellow; 325th FG: checkered; and 332nd FG: red. (From the collection of Arthur Fiedler)

more officers in the Royal Hungarian Air Force in the relevant period; consequently, there were also greater numbers of officers among the pilots who were deployed to the frontline units.

The oldest Hungarian ace was 40 on achieving his fifth air victory in 1944, but the majority of these airmen were aged between 21 and 24 when they achieved their air victories. A number of these aces came from old noble families – although until 1945 the favored, traditional army branch for the aristocracy was the light cavalry (the Hussars) – and many of these families had traditional military backgrounds. The fathers of some of the aces were engineers or doctors, and some came from a railroad worker family, but there were also some who were the offspring of poor agricultural families. It is interesting, however, that the highest percentage came from families of teachers and educators (nine of them, or almost a quarter of their overall number).

Of the 38 aces, 10 (that is, more than a quarter) were born outside the Trianon borders, and one of them lived there originally. The Treaty of Trianon, the Hungarian peace agreement at the end of World War I was signed in 1920. Under this punitive treaty (or more correct to call it as a dictate), Hungary lost over two thirds of its territory, about two thirds of its inhabitants, including one third of the ethnic Hungarian population (the right of self-determination and plebiscites were not implemented and allowed related to the Hungarians). After the Treaty of Trianon, nearly all aces who were born in the lost territories were forced to relocate within the new borders. Of the individuals in question, only one was brought up as a child in these ceded territories (in Transylvania), where (according to the recollection of his family) he was constantly subjected to harsh treatment because of his ethnicity.

A third of the 38 aces (13 individuals) were killed in combat during the Second World War. Of these 13, five were killed while fighting against their most powerful opponents, the Americans (four were killed in air combat, two of whom were shot after having bailed out by parachute, and one died as a result of an American strafing run). Of the eight remaining killed aces, one died as a result of an air accident due to bad weather, while two died of wounds inflicted during air combat with their Soviet opponents: one was shot down after bailing out of his aircraft; and the other died of internal wounds inflicted during a crash-landing after air combat. A further five aces died from anti-aircraft fire; however, one – according to research by the author – was probably shot down by his own anti-aircraft defense forces by accident, and not by the Soviets.

It can therefore be concluded that almost 40 percent of those killed in combat were shot down by American aircraft, and equally that 40 percent were shot down by Soviet anti-aircraft defense. The Soviet fighter pilots, with whom the Hungarian aces were engaged in air combat for the largest amount of time and against whom the Hungarians reported the largest number of aerial victories (more than 150), only caused approximately 15 percent of the deaths among the Hungarian aces: two individuals killed. It must be added that Soviet fighter aircraft pilots shot down the Hungarian aces much more frequently – some more than once – although without lethal consequences. It should also be mentioned that three individuals (almost a quarter of those killed in action) were killed by enemy fighter aircraft after they bailed out from their aircraft.

Four of those who were killed in combat (30 percent) never had an officially registered grave. The grave of an ace killed in combat was abolished of in the 1980s, and one ace, whose remains were relocated more than once, has two gravesites even to this day.

The end of the war was a major breaking point in the lives of the majority of the surviving aces. After the war, only a very small portion of them were lucky enough to secure an occupation for themselves as a pilot. In Hungary, the *Magyar–Szovjet Polgári Légiforgalmi Részvénytársaság*

(*Maszovlet,* or the Hungarian-Soviet Civil Air Transport), the *Országos Magyar Repülő Egyesület* (*OMRE*, or the Hungarian Aviation Association) and the military aviation (which continued operating in later years) needed trained and experienced pilots. To the new Soviet influenced regime, however, the former aces were untrustworthy, and therefore most of them flew rarely at best, even though aviation meant everything for them. In civilian life, these commissioned officers did not have any civilian jobs or qualifications, and their military past was considered to be a serious hindrance for a considerable period of time – they were not able to find any jobs or they were just given the most basic, unskilled laborer's work. Often they were dismissed from work soon after starting based on false allegations, and they were not admitted to higher education either to educate themselves further. For them, police harassment happened daily.

It is therefore understandable that, of the 25 Hungarian aces who survived the war, 17 (more than 70 percent of them) emigrated, most of them to the American continent (to Canada, the USA, Venezuela, Argentina, Brazil or Chile). The most successful Hungarian fighter pilot, Dezső Szentgyörgyi, was among the eight individuals who chose to remain at home. He spent six years in prison between 1950 and 1956, convicted on false accusations; however, before and after this, he was still able to work in the field of civilian aviation and later lost his life in 1971 in an air disaster. One of the most successful pilots, Lajos Tóth, was employed for a short period by the reorganized Air Force; he was later convicted in a show trial and was hanged in 1951. He undoubtedly 'earned' his fate from Mihály Farkas, Minister of Defense in the communist regime, through his wartime achievements. Although there were a few individuals among the aces – almost exclusively after emigration – who succeeded in pursuing an outstanding career in their civilian lives and established a stable existence for themselves, many became bitter and later suffered from serious alcohol abuse problems and private issues. Some died in very undeserving conditions: at home, one ace lived in a stable for the last few years of his life, but there was also one emigrant who died in a poorhouse run by nuns and received a funeral at public expense. In this country it meant he was buried in an unmarked pit, and he therefore does not even have a registered grave.

Of the aces of the former Royal Hungarian Air Force, only one is still living at the time of submitting the manuscript: László Dániel, in Chile.

A Short History of Hungarian Air Victories

Although the aim of this book cannot be a detailed description of the history and activity of the Royal Hungarian Air Force, it is nevertheless useful to provide a short summary of the air victories achieved by the Hungarian aviators of the Second World War.

The fighters of the Royal Hungarian Air Force achieved their first air victories before the Second World War broke out, during the border conflicts with Czechoslovakia, later Slovakia. The first Czechoslovakian aircraft to be brought down was a Letov Š.328 type double-seated short-range reconnaissance aircraft, shot down on 25 October 1938 over Csallóköz by an aggressive, excellently trained airman, *főhadnagy* László Pongrácz, of the 1/2 Fighter Squadron (which was equipped by Fiat CR.32 biplanes). This was the first Hungarian air victory since 12 June 1919, when a Romanian aircraft had been shot down by the fighters of the Hungarian Soviet Republic.[1]

Főhadnagy László Pongrácz (1907–1986), of 1/2 Fighter Squadron, scored the first air victory of the Royal Hungarian Air Force on 25 October 1938 against a Czechoslovakian Letov Š.328. (*HM HIM* Military Archives)

This first air victory was followed by the achievements of 1/1 Fighter Squadron, which reported having shot down nine single-engine Slovak aircraft at the western borders of Carpathian Ruthenia on 24 March 1939 (in reality, they shot down seven aircraft with their CR.32s: five Avia B.534 fighter aircraft and two Š.328s).[2]

The next air combat activities took place in 1941 during the first year of the war against the Soviet Union. According to a summarized report created at the end of the year, the Hungarian units altogether achieved 30 air victories against Soviet aircraft in 1941, although because of the fragmentary nature of the unit documentation, and according to a few other contemporary documents, we know that a few more air victories were also achieved. During this year, the majority of the air victories (as always) were achieved by the fighters, now

1 Csaba, B. Stenge, *Baptism of Fire: The First Combat Experiences of the Royal Hungarian Air Force and Slovak Air Force, March 1939* (Solihull: Helion, 2013), pp. 7–8; Zoltán Czirók, 'Az első légi háború Magyarország felett – 1919,' *Hadtörténelmi Közlemények*, 2011:2, pp. 352–353.

2 For the conflicts, see Stenge, *Baptism of Fire*, p. 136.

The wreck of the burned-out Letov Š.328.237 shot down by László Pongrácz near Zsemlékes (today Lipové, Slovakia) in the Csallóköz (in the denomination of the Letov, the numbers after the second dot designate the serial number of the aircraft). The aircraft served in the Czechoslovakian 10 Reconnaissance Squadron; its pilot, Ján Kello, was wounded, and the observer, Jaromír Šotola, was killed. (From the collection of Jiří Plachý)

flying CR.42s and Reggiane Re.2000s (*Héja*); four victories were, however, also reported by the Caproni Ca.135s, and another by a gunner of a Ju 86 bomber; one further victory was reported by a Heinkel He 111 long-reconnaissance aircraft. The Soviet aircraft shot down were all single-engine aircraft, and (apart from a short-range reconnaissance biplane) all were fighter aircraft, the majority of which were I-16s.

In 1942, the supporting air force units of the Hungarian 2nd Army achieved approximately 35 air victories over the Don river. The long-range reconnaissance airmen with their He 111s achieved 12; the short-range reconnaissance crews flying their Heinkel He 46s achieved three; and the bombers with their Ca.135s achieved one air victory. The remaining victories were achieved by the fighters, who, from the end of the year, were also flying Messerschmitt Bf 109 F-4s besides the *Héja*s. The Soviet aircraft shot down in this year were all single-engined ones, similarly to the previous year; the majority of them were fighter aircraft and Ilyushin Il-2 ground-attack aircraft. The latter were all shot down by the fighters, and these were still the single-seated type. The double-seated Il-2m3 subtype, reinforced with a rear gunner, appear among the victories of the Hungarian fighters from the summer of 1943.

The Il-2s were one of the most important targets for the Hungarian fighters from 1942 until the end of the war (more than 80 of the air victories of the Hungarian aces were achieved against this type). The heavily armored Soviet aircraft were not easy prey before the fighters gained extensive knowledge about them. In 1942, the *Héja* pilots experienced major difficulties destroying even the single-seated Il-2s because of their own insufficient firepower and speed. Those pilots flying Bf 109s equipped with 2cm automatic cannon had further difficulties because of the strong armor of the Soviet aircraft, until they began targeting this type at their most vulnerable spot – the oil cooler. Later, from the autumn of 1944, the newly acquired 3cm automatic cannon of the Bf 109s no longer forced pilots to exclusively target the oil cooler, although the aircraft equipped with that powerful weapon still favored the same spot when attacking the

A memorial erected in Voronezh from a Ilyushin Il-2m3 subtype ground-attack aircraft. Under the fuselage of the aircraft, the oil cooler can clearly be seen; this was the preferred target for the attacking fighters (photographed by the author, 16 May 2014)

Soviet ground-attack aircraft. György Debrődy achieved nine confirmed air victories against Il-2s 1943–1944, but theoretically he can be the only ace who may have surpassed this number and thus was probably the most successful Hungarian pilot in fighting against this type (the details of the victories of *hadnagy* Kenyeres achieved during the same period are mostly not known). Debrődy remembered the challenges of fighting these aircraft:

> In earlier times, our encounters with the Il-2s were pretty unsuccessful. Generally, you shot the rear gunner at first pass [his machine gun was motionless and pointed to the sky], and the cannon and machine gun fire of the successive passes ripped off parts from the aircraft, but the pilot within just made his way home to safety.
>
> Once an Il-2 crash-landed near Kharkhiv [probably this was one of the aircraft that was lost on 5 July 1943]. When we all went to take a look, we realized that this was a flying tank. The pilot and the engine were completely armored. An old and experienced German pilot called our attention to the oil cooler on the underside of the fuselage, which was around 20x80cm in size. From that moment, to notice and to shoot down Il-2 took just a short time. According to our armourers, I had an Il-2 kill for which I only used four cannon shells. After the target was hit – and of course you needed to shoot from close range – the

> oil of the enemy aircraft messed up the cockpit windshield; so you just pulled off to the side, and all you could see was an aircraft plummeting from the air downward, which crashed and blew up. Because they preferred low-altitude missions, their pilots [and gunners] had no chance to bail out of the aircraft.[3]

By 1943, the activity and efficiency of the Hungarian Air Brigade deployed to the Eastern Front had increased considerably, thanks to the modern German aircraft types that were put into service and to the fact that, during the battle of Kursk, they were deployed in the main course of the attack. In this year, the squadrons of the Royal Hungarian Air Force shot down more than 120 Soviet aircraft, and a further significant number of air victory claims have remained unconfirmed. Of these, 11 victories were attributed to the Junkers Ju 88s of the long-range reconnaissance units (there was a twin-engined Soviet long-range reconnaissance aircraft among these, and the others were all single-engine fighters). The short-range reconnaissance units' Focke-Wulf Fw 189s achieved approximately five to six air victories, while the achievements of the Junkers Ju 87 and Ju 88 bombers could be estimated at more than 10 air victories (in general, all of these aircraft were single-engine fighters). The Hungarian fighters flying the Messerschmitt Bf 109s achieved approximately 100 confirmed, and a large number of unconfirmed air victories during the year, shooting down single-engine fighters and Il-2s in most cases, but they also succeeded in destroying a number of twin-engined Boston and Pe-2 bomber aircraft, the latter mostly during the battle of Kursk.

The first heroes of the fighter arm of the Royal Hungarian Air Force: the pilots of 1/1 'Íjász' Fighter Squadron, 24 March 1939. (From the author's collection)

3 Recollections of György Debrődy, in manuscript, February 1976 (owned by the author).

The year 1944 was the most successful for the Royal Hungarian Air Force in terms of air victories, although, at the same time, the units suffered the most serious losses in air combat during that year. The air combat activity against the Americans in home defense during the late spring and summer (unlike anything they had seen before in terms of intensity and fierceness) also caused enormous personnel and material losses. In the year of 1944, the Hungarian air units reported approximately 280 air victories.

The achievements of the bombers, the ground-attack aircraft and the short-range reconnaissance units are unknown to a large extent, but these units achieved at least 20 air victories in 1944. Apart from one Il-2, all the air victories occurred against fighter aircraft.

The 102 Fighter Group, which fought against the Soviets from the beginning, achieved 85 air victories against aircraft and two against observation balloons during this year. The majority of the downed aircraft were single-engine fighters and Il-2s.[4]

The twin-engined destroyer and night fighter squadrons deployed for home air defense reported approximately 10 air victories against American units, mostly four-engined bomber aircraft. Of these, seven were included in the air force confidential order nr.1944/63. These air victories occurred in April, during the daytime, against American units; regarding the night combat missions of the night fighters, we have no data of confirmed victories.[5]

The 101 Fighter Wing and its predecessor units reported more than 160 air victories during the

A tale to tell after a harrowing air combat with the Americans during the summer of 1944 in Veszprém, in front of the Bf 109 'Red 2' of 101/1 Fighter Squadron. (From the collection of László Hemmert)

Two hits from an American fighter's .50 caliber (12.7mm) Browning machine gun on the starboard wing of the Messerschmitt Bf 109 G-6 'Red 11' of 101/1 Fighter Squadron in 1944. (From the collection of László Hemmert)

4 *HM HIM Hadtörténelmi Levéltár* (Military History Archives, *HM HIM HL*), documents of the 101 Fighter Wing, box nr. 112, summarized score report of the 102 Fighter Group until 31 December 1944.

5 *HM HIM HL*, documents of the 101 Fighter Wing, box nr. 110, air force confidential order, nr. 1944/63, 23 September 1944; Csaba Becze, 'A magyar királyi 1. honvéd éjjeli vadász repülőszázad', *Magyar Repüléstörténeti Társaság Konferencia Közleményei*, 1999, pp. 53–56.

year, more than 120 of them against American aircraft. More than 70 air victories were reported against four-engined heavy bombers; the remaining numbers were against single and twin-engined fighters (not all of which were later confirmed). Of the Soviet aircraft shot down during November and December, one was a twin-engined bomber, and the others were single-engine ground-attack and fighter aircraft.

In the first four months of 1945, the Hungarian air force units achieved approximately 135 air victories, but a number of these remained unconfirmed, among them a significant number of kills that were attested to by witnesses (this was due to the general collapse of the administrative and confirmation system at the end of the war). Two squadrons of the Ground-Attack Group shot down at least 10–15 Soviet and two American aircraft, while the Fast Bomber Group reported at least one air victory against a Soviet fighter.

The 101 Fighter Wing achieved approximately 120 confirmed and a good number of unconfirmed air victories from the beginning of January to the second half of April 1945. Of their reported kills, six were American; the others were Soviet aircraft.

The very last officially confirmed Hungarian air victory of the Second World War was achieved by *főhadnagy* Elemér Kiss, a pilot serving on the staff of the 101/II Fighter Group, who reported shooting down a Yak-9 on 17 April 1945 at 11:15 over Czech territory, south of Milovice. Individual registry documents give a description of a later victory in the logbook of *zászlós* Tibor Murányi: a kill of an Il-2 on 19 April 1945. However, this is undoubtedly a fictitious claim, together with a number of other notes from April regarding other sorties; the mission log and the after-action report of the 101 Fighter Wing for the given time do not confirm these kills.

According to the author's research, the reason for these fictitious notes could be that, in some cases, unauthorized personnel with access to the logbooks kept in the squadron offices (in which squadrons kept track of individual flights) added some invalid data, perhaps out of fun at the very end of the war. In the case of the individual registry of missions and flights, it is important

The airfield at Veszprém-Jutas, home base for 101 Fighter Group (later Wing). The picture was probably taken in the first week of July 1944, directly before the American bombing raid against the airfield. The aircraft on the left is the covered V.805 Messerschmitt of *hadnagy* Mihály Karátsonyi (serial number 95211), on which the white cross insignia has already been painted over with gray to prevent it being so clearly visible. (From the author's collection)

A Messerschmitt that belly-landed with a running engine during the winter of 1944–45 in North-Western Transdanubia (*Dunántúl*). (From the collection of János Pocskai)

to note that, in many cases, the pilots also registered their flights and sorties into the flight log originally used by sports pilots started at the *HMNRA*, and that they sometimes did this even after completing their training. This document was not tampered with and was only filled in by the pilots themselves; sometimes this document was also stamped at the squadron office to validate the data. Therefore, these documents at the *HMNRA*, if they were not destroyed, are in many cases more accurate than the logbooks – for example in the case of Tibor Murányi.[6]

In summary, the squadrons of the Royal Hungarian Air Force achieved more than 600 air victories during the war, but it is impossible to provide an exact number. Because of the destruction of the majority of the relevant primary documents, the details in many cases are completely missing; the summarized data for certain time periods also differ from earlier data, and from the fragmentary details that still emerge from time to time. In the case of a number of surviving air victory claims, it is not even possible to decide whether they were at last confirmed or not because of the loss of the related documents. Furthermore, if these claims were eligible for the confirmation criteria but are missing from later summary documents, the question remains: does this constitute an administrative mistake, or something else?

What is certain is that more than 50 percent of all Hungarian aerial victories in the Second World War were achieved by pilots featured in this work.

6 *HM HIM HL*, documents of the 101 Fighter Wing, box nr. 113, combat mission log and combat reports of the 101 Fighter Wing; also based on Tibor Murányi's logbook and *Repülési napló motoros sportrepülők számára* (flight log for sport aviators of powered aircraft) (the full copy of the latter is owned by the author).

Definition of an Air Victory: The System of Confirmation for Air Victories in Hungary

Following the successful air combats against the Slovaks on 24 March 1939, there was an emerging need for rules outlining the definition of the aerial victory and the criteria for confirming it. The *Magyar Királyi Honvéd Légierők Parancsnoksága* (Royal Hungarian Air Force Command) defined these in detail in a document issued during the summer of 1939:

> Budapest, 7 July 1939
> Regarding the recent air victories
> To be able to define and confirm aerial victories in the future, I hereby order the following:
>
> I. A success is to be considered air victory if the enemy aircraft or the enemy aircraft's crew is put out of combat to such an extent that the aircraft is not usable in combat anymore.
>   *Air Victory occurs, therefore, in air combat*:
>   a. if the enemy aircraft crashed into the ground and is in flames;
>   b. if the pilot of the enemy aircraft is wounded and not able to fly his aircraft and the aircraft crashes or crash-lands; or
>   c. if the enemy aircraft's airframe or engine is damaged to such an extent that the aircraft crashes or crash-lands.
>
> II. The confirmation of air victories is to be defined as follows:
>   A. if the shot-down (crash-landed) enemy aircraft has landed behind own lines, the air victory may be confirmed by:
>   a. two eyewitnesses officers (creditable persons) on the ground who confirm it unequivocally and the confession is stated in the record;
>   b. pilots flying in formation;
>   c. the crew of two escort aircraft;
>   d. the crew of one escort aircraft and an eyewitness officer on the ground, who confirm the fact unequivocally and the confession is stated in the record;
>   e. (for certain – for example reconnaissance – aircraft where there are no eyewitnesses available) the documented and reported interrogation of the crew of the aircraft claiming the air victory, and the enemy aircraft wreck found on own territory; or
>   f. the confirmation of the direct superior command which initiated the investigation.

B. If the shot down (crash-landed) enemy aircraft has landed on enemy territory behind enemy front, the air victory may be confirmed by:
   1. the crashed enemy aircraft if it is still visible in a place where it can be observed via binoculars, and
      a. two eyewitness officers on the ground, who confirm it unequivocally and the confession is stated in the record;
      b. pilots flying in formation, as in A/b); or
      c. (for certain – for example reconnaissance – aircraft where there are no eyewitnesses available) the documented and reported interrogation of the crew of the aircraft claiming the air victory, and the enemy aircraft wreck photographed from the air, or (in the case of reports received from intelligence personnel) if other information received from trustworthy sources confirms the statement of the crew.
   2. In the case of aircraft shot down over enemy territory deep behind enemy fronts:
      a. in case of single aircraft, air victory is confirmed by aircraft crew in the case of formation flight by the crew of two escort aircraft based on the documented and reported interrogation, if 'H' (intelligence) personnel confirm the statement of the crew; or
      b. such air victories may be confirmed at a later point in time (in some cases, after months) through the interrogation of civilian residents of the occupied territory, the examination of graves in cemeteries, etc. The relevant command is to confirm the air victory following a thorough and detailed investigation.

III. The reported interrogation of military personnel is to be conducted by the superior command of such personnel. In the case of civilian persons interrogated, the interrogation is to be conducted by the superior command of the crew in air combat.
The report for the confirmation of air victories should generally contain the following data:
1. subject, date and those present, as in the case of any other reports;
2. time and place of the air combat;
3. number of aircraft in the air combat (enemy and own aircraft);
4. a detailed description of the air combat;
5. how far the spot where the enemy aircraft crashed, seemingly crash-landed or was set on fire is from our front (place, direction, time, in own and in enemy territory as well);
6. whether the enemy aircraft shot down landed normally, or crashed or burned out;
7. a description of the area (open space, vineyard, gardens, forest or rock surface);
8. whether any air defense units or other units intervened in the air combat (either on our own or on the enemy's side), and, if so, in what way and with what effect; and
9. other observations in relation to the air combat, with special attention to the behavior of the aircraft that achieved the air victory.

A clause is to be attached to the record in which the superior commander explains his opinion on the confirmation (or non-confirmation) of the air victory.

The photograph of the shot-down aircraft (wreck), if available, is also to be attached to the report.

IV. Guidelines regarding the confirmation of a air victory, depending on whether one or more aircraft took part in the air combat:

a. in cases of dogfights, where single aircraft were involved, the confirmation of the air victory does not require any further proceedings;

b. in cases where the enemy aircraft was shot down in flight formation, the air victory will be confirmed according to the decision of the unit (flight) commander;

c. in cases of squadrons or larger units, the confirmation of air victories is to be decided by a committee. The chair of the committee should be the commander of the unit (squadron, group), or his deputy; the members of the committee will be one or two officer pilot from each squadron (flights);

d. in cases where ground defense (anti-aircraft artillery) also contributed to the combat, and where interrogations contradict each other and do not make it clear whether the enemy was shot down by aircraft or anti-aircraft units from the ground, the credit for the kill will belong to the relevant person upon the joint decision of the unit commander and the ground defense unit commander based on the reports. This would be on most occasions an army commander or commander-in-chief; and

e. there has been no air victory in cases where the aircraft have been destroyed on the ground, either by machine gun fire or bombs.[1]

For comparison, a slip of paper among the documents of the 101 Fighter Wing from the end of the war deals with the confirmation of air victories as follows:

In our own airspace: either an air or a ground eyewitness, and the wreck or its traces.

In enemy airspace:

a. own confession and an air witness, and either the traces of the crash or the extent of damages inflicted on the enemy aircraft;

b. the same in the absence of own confession, where the confession of the eyewitness is sufficient; or

c. own confession and the observation of a *Frontflugmeldedienst* (ground witness).[2]

It was not necessary to change or adjust the definition of the air victory again after 1939. In connection to what may have counted as a air victory in the Royal Hungarian Air Force, it is important to note that, for the Hungarians, unlike many other armed forces, probable air victories and damaged aircraft were not registered and nothing was noted in the personal statistics of the airmen (probable victories were scarcely mentioned in contemporary documents, and only listed as 'unconfirmed', on which record no personal statistics could be based). This only changed at the end of the war, with Wing Order Nr. 1945/48, issued 13 March 1945, which contained instructions regarding the inclusion of probable air victories. Some of these probable victories were later upgraded and confirmed as full air victories, as will be seen below.

1 *HM HIM HL*, Vkf. 1939. 1. oszt. 4281/eln.
2 *HM HIM HL*, documents of 101 Fighter Wing, box nr. 113, document with no number or date.

Two officers of the German Liaison Staff (*Verbindungsstab*) with Hungarian officers in front of the code-map at the Air Defence Command Centre ('*Szikla*', which means Rock) during the late spring of 1944. (From the author's collection)

As Section IV(e) in the document from July 1939 mentioned, enemy aircraft destroyed on the ground were also not counted as part of the personal statistics of the airmen in terms of air victories. This system remained unchanged until the end of the war, nor was it altered in the spring of 1945.

IIn few cases the author found data from the first half of the war - for example one case in 1941 and one in 1942 – which suggests that the Royal Hungarian Air Force did not even count a case as an air victory when an enemy aircraft crash-landed over its own territory and was deemed repairable.

From 1943 on, a points awarding system was also put in place, similar but not identical to the German points system used in connection with confirming air victories. According to this, one point was awarded for shooting down a single-engine aircraft, two points were awarded for a twin-engined aircraft, and four points were awarded for a four-engined aircraft. There were, however, at least two instances where incorrect data was recorded: Air Force Orders Nrs. 1944/3 and 1945/1 awarded four points for air victories involving both single-engine and four-engined enemy aircraft.[3]

During 1944 and the air combat against the Americans, a formerly new category re-emerged – the shared air victory – which had been given for the last time in 1941. This was mainly due to the fact that the four-engined heavy bomber aircraft were considerably harder to shoot down, and in many cases both members of an element actively took part in taking down these bombers. However, the shared victory cannot be clearly attached solely to the four-engined aircraft, as some of such victories were also scored against twin-engined fighters, and one shared victory was even credited against a single-engine fighter. The shared victories – similarly to the First World War, the period until the end of 1941 and the practices of many other countries during

3 *HM HIM HL*, documents of 101 Fighter Wing, box nr. 110, collection of orders.

the Second World War – were confirmed in a way that awarded each of the contributors an air victory, rather than allocating a percentage of the air victory to each contributor, which was an unknown practice in Hungary. However, with a decreased points value, when the system of shared victories was introduced, the statistical data remained correct in terms of enemy aircraft shot down, but the number of aerial victories increased in terms of personal achievements. The shared air victories (with one single exception) were credited to two pilots, and some shared air victories against four-engined bombers were also credited partly to the anti-aircraft artillery (some of these cases were only 'point-thefts' from the fighter aircraft).

The exception to this occurred on 30 July 1944, when a flight of four aircraft claimed to have separating two Liberators from their formation. This claim was at first deleted, then, on the recommendation of Aladár Heppes, one of the four-engined aircraft was confirmed for *hadnagy*s Molnár and Dániel with two points each; another was confirmed for *őrmester* Kovács and *szakaszvezető* Boldizsár, also each awarded two points. This case was not clarified satisfactorily until the end of the war, and the author feels obliged to mention it in detail because this issue also affected the personal statistics of three aces. As the case remains unclear, the author will mention two air victories, marking the cases as shared successes along with the three other pilots.[4]

The points allocated for shared victories were halved: two points each for four-engined aircraft, and one point each for twin-engined aircraft. The only shared air victory against a single-engine aircraft during this period ended with each pilot being awarded one point each (for a P-51; there is no indication of this allocation system being in use earlier).

Confirmation of shared air victories was suspended in the autumn of 1944, when the units received an order stating that if more than one pilot targeted the same aircraft, the victorious airman would be chosen either based on who had carried out the first successful pass or – if that were not possible – by lottery! (There was one example of such a lottery from 1945.) Despite all these regulations, the last shared air victory was reported on 17 December 1944, after the category had already been revoked, by an element from 101/4 Fighter Squadron against a Liberator. Their claim was confirmed as shared despite earlier regulations (one of the relevant individuals in this shared air victory was Béla Füleky, and more details are included in his biography).[5]

Besides the abovementioned double claim of a four-aircraft flight, among the air victories confirmed against American four-engined heavy bombers at the end of the war, three ace pilots received four instances of a new category of victory that was unknown in Hungary, although it existed for the *Luftwaffe*: the '*kilövés*' (the *Herausschuss* [HSS] or 'shoot out').[6] In Germany, this category was created for separating four-engined bombers from their closed combat flight formations – an extremely difficult task – and was viewed as a complete victory. This category was employed to increase the morale of the *Reichsverteidigung*, the home defense pilots, who were constantly fighting the most difficult battles in the air. (It must be added that many such four-engines did not crash in reality and were able to return to base).

A distinct and very interesting category consists of the air victories scored by aircraft flown by multiple crewmembers. On rare occasions, an air victory was only confirmed for the gunner who practically scored the kill (although this could also have been an administrative mistake); more

4 *HM HIM HL*, documents of 101 Fighter Wing, box nr. 110, Wing Order Nr. 1945/27; box nr. 112, 329. biz. 101 v. rep. e. 45. II. 11.
5 *HM HIM HL*, documents of 101 Fighter Wing, box nr. 110, Wing Order Nr. 1945/62.
6 *HM HIM HL*, documents of 101 Fighter Wing, box nr. 110, Wing Order Nr. 1945/62.

often, such a kill was confirmed for the whole crew, and this is why two pilots from long-range reconnaissance units flying twin-engined aircraft and one pilot from a bomber are also featured in this work. In the case of the long-range reconnaissance pilots, the same air victories applied to both airmen because they flew in the same crew as pilot and observer, as will be explained later in detail.

The Hungarian fighters, who flew Messerschmitt aircraft from October 1942, indicated the location of their air victories on the basis of the German map code system, mainly because their unit was partially subordinated to the Germans. However, the author has not used this system (which was employed on the Eastern Front) in this present work because the precise code-based air victory reports are not available as a result of the loss of contemporary documents, and readers might not find these reports so easy to interpret. In the context of this work, however, the author has occasionally also indicated Hungarian fighter aircraft losses using the system of the German map squares (*Planquadrat*, *Plq*.), indicating the exact location where there was any remaining data in contemporary German casualty reports regarding the Hungarian aces. Later during the war, during the period of the home defense combats when the air force units operated on the basis of the same map system, it could even happen that this code was given instead of the location itself. For example, in Air Force Order Nr. 1945/13, containing the victories scored during the month of December 1944, most of the locations were described only using the relevant map section (for the sake of better orientation, I have given these locations using the names of the nearest town or village). This protocol was abandoned with Wing Order Nr. 1945/39, according to which air victories were to be reported by naming the exact location rather than using map-codes.[7]

On the Eastern Front, the number of aerial victories increased from the summer of 1944 onward. The reports pertaining to the regulations on air victories were introduced by the squadron commanders to the group commander, who forwarded them after verification and confirmation to the brigade command. This step practically meant confirmation of the air victory. From the brigade command, the documentation was transferred to the personnel department of the Air Force High Command, where administrative work was delayed for some time before the confirming air force order officially published the air victory as a fact. The author has, unfortunately, not discovered any surviving air force orders from 1943 that might have contained these kinds of confirmations, only the registry numbers of

The Messerschmitt Bf 109 G W-078 of 101/3 Fighter Squadron on the airfield at Tapolca, in the autumn of 1944. The aircraft was destroyed in an accident by *őrmester* Pál Domján while landing on the afternoon of 4 January 1945 at Veszprém-Jutas. (From the collection of János Pocskai)

7 *HM HIM HL*, documents of 101 Fighter Wing, box nr. 110, Wing Order Nr. 1945/62.

Messerschmitt Bf 109 G-6 V.804 (serial number 95208) of *hadnagy* László Hemmert, which belonged to 101/1 Fighter Squadron. It belly-landed and partially burned out after a dogfight in June 1944. (From the collection of László Hemmert)

these orders. This is how we know, for example, that a number of aerial victories claimed at the beginning of July 1943 were confirmed in the Air Force Order Nr. 1943/42.

The home air defense situation was different during the summer of 1944. It was often impossible to exact spot where enemy aircraft crashed after being hit at extremely high altitudes (approximately 7–9,000 meters high). At such altitudes, even a very badly damaged aircraft might be able to leave the country's airspace, but it was not always possible to follow and check the fatally damaged aircraft because of the large number of escort fighters. The task of the home defence fighters was not to look for personal glory either to follow already shot down enemy aircraft to see their exact crashing places for the confirmation procedure. It is very important to emphasize in connection with the confirmation of air victories that, in the above-mentioned cases, the claims were handled and processed by the committee of the Hungarian 103. Anti-Aircraft Artillery Group, which was understandably biased toward anti-aircraft artillery personnel. The criteria for confirmation in these cases were extremely strict: the committee compared the Hungarian–German anti-aircraft artillery claims and the fighter aircraft air victory claims with the examination results of crashed aircraft over the given period, the observations of civilian residents in the area and sometimes also the confessions of captured enemy airmen. The claimed air victories were confirmed based on a consideration of all these factors. (The practice of deleting air victory claims was not then in use, but some were not confirmed, and these in turn were not included in the confirmation orders.) This is also the reason why in many cases the exact locations of the crash of American aircraft were known and indicated in the air victory confirmations. In many cases the confirmations were granted based on the locations of examined aircraft wrecks in the given area rather than on the reported approximate locations of crashes, which could differ to a lesser or greater extent from the actual location.

There were sometimes, however, incorrect dates found in the confirmation air force orders issued regarding the home air defense and the combat missions flown in Hungarian airspace. There were also instances in connection with air defense where aircraft that crashed on the same day and close to each other were mixed up; there were also known cases when aircraft that crashed close to each other within a few days were also mixed up, and the air force orders did not contain the actual aircraft that was shot down.

Regarding the biased behaviour of the anti-aircraft artillery crews toward their own when processing the confirmations, it is worth mentioning, that according to his memories, Aladár Heppes met a former Hungarian anti-aircraft artillery commander in 1970 who refused to believe that home air defense had had Hungarian fighter aircraft at all and who complained about 'those German Messerschmitt fighters who claimed all air victories for themselves'.[8] Although it is evident that this particular group commander had a very bad memory, both the Hungarian and German anti-aircraft crews and the German (and of course the Hungarian) fighters preferred their own, and of course everyone wanted to secure more air victories over enemy aircraft for themselves. This topic will be discussed later in detail.

In any case, the extremely strict system of confirming air victories (even according to international standards) resulted in the abandoning and, later, the deletion of many formally approved air victories for the Hungarian fighters (this never happened for the German fighters; according to surviving documents, confirmation from the German authorities arrived instantly and without further comment for air victories claimed by Hungarian fighters over Austria). Aladár Heppes voiced his concerns about this: 'I have to mention that the higher air force command never turned down any air victory claims that were formally acceptable, and which were forwarded by group or wing command (however, many were not processed for of administrative reasons). The former only occurred at the Home Air Defence Command.'[9]

Many air victory reports were lost during the encirclement of Budapest, in which the archives in the air force command building were destroyed; in February 1945, therefore, the commander of the 101 Fighter Wing again reported the air victories based on the remaining copies of previous reports. This also took place because, from February 1945, air victories were assessed by the command of the air division who pointed them out to the personnel department of the air force, and not by the air defence command. (This change was communicated in Wing Order Nr. 1945/17, issued 22 January 1945, and Air Force Order Nr. 1945/5, issued 25 January).[10] At the end of the war, *alezredes* Aladár Heppes, commander of the 101 Fighter Wing, also confirmed air victories in wing orders within his own scope of authority, even though he did not possess the official authority to do so. He gave the reasons behind his actions (which were undeniably correct at that particular time, given the circumstances) in the 1970s in his explanation of Wing Order Nr. 1945/62, issued 19 April 1945. In Section 5 of the order, he confirmed 125 kills as air victories; these claims had been registered before, but their assessment had not been completed earlier. He explained:[11]

8 Recollections of Aladár Heppes, in manuscript (copy owned by the author).

9 Recollections of Aladár Heppes.

10 *HM HIM HL*, documents of 101 Fighter Wing, box nr. 110, Wing Order Nr. 1945/17 and Air Force Order Nr. 1945/5.

11 *HM HIM HL*, documents of 101 Fighter Wing, box nr. 110, Wing Order Nr. 1945/62. There were 126 victories confirmed in the order, but for two pilots one shared air victory was included that has already been mentioned as the last shared victory of 101/4 Fighter Squadron reported on 17 December 1944. The author has therefore listed the 125 air victories included in the list of the Wing Order as 126 confirmed air victories, with one victory listed for both pilots who achieved the kill.

> In April 1945, toward the end of the war, it became evident that we could not wait for the air victory confirmation system, as it had either not worked solidly or not worked at all over the past few months to solve the issue of the large numbers of claims still in progress. I therefore ordered that, on our last airfield in use in Raffelding, Austria, the group commanders were to provide us with copies of all the unconfirmed air victory claims that remained. A committee of the wing would examine these documents, and if they complied with the requirements, I confirmed them in this wing order. It is true I did not have an explicit authorization to do so, but there was no precedent for any claims introduced by me to the 102 Brigade or 1 Air Division being turned down; therefore, my action voluntarily took on an administrative duty that was otherwise not working anymore to ensure that this data would not be lost to military history. It is indicative of the complete failure of the air victory confirmation system that, in this order, I had to confirm 23 victories for the year of 1944 following 16 June 1944, and 100 air victories for 1945, for which claims had been submitted in full compliance to requirements, but which had not been confirmed, rejected or arranged for at all.[12]

Crash-landed, broke in two and partly burned out Hungarian Messerschmitt Bf 109 G-6 V. 823 (serial number 95265), summer 1944, in North-Western Transdanubia. The aircraft belonged to 101/2 Fighter Squadron. (From the collection of László Hemmert)

The US 15th Air Force suffered considerable losses at the hands of the Hungarian–German fighters and anti-aircraft artillery. The image shows the first Liberator shot down by Hungarian anti-aircraft artillery on 22 February 1944; it has been disassembled for transport. The B-24 of 450th BG (serial number 41-28604) was shot down by the 8cm Bofors anti-aircraft guns of the Hungarian anti-aircraft defense at Lispe, and crash-landed in the Muraköz, near Kristóffalva (today Krištanovec, Croatia). (From the collection of János Pocskai)

The staff officer, who was 41 years old at the time, not only saved invaluable data for the future through this decision, but also with his other action at the end of the war when, despite receiving orders to do so, he did not destroy the still partially-existing documents of the fighter wing but placed them into the safekeeping deposit of the archives of the town major's office at Wels, Austria, where the documents remained for decades before they were able to return to Hungary. The war had already ended in

12 Recollections of Aladár Heppes.

Europe when, on 12 May 1945, *alezredes* Heppes was still confirming air victories for the pilots of the 101/8 Squadron in Wing Order Nr. 1945/75.[13]

The situation of 101/III Fighter Group was particularly difficult because their ground support had lost many of the vehicles carrying the group's documents when crossing the Austrian borders. These documents were thus destroyed or lost when these vehicles had been confiscated by armed *Waffen-SS* soldiers by force. Because of this, not all the documents of the group were preserved, and not all of their air victories were submitted and confirmed in the wing orders at the end of the war. Therefore, in the case of many ace pilots of 101/III Fighter Group, the author has added some additional air victory claims (confirmed by witnesses) to the summary after examining the fragmentary documents of the wing, or other documents that have survived in private ownership.

A unique case of confirmation can be linked to 102 Fighter Group (the future 101/III Fighter Group), which perfectly describes the extent of the destruction of documents during 1944 and earlier, even before the vast majority of documents were destroyed in the last few months of the war. The destruction occurred, partly in the capital, and partly at the hands of troops being evacuated or retreating. The victory claim of László Pottyondy from 12 July 1941 was confirmed in Wing Order Nr. 1945/4 on 19 January 1945 (this had evidently been confirmed for the second time, as the air victory had been registered as a confirmed kill earlier). Unfortunately, we do not have any information regarding why this step was necessary, but it seems that the case can be linked to the destruction of the documents. In any case, a secondary confirmation coming three and half years after the first must have been unique (the air victories confirmed in this air force order were based on claims submitted by 102 Air Brigade from 15 November and 1 and 16 December 1944).[14]

The author wishes to emphasize once more: the most important factor in the confirmation of air victories was the presence of an air or ground eyewitness. In the case of Hungary, the author would like to pinpoint two problematic periods that relate to this. The first was August 1943, during the second phase of the battle of Kursk. While the first lines were stable, and while the Germans gained minimal ground during the battle, the work of the German observer and reporter service, as well as its connection to the air units, was uninterrupted. In the case of air victories scored at the fronts, therefore, there were usually many more verifications available than were necessary; even if the Hungarian elements did not see each others' successes, there were plenty of ground eyewitnesses and verifications necessary for the confirmation of the victory. From 3 August 1943, when the Soviet forces launched their counteroffensive in the southern sector of Kursk, the situation changed drastically. This is adequately described by the summary of the heavy fighting that occurred that day involving the 1/1 Fighter Squadron, the pilots of which reported 14 victories during the day. Of these, only four were later confirmed by the Hungarian authorities (5/2 Fighter Squadron also scored a number of aerial victories during the day, and therefore if we only take into account the number of claims submitted, this was the most successful day for Hungarian fighter pilots during the Second World War). Until 9 August, a further 17 unconfirmed aerial victory claims were submitted by the pilots of the 1/1 Fighter Squadron. This situation perfectly describes the heavy fighting and also the collapse of the earlier observer and reporter system.[15]

13 *HM HIM HL*, documents of 101 Fighter Wing, box nr. 110, Wing Order Nr. 1945/75.
14 *HM HIM HL*, documents of 101 Fighter Wing, box nr. 110, Air Force Order Nr. 1945/4.
15 Excerpts from the logs of 1/1 Fighter Squadron prepared by *százados* Ujszászy (owned by the author).

The other difficult period was the first half of the winter of 1944–45 for 101/II Fighter Group. During this period, the number of claims without eyewitnesses increased considerably, partly because of the bad weather and partly because there were large numbers of pilots in the Group who did not have any combat experience. This drew an angry appeal from Major Heppes on 5 January 1945:

> Regarding the confirmation of air victories.
> My observation regarding reporting and confirming air victories is that, especially for II Group, almost all air victories are achieved without eyewitnesses and the exact location is missing. At the same time, the action report does not mention the dispersion of the unit, and the air victory is claimed as the joint combat effort of the unit.
>
> I order, therefore, that any claims that fail to comply with the standard requirements for confirmation (including the exact location of the air victory and eyewitness reports from the air and from the ground) can only be mentioned in the combat action report as claims that do not comply with the standard; and the *Schwalbe* [literally swallow, codename of the German liaison staff] may also only receive such reports. The units shall make all reasonable efforts (search for witnesses; photos) to be able to confirm these claims.
>
> Any claims that fail to comply with the standard requirements of the confirmation process will be returned by me immediately because I am not going to endanger the good reputation of the wing with air victories that have been achieved while flying in formation but which were not seen by anybody. I am referring to the fact that an element is a unit that must never, under any circumstances, leave each other, and that means the air victories claimed should have at least one eyewitness. In compliance with my first order, I hereby order the commander of II Group to start legal proceedings against any who may leave their formation or their element members. In the present case, the report of two air victories clearly shows that *zászlós* Murányi on 2 and *tizedes* Nagy on 3 were left alone [*zászlós* Tibor Murányi and *tizedes* József Nagy (not to be confused with the pilot of the same name serving in 101/1 Squadron) both reported shooting down a Yak-9 on the given dates in January, which was not confirmed due to the lack of witnesses]. The case should immediately be investigated to discover whose fault it was that the two abovementioned pilots remained alone, and to report on what kind of measures were taken against the offenders. At the same time, the commander should report on the kind of punishments inflicted earlier against the perpetrators according to my orders; or, if nothing has happened, to report on why my order was ignored.
>
> To be received by: II Group for execution, I Group for notification.[16]

The author also wishes to call attention to a tendency that, however faintly present, was an observable problem in connection with confirmation of air victories. A feature of the conservative Hungarian military forces was that, comparing the air victory claims submitted by the officers and those submitted by non-commissioned officers and enlisted pilots, the claims of the latter were more often refused in cases where there was any doubt.

16 *HM HIM HL*, documents of 101 Fighter Wing, box nr. 112, 22/101 v. rep. e. pk. 45. I. 4. 4.

In connection with the assessment of the air victory claims, it is worth doing a short comparison with the similar system of the comrades in arms, the *Luftwaffe*, which achieved extraordinary successes during the war. The *Luftwaffe* pilots exceeded all other sides in the war in terms of performance during their long front service, which involved hundreds of combat sorties. No other nations managed to achieve 100 confirmed air victories, whereas more than 100 fighter pilots in the *Luftwaffe* reached that number; two of them achieved more than 100 air victories at night. It also needs to be added that there were 15 pilots in the *Luftwaffe* who exceeded 200 air victories, and two of them had even more, had even exceeded 300 air victories.

According to the information of *Major* Ernst Düllberg, commander of the *Jagdgeschwader* (JG) 76, a 7 March 1945 document lists the following requirements for an air victory to be eligible for confirmation and verification:

> Regarding the confirmation of air victories.
> I report that the confirmation of v air ictories on the German front is to be executed along the following guidelines (based on information received from the commander of JG 76, because of lack of any further orders).
>
> 1. Documentation in writing should detail the circumstances of the kill: task, location and time of the air combat, against what kind of unit, the method of air victory, the fate of the enemy aircraft, the damage done, whether there was a crash, the fate of the enemy air crew, the damage done to own aircraft and the wounds inflicted on own air crew.
> 2. It is necessary, in addition to the air crew that scored the air victory, to have at least one eyewitness on the ground or in the air capable of providing the data listed in Item 1, even if the wreck can be found (to compare the date and time of the kill to avoid anybody claiming an old wreck).
> 3. It is preferred that the exact location of the crash should be pinpointed, but this is not essential, because in many cases this is not possible due to the circumstances of the air combat.
> 4. The air victory can also be confirmed as an exception if the airman who scored the air victory did not actually see the air victory and therefore cannot give a statement, but if an air or ground witness is able to offer a reliable statement regarding the air combat, the outcome thereof and the exact fate of the enemy aircraft; or if there is more than one witnesses.
> 5. The air victory can also be confirmed based on gun camera footage (reliably developed) in the absence of witnesses.
> 6. The introduced claims with the attachments will be submitted by the squadron commander, and at the same time he will provide his opinion regarding the claim. The group commander and the wing commander will agree, reject or return the claim to be further supplemented.
> 7. In extraordinary circumstances, after careful and extensive examination, air victories can be confirmed in the absence of the above details based on prisoner-of-war confessions, victories not claimed at all because of lack of witnesses, etc.[17]

17 *HM HIM HL*, documents of 101 Fighter Wing, box nr. 112, 726 biz/101 v. rep. e. 45. III. 7.

The German confirmation system was famously strict, but it must be added that it was not as strict as the Hungarian counterpart in some cases. The similar systems of other nations fighting alongside the Germans on the Eastern Front (excluding the Finns) were even less strict, based on the author's knowledge gained by reviewing large numbers of air victory reports (*Abschussmeldungen*) in Freiburg in the *Bundesarchiv-Militärarchiv*. Furthermore, the German system became devalued at the end of the war (although this was partly true for the Hungarian system too), and Point 7 of the text quoted above can be applied very loosely in many circumstances.

From the summer of 1943, confirmations of air victories for German fighters were not attested to by air or ground witnesses and were scored in enemy airspace (although the number of these was not exceptionally high). By the end of the war a new category had emerged that was not easily definable: the '*wirksam beschossen*', which was also seen as an air victory. The literal translation of the German expression is 'fired upon effectively', and this also appears a few times in the Hungarian combat reports as '*hatásosan lőve*', although not as a full value air victory. (As an exception, not for the aces but for the less experienced pilots of 101/II Fighter Group, the author has found two such reports dated 19 March 1945, which were later upgraded, submitted and confirmed in the wing orders.) The author records this as 'damaged aircraft' in connection with László Máthé, the only Hungarian ace who reported one.

The emergence of the 'probable' and 'fired upon effectively' categories discussed above can be linked to an order issued at the end of the war. Point 11 of Wing Order Nr. 1945/48 of 101 Fighter Wing, dated 13 March 1945, features the two expressions, although the latter appears slightly differently as '*hatásos lövés*' ('effective shot'), with an explanation:

> To avoid any misunderstanding, I hereby state that, after any combat missions, airmen are to report any probable kills or any effective shots, but these are not to be included in any air victory shortlists of the squadron or group apart from the daily result report (and thus cannot be part of the pilot's result statistics), until other data for the proof and confirmation are provided and the request for the confirmation of the air victory is submitted.[18]

This means that, from then on, these categories were officially present in the documents of 101 Fighter Wing as probable cases for

An La-5F type fighter aircraft of 31st IAP, with a group of pilots from the regiment in front of the aircraft. The 295th IAD (31st, 116th and 164th IAPs) lost 23 aircraft and 14 pilots during the battles fought for Budapest. Standing, second from the right is the commander of 31st IAP, *podpolkovnik* Grigori Denisovich Onufriyenko (1916–1998), Hero of the Soviet Union, who achieved 17 individual and 10 shared air victories prior to the end of the war. The photograph was probably taken at Zombor (today Sombor, Serbia) airfield in the autumn of 1944. (From the collection of Dmitri Karlenko)

18 *HM HIM HL*, documents of 101 Fighter Wing, box nr. 110, Wing Order Nr. 1945/48.

A great-looking Yak-3 fighter of 897th IAP in the spring of 1945 on a Hungarian frontline airfield. (From the collection of Dmitri Karlenko)

future upgrading to full value air victories. The author would like to take the opportunity to offer a more detailed picture here, as from the end of the war the inflation of reports can also be observed on Hungarian side: the last reported air victory of Dezső Szentgyörgyi on 16 April 1945 is a good example of this (see the detailed explanation in the biography of Szentgyörgyi).

The central authorities in Berlin did not confirm claimed air victories after the autumn of 1944, but it was a practice until the end of the war to consider those air victories that complied with all necessary requirements as confirmed. (The author would like to refer here to some other air victories mentioned before, which the author has added to the achievements of 101/III Group based on this practice.)

An especially important – and sensitive – topic is overclaiming. The existence of overclaiming in Hungarian and German combat reports was partly due to the fact that, during air combat of large formations, it was very difficult to follow the fate of the enemy aircraft exactly, but it also depended largely on the habits of the given pilot. It is true that, as competition and the desire for achievements have been ever-present traits since the dawn of humankind, the more ambitious pilots tended to exaggerate; according to the available data, Erich Hartmann, the most successful fighter pilot of the war, was such a person.

On the other side, too, during 1944–45, each American fighter aircraft had a 16mm gun camera installed, which was a great help when air victories needed to be confirmed. Developing the films could help confirm air victories with no air or ground witnesses. On the control panel of the aircraft there was a multi-position switch so the pilots could use the gun camera in 'camera only' mode without using their weapons; this way bailed-out enemy pilots or burning wrecks could be photographed without wasting ammunition. The overclaiming among the American fighters could be traced back on one hand to the above-mentioned circumstances of air combat in large formations, the difficulty of forming an overview and the challenges of confusing dogfights. On the other hand, in the author's opinion, personal ambition was another increasingly present key factor. Most American pilots flew around 50 combat sorties, after which they were sent home and replaced by new arrivals in a rotating cycle. All pilots wanted to achieve the highly appreciated 'ace' status during this period (and they were more preoccupied with this than anybody else, even at official levels.) This is why

A P-38J Lightning fighter aircraft of 1st FG's 94th Fighter Squadron on the airfield at Salsola, at the beginning of June 1944. Three aircraft of the Squadron have been shot down on 16 June 1944 by Hungarian fighters. (From the collection of Michael Hoffman)

their ambitious pilots sometimes 'had seen more' in air combats. Regarding the Americans, it has to be noted that the gunners of their heavy bombers had one of the highest overclaiming rate during the war: most of the fighter aircraft that dived through their formations were seen as having been shot down. Although they did score many hits, of course, these facts render a large portion of their reports unreliable.

As for the Soviet fighters, the tendency to overclaim air victories can also be observed, mostly linked to large dogfights. A couple of actual examples are described below.

On 14 June 1944, 101 Fighter Group was engaged in air combat with 49th Squadron of 14th Fighter Group (in the last part of the combat, one *Staffel* of the German I./JG 302 also arrived and joined the fight).

In the swirling air combat, two Hungarian and one German Messerschmitt were destroyed, five P-38s crashed, two returned to their base with extensive damage and many more experienced minor damage. The American fighters claimed to have shot down 15 Messerschmitts and reportedly damaged some more, and all their air victories were verified and confirmed, which amounted to exactly five times the number of actual Hungarian and German fighter losses (the returning pilots claimed 13, while one of their shot-down comrades claimed to have scored a victory over two more Bf 109s). The Hungarians reported having shot down 12 Lightnings, and the Germans claimed one. Exaggeration is also an issue here but due to the extremely strict air victory confirmation system in Hungary and the presence of only five Lightning wrecks; of the 12 reported kills, four were later deleted, three were confirmed individually and four others confirmed a shared victory – in other words, five victories were verified in 1944. In one of the cases it is not entirely clear whether it was an individual or shared victory confirmation, although the latter is more probable, but for more details see the biography for István Fábián.

The results of the 12th pilot were confirmed at the end of the war, in a wing order issued in 1945 based on the statements of witnesses. The seven air victories on the Hungarian–German side thus matched the number of the crashed or seriously damaged American fighter aircraft (one of the seriously damaged P-38s, for example, returned home having been hit 49 times and was probably written off immediately).[19]

On 30 June 1944, 14 four-engined heavy bombers were credited to the German twin-engined destroyers attacking the American Liberators jointly with the Hungarian fighters. The Hungarians were credited with only three, while the fourth claim was deleted (in fact, six Liberators crashed altogether). On the same day, another case arose, this time from a dogfight against P-38s, during which the fighters engaged in a short air combat. On the Hungarian side, *főhadnagy* József Bejczy and *őrmester* Pál Kovács both reported a victory against one Lightning each, but these claims were not confirmed and were subsequently deleted because no P-38s had crashed and there was thus no wreck to account for. On the German side, however, *Hauptmann* Richard Lewens, commander of I./JG 302, also reported having shot down a P-38 north of the Balaton, which was credited to him without question.[20]

On 27 July 1944, the Hungarian and German fighters engaged in combat with the heavy bombers attacking the Hungarian capital. The fighter pilots of the JG 300 were credited with shooting down 16 four-engined bombers and one that became separated from its unit; of these, 12 kills were confirmed for II./JG 300, which was equipped with Fw 190s, even though the real losses – according to the American reports – were inflicted on them mostly by Messerschmitts (thus by the Hungarians and I./JG 300). A Focke-Wulf-pilot, *Feldwebel* Konrad Bauer, reported shooting down three B-24s over Székesfehérvár within the timespan of one minute, all of which were confirmed to him. This day is a very good example of how bigger firepower is not everything, and that shooting down four-engined bombers also required good marksmanship.[21]

Hungarian mechanic working on the spinner of a Messerschmitt Bf 109. (From the author's collection)

19 *HM HIM HL*, documents of 101 Fighter Wing, box nr. 110, Wing Order Nr. 1945/62; Jon Guttman, 'P-38s vs. Pumas: Dogfight over Hungary', *Aviation History March*, 2001, p. 54.

20 *HM HIM HL*, documents of 101 Fighter Wing, box nr. 110, Wing Order 1945/27; Willi Reschke, *Jagdgeschwader 301/302 'Wilde Sau'* (Stuttgart: Motorbuch Verlag, 1999), pp. 81–83; Nándor Mohos, 'A 460. Bomber Group légi harca Magyarország felett 1944 június 30-án', *Magyar Repüléstörténeti Társaság Konferencia Közleményei*, 1996, pp. 33–39. For the German victories until the end of 1944, please see the database of *Luftwaffe* victories compiled by Tony Wood based on the primary sources of the Bundesarchiv/Militärarchiv: https://web.archive.org/web/20130928070316/ http://lesbutler.co.uk/claims/tonywood.htm (accessed 30 April 2015).

21 National Archives and Records Administration (NARA), Missing Air Crew Reports (MACR) 6999, 7025, 7031, 7140, 7198, 7527, 12390; Jean-Yves Lorant and Richard Goyat, *Jagdgeschwader 300. A Chronicle of a Fighter Geschwader in the Battle for Germany, Volume 1: June 1943–September*

As the above example from the summer of 1944 also shows, sometimes there were multiple overclaims within a given airspace, making it difficult to decide what exactly happened in the air combat. Even the question of who shot down a particular aircraft was not unambiguous, for example due to overclaiming, the same aircraft being targeted by more than one pilot at the same time or not knowing the achievements of pilots in their last dogfight if they were killed.

It is also easy to see that, although all the opposing forces tried to monitor the claimed air victories as strictly as possible, frequent overclaims were an unavoidable aspect of air combat. Overclaiming and over-confirmation were also issues in the later conflicts of the 20th century, and one might even consider them to be everyday cases.

1944 (Hamilton, MT: Eagle Editions, 2005), pp. 252–254. The preliminary condition for filling in the MACR was loss of personnel, not loss of aircraft. It was prepared in cases where at least one person of the crew was missing, but if only the aircraft was destroyed and the whole crew returned immediately, the document was not filled in.

Tactics and Combat Methods in Air Combat

Hungarian fighter pilots had engaged in their first air combats in 1938–39 in small, easily maneuverable Italian biplanes, the Fiat CR.32s, which were armed only with two Hungarian-manufactured Gebauer 8mm machine guns. The main formation adopted by the fighter squadrons was then a wedge formation of flights of three planes. On 24 March 1939, the fighters achieved a major success against the Slovaks; the fact that they were able to overcome the technically more advanced and more modern aircraft of their opponents, and that there were no losses on Hungarian side, was thought to be the consequence of their combat method of dogfighting, which was more favorable for the CR.32s.[1]

Deputy commander *főhadnagy* Aladár Negró (who changed his name officially to Szobránczy in 1940) from the victorious unit, 1/1 '*Íjász*' Fighter Squadron, shot down personally two Avia B.534 fighter aircraft. He later explained the cause of these successes:

> The Slovak fighters, in air combat, forced their Avias – which were 100 km/h faster and better in climbing by approximately 4 minutes until 5,000m than the CR.32 – to follow the turning arc of the CR.32 Fiat in air combat. Thus the situation quickly evolved into this: while the CR.32 turned in a stable manner with an approximate speed of 150 km/h, even ascending slightly, the Avia struggled helplessly at this speed and descended heavily because of its entirely different flight characteristics. The consequence was that they lost their air combats. They made the mistake of not conducting the air combats in a way that would have been favorable to the characteristics of their aircraft, and they let themselves be led by other aircraft with inferior and different capabilities.[2]

Aladár Negró refers to the fact that the stalling speed of the Avia was higher (30–40 km/h) than that of the CR.32, and that the Slovaks should have exploited the height advantage that could have been achieved by the better climbing rate of their aircraft. Of course one should not forget the excellently qualified Hungarian pilots, although the Slovak fighter pilots also had extensive experience.

It is interesting to note that, in assessing these first combat engagements, the most successful Hungarian pilots wanted more ammunition and the less successful ones wanted machine guns with a larger caliber.

1 Stenge, *Baptism of Fire*, pp. 40–44.
2 Aladár Szobránczy, 'A vadászrepülőgép kérdése', *Magyar Katonai Szemle*, 1941:4, p. 131.

In the short campaign against the Kingdom of Yugoslavia, already under dissolution in April of 1941, the Hungarian fighter aircraft were not engaged in dogfights and therefore did not gain any additional air combat experience.

In 1941, the Hungarian fighters used the Fiat CR.42 biplanes in combat against the Soviet Union, and for a short period they sent seven Re.2000 *Héja*s to Ukraine for testing. The armament of both aircraft consisted of two 12.7mm heavy machine guns. The CR.42s were engaged in air combat mostly when escorting Hungarian short-range reconnaissance and bomber aircraft, and also during protective missions patrolling over the Hungarian and German ground forces.

The CR.42 was considered to be slower than Soviet aircraft, but the Hungarian fighters were better at exploiting their excellent turning abilities. *Százados* László Tomor, commander of the 1/3 '*Kőr Ász*' Fighter Squadron, which was supporting the Hungarian Ist Rapid Corps, expressed his opinion in his diary (which was later published as *Harcok az orosz égen*) about the differences between the Hungarian and the German aircraft and combat methods in the middle of August 1941, when they were stationed at Voznesensk airfield with Messerschmitt Bf 109s from JG 77:

> These Germans are lucky to possess the fastest fighter aircraft in the whole war. Their superior speed gives them the advantage that they can attack when they want and cease fighting when they want. The enemy fighters cannot even reach them. This is why the German fighter can dare to go into missions deep behind enemy lines, even if there are only two of them.
>
> Our aircraft are not the most advanced ones. They were constructed along the guidelines and requirements of dogfighting. Many of the Russian *Rata* fighter aircraft are faster than ours. They are much faster than the Hungarian aircraft, just as the German ones are swifter than the Russian ones. This was known to us and we also knew that we could only succeed against the Russians if we could force them into dogfighting. But if the training of the Russian pilots is at least as flawless as that of the Germans, we would be in a very difficult situation. If the Russians were able to use their weapons in the best way, and if their flying skills were accompanied by knowledge coming from tactical training, they might use the German method of passes and then I would also swiftly end my diary here.
>
> Thus, and also because of the characteristics of our aircraft, we are compelled to do what our blood dictates: we can only attack and end the air combat when we are victorious. So long as we have not defeated the enemy, we cannot disengage from combat. We cannot even fake an escape, because our fleeing aircraft would be swiftly caught up by the Russians. Therefore, we always strive to either surprise the enemy with a pass from dead astern and using the advantage of height, or, if that is not possible, force them into a dogfight, and in this case, get into their backs with our better maneuverability. This surely gives us an opportunity to shoot them down.
>
> We know that if we run out of ammunition during air combat, or if any hindrances render us unable to use our machine guns, the Russian might as well shoot his initials into our backs. In similar cases, our German comrades just speed up as much as possible and disappear, so the Russian will again meet them only with weapons in perfect condition and full of ammunition.
>
> Just one German fighter can attack 10 Russian fighters. He pass them once, hopefully shoots out his own Russian, and then waves goodbye, because the other nine would not even be able to reach him. For us, we need to think twice before going into an air combat

> with an enemy in superior numbers, because we have to fight until the very end, and the great question there is: will our ammunition be enough?[3]

Százados Tomor was correct in stating that the Soviet pilots, instead of exploiting the greater performance of their aircraft against the Hungarians, tried to force the dogfight tactics they used to employ against the Germans, with disastrous consequences.

Of course, training also played a part in this, and in the period in question, the average Hungarian pilot was much more trained and experienced than an average Soviet pilot. The reason for this was that the Soviets had quickly increased the number of the pilots in their air force build-up and were unable to provide them with the necessary training. Training times were further curtailed by the need to counter the tragic losses at the beginning of the war. The difference between the Hungarian and the Soviet pilots was, therefore, more significant in the first half of the war, but lessened gradually over the course of the war, even vanishing toward the end of the conflict.[4] Naturally, this comparison is only very sketchy when made with such vast air forces as those belonging to the Americans and the Soviets; the Soviet air force, for example, had numerous very experienced fighters among the poorly trained masses, even at the most dramatic times.

Nevertheless, the crews of the Hungarian CR.42s reported shooting down approximately 24 enemy aircraft that were faster and partly more modern than their own, while they lost only two Fiats in air combat, both of which were only destroyed because the Soviet I-16s used the tactic of aerial ramming (*taran* in Russian). The first of these two cases, on 12 July 1941, will be discussed in detail in the biography of László Pottyondy; the second case took place on 27 August 1941, when a pilot of 88th IAP, *starshiy leytenant* P.N. Maltsev, forced the CR.42 of *zászlós* Márton Szőnyi of 1/3 Fighter Squadron to the ground (the Hungarian pilot became a prisoner of war).[5]

Héja aircraft only took part in air combat once in 1941, when they shot down three I-16 aircraft without sustaining any losses themselves. Against this type of aircraft, the *Héja* was undoubtedly superior.

In the same year, Hungarian fighters flew in a basic formation of three aircraft; elements were only sent on missions out of necessity, when they were called 'incomplete flights'.

It is also important to notice for 1941 that a fundamental and very serious problem still remained unsolved – Hungarian aircraft did not have radio transmitters. Communication with each other or with ground control was therefore impossible, which was a serious hindrance. This was also why there were no successful aerial interceptions of enemy aircraft after reports of enemy aircraft arrived into their own airfields due to late notifications, slow fighter aircraft and the lack of communication with aircraft already in the air.

In the summer of 1942, the two fighter squadrons deployed to the Eastern Front to support the Hungarian 2nd Army were equipped with *Héja*s, but this type was already obsolete. Its radio transmitter was not reliable – and it was only found in the flight leaders' aircraft; the other aircraft were equipped only with receivers. Nevertheless, new developments in tactical methodology had been drawn from the experiences on the front. From 1942, the Hungarian fighters also flew in elements and four-aircraft flights like the Germans, rather than in three-aircraft flights. Although the 1943 Hungarian flight regulations still contained the three-aircraft

3 László Tomor, *Harcok az orosz égen* (Budapest: Stádium, 1942), pp. 80–81.
4 Mikhail Aleksandrovich Zhirohov, *Istrebiteli na vzlet!* (Moscow: Veche, 2013), pp. 28–38.
5 Csaba Becze, *'Kőr Ász', Egy vadászrepülő század története 1936–1941* (Nagykovácsi: Puedlo, 2007), p. 56.

Three Hungarian fighter pilots who later became aces scored their very first air victories on the first day of the battle of Kursk, 5 July 1943. The Ilyushin Il-2 ground-attack aircraft in the picture was shot down on this day by German fighters near the airfield at the Hungarian 3/1 Short-Range Reconnaissance Squadron at Kharkhiv-Grobly. The pilot standing next to the aircraft with his eye bandaged is *őrmester* János Koppány Suttai, one of the most experienced pilot of the squadron. (From the collection of János Koppány Suttai)

flight as a basic formation, the Fighter Combat Training Group was already training using the 'German-style' of four-aircraft flights as early as the autumn of 1942. From this time, elements of two aircraft became the basic formation for the Hungarian air force, too – the element leader and the wingman, called '*Katschmarek*' in humorous German aviator slang.

With the slow *Héja*s possessing less firepower, the Hungarian pilots needed to enforce the dogfight type of combat against the Soviet fighters who were faster and had better climbing and heavier firepower – the LaGG-3, the Yak-1, the La-5, the P-39 Airacobra and the Hurricane Mk. II. The *Héja*s enjoyed very limited success during this year, both against the Soviet fighters and against the heavily armored Ilyushin Il-2 ground-attack aircraft, and their limited losses are probably owed more to the considerable inexperience of the Soviet pilots.

It is also not a coincidence that, in 1941 and 1942, the Hungarian pilots with their slow fighter aircraft were unable to shoot down any swift twin-engined bombers, as has already been mentioned earlier in connection with air victories.

In October 1942, the long-awaited Messerschmitts arrived at last for the 1/1 '*Dongó*' Fighter Squadron on the front, more specifically the Bf 109 F-4 subtype. The aircraft's 1350 HP, liquid-cooling Daimler-Benz DB 601E type engine did not only perform better than the Italian 1000 HPs Piaggio radial engine of the *Héja*; it was also immensely more reliable. The armament of the Bf 109 F-4 consisted of one 2cm automatic cannon and two 7.9mm machine guns. The firepower of the cannon also proved enough to destroy the hard-to-conquer Il-2s: after the soft spots of the Soviet ground-attack aircraft had been recognized, the method used against them was mostly to descend beneath them and target their vulnerable oil cooler. Of course, all

The first Messerschmitt Bf 109 G-4s manufactured by the *Magyar Waggon és Repülőgépgyár Rt* in Győr and arrived for the Royal Hungarian Air Force in 1943. (From the author's collection)

Messerschmitts was provided with a reliable, working radio transmitter, and this was an invaluable help for the future.[6]

The disadvantage of all this was that the Hungarian squadron began to be used for fighter-bomber tasks, and therefore had less opportunities for air combat while searching for ground targets. Their combat missions were usually carried out by two Messerschmitts.

The first four confirmed air victories for the Hungarian Messerschmitts were scored on 16 December 1942, when Hungarian fighters shot down four Il-2s. However, they had to wait more than four months for their next successes; bad weather, the winter retreat, the constant fighter-bomber tasks assigned to them and the limited activity of Soviet aircraft in the region all increased their difficulties, and air combat was scarce.

At the end of April 1943, the Hungarian fighters again succeeded in scoring air victories. One was achieved after an airfield defending scramble leading to the first Soviet twin-engined bomber shot down by the Hungarians, and two aircraft were shot down while flying with the Germans deep beyond the Soviet front. These air victories were only followed by more at the end of May, and then from the middle of June onward. As the Hungarian Messerschmitts gradually decreased the number of their fighter-bomber missions, they were also deployed in increasing numbers for fighter escort missions to defend Ju 87, Ju 88 and He 111 bombers, and sometimes to escort Fw 189 short-range reconnaissance aircraft.

The number of aerial victories scored by the Hungarian fighters started to increase radically from 5 July 1943, the first day of the battle of Kursk. From this date, they flew for increasing amounts of time of free hunt missions, their most preferred type of mission. During these tasks, while patrolling the assigned airspace, they also attacked Soviet aircraft, which they either discovered by themselves or had notified to them by the efficient German ground radio control. There were many such Soviet aircraft present because the area in which they were stationed was the main direction of the strategic offensive.

From July onward, the Hungarian fighters also started to employ the Messerschmitt Bf 109 G-2 subtype in ever-increasing numbers. This type, with its 1475 HP DB 605A-1 engine, performed better than the Bf 109 F-4, although their armaments remained the same.

6 Csaba B. Stenge, '70 éve történt: Az első magyar Messerschmitt pilóta', *Katonaújság*, 2012:5, pp. 29–31.

A Hungarian-manufactured Messerschmitt Bf 109 G-4, V.753 (serial number 91008) in 1943. (From the collection of László Hemmert)

The main four-engined opponents of the Hungarian fighters were the Liberators. Pictured here are the B-24s of 460th BG's 760th Squadron, stationed at Spinazzola airfield, approaching their target in the early summer of 1944. (From the collection of Nándor Mohos)

At the end of July and at the beginning of August 1943, the F-4s were withdrawn from service in the two fighting squadrons and were henceforth only used as training aircraft. Around the same time, a number of Bf 109 G-2/R6 aircraft were received by the Hungarian fighters, with one 2cm automatic cannon in both of the gondolas under the wings. Although these weapons considerably worsened the flight performance of the aircraft, their firepower was much increased, and so the gondolas with the extra cannons were not removed. Later, during 1944 and 1945, the Hungarian fighters no longer received Messerschmitts equipped with this additional armament, and only one memoir mentions a flight of received aircraft from the summer of 1944 (although such aircraft were also manufactured in Győr and the *Luftwaffe* was extensively using them as well, mainly in the units of the *Reichsverteidigung*).[7]

7 The flight consisting of Bf 109s with cannon gondolas under each wing from 101 Fighter Group in the summer of 1944 features in the manuscript memoirs of Pál Forró (copy owned by the author).

The Hungarian fighters were still sent on combat missions in small formations, mainly in elements. As the Soviet air force was also very active in the area, the situation resulted many times in the members of the elements being so occupied by the air combat itself that they did not have time to notice the air victories of others; thus, in the absence of witnesses, many such air victories were not confirmed.

The combat method they used was similar to that employed by the Germans, and remained so until the end of the war. The majority of the air combats on the Eastern Front were conducted at a low or medium height. Because the Messerschmitts were better at climbing than the Soviet aircraft, the Hungarians tried to gain an altitude advantage, from which point they usually dived on their enemy. However, Hungarian fighters always had a tendency to start a dogfight with the Soviets, and this remained so even after the arrival of the Messerschmitts. This was referred to by some German pilots as 'chivalrous, but suicidal', because most Soviet fighter aircraft had better turning abilities than the Messerschmitts and the growing number of experienced Soviet pilots in the area were quick to exploit this. From January 1944, the Bf 109 G-6 subtype began to be utilized by the Hungarian fighters on the Eastern Front. This brought about changes, not in combat methodology but in effectiveness. The aircraft subtype had 2cm automatic cannon as its main armament along with two 13mm MG 131 heavy machine guns, instead of the 7.9mm MG 17 machine guns that had been installed on earlier subtypes. The MG 131 proved much more effective against the Soviet aircraft.

In general, we may conclude that, from this point on, the combat methodology against the Soviets did not change considerably until the end of the war. During the air combat over Hungary, the Hungarian fighter forces usually deployed one or two flights against the Soviets, and sometimes even bigger units. The Soviet fighters flew at a slightly higher altitude by that point, and thus the general altitude of the air combat activities also increased, although the Il-2s continued operating at lower altitudes. Compared to what had come before, it became more and more difficult to score a victory against Soviet fighters because they used increasingly better aircraft with more and more experienced pilots.

At the end of the summer of 1944, the first Messerschmitts arrived for the Hungarian fighters with the powerful 3cm MK 108 type automatic cannon (Bf 109 G-6/U4 subtype), instead of the 2cm automatic cannon, both were firing through the propeller hub. The MK 108 produced effective and destructive results when targeting even such heavily armored targets as the Il-2s; there was thus no need to aim at the oil cooler anymore. As a result of the introduction of this powerful weapon, there were an increasing number of reports at the end of the war describing enemy single- or twin-engined aircraft that had practically exploded mid-air. Such accounts had previously been very rare.

During the spring of 1944, the Hungarian fighters came across a new enemy flying over their home bases: the American air force. The need emerged for a different type of combat method against the waves of hundreds of attacking American aircraft. The differences between the combat methods applied on the Eastern Front and on the home front were detailed by *őrnagy* Aladár Heppes, commander of the 101 'Puma' Fighter Group, in a radio interview in June 1944:

> The Russian pilot is of inferior status, and the quality of the aircraft is much lower than that of the Americans or the English. There are also differences in the fact that the romantic notion of fighter combat was fully observable on the Eastern Front, and the combat was

> strictly conducted among individual aircraft and people. Now, at home, we observe the organized deployment of huge numbers.[8]

Százados Miklós Scholtz and the unit commanded by him, 2/1 Fighter Squadron, was first stationed at Ferihegy airfield, then incorporated into 101 Fighter Group. They were the first to gain an impression of the Americans and the nature of the air combat against them. One and a half decades after the war, he wrote:

> While in Russian territory the basic unit was the element [*Rotte* in German], here the units began with the squadron. In short: a squadron deployed against a larger bomber unit needed to be as swift and maneuverable as an element. Furthermore, it was necessary to gain control over the unit again after the first attacks as swiftly as it was with the flight. Because assembling was not that easy. Well-protected bomber units were escorted by large numbers of fighter aircraft, and usually these came down on us right after the first pass. The question, therefore, was the following: what does the most effective unit look like? Wedge, echelon, battle spread or trail; or (and this was our own invention) the so-called assault spread – flights behind each other in a line? We experimented a lot; we even executed some joint exercises with German units flown over from Vienna. It was not easy to stay together, I must say. But before a unified picture could be formed, the bombing of Hungarian targets began. During the first missions – even before we realized what was happening – we already lost two fallen comrades [on 17 March 1944]. Thus we paid a very high price for the first air victories.[9]

Against the huge combined American formations, the squadron was indeed the smallest usable and effective unit, but the experience of the summer of 1944 showed that a group formation (rather than a squadron) was the smallest effective unit. Together with the units of the German *Reichsverteidigung*, only several groups flying together at the same time could achieve significant successes, force fighters to disengage from their escorted aircraft and inflict heavy damage on the bombers themselves.

The four-engined heavy bombers were particularly difficult to overcome, especially when flying in close formation and defending themselves and each other with the fire of their double-barreled 12.7mm heavy machine guns. Of the two types of four-engined heavy bombers employed, the B-17 Flying Fortress and the B-24 Liberator, the B-17 was more robust.

Messerschmitt of 101/1 Fighter Squadron marked 'Red 9' on the airfield at Veszprém-Jutas, during the early summer of 1944. (From the collection of László Hemmert)

8 István László, 'Két bevetésen 27 légigyőzelem', *Magyar Szárnyak*, 1 July 1944, p. 9.
9 Letter of Captain Miklós Scholtz, 1961 (copy owned by the author).

The swiftly formulated Hungarian tactics may be summed up as an 'air victory, then flee as fast as you can, or you'll be shot down'. They tried to find bomber formations where the escort was not in the immediate vicinity and shot down as many bombers as possible before retreating immediately from the approaching American escort fighters. To remain in the vicinity of the bomber formations meant that the Hungarians would almost always be destroyed by the incoming American fighters.

During the summer of 1944, the Hungarian 101 Fighter Group was equipped with Hungarian-manufactured Messerschmitt Bf 109 G-6s, with an armament of one 2cm cannon and two 13mm heavy machine guns. As discussed earlier, apart from a flight in reminiscence, no other Hungarian aircraft during this summer had 2cm cannons fitted in the gondolas under the wings. This armament was not particularly effective against four-engines; it was difficult to shoot down a heavy bomber in one pass with it, and (in most cases) multiple passes were impossible to carry out simply because there was no time as the American fighters were already coming in. The Hungarian fighters, after their initial successes against American escort fighters in June, flew a number of altitude escort missions for units consisting of the heavy-armed German Bf 110 (II./ZG 1), Me 410 (II./ZG 76) and Bf 109 (I./JG 302 – the latter partly equipped with 3cm cannon, and sometimes even with armament in the gondolas under the wings). During these missions, the task of the Hungarian Messerschmitts was to hold the enemy fighters at bay until the more heavily armed German aircraft attacked the four-engines.

However, the situation for the Hungarians was not worsened solely by the Americans.

The Hungarian Air Defence Command Centre, the *Szikla* under Mount Gellért, could not deal with the situation effectively. When dealing with reports of the detection of American formations, they neither took into account the

Missing in Action Over Hungary

LT. JOHN J. SHEPARD, JR.

Lt. John J. Shepard, jr., 26, a P-38 pilot, has been missing in action over Hungary since June 16, according to a telegram sent by the war department to his wife and son, John J., III, 3220 E avenue NE. He is the son of Mr. and Mrs. J. J. Shepard, 501 Thirty-third street NE.

It was on June 16 that The Gazette printed a story from the Fifteenth army air force that Lt. Shepard led a daring low-level strafing attack to the Reggio-Emilia airdrome in Italy, destroying one enemy fighter on the ground and damaging eight others.

Lt. Shepard, a reserve officer, reported for active duty in January, 1942, and was assigned to artillery, later transferring to the air forces. He had been farming for two years near Boxholm prior to entering service and after being graduated from Iowa State college.

Stationed in Italy, he is believed to have been making shuttle raids over enemy territory between Italy and Russia.

A brother, Lt. Robert Shepard, 29, participated in the invasion of France with the airborne infantry, according to word received by his parents Saturday.

Another brother, Louis Edward, 18, is a navy V-12 student at St. Ambrose college in Davenport.

Article in the *Gazette* (Iowa) about the disappearance of 1st Lieutenant John J. Shepard (born 24 June in 1917) over Hungary, on 16 June 1944. He was an experienced pilot, serving in 1st FG's 71st Fighter Squadron, and had already completed 42 combat sorties. When the Hungarian fighters shot his aircraft down, he bailed out of his burning aircraft; upon landing, he broke his ankle and was taken POW. After the war he returned home and was employed in civilian professions. He passed away on 3 December 1998. (From the collection of the Shepard family)

delayed arrival, nor the high speed with which they were approaching; thus the Hungarian fighters were ordered to areas that had already been left by the approaching attackers. The Hungarian unit commanders needed to learn how to estimate the real position of the American formations before the actual point appointed by the *Szikla*. The inflexibility and the scope of maneuvers for the Hungarian units confined by the ground control also posed problems. The unit commanders many times received impractical orders that were impossible to carry out even with a better overview of the situation from the air, instead of having been entrusted with the tactical decisions. For example on 16 June 1944, when the overpowered Hungarian group was scattered and was literally fighting for their lives after an American attack of P-38 Lightnings, ground control ordered them to detach themselves from the fighters and attack the bombers. On 7 August 1944, another incorrect decision had a particularly serious impact as ground control did not let the Hungarian formation turn against the Mustangs that were appearing from astern; thus the American fighters were able to shoot down as many of the German-Hungarian formation as they wished.

The Hungarian fighters had absolutely no means of communication with the German fighter formations in the air because they used different wavelengths. The Hungarians received their orders from Budapest in Hungarian; the Germans received their orders from Austria in German, and although there was a German liaison staff in the *Szikla*, the alignment and synchronization of the formations proved problematic.

A few cases during the early missions in June suggest that German ground control (still not perfect but improving, and still more experienced and flexible than its Hungarian equivalent) employed the tactic of waiting until the Hungarian fighters did the 'dirty work', treating them as '*Kanonenfutter*' (cannon fodder). On 16 and 26 June 1944, the German ground control units of *8 Jagddivision* stationed near Vienna waited until the Hungarian fighters had attacked the four-engines alone, drawing the fighter escort on themselves and becoming seriously outnumbered. The fighter escort, after consuming too much fuel in the air combat and having jettisoned their drop tanks at the beginning, soon needed to turn back, giving the German fighters a relatively undisturbed opportunity to attack the four-engines.

In contrast with the fighters, the Hungarian reconnaissance and bombers fought their air combats only in cases of dire need or in self-defense, and used no spectacular or unique tactics. The He 111 and Ju 88 long-range reconnaissance crews, entering enemy airspace alone, at high altitudes and hundreds of kilometers beyond the enemy front, could only count on themselves. The Soviet fighters sent against them were either avoided by maneuvers (for example, by flying right into the course of the sun or into the clouds), or the crew defended themselves with their machine guns.

The short-range reconnaissance crews could exploit the excellent maneuverability of their He 46 and Fw 189 aircraft and fight air combats forced on them at low altitudes.

The Ju 87 single-engine dive bombers and the fighter escort of the various types of twin-engined bombers were in many cases insufficient for containing the Soviet fighters who outnumbered the Hungarians, and many times they, too, were forced to engage in air combat. In their case, the main objective was to try to keep the formation united and to repel the attackers using the concentrated fire of their defensive machine guns. In the case of the Ju 87, the excellent maneuverability of the aircraft also helped a great deal against the fighters.

The Royal Hungarian Air Force had one more single-engine aircraft 'of fighter origin' type, the modern Focke-Wulf Fw 190 type ground-attack aircraft, which (mainly the Fw 190 F-8 variant) was used by two Hungarian squadrons in combat missions between November 1944 and April 1945. The robust, massive aircraft with significant firepower (2x2cm cannons and 2x13mm heavy machine guns) were slowed down by the built-in supplemental armor, and the bomb racks under the fuselage and wings (all these alterations were due to their original function as ground-attack aircraft); however, with an experienced pilot, this aircraft could also be used effectively in air combat. The ground-attack Fw 190 was practically the subtype of an originally fighter-type aircraft, developed and used against ground targets. The Hungarian ground-attack aircraft usually carried out their combat tasks at low altitudes, and they did not even receive escort from the Messerschmitts on a number of missions; in these cases, a flight usually went higher behind the others to observe the surroundings and act as a defense against fighter attacks. They were equipped with bombs just like the other aircraft; these were instantly released without activating them, or (if they did not meet enemy fighters) they carried out attacks against ground targets themselves. After the release of the bombs, the aircraft could defend themselves. Of course, when highly outnumbered, their task was not at all easy, and the Hungarian ground-attack aircraft also got a taste of the lesson already experienced by the *Luftwaffe* pilots – many of the bomber pilots who had retrained from large twin-engined aircraft could not get used to fighter tactics in time and could not handle efficiently the small and maneuverable aircraft, as a result of which they were shot down even before they could learn to exploit all the opportunities offered by the Fw 190.

Hadnagy Lajos Vargha, the most successful pilot of 102/2 Ground-Attack Squadron, at the beginning of 1945, on the nose of the belly-landed Fw 190 F-8 'Ági'. (From the author's collection)

The Hungarian Fw 190s scored their victories usually at low altitudes, sometimes while in a dogfight with the enemy fighters, but they also shot down a number of the Il-2s belonging to their Soviet ground-attack 'colleagues'. The fact that the Fw 190 was such a deadly weapon in the hands of an experienced pilot can be demonstrated through the example of János Róza (detailed later in this work) or through *hadnagy* Lajos Vargha, one of the flight leaders and the most successful pilots of 102/2 Ground-Attack Squadron. Vargha, over the relatively short timespan of 24 combat sorties (and in addition to his successes against ground targets), shot down four enemy aircraft: one P-51D (a fact also confirmed by American sources), two Yakovlev fighters and an Il-2.[10]

10 For Lajos Vargha (Kópháza, 22 December 1918–Sopron, 6 January 2001), see Csaba Becze, 'A 102 vadászbombázó osztály története II 1945', *Magyar Szárnyak Évkönyv*, 2001, pp. 32–39.

Decorations

The topic of decorations usually interests many readers, but until now has been given less publicity than other topics regarding the air force. The author has thus striven to discuss this topic in detail within the biographies of each ace. For each combat decoration, the author has also given the most accurate awarding date of the decoration he has discovered. These have been extracted either from issues of the contemporary *Honvédségi Közlönyök és Rendeletek (Személyes ügyek)* (Army Bulletin and Regulations [Personal matters]), or from the documents of 101 Fighter Wing at the end of the war (including the air force orders preserved by the wing, which are not only related to the fighters). Apart from these, there was only one case where the author was able to find an awarding document of a decoration in April 1945 that had been preserved by the family; the night fighter's case had not been included in the documents of 101 Fighter Wing because he had not been a daytime fighter. In the case of the German Iron Crosses (1st and 2nd Classes), the dates provided were almost exclusively copied from the original awarding documents, or from documents accurately referring to the date of awarding, because in this case, the *Honvédségi Közlöny* only recorded the permission to wear these decorations and not the awarding date itself.

The author has noted all decorations in the order in which they were worn.

In connection with military decorations it is important to note that Ferenc Szálasi, head of the Arrow Cross Party - Hungarist Movement, 'Leader of the Nation', issued an order on 17 November 1944 entitled *Hadikitüntetések adományozási jogának további átruházása és egyéb kitüntetési kérdések szabályozása* ('Assignment of the right of endowment of decorations and the regulation of other questions on military decorations'). Based on this, the denomination of the former *Kormányzói dicsérő elismerés Magyar Koronás Érdemérme* ('Sign of Praise of the Regent Hungarian Medal with the Holy Crown', or '*Signum Laudis*', as these decorations were known) was changed, although the order of wearing it remained the same. After the order, the military merit medal was renamed the *Magyar Koronás Érdemérem* ('Hungarian Medal with the Holy Crown'), with the *Kormányzói dicsérő elismerés* ('Sign of Praise of the Regent') part removed. The bronze medal could be awarded only once, but the silver and gold medals could be awarded more than once, and it became possible for these to be awarded independently of each other; having a bronze medal was therefore not a prerequisite for receiving the silver medal. From this time on, also, the merit medals could be awarded to foreign nationals, whereas earlier this had been impossible.[1] This is why the author has referred to the merit medals by their new name for later awards, as the decoration itself did not change.

1 *HM HIM HL*, HM 93986/eln. 8/e.-1944.

The multiple awards the author mentioned earlier were indicated on the given decoration by clasps.

In connection with the Arrow Cross (*'nyilaskereszt'*) era, it is important to note the desire to create a separate set of military merit medals and decorations because of the intention to establish complete distance from the Horthy era and the past in general. The plans for an Arrow Cross Order for military service and a Star Cross Order for civilian service were therefore planned, and there was even a competition for designing the medals in late February 1945. However, these new types of decorations were never realized because of the shortage of time and the historical context.[2]

Apart from the military merit medals, the author has also indicated the *Tűzkereszt* (Fire Cross), an award instituted at the end of 1941, the 1st Class of which (with swords and wreath, that is, *I fokozata a kardokkal és koszorúval*) was awarded for 12 weeks of front-line service and for 10 completed combat sorties for aircraft crews.[3] All the pilots introduced in this work except Béla Lipcsey received this medal. The clasps on the ribbon of the *Tűzkereszt* represented the wounds of the servicemen suffered in combat. The author also mentions the merits and award related to territorial revisions – *Felvidék* (Upper Hungary), *Erdély* (Transylvania) and *Délvidék* (Southern Hungary). The criteria for these were the mobilization of one's unit and leaving peacetime garrison. The squadrons of the Royal Hungarian Air Force flew combat missions against all three former Little Entente countries (as will be elaborated in detail later), even the reconnaissance units also completed missions over Romania in August 1940. The *Felvidéki Emlékérem* (Commemorative Medal for the Liberation of Upper Hungary) was awarded in 1939, while the *Délvidéki Emlékérem* (Commemorative Medal for the Return of Southern Hungary) and the *Erdélyi Emlékérem* (Commemorative Medal for the Liberation of Northern Transylvania) were awarded in 1941 to pilots featured in the present work. The author has not detailed the issue of *Tiszti Szolgálati Jel* (Officer Service Decoration), which did not depend on one's front-line actions and was awarded only for honoring time spent in service. *Tiszti Szolgálati Jel* was only awarded to Aladár Heppes among those featured in this work; his medal was a Class III/A *Tiszti Szolgálati Jel*, awarded after 15 years of service. If one is interested, it is easy to calculate that the 2nd and 3rd Class non-commissioned officer service decorations were awarded after 10 or six years of military service. The author has not discussed other medals and decorations in detail that were not awarded to honor airmen's front-line service or air force actions, such as the sport qualification badges awarded to Heppes, Krascsenics and Lőrincz, or the *Nemzetvédelmi Kereszt* (National Defense Cross) awarded to Heppes.

Among the decorations and medals received from the Germans, apart from the Iron Crosses, the author has also mentioned the *Frontflugspange* (Front Flying Clasp of the *Luftwaffe*, *frontrepülő jelvény*). This was a performance badge awarded in bronze, silver and gold grades according to the number of individual combat sorties flown, and pennants were hung on the gold clasp after each set of 100 completed sorties (the bronze was awarded after 20, the silver after 60 and the gold after 110 combat sorties). Although this was a performance badge and not an actual award for valor or outstanding military actions, it was certainly treated with respect. A gold *Frontflugspange* was much more valuable for a contemporary pilot than an Iron Cross 2nd Class, because it was much more

2 *Nemzetvédelmi Tudósító*, 20 February 1945, pp. 1–2.
3 *Honvédségi Közlöny (Személyes ügyek)*, nr. 1941/57 (2 December 1941), pp. 759–762.

difficult to earn. *Frontflugspanges* were given in the Royal Hungarian Air Force to the fighter pilots (or at least a number of them), and also to Ju 87 and Fw 190 pilots. The pilots of short- and long-range reconnaissance aircraft and twin-engined bomber aircraft did not receive the badge as far as the author knows. As a matter of interest, the author also mentions pilot and observer badges received from foreign states; for example, everybody who completed the *Dél-olasz Repülő Tanfolyam* (*DRT*, or the South Italian Flight Training Course) wore the Italian pilot badge. Those who had reached the rank of *hadnagy* on 20 August 1939 took part in an excursion in Bulgaria with the class to be initiated in 1940; the 1939 class received the Bulgarian Pilot Badge, while the 1940 class received the Bulgarian Observer Badge. Aladár Heppes received the Croatian Pilot Badge when, in 1942, a delegation of the Croatian Air Force visited Hungary.

At the end of the war, the issue of decorations was afflicted by the problem of missing data and uncertainty; there are controversies and many obscurities. The *Honvédségi Rendeletek*, which published the awarded decorations, was not issued after the middle of March 1945, so this data is missing, but the same award was sometimes mentioned twice in different documents with

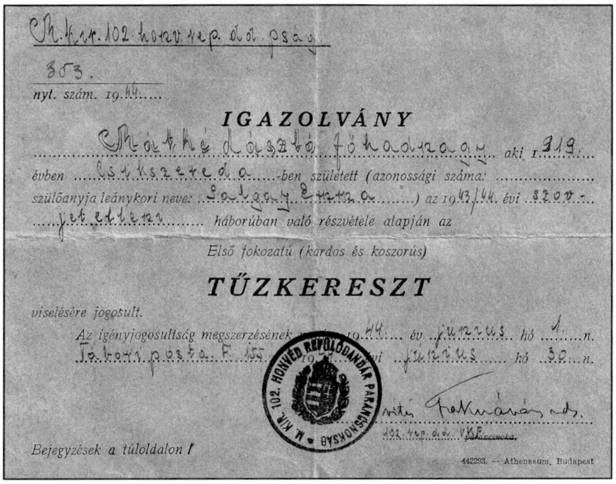

853.

nyt. szám. 19.44.....

IGAZOLVÁNY

Máthé László főhadnagy aki 1919. évben Csikszereda-ben született (azonossági száma: ... szülőanyja leánykori neve: ...) az 1943/44. évi ... háborúban való részvétele alapján az

Első fokozatú (kardos és koszorús)

TŰZKERESZT

viselésére jogosult.

Az igényjogosultság megszerzésének 1944. év június hó 1. n.

Tábori posta F. 155 ... június hó 30. n.

M. KIR. 102. HONVÉD REPÜLŐDANDÁR PARANCSNOKSÁG

Bejegyzések a túloldalon!

442293. — Athenaeum, Budapest

Certificate of the Fire Cross (*Tűzkereszt*) belonging to *főhadnagy* László Máthé, summer 1944. (From the collection of László Máthé)

Verleihungsurkunde

Im Namen des Oberbefehlshabers der Luftwaffe

verleihe ich dem

Oberleutnant

Ladislaus M á t h é

die

Frontflug-Spange für Jäger in Gold

Gefechtsstand, den 17. Februar 1945

Der Oberbefehlshaber der Luftflotte 4

Generaloberst

Award certificate of the Gold *Frontflugspange* belonging to László Máthé. (From the collection of László Máthé)

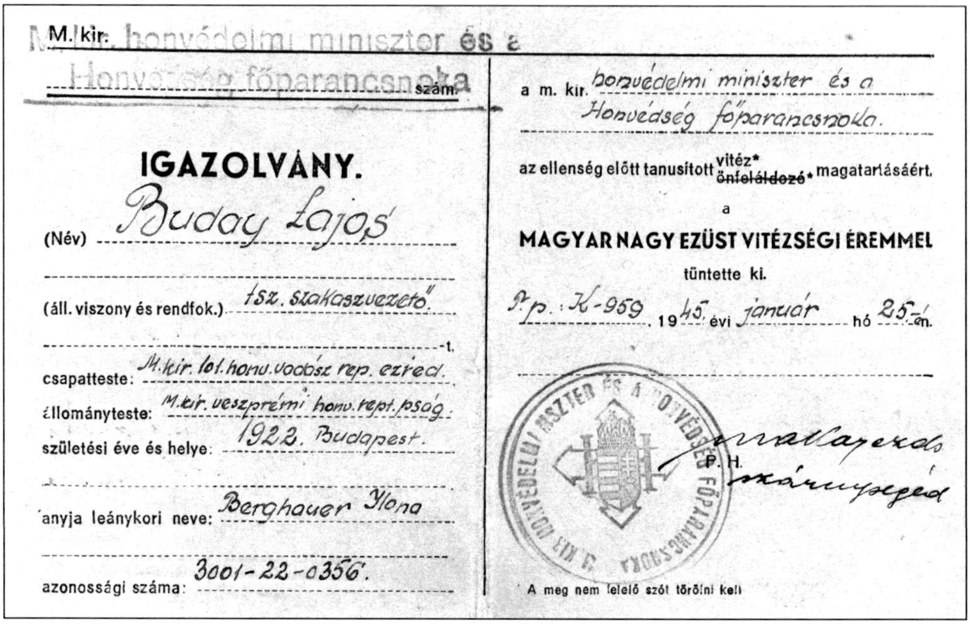

M. kir. honvédelmi miniszter és a Honvédség főparancsnoka szám.

IGAZOLVÁNY.

(Név) Buday Lajos

(áll. viszony és rendfok.) tsz. szakaszvezető.

csapatteste: M. kir. 101. honv. vadász rep. ezred.

állományteste: M. kir. veszprémi honv. rept. psóg.

születési éve és helye: 1922. Budapest.

anyja leánykori neve: Berghauer Ilona

azonossági száma: 3001-22-0356.

a m. kir. honvédelmi miniszter és a Honvédség főparancsnoka.

az ellenség előtt tanusított vitéz* ~~önfeláldozó~~* magatartásáért,

a

MAGYAR NAGY EZÜST VITÉZSÉGI ÉREMMEL

tüntette ki.

B.p. : K-959 1945. évi január hó 25-én.

P. H.

* A meg nem felelő szót törölni kell

The certificate of the first Hungarian Great Silver Medal for Bravery belonging to Lajos Buday from January 1945, signed by the adjutant of Minister of Defense and Commander in Chief Károly Beregfy, *vezérkari ezredes* Ferenc Makay-Hollósy. Because of this, and because of the stamp of the Arrow Cross Minister of Defense and Commander in Chief of the Royal Hungarian Armed Forces, this is an exceptionally rare document. (From the author's collection)

different dates attached. This did not indicate a double award, but the same decoration; in such cases, the author has only mentioned one of the dates. To mention one particular example regarding missing dates at the end of the war, Wing Order Nr. 1945/33, issued 13 February 1945, published a long list of the freshly decorated enlisted airmen, noting that 'the decree on the award of decorations is delayed due to certain printing issues'.[4] The author has therefore marked the date of the Wing Order (that is, 13 February 1945) as the date of the decorations awarded.

The biographies of two pilots, written at the beginning of the 1950s for the communist authorities, mention certain decorations that have not been documented anywhere. The biographies written in this period can be fully exempt from any accusations of exaggeration because any wartime or military decorations were deemed a major hindrance in the eyes of the authorities. One was the second *Magyar Koronás Ezüst Érdemérem hadiszalagon a kardokkal* (Hungarian Silver Medal with the Holy Crown, on a war ribbon with swords) awarded to Lajos Tóth; the other was the *Magyar Érdemrend lovagkeresztje hadiszalagon a kardokkal* (Hungarian Knight's Cross of the Order of Merit on a war ribbon with swords) awarded to Tibor Papp. These uncertain decorations have not been mentioned in the biographies for the respective pilots given in this work.

The author wishes to go into detail regarding the case of the *Magyar Tiszti Arany Vitézségi Érem* (Hungarian Officer's Gold Medal for Bravery) destined for Dezső Szentgyörgyi. Szentgyörgyi

4 *HM HIM HL*, documents of 101 Fighter Wing, box nr. 110, Wing Order Nr. 1945/33.

was recommended for this decoration more than once, but despite his outstanding achievements, he never received it (although certain publications indicate otherwise).[5] The author's opinion is that a decoration can be deemed as having been awarded if the fact of the award was publicly announced, or if the soldier himself received the decoration in its physical form. In the case of Szentgyörgyi, neither occurred, and he himself did not count the *Magyar Tiszti Arany Vitézségi Érem* among his decorations. Although in theory the decision to award the decoration was made on 25 March 1945, it was not officially announced and the decoration itself was not awarded. The last wartime decoration Szentgyörgyi actually received was a *Magyar Koronás Bronz Érdemérem hadiszalagon a kardokkal* (Hungarian Bronze Medal with the Holy Crown on a war ribbon with swords), which was received by him upon an introduction to the *Magyar Érdemrend tisztikeresztje hadidíszítménnyel és kardokkal* (Hungarian Officer's Cross of the Order of Merit on war decoration with swords) on the previous day, 25 April 1945.

This was not the only case in the Air Force where the award of a *Magyar Tiszti Arany Vitézségi Érem* did not taken place after a positive theoretical decision was made. In the case of *főhadnagy* László Herder, an outstandingly effective commander of 3/1 Bomber Squadron, a positive decision was made in the summer of 1944, which meant there was still plenty of time to announce and to award the decoration; however, this did not happen. In the case of Herder, an excellent commander who flew 250 missions in twin-engined bombers and had at least two confirmed air victories, one of his comrades, *százados* Imre Homér, remembers that the unofficial response to an enquiry about why the award had been delayed was: 'Herder will not receive the *Magyar Tiszti Arany Vitézségi Érem*, because we cannot put all decorations on one Air Force *főhadnagy*'![6]

The author's personal opinion regarding this situation is that where one really wants to differentiate between performance and performance, knowing well why others have received this decoration, then both Szentgyörgyi and Herder were eligible to receive at least two *Magyar Tiszti Arany Vitézségi Érem*, both for their bravery on the front as well as based on the multiple recommendations: one for their overall achievements on the front, and one for their heroic actions, of which both had a number.

The fighter arm of the air force had two pilots who were actually awarded the *Magyar Tiszti Arany Vitézségi Érem*; one of them, László Molnár, was recommended twice (17 June 1944 and 8 August 1944) and finally received the decoration posthumously, while György Debrődy was also recommended twice (on 17 June 1944 and 9 September 1944) and finally received the decoration after he sustained life-threatening injuries. They too could have received their decorations considerably earlier. Apart from them, many others in the air force were reasonably recommended for this decoration based on their outstanding service, but these recommendations were ignored (see, for example, the case of ace Miklós Kenyeres).[7]After 24 October 1944 Szentgyörgyi was recommended again for *Magyar Tiszti Arany Vitézségi Érem* on 13 March

5 For example, the following work mentions the decoration as having been awarded: Péter Illésfalvi, Vilmos Kovács, and Roland Maruzs, *'Vitézségért'. A Magyar Tiszti Arany Vitézségi Éremmel kitüntetettek a második világháborúban* (Szeged: HK Hermanos Kiadó, 2011), p. 160.

6 Tibor Nagymarosy, Zoltán Guthy, and Imre Homér, 'Tovább zuhannak a "Boszorkányok"', *Magyar Szárnyak Évkönyv*, 1987, pp. 67–68. For Herder's *Magyar Tiszti Arany Vitézségi Érem*, see Csaba B. Stenge, 'Majoros Kornél repülő főhadnagy emlékezete', *Katonaújság*, 2012:6, pp. 5–6.

7 *HM HIM HL*, documents of 101 Fighter Wing, box. nr. 113, registry of decorations. In the case of Debrődy, a contemporary article mentioned four recommendations for decoration, but this cannot be confirmed based on the surviving fragmentary documents.

1945 after his 25th victory, following which a theoretically positive decision was made; however, the actual award was not granted, and naturally no announcement was made. The reason for this, based on the data found by the author, could be that from May 1943 the official number of air victories for pilots to be eligible to receive this military decoration was set at 30. At the end of the war, on 24 April 1945, Lajos Tóth was also recommended for this decoration for the second time after 24 November 1944. At the end of April 1945, Tóth had 26 confirmed air victories, but he did not receive the decoration either, probably for the reason detailed above (and perhaps because the case did not reach the 'Leader of the Nation', who could award a decoration).[8]

In the case of Dezső Szentgyörgyi, the case of awarding a *Magyar Koronás Bronz Érdemérem* instead of a *Magyar Érdemrend tisztikeresztje* on 25 April 1945 can be traced back to the following. On 24 April 1945, an exceptionally large number of recommendations to various decorations (157) were forwarded to Air Force Command from 101 Fighter Wing. Among these were 46 officer pilots of the wing, along with enlisted pilots, members of the ground crew and two KIA pilots who had been flying with squadrons that had not been part of the regular wing at the time of their deaths. According to the previously mentioned order (the *Hadikitüntetések adományozási jogának további átruházása és egyéb kitüntetési kérdések szabályozása* issued on 17 November 1944), the commander in chief of the air force – together with other commanders in chief – had been declared able to award the *Magyar Koronás Bronz Érdemérem* (earlier only decorations for the enlisted servicemen could be awarded by granted authorities, but this was not the case for officers). Thus, with exceptional speed, all the recommended decorations were assessed and awarded the next day by the commander in chief of the air force in the name of the 'Leader of the Nation'. In this case, Dezső Szentgyörgyi received a decoration that was of much lower level than what had originally been intended for him, because the commander in chief of the air force was only eligible to award the *Magyar Koronás Bronz Érdemérem* through his own authority and was not able to award any classes of the *Magyar Érdemrend*. Another particular aspect of this group award was that, during this single event, 23 *Magyar Koronás Bronz Érdemérem hadiszalagon a kardokkal* and 28 *Magyar Koronás Ezüst Érdemérem hadiszalagon a kardokkal* were awarded at the same time. The previously-mentioned order of 17 November 1944, however, only allowed for the Bronze class decorations to be awarded through the granted authorities of the commanders in chief of the armies, and the Silver classes could not be awarded in this way (the order only allowed these to be awarded by the Minister of Defense and the commander in chief of the armed forces). No later decrees regulated the awarding of decorations; in theory, it is possible that such a document was issued at the end of the war and has not survived, but it is highly unlikely that anyone could have spared time to regulate such issues. Based on this, it is possible that the award of the *Magyar Koronás Ezüst Érdemérem* by the commander in chief of the air force on 25 April 1945 exceeded his powers. This concerns nine airmen featured in this work, among them seven aces (István Kálmán, László Máthé, László Dániel, Kálmán Nánási, György Michna, Ervin Flóznik, Béla Füleky, Tibor Tobak and Gyula Pintér).[9]

8 *HM HIM HL*, documents of 101 Fighter Wing, box. nr. 113, registry of decorations; see also the wartime diary of *őrmester* Ferenc Nyakas from 1943 (full copy owned by the author).

9 *HM HIM HL*, HM 93986/eln. 8/e.-1944; documents of 101 Fighter Wing, box nr. 110, Wing Order Nr. 1945/69. For this question, see also Gergely Sallay, 'Magyar hadikitüntetések posztumusz adományozása a második világháború idején', in: Roland Maruzs, *Vitéz és önfeláldozó magatartásért.*

Tizedes Tibor Varjas (1924–2006) with his Messerschmitt Bf 109 G-6 in the autumn of 1944. *Tizedes* Varjas was the wingman of Dezső Szentgyörgyi from the end of 1944 until January 1945, when he suffered an accident and was injured while taking off in the aircraft W-177, borrowed from Szentgyörgyi. The accident happened because the pilot, who was much shorter than Dezső Szentgyörgyi, was almost unable to reach the rudder pedals from the seat, which was adjusted to Szentgyörgyi's height. (From the collection of Tibor Varjas)

It is also important to note that only one of the *Magyar Arany Vitézségi Érem* (Hungarian Golden Medal for Bravery) awarded to the non-commissioned officers and the enlisted pilots was received by a pilot of the air force – Sándor Szoják (Szobránci) – and this, too, was awarded to honor his deeds during the combat activities of March 1939. Despite the large numbers of recommendations during the Second World War, no more awards were received by any individual in the air force. According to the previously mentioned diary from May 1943, the criteria for awarding the *Magyar Arany Vitézségi Érem* were raised to unreasonable levels, and irrationally high demands were set in contrast with earlier regulations. This meant 30 air victories in the case of fighter pilots, and similarly for the officers. As a comparison, it is interesting to mention that Sándor Szoják received his decoration for two victories on 24 March 1939.[10]

As I have already noted in connection with the award of the *Magyar Arany Vitézségi Érem*, the aircraft crewmembers and pilots were markedly ignored in terms of decorations. In Hungary, between 1941 and 1945, relatively few *Magyar Arany Vitézségi Érem* were awarded, and the procedure itself was also very slow – only in the Arrow Cross era was it sped up and simplified to boost morale – but the air force servicemen seemed to have been ignored then too.

As late as the Szálasi era, on 25 January 1945, *vezérezredes* Károly Beregfy, Minister of Defense and commander-in-chief of the armed forces, who was visiting the 101 Fighter Wing stationed at the Veszprém airfield, personally awarded decorations to 10 pilots, nine of whom were aces (Lajos Tóth, László Pottyondy, József Málik, Béla Füleky, László Máthé, István Fábián, Lajos Buday, Pál László Szikora and Lajos Krascsenics). The tenth pilot receiving an award was *főhadnagy* Sándor Halasi, who successfully commanded 101/3 Fighter Squadron from 17 November 1944 until the end of the war. At the same time, three German pilots were also decorated; there had been no precedent for such an action before. Although the decorations were awarded in groups, on this day an exceptionally high ranking decoration was also awarded without any recommendation: Lajos Tóth was awarded the *Magyar Érdemrend tisztikeresztje*.[11]

Hősi halált halt és posztumusz kitüntetett katonáink adattára 1939–1945 (Nagykovácsi: Puedlo, 2009), pp. 5–9.

10 Wartime diary of *őrmester* Ferenc Nyakas.

11 *HM HIM HL*, documents of 101 Fighter Wing, box nr. 113, registry of decorations.

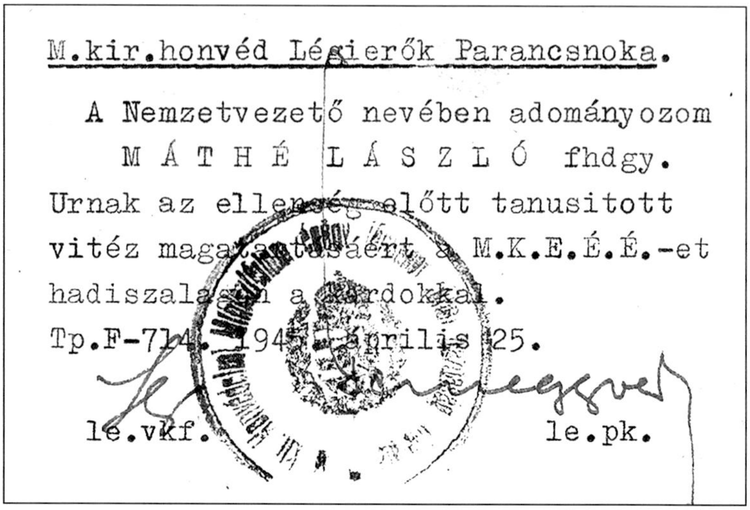

M.kir.honvéd Légierők Parancsnoka.

A Nemzetvezető nevében adományozom
M Á T H É L Á S Z L Ó fhdgy.
Urnak az ellenség előtt tanusitott
vitéz magatartásáért a M.K.E.É.É.-et
hadiszalagon a kardokkal.
Tp.F-714. 1945. április 25.

le.vkf. le.pk.

Awarding certificate of the last Hungarian military decoration belonging to László Máthé, 25 April 1945. As the paper supply was running out, this document gradually shrank in size, and it was only card-sized at the end of April 1945. (From the collection of László Máthé)

The bomber and reconnaissance crews were exceptionally affected by this neglect because their continuously outstanding performance was rarely rewarded – probably those with the power to decide regarding these matters were not even been aware of the full value of their service. This contrasts strikingly with the procedure of the *Luftwaffe*, where airmen were frequently rewarded based on a very realistic and flawless point-based system. In Hungary, it often happened that reconnaissance crew members and bombers received decorations only after their air victories – if they received anything at all – even though fighting in air combat was not among their main duties. In most cases, they were engaged in such actions solely because they had no other option left. The points system that was introduced in May 1943 met with general disapproval because it set irrational requirements, and not only for the fighters. For example, 300 points were needed to earn the *Magyar Arany Vitézségi Érem* for reconnaissance pilots, but a combat sortie that was shorter than two hours (and short-range reconnaissance sorties were almost always shorter than two hours) were only worth one point; it would therefore have been necessary to complete 300 of these sorties to earn this decoration. As one of the short-range reconnaissance pilots wrote in his diary, 'If, for example, we would like to earn the gold medal, two aircraft should be flown to war-veary [by sheer flight hours]. Impossible.'[12] Probably there were also two other problems regarding the neglect of air force units when awarding decorations. One of these concerned the period between spring 1943 and spring 1944, when, although considerable forces were deployed to the Eastern Front, only the combat squadrons of the Air Brigade fought on the front lines, equipped with a German aircraft fleet capable of considerably increased performance, and mainly in the principal strategic direction. As a consequence, the combat squadrons of the brigade, compared to their size and relative percentage within the whole fighting force, submitted a large number of recommendations for decorations. The superiors, who might not have realized all the circumstances that had led to this situation, may have been suspicious of this large number of recommendations. The other factor was mistakes committed at the troop level:

12 Wartime diary of *őrmester* Ferenc Nyakas.

in the author's opinion, a number of errors were made while filling in the recommendation papers, which did not emphasize enough the hardships and dangers of combat missions. There was also a considerable jealousy from the ground troops toward the air force troops, probably because of their large proportion of German decorations. This is exactly why the Royal Hungarian Air Force had a number of officers, ranking from *zászlós* to *százados*, who had their Iron Cross 1st Class already but were recommended for the *Magyar Érdemrend lovagkeresztje* in vain. For a number of them, this remained a bitter memory for the rest of their lives.

Mascot bunnies on the port wing root of a Hungarian-manufactured Messerschmitt Bf 109 G-6 in Veszprém in 1944. (From the collection of László Hemmert)

It is especially worth mentioning the situation of those who went missing in terms of their decorations. In theory, anyone who went missing could receive a military decoration only when their death had been proven, or if they had returned from captivity and proved their proper behaviour in the prisoner of war camp. During the first year of the war on the Eastern Front, in 1941, three Hungarian fighter pilots went missing: *hadnagy* János Pettendi (on 5 August), *főhadnagy* Gyula Lasztóczy (on 11 August) and *zászlós* Márton Szőnyi (on 27 August). At first, all were considered to have been killed, and it was planned to decorate them posthumously with the *Magyar Érdemrend lovagkeresztje hadiszalagon a kardokkal*; but then it turned out that Szőnyi had been captured and was alive, and was even attending a Soviet Partisan school.[13] This case probably convinced the decision makers to put aside all the recommendations of individuals who were missing for decorations until the end of the war, when no decisions were made because of the drastic changes in political circumstances. There were, however, exceptions: pilots who were known to have been captured nevertheless received decorations for which they had earlier been recommended (see, for example, the case of Miklós Kenyeres). At the end of the war, several individuals who went missing received a military decoration, even though their fate was unknown or uncertain (for example *főhadnagy* Béla Füleky).

In addition to decorations, the author would also like to mention the issue of promotions made out of turn, which was also a method of rewarding the soldiers for their exceptional combat achievements. Here again, the Hungarian practice was very problematic for a number of reasons. Rising to a higher rank was an exceptionally slow process, and promotion out of turn was almost nonexistent; only a few cases exist from the Arrow Cross era. Readers should not be misled by the fact that two of the pilots mentioned in this work were promoted out of

13 Szőnyi, the leader of a 13-member Hungarian–Soviet Partisan group, was airdropped on 8 August 1944 in the hills between Ózd and Pétervására. The Hungarian police force raided their place on the Macskás farm southeast of Kissikátor on 7 September 1944, where he was shot dead. Pál Földes, *Két ugrás az ismeretlenbe* (Budapest: Zrínyi Kiadó, 1975), p. 268; Becze, '*Kőr Ász*', pp. 57–58.

turn (György Debrődy and Aladár Heppes); apart from them, promotions out of turn, even for staff officers of the whole army, only happened a handful of times. The situation was not much better for the non comissioned officers and enlisted servicemen; some cases of promotion from *szakaszvezető* to *őrmester* only happened because the wing commander was able to decide on this within his own scope of authority.

Béla Lipcsey reached the rank of *Oberleutnant* after several months in the *Luftwaffe*, for which he would have needed to serve for a number of years in Hungary. The outstanding enlisted pilots in the *Luftwaffe* could even achieve staff officer ranks, for example Heinz Bär,[14] who was an *Unteroffizier* at the beginning of war. Dezső Szentgyörgyi was the same rank at the beginning of the war, but by the end of the conflict Bär had become an *Oberstleutnant*, whereas Szentgyörgyi had only risen to the rank of *zászlós*. The Americans and the Soviets also had a swifter and easier promotion system for their pilots. For example on the American side, after the outbreak of the war, youths who had completed their high school exams went to a short but intensive training course before being given their aviator badges and promotions to the rank of 2nd Lieutenant, without having to spend years at a military higher education institute. Other promotions followed quickly, which explained why Captains hardly above the age of 20 were serving in the US Air Force.[15]

14 For Heinz Bär (Sommerfeld, 25 May 1913–Braunschweig, 28 April 1957), see Ernst Obermaier, *Die Ritterkreuzträger der Luftwaffe 1939–45: Band 1, Jagdflieger* (Mainz: Verlag Dieter Hoffmann, 1989, 2nd edition), p. 30.

15 For the different training and promotion systems in use in the American and Hungarian armies, see Csaba Becze, *Az Arany sas nyomában. Szilaj Varga Gyula és a magyar gyorsbombázók a II. világháborúban* (Nagykovácsi: Puedlo, 2008), pp. 18–19.

Comparative Table of Ranks

Below is a short comparative table of the most important ranks used in the troops of the Hungarian, German, Soviet and American air forces. In the case of the rank '*zászlós*', it should be noted that the nearest rank in the air force of the US Army Air Force was Flight Officer, which is not equivalent but only the closest in correspondence; therefore, if this rank needs to be translated, it is perhaps more appropriate to use *zászlós* than *hadnagy*. Of the American pilots featured in this work, Richard A. Troutt was a Flight Officer. If translating the Hungarian '*zászlós*' into English, the author would use the US Navy's rank of 'Ensign', although, again, this is not an exact equivalent because such a rank did not exist in the British and American Air Forces. For a similar anomaly regarding the ranks of the Soviet Air Force, see the explanatory note for the rank '*alhadnagy*'.

Hungarian rank	German rank	Russian rank	American rank
vezérőrnagy	*Generalmajor*	*генера́л-майо́р (general mayor)*	Brigadier General
ezredes	*Oberst*	*полко́вник (polkovnik)*	Colonel
alezredes	*Oberstleutnant*	*подполко́вник (podpolkovnik)*	Lieutenant Colonel
őrnagy	*Major*	*майо́р (mayor)*	Major
százados	*Hauptmann*	*капита́н (kapitan)*	Captain
főhadnagy	*Oberleutnant*	*ста́рший лейтена́нт (starshiy leytenant)*	1st Lieutenant
hadnagy	*Leutnant*	*лейтена́нт (leytenant)*	2nd Lieutenant
zászlós/alhadnagy[1]	*Oberfähnrich*	*мла́дший лейтена́нт (mladshiy leytenant)*	
zászlóshelyettes			
főtörzsőrmester	*Stabsfeldwebel*	–	Master Sergeant
törzsőrmester	*Oberfeldwebel*	*старшина (starshina)*	Technical Sergeant
őrmester	*Feldwebel*	*ста́рший сержа́нт (starshiy serzhant)*	Staff Sergeant
szakaszvezető	*Unteroffizier*	*мла́дший сержа́нт (mladshiy serzhant)*	Sergeant
tizedes	*Obergefreiter*	–	Corporal
őrvezető	*Gefreiter*	*ефрейтор (yefreytor)*	Private 1st Class
honvéd	*Flieger*	*красноармеец (krasnoarmeyets)*	Private

Notes)

1 The rank of '*alhadnagy*' had existed earlier in the Hungarian army. With the adoption of the Soviet regime and the discontinuation of the rank of ensign (in Hungarian, *zászlós*) after 1945, the rank of *alhadnagy* was used in lieu as a matching rank. The old rank of *zászlós* was also referred to as *alhadnagy* from this time onward, but in the author's opinion the two ranks were not completely equivalent because the requirements for them were not the same. The Soviet rank of *mladshiy leytenant* was the equivalent to *alhadnagy* after 1945; the author has therefore used this rank throughout the text for this fairly common Soviet rank, rather than *zászlós*. In the corresponding row, therefore, the exact equivalent of ensign is *Oberfähnrich*, while the *mladshiy leytenant* is equivalent in the post-war period to *alhadnagy*. At the same time, ensign and *Oberfähnrich* are, according to the author, not to be translated as *mladshiy leytenant*.

Expressions and Abbreviations

Within the text, the names of the contemporary foreign air force units have been left unchanged, mainly because not all of them could be exactly translated into each language and this might mislead a reader who is not familiar with the real strength and combat force of these units (this is especially true for the American units). The author has summarized the respective names for each unit. Without going into too much detail due to lack of space, the German and Hungarian units generally had similar combat strength, whereas their American counterparts had a much larger combat strength and the Soviets a much smaller one (for example, a Soviet Regiment can be matched in terms of combat strength to a German or Hungarian group). It needs to be added that, although the American term 'group' is usually translated as *csoport* in Hungarian, this is entirely incorrect: the denomination *csoport* was usually used by the Hungarian military language for temporary combat groups known by the names of their commanders, and there was only one such unit among the contemporary air force unit at the end of the war.

German

Jagddivision: *vadászrepülő-hadosztály*/Fighter Division
Jagdgeschwader (JG): *vadászrepülő-ezred*/Fighter Wing
Kampfgeschwader (KG): *bombázórepülő-ezred*/Bomber Wing
Schlachtgeschwader (SG): *csatarepülő-ezred*/Ground-Attack Wing
Sturzkampfgeschwader (St.G): *zuhanóbombázó-ezred*/Divebomber Wing
Transportgeschwader (TG): *szállítórepülő-ezred*/Transport Wing
Gruppe: *repülőosztály*/Group
Rotte: *géppár*/element
Schwarm: *raj*/flight
Staffel: *repülőszázad*/Squadron

American

Army Air Force (AAF)
Bomber Group (BG)
Fighter Group (FG)
Fighter Squadron (FS)

Fighter Wing (FW)
Photographic Reconnaissance Group (PRG)

Soviet

ва: Air Army (VA)
бад: Bomber Aviation Division (BAD)
бап: Bomber Aviation Regiment (BAP)
иад: Fighter Aviation Division (IAD)
гиад: Guards Fighter Aviation Division (GIAD)
иап: Fighter Aviation Regiment (IAP)
гиап: Guards Fighter Aviation Regiment (GIAP)
орап: Independent Reconnaissance Aviation Regiment (ORAP)
шад: Shturmovik (Ground-Attack) Aviation Division (SAD)
шап: Shturmovik (Ground-Attack) Regiment (SAP)
гшап: Guards Shturmovik (Ground-Attack) Regiment (GSAP)

Additional List of Abbreviations

Hungarian translation added where applicable

acc. nr.: accumulation number (*folyószám*, as in *fsz.*)
ADGB: Air Defence of Great Britain
ÁVH: State Protection Authority (*Államvédelmi Hatóság*)

BEAC: Budapest University Athletics Club *(Budapesti Egyetemi Atlétikai Club)*
biz.: confidential (*bizalmas*)
BSZKRT: Budapest Public Transport Plc. (*Budapest Székesfővárosi Közlekedési Részvénytársaság*)

TsAMO RF: Central Archives of the Ministry of Defence of the Russian Federation (*Центральный архив Министерства обороны Российской Федерации*)
cmdr.: commander (*parancsnok*)

DRT: South Italian Flight Training Course (*Dél-olasz Repülő Tanfolyam*)

E: East (*kelet*)

fhdgy.: 1st Lieutenant (*főhadnagy*)
fsz.: (see acc. nr.)

GAE: Foreign Auxiliaries (*Groupe d'Auxiliaires Etrangers*)
GP: general practitioner, local doctor (*körzeti orvos*)

hdgy.: 2nd Lieutenant (*hadnagy*)
HM HIM HL: Military Archves of the Institute and Museum of Military History of the Ministry of Defence (*Honvédelmi Minisztérium Hadtörténeti Intézet és Múzem, Hadtörténeti Levéltár*)
HMNRA: Miklós Horthy National Aviation Fund, MHNAF (*Horthy Miklós Nemzeti Repülő Alap*)

IR: instrument rating (*műszerrepülő kiképzés*)
IRO: International Refugee Organization (*Nemzetközi Menekültügyi Szervezet*)

ISZKI: NSZSZK: Network of Forensic Science Institutes / Hungarian Institute for Forensic Sciences (*Igazságügyi és Szakértői Kutató Intézetek / Nemzeti Szakértői és Kutató Központ*)

JPAC: Joint POW/MIA Accounting Command

KIA: killed in action (*hősi halált halt*)

LASE: Ludovika Academy Sport Club (*Ludovika Akadémia Sport Egylet*)

MACR: Missing Air Crew Reports
Malév: Hungarian Airlines (*Magyar Légiforgalmi Vállalat*)
Maszovlet: Hungarian-Soviet Civil Air Transport Joint Stock Company (*Magyar–Szovjet Polgári Légiforgalmi Részvénytársaság*)
MÁVAG: Hungarian Royal State Railroads' Machine Factory *(Magyar Királyi Államvasutak Gépgyára)*
MNL: Hungarian National Archives (*Magyar Nemzeti Levéltár*)
MOVERO Hungarian Defence Association Aviation Department (*Magyar Országos Véderő Egylet Repülő Osztály*)
MSRE: University Sports Aviation Club (*Műegyetemi Sportrepülő Egyesület, MSRE*)
MWG: Hungarian Wagon and Machine Factory (*Magyar Wagon és Gépgyár*)

N: North (*észak*)
NARA: National Archives and Records Administration
n.d.a.: no data available
NE: North-East (*északkelet*)
NKVD: People's Commissariat for Internal Affairs
NW: North-West (*északnyugat*)

OMRE: National Hungarian Aviation Association (*Országos Magyar Repülő Egyesület*)
őrgy.: Major (*őrnagy*)
őrm.: Staff Sergeant (*őrmester*)

POW: prisoner of war (*hadifogoly*)

Regvi: pilot training group (*repülőgépvezető iskolaosztály*)
RKI: Aviation Experimental Institute (*Repülő Kísérleti Intézet*)

SE: South-East (*délkelet*)
SW: South-West (*délnyugat*)

TAF: Tactical Air Force
tbn: to be noted
téesz: collective farm (*termelőszövetkezet*)
tj.: officer candidate (*tisztjelölt*)

UNRRA: United Nations Relief and Rehabilitation Administration (*Egyesült Nemzetek Segélyezési és Helyreállítási Hivatala*)

vkf.: Chief of Staff (*honvéd vezérkar főnöke*)
vol.: volume
v. rep. e. pk.: Fighter Wing commander (*vadászrepülő-ezred parancsnok*)
v. rep. e.: Fighter Wing (*vadászrepülő-ezred*)

WM: Weiss Manfréd, either referring to the WM-21 'Sólyom' aircraft or to the factory '*Weiss Manfréd Acél- és Fémművek*' (Manfréd Weiss Steel and Metal Works) itself
WNr.:serial number (on German aircraft)

zls.: *zászlós*

Explanation of Hungarian Names and Denominations of Personnel and Units in Alphabetical Order; Foreign Expressions

---

Units (as mentioned in the work)

101 'Puma' Fighter Group – Puma means cougar
1/1 'Íjász' Fighter Squadron – Íjász means archer
1/2 'Ludas Matyi' Fighter Squadron – Ludas Matyi is a traditional Hungarian folk hero
1/3 'Kőr Ász' Fighter Squadron – Kőr Ász means ace of hearts
1/4 'Szent György' Fighter Squadron – Szent György is Saint George
II 'Lucifer' Short-Range Reconnaissance Squadron
1/1 'Dongó' Fighter Squadron – Dongó means bumblebee
2/1 'Zongora' Fighter Squadron – Zongora means piano, it was a code-name, not an official squadron name
2/3 'Ricsi' Fighter Squadron – Ricsi is short for Richárd/Richard, after the squadron commander's Great Dane
3/4 'Bomba Matyi' Squadron – Matyi is short for *Mátyás*; *bomba* means bomb
4/1 'Boszorkány' Squadron – Boszorkány means witch
101/2 'Retek' Squadron – Retek means radish, it was a code-name, not an official squadron name

Nicknames of personnel (with explanations in brackets wherever applicable)
(in alphabetical order based on their family name)
József Bejczy – 'Dzsó' (*Dzsó* is equivalent to 'Joe', short for József)
Pál Bélavári – 'Spulni' (*Spulni* means a spool of thread)
László Boldizsár – 'Boldi' (*Boldi* is short for his family name, Boldizsár)
Lajos Buday – 'Lali', 'Lojás' (*Lali* is short for Lajos)
László Dániel – 'Dani', 'Laci' (*Dani* is short for Dániel)
György Debrődy – 'Debcsi', 'Gyurka', 'Mandula' (*Gyurka* is short for György; *Mandula* means almond)
István Fábián: 'Koponya' (*Koponya* means skull)
Ervin Flóznik – 'Pierre'
Béla Füleky – 'Béci', 'Fülcsi' (*Béci* is short for Béla, *Fülcsi* means 'little ears', and is a wordplay on his family name)
Aladár Heppes – 'Ali', 'Öreg Puma' (*Öreg Puma* means 'Old Cougar', an affectionate name for the commander, *Ali* is a short version of Aladár)
András Huszár – 'Pufi' (*Pufi* generally means fat, corpulent)

Pál Irányi – 'Cuni', 'Pali' (*Pali* is short for Pál)
Mihály Karátsonyi: 'Miska', 'Misu' (*Miska* and *Misu* are both short for Mihály)
István Kálmán – 'Pista' (*Pista* is short for István)
Miklós Kenyeres – 'Miki', 'Nikó', 'Nikoláj'
Ernő Kiss – 'Balbó', 'Sheriff'
Pál Kovács – 'Paja'
Lajos Krascsenics – 'Tülök' (*Tülök* means horn)
Mátyás Lőrincz – 'Matyi' (*Matyi* is short for Mátyás)
József Málik – 'Jóska', 'Józsika', 'Félbefűrészelt Óriás' (*Jóska* and *Józsika* are both short versions of József; *Félbefűrészelt Óriás* means 'a giant sawn in half')
Ferenc Málnássy: 'Frici', 'Málna Franci' (*Frici* and *Franci* are both short for Ferenc; *Málna* is a variation of his family name and means raspberry)
László Máthé – 'Dazser', 'Laci', 'Mazsola' (*Mazsola* means raisin)
György Michna – 'Gyuri' - (*Gyuri* is short for György)
László Molnár – 'Laci', 'Oroszlán', 'Paszulyos' (*Laci* is short for László; *Oroszlán* means lion; *Paszulyos* means either a bean, or a very little amount)
József Nagy – 'Juju'
Kálmán Nánási – 'Nána' (*Nána* is a shortened version of his family name)
Endre Németh – 'Bandi', 'Spahi' (*Bandi* is a variation of the name Endre)
László Pajtás – 'Laci' (see above)
Imre Pánczél – 'Pufi' (see above)
Tibor Papp – 'Tibci' (*Tibci* is a variation of the name Tibor)
László Pottyondy – 'Laci' (see above)
János Róza – 'Jani' (*Jani* is short for János)
Dezső Szentgyörgyi – 'Dezske' (*Dezske* is short for Dezső)
Kálmán Szeverényi – 'Szever' (*Szever* is a shortened version of his family name)
László Szikora – 'Laci', 'Sziporka' (*Sziporka* is a wordplay on his family name and means bright, sparkly, sparks)
Tibor Tobak – 'Cica' (*Cica* means kitten)
Lajos Tóth – 'Drumi'
György Ujszászy – 'Apuka', 'Gyurka' (*Apuka* means Daddy; for *Gyurka*, see above)

Aircraft types

R07a 'Tücsök' glider aircraft – *tücsök* means cricket
'Rata' – Polikarpov I-16 fighter aircraft
Reggiane Re.2000 'Héja' fighter aircraft – *héja* means hawk
WM–21 'Sólyom' reconnaissance aircraft – *sólyom* means falcon

Decorations

(in alphabetical order)
Délvidéki Emlékérem (Commemorative Medal for the Return of Southern Hungary)

Erdélyi Emlékérem (Commemorative Medal for the Liberation of Northern Transylvania)
Felvidéki Emlékérem (Commemorative Medal for the Liberation of Upper Hungary)
Kormányzói dicsérő elismerés (Sign of Praise of the Regent)
Újólagos Kormányzói dicsérő elismerés (Repeated Sign of Praise of the Regent)
Kormányzói dicsérő elismerés Magyar Koronás Érdemérme (Sign of Praise of the Regent Hungarian Medal with the Holy Crown) (*'Signum Laudis'*)
Kormányzói dicsérő elismerés Magyar Koronás Bronz Érdemérme hadiszalagon a kardokkal (Sign of Praise of the Regent Hungarian Bronze Medal with the Holy Crown on war ribbon with swords)
Magyar Bronz Vitézségi Érem (Hungarian Bronze Medal for Bravery)
Magyar Érdemrend lovagkeresztje hadiszalagon a kardokkal (Hungarian Knight's Cross of the Order of Merit on war ribbon with swords)
Magyar Érdemrend tisztikeresztje (Hungarian Officer's Cross of the Order of Merit)
Magyar Kis Ezüst Vitézségi Érem (Hungarian Small Silver Medal for Bravery)
Magyar Nagy Ezüst Vitézségi Érem (Hungarian Large Silver Medal for Bravery)
*Magyar Népköztársaság Érdemérem arany fokozat*a (Medal of the Merit of Hungarian People's Republic, Golden Class)
Magyar Koronás Ezüst Érdemérem hadiszalagon a kardokkal (Hungarian Silver Medal with the Holy Crown on war ribbon with swords)
Magyar Koronás Érdemérem (Hungarian Medal with the Holy Crown)
Magyar Tiszti Arany Vitézségi Érem (Hungarian Officer's Gold Medal for Bravery)
Nemzetvédelmi Kereszt (National Defense Cross)
Tiszti Szolgálati Jel (Officer Service Decoration)
Tűzkereszt I fokozata a, kardokkal és koszorúval (Fire Cross 1st Class with swords and wreath)

Further decorations

Bátorsági Érem – Medal for Courage, also *Magyar Arany Bátorsági Érem* (Hungarian Golden Medal for Courage)
*Kossuth-díj ezüst fokozat*a (Silver Grade of the Kossuth Prize)
Népi Repülésért Érdemjelvény (Medal of Merit for the People's Aviation)

Others expressions

(in alphabetical order)
alreáliskola – elementary level military cadet school
B listázás (B-listing) – a compilation of names during the Communist regime in Hungary, containing those persons who were deemed unfaithful to the system or otherwise sentenced for dismissal from jobs and other forms of negative discrimination
altábornagy – Lieutenant General
hadapród – cadet
cőger – military personnel who is a student in a military high school
delo – file, a basic classification unit within a fond (Russian)

fejedelem – prince
fond – document collection, record group; a basic organizational unit of archival materials
főreáliskola – secondary level military cadet school
hadiszalag - war ribbon
hadidíszítménnyel/hadiékítményekkel – with military decorations
hadiműszaki törzskar – staff engineers
karpaszományos – high school graduate
Kárpátalja (Zakarpattia Oblast) a territory in the former North-Eastern sections of Hungary that was lost with the Treaty of Trianon and was annexed to Hungary in the First Vienna Award, then the remaining sections were seized back by the Hungarian Armed Forces in 1939
kilövés (*Herausschuss*, HSS, or 'shoot out')
levente – paramilitary youth organization in Hungary
munkástanács – workers' committee: during the 1956 revolution, workers in factories, plants and workshops united and formed such organizations to represent themselves instead of Communist organizations doing the same
muszka – the Soviets or Russians, in Hungarian (military) jargon
nemes ('noble'), as from the ranks of the nobility, either born or the nobility being bestowed upon the person for his/her merits
nemzetőr – armed militiaman during the Hungarian Revolution of 1956
nyilaskereszt – Arrow Cross, the symbol of a extreme right wing nationalist party in Hungary
opis – inventory; unpublished inventory of a fond, a list of *dela* (pl. *delo*) a basic finding aid
páncélos zászlós – armored ensign
Planquadrat – *Plq.*, German map code unit
polgári iskola – state civic school, non military based institution
Repülő csapatminősítés – Aviation Unit Qualification (document)
tisztjelölt – officer candidate
vezérezredes – General
zubó (*zuhanóbombázó*) – dive bomber

List of Hungarian Organisations and Institutions

In alphabetical order (Hungarian)

I repülőtér-gondnokság (I Airfield Logistics Board)
II Magyar Központi Katonai Temető (2nd Central Hungarian Military Cemetery)
II Rákóczi Ferenc Reáliskolai Nevelőintézet (Royal Hungarian 'II Rákóczi Ferenc' Honvéd Military Cadet School)
18 kiegészítő parancsnokság (18th Auxiliary Command)
Állambiztonsági Szolgálatok Történeti Levéltára (Historical Archives of the Hungarian State Security)
Államvédelmi Hatóság (*ÁVH*, State Protection Authority)
Árpád Reálgimnázium (Árpád High School – now an obsolete term)
Aszfaltozó és Kövező Vállalat (Asphalt and Gravelworks Company)
Bonyhádi Evangélikus Reálgimnázium (Evangelical High School in Bonyhád)
Budapest Székesfőváros Közlekedési Részvénytársaság (*BSZKRT*, Budapest Public Transport Plc.)
Budapest Főváros Levéltára (Budapest City Archives)
Budapesti Katonai Törvényszék (Military Tribunal at Budapest)
Budapesti Műszaki és Gazdaságtudományi Egyetem (Budapest University of Technology and Economy)
Budapesti Műszaki Egyetem, Vízépítéstani Tanszék (Department of Hydraulic Engineering at the Budapest University of Technology)
Budapesti Piarista Gimnázium (Piarist High School in Budapest)
Ciszterci Rend Nagy Lajos Gimnáziuma ('Nagy Lajos' High School of the Cistercian order)
Délvidéki Aero Club (Southern Hungarian Aero Club)
Dunántúli Református Egyházkerület Pápai Főiskolája (College of the Reformed Church of the Transdanubian Diocese at Pápa)
Eötvös József Gimnázium és Kollégium (József Eötvös High School in Tata, another high school bears the same name in Budapest)
Érseki Katolikus Gimnázium (Archiepiscopal Catholic High School).
Ganz Villamossági Gyár (Ganz Electric Factory)
Forgácsoló Szerszámok Gyára (Metal Cutting Machinery Factory)
Független Kisgazda-, Földmunkás és Polgári Párt (Independent Smallholders, Agrarian Workers and Civic Party)
Gróf Széchenyi István Katolikus Gimnázium (Gróf István Széchenyi Catholic High School)
Gyulai Római Katolikus Gimnázium (Roman Catholic High School in Gyula)

Gyűjtőfogház (Budapest Strict and Medium Regime Prison)
HM Hadtörténeti Intézet és Múzeum (*HM HIM*, Museum and Institution of Military History)
HM Hadtörténeti Intézet és Múzeum Fotóarchívuma, Hadtörténelmi Levéltára és Központi Irattára (Photographic Archives, Military History Archives and Central Record Office of the Institute and Museum of Military History)
HM Személyzeti Osztálya (Human Resource Department of the Ministry of Defence, Budapest)
Honvédségi Közlönyök és Rendeletek (Személyes ügyek) (Army Bulletin and Regulations, Personal Matters)
Horthy Miklós Nemzeti Repülő Alap (*HMNRA*, Miklós Horthy National Aviation Fund)
Hunnia Filmstúdió (Hunnia Film Company)
Hunyadi Mátyás Reáliskolai Nevelőintézet (Mátyás Hunyadi Military Cadet School)
Igazságügyi és Szakértői Kutató Intézetek (*ISZKI*, Network of Forensic Science Institutes)
Kassai Repülőakadémia (Aviation Academy at Kassa Hungary - Kassa is today Košice, Slovakia)
Kerkápoly Károly Felsőkereskedelmi Iskola (Károly Kerkápoly High School of Commerce)
Kilián György Repülő Hajózó Tiszti Iskola (György Kilián Officers' Flight Technical College)
Kinizsi Pál Honvéd Altisztképző és Nevelőintézet (Pál Kinizsi Honvéd Non-Commissioned Officer Training School at Jutas)
Kinizsi Sportközpont (Kinizsi National Sports Club)
Magyar Aero Szövetség (Hungarian Aero League)
Magyar Ásványolaj és Földgáz Kísérleti Intézet (Hungarian Oil & Gas Research Institute)
Magyar Királyi Államépítészeti Hivatal (Royal Hungarian Bureau of Architecture)
Magyar Királyi 'Csaba királyfi' Honvéd Gyors-fegyvernemi Hadapródiskola (Royal Hungarian 'Prince Csaba' Rapid Reaction Forces Cadet School)
Magyar Képzőművészeti Akadémia (Hungarian Academy of Fine Arts)
Magyar Köztársaság Legfelsőbb Bírósága (Supreme Court of the Hungarian Republic)
Magyar Nemzeti Levéltár (National Archives of Hungary)
Magyar–Szovjet Polgári Légiforgalmi Részvénytársaság (*Maszovlet*, Hungarian-Soviet Civil Air Transport Joint Stock Company)
Magyar Waggon- és Gépgyár (*MWG*, Hungarian Wagon and Machine Factory)
Malért (Hungarian airlines, predecessor of *Maszovlet*)
Mátravidéki Fémművek (Mátra Iron Works)
Mélyépítő Teherfuvarozó Vállalat (Civil Engineering Construction and Transport Company)
Magyar Országos Véderő Egylet Repülő Osztály (*MOVERO*, Hungarian Defence Association Aviation Department)
Műegyetemi Sportrepülő Egyesület (*MSE*, Poytechnic University's Sports Aviation Group)
Nemzeti Emlékhely és Kegyeleti Bizottság (National Memorial and Piety Committee)
Nemzeti Számonkérés Szervezete (National Impeachment Organization).
Nemzeti Szakértői és Kutató Központ (*NSZKK*, Hungarian Institute for Forensic Sciences)
Néphadsereg (Hungarian People's Army)
Népi Repülésért Érdemjelvény (Medal of Merit for the People's Aviation)
Pápai Református Kollégium (Reformed College at Pápa)
Piarista Általános Iskola, Gimnázium és Kollégium in Kecskemét (Piarist Elementary School, High School and Boarding School)
piarista Gróf Esterházy Miklós Reálgimnázium (Gróf Miklós Esterházy Piarist High School)
Repülő Kísérleti Intézet (*RKI,* Aviation Experimental Institute)

Repülőgép és Motorszerelő Szakiskola (*REMOSZ*, Aircraft and Engine Mechanic School)
Somssich Pál Gimnázium (Pál Somssich High School)
Szent István Felsőkereskedelmi Fiúiskola (Szent István Boy's School of Commerce)
Szombathelyi Erdészeti Zrt. (Szombathely Forestry Plc.)
Táncsics Mihály Gimnázium (Táncsics Mihály High School)
Új köztemető (New Public Cemetery of Budapest)
Veszprémi Piarista Gimnázium (Veszprém Piarist High School)
Weiss Manfréd Repülőgép- és Motorgyár (Manfred Weiss Aircraft and Engine Factory)
Zrínyi Miklós Reáliskolai Nevelőintézet (Royal Hungarian 'Zrínyi Miklós' Honvéd Military Cadet School)

Branches of the National Archives in Hungary

MNL Vas Megyei Levéltára (National Archives, Vas County Archives)
MNL Zala Megye Levéltára (National Archives, Zala County Archives)
MNL Borsod-Abaúj-Zemplén Megye Levéltára (National Archives, Borsod-Abaúj-Zemplén County Archives)
MNL Győr-Moson-Sopron Megye Győri Levéltára (National Archives, Győr-Moson-Sopron County Archives at Győr)
MNL Csongrád Megye Hódmezővásárhelyi Levéltára (National Archives, Csongrád Country Archives at Hódmezővásárhely)
MNL Szabolcs-Szatmár-Bereg Megye Levéltára (National Archives, Szabolcs-Szatmár-Bereg County Archives)
MNL Jász-Nagykun-Szolnok Megye Levéltára (National Archives, Jász-Nagykun-Szolnok County Archives)
MNL Hajdú-Bihar Megye Levéltára (National Archives, Hajdú-Bihar County Archives)
MNL Baranya Megye Levéltára (National Archives, Baranya County Archives)
MNL Bács-Kiskun Megye Levéltára (National Archives, Bács-Kiskun County Archives)
MNL Veszprém Megye Levéltára (National Archives, Veszprém County Archives)
MNL Fejér Megyei Levéltára (National Archives, Fejér County Archives)
MNL Tolna Megye Levéltára (National Archives, Tolna County Archives)

Fighter Aces With More Than 20 Air Victories

ZÁSZLÓS VITÉZ[1] DEZSŐ SZENTGYÖRGYI

Number of aerial victories: 30 (+5)
Successes against ground targets: 10+ vehicles, 10+ sleighs and carts, a number of guns, and numerous further targets
Number of flown combat sorties: 220 (20 or 22 against Americans)
Number of hours flown in the air force: 1,400
Nickname: *Dezske*
Identification number: 1741-15-0004

Decorations

- *Magyar Érdemrend lovagkeresztje hadiszalagon a kardokkal* (1 November 1944)
- *Magyar Koronás Ezüst Érdemérem hadiszalagon a kardokkal* (16 January 1945)
- *Magyar Koronás Bronz Érdemérem hadiszalagon a kardokkal* (25 April 1945)
- *Magyar Nagy Ezüst Vitézségi Érem* (11 September 1943)
- *Magyar Kis Ezüst Vitézségi Érem* (18 April 1939)
- *Magyar Kis Ezüst Vitézségi Érem* for the second time (19 December 1942)
- *Magyar Kis Ezüst Vitézségi Érem* for the third time (25 April 1943)
- *Magyar Bronz Vitézségi Érem* (12 October 1943)
- *Tűzkereszt I fokozata a kardokkal és koszorúval*, with one wound clasp
- *Felvidéki Emlékérem*
- *Erdélyi Emlékérem*
- *Délvidéki Emlékérem*
- German Iron Cross 1st Class (17 March 1945)
- German Iron Cross 2nd Class (12 January 1943)[2]

1 The Hungarian *Vitézi Rend* (Knightly Order of Vitéz) was founded in 1920 to reward outstanding soldiers for their performance in the First World War; and later in the Second World War as well. '*Vitéz*' means 'valiant' in English. There were different award requirements for officers, non-commissioned officers and privates for this title.

2 The actual award of the decoration took place on 13 March 1943 in Poltava. A surviving awarding document (belonging to his comrade, who was decorated at the same time, *zászlós* Ottó Lukács) gives the date as 12 January 1943; therefore, as this event was a mass decoration, Dezső Szentgyörgyi probably received the Iron Cross 2nd Class on the same day. Stenge, '70 éve történt: Az első magyar Messerschmitt pilóta', p. 33.

- Gold *Frontflugspange* with the 200-pennant (20 April 1945)

Victories

No.	Date	Aircraft	Location
1	26 June 1943	Yak-1 (Yak-7B)	Graznoye SW
2	7 July 1943	La-5	Belgorod–Volchansk
–	20 July 1943	Soviet single-engine	
3	3 August 1943 at 07:30	Il-2	Belgorod W
4	3 August 1943 at 17:00	La-5	Chuguyev S
–	3 August 1943	La-5	
5	4 August 1943	Pe-2	Belgorod S–SE
6	4 August 1943	La-5	Kharkhiv NW, Udi
–	5 August 1943	Soviet fighter	
–	6 August 1943	Soviet single-engine	
–	7 August 1943	Soviet single-engine	
7	14 June 1944	P-38	Vérteskozma
8	27 June 1944	P-51	Győr (Márianosztra N, Nagyirtáspuszta)
9	2 July 1944	B-24	Etyek–Ödönmajor
10	16 July 1944	B-24	Gálos (Gols, Austria)
11	27 July 1944	B-24	Oroszlány
12	22 August 1944	B-24	Zalaerdőd N
13	13 November 1944 at 14:48	Yak-9	Jászkisér N
14	16 November 1944	Il-2	Apatin
15	8 December 1944	Yak-9	Érd, Martonvásár
16	20 December 1944 at 10:00	Il-2	Meggyespuszta
17	4 January 1945	La-5	Bicske SE
18	8 January 1945	La-5	Szabadbattyán
19	18 January 1945	La-5 (Il-2?)	Aba E
20	18 January 1945	Il-2	Polgárdi E
21	28 January 1945	Yak-9	Kiskunlacháza
22	30 January 1945	Yak-9	Buda N (S?)
23	12 February 1945	Il-2	Budapest NW
24	9 March 1945 at 14:36	Yak-9	Káloz (Sárbogárd NW)
25	11 March 1945 at 14:40	La-5	Seregélyes E (Sárbogárd E)
26	19 March 1945 at 15:15	Il-2	Nádasdladány N
27	19 March 1945 at 15:46	La-5	Balatonfűzfő, Ságvár
28	20 March 1945 at 12:00	La-7	Sárkeresztes NW
29	23 March 1945 at 11:34	Yak-3	Tarján NE
30	16 April 1945 at 13:05	Yak-9	Hofstetten E (Guttenbrunn)

Hours flown in the Hungarian Air Force, by year

1935: 30; 1936: 20; 1937: 30; 1938: 100; 1939: 90; 1940: 100; 1941: 120; 1942: 180; 1943: 250; 1944: 350; 1945: 130[3]

Aircraft types flown in the Hungarian Air Force
Hungária, Udet, WM 10, Heinkel HD 22, Fokker CVD, Fw 56, Fiat CR.30, Fiat CR.32, Bü 131, Ar 96 (A, B), Re.2000 (Italian, Hungarian), Bf 108, Levente II, Fw 58, Bf 109 (F-4, G-2-4-6-10-14)

Aircraft types flown after the war in civilian aviation
Po-2, Li-2, Il-14, Il-18[4]

Aircraft flown
Re.2000: V.444 (20 August 1942), Bf 109 F-4: V-07 (winter of 1942–43), Bf 109 G-14/U4: W-115 (9 December 1944), W-092 (1 January 1945), W-177 (end of December 1944–very early January 1945), Bf 109 G-10/U4: 'Yellow 1' (27 March 1945)

Dezső Szentgyörgyi was born on 6 January 1915 in a small village, Kőkúttapazd, in Somogy County. The village was at that time part of the nearby Hencse, and only became independent in 1925 (its name today is Kőkút).[5] His birth name was Dezső Szánti, but he and his father changed their name to Szentgyörgyi in 1924.[6] This change of name to a more Hungarian-sounding version took place at his father's admitting ceremony into the Hungarian *Vitézi Rend*: he was a *őrmester* serving in the k.u.k. 48th Infantry Regiment in the First World War and had shown exceptional bravery on the Italian front, for which he received a number of military decorations. This earned him the title *vitéz*, which was also inherited by his son (his son graduated as *vitéz* in 1934). The new family name was inspired by the Szent György hill in the Tapolca Basin. At this time the family was already living in Enying, where his father worked as a shopkeeper, and where Dezső Szentgyörgyi lost his mother in a tragic traffic accident. After the second marriage of his father his only brother, Kálmán, was born.[7] Originally, Dezső Szentgyörgyi trained to be a locksmith, as the family financial situation did not allow him to attend higher education. Later, when their financial situation improved, his brother was able to attend high school; in Dezső's case, high school graduation was left until after the end of the war. In 1969, he gave an interview celebrating his 5,000,000th completed kilometer in the air. During the interview, he summarized what started him off in the direction of aviation:

3 Dezső Szentgyörgyi's flight service logs and flight logs after 1945 (full copies owned by the author).
4 Dezső Szentgyörgyi's flight service logs and flight logs.
5 *MNL Somogy Megyei Levéltára* (National Archives, Somogy County Archives), XXXIII/1, Kadarkút state birth registry from 1915, counterpart, acc. nr. note 4.
6 *MNL Somogy Megyei Levéltára*, XXXIII/1 Kadarkút state birth registry from 1915, counterpart, acc. nr. note 4, post-notes 1/1925 and 7/1936, based on Home Secretary Regulation 94988/1924, nr. IX.
7 The son of Kálmán Szentgyörgyi (Enying, 9 October 1921–Szekszárd, 2 July 2011), György Szentgyörgyi, is also a professional aircraft pilot, who flew with MALÉV from 1996 until the company's bankruptcy in 2012. At present, he is the captain of a Boeing 737 CL with ASL Airlines Hungary Kft. For the family, see Kálmán Szentgyörgyi, *Pilóták egy családban* (Szekszárd: Babits Kiadó, 2000).

> It all began with Lindbergh flying across the ocean. … When I was a kid, my only goal in life was to become a professional football player. There were quite a number of encouraging signs in this direction … but the desire to fly spread through my veins like a poison … and it was so efficient that I have never been able to free myself from its effects – nor do I want to do that! One can't live without aircraft, without aviation.[8]

In Dezső Szentgyörgyi's life, the love of football and sports has remained beyond his love of aviation, and he won a number of medals in sports competitions within the army for football and athletics.

When he was 18, Dezső Szentgyörgyi enlisted in the Royal Hungarian Air Force at the airfield of Székesfehérvár-Sóstó. He took the military oath on 3 September 1933, and on 5 October he had been entered among the personnel of the then-secret air force as 'aviation sub-assistant' (the denomination of the rank or private during the time of the Hungarian air force's secret period – it lasted from the Treaty of Trianon, which forbade the military aviation to Hungary completely until the autumn of 1938). He worked until 1935 as an aircraft and engine mechanic after obtaining qualifications at the *Repülőgép és Motorszerelő Szakiskola* (or *REMOSZ*, the Aircraft and Engine Mechanic School). Naturally, he was later able to exploit his acquired skills. At the beginning of 1935, he began his pilot training (which he completed in 1938), as well as Air Force non-commissioned officer training, with excellent results.[9] On completion of his fighter training, he started his official pilot service on 1 May 1938 in the 1/2 *'Ludas Matyi'* Fighter Squadron, which was equipped with CR.32s and stationed at Székesfehérvár-Börgönd. It was led by *százados* István Tímár.

He took part in frontier patrolling missions with his unit during the autumn of 1938, and on 24 March 1939 experienced his first combat. Along with the rest of his squadron, he was part of the escort of Ju 86 bombers raiding Spišská Nová Ves. He received his first military medal for this mission, a *Magyar Kis Ezüst Vitézségi Érem*. (The March 1939 combat missions were later not counted as part of actual number of combat sorties flown by the concerned pilots, the author just added this particular mission to the total number of combat sorties flown by Szentgyörgyi till the end of the Second World War.)[10]

Throughout constant relocations and reorganizations, he served in Szolnok from 1 September 1939. When war broke out with the Soviet Union at the end of June 1941, 1/I Fighter Group – still equipped with the obsolete CR .32s and before the re-equipping to Re.2000 *Héja* – relocated to Felsőábrány (today Bükkábrány) to defend the industrial sites around Diósgyőr before returning to Szolnok. During these operations, Szentgyörgyi was assigned to 1/1 *'Dongó'* Fighter Squadron, under its commander *főhadnagy* Zoltán Kiss.

In 1942, his squadron was relocated to the Eastern Front to support the Hungarian 2nd Army. When their deployment was decided, the Deputy Regent, reserve *főhadnagy* István Horthy, also asked to be served with this squadron and joined the squadron in May. The 1 Fighter Group supporting the army consisted of the staff and 1/1 Squadron of the Szolnok Group, along with 2/1 Fighter Squadron from Kolozsvár (today Cluj-Napoca, Romania). Because of the service of the Deputy Regent, the leadership of the unit had been transferred from the earlier group commander

8 'A megtett út hossza: 5,000,000km', *Ország-Világ*, 3 December 1969, p. 15.
9 *HM HIM Központi Irattár* (Central Record Office, *HM HIM KI*), document folder nr. 33104.
10 Stenge, *Baptism of Fire*, p. 136.

Pilots of 1/2 '*Ludas Matyi*' Fighter Squadron on 5 April 1939, on the airfield at Székesfehérvár-Börgönd, in front of one of their CR.32s. Third from the left is Dezső Szentgyörgyi and second from the right is László Pottyondy, the two prospective aces. The commander of the squadron, *százados* István Tímár (1902–1944), fifth from the right, was killed on the ground on 19 November 1944 during an American strafing attack in Devecser. At the time of his death, he was already *őrnagy*. (From the author's collection)

The table of the non-commissioned officer school with the candidates who completed the courses run between 1936 and 1938. The portrait of Dezső Szentgyörgyi can be seen on the right side, the outer portrait in the second row. Above him on the left is Imre Harangi (1913–1979), champion in lightweight boxing at the Berlin Olympics in 1936. (From the collection of the Harangi family)

at Szolnok, *százados* Mátyás Szabó, to *vezérkari őrnagy* Kálmán Csukás, and the command of 1/1 Squadron has been transferred from Zoltán Kiss to *százados* Mátyás Szabó. Kálmán Csukás chose Szentgyörgyi as his wingman, has he had already served as a wingman for *főhadnagy* György Bánlaky, the deputy commander for 1/1 Squadron. A squadron strength unit of the group took off for the Eastern Front on 1 July 1942, in which Szentgyörgyi took part. They arrived at Konotop on 2 July, and next day were deployed to their military airfield south of Kursk. *Őrmester* Szentgyörgyi flew his first combat sortie on 8 July 1942, and the 10th as early as 20th July: *vezérkari őrnagy* Kálmán Csukás tried to complete as many missions as possible and fly more hours than anyone else, so Szentgyörgyi, his wingman, flew more than the other pilots of his unit.[11]

Szakaszvezető Dezső Szentgyörgyi in April 1939, in the company of *százados* István Tímár and *őrmester* László Antal, in front of a Fiat CR.32 fighter aircraft (the V.114) of 1/2 '*Ludas Matyi*' Fighter Squadron. (From the author's collection)

Among the combat sorties he completed during this period were the two missions undertaken on 18 July covering the Hungarian troops (mainly 1 Field Armored Division) that were eliminating the Uriv–Storozhevoye bridgehead. For the day's successful combat activities, Szentgyörgyi received a laudatory document from the commander of the division, *altábornagy* Lajos Veress.

Szentgyörgyi shot down his first aircraft on 7 August 1942 on his 18th *Héja* sortie, but this was a fairly unpleasant incident. While escorting *vezérkari őrnagy* Csukás, they were patrolling their own lines when they spotted three twin-engined bombers who immediately opened fire on them. Csukás led his element into attack, and his wingman shot down one of the bombers, which crash-landed beyond the Hungarian lines at Korotoyak. Szentgyörgyi's *Héja* was also damaged in the air combat. The shot-down aircraft, however, was not a Soviet bomber aircraft but a Heinkel He 111 H-6 (WNr. [German serial number] 7578) of the German 7./KG 27. The aircraft suffered 50 percent damage, and two of its crew were wounded: *Unteroffizier* Franz Bartsch, the aircraft mechanic, and *Unteroffizier* Alois Kriegel, a gunner. The aircraft – whose aircrew reported that they had been attacked by three Soviet fighters, and had shot down one – was later flown back to Kursk, and the unpleasant incident was resolved with an apology. This incident luckily proved no threat or hindering force to Szentgyörgyi's military career. It is particularly interesting to note that, even though the real cause was immediately revealed, the German reports explained the damage inflicted on the aircraft as '*Jägerbeschuss*' – an attack by an enemy fighter – and not as '*Beschuss durch eigener Jäger*' – an attack by own fighter – which was usual for reporting such cases (which were absolutely not uncommon).[12]

11 Log excerpts of 1/1 Fighter Squadron compiled by *százados* Ujszászy (owned by the author). The mission data regarding 1/1 Fighter Squadron is always taken from the above source, even if it has not been noted elsewhere.

12 Bundesarchiv-Militärarchiv, RL 2 III/762/226.

Őrmester Dezső Szentgyörgyi with one of his comrades in front of his Focke-Wulf Fw 56 Stösser (the G.125). This aircraft was used for combat training and exercise purposes by the Hungarian fighters. The photograph was probably taken in 1940. (From the collection of the Szentgyörgyi family)

Dezső Szentgyörgyi – on the far left – jokingly wears his cap in reverse with three of his non-commissioned officer comrades in July 1941, at Felsőábrány (today: Bükkábrány) airfield. (From the author's collection)

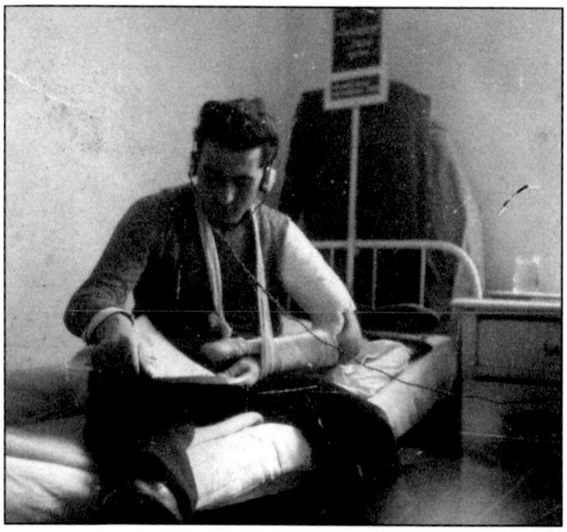

Dezső Szentgyörgyi broke his arm in a ground accident at the beginning of 1942. The picture shows him killing idle time by reading and listening to the radio. (From the collection of the Szentgyörgyi family)

Dezső Szentgyörgyi in Szolnok, next to the hangar, probably in 1942. (From the collection of the Szentgyörgyi family)

Five days later Szentgyörgyi completed his 20th combat sortie, and completed his 25th on 23 August. In the meantime, the Deputy Regent crashed with his plane on 20th August and died; after this, Kálmán Csukás appeared at the unit on fewer and fewer occasions, so Szentgyörgyi did not fly with him anymore. Szentgyörgyi then found himself for the first time in firing position dead astern to a Soviet aircraft on a mission during the second half of August. The Soviet long-range reconnaissance aircraft were fairly active in the region – as were the German–Hungarian units – but intercepting them was difficult due to the limited performance of the *Héja*. On this occasion, Szentgyörgyi succeeded in getting into firing position dead astern to the Soviet long-range reconnaissance aircraft at an altitude of 6,500 meters; however, he had to disengage from the air combat a few moments later because the Soviet gunner hit the propeller of his aircraft.[13]

M. kir. 1. honvéd páncélos hadosztály parancsnokság.
60./21. szám.
egl.-1942.

A Szovjet elleni hadjárat során
vitéz Szentgyörgyi Dezső
az 1. V. repülő osztály állományába tartozó ht. őrmestert
a julius 18.-i Uryw-i ütközetben
az ellenség előtt tanusitott vitéz magatartásáért
páncélos hadosztály parancsnoki dicsérő elismerésben részesítem.
Tábori posta, 241/01 1942. évi augusztus hó 6.-án.

páncélos hadosztály parancsnok.

The laudatory certificate for Dezső Szentgyörgyi from the commander of the Hungarian 1 Field Armored Division, *altábornagy* Lajos Veress, for the covering missions on 18 July 1942 during the first battle at the Uriv–Storozhevoye bridgehead. A similar certificate was also given to another ace, *hadnagy* Imre Pánczél. (From the collection Szentgyörgyi family)

He took a brief period of leave in September, and shortly after his return to the troops in October he was relocated from Ilovskoye to Stary Oskol for a brief retraining course to fly Messerschmitt Bf 109 F-4s. Following this, 1/1 Squadron was deployed as a fighter-bomber unit. Up to the deployment, Szentgyörgyi had flown 28 sorties with the *Héja*. He completed his first sortie mission in his new modern aircraft on 25 October, and on 27 October he also completed his first fighter-bomber mission using four 50kg bombs carried in the racks under the fuselage of the aircraft.

Over the following period, the main task of the squadron was to support directly the ground troops. On 1 December, Szentgyörgyi was promoted to *törzsőrmester*. Six days later the unit was relocated to the Rossosh airfield and actively supported the combat activities of Italian 8th Army. Szentgyörgyi completed his 50th combat sortie on 12 December. Around this time an incident happened: at 09:00 in the morning he scrambled to engage a Soviet long-range reconnaissance aircraft flying over the airfield, but even before he could reach the enemy twin-engined aircraft his engine failed and he had to crash-land near Starobilsk in deep snow.[14]

13 Béla Nagy, 'Egy magyar vadászrepülő leküzdi a balszerencsét', *Egyedül vagyunk*, 25 February 1944, p. 7.
14 Nagy, 'Egy magyar vadászrepülő leküzdi a balszerencsét', p. 7.

During January and February in 1943, when the Hungarian 2nd Army had suffered serious losses during the Soviet offensive, Szentgyörgyi completed 10 combat sorties – two in January and eight in February – during which he destroyed one artillery piece, four vehicles and eight sleighs.[15]

In March, the squadron supported the combat activities around Kharkhiv. This city and its surroundings were successfully recaptured by the Germans; following this, the Hungarian fighters also moved to this area. One of the comrades of Szentgyörgyi in the squadron, János Kőhalmy (promoted to *főhadnagy* on 1 May 1943, who was in the same class with László Máthé and László Pajtás and who was killed on 16 June 1944 in a dogfight with the Americans) recalled one of the characteristic missions in March:

> During the offensive toward Kharkhiv, we were strafing a column at low altitudes and destroying sleighs. At once, one of our friends, Sándor Tarnay [*őrmester* Sándor Tarnay, killed on 9 May 1943 when his wingman collided with him], informed us via radio that right ahead of us there was Soviet artillery marching forward. The weather was foggy, and most of the terrain below was covered with snow. Here and there patches of forested areas could be seen. I had not seen the artillery, and therefore asked Sándor to go and attack them. His aircraft flew past mine and I finally spotted the *muszka*. I ordered at once:
>
> 'Into formation! Attack in right echelon!'
>
> The Soviet soldiers jumped off their artillery guns and horses and ran away in every direction. I opened fire on the horses of the first gun and, in the heat of that intense moment, I did not realize that a few brave Russians were shooting at us while standing or lying on their backs. ... This mate [*törzsőrmester* Dezső Szentgyörgyi] was, however, watchful; flying in directly above ground, he killed the most dangerous Russian that was threatening me. My other two flight member attacked the next two guns in the meantime. Then, with a sharp turn back, we swept the confused artillery column again with our machine guns. I was almost laughing when I saw that one of the Russians was fleeing on horseback and one of us had hit the horse. It jumped suddenly, and the Soviet soldier just flew from its back and fell to the ground with a spectacular thud.[16]

Törzsőrmester Dezső Szentgyörgyi with a comrade (probably his chief mechanic) in front of his Messerschmitt Bf 109 F-4 fighter aircraft (the V-07) at the beginning of 1943. (From the collection of the Szentgyörgyi family)

Dezső Szentgyörgyi in the cockpit of the V-07. (From the collection of the Szentgyörgyi family)

15 *HM HIM HL*, documents of the 2nd Army, box nr. 17, log excerpts of 1/1 Fighter Squadron from 1 January to 28 February 1943. Based on data summarized by the author.

16 Gyula Kádár, *Sasok harca* (Budapest: Magyar Repülő Sajtóvállalat, 1943), pp. 81–82.

Freshly decorated airmen from the 1/1 Squadron at Poltava, 13 March 1943. From left to right: *hadnagy* János Kőhalmy, *zászlós* Ottó Lukács, *főhadnagy* György Bánlaky and *törzsőrmester* Dezső Szentgyörgyi. Kőhalmy, Lukács and Szentgyörgyi also received their Iron Crosses 2nd Class on this day. (From the collection of the Lukács family)

After the recapture of Kharkhiv, the intensity of fighting subsided and the squadron flew fewer ground support missions. Other types of missions, mostly bomber escort, were more frequent. At the end of April, the retraining of the group staff and the other squadron (5/I Group Staff and 5/2 Fighter Squadron) to fly Messerschmitts came to an end and they joined Szentgyörgyi's squadron.

Szentgyörgyi completed his last fighter-bomber mission on 9 June; he had by then completed more than 30 fighter-bomber combat sorties.[17]

The most difficult problem for Szentgyörgyi was that the Soviet aircraft seemed to avoid him throughout the spring. At last, in the early summer, during an escort mission with German dive bombers, he met Soviet La-5s, but came into firing position from astern of one of the Soviet aircraft in vain as one of the other members of the mixed escort, a German aircraft, was swifter and shot down the Soviet opponent first. Szentgyörgyi was frustrated because his long front-line service seemed pointless and ineffective in the absence of air victories; he therefore requested to be replaced by his squadron commander, *százados* György Ujszászy (who started to fly combat sorties at the end of April) at the beginning of summer 1943. He felt that he was not a worthy descendant of the famous Hungarian fighter aces of the First World War and that he was not worthy of the title of *vitéz* inherited from his father.[18] His squadron commander, however, talked extensively with Szentgyörgyi and finally convinced him to stay.

The situation soon changed. On the morning of 26 June 1943, Szentgyörgyi was escorting the Hungarian 4/1 Bomber Squadron's five Ju 88 dive bombers with *szakaszvezető* Fábián on a raid against the Graznoye fighter airfield 42km east of Belgorod. This was his 92nd combat sortie. He later recalled this particular action:

> The bomber formation was raiding Graznoye airfield approximately 40km from the front. A very heavy anti-aircraft fire greeted them. One or two minutes after the bombing ended,

17 Excerpts from the logs of 1/1 Fighter Squadron.
18 Nagy, 'Egy magyar vadászrepülő leküzdi a balszerencsét', p. 7.

> eight or 10 Yak-1 type Soviet fighters engaged our bombers. After a short air combat, I shot down the first Soviet fighter from the back of one of our bombers. The pilot bailed out; the aircraft was burning out. I engaged another attacking enemy fighter, and when the Russian tried to flee with a sharp right turn, *szakaszvezető* F finished him so perfectly that the Soviet aircraft went into a spin and crashed with its pilot. After that, one of the Soviet fighters attacked me from dead astern, but the *szakaszvezető* chased him away with his accurate fire.[19]

It would be useful to elaborate on Szentgyörgyi's first real air combat in a little more detail. The target, the Graznoye airfield, had earlier been a Soviet fighter airfield, but at this time it was empty and serving as a decoy airfield (the Soviets have always been masters of military deception, or '*maskirovka*'). The attacking fighters were Yak-7B type aircraft of 508th IAP, and two aces of the unit, Vasiliy Pavlovich Mikhalev and Alexander Vasilievich Gaidukov, reported shooting down one bomber each (the former scored a total of 23 individual and 16 shared victories during the war and received the title of Hero of the Soviet Union; the latter scored eight individual and 13 shared victories).[20]

In reality, the Soviet fighters succeeded in shooting down one Hungarian Ju 88 bomber, from which the observer – the badly wounded *zászlós* Tibor Sármási and the aircraft mechanic *őrmester* Béla Karácsony – were able to bail out over Soviet territory; both became prisoners of war.

According to data collected by the author, only Sármási returned home after the war badly wounded: his left arm had been hit a number of times and was partially paralyzed, the left side of his body was badly burned and he was almost completely blind in his left eye. He returned from captivity in 1947 a broken man, and after all this ordeal was sentenced to eight years in prison by the communist authorities following a show trial for spying in 1953. He spent six years in prison, and the innocently imprisoned man crippled in the war died in 1985. Karácsony suffered serious head injuries in the aircraft and lost consciousness a number of times during his short interrogation, according to the memories of Vasiliy Pavlovich Mikhalev, who was present. These injuries probably caused his death in captivity.[21]

It was most likely that one of their parachutes had been taken as a Soviet one by Szentgyörgyi, because no Soviet fighter aircraft were downed during the combat, although probably few were damaged (Gaidukov's for sure, whose wings were damaged by the machine gun fire of the Hungarian fighters).

As can clearly be seen from the detailed description of the event, it was extremely difficult to follow the actual fate of claimed aircraft in the chaos of air combat, and mistakes, overclaims and overconfirmations happened every day. It was also usual to mix up the different subtypes of Yakovlev fighters for each other.

Operation '*Zitadelle*', the German summer offensive in 1943, opened on 5 July, and the immense battle of Kursk began. From this time the number of Hungarian fighters' air victories also began to increase considerably.

19 Kádár, *Sasok harca*, p. 120.

20 For the two Soviet pilots, see Mihail Bikhov, *Sovetskie Asy 1941-1945. Pobedy Stalinskich sokolov* (Moscow: Eksmo, 2008), p. 106 (Gaidukov) and p. 346 (Mikhalev).

21 *HM HIM KI*, document folder nr. 107114; the interview of the widow of Tibor Sármási by the author (8 July 2004); recollections of V.P. Mikhalev (in possession of Dmitri Karlenko).

Törzsőrmester Szentgyörgyi with *főhadnagy* György Bánlaky, a short man, the provisional commander of 1/1 Fighter Squadron, in the spring of 1943 in front of the Hungarian Messerschmitt Bf 109 F-4 'Yellow 7'. (From the author's collection)

Szentgyörgyi took off on his 100th sortie on 7 July as a wingman of *főhadnagy* Tibor Papp. Their task was to cover the airspace over the German forces, thrusting forward toward the area of Belgorod–Volchansk. At first, they met two La-5s, one of which was shot down by *főhadnagy* Papp; then another Soviet Lavochkin element appeared, one of which was eliminated by *törzsőrmester* Szentgyörgyi. His opponent crashed to the ground among the armored fighting vehicles of the thrusting German column, who all testified to the victory.[22] During the remaining part of July, luck seemed to abandon Szentgyörgyi again and he did not succeed in scoring another confirmed air victory, even though on 20 July he reported having shot down an enemy aircraft on one of his sorties of that day. Soon after this, he was wounded, probably on 1 August 1943. On this day he flew three sorties. In the morning he flew deep within Soviet territory and engaged in air combat with five Boston bombers and their fighter escort; however, because his fuel was running dangerously low, he disengaged from combat without any apparent results. Early in the afternoon, on his second sortie, he again met a Soviet Boston, but it dived quickly into the cloud below them, and the opportunity was lost. On the third sortie, at 18:00 he took off in the direction of Izium for a free hunt. He flew at a low altitude of about 300 meters,

22 Nagy, 'Egy magyar vadászrepülő leküzdi a balszerencsét', p.7.

not knowing the Soviets had created a bridgehead a few kilometers north of Izium. He was therefore surprised by heavy anti-aircraft fire when he reached the Donets. He dived instantly, but was already too late. The starboard side of his aircraft was hit by shrapnel near the cockpit, wounding Szentgyörgyi himself on his right side.

Luckily, neither his wounds nor the damage to his aircraft was serious, and he brought his aircraft back to the airfield without problems. The few shrapnel pieces were removed by the medical staff; Szentgyörgyi got away with a moderate fever, and two days later he was again in the air.[23] This was the wound that earned him the wound clasp (*'sebesülési pánt'*) for his *Tűzkereszt*.

On August 3, the large-scale counterattack by the Soviets began in the southern sector, and the Hungarian fighters were especially active in the combat. The 1/1 Squadron flew 58 individual combat sorties – seven by Szentgyörgyi – resulting in intensive air combats. During the sorties that did not engage enemy aircraft, the Hungarians emptied their magazines in strafing runs on the Soviet units advancing forward.[24] During the day, Szentgyörgyi reported shooting down three enemy aircraft. This was the day on which he has scored his first Il-2 kill. In the morning, not much later than 07:00, west of Belgorod, with *főhadnagy* Tibor Papp, he stumbled upon a formation of 12 Soviet ground-attack aircraft. Szentgyörgyi immediately attacked the aircraft on the far right. He descended to the altitude of the trees and attacked from below, engaging the Soviet aircraft at close quarters; he managed to target the vulnerable oil cooler of the enemy aircraft and set it aflame; the aircraft turned upside down and crashed headlong into the ground. The second air victory of this day was scored in the afternoon, after 17:00, when Szentgyörgyi was covering a Hungarian Fw 189 from 3/1 Short-Range Reconnaissance Squadron south of Chuguyev. Szentgyörgyi noticed, while still flying over his own territory, that three La-5s are trying to attack the reconnaissance aircraft from below in accordance with their preferred method. Dezső Szentgyörgyi attacked the one on the right; the Soviet aircraft reacted by fleeing to a lower altitude, but when he pulled up his aircraft, Szentgyörgyi was only 30–40 meters behind him, and he shot him down with a short burst of cannon fire. The burning La-5 crashed into the ground in own territory; a German radio observer unit immediately reported the case and confirmed the kill.[25] On the same day, as a wingman of *százados* György Ujszászy to escort He 111s, Szentgyörgyi shot down yet another La-5 aircraft, although this kill was not confirmed by the Hungarian authorities in the absence of eyewitnesses. *Százados* Ujszászy was too preoccupied with the overwhelming Soviet force and did not see Szentgyörgyi's victim crashing (he himself had shot down a Soviet fighter, but this was not confirmed either). It might be possible that German bombers saw one or both of kills, but the author has not been able to find any evidence due to the destruction of the detailed German documents.

The next day, Szentgyörgyi officially reached ace status when four Bf 109 G-2s from the squadron were deployed from Kharkhiv-Voychenko to Varvarovka to establish better cooperation with the Germans. Szentgyörgyi flew three combat sorties this day, ending all three with strafing runs. During his morning sortie he was engaged in heavy combat with approximately a dozen Soviet fighter and ground-attack aircraft; however, there were only two fighters – Szentgyörgyi and his wingman, *őrmester* Károly Kereki – to counter them, so he was not able

23 Nagy, 'Egy magyar vadászrepülő leküzdi a balszerencsét', p. 7.
24 Excerpts from the logs of 1/1 Fighter Squadron.
25 Nagy, 'Egy magyar vadászrepülő leküzdi a balszerencsét', p. 7.

to score a victory. In the afternoon he had better luck. On his first afternoon sortie, he was meant to escort *zászlós* Sándor Hautzinger, but his engine did not start properly and delayed his takeoff, so by the time he got up into the air he saw neither the reported Soviet aircraft nor his element leader (who had taken off after a scramble to meet them). Flying at low altitudes south of Belgorod, he spotted 12 Soviet Pe-2 twin-engined bombers as they crossed the Donets river, which was serving as the front. The Soviet aircraft were right down, releasing their bombs on the German positions. Seeing the attackers, Szentgyörgyi pulled up and engaged the Pe-2 flying on the far left of the formation. He came in from astern and attacked the aircraft in the blind spot left of the vertical stabilizer. He opened fire at 100m from the three 2cm cannons and two machine guns of his Bf 109 G-2/R6 at the Soviet aircraft's wing root. He approached his victim to 10–15m; the port wing of the Soviet aircraft was engulfed in flames. It lurched to the side, plummeted and crashed into the ground on Soviet territory.[26] The victory – during which Szentgyörgyi's aircraft sustained a number of hits from the defending rear gunners of the Soviet formation – was confirmed by the commander of the German fighter aircraft element that arrived during the latest stage of the combat. This was, it seems, *Leutnant* Günther Kurz from II./JG 52. The Pe-2 aircraft shot down by Szentgyörgyi was probably from the 202nd BAD (2nd Air Army).[27]

Dezső Szentgyörgyi with Fábián '*Koponya*' in the summer of 1943 in Kharkhiv, in front of Szentgyörgyi's Messerschmitt Bf 109 G-2/R6 subtype aircraft. (From the collection of Szentgyörgyi family)

On his last sortie on this day – his 133rd – Szentgyörgyi was engaged as element leader in air combat 50km northwest of Kharkhiv, over Udi, during a mission covering German dive bombers. Four Hungarian Bf 109s flew together with the German fighter escort. The attackers had been cut off from the bombers by the escort, and when the Soviet aircraft turned back, Szentgyörgyi engaged the wingman of the second element of a formation of six Soviet La-5s from 3,000 meters. The rounds of the three cannons hitting the aircraft tore pieces out of the Soviet fighter; it burst in flame and crashed into the ground near Udi.[28]

Altogether, Szentgyörgyi flew eight further sorties over the next three days and was involved in air combat on all three of those days, reporting a victory against Soviet aircraft each day. These air victories, however, remained officially unconfirmed by the Hungarian authorities.

26 Nagy, 'Egy magyar vadászrepülő leküzdi a balszerencsét', p. 7.
27 Nagy, 'Egy magyar vadászrepülő leküzdi a balszerencsét', p. 7. The 21-year-old *Leutnant* Kurz was shot down on 11 October 1943 by an La-5 at Uzhin. Up to his death, this German pilot achieved 33 victories. For Günther Kurz, see Bernd Barbas, *Die Geschichte der II. Gruppe des Jagdgeschwaders 52* (Überlingen: Traditionsgemeinschaft JG 52, 2003), pp. 134, 314.
28 Nagy, 'Egy magyar vadászrepülő leküzdi a balszerencsét', p. 7.

His last two sorties were flown on 2 August, after which he received leave. In September, he was redeployed to Szolnok. With this, his front-line service on the Eastern Front ended, with 142 combat sorties and six confirmed air victories. Although the majority of this data is included in the surviving documents, two contemporary sources list seven air victories for Szentgyörgyi in this period. These were the 3 November 1943 issue of the field magazine *Üvölt a Puma* ('The Puma Howls'), which showed a summary of victories achieved so far on its front page; and an introduction to decorations issued on 9 September 1944. The author did not manage to identify this seventh aircraft. The squadron log contains five more claimed air victories for Szentgyörgyi, but just lists six confirmed air victories.[29] When he arrived home, he received his well-deserved *Magyar Nagy Ezüst Vitézségi Érem*.

Törzsőrmester Dezső Szentgyörgyi in the autumn of 1943, after he returned home from the frontline. (From the collection of Szentgyörgyi family)

Szentgyörgyi's squadron (withdrawn in the middle and in the second half of August) also returned with him to Szolnok, and the next few months were spent in relative calm until the spring of 1944 when the American air attacks against Hungary started. In the meantime, Szentgyörgyi completed the chief non-commissioned officer course and was promoted to *zászlóshelyettes* on 15 March 1944, with a rank backdated to 1 January.

As the American air raids started in April 1944, 101 Fighter Group was created on the Jutaspuszta airfield directly north of Veszprém from the scattered units deployed in various airfields. The group's 101/2 Squadron consisted of Szentgyörgyi's former squadron from Szolnok, so the experienced fighter pilot came to be stationed in Veszprém for over a year.

Zászlóshelyettes Dezső Szentgyörgyi in 1944. (From the collection of Szentgyörgyi family)

His first victory in the course of the combat missions for home defense was achieved on 14 June 1944, when the 'Pumas' engaged the P-38J Lightnings of 14th FG's 49th Fighter Squadron. Szentgyörgyi's victim was among

29 Excerpts from the logs of 1/1 Fighter Squadron; Nagy, 'Egy magyar vadászrepülő leküzdi a balszerencsét', p. 7, also mentions seven aerial victories, although this is a mistake – this work mentions the twin-engined Pe-2 as a double victory (no double air victories for such aircraft were confirmed in the Royal Hungarian Air Force; in some cases, however, more points were allocated for them).

them; four Lightnings crashed so close to each other that it was impossible to determine which was shot down by whom. The air victory was confirmed (with the location of Vérteskozma) for Szentgyörgyi as a shared victory with *hadnagy* Pál Bélavári serving in 101/3 Squadron; instead of two points, therefore, Szentgyörgyi received only one.

I was able to identify surely Szentgyörgyi's second American victim. In this case, the officer in question had led a very interesting life and career. On 27 June 1944, the Hungarian fighters first flew off to Győr, where they had been engaged in heavy air combat the day before. They then turned back to engage the B-17s raiding Budapest. Szentgyörgyi shot down the Mustang of 1st Lieutenant Howard Baetjer of 31st FG's 309th FS (flying a P-51B, serial number [American] 42-106498) in the vicinity of Győr. Luckily the American pilot managed to bail out of his airplane without injury and went into captivity. The air victory was mistakenly confirmed with a location of Márianosztra, Nagyirtáspuszta, but according to the author's research, the airmen who jumped out of the aircraft over the Börzsöny were crew members of a B-17; the American fighter crashed near Győr.[30]

Howard Baetjer was born on 15 September 1919 in Baltimore. He majored in biology at Princeton University in 1942 (his thesis was written on hawks). After this, he enlisted in the army and received the rank of reserve artillery 2nd Lieutenant. Thereafter he began his training in the Air Force. He arrived to 31st Fighter Group in October 1943 and began completing combat missions. Baetjer was a skilled, but not a very fortunate pilot: the unit, which was then equipped with Spitfires, rarely met German aircraft, and he had therefore only completed approximately 100 sorties by spring without scoring any victories. After the Fighter Group was re-equipped with Mustangs, his first combat mission ended with him being shot down by the gunners of a Liberator on 16 April 1944 because the new aircraft type was not recognized by the bomber crew. Baetjer bailed out over Yugoslavia, southwest of Kruševac (today Serbia), and avoided captivity with the help of the Yugoslavian resistance fighters. After an exciting and adventurous escape, he was able to return to Italy on 28 May. Such pilots were not usually allowed to go on combat missions again – so that, in case any of them were captured, the German *Abwehr* could not retrieve information from them about previously used escape routes – but Howard Baetjer wished so badly to prove himself that he was allowed to fly again in June. On 23 June he reported having damaged an Fw 190 over Romania, although it was, in reality, an IAR-80 (the American fighters did not recognize this Romanian aircraft type, and therefore always reported them as the similar radial engine powered German type). Four days later, this experienced flight leader lost his last combat to Szentgyörgyi and was taken POW. His experiences in captivity were harsh; he returned to Maryland after the war and had a civilian jobs afterward. He died on 23 May 1992.[31]

Szentgyörgyi destroyed his first four-engined heavy bomber on 2 July 1944; the Liberator was confirmed to him with the location of Etyek–Ödönmajor. Probably this was the same four-engined bomber that was confirmed with two points as a kill shared with the anti-aircraft artillery; the B-24 was, probably, one of the aircraft from the 456th BG that were lost on that day.

30 NARA MACR 6393, 6467. The American pilot himself wrote after the war that he had left the formation over the area of Győr when he was shot down, and this statement is reinforced by a letter sent by the high command of 15th AAF to the Baetjer family in July 1944 (based on eyewitness evidence).

31 The author managed to find the family of Howard Baetjer in the United States, and the related bibliographical data was provided by them.

On July 16, Szentgyörgyi shot down his next white-starred enemy; the air victory over the Liberator was confirmed with the location of Gálos (Gols) in Burgenland, east of the northern end of Lake Fertő. The kill was confirmed with two points for Szentgyörgyi, as a shared victory with one of his squadron members, *hadnagy* Gellért Barsi. East of Lake Fertő, two Liberators of 464th BG's 779th Squadron crashed as a result of German and Hungarian fighter attacks. Of these two, the aircraft that crashed to the north closer to Gols, southeast of the village near Andau, was a B-24H (serial number 41-29398) flown by 1st Lieutenant James E. Jatho. The 10-member crew, among them three badly wounded gunners, went into captivity.[32]

Szentgyörgyi scored his next air victory against Americans on 27 July, against a Liberator, when, as a member of a smaller Hungarian formation, he was attacking four-engines west of Budapest frontally and shot down an aircraft of 455th BG's 743rd Squadron flown by 2nd Lieutenant Eugene D. Potucek. This aircraft crashed east-southeast of Oroszlány and was credited to Szentgyörgyi. Of the 11-member crew, four, among them the pilot himself, were killed; the other seven crew members were captured (B-24H, serial number 41-28952).[33]

Szentgyörgyi's last air victory against Americans was scored on 22 August 1944, on which day the bomber formations of 15th AAF mostly raided Silesian targets and suffered heavy losses during the attacks of the German–Hungarian fighters. The Hungarian formation engaged the Liberators above the western sector of the *Dunántúl* and attacked the American bombers for an extended time in multiple raids, shooting down a number of them. One air victory was scored by Szentgyörgyi. The Air Defense Force Command Order Nr. 31 (*31 számú légvédelmi erők parancsnoksági parancs*), issued 12 September 1944, contained confirmation of the air victories of 22 August, but has been destroyed, along with many other wartime documents; we only have information of its numeration, not of its actual contents. The actual location for Szentgyörgyi's confirmed fourth four-engined victory was preserved in the recommendation to the *Magyar Tiszti Arany Vitézségi Érem* from October 1944:

> Since his last recommendation, he has taken part in 19 home defense fighter missions and fought against superior forces with bravery and heroism. During these missions, he has shot down (on 27 June 1944) one Mustang fighter aircraft at Márianosztra and four four-engined Liberator bombers at the following locations: on 2 July 1944, at Etyek; on 16 July 1944, at Gálos; on 27 July 1944, at Oroszlány; and on 22 August 1944, Zalaerdőd.[34]

A police report issued on 22 August also includes a Liberator; according to this, the aircraft crashed in the vicinity of Zalaerdőd, and eight crew bailed out. The report of the national architecture office at Szombathely is more accurate: 'Between the villages of Keléd and Zalaerdőd [north of Zalaerdőd], near the Nr. 751 Jánosháza–Türje road, a four-engined enemy aircraft has crashed and burnt out. Its 10-member crew has been arrested and detained at Jánosháza.'[35]

32 NARA MACR 6903.

33 NARA MACR 12 390, MNL Komárom-Esztergom Megyei Levéltára (*National Archives, Komárom-Esztergom County Archives*), XXXIII/1 state death registry counterpart of town Oroszlány in year 1944; acc. nr. notes 18–21.

34 *HM HIM HL*, documents of 101 Fighter Wing, box nr. 113, recommendation for a decoration for Dezső Szentgyörgyi, 20 October 1944.

35 *HM HIM HL*, Personalia nr. 249, temporary summary of incident reports of the central command of investigation of the Royal Hungarian "*csendőrség*" (police force), 23 August 1944, *Ellenséges gépek*

A number of Liberators crashed in that area, relatively close to each other, and in a few cases 10 crew members were all captured. It is therefore extremely difficult to identify this aircraft. In the author's opinion, this heavy bomber might have been a B-24J of 98th BG (the aircraft of 1st Lieutenant William J. Patton, serial number 44-41160), or probably one of the B-24H's of 461st BG (2nd Lieutenant Robert G. Swinehart, serial number 42-28681).[36]

2nd Lieutenant Eugene D. Potucek (1922–1944), the pilot who flew the Liberator of 455th BG's 743rd Bomber Squadron that crashed at Oroszlány, and who was killed with his three crew members when the aircraft was destroyed. The victory was confirmed to Dezső Szentgyörgyi (Roosevelt High School Alumni Association of St. Louis, MO)

Szentgyörgyi received his first officer's decoration (the *Magyar Érdemrend lovagkeresztje hadiszalagon a kardokkal*) for his home defense air victories during the summer of 1944 with a reception date of 1 November 1944. He had flown 20 (some sources claim 22) combat sorties against American opponents, which were separately registered in the Royal Hungarian Air Force. It is necessary to mention that in the official army bulletin this decoration is mistakenly recorded as having being awarded posthumously, as Szentgyörgyi is mentioned together with the officers of the group who were killed in combat.[37]

His next air victory was scored nearly three months later, on 13 November, when six aircraft of his squadron defeated a Soviet Yakovlev fighter formation of superior forces and forced them to flee after an intensive dogfight (their opponents were most probably the Yak-9s of 149th GIAP; for more detail on this event, see the biography for Lajos Tóth). In the meantime, on 1 November, as a result of the abolition of the rank of *zászlóshelyettes*, all of that rank's holders, including Szentgyörgyi himself were officially promoted to an officer's rank: *zászlós*.

In December 1944, Szentgyörgyi first reported a victory over a Yakovlev fighter aircraft (this cannot be identified based on Soviet sources). On the 20th of the same month he destroyed another Il-2, but he was not the only one who claimed this air victory, and as a result he developed a short resentment against a few certain German pilots. His wingman, *tizedes* Tibor Varjas, remembered the particular mission in one of his letters to the author:

> We flew along the northern shore until Keszthely, and then we flew over to the southern shore and returned back. At Siófok we crossed the wide Balaton bay in the direction of Kenese. I noticed three aircraft coming toward us. Dezső was waving from his aircraft to find out whether I had seen what was happening. I waved back and confirmed.

berepülése nr. I/3/12; *MNL Vas Megyei Levéltára* (National Archives, Vas County Archives), *M. Kir. Államépítészeti Hivatal* (Royal Hungarian State Bureau of Architecture), Szombathely, Report on events during enemy aircraft entering airspace, 22 August 1944, pt. 3.

36 NARA MACR 10 643, 8096; letter of Robert G. Swinehart to the author (20 May 2014).

37 *Honvédségi Rendeletek* (*Személyes ügyek*), nr. 1944/54 (21 December 1944), p. 1,103.

> The two aircraft behind made several passes. After at least four, they turned right and disappeared in the direction of Veszprém. During this time the distance between us diminished so we could see an Il-2 coming toward us. It must have got lost and flown too far north. We were aligned with the Soviet aircraft when Dezső made a left turn, got dead astern to the Soviet and, pushing the aircraft, shot a burst into him. A huge pile of smoke burst out from the Il-2 and it plummeted, then crashed and burnt to ashes. The Soviet pilot bailed out from the aircraft, but his parachute did not deploy because he did not have the necessary altitude – the whole air combat took place at approximately 150 meters altitude. ... We made a few turns around the burning wreck, then off we flew toward Veszprém. After landing, Dezső reported to the commander of the command post, *százados* Scholtz, that he had shot down an Il-2 in the airspace of Szentkirályszabadja and Veszprém. To this, the *százados* smilingly replied that the two German pilots who had just landed had reported an air victory over the very same aircraft.[38]

In the death certificate registry of Szentkirályszabadja, the author found the following information regarding the crew of the crashed Il-2: a tall, slender man of approximately 30 years of age, reddish blonde hair, with blue eyes, died from a fall, while another male, short and plump, around 16 years of age, reddish blonde hair, with blue eyes, died as a result of burns. Their names were impossible to obtain. To record such detailed and prompt information about deceased enemy air crews – or even Hungarian air crews – of crashed aircraft on combat missions was extremely rare, as the local authorities had virtually ceased to exist due to the military operations; making registry entries postponed during the intensive ground combat. The aircraft in question was an Il-2 (serial number 1888103) of the Soviet 707th SAP, and the crew members killed were the pilot, *leytenant* L. N. Solomentsev (the younger, at the age of 23), and the gunner, *starshiy serzhant* N. F. Loginov (the elder by five years).[39]

The German pilot who too hastily reported victory over this aircraft was one of the pilots of I./JG 53, probably *Unteroffizier* Siegfried Göbel (or maybe *Unteroffizier* Heinz Hommes).[40]

January 1945, despite the weather being extremely bad and greatly restricting the combat activity, was the most sufficient month for Szentgyörgyi. During Operation *Konrad*, aimed at relieving Budapest, he achieved six confirmed air victories over a period of no longer than four weeks: he reported three Lavochkin and two Yakovlev fighters and a ground-attack aircraft. He scored two of his victories on 18 January, on the first day of *Konrad* 3.

His first victory of the month was scored on 4 January against an La-5 of 530th IAP, south-east of Bicske. At the same time, Lajos Tóth shot down another Lavochkin in the same area. His victim of 8 January cannot be identified based on the Soviet sources (there were no total losses of any Lavochkins on that day). Of the air victories on 18 January, the one east of Polgárdi was an Il-2, probably of 136th SAD – 715th or 989th SAP – although it is not possible to identify it due to the scarcity of data and the large number of losses sustained on that day. A Soviet

38 Letter from Tibor Varjas to the author (5 July 2004).

39 *MNL Veszprém Megyei Levéltára* (National Archives, Veszprém County Archives), XXXIII/1, state death registry counterpart of town Szentkirályszabadja for 1944, acc. nr. notes 34. and 35; Gábor Horváth, *Bostonok a magyar égen és földben (1944–1945)* (Szolnok: privately published, 2013), p. 81.

40 Jochen Prien, *PIK-AS Geschichte des Jagdgeschwaders 53. Teil 3* (Eutin: Struve Druck, 1991), pp. 1204–1205, 1682.

fighter aircraft definitely crashed following an air combat near Aba, although it was not an La-5, but an Il-2 of 639th SAP (serial number 11311). It might be that the confirming Air Force Order was mistaken in recording the aircraft type. As for the last two air victories reported for that month (assuming the date is correct), the Yak-9 shot down on 28 January in the area of Kiskunlacháza cannot be identified, because, according to Soviet sources, there were no such losses reported on that day. The Yak-9 credited to Szentgyörgyi on 30 January north of Buda could possibly be the long-range Yak-9DD belonging to 659th IAP (serial number 0115345) that was damaged on that day, but it is more probable that it was the Yak-9D of 897th IAP (serial number 181539). This aircraft was part of a six-member formation deployed in the area of Adony–Pusztaszabolcs, and was shot down by a Bf 109 element at 13:25, probably in the area of Szigetújfalu. The pilot, *mladshiy leytenant* I.A. Prozorov, was lightly wounded on his arms and legs. As the author has not found any other registered German or Hungarian air victories over a Yak-9 in the area, it can be assumed that the location was south of Buda, and the direction was mistyped in the wing order.[41]

February was not particularly eventful for Dezső Szentgyörgyi, mainly because of the bad weather, which was unsuitable for flying missions. He completed six combat sorties in this month and scored one confirmed victory when, on 12 February, he shot down an Il-2 while on a covering mission to protect the defenders breaking out from the besieged Buda. There were no reports of Soviet ground-attack aircraft total losses to fighter aircraft for this day, although the flights of 130th and 131st GSAP reported fighter attacks during the afternoon. The aircraft of *mayor* Samodelkin from 130th GSAP was badly damaged in an air combat in the area reported by Szentgyörgyi; most probably, therefore, Szentgyörgyi was responsible for the damage inflicted on the Soviet aircraft (although attackers of Fw 190 type were mentioned, this might well have been a case of mistaken type identification, which was not at all rare).[42]

Viktor Mikhailovich Samodelkin (1921–1999) was an outstanding shturmovik pilot who served throughout the war and completed 211 combat sorties. He enjoyed numerous successes against ground targets and scored six air victories with an Il-2. For his achievements during the war, he was awarded the title of Hero of the Soviet Union in 1946.

A recommendation for decoration filled in later but referring to this period appraises Szentgyörgyi's achievements (who, at that time, had not yet surpassed Debrődy in terms of the number of confirmed air victories):

> *V. zászlós* Dezső Szentgyörgyi has stood out among his fellow pilots with his comradeship, his readiness to sacrifice himself, his bravery and his skilled combat leadership in every mission in which he has taken part. As the second most successful fighter pilot and as a comrade, too, his deeds and combat actions make him an excellent example to all his younger comrades.[43]

41 Horváth, *Bostonok a magyar égen és földben*, p. 99; the correspondence of Gábor Horváth based on the documents of TsAMO disclosed by Boris Davidov (henceforth 'Gábor Horváth on documents of TsAMO').

42 Gábor Horváth on documents of TsAMO.

43 *HM HIM HL*, documents of 101 Fighter Wing, box nr. 113, recommendation for the decoration of Dezső Szentgyörgyi (undated).

Around this time, at the beginning of March, he completed his 200th combat sortie. This month was again very productive and successful for him.

At 13:56 in the afternoon of 9 March 1945, eight Hungarian fighter aircraft took off from Veszprém for a free hunt mission, led by *százados* Pottyondy. The target area was the sector south of Lake Velencei, where they were engaged in air combat with eight Yak-9s. *Zászlós* Szentgyörgyi reported shooting down one of them at 14:36, northwest of Sárbogárd, thus scoring his 24th air victory; this was confirmed by the Hungarian authorities. The Soviet pilot, according to the reports, was not able to bail out, and the victory was confirmed by *hadnagy* Károly Sipos. According to the Soviet sources, the aircraft cannot be identified; it was probably damaged and returned to base.[44]

Two days later, Szentgyörgyi took off at 13:59 to lead the four aircraft of his flight for a free hunt in the area of Káloz–Simontornya. The Hungarian flight met 14 Il-2s and six escorting La-5s. In the ensuing fight, the flight leader reported shooting down an La-5 east of Seregélyes at 14:48; the air victory was again witnessed by *hadnagy* Sipos and *zászlós* Géza Bartos. The nearest known loss on that day was an La-5F (serial number 39214947) of 164th IAP flown by *mladshiy leytenant* P.M. Taikov, which was damaged over Seregélyes during the afternoon, according to the Soviet reports by anti-aircraft artillery fire at 13:25, following which the pilot performed an emergency landing at the base. Although the aircraft itself burnt out completely, the pilot was unharmed. The destruction of this aircraft was definitely not caused by Szentgyörgyi, as his opponent's aircraft might just have been damaged in the air combat. This was Szentgyörgyi's 25th air victory. Two days later, his wing commander recommended him for the *Magyar Tiszti Arany Vitézségi Érem* (his second recommendation since 24 October 1944). His commander wrote: 'With his great number of air victories, he is one of the most successful Hungarian fighter pilots, and as such he is an example to be followed.'[45] On 25 March 1945, there was a theoretically positive assessment regarding this award, although this was not announced to the unit and the decoration itself was not awarded to the pilot.

On 19 March 1945, Szentgyörgyi started flying at 14:59 against continuously reappearing Soviet aircraft in the area of Berhida. One aircraft of the flight was not able to retract his landing gear and so returned to the airfield; the other three aircraft flew into the combat airspace. Once there, at first they only spotted two Il-2s north of Nádasdladány; they were flying at an altitude of only 50 meters. The Soviet ground-attack aircraft were flying without escort and had practically no chance; the opponent of Szentgyörgyi was blown up mid-air between a manor house and the forest at 15:15 due to the multiple hits inflicted upon it. The crew was killed. This aircraft was probably one of the missing aircraft of 715th SAP (serial number 18819118) flown by the crew of *starshiy leytenant* P.T. Grebenko. The kill was testified by *őrmester* István Fábián, who shot down the other Il-2. Thereafter, they also met Bostons, Yakovlev and Lavochkin fighters in the area of Balatonfűzfő and Balatonkenese, which they engaged in combat. During these combat actions, both Szentgyörgyi and *hadnagy* Sipos reported shooting down a fighter aircraft each. Szentgyörgyi's opponent was an La-5 shot down at 15:45; *hadnagy* Sipos reported a victory over a Yak.

44 *HM HIM HL*, documents of 101 Fighter Wing, box nr. 113, after-action reports and mission logs of 101 Fighter Wing, 9 March 1945; Gábor Horváth on documents of TsAMO.

45 *HM HIM HL*, documents of 101 Fighter Wing, box nr. 113, telegram to the high command of 1 Air Division, 13 March 1945.

In the combat mission log, this was at first listed as Szentgyörgyi's 27th air victory, but it was crossed out. In the end, for unknown reasons, this instance did not count among his air victories confirmed by the Hungarian Air Force, although the combat mission log states that the aircraft was seen to crash to the ground in billowing smoke. The combat report lists the aircraft as a probable kill, with a time of 15:46. Although the Soviet sources do not contain any data about a lost La-5 in this area at this time, the author interprets this air victory, which is stated in an official Hungarian source, as a claimed and registered kill conforming to the criteria based on which it can be added to the official victory list of the pilot (perhaps due to an administrative error it was not included in Wing Order Nr. 1945/62, issued at the end of the war). Therefore, this work will indicate one more air victory for Szentgyörgyi than the officially registered number.[46]

Zászlós Szentgyörgyi flew one of his last successful combat sorties from Veszprém on the next day, before the evacuation of the airfield. Eight aircraft of his squadron took off at 11:37 east of the airfield for a free hunt. Szentgyörgyi flew at an altitude of 3,000 meters between Sárkeresztes and Pátka and reported shooting down an La–7 at 12:00, the pilot of which, according to the report, bailed out and survived the destruction of his aircraft, which fell into a spin and went down due to several hits around the engine and the cockpit. The kill was attested to by *zászlós* Bartos although, according to the mission log and the combat report, the Hungarian fighters engaged in combat with 20 Bostons and 20 Soviet fighters. On this day the La-7s of the Soviet 179th GIAP were escorting bombers raiding Győr and lost two aircraft: one element escorted a Boston that was lagging behind because of an anti-aircraft artillery hit when two Bf 109s came down on them dead astern. The two Lavochkins collided while pulling into the clouds, and both pilots needed to bail out: the aircraft of both *starshiy leytenant* V.S. Piselko (serial number 45210501) and *mladshiy leytenant* P.P. Harlamov (serial number 45210353) were destroyed. These losses might well be linked to Szentgyörgyi's victory, but according to the report of the Soviet formation the two aircraft were lost at 16:20, and the time difference is too big to credit them to him (if the Soviet's recorded time is correct).[47]

Zászlós Szentgyörgyi's last victory of the month was scored on 23 March; it was also his last combat mission from Veszprém. On this day, a four-aircraft flight took off at 11:07 for a free hunt, during which they met two Yak-3s. After engaging them between 11:30 and 11:35, Szentgyörgyi reported shooting down one of the Yak-3s at 11:34. Its crash was clearly seen according to the combat report and the mission log; the witness was Szentgyörgyi's squadron commander, *hadnagy* Lajos Tóth. The aircraft cannot be identified based on Soviet sources, as no total losses were reported from the area on that day. After these events, between 11:40 and 11:42, the flight also engaged six to eight American Mustangs, but then disengaged from the combat due to shortage of fuel. Although Yak-3s were mentioned as Soviet fighters in both the combat report and the mission log, Wing Order Nr. 1945/62 confirmed the aircraft as a 'Yak-11' (the Yak-11 subtype, a special training aircraft developed after the war, did not then exist, but it is characteristic of the

46 *HM HIM HL*, documents of 101 Fighter Wing, box nr. 113, after-action reports and mission logs of the 101 Fighter Wing, 19 March 1945; Horváth, *Bostonok a magyar égen és földben*, pp. 185–186; the correspondence of Nikita Yegorov, based on the documents of TsAMO disclosed by himself (henceforth 'Nikita Yegorov on documents of TsAMO').

47 *HM HIM HL*, documents of 101 Fighter Wing, box nr. 113, after-action reports and mission logs of the 101 Fighter Wing, 20 March 1945; Horváth, *Bostonok a magyar égen és földben*, p. 144.

uncertainties surrounding the denomination of the new Yakovlev fighters that this Yak-11 appears a number of times in the Hungarian aviation documents at the end of the war).[48]

Zászlós vitéz Szentgyörgyi scored his last confirmed (29th – per the author's numbering, 30th) air victory on 16 April 1945 after taking off from the final base airfield at Raffelding. Under Szentgyörgyi's leadership, eight aircraft took off at 12:18 for a free hunt in the area of Sankt Pölten. One aircraft was forced to return because of mechanical problems, but the other seven were engaged in air combat in the airspace east of Hofstetten at an altitude of 4,000 meters between 13:00 and 13:08 by approximately 10 La-5 and Yak-9 fighters, of which Szentgyörgyi reported shooting down one Yak. The kill was mentioned as a probable one in the combat report as there were no eyewitnesses, although this sounds highly unlikely, as Szentgyörgyi was the formation leader. Later, however, the claim was upgraded and resubmitted as a complete kill, and was confirmed officially in Wing Order 1945/62 (Soviet sources do not confirm this loss).[49]

Szentgyörgyi last took off as a formation leader on 19 April 1945 at 07:57, leading five aircraft to the area of Brno and the areas southeast of the city. The formation met no opponents and landed at 09:40. During the afternoon, two different four-aircraft flights were deployed on a mission from the first group, but probably Szentgyörgyi did not take part; nor did he take off during the few days that followed, thus ending his military career.[50]

Of Szentgyörgyi's 30 air victories, the first six are included in the log of 1/1 Squadron, together with additional five claims, all without witnesses. His first five air victories against Americans are also included in Confidential Order of the Air Force Nr. 1944/63, and the sixth is featured in a decoration recommendation (probably confirmed in Air Force Command Order Nr. 1944/31, which did not survive). His first air victory in November was confirmed in Air Force Order Nr. 1945/1, and the two air victories in December were confirmed in the Order Nr. 1945/13. His second air victory in November and his 13 air victories from 1945 were confirmed in Air Force Order Nr. 1945/62; a further victory is included among the documents of the unit.

Along with other comrades in his wing, Szentgyörgyi was taken prisoner at Raffelding in Austria on 3 May 1945 by the US troops. Subsequently, he worked in an American workshop as an engine mechanic.

After being released from captivity, he returned home of his own free will, on foot, at the beginning of November. On 7 December, he was registered in Székesfehérvár, and he was discharged from military service as of 1 September the next year.

Szentgyörgyi worked as a pilot for *Maszovlet (*Hungarian–Soviet Civil Air Transport Joint Stock Company, *Magyar–Szovjet Polgári Légiforgalmi Részvénytársaság*) from 1946, at first as a Po-2 taxi pilot, then as a co-pilot on Li-2s, and later as a pilot. Until 7 December 1950, he flew 2,175 hours in Li-2;[51] on 7 December, he was arrested following false accusations of

48 *HM HIM HL*, documents of 101 Fighter Wing, box nr. 113, after-action reports and mission logs of 101 Fighter Wing, 23 March 1945; Gábor Horváth on documents of TsAMO.

49 *HM HIM HL*, documents of 101 Fighter Wing, box nr. 113, after-action reports and mission logs of 101 Fighter Wing, 16 April 1945, box nr. 110, Wing Order Nr. 1945/62; Gábor Horváth on documents of TsAMO.

50 *HM HIM HL*, documents of 101 Fighter Wing, box nr. 113, after-action reports and mission logs of 101 Fighter Wing, 19 April 1945.

51 Dezső Szentgyörgyi's flight service logs and flight logs.

spying activities. His trial was known as 'Dr. János Lenk and his accomplices', in which Dezső Szentgyörgyi was the seventh-degree defendant. This trial did not only target air force pilots; among the defendants were also three lawyers.[52] Upon the sentence of the *Budapesti Katonai Törvényszék* (Military Tribunal at Budapest) as per Kb.XII.051/1951 on 25 April 1951, the Military Head Tribunal as a secondary court of justice declared the sentence final and binding on 20 October 1951 (II.0238/kat.ftszék.-1951) and sentenced Szentgyörgyi to seven years in prison, 10 years of being banned from exercising his civil rights and full confiscation. He was also demoted of his rank of *alhadnagy* (the equivalent of *zászlós* in the *Néphadsereg*, or the Hungarian People's Army – on account of his false treason charge. It was very characteristic of Szentgyörgyi that, although his captors tried to force a confession out of him, the brutal beatings did not make him change his mind and sign the confession. He held out until he heard his wife crying from the next room; the authorities had begun brutalizing her, and only then did Szentgyörgyi sign everything.

The following years were extremely difficult for Szentgyörgyi and his family. They were forced out of their home ('*kitelepítés*') and made to live under inhuman conditions. This excellent pilot was freed from prison at last on 18 August 1956.

On 18 March 1957, the Supreme Court abrogated the above sentences with judicial decision *Kat.Törv.*30/1957 as the result of a legal appeal. It also relieved Szentgyörgyi and provided him with financial compensation for the years spent in prison. The successor of *Maszovlet*, *Malév* (*Magyar Légiforgalmi Vállalat,* or Hungarian Airlines), took him back as an active pilot as early as 1 November 1956.

His sense of justice was, however, deeply troubled by what had happened to him. In one of his proceedings Szentgyörgyi wrote the following:

> The data and facts contained in the reports are not valid; they were forced on me during the interrogations. I signed them after what happened to my wife and my brother, but I never accepted them under pressure during the 48 days of my interrogation, nor in court. From … 1950 to December 1953 I did not have a chance to notify my family of my whereabouts or that I was still living. In the summer of 1951, my innocent wife, my three-year-old child and my brother were displaced by force to Jászkarajenő, and our flat was confiscated. My wife, who understood I was no longer living, married again. All my relatives underwent terrible pains and sufferings because of me.[53]

During his later years, Szentgyörgyi was not put through such an ordeal again. After completing the type training in 1957, he flew as an Il-14 pilot for *Malév.* Soon news began to emerge that he might receive his reserve rank back.

Sándor Hűvös, managing director of *Malév*, described Szentgyörgyi in a certification in April 1959, written in connection with a request to reinstate him to his officer rank: 'He has excellent capabilities with the aircraft; he has earned the acknowledgments of his colleagues and superiors alike with his trustworthiness and good work.'[54] His demotion was abrogated on 26 May 1959. A document issued six years later, concerning his promotion, describes him as 'one of the

52 *HM HIM HL*, Bp. KB. B.051/1951.
53 *HM HIM HL*, Bp. KB. B.051/1951.
54 *HM HIM KI*, document folder nr. 33104.

most experienced pilots of the company. He is exact and disciplined and this is what he demands from his crew as well. He is an exceptionally good pilot with an excellent sense for aviation.'[55] Szentgyörgyi was at last promoted to reserve *főhadnagy* on 24 December 1965.

During the winter of 1959–60, he retrained to fly the Il-18 type in the Soviet Union, and afterward he exclusively flew this type of aircraft. Between 1957 and 1959, he flew 2,463 hours; after the retraining, he completed more than 7,600 hours in Il-18.[56]

The memorial plaque on the community house at Enying dedicated to the memory of Dezső Szentgyörgyi in 1995. (From the author's collection)

Sadly, Szentgyörgyi did not see his peaceful retirement. On 28 August 1971, Malév flight MA-731 (registration HA-MOC, type Il-18, serial number 181002903), flying from Oslo to Copenhagen in extremely bad weather conditions and approximately 10 kilometers away from the airfield at Kastrup, plunged into the sea at 18:52 hours at a 15–20° angle, probably because of an exceptionally dangerous microburst. The fuselage broke in at least two places and sank rapidly. There were only three foreign passenger survivors, two women and one man, all from the rear end of the plane.[57] The nine-member crew and 22 passengers – including two Hungarians, one of them a Malév colleague, the managing director of the Malév office at Copenhagen – died in the accident. The airplane was flown by Szentgyörgyi, who was an excellent pilot and sportsman even in his older years; the forensic examination clearly stated that his internal injuries were not directly caused by the crash itself, and they were not inflicted on him on impact. Dezső Szentgyörgyi, who was his whole life an exemplar of duty and gallantry, remained so also in death: he tried to pull the control yoke up with such inhuman force that he suffered fatal muscle tears in his chest.

The remains of Dezső Szentgyörgyi were laid to rest on 13 September 1971 in the Farkasréti Cemetery at Budapest, together with the crew members of his last flight.[58]

Until the day of the catastrophe, Dezső Szentgyörgyi had flown altogether 12,334 hours in civilian aviation after the war. On 14 May 1990, the Budapest Military Tribunal abrogated his 1951 sentence. From 28 April 1990, 59 Air Base at Kecskemét officially took the name of Dezső Szentgyörgyi. Upon the 100th anniversary of his birth, at Enying, 2015 was nominated as a memorial year dedicated to Szentgyörgyi; on 5 September, the square in front of the community house was named after him.

He was the most successful pilot of the Royal Hungarian Air Force, with excellent skills. He was an extremely capable soldier and, at the same time, he was very humble. His 'wings' were

55 *HM HIM KI*, document folder nr. 33104.
56 Dezső Szentgyörgyi's flight service logs and flight logs.
57 'A KPM és a Malév tájékoztatója a koppenhágai légi katasztrófáról', *Népszabadság*, 31 August 1971, p. 9; 'Hivatalos tájékoztató a koppenhágai légi szerencsétlenségről', *Népszabadság*, 5 September 1971, p. 9.
58 'Eltemették a koppenhágai légi szerencsétlenség áldozatait', *Népszabadság*, 14 September 1971, p. 8.

also inherited by his offspring. His son, of the same name, retired from *Malév* with more than 18,600 hours of flight time; and the youngest Dezső Szentgyörgyi, the ace's eldest grandson, still works in the field of civilian aviation. He has already flown over 10,000 hours, and is currently flying an A330 Airbus in the Kuwait Airways Corporation.

SZÁZADOS VITÉZ GYÖRGY DEBRŐDY

Number of aerial victories: 26 (+1)
Successes against ground targets: n.d.a.
Number of flown combat sorties: 199 (20 against Americans)
Number of hours flown in the air force: 582 hours 35 minutes
Nicknames: *Debcsi*, *Gyurka*, *Mandula*
Identification number: 2522-21-0002

Decorations

- *Magyar Tiszti Arany Vitézségi Érem* (17 December 1944, the 14th award in the Royal Hungarian Armed Forces)
- *Magyar Érdemrend tisztikeresztje hadidíszítménnyel és kardokkal* (1 November 1944)
- *Magyar Érdemrend lovagkeresztje hadiszalagon a kardokkal* (9 March 1944)
- *Újólagos Kormányzói dicsérő elismerés Magyar Koronás Ezüst Érdemérme hadiszalagon a kardokkal* (24 April 1944)
- *Kormányzói dicsérő elismerés Magyar Koronás Bronz Érdemérme hadiszalagon a kardokkal* (20 September 1943)
- *Tűzkereszt I fokozata a kardokkal és koszorúval*, with three wound clasps
- German Iron Cross 1st Class (June 1944)
- German Iron Cross 2nd Class (1943)
- Gold *Frontflugspange* with the 200-pendant (20 April 1945)

Victories

Number	Date	Aircraft	Location
1	5 July 1943	La-5	Kharkiv
2	7 July 1943	Il-2	
3	3 August 1943	Il-2	Belgorod N
4	5 August 1943	Yak-1	
5	6 August 1943	Il-2	
6	8 August 1943	Yak-1	
–	25 September 1943	Yak-9	
7	29 November 1943	Il-2	Zhitomir E
8	1 December 1943	Yak-9	
9	14 December 1943	Il-2	
10	1 January 1944	Il-2	Near Vinnytsia
11	5 January 1944	La-5	
12	11 January 1944	Il-2	

Number	Date	Aircraft	Location
13	11 January 1944	La-5	
14	25 January 1944	Yak-1	
15	27 January 1944	La-5	
16	3 February 1944 at approximately 09:45	La-5	Cherkasy W
17	16 February 1944	Il-2	
18	16 February 1944	Il-2	
19	14 June 1944	P-38	Dudar E
20	16 June 1944	P-38	Kapoly
21	2 July 1944	P-51	Pilisvörösvár (Mogyoród)
22	7 July 1944	B-17	Megyercs (Cerová, Slovakia)
23	27 July 1944	B-24	Mór
24	5 November 1944	B-24	Balaton SW
25	16 November 1944	La-5	Jászberény SE
26	16 November 1944	Yak-9	Nagykáta N

Aircraft flown

Bf 109 G-6: V.780 (early summer of 1944)

György Dieber was born on 1 January 1921 on Újhódospuszta, north of Lajoskomárom in Fejér County, (the small Újhódospuszta was attached to the village of Lajoskomárom in terms of public administration). Because of this, a number of documents states his birthplace as Lajoskomárom. He was the oldest boy from two (his father, Rezső Dieber, was a teacher in a state school).[59] During the summer of 1928, the family changed its name when his father was admitted to the *Vitézi Rend* and received the respective title of *vitéz* as an acknowledgment of his heroic service and feats during the First World War within the 20th Infantry Regiment. His title was inherited by his eldest son. The family later moved to Herend. Debrődy, who was an enthusiastic scout (*cserkész*), completed the first three years at a high school in Bonyhád (*Bonyhádi Evangélikus Reálgimnázium*), then attended another high school in Veszprém (*Veszprémi Piarista Gimnázium*). He graduated from here in June 1938, with good results. In Veszprém, among his classmates was the brother of Dezső Szentgyörgyi, Kálmán.[60] After graduating, he enlisted in the *Kassai Repülőakadémia* (the *'Akadémia'*, or the Aviation Academy at Kassa), where he

59 Debrődy's birth date is erroneously given on his personal registry file as 7 January 1921 (*HM HIM KI*, document folder nr. 14047). The incorrect date is used in the officer ranking documents for 1942 and 1944, and in all publications that take these original documents as a basis: for example, Illésfalvi, Kovács, and Maruzs, *'Vitézségért'*, p. 117. For the exact birth date, see *MNL Fejér Megyei Levéltára* (National Archives, Fejér County Archives), XXXIII/1, birth registry counterparts of Lajoskomárom in year 1921, acc. nr. note 2. The postnote referring to the Hungarianization of the name refers to the Decree of the Ministry of Interior Nr. 254802/1928.

60 *MNL Veszprém Megyei Levéltára* (National Archives, Veszprém County Archives), VIII/52/5 Matriculation register of the *Piarista Gimnázium* (Piarist High School) in Veszprém, 1939, certificate numbers 4 (György Debrődy) and 35 (Kálmán Szentgyörgyi), also according to the kind correspondence of Kálmán Szentgyörgyi (16 November 2006).

was promoted to *hadnagy* on 18 June 1942, as of 1 July 1942, with rank number 9 (altogether 65th).[61] During his years at the *Akadémia,* he formed a lifelong friendship with his classmate, Miklós Kenyeres. Immediately before graduation, he completed his instrument rating (IR, *műszerrepülő kiképzés*): the pretraining and the Link Trainer course was completed in Kassa, and the instrument rating was completed in Debrecen. On 6 July, he enlisted at Tapolca in the Fighter Combat Training Group, where he graduated on 27 November as an 'A' category pilot (a very capable fighter aircraft pilot ready for the front) with excellent shooting skills.[62] Thereafter, he was transferred to his parent unit, 5/I Fighter Group in Mátyásföld. From here he, with many of his comrades, was sent to the Eastern Front in the middle of December 1942 as part of 5/2 Fighter Squadron. The *Héja*s were already obsolete and in particularly bad mechanical condition, and some were not serviceable during the winter combat period and the ensuing retreat; thus Debrődy was not able to take part in combat sorties during the winter. He and his squadron retrained to Bf 109 in Uman during the spring. He completed his first flight with the new type on 15 April; during the test flight, it became apparent that there were still many problems with the old Bf 109 F-4s, which were used both during training and during the missions. *Hadnagy* Debrődy himself crash-landed with a Bf 109 F-4 on 5 May 1943 because of mechanical problems (the exact cause was the breakage of the power cylinder; the landing gear also was not released).[63] It should also be noted that, in July, when the Hungarian units were still operating in Bf 109 F-4s, the German fighter units deployed to the same area were already equipped with Bf 109 G-6-s, which were only sent to the Hungarian units in January 1944.

After the completion of his training, Debrődy's squadron was redeployed from Uman to Kharkhiv, and Debrődy completed his first combat sortie on 27 May 1943. He completed a number of fighter-bomber missions in June; in July, at the time of the battle of Kursk, his series of air victories began. At this time his wingman was usually *szakaszvezető*, later *őrmester*, Pál Kovács.[64]

Regarding the subtypes he was flying at this time, Debrődy completed his first training flight with a Bf 109 G-2 on 20 June 1943, but he used both subtypes alternately in July (he flew his last combat sortie on a Bf 109 F-4 on 3 August).[65]

At dawn on 5 July 1943, when the Soviet air force launched their first preventive air strikes against the German aircraft crowding the airfields around Kharkhiv, Debrődy (still flying a Bf 109 F-4) scored his first air victory: he came across a lone La-5 and, after a short dogfight, shot his enemy down with a short burst of cannon fire from below (dead astern).[66] His opponent might have been an aircraft of 295th IAD that went missing at the same time in approximately the same area. This Soviet Fighter Aviation Division met and engaged Hungarian Bf 109s numerous times until the end of the war.[67]

61 *Honvédségi Közlöny* (*Személyes ügyek*), nr. 1942/24 (16 June 1942), p. 613.
62 Based on the logbook (partial copy owned by the author), and on the evaluation report of György Debrődy (copy owned by the author).
63 Evaluation report of György Debrődy.
64 Recollections of György Debrődy, February 1976.
65 Logbook of György Debrődy.
66 'Kétszázötven magyar légigyőzelem. Helyszíni szemle a "Pumáknál" – a legeredményesebbb Magyar vadászrepülők névsora', *Egyedül vagyunk*, unknown issue, December 1944, p. 5.
67 For the use of the Soviet air force at Kursk, see Vitaliy Gorbach, *Nad Ognyennoi dugoi. Sovietskaya aviatsiya v Kurskoy bitve* (Moscow: Eksmo, 2007).

Two days later, on 7 July, Debrődy shot down an Il-2. After the anti-aircraft fire hit his aircraft's oil tank, he crash-landed near Varvarovka with his Bf 109 F-4. Less than two weeks later, on 19 July, his Bf 109 F-4 was again hit multiple times by anti-aircraft artillery. The aircraft was hit in its engine, wing, and fuselage, and the pilot belly-landed beyond his own lines.[68]

The day the Soviet counterattack was launched in the Belgorod sector (3 August 1943) was also a very eventful day for Debrődy. During one of his combat sorties completed on that day, while flying with *szakaszvezető* János Mátyás az a wingman, he noticed anti-aircraft fire north of Belgorod, and a little later also noticed an Il-2 formation flying without a fighter escort. His first pass against an Il-2 had no effect, but his shots during his second attack were well placed against another ground-attack aircraft, although it did not crash. Debrődy pushed his opponent continuously downward until the aircraft crashed into the ground. At the same time, Debrődy's cannon was stuck; as a result, and because of a large number of Soviet fighters in the vicinity, they disengaged and returned home. On the way back they again met Soviet ground-attack aircraft and Debrődy attacked one of them twice, but his 7.9mm machine gun rounds were of little effect on the heavily armored aircraft.

Later that day, while taking off on one of his sorties, he ran into a fresh bomb crater and his landing gear broke off.[69]

Two days later he succeeded in shooting down a Yak-1, and on 6 August he managed to achieve his fifth kill, against another Il-2. On 8 August, he shot down another Il-2 and achieved his sixth air victory – the last for him during the battle of Kursk. Following these achievements, a somewhat less successful period started in his service. On top of this, during a sortie on 25 September 1943 – after he had shot down a Yak-9, when the sight of the burning wreck had made him less aware of his surroundings – a Soviet Yakovlev fighter unexpectedly attacked him from the clouds. He was shot down and had to crash-land with his burning aircraft 20km behind enemy lines, east of the Dnieper River. Based on his own memories, the following description was published in the field magazine, *Üvölt a Puma*:

> Beyond the front, a heavy dogfight was going on; I was proudly watching the Yak-9 that I had just shot down catching fire, when suddenly something happened and my armor was falling down into my lap in pieces, smoke filling the cockpit. I was being shot down – it dawned on me suddenly. With thunderous crashing sounds I bellied to the ground while crashing into trees, finally stopping near a forest. I jumped out and ran as I had never run before toward the woods. A Soviet anti-aircraft battery crew was after me! I lay low in the bushes, grass and sedge thrown over me, and I listened, frightened, as the Soviets encircled the forest to look for me. Just two meters away two Soviets stopped to talk, while I grappled with a coughing fit. At last, they went away. I lay motionless for six hours in one place before I could begin moving westward slowly and very cautiously. The place was busy with people, so I hid in a haystack. At that time, I hadn't eaten anything for 20 hours, so I was really hungry. Then, a badly clothed Russian soldier came and started to carry away the hay from the stack over my head. On his second round, he spotted my leg, started yelling, and

68 Evaluation report of György Debrődy.
69 Evaluation report of György Debrődy.

ran away. So do I, but in the opposite direction. Then a German bombing raid came to my aid, which made the surroundings extremely noisy. Under this coverage, I made my escape. I fell over a telephone wire, so I quickly cut it with my knife. I almost stumbled upon a guard; he shot in my direction, then slowly slipped back to relax, because there was no movement anymore. One hour later the guard was changed, so at last I could move too and continue my escape. At length I reached the riverbank. I undressed, tied all my clothes and equipment on a grave cross I found, and at the end of September, at 02:00 in the morning, I forced myself into the icy cold water. I reached the other riverbank very slowly. Then I realized this was not the other bank, but a large island, and that there were still Russians there preparing for the river crossing. With chattering teeth, I descended again into the water and started off for the other bank. Soon I let my clothes float down the stream because they were too much hindrance. The Russians started shooting at me; these were dreadful moments, as I was at my strength's end. Everything was beginning to fade in front of me by the time I finally reach the riverbank. A Russian house was in front of me, with smoke curling out of the chimney. I fell through the door and lost consciousness.[70]

Two good-hearted women in the house dressed the pilot in old ragged pants and nursed him back to life by giving him a cup of goat's milk. The Germans on the front cried out when they heard his story: '*Schweineglück!*' (great luck – Schwein means pig, its a lucky symbol). He was indeed lucky – and exceptionally determined – to return to the squadron's airfield only three days later. The precise location of the Yak-9 he shot down, or its fate, was not possible to determine, therefore this kill was not confirmed.

Almost exactly a month later, Debrődy again found himself in a very dangerous situation behind enemy lines. On 22 October, the engine of his Bf 109 G-4 (WNr. 16124) (manufactured in Regensburg) stopped working. Luckily he was able to glide from a high altitude to own territory and crash-landed 57km west of Cherkasy, while his aircraft suffered 30 percent damage.[71]

He scored his seventh air victory after a long pause, on 29 November, near Zhitomir.

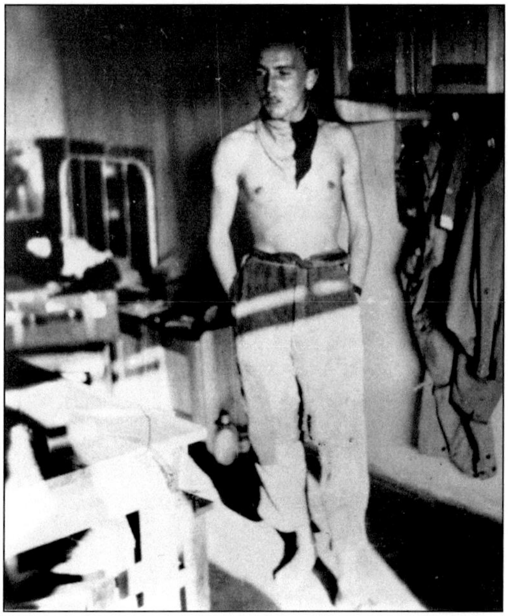

After he was shot down on 25 September 1943, Debrődy returned in shabby trousers, held round his waist by a string, that had been given to him by two warm-hearted local women. (From the author's collection)

70 *Üvölt a Puma*, 3 November 1943, p. 2.
71 Bundesarchiv-Militärarchiv, RL 2 III/1195/139; evaluation report of György Debrődy. In the original German loss record, the version of the Bf 109 is incorrectly recorded as G-2, but in reality (according to the serial number block and the Hungarian registry) this aircraft was a G-4.

Hadnagy László Molnár and *hadnagy* György Debrődy in the company of *Oberleutnant* Horst-Günther von Fassong (1919–1945), who scored at least 75 kills and was the commander of 10./JG 51 at this time. Picture was taken in the Ukraine, at the beginning of 1944. (From the author's collection)

A group of pilots from 5/2 Independent Fighter Squadron at the beginning of 1944. From left to right: *szakaszvezető* Ferenc Csikós, who scored one victory and was killed on 14 September 1944; *szakaszvezető* Sándor Tanács (three victories); *százados* József Kovács (four victories); *hadnagy* Kálmán Szeverényi; *őrmester hadnagy* György Debrődy; and *őrmester* János Mátyás. (From the author's collection)

The victim was again an Il-2. On 1 December, he was on a bomber escort mission, combined with a free hunt when he scored a victory against a Yak-9. On 14 December he was again successful in shooting down another Il-2, but came very close to being shot down himself by the Soviet air defense. Due to the low cloud, he was flying at a low altitude over the first lines when he was greeted by heavy fire. Debrődy's aircraft got away with being hit only twice, but his wingman, *karpaszományos honvéd* Count Dénes Wenckheim, was shot down, crashing beyond their own lines in his burning aircraft, and was killed.[72]

The most successful month for György Debrődy was January 1944, when he scored six confirmed air victories. Of these, the first aircraft, again an Il-2, was shot down on 1 January (his birthday) in the morning, after a scramble from the Vinnytsia airfield. Over the course of the month, this aircraft was followed by one Il-2, three La-5s and one Yak-1 on Debrődy's

72 Logbook of György Debrődy, and recollections of György Debrődy, February 1976. Wenckheim's original rank was *zászlós* but he had been demoted as a punishment. Following his death, he received his rank back posthumously and was decorated with the *Magyar Nagy Ezüst Vitézségi Érem*. For Wenckheim, see Csaba Becze, 'Vadászpilóta "komiszban"', *Magyar Szárnyak Évkönyv*, 1999, p. 258.

victory list. On 1 February 1944, however, Debrődy was again shot down by a Soviet fighter and he crash-landed west of Schpola (10km beyond enemy lines) with his burning Bf 109 G-6. This was a hopeless situation, but his friend, *hadnagy* Miklós Kenyeres, came to his rescue. Kenyeres shot down the Soviet fighter who had shot Debrődy, landed near him and, in an amazingly brave act that was unprecedented in the history of Bf 109s, brought him out in the cockpit of his aircraft (which was very small even for one person – for more details see the biography for Miklós Kenyeres).

Two days later they were flying over the cauldron in the Korsun–Shevchenkovsky area to escort transport aircraft headed for the encircled units. The flight of four aircraft, led by *hadnagy* Kenyeres with *hadnagy* Debrődy as the element leader, succeeded in defending the Ju 52s of the German TG 3 while shooting down three La-5s; but the aircraft of *hadnagy* Kenyeres was hit by an anti-aircraft artillery shell while flying over the cauldron and the pilot had to bail out over a forest. Debrődy circled overhead in vain; he was not able to help. With his severe lack of fuel he did not even reach his own airfield, but Debrődy managed to reach his own territory before landed with a released landing gear at Novo Arkhangelsk.

Hadnagy Debrődy scored his last two victories on the Eastern Front on 16 February 1944, during a free hunt mission against two Il-2s. He was then redeployed home at the end of the month. At the time of his departure from his squadron, with his confirmed 18 kills during 172 sorties, he was the most successful pilot who remained active, together with László Molnár. Miklós Kenyeres also had 18 air victories but, as he was a prisoner of war, he was not able to gain more.

Hadnagy László Molnár and *hadnagy* György Debrődy in June 1944 in Veszprém. (From the author's collection)

Debrődy's squadron commander, *százados* József Kovács, wrote when Debrődy was redeployed:

> From 15 December 1942 to 24 February 1944, he was in service on the front as a fighter pilot and flight leader. During this time, he completed 172 sorties, including three strafing runs and 16 fighter-bomber attacks, and scored 18 confirmed air victories. He is outstandingly brave, ingenious and successful. He will be excellent as a squadron commander.[73]

73 Evaluation report of György Debrődy.

György Debrődy with his father in Veszprém in June 1944, who, as a reserve artillery *százados*, was the commander of an anti-aircraft battery. (From the author's collection)

Not long after his return home, Debrődy was assigned to the newly created 101 Fighter Group for home defense, specifically into 101/3 Squadron.

After the combat missions against the Americans started, Debrődy scored his first air victory on 14 June 1944, when he shot down the P-38J (serial number 42-104229) fighter aircraft of 1st Lieutenant Louis Benne east from Dudar – Benne was the commander of the 14th FG's 49th Squadron on his 52nd combat sortie. The American pilot, who scored his fifth aerial victory during this mission, was wounded and captured after bailing out of his burning aircraft.[74]

Louis Benne was born on 28 July 1921 in Harrison, Pennsylvania. After he graduated from high school in Somerset, he enlisted at the recruiting office of the air force. After his fighter pilot training was completed, he was sent to Italy and flew his first combat missions in January 1944 in 14th Fighter Group. On 17 April, he shot down two Bf 109s over Italy; on 24 May, he shot down an Me 410 over Austria; and his last two victories

The aircraft of 1st Lieutenant Louis Benne was shot down by György Debrődy on 14 June 1944; the American ace was wounded and taken POW. (From the collection of the Benne family)

74 The recollections of Louis Benne can be read in Raymond F. Toliver and Trevor J. Constable, *Fighter Aces of the USA* (Fallbrook, CA: Aero Publishers, 1979), pp. 130–131; see also the mission summary of Louis Benne (copy owned by the author).

were reported during the 14 June air combat, before Debrődy shot him down. The Hungarian pilots visited him in the hospital and begged for the doctors not to amputate his badly wounded arm, for which he was forever grateful to them. Luckily, his wounds healed completely and the well-decorated ace (Silver Star, Distinguished Flying Cross, 13 Air Medals, Purple Heart) continued to serve in the USAAF, from which he was discharged in 1960 as a Lieutenant Colonel. His last mission was to command 29th Tactical Reconnaissance Squadron equipped with RF 101 Voodoo reconnaissance aircraft; this unit played an important role during the Cuban missile crisis. After his discharge, he worked in civilian life as a test pilot, and he died on 12 May 1978. He is buried in Arlington National Cemetery.[75]

Two days later, on 16 June 1944, Debrődy shot down another P-38 (serial number 43-28665). This time his opponent was a pilot of 1st FG's 94th Fighter Squadron, a Texan named 2nd Lieutenant George J. Loughmiller, who had been a B-17 pilot before and volunteered to serve with the fighters. This was his first P-38 combat sortie; he was not able to bail out from his burning aircraft and was killed when his plane crashed in the vicinity of Kapoly.[76]

On the next day, Debrődy was first recommended for the *Magyar Tiszti Arany Vitézségi Érem*.[77]

On the morning of 26 June 1944, *hadnagy* Debrődy participated in the large-scale air combat over Győr, but in the face of the superior force of the Mustangs he was not able to score any new victories. His wingman, *szakaszvezető* János Ájben, was shot down and killed.[78]

His third American opponent was shot down during the 2 July large-scale air combat over Budapest. This time the aircraft was a P-51B Mustang (serial number 43-6650), according to the author's identification an aircraft of 4th FG's 336th Fighter Squadron piloted by the 24-year-old 2nd Lieutenant John Calvin Norris. He bailed out and was captured; his aircraft crashed near Mogyoród.[79]

2nd Lieutenant Norris, who was born on 6 September 1920 in Lamesa, Texas, was not a particularly experienced pilot. He had arrived with his squadron on 3 June in England (the famous 4th FG was stationed in England, and had only been in Italy because of the shuttle bombing operations). Norris lost his unit in the air combat and was alone when Debrődy attacked him, aimed carefully at the engine – so the pilot would not be hurt – and shot his aircraft down from below and behind. The furious American pilot was able to bail out without being wounded and was captured. After the war, John Calvin Norris returned to civilian life and worked in the field of commerce, but when the Korean War broke out, the USAAF called him back to San Angelo to work as an instructor pilot. After the war, he worked as an agricultural pilot until 1958, settling into the cotton farming industry in Texas until his retirement in 1980. John C. Norris died on 25 March 1991 in his hometown, and he is also buried there.[80]

75 Frank Olynyk, *Stars and Bars. A Tribute to the American Fighter Ace 1920–1973* (London: Grub Street, 1995), p. 141; also based on documents preserved by the family of Louis Benne.
76 NARA MACR 6811.
77 *HM HIM HL*, documents of 101 Fighter Wing, box nr. 113 registry of decorations.
78 Letter of 2nd Lieutenant László Molnár to his parents, 28 June 1944 (copy owned by the author).
79 NARA MACR 6802.
80 Debrődy's air victory is wrongly located to Pilisvörösvár in the surviving Air Force Confidential Order 1944/63, because, according to the author's identification, the confirmation committee mistook Norris's aircraft as the crash-landed aircraft of Captain George I. Stanford. *HM HIM HL*, documents of 101 Fighter Wing, box nr. 110, Air Force Confidential Order Nr. 1944/63.

The local GP from Kapoly examines the remains of 2nd Lieutenant George J. Loughmiller, pilot of 1st FG, who was covered by his own parachute after being killed. Around them are curious soldiers, *leventes* and civilians. Loughmiller's aircraft was shot down by *hadnagy* Debrődy at Kapoly. (From the collection of Péter Tarr)

2nd Lieutenant John C. Norris with his Mustang. According to the author's identification, his aircraft was shot down by *hadnagy* Debrődy on 2 July 1944. (From the collection of the Norris family)

The Mustang of Captain George I. Stanford (P-51D, serial number 44-13402) crash-landed at Pilisvörösvár; the victory was erroneously credited to Debrődy (Botzheim via Soóky)

Debrődy's first American four-engined heavy bomber, a B-17, was shot down on 7 July: the aircraft brought him only two points instead of four, as it was confirmed as a shared kill with *zászlós* András Huszár, even though *zászlós* Huszár had been firing at another aircraft. The bomber was confirmed with a location of Megyercs (today Čalovec, Slovakia) in the *Csallóköz* (Žitný ostrov). Some misidentification must have happened again at the confirmation committee, because five days earlier, on 2 July, one B-17 (serial number 42-5946) of 340 Squadron/97th BG's 340th Squadron had crashed at Megyercs. The B-17 shot down by Debrődy and Huszár might have been the B-17G flown by 1st Lieutenant Ira B. Corpening (serial number 42-97183), belonging to 2nd BG's 96th Squadron; this aircraft crashed into the ground on Slovak territory, near Cerová. Nine crew members were captured, while one person successfully avoided this fate. [81]

During this sortie, Debrődy's aircraft was also hit a number of times by the gunners of the heavy bombers. One hit went through his oxygen tube, and the pressure blew onto his belly. Because of this, he landed on the nearest available airfield, at Győr, where he was transported to hospital. The examination revealed that he had luckily not sustained any injuries worth a mention. His last air victory against the Americans during the summer occurred on 27 July, when, as a member of a small formation, he shot down a Liberator west of Budapest, probably from 455th BG. On 30 July, György Debrődy was transferred to 101/1 Squadron; he was probably expected to inherit the squadron commander position after *főhadnagy* Irányi.[82]

On 7 August, his classmate and good friend László Molnár was killed, so György Debrődy remained alone for a time in the competition for the title of the most successful Hungarian fighter pilot. On 21 August, during one of the last combat missions against Americans in the summer, he was again forced to crash-land his aircraft because of mechanical problems (the engine stopped) even before the actual air combat had begun. Most probably he landed his aircraft near Márkó.[83]

György Debrődy was again recommended for the *Magyar Tiszti Arany Vitézségi Érem* on 9 September 1944, again without result. His commander, Aladár Heppes, wrote of him: 'With his 23 confirmed air victories, after the death of *hadnagy* László Molnár, he is the most successful Hungarian fighter pilot. An outstanding personality among his comrades, he is an instructor and a role model for those who serve with him.'[84]

After the end of the combat missions during the summer, the following description was written into his logbook: 'Until 31 October 1944, he served in the Home Air Defense as flight leader. He took part in 21 missions. During the air combats, he achieved six confirmed air victories (2 Lightnings, 1 Mustang, 2 Liberators, 1 Böing [sic!] Fortress II).'[85] The number '1' is crossed out and rewritten as '2' for the Liberators, which suggests the later addition of his 5

81 NARA MACR 6617, 6568; Peter Kaššák and Marián Hrodegh, *Konečná Zastávka: Slovensko!* (Martin: Klub Priateľov Vojenskej Histórie Slovenska, 2007), pp. 45–47; Robert F. Amos, Rudolph C. Koller, Alwyn T. Lloyd, and Earl W. Martin, *Defenders of Liberty 2nd Bombardment Group/Wing* (Paducah, KY: Turner, 1996), p. 240.

82 Based on the logbook of György Debrődy.

83 *HM HIM HL*, Personalia nr. 249, 23 August 1944, I/2/7; also based on the logbook of György Debrődy.

84 *HM HIM HL*, documents of 101 Fighter Wing, box nr. 113, telegram to the high command of the 1st Air Division, 307/101/I v. rep. oszt. pk (commander of the fighter group) 44. IX. 9.

85 Based on the logbook of György Debrődy.

November kill. Interestingly, however, the summary number '6' has not been rewritten from '5' but was written as such in the original.

On 1 November 1944, György Debrődy was promoted to the rank of *főhadnagy*.

When *százados* József Bejczy was killed on 4 November 1944, the next day György Debrődy was reassigned to 101/3 Fighter Squadron and take over the command.[86] He took off to his last combat sortie against the Americans on 5 November 1944; during the sortie, he reported shooting down a Liberator in the course of multiple passes southwest of the Lake Balaton.

On 12 November 1944, his commander recommended him to be promoted out of turn as *százados*. The recommendation, in which his last two air victories were not included (as they were scored four days later), praises Debrődy as follows:

> Said person has served almost two years on the front, partly on the Russian front, partly at home on the home defense front, and showed exceptional aviator skills and outstanding personal bravery – as a result of his combat actions he has scored 24 air victories (23 confirmed victories, 1 in the process of being confirmed), among them three four-engined bombers. As such, he has become the most successful fighter pilot in the Hungarian Air Force.
>
> He has served as deputy commander and squadron commander to the fighter squadron in the rank of *hadnagy*; he fulfilled the task of leading a squadron force formation and, on few occasion, a group force formation into combat with such excellence that, apart from his personal achievements, he provided the conditions for his unit to act successfully under his watchful leadership, thus contributing greatly to the unit's successes.[87]

It is extremely interesting to read the description of the last combat mission of Debrődy against the Americans on 5 November in the copy of the above-mentioned document, dated 1 February 1945:

> On 5 November 1944, he led a squadron of the fighter formation deployed against powerful American bomber units. Upon meeting the enemy, his formation commander assigned a separate group of targets to him, toward which he led his squadron bravely and so skillfully that they were fully able to exploit the element of surprise and gain the advantage. He noticed at the beginning of the attack that the releasing mechanism on his drop tank was not working, but he did not want to leave his squadron without a leader; therefore, fully aware of the dangers of fighting with the drop tank, he led his squadron and carried out the attack, making more than one pass at the enemy, during which he personally shot down a Liberator.
>
> During the combat against the enemy bomber units, he noticed that an overwhelming force of enemy fighter aircraft were arriving to join the fight, so he alone went down to the fighters and engaged them in combat to preoccupy them, succeeding in helping his squadron complete the attack against the bomber – during which one of his subordinates shot down a Liberator – and then disengaged the enemy bombers.[88]

86 Based on the logbook of György Debrődy.
87 *HM HIM HL*, recommendations for decorations, box nr. 13, group 510.a.
88 *HM HIM HL*, recommendations for decorations, box nr. 13, group 510.a.

The copy was made on 12 February 1945, a few days after Wing Order Nr. 1945/31, which, 'in the lack of eyewitnesses' deleted the Liberator from the kills Debrődy achieved on 5 November. There is thus some misunderstanding regarding this event; it is even stranger that his wing commander, who deleted the air victory a few days earlier, spoke about the exact same aircraft being shot down by Debrődy. In Debrődy's logbook, the aircraft is indicated as having been shot down, and he always counted it among his confirmed air victories. Because of the uncertainty, the author has also counted the aircraft as part of the airman's confirmed air victories, because it is impossible for a squadron commander leading his unit not to have any eyewitnesses for his victory, and this particular kill could not have been counted as a victory earlier if it had not been confirmed by at least one eyewitness. (The contradictions surrounding the deleted air victories will be detailed later.)

During the day, Hungarian fighters significantly overclaimed aagainst the American four-engines, but on one occasion for example a seriously damaged Liberator from 451st BG's 727th Squadron was hit multiple times by five attacking Bf 109s. At last, the bomber landed on Vis island's emergency airfield near the Yugoslavian coast, which was frequently used by the Americans, where the aircraft's nose landing gear collapsed. The crew flew back to their base with another aircraft, and the one left on the island was presumably written off. This one could well have been Debrődy's victim; on that day, there were no German fighters in the air combat against the 15th AAF, only Hungarians.[89]

Főhadnagy Debrődy took off on his last combat sortie on 16 November 1944 and led two flights of his squadron over the Jászság to a free hunt mission. First, they met a Lavochkin formation frontally, at a high altitude. *Főhadnagy* Debrődy carried out a head-on attack on the leading La-5; due to the hits received, the seriously damaged enemy aircraft went into a nose-dive. Debrődy did not follow it; he saw that fatal damage had been inflicted on the enemy aircraft. By comparing the Soviet and Hungarian sources, it seems that the victim this time was *starshiy leytenant* Boris Vasilievich Zhigulenkov, an excellent pilot and deputy squadron commander of 178th GIAP.

Starshiy leytenant Boris Vasilievich Zhigulenkov (1922–1944), ace of 178th GIAP with 20 air victories, Hero of the Soviet Union. On 16 November 1944, he was shot down by György Debrődy and was killed in his crash-landed La-5 (TsAMO)

Zhigulenkov was similar in skills to Debrődy; he was born on 2 May 1922 in Vasilevo. He had served on the front since June 1943 and fought 57 air combats during his 219 combat sorties, during which he scored 20 air victories – 11 against Bf 109s, and three against Fw 190s over Hungary. This is why he had been decorated with the golden star of the Hero of the Soviet Union on 26 October 1944. He also received the Order of Lenin, two Orders of the Red Banner and the Order of the Patriotic War 1st Class. The Soviet pilot was seriously wounded and, although he managed to crash-land near Besenyszög, he

89 Recollections of Delore Athmann, the radio operator of the aircraft, in manuscript (copy owned by the author).

was dead by the time he was pulled out of the cockpit of the wreck of his La-5FN (serial number 39212952) aircraft.[90]

After bringing down the Lavochkin, Debrődy engaged a Yakovlev fighter in the airspace of Nagykáta. The two pilots decided on a head-on attack, which resulted in serious consequences for both. The two aircraft, approaching each other with extreme speed, shot each other down: the Soviet pilot (probably *mladshiy leytenant* I.S. Rulev from the 85th GIAP with his Yak-9D [serial number 2015329], who, according to Soviet documents, went missing) was killed when his aircraft was blown up by the hits from Debrődy's 3cm cannon rounds. At the same time, however, he also managed to seriously damage the Hungarian pilot's aircraft, and a 20mm cannon round tore through Debrődy's belly near the spine. In spite of his grave injury, Debrődy managed to fly his aircraft back to the area behind his own lines and belly-landed near Hatvan, where he was rushed to hospital and his life was saved.[91]

The 26-year-old Ismail Semenovich Rulev was an ace in his own right with five air victories; one was achieved at Torda (today Turda, Romania) and three over the Great Hungarian Plains (*Alföld*), so Debrődy, although it almost cost him his life, fought his last air victories against exceptionally skillful and successful opponents.[92]

Because Debrődy had been flying without a dog tag, at first he could not be identified at the 11th Army Hospital (*helyőrségi kórház*) where he had been taken, unconscious. Wing Order Nr. 1944/44, therefore, issued 18 November, mentions him as missing in action; in the chaos of the dogfight against the Soviet fighters, his wingman had lost sight of his element leader, and was thus unsure of his fate.[93]

György Debrődy was an exceptional pilot in that he had excellent instructing skills; his less experienced comrades always received good advice from him. However, when in the air, Debrődy himself usually acted against his own advice and was courageous to the brink of fearlessness. He did not heed bad tactical position or superior numbers, but always rushed in and engaged the enemy at once. The last time his fearlessness almost cost him his life.

After his extremely serious injuries, Debrődy was again recommended for the *Magyar Tiszti Arany Vitézségi Érem* (it is not completely clear whether the previous recommendation was used again, or whether a new one was written), and at last he was decorated with this medal on 17 December 1944 as the 14th officer in the Royal Hungarian Armed Forces (*magyar királyi honvédség*).[94] Not long after this, as of 1 January 1945, he was promoted out of turn to *százados*.[95]

Debrődy was later transferred to the hospital in Balatonfüred, then to Veszprém, and he recovered miraculously swiftly from his grave injuries. His first flight with an Arado was on 20 March 1945, and on 14 April 1945 he completed a flight with a Bf 109, although he was not sent on a combat mission again until the end of the war (he did nevertheless execute some aircraft transfer

90 In a number of Soviet sources, the date Zhigulenkov's death is completely mistaken and stated as 7 February 1945: for example in *Geroi Sovietskovo soyuza* (Moscow: Vojenizdat, 1987), Book 1, p. 502. In the new Russian literature, the date is correct: Bikhov, *Sovetskie Asy 1941–1945*, p. 175; Horváth, *Bostonok a magyar égen és földben*, p. 53.

91 *HM HIM HL*, HM 47.118/8. ny.v.-1945; Horváth, *Bostonok a magyar égen és földben*, p. 53.

92 For Rulev, see Bikhov, *Sovetskie Asy 1941–1945*, p. 432 (although this source gives an incorrect date, 17 November, for the disappearance of Rulev).

93 *HM HIM HL*, HM 30.470/8. ny.v.-1945; documents of 101 Fighter Wing, Wing Order Nr. 1944/44.

94 *Honvédségi Rendeletek* (*Személyes ügyek*), 1945:7 (31 January 1945), p. 1.

95 *Honvédségi Rendeletek* (*Személyes ügyek*), 1945:7 (31 January 1945), p. 3.

flights with Bf 109s). By the end of the war, Debrődy had completed a total of 199 combat sorties and fought 57 air combats, during which he scored the victories detailed above. Apart from this, he also completed 18 fighter-bomber missions and at least six strafing runs. [96]

György Debrődy in a hospital bed at Balatonfüred on 30 November 1944. (From the author's collection)

Debrődy was captured with his wing in Austria at the beginning of May. He came home for a short time in December 1945, but decided fairly quickly that he did not want to stay in the country in its present state, occupied by the Soviets. Together with his many comrades – among them Miklós Kenyeres – he went first to Italy, where Debrődy worked as an unloader, a travel agent, a walk-on man and then a sign-painter. In 1947, with Miklós Kenyeres, he traveled to Spain, where he worked in a heavy steel factory as an assistant engineer; at the weekends it was also possible for him to fly as part of a Barcelona aviation club. Here he contracted heavy metal poisoning, and an X-ray revealed that the cause was a 12.7mm Soviet heavy machine gun round that had been lodged in his body since 16 November 1944. It was only removed in 1967 in North America. In 1957, he went with Miklós Kenyeres to Canada, where he worked for the Westinghouse Company until 1968 as a draftsman and designer. In 1968, at the behest of Pan American Airways, he moved to the USA, where he edited technical books for passenger airplanes, but his department was dismissed four years later and for a while he was without work, experiencing difficulties in finding a new job. At last, he worked for ETL Testing Laboratories as a draftsman and designer.[97] In 1983, he was diagnosed with lung cancer, and it brought him down very quickly. György Debrődy, one of the most prominent Hungarian fighter pilots, died on 2 February 1984 in Cortland, New York. His ashes were brought back to Spain and interred at Montjuïc Cemetery in Barcelona. His grandson, Tyler, works for the US Air Force today. The author is now working on György Debrődy's proper reburial in Hungary.

HADNAGY VITÉZ LAJOS TÓTH

Number of aerial victories: 26
Successes against ground targets: n.d.a.
Number of flown combat sorties: 181 (22 against Americans)
Number of hours flown in the air force: 800[98]
Nickname: *Drumi*
Identification number: 2054-22-0416

96 Based on the logbook of György Debrődy.
97 'Debrődy civilben' (1946–1984), *Magyar Szárnyak Évkönyv*, 1984, pp. 6–7.
98 This number is found in a document from after the war and was probably rounded up considerably. According to the author's estimation, Tóth flew 200 hours less of flight service time.

Decorations

- *Magyar Érdemrend tisztikeresztje hadidíszítménnyel és kardokkal* (25 January 1945)
- *Magyar Érdemrend lovagkeresztje hadiszalagon a kardokkal* (24 April 1944)
- *Újólagos Kormányzói dicsérő elismerés Magyar Koronás Ezüst Érdemérme hadiszalagon a kardokkal* (1 November 1944)
- *Kormányzói dicsérő elismerés Magyar Koronás Bronz Érdemérme hadiszalagon a kardokkal* (9 March 1944)
- *Tűzkereszt I fokozata a kardokkal és koszorúval*, with two wound clasps
- German Iron Cross 1st Class (17 March 1945)
- German Iron Cross 2nd Class (February 1944)
- Gold *Frontflugspange* (20 April 1945)

Victories

Number	Date	Aircraft	Location
1	5 September 1943	La-5	Senkov
2	25 September 1943	Yak-1	Kiev
3	28 September 1943	Il-2	Pereiaslav
4	28 September 1943	Il-2	Pereiaslav
5	5 November 1943	Il-2	Kiev
6	5 November 1943	Il-2	Kiev
7	29 November 1943	Il-2	Zhitomir E
8	15 January 1944	La-5	Sosovo–Vahnovka E
9	27 February 1944	P-39	Kirovograd S
10	16 June 1944	P-47	Felsőireg W
11	27 June 1944	B-17	(*HSS*) Szentendre
12	7 July 1944	P-38	Tét
13	5 November 1944	B-24	(*HSS*) Iharos N
14	13 November 1944 at 14:47	Yak-9	Tápiószele S
15	16 November 1944	Il-2	Apatin
16	5 December 1944	Yak-9	Örkény N (HT-3)
17	9 December 1944	Yak-9	Györköny (KS-5)
18	4 January 1945	La-5	Bicske SE
19	21 January 1945	Yak-9	Pusztaszabolcs
20	23 January 1945	La-5	Lovasberény
21	23 January 1945	La-5	Ercsi S
22	9 March 1945 at 10:22	La-7	Gárdony SE
23	20 March 1945 at 11:35	Yak-9	Csór N
24	13 April 1945 at 17:35	La-7	Vienna N
25	14 April 1945 at 12:27	Il-2	Vienna NE
26	14 April 1945 at 12:35	Il-2	Hausleiten

Aircraft flown
Bf 109 G-6: V-373 (at the beginning of 1944), V.863 (7 August 1944)

Lajos Tóth was born in Újfehértó, Szabolcs County, on 25 August 1922. His father was an infantry *főhadnagy* (he retired in 1923 and thereafter served at auxiliary headquarters). His only brother, Zoltán,[99] who was two years younger, also chose a military career: he was promoted to *páncélos zászlós* (armored ensign) on 15 November 1944 at Vasvár, at the *Magyar Királyi 'Csaba királyfi' Honvéd Gyors-fegyvernemi Hadapródiskola* (Royal Hungarian 'Prince Csaba' Rapid Reaction Forces Cadet School), which was relocated from Marosvásárhely (today Târgu Mureș, Romania). They also had two older sisters, from their mother's first marriage. The early years of his childhood were spent in Eger, and later he lived in Pécs, where he attended the *Zrínyi Miklós Reáliskolai Nevelőintézet* (Royal Hungarian 'Zrínyi Miklós' Honvéd Military Cadet School); he was considered to be among the most talented students. József Málik, who gave him his nickname '*Drumi*' and with whom he chose the air force officer as a future path, was his classmate and best friend at Pécs.

After he has graduated as *cőger* (one who had attended military high school) in the summer of 1940, he received his primary flight training at the Debrecen (Nyulas) training site of the *HMNRA* on Bü 131 D–2 type. In the autumn, he went to Kassa to the *Repülőakadémia* as of 16 November 1940, where he was promoted to *hadnagy* on 6 December 1942 (as of 1 December 1942) with rank number 1, the first in his class. He was a real natural leader, a bold personality always hungry for success.[100]

After his promotion, he was deployed to 1 Fighter Training Group at Szolnok. He was retrained to the Messerschmitt type in the spring of 1943 from the German training detachment stationed in Székesfehérvár-Börgönd – he had been forced to emergency landing three times with the old Bf 109s because of engine problems, although he did so each time without damaging the aircraft. He was then reassigned to Szolnok to his own unit, and from here he took off for the Eastern Front (from 1 July 1943), where he was assigned to 5/2 Fighter Squadron.

Ventilating the parachutes in front of the hangar at the airfield at Debrecen-Nyulas in the summer of 1940. The seventh from left in the line is Lajos Tóth. Behind the *HMNRA* students, in front of the hangar, one of the Bü 131s of II '*Lucifer*' Short-Range Reconnaissance Squadron can be seen, used for training purposes. (From the author's collection)

99 After the repression of the 1956 revolution, Zoltán Tóth emigrated to (West) Germany. He became an embittered man and changed his family name. The author has tried to contact him in vain; he has since passed away.

100 *Honvédségi Közlöny* (*Személyes ügyek*), nr. 1942/50 (4 December 1942), p. 1265.

Lajos Tóth (far right) with his classmates in front of the building of the *Repülőakadémia* in Kassa. In the middle stands *százados* Ernő Kistelegdi, one of their teachers. (From the author's collection)

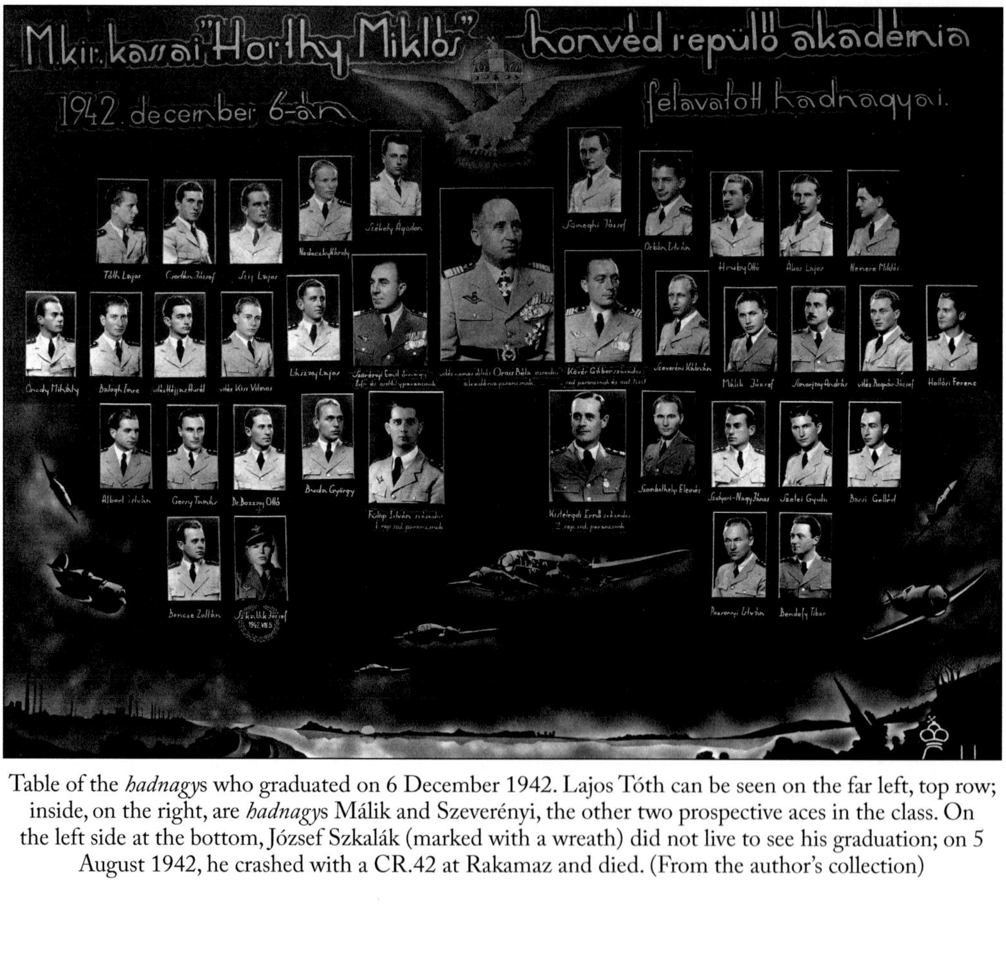

Table of the *hadnagy*s who graduated on 6 December 1942. Lajos Tóth can be seen on the far left, top row; inside, on the right, are *hadnagy*s Málik and Szeverényi, the other two prospective aces in the class. On the left side at the bottom, József Szkalák (marked with a wreath) did not live to see his graduation; on 5 August 1942, he crashed with a CR.42 at Rakamaz and died. (From the author's collection)

Lajos Tóth achieved his first air victory on 5 September 1943. *Hadnagy* Tóth was escorting Ju 87 dive bombers with *tizedes* Sándor Tanács in the area of Senkov. They noticed enemy aircraft flying at a low altitude; the other fighter element (Germans) escorting the *Stuka*s were right upon them. The Hungarian fighters also went after the enemy and they were separated. *Hadnagy* Tóth engaged an La-5 in a dogfight that lasted a few minutes, after the opponent tried to disengage northward as Tóth continued to chase him. The Soviet aircraft was forced to turn back and engage the Hungarian; following a short dogfight, he was hit and crashed into a meadow, where the aircraft instantly burst in fire. A German radio observer unit saw the whole action and confirmed the air victory.[101]

On 25 September, *hadnagy* György Debrődy was shot down east of the Dnieper on Soviet territory. His wingman, *őrmester* Pál Kovács, lost him in the very cloudy weather and declared him missing in action (he was seriously reprimanded for this by *hadnagy* Miklós Kenyeres, who feared for his dear friend).[102] *Hadnagy* Tóth led an element that took off to discover what had happened to Debrődy. While they were not able to uncover the fate of this excellent pilot, *hadnagy* Tóth took revenge on the Soviet fighters, achieving his second air victory. Later he remembered this combat sortie as follows:

> We searched for the missing *hadnagy* Debrődy in a free hunt mission. Beyond the Dnieper, I noticed Soviet fighters and we attacked them at high speed. One of the Yak-1s was showing me his underside; it was an excellent target. A short burst and the Soviet nose-dived with a spin and crashed into the ground. But after this, all the others were upon us, so down we went and sped away with a dive.[103]

Hadnagy Debrődy came back after more than 40 hours after he had fought himself through the front and even swam across the Dnieper. *Hadnagy* Tóth did not suspect that soon he, too, would be swimming. Before that, however, on 28 September, he also achieved a double air victory, again during the course of a favored type of combat mission (the free hunt), while leading a flight to the frequently visited Pereiaslav area:

> On 28 September we were again on a free hunt in the Pereiaslav area. We were at 300 meters and below us was an almost perfectly closed cloud surface. Suddenly, I saw a shadow gliding away on one of the clouds. We instantly fell through the clouds, and before us we saw 20 Il-2 heading westward. I engaged the one on the far right and shot it down from behind and from below; then I turned on the next one beside him, and set it aflame too. Both aircraft crashed. *Őrmester* Fábián, my wingman [more accurately, the leader of the second element in the flight] also got one, and also a LagGG-5 that was attacking us. I felt very happy that the surprise turned out to be that excellent. This way we managed to take out two aircraft each.[104]

101 Gyula Gaál, 'Egy önálló vadászszázad életéből', *Magyar Szárnyak Évkönyv*, 1991, p. 54; logbook of Sándor Tanács (full copy owned by the author).
102 Recollections of György Debrődy, February 1976.
103 *Üvölt a Puma*, 3 November 1943, p. 4.
104 *Üvölt a Puma*, 3 November 1943, p. 4.

On 3 October, it was *hadnagy* Tóth's turn when he was shot down during a surprise attack by a Yakovlev fighter behind enemy lines. His burning Messerschmitt Bf 109 G-2(manufactured at Wiener Neustadt, WNr. 13754) belly landed near Pereiaslav (Plq. 1176).[105] It took two days for the Hungarian pilot to get back to the German troops, and he even had to swim across the Dnieper. On crash-landing, he injured his head above his right eye, and on the next day, during his escape, he was wounded in his left hand by a Soviet submachine gun's bullet. He therefore received two wound clasps for his *Tűzkereszt*, because the two received wounds were counted separately. He remembered the adventurous story in *Üvölt a Puma*:

> I could barely believe it: they surprised me! By the time I realized what was happening, my aircraft was already burning. On crash-landing, I knocked my head and got a wound on my eyebrow. I was slightly dizzy when I jumped out of the seat and ran toward the forest. I had a whole howling army after me! I rushed through thick undergrowth and I arrived at a river approximately 40 meters wide – I plunged into it at once and swam across. Those after me were at the bank too and were poking at the bushes to find me. I hid until nightfall. At last, I could start off for the suspected border river, which I reached without any problems. Now I was only in my riding pants – the water was dreadfully cold, but I had to go in. I swam slowly, when suddenly a signal rocket was fired from the riverbank. I dived under water and let the drift carry me. At last, I reached the other riverbank and hid in the cold mud. A sentry was coming to and fro and I, trying my luck, shouted at him: 'Don't shoot, a Hungarian officer here!' The answer was a wild shooting in my direction. So I arrived at a bridgehead! I was running in a southwestern direction as fast as I possibly could. I suddenly thought I heard German words; come what may, I shouted toward that direction in German. The answer came in Russian: 'Come forward at once!' I responded with all my Russian knowledge: '*Ponimayu, harasho!*' – and I jumped in the other direction! Rockets, then a wild shooting after me from at least 20 weapons. I felt a hit on my left arm – I was wounded! Just a little more effort and I reached a forest. I was very cold and very weary; I just sank into a deep sleep. At dawn, I regained my consciousness and continued my journey. Hiding at the edge of the forest, I saw a Russian Ford going slowly up the hill. So I was still at the bridgehead! Not long after, a desert yellow Opel Blitz car followed the Ford. I ran onto the road – they aimed at me and could hardly believe that this naked, mud-covered and bloodied chap was a Hungarian officer pilot.[106]

Hadnagy Lajos Tóth tells his escape story to *százados* Gyula Horváth after being shot down on 5 October 1943. (From the author's collection)

The pilot who shot down Lajos Tóth on 3 October 1943 was the 24-year-old Soviet ace, *starshiy leytenant* Vasily Markovich Voronyuk, who served

105 Bundesarchiv-Militärarchiv, RL 2 III/1194/155.
106 *Üvölt a Puma*, 3 November 1943, pp. 2–3.

in 112nd GIAP and was flying a Yak-1; he reported his victory over a Bf 109 south of Pereiaslav (there were no other victories over a Bf 109 in the area on that day). This was Voronyuk's 11th victory; he finished the war with 15 individual and three shared air victories.[107]

Hadnagy Tóth achieved ace status by shooting down his fifth aircraft in November 1943, in which month he proved very sucessful against Soviet ground-attack aircraft. He achieved his fifth and sixth air victory on 5 November when he shot down Il-2s in the Kiev area during a free hunt. The air victories were attested by his wingman, *szakaszvezető* Sándor Nagy, who himself shot down an Ilyushin ground-attack aircraft. The wingman remembered his own air victory and the double kill achieved by his element leader:

> Smoke clouds were below us, pillars of fire. This was Kiev; most of it is in flames. We were circling around the smoke, pushing our way forward. The soldiers were like big ants running to and fro on the ground. The road to Zhitomir was like a fully packed vein. Thousands of cars ran through it, and each and every one of them was fully packed with soldiers. But listen! Small black dots going eastward. And getting bigger! This was the enemy! I pushed the radio button on the control column and warned my commander:
>
> 'Aircraft in front of us at 12 o'clock!'
>
> 'I see them!' The microphone clicks. They were getting closer as we moved in. They could be seen much better now. …
>
> On a wide arc, we got dead astern to them. My commander was already attacking; the Il-2 was burning. Poor guys, it seems they didn't know what had got them. But there were no fighters to be seen anywhere. We were free to do what we liked! … I hurled myself onto the neck of the Soviet Il-2. He

Hadnagy Lajos Tóth after he was wounded on 5 October 1943. (From the author's collection)

Hadnagys Tóth and Molnár and *zászlós* Kovács-Nagy in the early autumn of 1943, on a military airfield at the Eastern Front. Behind them is one of the Ju 87 D-3s of the Hungarian 2/2 Dive Bomber Squadron. (From the author's collection)

107 Bikhov, *Sovetskie Asy 1941–1945*, pp. 102–103; Nikita Yegorov on documents of TsAMO.

> tried to escape. No use, mate! I aimed calmly. ... My hits are nice, and the aircraft burst into flames.
>
> 'Bravo, Sándor!' I heard my commander's voice. So indeed the Soviet had crashed! I could not see it because I had pulled up promptly for another attack. I'm full with raging warrior fire. I saw yet another aircraft in the air – I started after him, but my commander got in before me and engaged it rapidly, throwing it down. The others fled in terror eastward.[108]

It would be interesting to share details about the *szakaszvezető*, Sándor Nagy, who also led an extraordinary life. He was shot down in an air combat on 1 April 1944 and was captured; after the war, in 1949, he was awarded the *Kossuth-díj ezüst fokozat*a (Silver Grade of the Kossuth Prize) for his writings on the poor agriculture class. In 1952, the Soviet Union awarded him the Stalin Prize for his short story entitled '*Megbékélés*' ('Atonement'); the award was presented to him on 25 October 1952 at the embassy of the Soviet Union in Budapest. Following this, however, in 1964 he was imprisoned for three years on charges of agitation and anti-state activity. This newspaper article is, to the author's knowledge, the first publication in a fundamentally different style from that of his later writings.[109]

Lajos Tóth scored another victory on 29 November against an Il-2, not far from the new airfield at Zhitomir in January.

After the end of November, following a fairly unsuccessful period, *Drumi* was again successful. In the middle of January 1944, which was an exceptionally successful month for Hungarian fighters, he shot down another La-5 fighter. Lajos Tóth scored his last confirmed victory on the Eastern Front on 27 February 1944 over Kirovograd, against an Airacobra. He described this last air combat in the contemporary aviation magazine, the *Magyar Szárnyak* ('Hungarian Wings'):

> For days I have been in a state of utter excitement. I have just come back from my leave, and the comrades greet me with good news. We are in a sector of the Russian air jungle where a few 'air snakes' are nesting – the proud, famous American aircraft, the Bell Airacobras. I slowly strap myself into my faithful aircraft, and I would like to whisper into its ear: 'Today we are going against big game!' We need to use all our cunning and wit. The night before my friend *Oroszlán* ['Lion', the nickname of *hadnagy* László Molnár], the great hunter, attacked two of them, but they got away. I need to succeed. ... No Cobra has been shot down before by Hungarian fighters.[110] The fronts are under us already. I call my wingman

108 Sándor Nagy, 'A győztes vadászok. Sanyi első légi győzelme', *Magyar Szárnyak*, 15 April 1944, p. 8.

109 For Sándor Nagy (Nagybaracska, 10 June 1922–Budapest, 4 April 1990), see Csaba B. Stenge, 'Horthy Miklós vadászpilótájából Sztálin-díjas író: Nagy Sándor élettörténete', *Katonaújság*, 2013:6, pp. 14–19; and *Kossuth-díjasok és Állami díjasok almanachja 1948–1985* (Budapest: Akadémiai Kiadó, 1988), p. 81.

110 This was not true; although the type was not recognized, the Hungarians had fought the first air combats with the Soviet P-39 fighter aircraft already in August 1942 against 153rd IAP, the first Soviet fighter unit equipped with Airacobras and deployed in the area of Voronezh. The Hungarian *Héja*s and the Soviet Airacobras first engaged in combat on 6 August, then again on 9 August. During the air combat on 6 August, although two engagements took place, it is difficult to decide if there were any claims against Airacobras because detailed information is scarce. This, however, can be followed quite well in Soviet sources, which always reported the Hungarian Re.2000 type as 'Macchi

on the radio: 'Aircraft on the right!' As I approach them, I realize these are Messerschmitt fighters out on a mission. So there will be no big game caught up in the net here; let's go elsewhere! But where will I find them? Which cloud path, which cloud clearance will show them to me? Suddenly the easiest, simplest, yet not the safest solution pops up in my mind: 'The big game needs to be caught in its den!' If he is not here, then he must be staying at home. That is a place not even the Germans dare to go to. They have their airfield near a big city, far behind the enemy lines, and the area is packed with heavy anti-aircraft defense. There won't be any problems, I try to convince myself; just bravely go forward! The German fighters disappear behind us, and we are in Soviet territory already, approaching the snowy city, the den of the cobra, bathing in the sun. ... All my senses are working; I am looking around with my whole body. So it is below us, the big city ... yes, there is the airfield ... and there are the Cobras. We fly past the airfield, which is packed with Soviet aircraft as if on parade. We hang ourselves on the glowing sun, and we watch from a balcony as the performance starts. The anti-aircraft defense is playing the overture. This is fishy ... they want to start off with some mass scene we guess. At this moment, eight aircraft took off at the same time from the airfield. They are coming for us! The curtains are drawn back, the first act has begun! The first piece: air acrobat show, presenters: *hadnagy* Lajos Tóth and *szakaszvezető* Ernő Kiss from Hungary. Also starring eight prominent members of the Stalin fighter regiment. The circus helpers are the Russian mechanics, who have already let the large beasts loose: six Airacobras took off in swift succession. The accompanying music is played by the various caliber anti-aircraft batteries playing in high-pitched 'C' major.

We are in the best of places. In the enormous cupola of the circus tent, in the sun itself, we are making our turns and preparing ourselves to enter the scene. The acrobats of the famous Stalin-regiment are already climbing up the rope ladder. They have almost reached the second floor when we hit them from the balcony. The distance is more than 1,000 meters. We are on them with hellish speed from the circus cupola, from behind a thin cloud cover. A wild dogfight begins; we are grappling with each other, presenting all formations of the acrobatics to the excited but not too grateful grounds spectators, who are not stopping with throwing large, burning heavy anti-aircraft artillery buckets of flower at us. I am right at the rear of the Yak-9. A sweet sense of revenge fills me – now I will pay back.

Perhaps this is the same Yak-9 that has shot me down three months earlier at P. [Pereiaslav], and I could hardly fight my way back to the German lines two days later, naked, wounded, having swum across the Dnieper. I already want to open fire when my wingman shouts in the radio: 'Cobras on the right... the Cobras!' Like a madman, I pull up my aircraft to the left into the sun again ... back to the balcony, to review the situation. The eight Yak-9s are far away now; they have lost us and they head down toward the first row of seats. The first act has ended. The upcoming second part of the show: snake-charming. Presenters: *hadnagy* Lajos Tóth with his exotic wingman, *Balbó* [the nickname of *szakaszvezető* Ernő Kiss], with six well-fed, shiny black skinned American Bell Airacobras. I don't know the method yet, am trying it out now. ... I sneak past over the Airacobras ... and I watch ... with heightened senses; I just watch and listen with all my

C.200'. During the air combat against P-39s on 9 August, *hadnagy* László Kázár from 1 Fighter Group reported shooting down two, while *őrmester* Sándor Tarnai reported shooting down one enemy aircraft. In reality, however, there were no P-39 losses on that day.

senses. The blood of the hunter is boiling in me; the big game I was waiting for so long is here … just carefully, not to scare them away. We know these must be attacked by the tail because they have poisonous stings at their noses: cannon and machine guns. Down below the play is being followed eagerly. The music has also stopped. No wind is blowing. I wait in anticipation, hanging from the cupola, for the right moment. The snakes are having hardships in locating me, the sun is blinding them. Over the houses of the city, two dishevelled Il-2 bear cubs are waiting for their turn.

Now! The tension reached its highest point in me. One of the cobras lagged behind. … The others have left him, and his distance from the formation is growing. It has paid off to wait! Like a dart I plunge upon him at high speed. … He still hasn't noticed me, even though I am right behind him. My finger is on the trigger. Suddenly he pulls up desperately, he wants to escape, and shows his whole backside to me. I only push the trigger once. … I see the tracing bullets hitting the cockpit. We almost clash as I disengage in close proximity. He helplessly shakes, pulls up, then quickly loses speed and dives down at an increasing speed to crash and shatter to a million pieces down below. The attraction has ended. Nobody is clapping and giving me compliments; the audience is watching in silent horror. It seems I did not gain too much success with this attraction here; let's go home then, they will surely appreciate the story. The curtains have fallen, the play has ended. I just glance at the smoking wreck down below once more and whisper to myself: 'Bell Airacobra, beautiful air snake!'[111]

On 27 June 1944, *hadnagy* Tóth was credited with an air victory against a B-17, shot out of formation north of Budapest. The photo shows the vertical stabilizer of a B-17 from 301st BG (serial number 42-30106), which crashed north of Budapest on that day at Márianosztra as a result of fighter attack. (From the collection of Péter Tarr)

It must be added to the above-described story that – if the surviving date is exact – the kill was not confirmed by Soviet sources, and the two fighter divisions in the area equipped with Airacobras (205th IAD and 304th IAD) did not report any total losses during the day.

On 10 March 1944, Tóth suffered an unpleasant accident. While taking off from Proskurov airfield on icy ground, the starboard landing gear of his plane was damaged and it collapsed while landing at Jasionka. The aircraft was 60 percent damaged, but the pilot was unharmed.[112]

On 14 March 1944, *hadnagy* Tóth was ordered back home after completing 95 (93 according to some sources) combat sorties and scoring nine

111 Lajos Tóth, 'Kobrát fogtam…', *Magyar Szárnyak*, 1 April 1944, pp. 8–10.
112 Based on his evaluation report: *Magyar Szárnyak Évkönyv*, 1992, p. 280. The original evaluation report was destroyed after the death of his two sisters.

confirmed air victories on the Eastern Front.[113] From 1 May 1944, he was reassigned from Szolnok to Veszprém as a flight leader, and then as the deputy commander of 101/2 Squadron of 101 Fighter Group, which was at that time being formed.

Hadnagy Tóth poses in his Messerschmitt in 1944. (From the author's collection)

During the summer combat missions, Tóth reported his first air victory against Americans on 16 June 1944, against a P-47. The Americans did not experience any losses of P-47s on that day, and these types did not take a significant part in air combat, so the case must be treated as a mistaken type recognition; in reality, he engaged a Mustang. A Mustang of 52nd FG indeed crashed in Hungarian soil on that day, but its pilot (who bailed out) remembered being shot down by Lightnings by mistake (for more details, see the biography for *hadnagy* Karátsonyi).[114]

On 27 June 1944, American B-17s raided Budapest, and *hadnagy* Tóth reported shooting a Flying Fortress out of its formation north of Budapest. A B-17F from 301st BG's 353rd Squadron (serial number 42-30106) crashed in the reported area that day after having been attacked by fighters. The aircraft was flown by 2nd Lieutenant Hugh J. McGee, and the nine-member crew was captured. Although the fatal hit on the aircraft was probably achieved by a twin-engined Bf 110 G-2 from the 6./ZG 1, *hadnagy* Tóth may also have engaged the same aircraft.[115]

Two weeks later, on 7 July, during their second air defence mission of the day, the Hungarian fighters first engaged the Lightnings of 82nd Fighter Group. The formation attacked the Lightnings once according to orders, then turned toward the arriving Liberators for one pass. *Hadnagy* Tóth remained alone among the Lightnings in a dogfight, and was at last shot down west of Tét, near Mórichida. The Hungarian pilot bailed out of his Bf 109 G-6 (manufactured in Győr) and landed without injury. Before being shot down, he had hit a Lightning, which nose-dived in front of him (although Tóth never stated that he saw the aircraft crashing, only that he saw it falling into a corkscrew). After landing, as both he and the American pilot were brought to Pápa airfield, he met the American pilot of the shot down P-38: 2nd Lieutenant Charles C. Walker, who crashed southwest of Tét at Szentkútpuszta. Tóth was confident that he had shot him and thus claimed the air victory, but in fact *szakaszvezető* Faludi had actually been responsible. As Faludi did not provide an exact location, however, the kill was not

113 *HM HIM HL*, documents of 101 Fighter Wing, box nr. 113, Royal Hungarian 101/I Honvéd Fighter Group 2 Squadron, summary of missions completed by the squadron against Americans and Soviets; and box nr. 112, Royal Hungarian 102 Honvéd Fighter Group, summary of decorated officers and enlisted, 29 January 1945.

114 MACR 5816; George Crawford, *Three Crawford Brothers: The WWII Memoirs of Three Pilots* (Bloomington, IN: AuthorHouse, 2008), pp. 411–424.

115 NARA MACR 6175.

A Hungarian Messerschmitt Bf 109 G-6 (V.863, serial number 95464) that belly-landed on 7 August 1944 after air combat. This was the aircraft of *hadnagy* Lajos Tóth, which belly-landed near Zalaszentgrót after being hit several times by Mustangs. (From the collection of János Pocskai)

confirmed to him during the summer, only at the end of the war. *Hadnagy* Tóth probably shot 2nd Lieutenant Lester J. Henry's aircraft from the same squadron; he was a newcomer who had only arrived to the 82nd FG's 95th Squadron on 26 June, and his aircraft was hit by a 2cm cannon round on the port fuselage.[116]

During the summer, Lajos Tóth did not succeed in achieving another air victory over the Americans.

During the tragic mission on 7 August, the Mustangs of 31st Fighter Group shot down *hadnagy* Tóth's Messerschmitt. He was hit several times and belly-landed near Zalaszentgrót, while his Bf 109 G-6 (manufactured in Győr, nr. V.863, serial number 95464) suffered 30 percent damage.[117]

In the autumn, the combat missions against the Soviets began, and on 11 October 101/I Fighter Group was deployed for a reconnaissance mission to the Tisza river to assess the situation on the ground, despite very cloudy weather. Among the received reports, the one with the most outstanding details was submitted by Lajos Tóth, although he did not have the best view from the cockpit of his Bf 109; nor was it easy to fly at a low altitude with high speed and making observations. Despite the terrible weather, storms and unfavorable visibility, and despite heavy Soviet anti-aircraft artillery fire, Tóth spent 100 minutes in enemy airspace, during which he obtained valuable information about Soviet armored formation movements and made other observations of tactical importance. This report offered the first clear picture of the situation at the Tisza, and for this *hadnagy* Tóth was specially commended by the commander in chief of the air force. According to the memories of Lajos Krascsenics, at the end of the mission the Hungarians also strafed the Soviet armored columns at a low altitude.[118]

116 *MNL Győr-Moson-Sopron Megye Győri Levéltára* (National Archives, Győr-Moson-Sopron County Archives, Győr), IV. B. 454/a, documents and administrative files of the *vicecomes* of Győr-Moson-Pozsony t. u. a. r. (*közigazgatásilag egyelőre egyesített* ['temporarily unified for administrative reasons'] – k. e. e) counties, box 388, report of the chief constable of the processus of Sokoróalja, 7 July 1944; NARA MACR 6573. For this aerial combat, see Steve Blake, 'Ambush over Hungary. A "Puma" pilot's revenge', *Fighter Pilots in Aerial Combat*, Fall, 1984, pp. 12–17.

117 Based on his evaluation report: *Magyar Szárnyak Évkönyv*, 1992, p. 280.

118 *HM HIM HL*, documents of 101 Fighter Wing, box nr. 112, 864 biz./101 v. rep. e. 45. III.16; Lajos Krascsenics, *Egy magyar királyi vadászrepülő visszaemlékezései* (Budapest: Tipo Kolor, 1990), pp. 44–46.

The Hungarian 101 Fighter Wing was again sent on a last combat mission against American heavy bombers on 5 November 1944. On this day, Tóth reported a air victory against a Liberator southwest of Lake Balaton. In summary, Lajos Tóth completed 22 sorties against the Americans in 1944, during which he reported four air victories.[119]

Aladár Heppes confirmed both of Tóth's four-engined kills (the B-17 of 27 June and the B-24 of 5 November) – as having shot out from the formation (*'Herausschuss'*) in Wing Order Nr. 1945/62. This category of air victory had not existed before in the Royal Hungarian Air Force. The same Wing Order confirmed his P-47 of 16 June: this air victory had not been confirmed during the strict examination over the summer, as no Thunderbolt wreck had been found in the area. However, as the claim met all formal requirements, including the existing witnesses, it was confirmed at the end of the war by the wing commander.[120]

With the redeployment of *főhadnagy* Tibor Papp, *hadnagy* Tóth led 101/2 Fighter Squadron from 9 November 1944 (initially as a commissioned commander). Under his successful leadership, the squadron became the most successful in the wing, even overtaking 101/3 Squadron, partly due to Tóth's and Szentgyörgyi's achieved air victories and partly due to the excellent leadership. Although he had often proved his ability, opinions on Tóth varied among his substitutes, and he was not unequivocally popular (the same was true of his good friend, József Málik, who also become a squadron commander). Tóth's overconfidence and his unbounded ambition might have contributed to this, and some of the pilots who were *cőger* – with their specific code of conduct and the privileges associated with them – were not very popular among the soldiers of civilian background. Of course, one cannot make generalizations, as former *cőger* Bejczy, Irányi and Papp had been exceptionally popular squadron commanders, and the heaviest conflict did not occur between a civilian and a *cőger* but between two *cőger*s, Irányi and Heppes. However, this very interesting aspect is unfortunately beyond the scope of this work.

As a commander, Lajos Tóth led his squadron into combat first time on 13 November, when he led a six aircraft formation to meet 16 Soviet Yakovlev fighter aircraft. Due to Tóth's leadership, the Hungarian formation reported five air victories, of which four were confirmed, without any losses of their own. One of the victories was reported by *hadnagy* Tóth. Their opponents were probably the Yak-9s of 149th GIAP, of which two were destroyed in the region at the specified time (one went missing and the other crash-landed). Three days later, the squadron reported shooting down two Soviet ground-attack aircraft at Apatin (these probably belonged to 165th GSAP). One was destroyed by the squadron commander.[121] Meanwhile, in the late autumn of 1944, Tóth was initiated into the *Vitézi Rend* based on his own merits.

In December, his number of air victories was increased when he shot down two Yakovlev fighters, the first reported on 5 December at Dabas, and the second on 9 December approximately in the area of Simontornya. Both were confirmed in Wing Order Nr. 1945/13 with the map code locations of HT-3 and KS-5 (the latter kill was probably an aircraft of 288th IAD).

119 *HM HIM HL*, documents of 101 Fighter Wing, box nr. 113, Royal Hungarian 101/I Honvéd Fighter Group 2 Squadron, summary of the missions executed by the squadron against Americans and Soviets; command of 101/I Honvéd Fighter Group, names on the 13th of current month as per Order Nr. 431/101 *v. rep. o. pk.* 44. XII. 13.

120 *HM HIM HL*, documents of 101 Fighter Wing, box nr. 110, Wing Order Nr. 1945/62.

121 *HM HIM HL*, documents of 101 Fighter Wing, box nr. 112, 864 biz./101 v. rep. e. 45. III.16; Nikita Yegorov on documents of TsAMO.

A group of pilots from 101/2 Fighter Squadron in November 1944 in Veszprém; to their left is a Bf 109 G-14/U4, manufactured in Wiener Neustadt, with a 300-litre drop tank under the fuselage. Pictured, left to right: *zászlós* Dezső Szentgyörgyi, *hadnagy* Lajos Tóth, *szakaszvezető* Lajos Krascsenics and *hadnagy* János Karcsai. János Karcsai was captured by the Soviet troops on 28 January 1945 after being hit by anti-aircraft fire; he died in captivity under unknown circumstances. (From the author's collection)

A humorous drawing from 1945 in which the leader of the flight, *hadnagy* Lajos Tóth, orders the Hungarian flight to 'Break through the fighter escort!' to reach the Soviet Boston bombers. (Drawing by Gyula Pintér)

Later, when geographical names were used in the registry instead of map codes, the locations of the two air victories were designated as Örkény North and Györköny.

During the heavy fighting in January 1945, *hadnagy* Tóth shot down four Soviet fighter aircraft, including a Lavochkin from 530th IAP on 4 January southeast of Bicske (similarly to Dezső Szentgyörgyi). On 23 January, he reported victories over two further Lavochkins; his victims were probably the two pilots of 31st IAP and 164th IAP who were killed on this day – *mladshiy leytenant* H.A. Abrarov and *starshiy leytenant* N.E. Grekhovodov. On 25 January, *vezérezredes* Károly Beregfy visited Veszprém airfield and awarded Tóth the *Magyar Érdemrend tisztikeresztje hadiékítményekkel és kardokkal*. This was a unique case, as this very high-grade decoration was received by Tóth despite the fact that 101 Fighter Wing had not yet recommended him.[122]

After a short, uneventful period, *hadnagy* Tóth reported his next air victory on 9 March 1945. On this day, he took off at 10:40 for a free hunt mission in the airspace of Seregélyes. After takeoff, the formation climbed steeply; soon they encountered nearly a dozen La-7s at an altitude of 3,500 meters in the Gárdony area. One was shot down by *hadnagy* Tóth at 10:22, southeast of Gárdony; the enemy aircraft crashed and exploded, according to his report. The kill was witnessed and attested to by *hadnagy* László Hemmert, and the formation was on the airfield again at 10:50. The air combat was probably fought against the La-7s of 179th GIAP, although the Soviet unit did not lose any aircraft that day.[123]

On 16 March 1945, *hadnagy* Tóth was recommended by his wing commander for promotion to *főhadnagy* out of turn. This recommendation was not, however, assessed until the end of the war. In the recommendation, *alezredes* Heppes credited the merits of *hadnagy* Lajos Tóth as follows:

> I recommend *hadnagy* Lajos Tóth to be promoted to the rank of *főhadnagy* based on his extraordinary combat merits on the battlefield.
>
> Said person has completed nearly two years of front-line service, partly on the Russian front, partly in home defense, and he has destroyed 22 enemy aircraft, thereby showcasing unmatched bravery and skills. Among his air victories, there were three multi-engined bombers [two four-engined bombers and one twin-engined fighter], making him one of the most successful fighter pilots of the Hungarian Armed Forces.
>
> His appointed positions as fighter squadron deputy commander, then squadron commander, have been fulfilled by him in the rank of *hadnagy*, but he has skillfully led squadrons and groups in combat with such efficiency that, beyond his own achievements arising from his personal bravery, he has also assured his unit's successful actions and thus contributed greatly to his unit's performance.[124]

The last air victory for Lajos Tóth from Veszprém was scored on 20 March 1945. He led a formation of eight aircraft for a free hunt, taking off at 11:37. *Hadnagy* Tóth reported a victory

122 *HM HIM HL*, documents of 101 Fighter Wing, box nr. 113, registry of decorations; Horváth, *Bostonok a magyar égen és földben*, p. 99; Gábor Horváth on documents of TsAMO.
123 *HM HIM HL*, documents of 101 Fighter Wing, box nr. 113, mission log of 101 Fighter Wing, 9 March 1945; Horváth, *Bostonok a magyar égen és földben*, p. 135.
124 *HM HIM HL*, documents of 101 Fighter Wing, box nr. 112, 864 biz./101 v. rep. e. 45. III.16.

over a Yak-9 over Csór airfield at 11:35; according to the report of the squadron commander, the enemy pilot was not able to bail out and crashed with his aircraft. The witness to the air victory was *hadnagy* Pál Forró, but this kill cannot be proven based on Soviet documents.[125] During the retreat to the west, Tóth was not engaged in air combat for a time; his last three air victories were scored in April while taking off from Raffelding.

Hadnagy Tóth took off on 13 April, in late afternoon, at 17:00 and led eight aircraft northeast of Győr on a free hunt. The Hungarian formation met superior numbers of Soviet fighters; approximately 30 to 40 Lavochkin and Yakovlev fighters engaged them north of Vienna. Tóth reported shooting down an La-7 at 17:35; according to the combat report, it was burning as it crashed headlong into the ground with its pilot. The kill was witnessed by *hadnagys* Sándor Csizmadia and Antal Szebeni, but sadly the Hungarian formation also lost two fighters. There was a loss of an La-7 on that day in the area, but that aircraft went missing at 08:45 in the morning, and so was definitely not Tóth's opponent, whom he fought in the afternoon. It must be added that the Lavochkins engaged in the air combat were more probably La-5s.[126]

The next day, Tóth took off at 12:10, leading an eight aircraft flight. The task was the same as the day before. The Hungarian formation engaged two Soviet ground-attack aircraft formations escorted by Yakovlevs, and *hadnagy* Tóth shot down one Il-2 from each group. His first victim, flying at a low altitude at 300 meters, crashed at 12:27, while his comrade, flying south of the Danube 200 meters higher than the first aircraft, followed suit at 12:35. According to the Hungarian report, neither pilot was able to bail out and both perished in their aircraft. The first kill was witnessed by *hadnagy* Mihály Karátsonyi, and the second was witnessed by *zászlós* Tibor Dinka. In the first case, the victim was probably the aircraft of 951st SAP (serial number 1880702) flown by the crew of *mladshiy leytenant* M.M. Satanovski that crashed northwest of Vienna; the other was the aircraft flown by *leytenant* V. N. Simanskiy of 210th SAP (serial number 1887210), which crashed with its crew near Stockerau, directly east of the reported Hausleiten. At this time, Hungarian aircraft repeatedly engaged La-7 formations of highly skilled pilots on the free hunt missions led by Tóth in the area of Sankt Pölten, but neither party could harm the other. Tóth called the missions the 'twilight gigs of Sankt Pölten' (he also called the combat missions against the Americans in the summer of 1944 the 'American season').[127]

The last known combat sortie of Lajos Tóth took place in the afternoon of 19 April 1945. At 15:06 he was leading a four-aircraft flight to escort German Hs 129 tank destroyers, but neither the German aircraft nor the enemy showed up in the appointed area, and the flight returned to base.[128]

125 *HM HIM HL*, documents of 101 Fighter Wing, box nr. 113, after-action reports and mission logs of 101 Fighter Wing, 20 March 1945; Gábor Horváth on documents of TsAMO.

126 *HM HIM HL*, documents of 101 Fighter Wing, box nr. 113, mission logs of 101 Fighter Wing, 13 April 1945; Gábor Horváth on documents of TsAMO.

127 *HM HIM HL*, documents of 101 Fighter Wing, box nr. 113, after-action reports and mission logs of 101 Fighter Wing, 14 April 1945; Horváth, *Bostonok a magyar égen és földben*, p. 206.

128 *HM HIM HL*, documents of 101 Fighter Wing, box nr. 113, mission logs of 101 Fighter Wing, 19 April 1945.

On 24 April 1945 (for the second time after 24 November 1944), Tóth's wing commander recommended him for the *Magyar Tiszti Arany Vitézségi Érem*, but this was not been awarded to him. The recommendation described Tóth as follows:

> With his high number of air victories, he is the second most successful Hungarian fighter pilot [Debrődy was not included]. *Hadnagy vitéz* Lajos Tóth as a squadron commander has successfully led his unit to become the fighter squadron with the greatest number of air victories. His performance has always been out of the ordinary, and his bravery has served as a role model for every Hungarian fighter pilot.[129]

He went into American captivity with his unit in May 1945, and returned to Hungary in May 1947 (according to his future wife, because 'he was not able to live without his home country, without his profession').[130] At first he had temporary jobs making mechanical drawings, then he worked for *OMRE* as a film propagandist on films promoting aviation. Meanwhile, he was 'B-listed' (deemed unreliable by the regime) on 23 September 1947. On 3 May 1948, he was called into service as a member of *I repülőtér-gondnokság* (I Airfield Logistics Unit) to Mátyásföld airfield and was employed as a pilot in the rank of *hadnagy*. On 2 May 1949, he was reassigned to Kecskemét as a squadron commander of *1/I honvéd repülőhajózó-kiképzőosztály* (1/I Honvéd Air Training Group) and was promoted to *főhadnagy*. As of 1 October 1949, he was promoted to squadron commander of *41 önálló repülőezred 3 század* (3 Squadron/41 Independent Wing), and soon after was promoted to deputy wing commander.[131] Tóth performed his instructor job with exceptional enthusiasm and was very eager to work; a February 1950 document described him as follows:

> He is very talented and has exceptional professional and blooming political skills. He very much likes his work and his comrades. His personality flaw can be seen in that he often overrates himself. An act of exaggerated ambition can be noticed very often in his conduct. He is prone to mention his world war air combats out of pure vanity.[132]

Tóth, like all the other former officers of the Royal Hungarian Air Force, was very much an annoyance for the new political regime, and was only considered good to train the first generation. The political description of him from March 1950 was markedly different in tone: 'His political commitment is not true. For example, in secret, he is learning English with his family [sic]. He is an exact example of a Horthy era pilot. He only flies "for the sake of aviation".'[133] He could not have received a more beautiful compliment from his enemies than that contained in the last two sentences.

129 *HM HIM HL*, documents of 101 Fighter Wing, box nr. 113, repeated recommendation of Lajos Tóth to receive the *Magyar Tiszti Arany Vitézségi Érem*, undated (according to the author's research, the document was created on 24 April 1945).
130 *HM HIM HL*, Bp. KB. 045/I. 1957, petition of his widow regarding his rehabilitation.
131 *HM HIM KI*, document folder nr. 211/493.
132 *HM HIM KI*, document folder nr. 211/493.
133 *HM HIM KI*, document folder nr. 211/493.

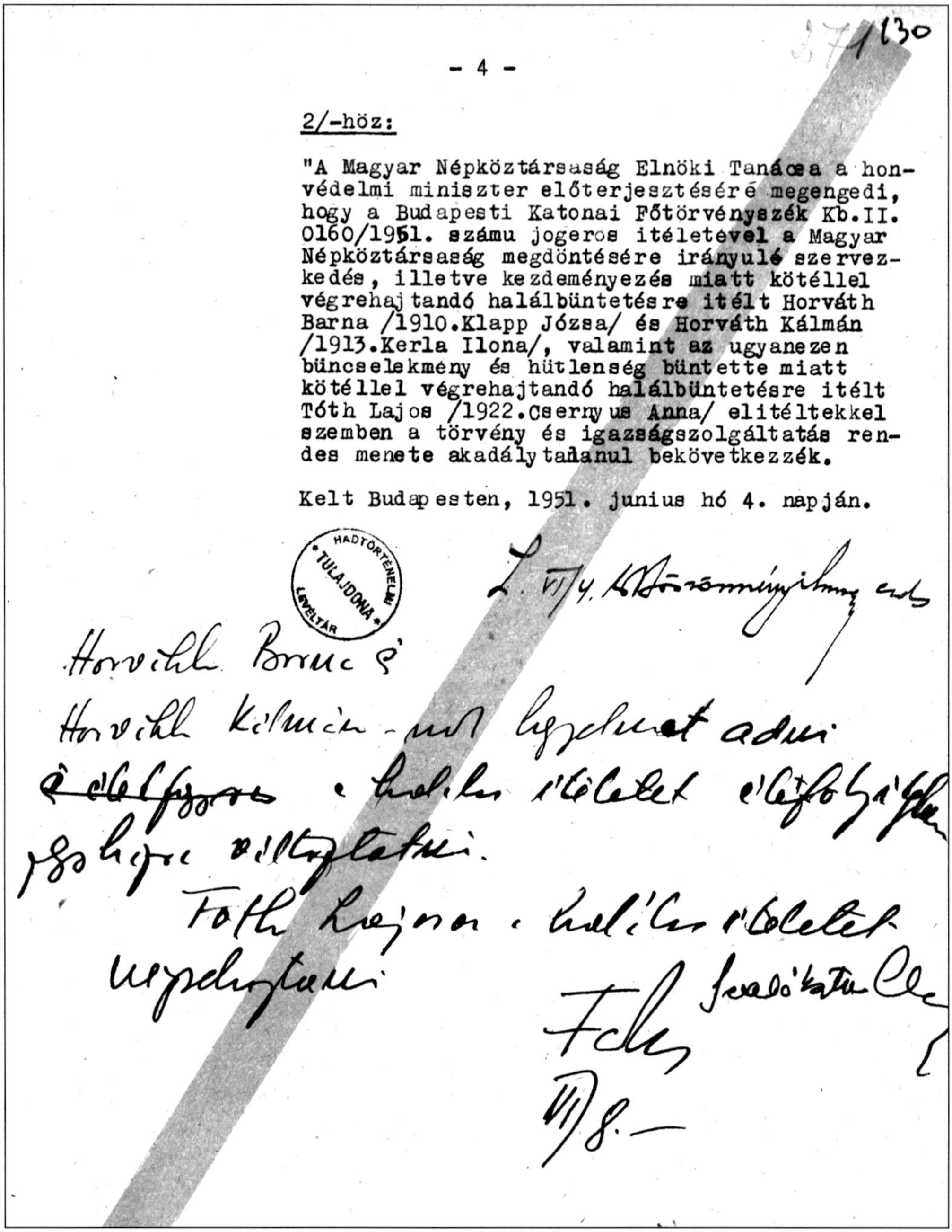

\- 4 -

2/-höz:

"A Magyar Népköztársaság Elnöki Tanácsa a honvédelmi miniszter előterjesztésére megengedi, hogy a Budapesti Katonai Főtörvényszék Kb.II. 0160/1951. számu jogeros ítéletével a Magyar Népköztársaság megdöntésére irányuló szervezkedés, illetve kezdeményezés miatt kötéllel végrehajtandó halálbüntetésre itélt Horváth Barna /1910.Klapp Józsa/ és Horváth Kálmán /1913.Kerla Ilona/, valamint az ugyanezen bünoselekmény és hütlenség büntette miatt kötéllel végrehajtandó halálbüntetésre itélt Tóth Lajos /1922.Csernyus Anna/ elitéltekkel szemben a törvény és igazságszolgáltatás rendes menete akadálytalanul bekövetkezzék.

Kelt Budapesten, 1951. junius hó 4. napján.

An astonishing document of historical importance. Minister of Defense Mihály Farkas added handwritten notes to the documents of the 'Barna Horváth and others' case stating that the first and second degree defendants, Mihály and Kálmán Horváth, should be pardoned and sentenced to life imprisonment, but he has also noted that 'the death sentence is to be carried out on Lajos Tóth', the third degree defendant (*HM HIM* Military Archives)

It is also worth citing a longer section from his contemporary professional description (the underscoring is from the original document):

> In a professional sense, he is exceptionally trained and has extensive experience. He is always interested in professional questions; moreover, he takes part in further developing topics by preparing articles and auxiliary material. Rules and regulations are well observed by him in practice, with which he increases the quality of the pilot training. He is prone to place the theoretical training behind the practical training. He is also much better in practice than in theory. He is always working on new helping materials, with success. In the course of pilot training, he has succeeded in bringing new practical approaches to training methods, according to which completing the traffic pattern in the training aircraft with dual controls will not bring out all the problems, only the main issue, and on the next round of the traffic pattern he is trying the resolve the main problem. In this way, he has sped up and at the same time increased the quality of the retraining of pilots to single-seated fighter aircraft, which, in its essence, embodies the application of dialectic methods. The result of his work has been that <u>five young cadres have been retrained for Yak-9 type fighter aircraft in the week of the congress</u> so that their first individual flight qualified as perfect. He is very good at enduring hardships and exertions; he is well-known for his bravery and his cool head.
>
> He can give orders perfectly in front of his unit or his subordinates and the training is organized well. However, he is not very good at taking care of his subordinates in private. He also shows development in this area, although this is quite slow.
>
> His political quality is medium; he does not have the theoretical intensity and needs considerable help. He is constantly reading political works and he tries to internalize these materials. There were problems with his party membership because in the autumn his membership book was stolen, so he was not allowed to enter party member meetings, which at the same time set him back in learning and also had a tremendous impact on his personal life. His only wish is to become a party member and lead a party-worthy life. He is talks happily about the Soviet heroes; they are a role model for him and he is constantly reminding himself of their brave heroic deeds. He talks about the enemy [that is, the Americans] full of hate, with words of revenge. In his personality, vanity can be traced.
>
> The appreciation of his performance at work is extremely important for him, and this has a considerable impact on his further work too. Considering his family life, he has just made a big step forward, because his wife has also moved in with him at his place of service after years of living apart. …
>
> <u>Summary:</u> His further success and his loyalty toward our system greatly [depends] on his sense of security, and this depends on how his direct and farther superiors express their trust in him.[134]

On 1 August 1950, he was promoted to *százados* and in autumn of the same year, he received the deputy commander position of the newly formed 25 Fighter Division. Meanwhile, he was decorated with the *Magyar Népköztársaság Érdemérem arany fokozat*a (Medal of the Merit of Hungarian People's Republic, Golden Class) on 12 October 1950.[135]

134 *HM HIM KI*, document folder nr. 211/493.
135 *HM HIM KI*, document folder nr. 211/493.

Identification of Lajos Tóth, using the portrait, the exhumed skull and the exposition of these on top of each other by the *Igazságügyi és Szakértői Kutató Intézetek* (*ISZKI*, Institutes of Forensic Sciences)

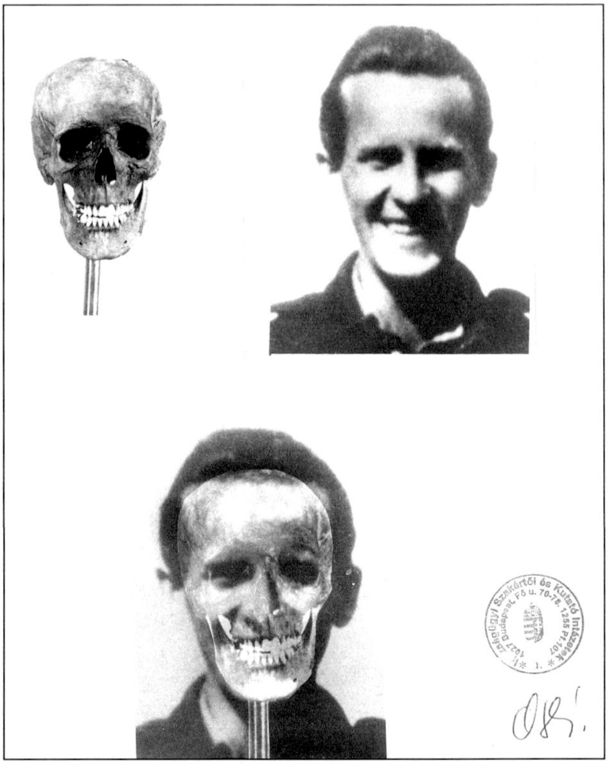

Memorial plaque of Lajos Tóth in its final location, between Plots 298 and 301, between the memorial plaques of István Kozma and Zoltán Kiss (photographed by the author, 24 July 2014)

Tóth's progressing career ended abruptly on 3 March 1951, when the *Államvédelmi Hatóság* (*ÁVH*, State Protection Authority) arrested him and sentenced him to death by hanging following a show trial for 'leading and organizing an attempt to put down the state of people's democracy and showing the sin of disloyalty'. The trial, which was entitled 'Barna Horváth and others',[136] targeted 13 defendants altogether, nine military personnel and four civilians (among the latter was Tóth's younger brother, Zoltán Tóth, and some of the other pilots featured in this work: Pál Forró, Béla Sűrű and Tibor Tobak).

Three hours after his arrest, his wife was also taken into custody by the *ÁVH*. She spent half a year in captivity and was interned for two years; she was freed in September 1953. The first- and second-degree defendants in the trial, *alezredes* Barna Horváth and *alezredes* Kálmán Horváth, were also sentenced to death, but their sentence was later changed to life imprisonment out of mercy; however, Tóth was not pardoned. The communist Minister of Defense, Mihály Farkas, wrote on the sentence that Tóth was not to be given absolution. Tóth had reportedly angered Farkas during an earlier military parade when he was introduced to the Minister, who was famous for his cruelty. When Farkas asked how many Soviet aircraft he had shot down during the Second World War, Tóth smiled as he told him the number.[137] This must have infuriated the powerful Farkas, and Tóth earned himself a deadly enemy.

Lajos Tóth was demoted to private on 4 June 1951 and was discharged from the military. He was hanged on 11 June 1951 in the *Gyűjtőfogház* (Budapest Strict and Medium Regime Prison).[138]

During the 1956 revolution, the revolutionary air force honored Lajos Tóth as their own honorary dead and initiated him among the martyrs. In 1958, the Military Judiciary in Budapest absolved Tóth of all the charges against him as 'lacking in evidence'; the decision was final and binding. On 12 June 1990, the *Magyar Köztársaság Legfelsőbb Bírósága* (Supreme Court of the Hungarian Republic) released *százados* Lajos Tóth and the other defendants with a verdict of 'in default of felony' in decision nr. I. 177/1990.

As a tribute to Lajos Tóth, on 11 June 1990, his former comrades erected a memorial plaque at Plot 301 of the *Új köztemető* at Rákoskeresztúr (New Public Cemetery of Budapest). The plaque was on the side of the plot because the exact location of his gravesite was not known. The Minister of Defense of the Republic of Hungary promoted him to *alezredes* posthumously as of 1 December 1990 in the issued order r. 217/1990.

The search for the body of Lajos Tóth led to an exhumation of Plot 298 of the *Új köztemető* (row 18, grave nr. 37) on 12 September 2002, revealing the so-called 'Ferenc Horváth', age 39, who died 13 June 1951 (in the Rákosi era it was not uncommon to bury executed persons under false names for political reasons). The body was identified as Lajos Tóth based on morphological similarities; the identification is highly accurate (DNS sample identification has not been carried out).[139] On 10 September 2003, Lajos Tóth was reinterred with full military honors at 11:30 in Plot 298 of the Rákoskeresztúr Cemetery, at the place of his earlier grave (row 18, grave nr. 37).

136 *HM HIM HL*, Bp. KB. 045/I. 1957.
137 Based on the interview of Gyula Pintér, 8 March 2002.
138 *HM HIM KI*, document folder nr. 211/493.
139 Based on data provided by the *Igazságügyi és Szakértői Kutató Intézetek* (*ISZKI*, Network of Forensic Science Institutes), which has, as of 1 January 2017, merged with the *Nemzeti Szakértői és Kutató Központ* (*NSZKK*, Hungarian Institute for Forensic Sciences). The author wishes to express his gratitude to Dr Éva Susa, former director general of the institution, for her kind help.

The memorial plaque erected in 1990 in the Rákoskeresztúr Cemetery honoring Lajos Tóth. At that time it was not known exactly where he was buried; therefore, the memorial plaque was erected beside Plot 301. This was replaced a number of times and now can be found between Plots 298 and 301. (From the author's collection)

Grave of the executed Lajos Tóth in Plot 298 (photograph of the author, 24 July 2014.)

FŐHADNAGY VITÉZ NEMES LÁSZLÓ MOLNÁR

Number of aerial victories: 25 (+3)
Successes against ground targets: n.d.a.
Number of flown combat sorties: 132
Number of hours flown in the air force: n.d.a.
Nicknames: *Laci*, *Oroszlán*, *Paszulyos*
Identification number: 1678-21-0289

Decorations

- *Magyar Tiszti Arany Vitézségi Érem* (14 September 1944 – posthumous, 6th award in the Royal Hungarian Armed Forces)

Regarding those burials that lack grave markers, see for example Éva Susa and Mária Molnos, 'Jeltelen eltemetések (1945–1962) kutatása', in *Trezor 3. Az átmenet évkönyve, 2003* (Budapest: Állambiztonsági Szolgálatok Történeti Levéltára [Historical Archives of the Hungarian State Security], 2004), pp. 245–254.

- *Magyar Érdemrend lovagkeresztje hadiszalagon a kardokkal* (3 February 1944)
- *Tűzkereszt I fokozata a kardokkal és koszorúval*, with one wound clasp
- German Iron Cross 1st Class (May 1944)
- German Iron Cross 2nd Class (February 1944)

Victories

Number	Date	Aircraft	Location
1.	16 August 1943 at 16:55	La-5	
–	6 September 1943	Yak-1	Novaya Vodolaga
2.	8 September 1943	La-5	
3.	24 September 1943	Soviet fighter (La-5?)	
4.	24 September 1943	Il-2	
5.	7 October 1943	La-5	
6.	9 October 1943	Soviet fighter (La-5?)	
7.	14 October 1943	Il-2	
8.	16 (17?) December 1943 at 10:10	Il-2	
9.	5 (8?) January 1944	Il-2	Sosovo–Vahnovka E
10.	5 (8?) January 1944	Il-2	Sosovo–Vahnovka E
11.	5 (8?) January 1944	Il-2	Sosovo–Vahnovka E
12.	5 (8?) January 1944	La-5	Sosovo–Vahnovka E
13.	9 January 1944	Il-2	Kalinovka
14.	9 January 1944	Soviet fighter	
15.	15 January 1944	Soviet single-engine	
	15 January 194	Soviet single-engine	
	25 January 1944	Soviet single-engine	
16.	25 January 1944	Soviet single-engine	
17.	25 January 1944 at 15:05	La-5	Beresovka E 3km
18.	16 February 1944	Il-2	
19	14 June 1944	P-38	Pusztavám N
20	7 July 1944 at 10:00	B-17	Kolozsnéma
21	7 July 1944	B-24 (B-17?)	Magyargencs
22	26 July 1944	P-38	over Austrian territory (between Graz and Wiener Neustadt)
23	27 July 1944	B-24	Csákvár
24	30 July 1944	B-24	Nádasdladány
25	30 July 1944	B-24	Nádasdladány

Aircraft flown

Bf 109 G-6: (V.3)66 (early 1944), V.818 (early summer of 1944), V.848 (26 July and 7 August 1944)

Soldier son of a soldier father: László Molnár as a *cőger* with his father on a Hubertus ride in 1934 (*HM HIM* Photographic Archives 106.719/052)

László Molnár was born on 1 May 1921 in Nagykőrös, into a military family. He was the youngest of three children, and the only boy (he also had a third half-sister from his mother's first marriage).[140] From Nagykőrös, they have moved to Sopron. The family had received a title of nobility from Empress Maria Theresa in 1758. After the family proved this with original documents, it was entered into his personal registry file on 22 June 1944, following which László Molnár has used his *nemes* ('noble') title.[141] Inspired by his family, Molnár attended a military school (*II Rákóczi Ferenc Reáliskolai Nevelőintézet,* Royal Hungarian 'II Rákóczi Ferenc' Honvéd Military Cadet School) in Sopron, from which he graduated. He attended the *Kassai Repülőakadémia* where he graduated as *hadnagy* on 18 June 1942 as of 1 July 1942, with rank number 8 (altogether 56th).[142] Following his graduation, he went to Szolnok to serve in 1 Fighter Training Group.[143] He was sent at first to Tapolca to a fighter school, then to Börgönd to train with Messerschmitt Bf 109.

After his training ended, he was reassigned to the fighter school as a instructor. He worked at first in Tapolca, then in Kecskemét (where he has trained, among others, the officer class graduated on 6 December 1943, a number of subsequent aces and many who later became his squadron mates). From here he was deployed to the front on 22 July 1943 to 1/1 Fighter Squadron led by *százados* György Ujszászy, *hadnagy* Molnár's cousin. The unit was soon ordered back home, but most of the pilots who had only had a short front service were automatically transferred to 5/2 Fighter Squadron, which remained at the front.

Molnár's first two combat sorties were completed on 16 August 1943. On the same day, during his second sortie, in his first dogfight he scored his first air victory over a La-5.[144] His fifth victory was achieved on 7 October around the great bend of the Dnieper. He later recalled this and the following (sixth) air victory:

140 For his family background, see Sándor Sarkady Jr., *Az Ász és a Polihisztor* (Feketeerdő: Mosonvármegye Könyvkiadó, 2016).
141 *HM HIM KI*, document folder nr. 66951; also based on documents preserved by the family.
142 *Honvédségi Közlöny* (*Személyes ügyek)*, nr. 1942/24 (16 June 1942), p. 613.
143 *HM HIM KI*, document folder nr. 66951.
144 Excerpts from the logs of 1/1 Fighter Squadron prepared by *százados* Ujszászy, 1942–43 (owned by the author); Sarkady, *Az Ász és a Polihisztor*, pp. 46–47.

> It was already dusk when we entered Russian airspace. My commander, *hdgy.* Kenyeres, soon signaled four enemy aircraft. We flew into a thin layer of clouds and thus placed ourselves behind to the Russians, who noticed us only when we were already engaging them. We attacked in a line formation; *hdgy.* Kenyeres went after the aircraft on the far right, and I found myself head-on with the enemy flight leader, who turned against me. He got my first burst frontally, and he started to plunge eastward. I turned after him and hit him again with another burst from behind. The aircraft began to burn and crashed into the ground; it was the end for him. My sixth aircraft was shot down after a bomber escort mission. The Soviet fighters were in superior numbers; we were engaged in a dogfight, and we were pretty much mixed up. With my new wingman, *őrmester* Pál Kovács, we were flying to and fro at 5,000 meters when I noticed a moving dot over the glistening Dnieper moving eastward. '*Paja*, we are attacking!' I shouted, and then we were already coming down on the Soviet. I got him at an altitude of 800 meters from behind and above; without noticing us, I opened fire with all my weapons. The aircraft went up in flames and crashed on the eastern bank of the Dnieper.[145]

On 7 October, the Hungarian fighters, together with the Fw 190s of II./JG 54, fought heavy battles against the La-5s of the Soviet 8th and 10th GIAD. The 8th GIAD lost seven, while the 10th GIAD lost another four La-5s during the day. At least one of these losses (in the late afternoon) cannot be verified with German victory reports: the La-5 of 113rd GIAP subordinated to 10th GIAD flown by *kapitan* Prilepsky was shot down during an air combat over the Jasniki area between 15:55 and 16:40. The Soviet pilot survived the crash of his aircraft; this was definitely a Hungarian air victory.[146]

Hadnagy Molnár scored his seventh air victory on 14 October, when he was on a free hunt with *hadnagy* Árpád Karnay, this time also around the great bend of the Dnieper. The two Bf 109's were flying at an altitude of 4,500 meters when Molnár, as the element leader, noticed an aircraft at a lower altitude over their own territory, heading westward. They dived and approached the aircraft at a speed of 750 km/h; it was soon identified as an Il-2m3. The gunner was already firing at them from half a kilometer's distance, but *hadnagy* Molnár nevertheless got closer to him and, within 100 meters, opened fire with all his weapons. The enemy aircraft was literally torn to pieces from the hits and crashed. One of the crew members was able to bail out and was captured by the German troops.[147]

As a fighter instructor, *hadnagy* László Molnár sunbathes on the nose of an Arado Ar 96 on Kecskemét airfield in the early summer of 1943. (From the author's collection)

145 *Üvölt a Puma*, 3 November 1943, p. 3.
146 Nikita Yegorov on documents of TsAMO.
147 *Üvölt a Puma*, 3 November 1943, pp. 3–4.

The young ace was given the short-lived nickname of '*Paszulyos*' (*paszuly* means 'bean' in Hungarian) over the winter of 1943–44, when got so drunk while celebrating one of his air victories that he went about camp with a hand grenade with its pin removed, looking for Soviet soldiers among the stationed aircraft. His squadron commander subsequently presented him with a custom-made 1 cubic centimeter cup from which to drink alcohol, which was as small as a '*paszuly*'.[148] His other nickname was more serious and future-proof of him: he was named '*Oroszlán*' ('Lion') by his mechanics for his bravery.

On 2 November, during a strafing run in the area of Kaniv, Molnár's aircraft was hit by an anti-aircraft artillery shell on its wing and then in the proximity of the cockpit; he suffered head injuries and crash-landed behind his own lines. He then received the wound clasp for his *Tűzkereszt*. He recuperated at home, although on paper he was reassigned to the Tapolca Fighter Training Group. *Hadnagy* Molnár immediately insisted to be sent back to the front; thus he was reassigned to his squadron, and he finished 1943 with eight air victories.

In the morning of the first day of 1944, his airfield was attacked by a strafing run carried out by Soviet Il-2s. *Hadnagy* Molnár, starting off from a scramble, had the chance to attack an Il-2 from behind, but his weapons malfunctioned and the opportunity was lost.

His dry spell ended on 5 January (according to a contemporary document on 8 January, but it must be an error).[149] On Molnár's 68th combat sortie, he and his wingman *szakaszvezető* Ernő Kiss attacked a large Soviet ground-attack aircraft formation protected by La-5s east of the Sosovo–Vahnovka area, over Soviet territory. They scattered the formation over Soviet territory, and reported shooting down six aircraft – four Il-2s and two La-5s. Four of the six kills were reported by *hadnagy* Molnár. He described the air combat as follows in a letter to his parents:

> Yesterday I went out on a free hunt. The weather, as well as my mood, was very unfriendly. The former was grey and cloudy, the latter resentful because I had not met the enemy for weeks. At first, I flew northward, but the cloud base was so low that soon I turned my aircraft eastward. Below me, the combat in the first lines was raging; I watched it from above. The cloud base slowly emerged to 600 meters. I was flying cautiously because I had a wingman who was new to the front. A railway line forked away below us; I followed the northern line and entered Soviet territory. I was even more eagerly looking around because we could meet the enemy at any time. Only a few minutes passed and little black dots appeared on the grey northern horizon. They grew rapidly and raced toward us; we could slowly make out their shapes. 'Enemy bombers, fighters behind them!' I announced to my wingman on the radio. Then I called him closer and we hid under the cloud base. The dots grew constantly. My nerves were strained; I turned the trigger down. Approximately 30 enemy bombers were carrying their deadly, destructive load toward our territories [in his letters to his parents, *hadnagy* Molnár consistently called the Il-2 ground-attack aircraft 'bombers']. Behind them, 10 red star fighters swarmed in the air to secure their thrust

148 János Domonkos, 'Egy Messerschmitt szerelő hadi- és "egyéb" tapasztalatai', *Magyar Szárnyak Évkönyv*, 1982, p. 39.

149 The date of 8 January originates from the victory registry of his wingman, Ernő Kiss, from the end of the war. However, this registry also contains other errors (for more, see the biography of Ernő Kiss). The date of 5 January originates from his own letter: Sarkady, *Az Ász és a Polihisztor*, p. 83.

forward. In the next moment they flew past us very close to each other, but in the opposite direction.

'Attack!' I ordered to wingman, and with a tumble turn I dived into the gap between the aircraft, just below the bombers. My wingman dived under me and went with me below the bombers. My finger was on the cannon button, and I placed the electronic light dot of the reflector sight on the underside of the closest of the bombers. The Soviet aircraft was constantly growing in my sight, my fingers were impatient, but I needed to control myself – closer… closer… just do not let the enemy turn out of the firing line – still so far away! By then I could see all the detail on the aircraft, I could see the red star on the wings, it felt as if we were going to collide at any moment… Now! I pressed the button of the cannon and the trigger of the machine guns… Fire!!

The small red projectiles hit the enemy aircraft; fire, smoke and soot gushed forth; his route turned toward the earth and he plummeted into the depths like a burning torch. I pulled my aircraft up; on the right, another Soviet aircraft was falling down, engulfed in flame.

The escorting enemy aircraft were swarming around me, and I wondered how come none of them had yet collided with me. With a turn, I was able to get dead astern to them and I was already diving under them. Another victim was in front of me, even closer than the first. I was greeted by a fierce rain of fire from everywhere, but I did not turn away because I was in an excellent firing position. I saw his cooler in my sights. Fire! The aircraft lurched a little, turned left, gushing flames … after him, lines black as soot; he turned upside down, and the whole aircraft was no more now than a flaming, plummeting torch. … I pulled up my aircraft over him and, as I watched it, I saw it hit the ground and almost splattered apart.

From behind, the Soviet fighters were bloodthirstily pouring fire on me from their cannons. With a sharp turn, I faced them. I pushed the control column down almost vertically to be able to target the area in front of them. One was flying directly toward me, and I managed to get my flaming torch of fire drawn across its back. … it disappeared. The others dived down at me from above. All around me the sky was full of smoke puffs; with a very sharp turn, I managed to slip through them and, with an immense pull, I got to their rear. They were squirting to both sides … this was what I needed! I again dived under the bombers; the closest one was a bit sideways, and his gunner was desperately firing at me. The rounds swept just past my cockpit. I was so close to him that I could even see his face distorted with anger. My fingers were fast on the trigger, and then only a sooty glimpse of light could be seen in the place of the Soviet bomber, which was plummeting on an ever steeping path toward the snow-covered ground. I pulled up toward the clouds again and tried to look for my wingman, but I could not see him anywhere. Above me, four Soviet fighters were pulling into the cloud base, but left of me there were still two more. I turned after them, upon which they tried to escape toward the ground. At this moment I still saw that, from somewhere, there were two other fighters turning on me. It is okay, I thought, you will not reach me! I dived to the right of one of them in front of me. My tracer rounds flying around his cockpit. In a panic, he started to squirming. He was turned away from my bursts a number of times; he tried to dive sharply… we almost collided… fire! The aircraft spun as it nose-dived toward the ground, unable to do anything, and it blew up in flames in front of my eyes.

> I took a deep breath of fresh air. My limbs and nerves are burning; I turned my head left and right, but I wasn't able to see any more aircraft in the air. ... I turned my eyes to the snowy ground beneath me, and I saw four burning wrecks scattered below ... and now all the anxiety was released, and I realized that I had scored four air victories in a row! I was so happy I cannot describe it to you – this was a record!
>
> But where was my wingman? I called him on the radio; he did not answer. ... I searched for him for some time, but then I needed to head back home because my fuel was running low. I flew over our airfield four times, waggling my wings. The comrades on the ground threw their caps up into the air, and when I landed, a whole crowd swarmed around. Hungarians, Germans alike. They had a multitude of questions, they complimented me, they congratulated me, they laughed and smiled. Then came the slender figure of the Knight's Cross of the Iron Cross-decorated commander of the Mölders fighter group [IV./JG 51]. I greeted him and proudly reported:
>
> '*Herr* Hauptmann, *ich melde gehorsamst, vier Abschüsse*!' (Sir, I report four kills to you!)
>
> He was smiling and congratulating me, asking me about the details. I was the first '*Vierling*' – until now the record had been two kills during one mission – and everybody was truly happy. To complete my happiness, my wingman also arrived, and he was waggling his wings too – he had scored two air victories.[150]

This was the only case during the Second World War of a Hungarian fighter pilot achieving four air victories in one combat sortie. The area of Sosovo–Vahnovka lies northeast of Vinnytsia and southeast of Kalinovka. During the period of the heavy air combats during the course of January 1944 in the area, in addition to *hadnagy* Tóth and *hadnagy* Molnár, *szakaszvezető* Kiss and probably the other aces of 5/2 Squadron – *hadnagy* Debrődy and *hadnagy* Kenyeres – also achieved air victories.

In mid-January, László Molnár again showed why he had been given the nickname '*Oroszlán*'. On 9 January, according to the author's identification, he was the only fighter to take off against the Soviet formation attacking the Kalinovka airfield, repulsed the attempt and shooting down two aircraft. In the same letter reporting these air victories, he also mentioned his next air combat six days later, when he shot down two aircraft while flying as a element leader against approximately 40 Soviet aircraft attacking in three waves. Of the two victories, however, only one was confirmed for him:

> Since I wrote last, we have been moved again and the Soviet has disturbed our quiet life on the airfield a number of times with strafing runs. However, the results were insignificant, so we did not pay too much attention. During the first raid, amid the largest cannon fire and bomb explosions, four lads helped me start my engine, but it must have had some problems because it would not start at all and our efforts were in vain. At the time of the second raid, I was more fortunate. Before this attack, a reconnaissance aircraft came over and I took off within 30 seconds, but to my great annoyance I was not able to get him because he sped right into the clouds before my eyes. This was just my luck!

150 'Két levél a frontról...', *Magyar Szárnyak*, 15 February 1944, p. 11.

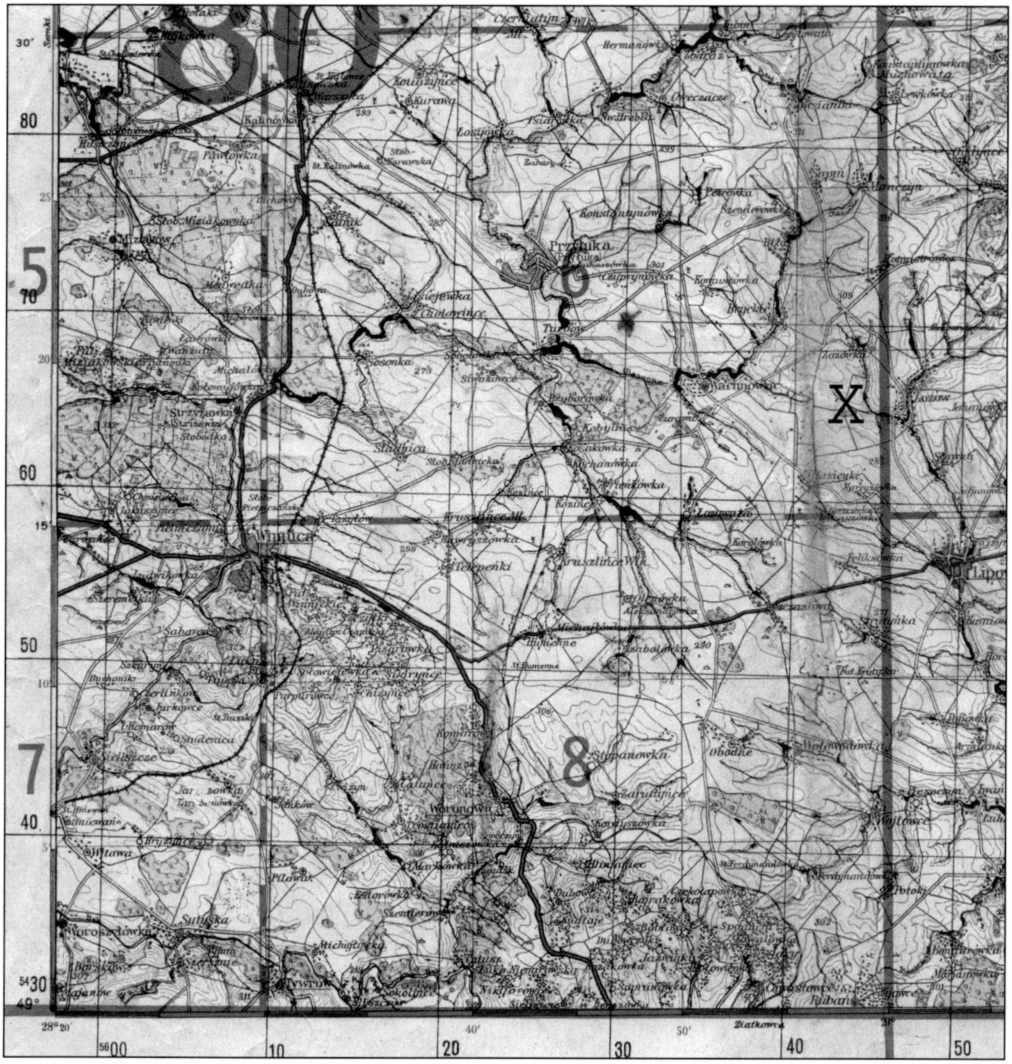

Detail of a Luftwaffe code-map of the Ovruch–Cherkasy area issued in 1943, scale: 1:300,000. Northeast of Vinnytsia, southeast of Kalinovka, an X marks the airspace above Sosovo–Vahnovka, where the Hungarian fighters were also engaged in heavy fighting in January 1944. West of the X is Vahnovka, while north of it is Zozovka; to the east is Zozov (the map uses names of Polish origin). Probably the name of one of the latter two locations has become Sosovo, because on the maps of Russian origin the Cyrillic 'z' was often read as 's'. (From the author's collection)

As I was returning toward our airfield, I was astonished to see cannon bursts puffing around our parked aircraft. As I looked more closely, I saw three Soviet bombers and five fighters diving in from above. I was the only one in the air, and there was no point thinking about what to do – I needed to attack, this was evident. To my great surprise, four fighters escaped immediately. Only one engaged me in combat, but I just left him there, because it was now much more important to ward off the bombers from our airfield.

I dived just beneath one of the bombers. His rear gunner hadn't even noticed me when I opened fire from close proximity. The fuselage burst into flames at that instant; his nose darted up toward the sky, the aircraft turned over and crashed into the ground near the airfield. I quickly slid under the next aircraft to engage it, but luckily I glanced behind me before targeting the Soviet, so I noticed the fighter from the previous encounter approaching fast. My persistent 'Raddy' friend was at a tactical advantage, so I had to leave my second victim and gather my wits together to scrape this fighter off me. After a short dogfight I managed to turn head-on to him through a swift maneuver; thus the dance began. I needed to work off the advantage he had, second by second. At last, I reached his altitude; this was even more difficult because his aircraft was much more maneuverable than mine. The dogged combat between us went on with alternating luck near our airfield. During the fourth minute of the air combat, I managed to get behind him. My weapons were wildly spitting fire into the aircraft dancing before me. At that time we were over the front. The 'Raddy' at last burst into flames and crashed to the ground. When I arrived back into the airspace of our airfield, the enemy aircraft were already long gone. Our crews watched the whole fight from the ground, which boosted their morale and their enthusiasm a great deal. These were my 13th and 14th air victories. Later, we went out to the wreck of the bomber aircraft, which lay quite close to our airfield. Its pilot was born in 1921 and was *leytenant* and political officer, as we managed to uncover from his papers. Poor lad was probably dead already in the air, as he was hit in his stomach through his back.

… I continue my letter today because I wasn't able to send it off by post. Yesterday I celebrated my 75th combat sortie. The air activity is increasing on both sides and there is heavy armored warfare going on at ground level, too. Our squadron is achieving more and more victories, and this is a sure sign of our rising experience. My commander has recommended me for the Iron Cross 1st and 2nd Class, but the Germans are not going to award them to me unless I am not awarded with Hungarian medals of equivalent rank – the *Signum*, for example. Yesterday, I was in an extremely tense air battle, where I shot down my 15th and 16th aircraft. My wingman fell behind me so only one of my kills was confirmed because it was witnessed by the Germans. The other is being searched for at the moment because this also crashed beyond our lines.

I have now completed 78 combat sorties.[151]

Hadnagy László Molnár is decorated with the Iron Cross 2nd Class in February 1944 in the operational area. (From the author's collection)

151 'Két levél a frontról…', p. 12.

The freshly decorated *hadnagy* Molnár with the chief mechanic of his aircraft, Ferenc Vásárhelyi, in front of '*Erzsike*'. (From the author's collection)

Soon after, Molnár achieved a further three confirmed and one unconfirmed air victories on the Eastern Front. His 17th air victory from this period is known in detail: on 25 January 1944, during a free hunt in the Sosovo–Vahnovka area and at an altitude of 2,500 meters, he attacked an La-5 from the rear and shot it down. His witness was a pilot from 11./JG 51, *Unteroffizier* Jörg Lastowsky, who was serving as Molnár's wingman, and who went missing two days later. According to Lastowsky's report, Molnár attacked the La-5 from a distance of 50 meters, upon which parts broke off the La-5's wings and it crashed while burning fiercely 3km east of Berezovka. *Hadnagy* Molnár's was probably an La-5 of 40th GIAP, with which *mladshiy leytenant* Lisikin had to crash-land.[152]

Unfortunately, due to the loss of the relevant documents, details of some of Molnár's victories on the Eastern Front are unknown. It seems nevertheless certain that all his victims were single-engine aircraft. According to the author's research, seven Il-2s, eight La-5s and three Yakovlev fighters were among his air victories, but he mentioned eight Il-2s in his letters. It is therefore probable that the real list of victories is eight Il-2s, seven La-5s and three Yakovlevs.[153]

At the beginning of 1944, *hadnagy* Molnár was already the deputy commander of 5/2 Fighter Squadron. He finally returned home from the front in the middle of March 1944; at this time he had scored 18 confirmed air victories during 113 combat sorties.[154] By that time, many considered him to be the best Hungarian Messerschmitt pilot.

Upon arriving home, *hadnagy* Molnár returned to Tapolca to serve as a fighter instructor. The surviving accounts differ regarding who flew with Ferenc Kass in a formation of three instructors in *Héja*s at dawn on 13 April 1944, when they met American Lightnings in combat. According to

152 Lastowsky's aerial witness report (copy owned by the author), and Nikita Yegorov on documents of TsAMO regarding the possible Soviet opponent.

153 The author has originally identified the types of aircraft shot down by László Molnár on the Eastern Front with the help of the aluminum silhouettes on his walking stick, which has been preserved by the family (the Il-2 and the radial engine powered La–5 and the inline engine Yak types can also be identified, all marked with a different but distinctive aluminum marker). See Sarkady, *Az Ász és a Polihisztor*, pp. 46–96, 107.

154 *HM HIM HL*, documents of 101 Fighter Wing, box nr. 112, Royal Hungarian 102 Honvéd Fighter Group, summary of decorated officers and enlisted men.

some accounts, *hadnagy* Molnár and *szakaszvezető* Szikora were there. On 19 April 1944, *hadnagy* Molnár crashed while landing with his student, Zoltán Szentgyörgyi (not a relative of Dezső Szentgyörgyi), freshly arrived from the officers' class to be graduated on 20 August 1944. They were flying in a WM-21 Sólyom; it was the student's fault, but luckily no one was injured.[155]

Hadnagys Debrődy, Molnár and Szeverényi in front of the *'Erzsike'* (66) in early 1944 (*HM HIM* Photographic Archives 106.719/109)

With the organization of 101 Fighter Group in May 1944, *hadnagy* Molnár was reassigned to this unit, more precisely to 101/3 Fighter Squadron. György Debrődy had also arrived back from the Eastern Front with 18 air victories, and he also joined this squadron, so a friendly rivalry went on between them for the title of the most successful Hungarian fighter pilot. László Molnár was initiated into the *Vitézi Rend* on 20 May 1944 based on his own merits; he then took part in a combat leader training course between 24 May and 8 June at Fels am Wagram, for I./JG 27.[156]

Hadnagy Molnár has scored his first air victory against the Americans on 14 June 1944 over a Lightning of 14th FG's 49th Squadron. At the same time, Debrődy also scored a kill. Two days later, on 16 June, the Hungarian fighters again deployed in air combat and were engaged in heavy fighting with the Americans, but Molnár was not present because he had a day off. György Debrődy was there, however, and shot down a Lightning, again earning the title of the most successful Hungarian fighter pilot. *Hadnagy* Molnár was very

Hadnagy Molnár at the beginning of 1944 with his walking stick decorated with thin aluminum aircraft silhouettes. All the silhouettes signified a victory (*HM HIM* Photographic Archives 106.719/117)

155 Jenő Farkas, *A m. kir. vitéz nagybányai Horthy István Honvéd Repülő Akadémiai évfolyamom története. Szombathely-Veszprém, 1943.09.15–1944.08.20* (Gödöllő: privately published, 2010), pp. 124–125. The work mentions Molnár and Szikora; according to Iván Pataky, László Rozsos, and Gyula Sárhidai, *Légi háború Magyarország felett*, vol. 2 (Budapest: Zrínyi Kiadó, 1990), p. 176, based on the recollections of Kass, the other two pilots were *őrmester* Tüske and *szakaszvezető* Szilágyi.

156 *HM HIM KI*, document folder nr. 66951; *HM HIM HL*, microfilm box nr. 1122, log of 101/3 Fighter Squadron.

keen for an opportunity to answer to his friend, but he had to manage his expectations for a while.

On 17 June 1944, Molnár's group commander recommended him for the first time (together with György Debrődy) to receive the *Magyar Tiszti Arany Vitézségi Érem*.[157]

One of the official portraits of *hadnagy* László Molnár, taken in Veszprém, probably in June 1944. (From the author's collection)

On 26 June 1944, *hadnagy* Molnár completed two missions. In the morning, he took part in the large-scale air combat over Győr, but was unable to score another victory. In the first air combat against Mustangs, the Americans – who flew in superior numbers and whose aircraft were capable of a better performance – shot down Molnár's wingman, *szakaszvezető* Illés Podoba, who was killed. Along with Molnár, Podoba had also been a fighter instructor at Tapolca, and they had known each other for a long time.[158] According to information collected by the author, this was the only occasion throughout the war when *hadnagy* Molnár lost his wingman.

Hadnagy Molnár flew his 115th combat sortie[159] on 30 June 1944, when he contributed to shooting down a four-engined Liberator. The kill was confirmed to his wingman, *zászlós* Huszár (for details, see Huszár's biography).

Hadnagy Molnár was the airfield's officer on duty on 2 July; he did not, therefore, take part in the large-scale air combat on that day. On 7 July 1944, during the first mission of the day, Molnár showcased his exceptional performance and shot down two four-engined bombers from the American formation flying over the *Dunántúl* toward Silesian targets, but György Debrődy was already on his fourth air victory against American aircraft, so *hadnagy* Molnár had not yet succeeded in matching his friend's number of air victories. He recalled the mission as follows:

> We gathered in the airspace above Győr, and the air battle with the enemy took place here. Because of the bad visibility, I lost the group, but remained with my wingman. We were flying at 8,500 meters when I noticed a formation of at least 200 Boeing Fortress IIs flying northward slightly west of Győr; the formation flew in four waves, each consisting of 50 to 60 aircraft. I immediately ordered my wingman to attack and I did so from the rear. The strength of the defensive fire is not even worth talking about. … There was a rain of fire! The air before me was full of tens of thousands of red dots! This, however, did not stop us.

157 *HM HIM HL*, documents of 101 Fighter Wing, box nr. 113, record of decorations.
158 Letter of *hadnagy* László Molnár to his parents, 28 June 1944 (copy owned by the author).
159 This was the number of sorties he himself recorded; in the fragmentary sources that survive, slightly different data is preserved. Based on the fragmentary remains of the statistics of 5/2 Squadron, he returned from the Eastern Front having completed 113 sorties; however, by 30 June he had completed at least four new combat sorties, so there is at least a difference of two sorties.

Forward! I switched my weapons on and, from approximately 100 meters, I opened fire at the four-engined at the rear in the far right of the formation. The rounds went a bit in front of him, so I corrected my aim calmly and shot again – Fire! At this time I was not more than 50 meters from the formation. My bursts now hit the enemy aircraft on its starboard wing and fuselage. The aircraft burst into flames and fell into a right spin. There was no time to watch it and follow its fate; we rushed past the last wave at the back and I was already aiming at the next target. The aircraft lurched and went up in flames while I dove out on the right. I pulled my aircraft from the formation and disengaged. The fire coming after me was the same as the fire that had greeted me. The aircraft I had shot down first was spinning downward below me; I saw one person bailing out. The others were probably already dead. The four-engined crashed and blew up north of Győr, near the Danube.

So, at last, I had achieved my 20th official kill. But there was no time for happiness now; the second aircraft I had engaged was losing altitude, but did a complete turn and started to flee westward. I flew down on him again, and shot out his port outer engine. We were constantly attacking on this aircraft from Győr to Veszprém; it already had two engines were knocked out when we attacked again over Veszprém. We were anxious to succeed! The damaged aircraft defended itself desperately. I was approximately 150 meters from him when I pressed the trigger … and then there was silence. Either it was stuck or I had no ammunition left. I didn't know. I tried again, and again there was silence. I rushed nevertheless forward toward the aircraft, hoping my wingman did not have such problems. I was only a few centimeters from the aircraft when I rushed past and dived to the right. At that moment I felt a strong jolt and the cockpit was filled with smoke. It was black as soot and choking. The control column hung lifelessly, its wires torn. The aircraft could no longer be controlled. The starboard side was in flames and I was plummeting already. *Jump or I'll burn alive*! I tried to jettison the canopy; it wouldn't come off. I opened the clasp that held it in its place – and it stayed right there! I cast away everything and tried to push it out of the cabin with both of my hands – and at last, it flew off! The smoke cleared; I took off my helmet and my breathing apparatus, unfastening myself – another glance at the panel: height 4,000 meters, velocity 550km – I pushed myself out of the cockpit with a huge kick, but then came the hardest part! I noticed that, from the south, other four-engined bombers were approaching in the company of fighters. If I opened my parachute now, they would surely shoot me right there. So, against all my instincts, I did not open my parachute, but let myself fall. I counted to 20 and, when I saw the earth very close – albeit I was making flips – I opened my parachute. An enormous pull – the parachute opened. It was a wonderful feeling – there was silence, and I was slowly drifting downward. Below me was Papod Hill and our airfield. I had done it; I bailed out exactly over our airfield! I stepped out of the aircraft at an altitude of 4,000 meters and fell for 2,000 meters. I was drifting in silence and I watched airfield cars speeding toward me. The wind was blowing toward the pinewoods and I tried to drift toward the airfield so that I could land nearer. I looked up and saw that two strings were torn and I was descending swifter than I should. Apparently I was too heavy for this 'umbrella'! … Meanwhile, I was descending further; I was approximately 80 to 100 meters from the ground. I tried to slide as much as possible; I reached the meadows by the forest – 60–50–40 meters – then I received a strong headwind from the opposite direction, which drifted me back over the pines. I prepared myself for arrival in the

> woods; a tall pine was before me, with one single bare branch at the top. I needed to catch this! I again tried to slide; the branch caught my feet, the parachute started to collapse on me, the branch snapped and the pine cracked. I was falling down the side; then came a pull, and I stopped somewhere mid-air.
>
> The tree-trunk was one centimeter from my nose. I looked up and saw that the top of the pine had gone right through the middle of my parachute. I looked down; I was only about one meter up in the air! What kind of luck is this! My comrades were already rushing forward – meanwhile, I untangled myself – they congratulated me, and helped me get on my feet. I jumped to the ground and quickly inspected myself – I felt a trickling of warm blood on the right side of my chin and neck – a small scar. It was so little I didn't even want to ask for a wouond clasp for it![160]

This was *hadnagy* Molnár's 118th combat sortie, and the first time he had been shot down by enemy aircraft. He had not even been hit before this, and only once (on 2 November 1943) had he been shot down by Soviet anti-aircraft defense. Of the two four-engines he shot down, the first was the B-17G (serial number 4297351) of 2nd BG's 20th Squadron flown by 1st Lieutenant Harold T. Tomlinson; the aircraft was burning when it crashed and it blew up together with its bomb load at Kolozsnéma (today Klížska Nemá, Slovakia) in the Csallóköz. Six of its crew were killed, and four of them (two of whom, the pilot and the navigator, were wounded) were captured. American eyewitnesses stated that the aircraft was shot down by a lone Bf 109, which performed only one pass and shot four or five bursts into the B-17 from close proximity. This American aircraft is featured in the Air Force Confidential Order nr. 1944/63, with its exact location (appearing as 'Kolozsnána'), but the type given in the order (B-24) is probably a typing error; presumably the same is true for the location, as there has never been a settlement named Kolozsnána. The same order records the second aircraft as a B-24, giving a location of Magyargencs: at that spot, a B-24H (serial number 42-52374) from the 460th BG indeed crashed as a result of an attack of Bf 109s, and 2nd Lieutenant Walton E. Metier with his 11-member crew was captured. However, this aircraft crashed more than two hours later on the way back from Silesia, after completing the bombing raid, at around 12:15; it could not, therefore, possibly have been *hadnagy* Molnár's victim, and consequently the aircraft must have been mixed up again. For the second aircraft, Molnár's letter quoted above suggests it was also a four-engined shot out of its formation, probably a B-17. Until now, the author has not been able to identify this aircraft unambiguously, but in fact on this day two four-engines have been credited to *hadnagy* Molnár.[161]

Hadnagy Molnár's destroyed aircraft was probably the Bf 109 G-6 V.818 (serial number 95250). According to the handwritten recollections of his comrade in the squadron, *hadnagy* Dániel, this was the aircraft *hadnagy* Molnár used at first while with the squadron.[162]

160 Letter of *hadnagy* László Molnár to his parents, 9 July 1944 (original owned by Krisztián Tóth; a copy is owned by the author).

161 *HM HIM HL*, documents of 101 Fighter Wing, box nr. 110, Air Force Confidential Order Nr. 1944/63; NARA MACR 6565, MACR 6593; Amos, Koller, Lloyd, and Martin, *Defenders of Liberty*, p. 239.

162 László Dániel, *Így kezdődött…* (recollections in manuscript, copy owned by the author).

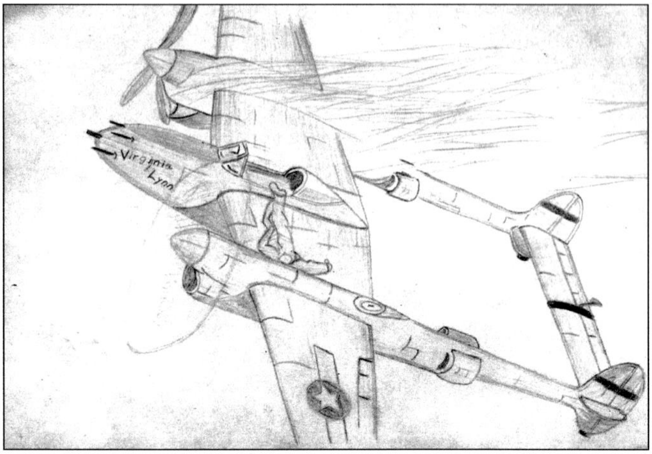

The drawing by Captain James C. Smyth of his own burning aircraft on 26 July 1944, which he left at the exact moment depicted. (From the collection of the Smyth family)

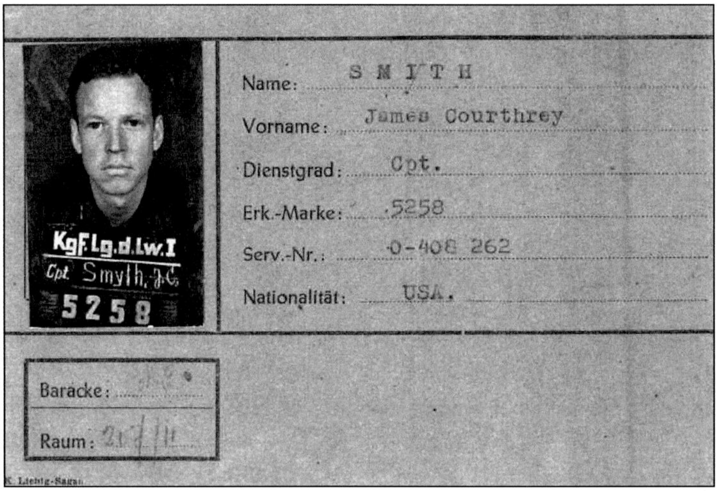

Captain James C. Smyth's POW card. (From the collection of the Smyth family)

The next day, 8 July 1944, a heavy American fragmentation bomb-raid was carried on Veszprém airfield, and two pilots of *hadnagy* Molnár's squadron were wounded: the deputy commander of the squadron, *főhadnagy* Tamás Gersy was seriously injured, and *zászlós* János Nyemecz was lightly injured. Gersy needed an urgent blood transfusion in the hospital; he received large quantities of blood from Molnár, which saved his life.[163]

Hadnagy Molnár took over the position of the deputy commander of 101/3 Squadron from Tamás Gersy, who was recovering from his wounds. On 26 July, the Hungarian fighters engaged the American formations together with the *Luftwaffe* between Graz and Wiener Neustadt. On this mission, Molnár reported shooting down a P-38. A Lightning (serial number 43-28260) of 14th FG's 37th Squadron indeed crashed in the area, having been attacked by

163 The interview of Tamás Gersy (Szolnok, 6 November 1918–Kistarcsa, 19 February 2013) to the author, 4 March 2003. For Gersy, see Csaba B. Stenge, '*In memoriam* Gersy Tamás', *Magyar Repüléstörténeti Társaság Évkönyve*, 2013, pp. 14–19.

a Bf 109 (German Bf 109s reported shooting down a further two Lightnings in the area, of which one was confirmed). The P-38J was hit on the fuselage and on its starboard engine; its starboard wing was set on fire too. The pilot was Captain James C. Smyth, who suffered a number of smaller shrapnel injuries, bailed out of his aircraft and went into captivity. Most parts of the aircraft crashed northwest of Fischbach, and one part near Gschaid. During the lengthy mission, *hadnagy* Molnár – who had matched Debrődy's number of air victories – used up too much fuel, landed in Szombathely and filled up his fuel tanks before returning to Veszprém in his new aircraft, the V.848 (serial number 95420).[164]

James Courtney Smyth was born in Bluefield, West Virginia on 17 September 1919. He graduated as a chemist from Virginia Polytechnic Institute and State University, so the American army enlisted him to work in the department of biological weapons in 1942. From this department, he volunteered with another chemist friend for pilot training because he wanted to do more for his country. He had completed 24 combat sorties before he was shot down and captured. After the war, he returned to his original profession and worked as a chemist; he occupied manager positions until his death on 29 June 1987.[165]

The next day, 27 July, Molnár shot down a Liberator west of Budapest, but György Debrődy also scored a victory. *Hadnagy* Molnár was credited with shooting down the B-24H (serial number 41-29266) of 455th BG's 741st Squadron flown by 2nd Lieutenant Maxwell B. Gates, which crashed near Csákvár. Of the 10-man crew, five – including Gates – survived the destruction of the heavy bomber.[166]

Three days later, on 30 July, Molnár flew in a very tight formation (a technique he had developed

Comrades congratulate *hadnagy* Molnár after a successful mission in the summer of 1944. Behind him, with his face covered, stands *hadnagy* Debrődy (*HM HIM* Photographic Archives 106.719/136)

Captain George G. Loving, who led the 31st FG on 7 August 1944 and ordered the attack against the Hungarian–German formation. He scored five victories in Second Wold War, and also took part in the Korean War; after an outstanding career, he retired as a Lieutenant General. (From the collection of George Loving)

164 NARA MACR 7190, microfilm box nr. 1122, log of 101/3 Fighter Squadron; the recollections of James C. Smyth (in manuscript, owned by the author).
165 The author is grateful to the daughter of James C. Smyth, whom the author managed to find in the United States, for the biographical data and the copy of his diary, as well as all related information provided.
166 NARA MACR 6999.

himself) and engaged the four-engines raiding Budapest frontally in multiple passes southwest of the capital. He shot two four-engines out of their formation; with this, he took the lead among the Hungarian fighters in terms of number of air victories.

On 7 August 1944, a Hungarian fighter formation was led by Molnár to escort and protect the heavily armed Bf 109s (partly carrying 2cm cannon gondolas under the wings) of the German I./JG 302. The two formations united west of Lake Balaton and started to circle the area, waiting for the Americans. Because of the communication problems discussed earlier (the different wavelengths used, separate ground control, etc.), the two formations were not able to talk to each other, and this soon led to tragedy.

On this day, the American bombers had been raiding targets in Silesia. One of the fighter units escorting the bombers, the 53 Mustangs of 31st Fighter Group, was led by Captain George Loving, who had celebrated his 21st birthday that day; it was his 145th combat sortie. The Mustangs had reached the Balaton area before the arrival of the bombers – the big lake was visually easy to identify and it was one of the favored spots for the Americans to orientate themselves – when they noticed the German-Hungarian Messerschmitt formation below them. Captain Loving faced a second of dilemma upon noticing the Messerschmitts, because his task had been to escort the bombers to Silesia; if they released their drop tanks now and engaged in air combat, they would not be able to complete their original mission. However, there was a solution to the dilemma: there were some extra aircraft in the formation, and he ordered the 12 Mustangs of this 'lawless squadron' to engage the Messerschmitts. The 'lawless squadron' consisted of one flight of four aircraft from all three squadrons of the Fighter Group, and its general task was exactly what they were ordered to do now: to attack the enemy fighters before (or instead of) joining the bombers. They thus had a much larger scope for movement, and more freedom to act.[167]

Thomas Hardeman, one of the flight leaders of 31st FG, who led a devastating strike on the German–Hungarian fighter formation on 7 August 1944; he shot down three Bf 109s and damaged another, for which he was decorated with the Silver Star (he ended the war with four confirmed air victories). The photo was taken a few years after the war and shows him as a pilot of the National Guard, with a P-80 Shooting Star type jet aircraft. (From the collection of Robert Goebel)

The Hungarian fighters saw the Mustangs circling overhead, and *hadnagy* Molnár (who was leading the formation) asked for permission to turn against the Mustangs. The response every time, however, was that the aircraft beyond him were German reconnaissance aircraft, and he was to continue escorting the German formation without attempting to turn against the Americans. The Germans – whom Molnár could not warn because of the different wavelength – noticed nothing of what was going on, and

167 George Loving, *Woodbine Red Leader* (New York, NY: Ballantine, 2003), pp. 237–238; letter of George Loving (Roanoke, 7 August 1923–Williamsburg, 31 December 2016) to the author, 4 May 2005. For Loving, see Olynyk, *Stars and Bars*, pp. 409–410.

they continued to fly with their drop tanks on, as though on a training course (the fighter control in Vienna was not operating at the height of its abilities, as the arriving Mustangs should have been noticed by them). Perhaps, if an older and more experienced officer – for example, *főhadnagy* Tibor Papp or Pál Irányi – had led the formation, they would have turned against the Americans despite the poor order of the ground control, but László Molnár – who was an exemplary soldier – obeyed his orders to his last breath.

The 12 aircraft of the 'lawless squadron' attacked fiercely and scattered the Messerschmitt formation in one pass – they were practically offering themselves up as an easy target. The Messerschmitts were partly destroyed; the Americans shot down at least a dozen of them. The Hungarians lost two pilots killed – László Molnár and *zászlós* János Nyemecz – and *hadnagy* Mihály Karátsonyi was seriously wounded; four aircraft suffered 100 percent damage, one suffered 30 percent damage and few more were damaged to a lesser extent as a result of the combat with the Mustangs. The Germans lost more than six aircraft, one pilot killed and three wounded.

Hadnagy Tibor Tobak, who was flying on his first sortie and was Molnár's wingman, remembered the tragedy:

> The seconds seemed to linger on endlessly. The Germans were very calm – as if they were flying circuit patterns! The radio messages were now getting out of control: 'The *pifke* [Germans] do not see the *Ami* [Americans]!' And surely they had not seen them. We were dancing in the air, literally, stressed out, without our drop tanks. Dramatic moments. Only the three commanders were talking. Mainly Laci. He tried to ask for approval to disengage and face the Americans at least four times. Each time, the response was that these were not Mustangs but German reconnaissance aircraft! Obey orders and cover the German unit! Laci was a soldier to his last breath. If he had not been, he might be alive today! He kept to the orders. I glanced aside; Jóska Málik was dancing as if a thermal column was pushing him, or was it me who was dancing? Who knew now? The pressure intensified; it seemed we were going to collide with Jóska, and I could not turn to the right, because there was Laci Molnár. And at that moment, I heard *Drumi* on the radio:
>
> 'The Mustangs are attacking from the sun!'
>
> Then the voice of Gyurka Debrődy, which was impossible to miss:
>
> 'Dogfight behind!'
>
> The dramatic events suddenly started to unfold very quickly, as if film reels had been sped up. Laci Molnár used up all the emergency performance of the aircraft so I lagged behind him from at least 50 meters, but I could keep this distance. The Germans were flying before us approximately a distance of 600 meters and 100–200 meters below, still with their drop tanks. Laci was trying to fly near them and warn them of what was going on above. I was also within 100 meters of the Germans when Laci began to waggle and let off a short burst in front of the Germans to warn them. At the same time, I saw tiny red flashes on the fuselage of his aircraft, and small patches of smoke. … The aircraft was pulling up a bit, then turned sharply to the right, began to dive toward the ground, trailing yellow and white smoke. But it was not burning! And then, a hail of yellow tracer bullets from behind. Striped tail, glistening fuselage, with a characteristic underside, 10 meters left of me and at least 80–100km/hour of extra speed, rushing past me. This was the one that had shot Laci down! I did not even look back. I saw him run into my gunsight's crosshairs, and not further

than 50 meters. Fire from all of my weapons! I saw others also opening fire; I saw the bursts hitting the aircraft and the tracers of the Messers, but I also saw that the German aircraft with the drop tanks were burning! They died without even knowing what had happened. The Mustang did not catch fire but dived sharply. I went after him, but now I could already see that it was doomed. A large town below me; further, the Rába. I was southwest of Jánosháza. At that moment, tracer bullets were whizzing near my cockpit. I was not hit, but I pushed the control column forward until 'the blackening', that is, the breaking point, where due to aerial forces in effect during freefall, all goes back in front of one's eyes. I was falling at full speed at a negative angle and I tried to twist and loop the aircraft; I was trimming meanwhile and exerting physical force like a locomotive – the pressure was so high. The tracers were dead astern to me, my ears are cracking like a machine gun. I needed to get the aircraft up. Now I saw not only blackness, but also white and red, usually the last sign for me. … I let the aircraft out and rushed past at least at 1,000km/h. Somló Hill was to my right; from this, I knew I was heading toward Veszprém. I turned my head, but I could not see any aircraft. I remained at a low altitude. I did not have the best feeling. … Where were the others, and Laci? Was it not an act of cowardice for me to dive toward the ground? Today I have my answers but then, those were very hard minutes. At last, I could do nothing else. … I hadn't even thought of achieving a Mustang kill because I had not seen it crash. And again, many more people were targeting that aircraft. From the direction of Papod, I arrived over Jutas. Upon landing, I saw that two aircraft are taxiing towards the line-up.

The wreck of the aircraft of *hadnagy* László Molnár in the Farkas-forest near Káld. (From the collection of János Pocskai)

This photograph also shows the wreck of Molnár's aircraft. (From the collection of János Pocskai)

I taxied my aircraft alongside the two aircraft as silently as possible; I felt beaten. Nobody was talking. Huszár and Boldizsár. Laci Boldizsár was shaking his head and we were smoking cigarettes, just smoking. We reported via telephone, but there were people still missing from all squadrons. We

> peeked anxiously at our watches; they could not come now, as the maximum operational time for the Messer was over. We are lowering our heads. From our squadron, the formation leader, Laci Molnár, did not come back; neither did Nánási, Nyemecz or Karácsonyi. … There was no news of *Drumi* Tóth from the *Retek* Squadron.[168]

László Molnár had tried to warn the Germans until the very last moment, when his aircraft was hit by the Mustang of 2nd Lieutenant Leoborn E. Richards, who was then immediately shot down by the other pilots flying behind Molnár. Molnár with his damaged aircraft went into a dive, but when he leveled his aircraft at a low altitude, another Mustang was again at his rear and opened fire. Molnár bailed out of his damaged aircraft but, as he was already at a low altitude, he had to open his parachute immediately. The Mustang behind him gunned down the defenseless Hungarian pilot; one of the most skilled and dedicated airmen of the Royal Hungarian Air Force, *vitéz nemes hadnagy* László Molnár, was hit several times in the chest and one of his lower arms was ripped off. He died instantly. His Bf 109 G-6, manufactured in Győr, the V.848, crashed into the forest of Farkas west of Káld, while the body of the pilot stuck on a short tree at the edge of the forest, almost 2km from his aircraft. It cannot now be established which of the seven successful Mustang pilots present at that time (together they reported 12 air victories) shot *hadnagy* Molnár, because the area was quite small and the air combat was intense with multiple claims; but it is highly probable that it was either flight leader 1st Lieutenant Thomas Hardeman, who reported three victories during this particular air combat and four altogether during the war, or one of the three other pilots who reported two air victories on that engagement. All were aces, or became so later: 1st Lieutenant Robert D. Thompson finished the war with five victories; 1st Lieutenant Robert E. Riddle had eleven victories; and 2nd Lieutenant Norman C. Skogstad reported his first air victory that day and ended the war with 12 victories.[169]

The author suggests that, where the death of *hadnagy* Molnár is concerned, it is very important to go into detail regarding the highly sensitive issue of targeting pilots who had bailed out of their aircraft and were descending on their parachutes. Although the majority of American pilots did nothing like this, of course, the practice of shooting airmen in this manner was not uncommon among the fighter pilots of 15th AAF; most of the combatant pilots considered it to be a barbaric act. (Actually the Article XX of the 1923 Hague Rules of Air Warfare, which never became legally binding emphasizes that when an aircraft has been disabled, the occupants when endeavoring to escape by means of parachute must not be attacked in the course of their descent.) The other pilot killed on that day, *zászlós* János Nyemecz, had also bailed out of his aircraft near Kisgörbő when two Mustangs attacked him and wounded him gravely; he was hit in his belly multiple times, and his spine was also injured. The ambulance did not dare to go out for him because of the air raid alert – earlier, a Hungarian ambulance had been strafed and riddled by Americans while carrying a wounded Hungarian pilot – so a German soldier brought

168 Tibor Tobak, *Pumák földön-égen* (Budapest: Háttér Kiadó, 1989), pp. 121–124.

169 For the three American ace pilots, see Olynyk, *Stars and Bars*, p. 521, (Riddle), pp. 556–557 (Skogstad) and p. 591 (Thompson). For Hardeman, see Robert J. Goebel, *Mustang Ace. Memoirs of a P-51 Fighter Pilot* (Pacifica, CA: Pacifica Military History, 1991), p. 228. The author has, unfortunately, tried to contact Hardeman in vain.

The *Szombathelyi Erdészeti Zrt.* has established a memorial site with a cross and a plaque on 7 October 2014 in the Forest of Farkas, at the exact location where László Molnár's body was found (photograph of the author, 18 December 2014)

him in his sidecar to the hospital at Tapolca, where he died of his extremely serious and painful injuries later that day, at half past one in the afternoon. He is buried at Gyöngyös.[170]

Between 24 May and 22 August 1944 (the intensive combat period against the Americans), of the Hungarian fighter pilots killed in air combat against the forces of 15th AAF, five were shot dead after bailing out of their aircraft, while opening their parachutes or when descending to the ground (this is more than 25 percent of the 19 fighter pilots who were killed during this period as a result of air combat with the Americans). One further pilot was shot dead on the ground after crash-landing; the gunner of a Hungarian Me 210 was killed in the same way in April 1944, and two more pilots of Hungarian Bf 109s were so seriously wounded during descent on their parachutes that they never returned to active service. A number of pilots were also wounded on the ground after crash-landing during the period under discussion, or later. To the author's knowledge, the last case of a Mustang targeting a Hungarian pilot who was bailing out of his aircraft happened in April 1945. Based upon this, therefore, it can be concluded that attacking the baled out pilots was a quite frequent act on the American side (the *Luftwaffe* collected similar experiences, in much larger scale).

It is also especially important to mention that one of the 15th AAF aces, Arthur Fiedler from the 325th FG, called the author's attention to a very interesting issue. In September 1944, his unit was visited by an officer's delegation from the Pentagon, who told them that the Germans had a number of very experienced pilots who could be shot down as many as 10–15 times, bail out and fly again to cause serious losses to American units. However, if they could

170 Based on the interviews of the older brother of János Nyemecz, Pál Nyemecz (Budapest, 19 February 1917–Budapest, 28 September 2017), who was also a fighter pilot and who worked as a test pilot during the summer of 1944. The squadron log incorrectly states that the pilot was transported to the hospital in Sümeg, but (besides his brother's recollections) the location of Tapolca is also reinforced by the fact that his death certificate was issued there.

be shot while descending on their parachutes, the 'problem would be solved'.[171] Naturally, the majority of pilots did not heed this suggestion, but the actual cases that happened angered the Hungarian pilots very much. We do not know whether this led to the direct consequence of mortally wounding American airmen in the same manner; however, we know of a case from 1945; for details, see the biography of Kálmán Szeverényi.

The wreck of László Molnár's aircraft was found on 7 August, but the body of the pilot could be found neither by the police nor by the airmen, and there was no news the next day, either. At the request of the desperate parents, civilians were also asked to join the search; at last, five days later, Molnár's body was found by a civilian, Lajos Németh. The part of the forest where the body was found has since been called *Pilóta* ('Pilot') Hill; the name was given to the place by the local residents.[172]

The grave of László Molnár in the heroes' cemetery in Sopronbánfalva. The grave was declared part of the National Cemetery in category 'A' by the *Nemzeti Emlékhely és Kegyeleti Bizottság* during its meeting on 16 January 2013, with decision nr. 1/2013 (photograph of the author, 23 October 2013)

László Molnár was buried with deep sympathy in the military cemetery of Sopronbánfalva on 14 August 1944.[173] His grave – which was created by his father, *ezredes* dr. *nemes* Gyula Molnár, who was also an acclaimed sculptor – is decorated with the twisted propeller of his aircraft, with the following inscription:

VITÉZ NEMES MOLNÁR LÁSZLÓ M. KIR. REP. HADNAGY
ÉLT 23 ÉVET
HŐSI HALÁLT HALT 1944 AUG. 7-ÉN
HALÁLA NAPJÁIG HAZÁNK ELSŐ VADÁSZREPÜLŐJE VOLT

The inscription reads:
Hadnagy vitéz nemes László Molnár of the Royal Hungarian Air Force, aged 23 years, was killed in combat on 7 August 1944. At his death, he was the first fighter pilot of his country.

Wing Order 1944/58, issued soon after Molnár's death, contains the following:

171 Letter of Arthur Fiedler (Oak Park, 1 August 1923–Oxnard, 11 May 2016) to the author, 27 December 2005. For Fiedler, see Olynyk, *Stars and Bars*, p. 267.
172 *Soproni Hírlap*, 17 August 1944, p. 2; also based on documents issued in connection with the finding of the body and the payment of rewards (copies owned by the author).
173 *Soproni Hírlap*, 17 August 1944, p. 2.

> He was outstandingly brave, always ready to sacrifice himself; a true warrior has left the the Hungarian airmen. The fighter arm has lost an exceptionally skilled pilot and a true comrade in the defense of the Hungarian homes. *Hadnagy vitéz* László Molnár already made himself known during the last year when his scoring four air victories in one combat sortie became one of the most beautiful achievements of the Hungarian Air Force. He scored 18 air victories in a matter of weeks on the Russian front, when he was ordered to serve on the home front; his series of air victories was then paused for some time. With the beginning of the American air raids, however, the successful series of this experienced and combat-hardened pilot was quickly resumed. He shot down his 25th opponent in fair combat when the Lord of the Battles took him.
>
> Hungarian flying comrades! May the heroic memory of László Molnár give us strength and endurance in our life-or-death fight to save our homeland! My young pilot comrades, look up at him as a role model, fight with such a fanatical fervor for victory as he did during his painfully short military career – but which has propelled him directly into immortality. The name and remembrance of *hadnagy vitéz* László Molnár will be counted among the heroes who will be blessed by all those coming after, as long as there are any Hungarians still in this land.[174]

On 8 August 1944, Aladár Heppes again recommended László Molnár to the *Magyar Tiszti Arany Vitézségi Érem*, and he received the decoration posthumously on 14 September 1944, as the sixth person in the Royal Hungarian Armed Forces. The decoration was physically presented to his parents on 2 February 1945 in Sopron.[175] Besides this decoration, on 1 November 1944, László Molnár was promoted posthumously – together with the pilots in the same year of the *Akadémia* – to *főhadnagy*.

A short excerpt from László Molnár's last letter to his parents perhaps shows most perfectly how dedicated a soldier he was. His last letter was finished on 4 August but was posted only one or two days later, so it was only delivered to his parents after his tragic death:

> Victory, growing, requires sacrifice. We have received territories back without shedding a drop of blood – now we have to pay, and now we have to ensure that whatever it takes, the country will be held from the moment of final victory to the end of days. … To be enthusiastic, to hope when luck is on our side, is not a big deal; but when the time of troubles comes, gathering our strength at the final hour, not faltering, encouraging others and being brave, and following the hard path – this is heroism, and this is how we fulfil our oath: for the Homeland, until death![176]

174 Air Force Order Nr. 1944/58, 12 August 1944, quoted in *Soproni Hírlap*, 17 August 1944, p. 2.

175 Diary of *vezérőrnagy* Aladár Szirmay (original owned by the author); *Soproni Hírlap*, 6 February 1945, p. 3.

176 The original copy of this letter has, to the knowledge of the author, been destroyed, and only fragments survive. For further parts of the letter, see the webpage of Dr János Szentváry-Lukács about decorations: http://rendjel.myhunet.com/templates/page_plus/molnar.htm (accessed 31 March 2015).

Fighter Aces With Over 10 Air Victories

FŐHADNAGY DÁLNOKI MIKLÓS KENYERES

Number of aerial victories: 18 (+1)
Successes against ground targets: n.d.a.
Number of flown combat sorties: 178
Number of hours flown in the air force: n.d.a.
Nicknames: *Miki*, *Nikó*, *Nikoláj*
Identification number: 2098-21-1185

Decorations

- *Magyar Érdemrend lovagkeresztje hadiszalagon a kardokkal* (17 February 1944, after he was captured by the Soviets)
- *Kormányzói dicsérő elismerés Magyar Koronás Bronz Érdemérme hadiszalagon a kardokkal* (20 September 1943)
- *Bátorsági Érem* (17 February 1944, after he was captured by the Soviets)
- *Tűzkereszt I fokozata a kardokkal és koszorúval*
- German Iron Cross 1st Class (1 February 1944)
- German Iron Cross 2nd Class (autumn 1943)

Victories

Number	Date	Aircraft	Location
1	5 July 1943	Il-2	Kharkiv
2	Summer of 1943	Soviet aircraft	
3	Summer of 1943	Soviet aircraft	
4	24 September 1943	La-5	
5	7 October 1943	La-5	
6	Winter of 1943–44	Soviet aircraft	
7	Winter of 1943–44	Soviet aircraft	
8	Winter of 1943–44	Soviet aircraft	
9	Winter of 1943–44	Soviet aircraft	
10	Winter of 1943–44	Soviet aircraft	
11	Winter of 1943–44	Soviet aircraft	

Number	Date	Aircraft	Location
12	Winter of 1943–44	Soviet aircraft	
13	Winter of 1943–44	Soviet aircraft	
14	Winter of 1943–44	Soviet aircraft	
15	Winter of 1943–44	Soviet aircraft	
16	Winter of 1943–44	Soviet aircraft	
17	1 February 1944	Yak-9	Schpola W
18	3 February 1944 at 09:45	La-5	Cherkasy W
–	1943–44	Soviet aircraft	

Aircraft flown
n.d.a.

Miklós Kenyeres was born on 27 September 1921 in Nyíregyháza. Later, his family lived in Gomba, Pest County. One of his three siblings – a brother, János, born on 31 October 1918 – also become a soldier and graduated as a *hadnagy* in the Hussars on 20 August 1939. He also survived the war and left the country in 1956; he died in Canada in 2006.

The family was given the title of nobility by *fejedelem* (Prince) Gábor Bethlen in 1615, but due to the modesty of Miklós Kenyeres's father, who retired as an *őrnagy* from the Hussars in 1924 and was a Member of Parliament from 1931, he usually did not use the title incorporated into his name.[1] Miklós Kenyeres graduated from high school (*Szent István Gimnázium*) in Budapest in 1939. It is important to mention that their family was distantly related to the Regent's family: the maternal grandmother of Miklós Kenyeres, Erzsébet Horthy, was the Regent's sister, so he was informally called by the family 'Papa Miklós'. According to the memories of his relatives, however, this relationship was always kept hidden by Miklós Kenyeres, and he never used it for protection or as a means of getting forward – nor would his father allow it – and he was admitted to the *Akadémia* without this assistance and only based on his own skill.

Miklós Kenyeres (far right), with three of his classmates from the *Repülőakadémia*, perhaps in 1941. (From the collection of the Kenyeres family)

Miklós Kenyeres was a natural aviation talent. As the student of *főhadnagy* Jenő Chirke (together with György Debrődy and László Molnár), he was the first to fly solo with a Bücker among his classmates. On 18 June 1942, he graduated as *hadnagy* as of 1 July 1942, with rank number 14 (altogether 121st).[2]

After the graduation, he was assigned to Tapolca with his friend, György Debrődy, to the fighter school, then to Mátyásföld as part of 5/I Fighter Group, with which he was deployed to the Eastern Front together with

1 Béla Kempelen, *Magyar nemes családok*, vol. 5 (Budapest: Grill Károly Könyvkiadóvállalata, 1913), p. 438; also based on the correspondence with the Kenyeres family.
2 *Honvédségi Közlöny* (*Személyes ügyek)*, nr. 1942/24 (16 June 1942), p. 613.

Miklós Kenyeres as an academy student in Kassa, with his Zündapp motorcycle. (From the collection of the Kenyeres family)

The table of the class of the *Repülőakadémia* that graduated on 18 July 1942. In the upper left corner are Miklós Kenyeres and László Molnár; in the middle inside, on the right, is György Debrődy. These were the three prospective aces in the class (*HM HIM* Photographic Archives 106.719/001)

Hadnagy Miklós Kenyeres – in a white shirt – tells a story after returning from a sortie, to two ground crew officers in the early summer of 1943. Behind him is probably the Bf 109 F-4 he flew, with unusual dotted camouflage painting. (From the collection of dr. Tünde Horváth)

Debrődy in the middle of December 1942. During the winter retreat, the false news started to spread at Mátyásföld that, apart from *hadnagy* Pánczél, *hadnagy* Kenyeres had also been killed in January, as he reportedly crashed with a *Héja* and burned to death during the retreat from Ilovskoye.[3] Luckily this was not true; *hadnagy* Kenyeres was safe and sound and did not even fly any combat sorties with a *Héja* during January. He retrained to Bf 109 in Uman, and his first combat sortie was completed at the end of May 1943. For the majority of combat sorties on the Eastern Front, *hadnagy* Kenyeres was accompanied by wingman János Mátyás.

After one of his early summer sorties, during which he was engaged in air combat, the following excerpt from a letter survives, written to his sister, Margaret. This sortie, according to the author's identification, probably took place either on 7 June or 21 June (*őrnagy* Aladár Heppes – based on his logbook – completed bomber escort missions and was engaged in air combat, but reported no air victories on these days):[4]

> Today I was on a big sortie; we were escorting three bombers with *őrnagy* Heppes 150km beyond the front. Suddenly, I noticed an aircraft below on the left. I noticed it was Russian, and what is more, a very good one, perhaps even better than our aircraft [*hadnagy* Kenyeres was most probably still flying with a Bf 109 F-4]. I turned on him and then the *őrnagy* was already talking on the radio, saying there was one more up on the right, and I noticed two more behind me. Hooray, the dance began; they were in superior numbers, so the only things that could be done were to attack to keep them harassed and occupied. I got one of them, targeted him and opened fire; unfortunately, he was more maneuverable than us and he always turned out of the way of our fire. It is better to save the ammunition, I thought then.

3 An enlisted pilot who completed his primary flight training in 1941 and who was serving in Mátyásföld wrote a letter in connection with this on 5 February 1943; the copy of the letter is owned by the author.

4 Based on the logbook of Aladár Heppes (partial copy owned by the author).

The chap dived; I pulled up, because there was fire coming from behind; the upper right side one was attacking the *őrnagy*, so I let out a long burst in front of this one and turned on the third. This escaped with a sharp turn, but then when I glanced back, I saw that a guy was sitting right behind me and he released the cicadas [a cicada is any kind of projectiles that pops or explodes; it is possible to kill with it, be it a bomb, an anti-aircraft shell, a cannon or machine gun round]. I could see the nose of the guy so there were no problems – it would be problematic only if I could see its underside while turning – it would mean he was keeping his distance and was ready to fire. I waited until he got into firing position and then left him standing with a climbing turn. And then came the most irritating minute of the day, because, until now, I really had been enjoying my life. A guy started a frontal attack against me, and we rushed against each other, firing like madmen. He didn't know where I would dodge and I didn't know either where he would; it was a bit hot in there! It was only a question of nerves, so whatever came next, I pushed to his left and dodged, and we flew past each other. The *őrnagy* was already going home; we had lost each other. I too turned toward home, and I saw that two were coming after me. We discussed with the *őrnagy* that I would lure them toward the front and the *őrnagy* would attack them from behind. I tried everything to lure them after me; I flew slowly and horizontally, but they were not keen on chasing me and returned home.[5]

His first air victory, like György Debrődy's, was achieved on 5 July 1943 against an Il-2, probably from the 237th SAP. He recalled his first success:

> I position myself beside a German fighter; he is out all alone too. All these German pilots are good comrades. We know them well; they are stationed at the airfield near us. We attack six Soviet fighters; they are scattered at once, so no result for us. One of them dives, with me after him, but he turns under me and I lose sight of him. A lonely white-crossed aircraft is flying past our airfield. This is our own – I think. 'Hallo, aircraft left of me, close up.' I read its number: 041. This is Paja [the nick-name of *őrmester* Pál Kovács]. 'Hallo Paja, Miki here, close up.' 'Roger, closing up.'

A group of pilots of 5/2 Fighter Squadron in the early summer of 1943. From left to right: *hadnagy* Miklós Kenyeres, *százados* Gyula Horváth, *főhadnagy* János Kőhalmy, *hadnagy* György Debrődy and *hadnagy* György Lipták. The aircraft is a Bf 109 F-4 with plug cooler intakes appearing on the engine cowling of the G-2, designed for its DB 605 engine (which had a better performance). (From the collection of dr. Tünde Horváth)

5 The copy of the original letter is owned by the author; after the death of Margaret Kenyeres, the original letter was also lost, and now only the author's copy remains. Unfortunately, the letter is undated.

> So now let's look after something. At the eastern edge of the city, huge numbers of anti-aircraft smoke puffs are appearing at about 20–30 meters. This is the best guidance. There is a red-starred aircraft here. 'Paja, follow me, I am attacking.' Four Soviet ground-attack aircraft are approaching the city. They have iron nerves for sure. They are flying in a calm, closed formation despite the killing fire upon them. We fly past a burning wreck. 'That was me,' says Paja, 'and the other one over village X'. Excellent, he already has two aerial victories.
>
> I dive into the Russian formation with my aircraft. The anti-aircraft artillery imperturbably continues firing. In the turmoil, having Soviet and own aircraft in the air in close proximity does not count. We are not bothered by the anti-aircraft fire now either; only the four Soviet stars. And now I notice I have not been entirely correct in assessing the situation. Because, there were four more aircraft behind the first four, and I have flown between the two formations. Then it seems I am lucky again: the aircraft on the left leaves the flight, and I rush after him. The dogfight begins. The Russian descends close to the ground and is trying to escape above the trees. We are after him everywhere. Left of me, three German comrades are also after him. One of them making a pass on him but he does not succeed in getting the Soviet down. Now it's my turn. I pull up a bit and, from the side, I aim exactly in front of the engine. I am not yet firing; he is too far. Now, now to pull all triggers! I pull up in an instant to avoid collision. I slide toward the right and turn to the left side of the Soviet aircraft and now firing at him from above, targeting his cockpit. The Russian gunner is not returning the fire anymore. Now, from very close, I open fire with the cannon as well. The aircraft shudders and crashes the ground with his starboard wing.[6]

Unfortunately, war correspondence could very rarely reach Kenyeres to tell such a long story, but he sometimes told such stories to his family.

Most of the combat sorties flown around the time of the battle of Kursk were of a similar type, although unfortunately the details of his next two air victories are lost.

On 8 July, *hadnagy* Kenyeres was on a bomber escort mission with his squadron when they were engaged in a dogfight with a larger La-5 formation. One of the Soviet pilots managed to get behind Kenyeres, who wasn't able to escape; at last, *százados* György Ujszászy, commander of 1/1 Fighter Squadron, saved him and shot his attacker down. The Hungarian and the Soviet aircraft were so close to each other that Ujszászy almost downed both of them with a single burst. Bullets were passing between Kenyeres's legs and, after they were removed from the engine block, they were found to have been fired by Ujszászy!

Hadnagy Miklós Kenyeres soon had another extraordinary experience during a very dark, cloudy morning with low cloud base, after a scramble. This happened on 27 July, according to the logbook of György Debrődy. As the other pilot of the element, *hadnagy* Debrődy remembered what happened:

> A rocket was fired from the control building of the airfield; the mechanics woke me up and, we were soon in the air. Low clouds; at the area marked by the radio, we discovered

6 Kádár, *Sasok harca*, pp. 118–119.

> the Il-2s, who, noticing our presence, started to circle us. Because of the low cloud base, it was not possible to break free upward, so the only thing we could do was to slip out of their circle at a very low altitude. I escaped with a very badly placed burst from a rear gunner, but one of the bombers turned frontally against Kenyeres. This happened at four or five meters from the ground. The Il-2 opened fire. Those who have not yet seen an Il-2 attacking face-to-face simply cannot assess the psychological effect it creates. You can only see the flashing muzzle fire all along the wings and nothing more, and it is not advised to pull through this curtain of fire. Kenyeres slowly pushed the aircraft downward, the Russian too, firing with all his guns. Glancing sideways to the right, I could see they were crossing each other's path; then, there was a huge cloud of dust. A few seconds later, I saw Lajos [Debrődy and Kenyeres called each other 'Lajos' during combat sorties] beside me, the tip of his wing curled upward. The Russian pushed him down to such extremes that he had hit the rooftop of a peasant house (hence the cloud of smoke). After the critical landing on the airfield, he very gladly commented on how lucky he was that the Ukrainian peasants did not use reinforced concrete to build their houses.[7]

The – albeit abbreviated – descriptions of *hadnagy* Kenyeres's fourth and fifth air victories from early autumn have survived; he himself described these victories in the newspaper as follows: 'Flight leader. Out of the clouds, down on the Russians. Laci [László Molnár] is screaming; he was firing too. Lag 5 falls down.'[8]

Not long after, on an extremely eventful 7 October for Hungarian fighters, Kenyeres scored another air victory: 'On 7 October: free hunt. Below us Parachuting Jani, a guy of *hadnagy* Szeverényi. Four Russians before me; they to the left, I am after them. The Russian is dumb, turns in front of me, and down he falls at once.'[9]

For the opponents of the Hungarian fighters on 7 October, see details at *hadnagy* Molnár. From the autumn of 1943, the three classmates – Miklós Kenyeres, György Debrődy and László Molnár – were a golden triumvirate competing for the title of the most successful Hungarian fighter pilot.

The most successful month for *hadnagy* Miklós Kenyeres – according to the partially surviving personal records of the pilots of the squadron – was probably January 1944, but no description of these air victories remains. According to the author's approximations, he must have achieved eight to 10 air victories during the course of this month.

On 1 February 1944, *hadnagy* Kenyeres performed a heroic and completely unprecedented deed in the history of Messerschmitt Bf 109s, saving his friend, György Debrődy, from Soviet captivity and bringing him back in his own aircraft. During that mission, *hadnagy* Debrődy had been shot down by a surprise attack of a Yakovlev fighter, and belly-landed approximately 10km behind the enemy lines with his burning aircraft west of Schpola. In Kenyeres's memoirs, an La-5 type was mentioned as the attacker, but this was probably a slip of his memory, because contemporary sources all mention a Yak-9 present as the enemy aircraft. Kenyeres shot down the fighter aircraft who had shot his friend, then landed on totally unknown, snowy and icy

7 Recollections of György Debrődy, February 1976; Gyula Gaál, 'A Pumák első nyara', *Magyar Szárnyak Évkönyv*, 1990, p. 86.
8 *Üvölt a Puma*, 3 November 1943, p. 4.
9 *Üvölt a Puma*, 3 November 1943, p. 4.

terrain, which even had a ditch across it. He released the canopy, threw away his parachute and emergency kit, sat Debrődy in the seat, sat himself in his friend's lap, took off and successfully landed at Uman airfield, despite witnesses commenting (on the arrival of this Bf 109 with such an enormous 'human bump') that he would kill himself on landing for sure after coming such a long way.

It is very characteristic of Kenyeres's modesty that, after this event and with the German and Hungarian war correspondents swarming around him, he said nothing of the case and only added that he would have done it for any of his comrades at any time. Later, however, the interested people managed to get him talking, and he let the history of the rescue story be recorded after the passage of some decades (thus, when remembering the type of the attacking Soviet aircraft, the veteran must have remembered incorrectly):

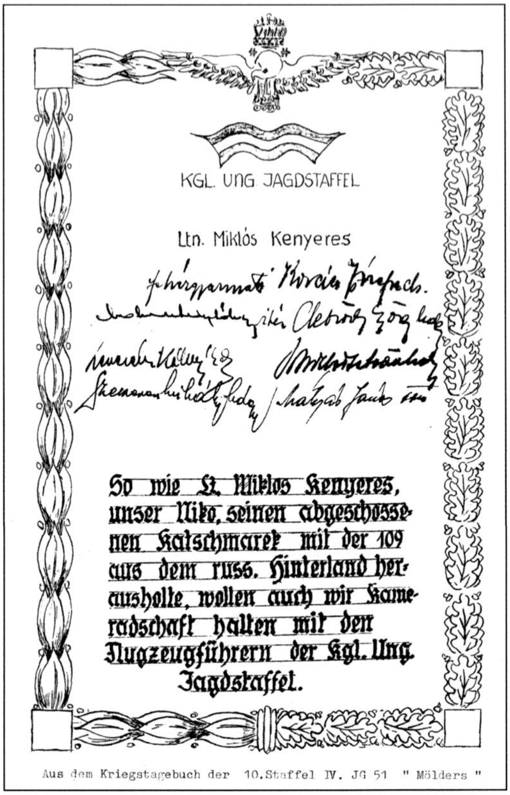
KGL. UNG. JAGDSTAFFEL

Ltn. Miklós Kenyeres

So wie Lt. Miklos Kenyeres, unser Miko, seinen abgeschossenen Katschmarek mit der 109 aus dem russ. Hinterland herausholte, wollen auch wir Kameradschaft halten mit den Flugzeugführern der Kgl. Ung. Jagdstaffel.

Aus dem Kriegstagebuch der 10.Staffel IV. JG 51 " Mölders "

Excerpts from the war diary of 10./JG 51 commemorating the heroism of Miklós Kenyeres who, on 1 February 1944, brought Debrődy back from behind enemy lines. The document was also signed by four Hungarian aces: László Molnár, György Debrődy, Kálmán Szeverényi and János Mátyás. (From the author's collection)

> On this particular sortie, we had just dived out of the clouds when I noticed that an La-5 had engaged Debrődy from dead astern. I shot down the Russian in vain, as he had already downed Gyurka. I saw his aircraft belching smoke, but it was still maneuverable. I followed him and saw that he landed on his belly … behind enemy lines, near a marching Russian division. … The whole area is right in front of my eyes even today; I could draw it from memory. A village in front of me, and I draw past a factory; on the left is a forest where batteries are stationed, and right in a steep ditch is the road, where the marching units are going past. I had enormous luck because those who were nearer to us were firing, and those who were further behind, started to run toward us; if that had been otherwise, we would have been caught in an instant. …
>
> So I saw the aircraft had belly-landed and Gyurka opened the cockpit. At that moment I released my landing gear instantaneously. When it was out, I was saying to myself, *What the hell are you doing? This can't be done, you fool*! He was on a bumpy plowed field, with a ditch across it and very limited space to take off or to land. The chances were one in a thousand or ten thousand, but the key to success was, I think, that then and there I was absolutely sure what I could do with a Messerschmitt! At that time I was flying six to eight hours a day and, in the end, I did not see it as flying, but that I had become the aircraft itself. … I flew

around with released landingg gears. I saw everything perfectly and I was absolutely aware of how utterly desperate our situation was. And here comes an interesting thing. Both of us had been raised and trained to be aware of our duty. We had taken the oath; we had been raised in the knowledge that our duties must be fulfilled. For a second, it flashed in my mind that nobody would know if I just retracted my landing gear and flew away from the area. But then, for the rest of my life, I would have to live with the weight of the knowledge that I should have tried. … And besides, I have an adventurer's soul, which whispered, *Goddamn it, let us try*!

During these situations, everything is only a matter of seconds. Because of the adrenalin rush, everything goes super quick. And however impossible the landing is, one concentrates with all of one's nerves and senses to land. That is, within 50 meters! I perfectly pulled the aircraft to the tail; I was hovering. It was not the aircraft that was hovering, it was me. I felt in my buttocks the least possible speed with which it was possible to fly. At the last second I cut off speed. A large bump, tail lifting up, and the aircraft stopped. The most difficult part was that I wasn't able to land exactly near Debrődy, so there was a good deal of distance between us, and the snow reached to our knees. All the way the Russians were firing like hell and the most nerve-wracking thing was to watch the bullets that kept hailing around me and any of which could hit us at any moment. Debrődy had iron nerves; he even tried to dismantle the radio with a small knife. But when he was targeted from the forest, he fled at once! By the time he got near me, I had already thrown the parachute out and released the canopy. We squeezed ourselves into the seat. I knew that our only chance was not to start slowly but at full speed. I pushed it to full speed and the aircraft did not have its tail raised up too much. The cross ditch was there, a pull, a thud and we were in the air. It was a hell of a difficult thing to fly with my face pushed to the glass, not seeing anything and having the terrible wind in our faces. It tore out half of Debrődy's hair.

After approximately half a minute, we reached the front and the armored vehicles. I knew what direction the front was in, and although I wasn't able to see the control panel, I knew we must fly in the direction where there was no sun. I did not have the faintest idea, though, where our airfield could be. We were incredibly lucky because we had seen an aircraft taking off and landing. It was a test flight. I thought that the airfield must be there somewhere. On landing, at first, we made a left circle, and when we came straight and I extended the flaps, I screamed into Gyurka's ears to rise when I pulled back the throttle. We started to glide; I screamed 'Now!' and he grasped two handles and rose; I fell into the seat, pulled back the throttle and we literally just fell to the ground from two meters.[10]

Debrődy recollected the events just after landing for an inquiring war correspondent:

All of a sudden we noticed six Yak-9 fighters. We engaged them instantly. I 'sat' behind one of the aircraft and fired burst after burst into him, but on that day somehow I did not have too much luck with this (admits the *hadnagy* who has already scored 16 air victories), and I was just about to attack the 'Jani' once again when another enemy fighter appeared out of the clouds. It attacked me at that instant. He was coming from behind; my cockpit filled

10 'A lelkiismeret súlyával fel lehet-e szállni?', *Top Gun*, 1992:4, p. 58.

> with smoke and I felt I was going to choke to death. I pushed the cockpit open. I wanted to bail out but luckily I noticed that I was only at 100 meters of altitude. I could not do anything; I had to land somehow. I saw that *hadnagy* Miklós Kenyeres was attacking the Soviet fighter who shot me down, and in the next moment I saw the enemy falling from the sky to the ground, burning. This was Miklós's 18th air victory.
>
> I managed to pull my aircraft out of the downward spin and belly-landed in a clearing surrounded by forest. I did not have a clue if I was in enemy territory or in our own, because at that time the German and Russian pockets were alternating along the front. As soon as I landed, I began dismantling the radio. I noticed, however, that *hadnagy* Kenyeres flew a few circles over me then released his landing gear and landed at the side of my aircraft. 'Come Debcsi, quick, we are going home' – and he was already pushing away the canopy.
>
> For the first moment, it seemed completely impossible to fit two people into the cockpit, which was already tight for one; but we did not have much time to think. Infantry bullets whistled over our heads, then there was a whistling sound and an impact. These were artillery shells, and the second and third impact was coming. But Miklós was not bothered. 'Throw the leather jacket away,' he said, and he did so himself. The artillery shells exploded nearer and nearer to us; we needed to hurry. I was the first to sit behind the seat, and then Miklós pressed himself into my lap. Even today I can't imagine how we managed to fit into that incredibly small place; all I knew was that I hugged [*hadnagy*] Kenyeres so gratefully.
>
> Then the engine started up. The pedals were operated by me, the control column and the throttle by Miklós. The ground started to move below us. Our fateful aircraft needed to jump over a ditch while starting up but, in the end, we were in the air. But the real struggle had just begun. With full force, I clasped the frontal armor, but after a few minutes I felt that my fingers could not hold it anymore. We flew at a speed of 400–450km/h and I feared the enormous draft would pull me out of the seat. In my agony, I held onto Miklós's helmet with my teeth; meanwhile, I had to pay attention to the control column. At last, we arrived home. It was an unforgettable moment when we got out and I could shake the hands of *hadnagy* Kenyeres and thank him for saving me from captivity.[11]

After this extraordinary adventure, *hadnagys* Kenyeres and Debrődy also completed another sortie during the day, tasked with bomber escort and free hunt.[12] In this case, their Soviet opponent can be clearly identified. The fighters of the Soviet 5th Air Army reported shooting down 15 Messerschmitts in the given area (14 by Yakovlev fighters from the 203rd and 294th IAD's; only one by an La-5 pilot). This is too many claims altogether; however, only one Soviet pilot went missing (was killed) after his claim was reported. This was a young *leytenant*, Grigori Bravov from 516th IAP, who at 07:57 (Hungarian time) reported shooting down a Messerschmitt near Jaroslavka, but then went missing and never returned. (Of the 14 victories against Bf 109s claimed by the Yakovlevs, eight were reported by 516th IAP.) It is highly probable that he was

11 Ferenc Gyulai Jankovits, 'Repülő bajtársak', *Magyar Szárnyak*, 15 April 1944, p. 9.
12 Logbook of György Debrődy.

the one who shot Debrődy down and subsequently became the victim of *hadnagy* Kenyeres right afterward (this was Bravov's first and only air victory).[13] Around that time, there was extremely heavy air combat activity going on in the area. During their increased air combat activity in the area of Korsun–Shevchenkovsky (which will be discussed soon) between 29 January and 3 February 1944, the fighters of the Soviet 5th Air Army reported shooting down 94 enemy aircraft altogether.[14]

After this heroic deed, *hadnagy* Kenyeres was immediately recommended for the *Magyar Tiszti Arany Vitézségi Érem* by the commander of the Hungarian 102 Air Brigade, *vezérőrnagy* Aladár Szirmay. The Germans were also impressed by the actions of *hadnagy* Kenyeres: over the winter of 1943–44, the independent 5/2 Fighter Squadron was subordinated to the German IV./JG 51 (commanded by *Major* Hans-Ekkehard Bob),[15] so usually they were in close connection with the Hungarians. After this action, *hadnagy* Kenyeres immediately received the Iron Cross 1st Class, and was also recommended for the Knights Cross of the Iron Cross, because the Germans were also much impressed by the extraordinary deed. Even though there were many experienced Messerschmitt pilots in IV./JG 51, doing anything like this had not even crossed their minds. One ace of the group, the commander of 10./JG 51, *Oberleutnant* Horst-Günther von Fassong,[16] often flew with Hungarian comrades and was very popular. He commented:

> I have spent a long time out on the front, but I have never seen anything like this before. Such a display of comradeship and heroism I haven't even heard of before. It was especially hard to carry out this rescue mission with a Messerschmitt aircraft because the cockpit is so narrow, and it is extremely difficult to land with a Messerschmitt on unknown ground; before this happened, we wouldn't even have dared to think of attempting such act. It is undoubtedly the highest level of bravery and heroism I can imagine.[17]

Unfortunately, *hadnagy* Kenyeres was not able to increase his number of air victories for long. Two days later, on 3 February 1944 his aircraft was shot down by a Soviet anti-aircraft gun and he had to bail out over a forest, where he was captured.

The records in connection with the capture of *hadnagy* Kenyeres have survived. In them, *hadnagy* Debrődy wrote:

13 The Soviet data is based on information kindly provided by Mikhail Bikhov regarding the documents of TsAMO, disclosed by himself.

14 S.M. Davtjan, *Pjataja vozdusnaja* (Moscow: Vojenizdat, 1990), p. 144.

15 For Hans-Ekkehard Bob (Freiburg, 24 January 1917–12 August Freiburg, 12 August 2013), see Hans-Ekkehard Bob, *Betrayed Ideals. Memoirs of a Luftwaffe Fighter Ace* (Bristol: Cerberus, 2004), p. 160; Obermaier, *Die Ritterkreuzträger der Luftwaffe 1939–45*, p. 90. Bob lived for most of his life in his home town. When the author spent three months researching in the German military archives (*Bundesarchiv-Militärarchiv* in 2004), he met with him to inquire about his wartime memories. Bob remembered his '*draufgänger*' (dare devil) Hungarian fighter pilots with fondness, but was not able to provide any details – understandably, given the time that had elapsed since the events.

16 He scored at least 75 victories, was promoted to *Hauptmann* and served as the commander of III./JG 11; he was shot down on 1 January 1945 during Operation Bodenplatte north of Maastricht, near Opglabbeek, by a P-47 of 366th FG, and was killed. For more on Horst-Günther von Fassong (Kassel, 27 April 1919–Opglabbeek, 1 January 1945), see Obermaier, *Die Ritterkreuzträger der Luftwaffe 1939–45*, p. 109.

17 Jankovits, 'Repülő bajtársak', p. 9.

> On 3 February, under the leadership of *hadnagy* Miklós Kenyeres as second element leader with *őrmester* János Mátyás and *szakaszvezető* László Varga as wingmen, we took off at 08:40 to secure the airspace over the airfield of the encircled German units. We escorted a Ju 52 transport formation that took off from Korsun at 09:30, when we noticed two waves of 20–20 Russian fighters in the air. The Russian fighters have attacked the Ju 52 formation, which tried to escape into the clouds, but the majority of the aircraft did not reach the clouds yet. We attacked the Russians immediately, and in the desparate air combat (which lasted approximately 15 minutes) *hdgy.* Kenyeres, *őrm.* Mátyás and I shot down one Russian fighter aircraft each. With our attack, we drew the Russians upon us and the transport aircraft flew away unharmed. After this, we met a further 20 Russian fighters, but we could not engage them as we lacked fuel and ammunition. We were heading out of the encirclement in the shortest way possible, in the direction of south–southeast. In airspace 10-7-5-3 at an altitude of 600 meters, I noticed that the aircraft of *hdgy.* Kenyeres had burst into flames. The aircraft was plummeting into a steep dive. *Hdgy.* Kenyeres released the canopy and bailed out at approx. 200 meters. A few seconds later the aircraft blew up in mid-air. *Hdgy.* Kenyeres was stuck up on a tree with his parachute in a forest in the area 10-7-5-3 (Kasazkoye West). I performed three passes near him and I saw that he tried to grab a tree to climb down. The aircraft of *hdgy.* Kenyeres was probably shot down by the anti-aircraft artillery stationed at the edge of the forest, because I myself faced extremely heavy anti-aircraft fire while approaching the location. During the low flight, I bitterly admitted that I was not able to help my comrade who had just rescued me from Russian captivity two days earlier, because there were no spots nearby that I could use as a runway. The three aircraft of the flight were unable to reach the airfield due to lack of fuel and two emergency landed on released undercarriages at Nowo-Archangelsk; the third aircraft's engine stopped mid-air and *őrm.* Mátyás belly landed.[18]

Hadnagy Kenyeres bailed out of his burning Messerschmitt Bf 109 G-6 67km southwest of Cherkasy, over the forest, west of Kozatskoye (*Plq.* 10753). He was soon captured by Cossacks, who gave him 'the biggest slap in the face he has ever received', and drove him away to captivity without his boots.

The Regent, Miklós Horthy, sent the following handwritten letter on 17 February 1944 to Kenyeres's mother:

> My dear Erzsike!
> I have received your letter. We are informed of the same as what you write: that he has bailed out of his burning aircraft and was captured by the Russians. The English radio proves he is all right. As far as I know, his last air victory was his 17th, and not his 16th. I am attaching the report of his last, exceptionally brave deed.
>
> He was recommended for the third time for a decoration. The first two have not yet reached me. According to this, he will get the Knight's Cross with swords and the most precious and rare decoration, Medal for Courage, which has never been given to anybody

18 'Évfolyamtörténetek – Az 1942 június 18-án felavatott évfolyam', *Magyar Szárnyak Évkönyv*, 1995, p. 237.

before on the Eastern Front. Let us rejoice that this has ended this way, and let us hope he will soon be home safe and sound. You can be very proud of him.
With loving regards,
Papa Miklós.[19]

It is necessary to add a few things to this already very interesting letter. The kill on 3 February was Kenyeres's 18th confirmed air victory; at least his squadron commander mentions 18 air victories in his summary report. *Hadnagy* Debrődy, however, strongly suggested in his report that Kenyeres's 18th air victory had been scored on 1 February; according to this, the one on 3 February was his 19th. Unfortunately, in the absence of proper documentation, this uncertainty cannot be settled without a doubt. Perhaps the *Luftwaffe* confirmed his 19th air victory as the one scored on 3 February, but the Hungarian authorities had not done so because he had not come back to claim it formally; the kill might also have concerned another aircraft, and his claim might have been confirmed on the Hungarian side too, because (according to the memories of his comrades) the Germans credited him with 19 air victories.[20]

The *Bátorsági Érem* (Medal of Courage) was awarded on many occasions on the Eastern Front, and in many cases not exactly for combat-related actions, but for example when somebody had saved a drowning man from a river. There were a few decorations also made in the Royal Hungarian Air Force for heroic actions performed on airfields, for example when soldiers risked their lives to save somebody from a burning aircraft. The more than two dozen awarded Medals of Courage were all of silver class, and there were plans for a golden one to be given; the Regent was possibly thinking about this when he spoke of a decoration that had never been given before. Unfortunately, however, this decoration was never bestowed, although Kenyeres's squadron commander, József Kovács, also mentioned the '*Magyar Arany Bátorsági Érem*' by mistake in his statistical documents for *hadnagy* Kenyeres.[21]

Kenyeres received the Medal of Courage instead of the *Magyar Tiszti Arany Vitézségi Érem*. The process of awarding him the German Knight's Cross of the Iron Cross was halted after his capture, so he never received the latter decoration either.

Kenyeres came home in the spring of 1945 with the first transport; during his captivity, emigrated communists had wanted to lure him into working for them, but Kenyeres was not at all supportive of the idea (they wanted to make him commander of the Győr police force). In the meantime, after being assessed, on 20 April 1945 he was promoted to *főhadnagy*, effective from 1 April 1945.[22] For a few months he worked for the newly established air police, an organization that did not even have any aircraft, then in December 1945 he decided it would be better for him to leave the country. From Austria, he went to Italy and then to Spain, where he attended the technical university in 1947; the university took into account some of the time Kenyeres had

19 A copy of the letter is owned by the author.

20 *HM HIM HL*, documents of 101 Fighter Wing, box nr. 112, Royal Hungarian 102 Honvéd Fighter Group, summary of decorated officers and enlisted; Jankovits, 'Repülő bajtársak', p. 9.

21 *HM HIM HL*, documents of 101 Fighter Wing, box nr. 112, Royal Hungarian 102 Honvéd Fighter Group, summary of decorated officers and enlisted.

22 *HM HIM KI*, document folder nr. 47209. As this was a promotion that took place just before the end of the war, and as it was directly connected to his service in the Second World War, the author has mentioned this rank on the first page near his name.

spent at the *Repülőakadémia*, and he managed to graduate in two years. From 1949, he tried to find work in France; then, in 1950, he emigrated to Canada, where he became an acclaimed development engineer at Westinghouse. In 1959, he fell in love with sailing boats – of which he knew nothing before – and gave up everything to go back to Spain, where he founded a shipbuilding company called Carabela. His beautiful wooden yachts were extremely popular, and his company was one of the most prominent in its kind. After a heart attack in 1986, he closed his shipbuilding company, retired and lived near Barcelona and in Buda, enjoying his well-deserved retired years in peace. After the democratic transformation in Hungary, on 30 June 1994, the Minister of Defense promoted him to *őrnagy* in Order Nr. 307/1994.[23]

Miklós Kenyeres died on 12 October 1997 at Cabrera de Mar, and was thus the last of the greatest Hungarian aces – an exceptional person – to pass away. According to his last wish, his cremated remains were scattered from a yacht made by him into the sea near Barcelona, a place he loved so much.

TJ. (TISZTJELÖLT) ŐRMESTER VITÉZ ISTVÁN FÁBIÁN

Number of aerial victories: 14 (+6)
Successes against ground targets: n.d.a.
Number of flown combat sorties: 122+ (13 against Americans)
Number of hours flown in the air force: 1,250
Nickname: *Koponya*
Identification number: 2287-18-0062

Decorations

- *Magyar Nagy Ezüst Vitézségi Érem* (20 March 1944)
- *Magyar Nagy Ezüst Vitézségi Érem*, second award (25 January 1945)
- *Magyar Kis Ezüst Vitézségi Érem* (20 January 1944)
- *Magyar Bronz Vitézségi Érem* (20 October 1943)
- *Magyar Bronz Vitézségi Érem*, second award (13 February 1945)
- *Tűzkereszt I fokozata a kardokkal és koszorúval*
- *Erdélyi Emlékérem*
- *Délvidéki Emlékérem*
- German Iron Cross 1st Class (17 March 1945)
- German Iron Cross 2nd Class (1943)
- Gold *Frontflugspange* (20 April 1945)
- Italian Pilot Badge (1939)

23 *HM HIM KI*, document folder nr. 47209.

Victories

Number	Date	Aircraft	Location
1	17 June 1943	Soviet fighter?	
2	26 June 1943	Yak-1 (Yak-7B)	Graznoye SW
–	7 July 1943	La-5	
3	13 July 1943	Il-2	Belgorod N
–	3 August 1943	Soviet aircraft	
–	4 August 1943	Soviet aircraft	
–	6 August 1943	Soviet aircraft	
–	9 August 1943	Soviet aircraft	
4	28 September 1943	Il-2	Pereiaslav
5	28 September 1943	La-5	Pereiaslav
6	14 June 1944	P-38	Pusztavám SE
7	30 June 1944	B-24	Veszprémpinkóc?
–	5 November 1944	B-17	
8	13 November 1944 at 14:48	Yak-9	Tápiószele N
9	21 December 1944	La-5	Seregélyes
10	16 January 1945	Pe-2	Pincehely N
11	16 January 1945	Yak-9	Sárszentmihály
12	19 February 1945	La-5	Tardos
13	13 March 1945 at 10:46	Il-2	Pázmánd SW
14	19 March 1945 at 15:15	Il-2	Nádasdladány N

Aircraft flown

Bf 109 G-10/U4: 'Yellow 5' (14 March 1945), 'Yellow 11' (17 March 1945), 'White 10' (21 April 1945)

István Fábián was born on 6 December 1918 in Tolna County at the Kölesdtengelic train station, where his family lived because his father was a railway signalman and switch operator. After three older sisters, he was the first and only boy in the family, as well as the youngest child.[24] Later, the family moved from Tolna to Somogy County, and they lived in Kaposvár. Due to the grave financial situation of the family, István Fábián left high school (*Somssich Pál Gimnázium* at Kaposvár) one year before graduation and started to work as a baker. In 1938, he heard about the call of the Hungarian Air Force to join them and train as pilots; he applied immediately, because aviation had been his dream from an early age.

He was one of the 200 students who received their complete training within the framework of the *DRT* in Italy, on the Grottaglie airfield near Taranto, between 1938 and 1940. His nickname,

24 *MNL Tolna Megye Levéltára* (National Archives, Tolna County Archives), XXXIII/1, Gindlicsalád state birth registry from 1918, counterpart, acc. nr. note 62. A settlement with the name Kölesdtengelic has never existed; there was only a joint railway station with this name. The railway station itself belonged to the Gindlicsalád birth registry district, so the birth was recorded there. The name of Gindlicsalád was officially changed to Tengelic in 1931.

Koponya ('Skull'), was used as early as this time, and the name followed him throughout his military career. In Italy, he was assigned to the fighter group, and on completing his training he returned home in 1939, where he was deployed to Szolnok. Like Dezső Szentgyörgyi, he also missed the type of the CR.42s, as he was serving with units equipped with the obsolete CR.32s until the end of 1941.

During the campaign against Yugoslavia, in April 1941, as a pilot of 1/I Fighter Group, he completed a few protective sorties over own territory, but the old CR.32s with a very high number of service hours were not quite suitable even for these tasks. Despite this, and in the absence of any other types of aircraft, his group was relocated to Felsőábrány in the summer of 1941 to defend the Miskolc–Diósgyőr industrial area still with the CR.32. In 1942, he was ordered for a short time to be an instructor in the *Repülőakadémia*; after being retrained to the slowly arriving Re.2000s, *szakaszvezető* Fábián arrived at last at the front as a replacement pilot in the middle of December 1942 as part of the 1/1 Fighter Squadron.

He did not take part in the battles of the winter breakout; due to the bad weather and the constant retreat, his retraining to Messerschmitts was delayed and only completed in the spring of 1943. After the completion of the training, he flew his first combat sortie with this type on 27 April 1943 on the Eastern Front. In the first weeks, he served mainly as the wingman for *főhadnagy* József Bejczy; he was officially promoted to the rank of flight leader from 15 May 1943, although most of the time he was still serving as element leader. In May, before the Hungarian fighters abandoned these types of missions, he also completed five fighter-bomber sorties, dropping the usual four 50kg bombs in each case.[25]

Fábián achieved his first two air victories on 17 June 1943, when he completed three combat sorties. Of these, the second – his 16th on the Eastern Front – probably saw him shoot down a Soviet fighter aircraft; however the details of the event have not been recoverable due to the loss of documents (the type of the Soviet aircraft and the location is unknown). On 26 June, on his 23rd sortie and acting as a wingman to *törzsőrmester* Dezső Szentgyörgyi, he reported a victory over a Yakovlev fighter (see the details of the event in the biography of Dezső Szentgyörgyi).

He achieved his third air victory during his 34th sortie during the battle of Kursk, on 13 July 1943. As a wingman to *százados* György Ujszászy, he shot down an Il-2 north of Belgorod, which crashed and burned out.

The Soviet counterattack that was launched in the Belgorod sector on 3 August meant a hectic and exciting period for him too: he has completed five sorties on that day, with a number of strafing runs. Between 3 and 9 August he has completed altogether 25 sorties and reported four air victories, but these have remained unconfirmed.[26]

While *százados* Ujszászy was still out at the front, he meticulously noted down the combat sorties of 1/1 Squadron up to 18 August 1943. According to these notes, Fábián '*Koponya*' had completed 62 combat sorties.[27] According to the documents of 101 Fighter Wing, a later summary mentioned that Fábián had flown 57 combat sorties on the Eastern Front altogether, but this was obviously incorrect.

25 Excerpts from the logs of 1/1 Fighter Squadron.
26 Excerpts from the logs of 1/1 Fighter Squadron.
27 Excerpts from the logs of 1/1 Fighter Squadron.

A group of non-commissioned officer students of the *DRT* in front of an Italian CR.32 fighter aircraft on the airfield at Grottaglie in 1939. The second from the right in the standing row, in front of the cockpit of the aircraft, is István Fábián. (From the author's collection)

On 28 September 1943, Fábián at last scored his fifth air victory. In the flight led by *hadnagy* Lajos Tóth, he was the leader of the second element when they were engaged in combat by Soviet aircraft in the area of Pereiaslav. Fábián remembered the mission:

> On 28 September, I prepared to fly to Zhitomir with the old Weihe [Fw 58], when a new order came in and I had to stay at home, to my great annoyance – this would have been my first independent Focke-Wulf flight. I was walking sadly back from the aircraft to the pilot bunker when I noticed a huge four-leaf clover: *I will be lucky today*! My luck did not make me wait long, because soon I received orders to took off on a free hunt into a freely chosen area as element leader with *őrmester* Kereki. Under command of *hadnagy* Tóth, we were hunting beyond the great bend of the Dnieper, some 45km within enemy territory, when out of the blue we noticed 28–30 Russian bombers and fighters, who did not notice us. An imminent energetic attack on them, a well-placed cannon burst and an Il-7 [following the German example, the Il-2m3 ground-attack aircraft with a reinforced rear gunner was called the Il-7 for a short time by the Hungarian fighters] was already burning and nose-diving to where he belonged. Now the Russians wake up and the gunners and pilots alike started firing like hell. In the chaos, I met another Il-7 head-on. We engaged each other with a long burst, but what became of it? It is a mystery to me; I still get itching

> if I remember him firing at me from his 27mm [in fact, only 23mm] cannons. Now the Russian fighters joined in the fray; late, luckily for us, and ineffectively, but with enormous recklessness. Two attacked me from dead astern, but with a strong push and turn I shook them off and became the hunter myself! Like lightning, it flashed for a moment in my mind that I had an opportunity: two successes on one occasion. So, not heeding the killer anti-aircraft batteries vomiting fire or the significant firepower of the Il-7s, I positioned myself at the rear, and from above in a left turn I shot until his fate could not be any more obvious. The aircraft crashed to the ground, burying its pilot with it. Meanwhile, the other element was also in heavy combat against the Soviets, and had also shot down two enemy aircraft. The four victims were burning like enormous torches in this gloomy, dark weather. After the dogfight was over, I sped home and waggled my wings twice with a double spin, very pleased with the day's achievements. The four-leaf clover had indeed brought me luck![28]

Soon after, during the autumn, *szakaszvezető* Fábián was redeployed to Szolnok, where he remained until the spring of 1944 when 101 Fighter Group was formed. Meanwhile, he was promoted to *őrmester*. As of 1 May 1944, he was reassigned to Veszprém as part of 101/2 Fighter Squadron.

On 14 June 1944, Fábián took part in the mission during which the Hungarian fighters engaged the Lightnings of 14th Fighter Group's 49th Fighter Squadron, and reported shooting down a '*létra*' ('ladder', the nickname of the Lightning among the Hungarian airmen). His air victory was confirmed as a shared kill with *hadnagy* József Málik in Air Force Confidential Order Nr. 1944/63. Later, however, Wing Order 1945/27 deleted the kill completely, and the whole air victory was confirmed to *hadnagy* József Málik. Again, the situation was not clear: this success was always later counted as an individual air victory for Fábián, and it is possible that an administrative error had been made resulting in the deletion at the beginning of 1945. There was no precedent before that a shared air victory, confirmed by an Air Force Order was later partly deleted on one claimant's side by a Wing Order, this only happened in Air Force Orders and only one of such cases remained in the surviving documents (for *hadnagy* Karátsonyi, regarding his Lightning victory from 16 June 1944). The supreme Air Force Order could not be overwritten by a lower level Wing Order; in the author's opinion, therefore, this air victory should still be counted as one of Fábián's successes.

On 30 June 22, Bf 109s of 101 Fighter Group (Fábián's aircraft among them) took off at 08:16. At 08:45, they joined the twin-engined Bf 110s of II./ZG 1 over Komárom. The weather was rainy and the formation started to loosen up when the aircraft noticed the Liberators of the American 460th and 465th BGs over Tapolca. Although the Hungarian fighters had already engaged the Lightnings of 82nd FG east from the area, there were no American fighters at this area, so the escort of the German destroyers – the Hungarian Bf 109s – also joined the fight. *Őrmester* Fábián reported shooting down a B-24 during the air combat against the aircraft of 460th BG. It is possible that, in this case, the location of the crashed aircraft is not correct in Air Force Confidential Order Nr. 1944/63 (Veszprémpinkóc), because the wrecks might have been mixed up, or the location might have been mistaken for that of another four-engined that crashed four days earlier.

28 *Üvölt a Puma*, 3 November 1943, pp. 4–5.

During the last mission of his unit against Americans in large formation on 5 November 1944, '*Koponya*' reported shooting down a B-17, but this claim was not confirmed and was deleted in Wing Order Nr. 1945/31 because there were no witnesses (no B-17s of the 15th Army Air Force were lost due to enemy action over enemy territory on that day).

Fábián participated altogether in 13 combat sorties against the Americans during the course of 1944.

Szakaszvezető István Fábián with *törzsőrmester* Dezső Szentgyörgyi, with the latter's Bf 109 G-2/R6 in Kharkhiv, in the late summer of 1943. (From the author's collection)

His next confirmed air victory was scored on 13 November 1944, when he shot down a Yakovlev fighter early in the afternoon (see the details in the biography of Lajos Tóth). This was followed by a Lavochkin fighter in December. During the combat efforts over Hungary, *őrmester* Fábián was most successful on 16 January 1945, when he scored two confirmed air victories: one Pe-2 and one Yak-9 were reported and credited to him. The Pe-2R belonged to 39th ORAP and was flown by *leytenant* P.S. Makarov; according to the crew, it was attacked at 09:45 near Székesfehérvár at an altitude of 5,000 meters by two Bf 109s, which chased him relentlessly and performed 14 passes on the Soviet long-range reconnaissance aircraft. During the air combat, which reached the airspace of Paks, the Soviet aircraft was hit 56 times and seriously damaged. It finally had to crash-land on only one landing gear at its base, the airfield of Madocsa, where it was repaired with great effort. The Soviet twin-engined probably survived because Fábián's cannon jammed due to quality problems with its shell casings, an issue that became more and more frequent toward the end of the war; but Fábián did not want to let go of the aircraft and chased him with machine gun fire. The other victim of the day was not so lucky: the air victory Fábián has reported over a Yak-9 was probably against a Yak-3 from 659th IAP. The pilot, *mladshiy leytenant* N.I. Galkin, was killed in his aircraft (serial number 2917).[29]

The veteran non-commissioned officer scored his next confirmed air victory on 19 February over an La-5. The aircraft was an La-5F of 164th IAP (serial number 39215021), which was seriously damaged during the air combat over Tardos and crashed at Tököl, at the airfield used by the pilot's unit. Its pilot, *mladshiy leytenant* J.M. Yemets, was killed.[30] *Őrmester* Fábián probably completed his 100th combat sortie a day or two later.

Fábián had a long and successful combat service; on 12 March 1945, therefore, his commander recommended him for promotion to the rank of *zászlós*. However, this promotion did not take

29 Horváth, *Bostonok a magyar égen és földben*, pp. 83, 108.
30 Horváth, *Bostonok a magyar égen és földben*, p. 127.

place because of the end of the war. Fábián was allowed to use the officer candidates badge from 1 February 1945, when he was admitted for the officer's training course, as an 'officer candidate', indicated by '*tj*' ('*tisztjelölt*', officer candidate) next to his name and behind his rank. This badge was a not a new complementary marking used on military uniforms, it was an older armband that had earlier been used to indicate graduation from high school.[31]

Fábián scored his last two air victories in the middle of March 1945, while stationed in Veszprém. On 13 March 1945, he took off at 10:10 as part of the flight led by *százados* Pottyondy to carry out a free hunt southeast of Lake Velence. The flight met an Il-2 formation escorted by La-5s southwest of the lake; in the ensuing air combat, *őrmester* Fábián shot down a Soviet ground-attack aircraft, which (according to his report) crash-landed at 10:46 engulfed in flames. The kill was witnessed by *százados* Pottyondy; the aircraft was probably the one flown by *leytenant* Tumashev from 951st SAP, with serial number 1877483. The crew was killed. Six days later, Fábián achieved his last air victory as his 14th confirmed kill. He was part of a four-member flight led by Dezső Szentgyörgyi, which soon met two Il-2s flying at 50 meters. One was shot down by *őrmester* Fábián, the other by Dezső Szentgyörgyi. Due to the damage inflicted to his aircraft, *őrmester* Fábián's victim crash landed crudely at 15:15, 800 meters north of Nádasdladány; during the landing, the aircraft's port wing was torn off. Fábián's possible victims were *mladshiy leytenant* I.K. Burakovsky and his gunner, who were killed (989th SAP, serial number 18835124; Burakovsky was also shot down on 8 March – see details at the biography of Pottyondy). The victory was witnessed by *hadnagy* Sipos. Fábián's five air victories in 1945, among them the two Il-2s from March, were confirmed by Wing Order Nr. 1945/62.[32]

Őrmester István Fábián in the summer of 1944 in Veszprém in front of his Bf 109. (From the collection of the Fábián family)

Fábián's last combat sortie was completed on 21 April 1945; he was captured by the Americans at the beginning of May, together with his unit.

Fábián was an extremely skilled, but very modest person who was loved by all who knew him. He was the most successful pilot who completed the DRT, and also the most successful non-commissioned pilot officer at the end of the war.

Despite his noted modesty, Fábián had huge self-confidence in the air, partly due to his excellent eyesight and quick reaction; he was always the one who spotted the enemy first. A number

31 *HM HIM HL*, documents of 101 Fighter Wing, box nr. 110, Wing Order Nr. 1945/47.
32 *HM HIM HL*, documents of 101 Fighter Wing, box nr. 110, Wing Order Nr. 1945/62; box nr. 113, mission log of 101 Fighter Wing, 19 March 1945; Horváth, *Bostonok a magyar égen és földben*, p. 186; Gábor Horváth on documents of TsAMO.

of his comrades confirmed that he flatly told his wingmen not to concern themselves with his escort, but if they had a good chance to shoot, then attack and shoot, as there would be fewer enemy aircraft in the air the next time.[33] His enemies were never able to shoot him down or damage his aircraft significantly, and the author has not found a single case where Fábián was hit in air combat. In all probability, this is why he had so many unconfirmed air victories: his wingmen did not remain by his side, and in many cases did not see the aircraft shot down by him to crash.

István Fábián returned to Hungary for a brief period in 1945, but he quickly decided he could not live in a country occupied by the Soviets, as he thought he would get little credit under the new regime. The last information from him of any military importance was on 31 August 1946, when he was reassigned to the *18 kiegészítő parancsnokság* (the 18th Auxiliary Command),[34] but he left the country that year with his fellow pilot, Károly Tass. They went to France and then to Brazil a year later, where Fábián worked as a transport company. At last, he moved to Canada in 1958, where he settled permanently and worked in the Hamilton glass factory as a tools crafter. He was not able to fly again after his emigration, which was very hard for him. His bitterness deepened when his only 22-year-old son with his Brazilian wife was killed in a tragic car accident.

István Fábián died on 6 May 1993 in Hamilton, Ontario, and his ashes are buried there.

ZÁSZLÓS ISTVÁN KÁLMÁN

Number of aerial victories: 14 (+1)
Successes against ground targets: n.d.a.
Number of flown combat sorties: 75+
Number of hours flown in the air force: n.d.a.
Nickname: *Pista*
Identification number: 2579-22-0005

Decorations

- *Magyar Koronás Ezüst Érdemérem hadiszalagon a kardokkal* (13 February 1945)
- *Magyar Koronás Ezüst Érdemérem hadiszalagon a kardokkal*, second award (25 April 1945)
- *Magyar Koronás Bronz Érdemérem hadiszalagon a kardokkal* (15 January 1945)
- *Tűzkereszt I fokozata a kardokkal és koszorúval*
- German Iron Cross 1st Class (2 April 1945?)
- German Iron Cross 2nd Class (January 1945)
- Silver *Frontflugspange* (1945)

33 For example Krascsenics, *Egy magyar királyi vadászrepülő visszaemlékezései*, p. 62.
34 *HM HIM KI*, document folder nr. 5705. Unfortunately, nothing but historically irrelevant data survives in connection with his military service in the files of István Fábián.

Victories

Number	Date	Aircraft	Location
1	14 September 1944, approx. at 11:20	Observation balloon	Sanok S 4km
2	14 September 1944, approx. at 11:25	Il-2	Sanok
3	16 September 1944 between 09:45 and11:00	La-5	Sanok
4	30 October 1944	La-5	Rákóczifalva
5	1 November 1944	Boston III	Cegléd
6	5 December 1944	Yak-9	Hatvan
7	14 December 1944	Il-2	Balatonkenese
8	14 December 1944	Il-2	Balatonkenese
9	22 January 1945	Il-2	Bugyi
10	22 January 1945	Il-2	Bugyi
11	22 January 1945	Il-2	Bugyi
12	8 March 1945 at 14:45	Yak-9 (Yak-3)	Dömsöd NE 1km
13	14 March 1945 at 13:20	'Marauder' (Boston)	Dabas E
14	13 April 1945 at 18:30	Boston III	Vienna SE
–	16 April 1945	P-51	Raffelding

Aircraft flown
Bf 109 G-6: V-391 (14 September 1944), V-387 (15–16 September 1944), V-392 (16 September 1944)

István Kálmán was born on 12 January 1922 in Bakonycsernye, to a teacher's family of four children. His father descended from an old family of the village and, at first, he was a choirmaster and a teacher in his home village; in 1925, however, he have moved to Budapest and the children grew up there. István Kálmán attended the high school at Óbuda (*Árpád Reálgimnázium*), where his sports career began. A very skilled sports instructor, Andor Takács (1905–1993, later master trainer at pentathlon and acclaimed university lecturer), inspired him to attend the agricultural high school in Zugló, where talented young sportsmen gathered. Kálmán graduated from here. He was an excellent athlete and wanted to become a professional pentathlon sportsman, but he also liked all forms of skiing. In this field, he achieved his most prominent sports successes: in 1944, he was the Hungarian champion for ski-jumping while a member of the *BEAC (Budapesti Egyetemi Atlétikai Club,* or the Budapest University Athletics Club – other members of the team included Dezső Kálmán, his younger brother, and Aba Szatmáry). His interest in aviation was sparked by one of his teammates, the excellent glider pilot Róbert Méray-Horváth.[35]

István Kálmán received his basic level engine training in 1941 at Ferihegy in the *MSRE (Műegyetemi Sportrepülő Egyesület,* University Sports Aviation Club). In the autumn, he was

35 The details of his younger years, his family background and his school years were provided by the family and based on the interview with István Kálmán recorded on 28 September 1991 (a copy of the latter on tape is owned by the author). Róbert Méray-Horváth (1922-1945) was an exceptionally talented glider pilot, who got the 2nd Hungarian (45th ISTUS) E badge (Gold Badge). On 7 January, 1945 in Budapest he was shot by a Soviet soldier while doing 'malenkiy robot' ('small labour' – forced labour for the Soviet troops).

Group photo, taken at Veszprém airfield in 1943, of the officer class graduating on 6 December 1943. Three of the airmen in the picture subsequently became aces: the first on the right in the standing row is István Kálmán; the second is András Huszár; and the second from the left in the kneeling row is László Dániel. (From the author's collection)

admitted to the *Repülőakadémia*, where he graduated on 6 December 1943 as reserve *zászlós*. His long-term plans were to work as a commercial airline pilot after the war. After graduation, he was assigned to 5/I Fighter Group at Mátyásföld, and from here he was deployed to the front on 7 June 1944 to 102 Independent Fighter Squadron, where he served until the end of the war. Until his deployment to the Eastern Front, he had spent 191 hours and 49 minutes in the air: 32 hours and 4 minutes at *HMNRA* and a further 159 hours and 45 minutes with the air force.[36]

His first combat sortie was completed on 3 July 1944 from the airfield at Zamość, as a wingman to an experienced German pilot. According to his memories, at that time the squadron had only one combat-ready Bf 109.[37]

Kálmán took part in his first serious air combat on 9 August 1944 while escorting a German tank destroyer aircraft; Soviet Airacobras damaged his aircraft, which he was able to fly back to the airfield at Radom, but the damaged fuselage of the Messerschmitt – one of the compressed air bottles had been blown up by a direct hit – was broke into two pieces behind the cockpit after landing.[38]

His first two air victories were scored on the morning of 14 September 1944 when he took off from Munkács: he shot down an observation balloon and an Il-2 in the

Graduation portrait of *zászlós* István Kálmán. Kálmán was a very handsome young man; besides, he was brave and daring, a perfect ideal for a fighter pilot. Unfortunately, Hungarian propaganda did not 'discover' him during the war, so very few photographs were taken of him, and only a few survive today. (From the author's collection)

36 The copy of the logbook of István Kálmán, owned by the author, ends here; unfortunately, the subsequent parts that might contain the most interesting data have not been found, as the original document has been removed from family possession.
37 Interview with István Kálmán, recorded on 28 September 1991.
38 Interview with István Kálmán, recorded on 28 September 1991.

Pilots of 102/1 Fighter Squadron resting in September 1944 in Munkács. In the foreground on the right sits *zászlós* István Kálmán, with his friend, *hadnagy* Csaba Szűts, by his side. Szűts finished the war with two air victories and suffered a long prison sentence as a result of the Lajos Tóth trial. (From the collection of the Kálmán family)

airspace of Sanok–Dukla during a free hunt combat sortie. *Szakaszvezető* Csikós, his wingman, was witness for the air victory against the observation balloon and for the Il-2; the latter kill was also attested by *főhadnagy* dr. Vajda. However, *szakaszvezető* Ferenc Csikós did not return from the mission; according to ground witnesses, he was hit by an anti-aircraft shell after shooting down an Il-2 and was killed. The squadron log contains the following note on their element's air combat:

> Upon entering the airspace, *zls.* Kálmán saw a tethered Soviet balloon 4km south of Sanok. He wanted to report this to the lead element but was unable to establish contact with *fhdgy.* Máthé. Therefore, he left the formation with his wingman and shot down the balloon. It fell down in flames. … In the meantime, *zls.* Kálmán … noticed two Il-2s. He engaged one of them, opened fire and shot it down, which was confirmed by *szkv.* Csikós on the radio with a loud 'Well done!' From this moment on, we know nothing of the fate of *szkv.* Csikós.[39]

The case with the tethered observation balloon is extremely interesting. During the First World War, the combatant forces counted such victories as full value air victories, as was the case for most of the combatant armies in the Second World War. During the war, there were only two such air victories against observation balloons within the Hungarian Air Force – in the Red Army, the balloonists were subordinated to the artillery and not to the air force. Both were scored in September 1944 at the Carpathian mountains. The other such case was that of *hadnagy* Galambos. There are some records of a third one, credited to *hadnagy* Holéczy in 1945, but the latter is (according to the pilot himself) an error and therefore not valid. Although the observation balloon is contained in the squadron log and is featured in the surviving statistics, according to the memories of *zászlós* Kálmán it was not credited to him as a full value air victory.[40]

39 Excerpts from the logs of 102/1 Fighter Squadron, 14–16 September 1944 (copy owned by the author).

40 Interview with István Kálmán, recorded on 28 September 1991.

On the basis of the above information (partly confusing and partly destroyed), based on the fact that the observation balloon was registered as destroyed and because air victories against observation balloons were registered as full value kills during the First World War and in other air forces during the Second World War, the author has therefore added this score to the air victories of *zászlós* Kálmán.

Two days later, *zászlós* Kálmán scored another air victory on a free hunt mission completed between 09:45 and 11:00 in the area of Sanok, where, as a wingman to *hadnagy* Szeverényi, he has shot down a Soviet fighter aircraft. In the squadron log, this event appears as follows:

> *Hadnagy* Szeverényi, with his wingman, attacked two Il-2s. *Hdgy*. Szeverényi attacked one of the Il-2's, but his cannon and machine guns malfunctioned. Meanwhile, the two La-5s escorting the Il-2s turned onto *hdgy*. Szeverényi. One of them, however, was shot down at a very low altitude by *zls*. Kálmán at the rear of *hdgy*. Szeverényi; the Russian aircraft crashed to the ground engulfed in flames.[41]

Zászlós István Kálmán with his German shepherd dog in the autumn of 1944. (From the collection of the Kálmán family)

This air victory was left out of the registered successes of the pilot, probably due to an administrative error.

During the combat activity over Hungary, *zászlós* Kálmán reported two further air victories taking off from Felsőábrány (today Bükkábrány) at the end of October, then at the beginning of November (30 October, an La-5, witnessed by *hadnagy* Szűts; and 1 November, a Boston, witnessed by *hadnagy* Szeverényi). These were confirmed by Air Force Order Nr. 1945/4. Of these, the Lavochkin probably served in the 279th IAD (92nd IAP?) and was identified in the Soviet technical documents as an La-5FN (serial number 39212274); the pilot was unharmed. The air victory reported on 1 November was scored in the air combat against the Bostons of 452nd BAP attacking Cegléd. On that day, two Bostons of 452nd BAP crash-landed; one, according to the reports, crashed because of a fighter attack and emergency landed without releasing the undercarriage, during which the aircraft was wrecked; as for the other case, anti-aircraft artillery damage was reported on the aircraft, but after crash-landing the aircraft itself was fixed and repaired. In contrast, two air victories were claimed against Bostons for *zászlós* Kálmán and *hadnagy* Málnássy (for the latter, see the biography of Málnássy for further details). Following these events, in December, Kálmán scored three further air victories. On 5

41 Excerpts from the logs of 102/1 Fighter Squadron, 14–16 September 1944.

December, he reported shooting down a Yak-9 at Hatvan, probably the Yak-9T equipped with 37mm cannon flown by *mladshiy leytenant* M.S. Erko of 122nd IAP, who went missing. The other two air victories in this month were scored during a single combat sortie on 14 December 1944, when, after taking off from the Csór airfield, *zászlós* Kálmán reported shooting down two Il-2s over the Balatonkenese area. His opponents were the aircraft of 715th SAP. The Yak-9 was witnessed by *hadnagy* Szűts; the two Il-2s five days later were witnessed by *hadnagy* Horváth. These three air victories were confirmed in Air Force Order Nr. 1945/10.[42]
The most successful day for István Kálmán was 22 January 1945. According to his memories, he shot down three Il-2s that day; two were scored on the same sortie and the third aircraft was downed during a later, second sortie. According to the surviving wing documents, the three air victories were registered, but the report was filled in with pencil. Between the two handwritten Il-2s, the third aircraft is written differently, resembling a U-2 (Po-2). However, Kálmán – based on the data in his logbook, that is, based on official documents and not only on his recollections – definitely mentioned three Il-2s, so I have listed these aircraft among his list of air victories.[43]

According to the recommendation of his group commander, by 29 January 1945, Kálmán had completed 57 combat sorties and shot down nine aircraft and the observation balloon.[44] The victory against the La-5 on 16 September is left out of this list, although it is described in detail in the squadron log (the cause of this omission is unknown). In February, *zászlós* Kálmán only flew four combat sorties because of the unfavorable weather conditions, so he did not score any kills; but in March he was again successful.

In the early afternoon of 8 March 1945, *zászlós* Kálmán was leading a four aircraft flight in the vicinity of Székesfehérvár for a free hunt. The flight took off at 14:15, and approximately

The Boston (serial number 43-21603) of 260th BAP shot down at Alsódabas on 14 March 1945, on a Soviet airfield. The second on the right is the pilot, *mladshiy leytenant* Pyotr Trofimovich Zakharov (Golovin-Kuzmin via Horváth)

42 *HM HIM HL*, documents of 101 Fighter Wing, box nr. 110, Air Force Orders Nrs. 1945/4 and 1945/10, 19 January 1945 and 22 February 1945; Horváth, *Bostonok a magyar égen és földben*, pp. 49, 79–80.

43 *HM HIM HL*, documents of 101 Fighter Wing, box nr. 113, 101/III Fighter Group, record of victories, Wels, 30 May 1945; interview with István Kálmán, recorded on 28 September 1991.

44 *HM HIM HL*, documents of 101 Fighter Wing, box nr. 112, Royal Hungarian 102 Honvéd Fighter Group, summary of decorated officers and enlisted.

20 minutes later they engaged a Soviet Yakovlev fighter formation of 16 aircraft southeast of Székesfehérvár. Of the 16, Kálmán shot down one aircraft at 14:45. The Soviet fighter – according to their report – crashed 1km northeast of Dömsöd; the witnesses were *hadnagy* Kovács and *hadnagy* Galánfy. *Zászlós* Kálmán's victim was probably a Yak-3 of 866th IAP (serial number 310099), the pilot of which, *leytenant* V.V. Yablochkin, was killed.

Six days later, *zászlós* Kálmán destroyed a Soviet bomber. He took off at 12:40 leading his flight for a free hunt, and half an hour later they met a Soviet bomber formation of 18 aircraft at an altitude of 3,000 meters. The bombers were escorted by 4 Yakovlev fighters. In the ensuing air combat in the area of Csepel South–Dömsöd, he managed to shoot down a bomber, which crashed into the ground engulfed in flames at Alsódabas (today part of Dabas). The witnesses were *hadnagys* Galánfy and Szűts. The bombers were registered as Marauders in the mission and combat logs, and the kill was confirmed as having been fought against Marauders. However, the Soviet twin-engined bomber formation was mistakenly identified; these were Bostons. Perhaps there was something unusual painted on them, which was why another, similar type was reported that was not in use by the Soviet bomber units deployed in the area. In his own memories, Kálmán mentioned Bostons, and it is possible that his logbook also recorded the type. His victim in this case was an A-20 G (serial number 43-21603) of 260th BAD's 1st Squadron, flown by *mladshiy leytenant* P.T. Zakharov. The aircraft belly-landed at Tatárszentgyörgy and was completely burned out; all four crew members were wounded. Kálmán's two air victories in March were confirmed in Wing Order Nr. 1945/62.[45]

The last air victory featured in official documents was scored on 13 April 1945, after taking off from Raffelding; this was against another Boston bomber. At 17:30, Kálmán led eight aircraft on a free hunt mission northeast of Vienna. In the cloudy weather, the Hungarian formation engaged three Bostons, seven Il-2s and many fighters southeast of Vienna. The Bostons flew one by one, probably because they were trying to exploit the cloudy weather. One of them, however, did not succeed: according to Hungarian reports due to the heavy damage inflicted on it by *zászlós* Kálmán, the bomber crashed southeast of Vienna at 18:30, and the crew members were killed (Soviet sources do not confirm the total loss). The kill was confirmed by the Germans, because the Hungarian formation had also been scattered among the clouds. *Zászlós* Kálmán returned to the airfield alone; nobody from his flight witnessed his air victory. Due to the lack of Hungarian witnesses, this air victory was not confirmed in the Wing Orders at the end of the war, along with a number of other claims made by 101/III Group; however, the kill was claimed and attested to by the required witnesses, so the author has counted it among the successes of the pilot. This was the last time *zászlós* Kálmán flew a combat sortie as a flight leader.[46]

His last sortie was completed on 16 April, when his aircraft was damaged in air combat over Raffelding by the Mustangs; he nevertheless managed to take the damaged Bf 109 back to the airfield. On this sortie, according to his memories, he successfully attacked a four-aircraft flight

45 *HM HIM HL*, documents of 101 Fighter Wing, box nr. 110, Wing Order Nr. 1945/62, 19 April 1945; box nr. 113, after-action reports and mission logs of 101 Fighter Wing, 8 and 14 March 1945; interview with István Kálmán, 28 September 1991; Horváth, *Bostonok a magyar égen és földben*, pp. 152, 165–166.

46 *HM HIM HL*, documents of 101 Fighter Wing, box nr. 113, after-action reports and mission logs of 101 Fighter Wing, 13 April 1945; Horváth, *Bostonok a magyar égen és földben*, p. 219.

of Mustangs chasing a German transport aircraft. The targetted Mustang was hit and emitting smoke before crash-landing near the Danube. This claim was not confirmed by the end of the war and is not included in any official documents.[47]

István Kálmán went into captivity with his wing at the end of the war; he remained in an Austrian prisoner of war camp for a longer time, before returning to Hungary at the end of 1948 to help two of his former comrades escape to the west. However, a communist son of an older aviation officer told everything to the *ÁVH*, which captured him. After he was brutally beaten for a time in the dreaded building at 60 Andrássy Street (he wore some marks of the beating on his back for his whole life), he was luckily transported to a barracks in Buda, because 60 Andrássy Street was too crowded. From this barracks he managed to escape when he went to the toilet one night from his cell on the first floor. He descended from the toilet window then jumped down using the wartime cracks on the double wall, even though the guards were firing on him and dogs were also sent to get him. After this, his uncle hid him in a farmhouse for two weeks until the turmoil caused by his escape settled, then brought him to Szombathely in a hay cart. From here, he crossed the Austrian–Hungarian border at Pinkafő. After his adventurous escape, he reached the British zone in Austria, bald and with grey skin, and seriously underweight. On reaching safety, he slept for two days in a row. Kálmán was wanted by the *ÁVH* after his successful escape; his name even surfaced in Dezső Szentgyörgyi's trial as a 'dangerous imperialist agent'.

István Kálmán was not only a very daring and brave pilot with excellent aviation skills; he was also very modest, and a man who always took on risks and dangers for his comrades. This is strongly proven by his rescue attempt. Although, according to his widow, he remembered scoring more than 20 air victories, he was not bothered too much by the fact that many of these remained unconfirmed. Kálmán was the most successful pilot of the officer class graduated on 6 December 1943.

From the Austrian prisoner of war camp, he emigrated to Chile in 1949 via an Italian port. He was employed in Chile in the textile industry as a designer. From there, he went to Canada in 1956 with his family, and after staying here for almost a year he moved to the USA in 1957, first to New Jersey and then in 1960 to California. He was not able to obtain a job in aviation here, mainly because these were 'protected jobs', like the helicopter test pilot job at Hiller, and he was not yet a citizen; partly, also, because he was 'too old'. Like István Fábián, he lost his only son at a young age to an incurable disease, which affected him very badly. At last, he retired in 1986 as a security chief of Kaiser Industries. After the war, he had to start his life over five times with his faithful wife, Daisy. In his later years, Kálmán suffered from many illnesses; he died on 23 February 1995 in Los Altos, California, where he is buried.[48]

47 Interview with István Kálmán, 28 September 1991.

48 Although István Kálmán has a personal document folder in the HM HIM Central Record Office (nr. 959/2052), it is not old, but new, and contains nothing but a letter created in 2008, after the first edition of the *Elfelejtett hősök* regarding various questions concerning him.

SZÁZADOS CSÁFORDI AND POTYONDI LÁSZLÓ POTTYONDY

Number of aerial victories: 13 (+1)
Successes against ground targets: n.d.a.
Number of flown combat sorties: 130+
Number of hours flown in the air force: n.d.a.
Nickname: *Laci*
Identification number: 3242-15-0946

Decorations

- *Magyar Érdemrend lovagkeresztje hadiszalagon a kardokkal* (25 January 1945)
- *Újólagos Kormányzói dicsérő elismerés Magyar Koronás Ezüst Érdemérme hadiszalagon a kardokkal* (26 August 1941)
- *Kormányzói dicsérő elismerés Magyar Koronás Bronz Érdemérme hadiszalagon a kardokkal* (18 April 1939)
- *Tűzkereszt I fokozata a kardokkal és koszorúval*
- *Felvidéki Emlékérem*
- *Erdélyi Emlékérem*
- *Délvidéki Emlékérem*
- German Iron Cross 1st Class (April 1945)
- German Iron Cross 2nd Class (1944)
- Gold *Frontflugspange* (1945)

Victories

Number	Date	Aircraft	Location
–	12 July 1941	I-16	
1	12 July 1941	I-16	Shatava (Dunayevtsi)
2	15 September 1944	Il-2	Mezőlaborc
3	9 October 1944	La-5	Tuchla
4	30 October 1944	Boston III	Kiskőrös
5	30 October 1944	Yak-9	Törökszentmiklós
6	1 November 1944	La-5	Szolnok
7	17 November 1944 at 14:30	Boston III	Ócsa
8	22 November 1944	Il-2	Csány
9	3 January 1945	Yak-9	Csabdi
10	14 January 1945	Boston III	Pilisvörösvár
11	22 January 1945	La-5	Ercsi
12	20 February 1945 at 10:35	Yak-9 (Yak-3)	Szendehely
13	8 March 1945 at 16:34	Il-2	Soponya, Káloz E

Aircraft flown

CR.42: V.245 (29 June 1941), V.251 (12 July 1941), Re.2000: V.424 (summer and autumn of 1942), Bf 109 G-6: 'Black 1' (summer and autumn of 1944)

László Pottyondy was born on 26 December 1915 in Pécs, the only child in the family. His family stemmed from the Tolna branch of the old noble Pottyondy family, but they did not use their title of nobility. His father (of the same name) was a pediatrician and general practitioner in Pécs; he was killed by a shot to the heart in the First World War in Oituz-Pass on 24 December 1916, where he was serving as the chief physician of the k.u.k. 7nd Hussar Regiment's second squadron.[49] Later, the family moved to Fehérvárcsurgó.[50] After graduating from a civilian high school, Pottyondy attended the *Ludovika Akadémia* (Ludovika Academy) at Budapest, where he graduated as *repülő hadnagy* on 20 August 1938.

His first unit was 1/2 Fighter Squadron stationed in Székesfehérvár-Börgönd, where he served with Dezső Szentgyörgyi. Like him, Pottyondy also took part in the escort of the Hungarian Ju 86s bombing Spišská Nová Ves on 24 March 1939; this was rewarded by his first decoration, a bronze *Signum*.[51]

Pottyondy won the hand and heart of Éva, the very pretty daughter of the commander of the *Ludovika Akadémia*, *tábornok* kisbarnaki Ferenc Farkas. With the help of his father-in-law, following his wedding in November 1939, he was reassigned to Mátyásföld and the sister unit of 1/2 Fighter Squadron – 1/1 Fighter Squadron – which was becoming famous after the air combats in March 1939. The squadron was led by the then legendary Aladár Szobránczy. Pottyondy became the squadron's deputy commander.

On 1 September, he was promoted to *főhadnagy*, and (following the Second Vienna Award) the squadron relocated to the airfield of Kolozsvár-Szamosfalva (today Someşeni, Romania), which became their base airfield. Here the unit was renumbered 2/3 Fighter Squadron, although the name '*Ricsi*' (after the enormous Great Dane of *százados* Szobránczy) and the squadron emblem did not change.

In the summer of 1941, they relocated to Kárpátalja, Bustyaháza (today Bustino, Ukraine) from Kolozsvár, and it was from here that they completed their first combat mission against the Soviet Union at dawn on 27 June 1941. Two days later, due to problems with the engine of his CR.42 (code V.245), Pottyondy was forced to crash-land near Tiszasásvár (today Trosnik, Ukraine). The aircraft suffered 50 percent damage, but the pilot was, luckily, unhurt.[52]

During the combat period from 27 June and until the middle of July, Pottyondy flew 14 combat sorties. Of these, the most remarkable was on 12 July, when his squadron engaged the aircraft of the Soviet 168th IAP and reported shooting down five I-16s.

Főhadnagy Pottyondy, who flew the V.251 aircraft on this mission, noted down the events in his diary:

> My opponent turned horizontally, completely narrowing down the turns, and I pulled up, stretching the aircraft to the ultimate limits of speed, trying to get to his rear. I succeeded with the third turn – he was already in the firing line! I pushed the trigger and opened fire on my opponent – correcting the aim with phosphorus, my bursts going around the enemy

49 *MNL Baranya Megye Levéltára* (National Archives, Baranya County Archives), XXXIII/1, birth registry counterparts from 1915 in the city of Pécs, note nr. 946. fsz; Béla Pottyondy, *Csáfordi és potyondi: A Pottyondy család monografiája* (Szombathely: Martineum Nyomda, 1937), pp. 7–15, 56–57.

50 *HM HIM KI*, document folder nr.79893.

51 Stenge, *Baptism of Fire*, pp. 60–66, 109.

52 *HM HIM HL*, Vkf. 1941 1. oszt. 5813/eln.

> aircraftt. At this point, my opponent took the aircraft out of the turn, and so did I. He flew in a straight line, with a slight descending glide. In front of him, there was another Fiat firing at it. The phosphoric projectiles disappeared into the Rata. Bravo! Then the Rata lifted his nose, and this was the most shocking sight during my entire aviation career! The Fiat did not expect the Rata to make this crazy move, and touched the Rata from above with his landing gear and starboard wing; they collided. I flew past them and there were fragments of aircraft everywhere. Only the wrecks of two proud aircraft and the two parachutes swinging in the air showed the tragedy that had happened here. But I did not have time to contemplate on whether my comrade was alive, because another Rata attacked me from above on my right. When I glance aside during the dogfight, I saw that two burning aircraft were gliding down in flames. Thank God, Ratas!
>
> My Rata was a hard case. It had a huge altitude advantage and this was why it was harder for me to deal with him. I glanced around and I saw a Fiat in the distance chasing a Rata. I couldn't see anything else; it seemed we had gone quite far. At last, I managed to 'sit' behind the Rata, and I said to myself, *You will not slip out of my hands like your comrade did*! I also aimed much more calmly. The first rounds hit his tail so I pulled a little on my aircraft and the phosphorus disappeared between the engine and the cockpit. The Rata pulled his aircraft out of the turn and started flying in a straight line. I was behind him. I felt that his aircraft was a little faster than mine. From time to time I found myself in its rear, firing at it endlessly. Suddenly, a narrow track of smoke appeared at both sides like a mustache; it got bigger and thicker. What a relief – I wouldn't go home without an air victory![53]

The first air victory of the two claimed that day was not credited to Pottyondy but to *hadnagy* Győző Vámos, who collided into the I-16 but was able to bail out of his aircraft and survive the collision. The Soviet pilot, however, was killed; probably it was Pyotr Shurmin, who served as the political officer of the unit. The second aircraft Pottyondy managed to shoot down became his first confirmed air victory. The pilot of the I-16 that crash-landed behind their own lines was probably Konstantin Alexandrovich Pilshikov, who himself reported shooting down a Fiat as his first air victory, then set his own aircraft aflame and returned to his unit. Pilshikov was a good friend of Alexander Ivanovich Pokryshkin, even before the war; they completed their aviation training together in the Perm during the first half of the 1930s. Pokryshkin later became one of the most famous and successful fighter pilots of the Soviet Union; he was made Hero of the Soviet Union three times, but, according to the latest research, he did not end the war with the 59 air victories often mentioned, but with 46 individual and six shared victories. During the war, Pilshikov achieved eight individual and thee shared air victories prior to 24 December 1944, when – as the commander of 523rd IAP – his La-5 was shot down over Lithuania by German anti-aircraft artillery during a reconnaissance mission. He spent the remaining time during the war in a prisoner camp, and was freed by the Americans on 22 April 1945.[54]

The 2/3 Fighter Squadron returned to Kolozsvár in the middle of July 1941, and the task of supporting of the Hungarian 1st Rapid Corps was transferred to 1/3 Fighter Squadron under the immensely ambitious *százados* László Tomor.

53 István Bognár, *A győzelmes repülés titkai* (Budapest: Jövő Nyomda, 1942), pp. 123–124.
54 Bikhov, *Sovetskie Asy 1941–1945*, p. 401 (Pilshikov), pp. 407–408 (Pokriskin); the correspondence of Dmitri Karlenko regarding documents of TsAMO disclosed by himself.

The Reggiane Re.2000 fighter aircraft (V.424) of *főhadnagy* László Pottyondy in Ilovskoye, October 1942. The white stripe on the aircraft's vertical stabilizer represents his confirmed air victory from 1941, and his personal markings is also visible under the cockpit (*HM HIM* Photographic Archives 97.841/038)

Close-up of the personal markings on *főhadnagy* Pottyondy's aircraft. This markings most probably featured already on his CR.42, and there are also photographs of the actual painting of it on the Re.2000 and the Bf 109 (*HM HIM* Photographic Archives 97.841/039)

On 1 November 1941, 2/II Fighter Group was disbanded and partly reorganized. Pottyondy was transferred to the newly formed *2 vadászgyakorló-osztály* (2 Fighter Training Group) as the deputy commander of 2/1 Fighter Squadron, under commander *százados* Béla Keresztes.

In 1942, 2/1 Fighter Squadron was sent to the Don, and Pottyondy again arrived at the front on 29 July 1942. Although he flew a number of sorties, the *Héja* he flew was already obsolete and too slow, and *főhadnagy* Pottyondy did not succeed in scoring another air victory. From the front, he returned in the late autumn of 1942 and served with 2 Group.

In 1943, although he was relatively young and did not possess high rank, he took part in the development of the new air force regulations, probably because of his extensive combat experience.

In this year, finally, his wish to be promoted to the fighter squadron commander was granted, and he took over command of 2/2 Fighter Squadron (which was still equipped with *Héjas*). As a tribute to his previous commander, Aladár Szobránczy, he chose the '*Ricsi*' head as the squadron insignia. In the new year, on 1 January 1944, Pottyondy was promoted to *százados*. His squadron was deployed in the early summer, and the pilots were transported on 7 June with a Ju 52 transport aircraft to the Eastern Front; they were still equipped with *Héjas*, and it was out of question to deploy the squadron with these obsolete aircraft. In the combat area, the squadron was renumbered to 102/2 Fighter Squadron, but they had not yet seen combat, as the unit still lacked Messerschmitts. At this time, they were still separate from the independent 102 Squadron, which was already on the front; this squadron was later renumbered 102/1 because of the arrival of Pottyondy's force.

Százados László Pottyondy with his Bf 109 G-6 with an Erla canopy manufactured in Regensburg in the autumn of 1944. The personal markings of the pilot can clearly be seen under the cockpit (*HM HIM* Photographic Archives 97.841/417)

Another photo of *százados* Pottyondy's aircraft. In this picture, one can also see the serial number of the aircraft: WNr. 167209 (*HM HIM* Photographic Archives 97.841/691)

Pottyondy asked for appropriate aircraft and besieged the *Luftwaffe* for weeks. At last, according to the memories of one of his subordinate pilots, he heeded the advice of a German female office clerk who introduced him to many high-ranking officials, and practically 'purchased' Bf 109s for the squadron with a Weihe-load of alcohol from the German supply service. At the beginning of July, therefore, the squadron at length received its keenly awaited aircraft.[55] The pilots in the unit started their combat missions on 9 July; from the middle of the month to the end of the month, the squadron was subordinated to IV./JG 51, under the command of *Major* Heinz Lange[56] (the JG 51 also suffered from a serious shortage of aircraft at this time).

In the face of the Soviet offensive launched in the summer, the squadron relocated to Hungary. The unit began their committed combat actions from the airfield at Munkács. Pottyondy scored his first air victory from here on 15 September against an Il-2. This victory seemed to be an icebreaker, as the squadron started to come alive and the new pilots, who had never before been in combat (apart from the commander and *őrmester* István Kárpáti, who in 1941 had served in 2/3 Squadron), started to get used to fighting in the air. Pottyondy scored a further three air victories in October; with his two air ictories on 30 October, he reached ace status. Of his victims of 30 October, the Boston was probably the A-20G of the 48th BAP, flown by *starshiy*

55 Géza Szenteleky, 'Emlékeim a 102/2 századnál eltöltött időmről', *Magyar Szárnyak Évkönyv*, 1992, pp. 59–60.

56 For Heinz Lange (Köln, 2 October 1917–Bergisch Gladbach, 26 February 2006), see Obermaier, *Die Ritterkreuzträger der Luftwaffe 1939–45*, p. 153. The author also contacted Heinz Lange a few years prior to his death to discover his memories of his subordinate Hungarian fighter pilots, but unfortunately he was not able to help.

Százados László Pottyondy with *Hauptmann* Erich Hartmann (1921–1993), then the commander of 4./JG 52, who achieved 352 air victories by the end of the war, thus becoming the single most successful fighter pilot in the Second World War. The photo was taken in November 1944 at Budaörs airfield in front of one of the aircraft of 102/2 Fighter Squadron; the emblem of the unit, the '*Ricsi*' head, can clearly be seen on the engine cowling, and on its band two words can be seen: '*Erő, Hűség*' ('Power, Loyalty'). (From the collection of Bernd Barbas)

leytenant I.M. Frolov (serial number 42-53856), which went missing with its whole crew on a reconnaissance sortie. On this day, one Boston went missing and another belly-landed after having been damaged by Bf 109s. For these two losses, there was a German and Hungarian fighter claim each. The Yak-9 reported on this day was probably the Yak-1b of 31st GIAP that was lost during the afternoon (serial number 21151, flown by *mladshiy leytenant* E.V. Erofitski). These victories were soon followed by a kill against another Soviet fighter; on 1 November, Pottyondy shot down an La-5F of 177th GIAP's 1st Squadron that was escorting a Boston formation. This was his sixth confirmed air victory. The aircraft, with serial number 39215336, crash-landed on its own airfield; it was wrecked and the pilot, *mladshiy leytenant* J.I. Batiunya, was wounded. Yevgeny Ivanovich Batiunya was a successful pilot who achieved five individual air victories (and one shared) before the end of the war. Of these air victories, two of the individual victories and the shared kill were achieved over Hungary, after he was wounded.[57]

Pottyondy's seventh air victory was achieved on 17 November 1944 in interesting circumstances. On this sortie, his wingman was *Hauptmann* Eric Hartmann, much younger than him, who was then the commander of 4./JG 52; he ended the war as the most successful German fighter pilot, with 352 air victories. During the free hunt, in the early afternoon, both reported shooting down one Boston each.

Frigyes Hefty, First World War ace and war correspondent, wrote about this mission:

> A pair like this is not found every day, where both pilots are considered to be big names. The great German fighter, *Hauptmann* Hartmann, who has 316 air victories, and *százados* Pottyondy, his newly emerged Hungarian comrade, whose unit has achieved great success and who has a swiftly increasing sortie/kill ratio, are covering each other.
>
> They are conducting a free hunt in the Gyöngyös area. Down below there is intense movements, indicating that the slopes of the Mátra mountains have become the location of heavy fighting; but they fly past the Hatvan–Aszód area in vain, because there is silence in

57 Horváth, *Bostonok a magyar égen és földben*, pp. 43, 49; Bikhov, *Sovetskie Asy 1941–1945*, p. 49.

> the air, and there isn't even a lone Yak or Shturmovik to be seen above the misty hills. They are flying southward to the area of Tura, Zsámbok, but they stared in vain at the vast greyness on the horizon; there is no movement either above or on the ground. … With reduced speed, their Messerschmitts are already doing over 400km/h and speeding toward the capital. Those are the big chimneys of Kőbánya and the Citadella can be seen sitting on top of Mount Gellért like a crown. *Százados* Pottyondy is flying at the front, Hartmann follows him to the right and rear. Both are very angry and condemning the weather. … Now how are we doing with the fuel? They still have enough for 20 minutes, so they can spend 10 of that with a little 'sniffing around'; maybe there will be something worthy to shoot at further down around Csepel Island. They turn their eyes toward the Danube. There, near the Kelenföld docks, directly next to Mount Gellért, large pillars of whitish grey smoke are rising from the ground. Their experienced eyes immediately know what these are: bomb impacts. Pottyondy glances through the air quickly; he notices an anti-aircraft smoke ring at the same altitude. The aircraft must be here! A sweet sense of excitement runs through his veins. At last! Via his throat microphone, he warns his German wingman, who at the same time signals that he is already aware of the enemy: two Boston bombers are flying over Kelenföld and heading south in the direction of Csepel.
>
> Gas to the engine; turn the trigger down. The fingers touch the trigger, the eyes stare to the gunsight's crosshair. They do not need to consult on this; each chooses an opponent – the 109s rush with superior speed toward the enemy. They are trying to pull up and disappear in the clouds in vain; one single move of the control column in the Messerschmitts and they are at the rear of the Bostons as if they have been lifted there by some magical mechanism. Now they have them! The Boston fires desperately from his rear gun to keep his enemy away, but they can't get rid of *százados* Pottyondy that easily. The bursts hit the fuselage of the Boston in rapid succession and the engines get their rounds too. The *tovarish* is defending itself; some of its bullets whirl through the cockpit. Pottyondy dives with a quick movement, but some seconds later he is up again at the back of his enemy; he finishes off the Russian on the second pass. They have still not reached Ócsa when fire spurts from one of the engines of the Boston and the thick black smoke is like an exclamation mark in the sky: the perpetrators of the harassing attack against the capital will not get away without revenge being exacted on them.
>
> Now the wings of the 109 are waggling over the airfield; but Hartmann also waggles his wings, as he has chased his enemy until Rákosrendező, where he finished him off with a final burst.[58]

The aircraft shot down by Pottyondy was the A-20 G type bomber of 453rd BAP's 1st Squadron (serial number 4253956) flown by *leytenant* N.S. Danielyan, who belly-landed north of Bugyi, west of Ócsa, where the Messerschmitts strafed and shot a few more bursts into the aircraft. Of the crew, the pilot and one of the gunners were wounded; their two other comrades were killed. On 17 November, this was the only combat loss of a Soviet Boston in the area; apart from this, there was another loss due to an accident 1km south of Kevermes, where a Boston crash-landed and was wrecked during a ferry flight. Probably, therefore, Pottyondy

58 Frigyes Hefty, 'Visszavágás', *Magyar Szárnyak*, 1 December 1944, pp. 5–6.

and Hartmann claimed the same Boston as their air victory. Unfortunately, there are no more surviving details, either German or Hungarian, regarding this event.[59]

On 15 November 1944, 102 Fighter Group was founded through the close-up of 102/1 and 102/2 Squadrons. The group commander became *őrnagy* József Kovács, the former commander of 102/1 Squadron. His position as squadron commander was taken over by his former deputy commander, *főhadnagy* László Máthé. Pottyondy remained as commander of 102/2 Squadron.

Photo from after the war of *mladshiy leytenant* Norayr Sumbatovich Danielyan, pilot of the Boston (serial number 42-53956) of 453rd BAP shot down at Ócsa on 17 November 1944. This victory was claimed by both Hartmann and Pottyondy (TsAMO via Horváth)

Százados Pottyondy achieved his eighth air victory over an Il-2 in the area of Csány on 22 November 1944. The date of the victory can be found in a registry of air victories of 101/8 Fighter Squadron compiled at the end of the war, which is among the documents of 101 Fighter Wing; the date here is incorrectly noted as 22 December 1944, probably because of a common typing error – instead of month XI, month XII was typed. This air ictory is registered as 22 November in Air Force Order 1945/4, and although this document also contains a number of typing errors, the date must be correct, because it contains the air victories of 102 Air Brigade introduced on 15 November and 1 and 16 December. None of the victories contained in this document could therefore have happened after 16 December. Other claims from 101 Fighter Wing included in the order also pre-date the above-mentioned date.[60]

The November date is further confirmed by the fact that there was heavy fighting in the area of Csány in November, but not in December (Soviet forces occupied the village on 27 November). Moreover, on 22 December there were no Il-2 losses in the area, while on 22 November an Il-2 belly-landed 7km from Csány. The aircraft belonged to 809th SAP (serial number 1878785; the pilot was *leytenant* F.S. Polunin, and the damaged aircraft was later repaired). Probably this was the aircraft confirmed to Pottyondy, although in this case, the Soviet casualty report records an anti-aircraft hit and not fighter attack.[61]

According to a summary created at the end of the year, from 9 July to 31 December 1944 the squadron completed 334 combat sorties and achieved 18 confirmed air victories, seven credited to Pottyondy. The squadron also knocked out a medium tank.[62]

59 Horváth, *Bostonok a magyar égen és földben*, pp. 53–54.
60 *HM HIM HL*, documents of 101 Fighter Wing, box nr. 110, Air Force Order Nr. 1945/4, 19 January 1945; box nr. 113, registry of the victories and decorations of the pilots of 101/8 Fighter Squadron.
61 Gábor Horváth on documents of TsAMO.
62 *HM HIM HL*, documents of 101 Fighter Wing, box nr. 112, high command of the Royal Hungarian 102 Honvéd Fighter Group, summarized score report of 102 Fighter Group until 31 December 1944.

Őrmester János Mátyás, with *hadnagy* György Debrődy and *hadnagy* László Molnár on the airfield at Veszprém-Jutas, during the summer of 1944. (Collection of László Dániel)

The Messerschmitt Bf 109 G-6 of *hadnagy* László Dániel, marked W-021, manufactured in Győr (WNr. 760381, serial number 95456) on the airfield at Veszprém-Jutas, September 1944. The W-021 was flown by *zászlós* András Huszár on 11 October 1944 when it belly-landed between Pálosszentkút and Kistelek after having been hit by anti-aircraft fire. (Collection of László Dániel)

A close-up photo of the vertical stabilizer of the W-021 of *hadnagy* Dániel, on which one can see the silhouettes of the first five victories he reported and claimed (three Lightnings and two Liberators). Victory markings were rarely painted on Hungarian Messerschmitts. (Collection of László Dániel)

A Hungarian Messerschmitt Bf 109 starts off on a combat mission during the summer of 1944. (Collection of László Dániel)

Főhadnagy László Pottyondy's Reggiane Re.2000 '*Héja*' fighter aircraft, marked V.424, during the summer of 1942 on the airfield at Ilovskoye. (*HM HIM* Photographic Archives, slide 1795)

The armorer loads ammunition into the MG 151/20 automatic cannon of one of the Messerschmitt Bf 109 G-2 fighters of the Hungarian 5/2 Fighter Squadron. The aircraft has recently arrived; the insignia has not yet been painted on it. Collection of Balázs Jásdi)

Engine maintenance on a frontline airfield on the Eastern Front in the early autumn of 1943. This Bf 109 G-2 was the aircraft of 5/2 Fighter Squadron. (Collection of Balázs Jásdi)

One of the mechanics of 101 Fighter Group with the Daimler-Benz DB 605 engine of a Hungarian-manufactured Messerschmitt Bf 109 G-6 on the airfield at Veszprém-Jutas, summer 1944. (Collection of László Dániel)

The second victory of Dezső Szentgyörgyi against the Americans was over the Mustang of 1st Lieutenant Howard Baetjer. Baetjer is still an air force cadet in this picture. (Collection of the Baetjer family)

Hadnagy László Dániel in the cockpit of a Messerschmitt in 1944. (Collection of László Dániel)

Hadnagy László Dániel, technical officer of 101/3 Fighter Squadron, in front of a Messerschmitt Bf 109 G-6 manufactured in Győr; taken in the summer of 1944 on the airfield at Veszprém-Jutas. The German jacket of the pilot can clearly be seen. (Collection of László Dániel)

Two good friends from 101/3 Fighter Squadron on the wing of a Messerschmitt in the late summer of 1944: *hadnagy*s Pál Bélavári (1923–1944) and Dániel. Bélavári, nicknamed '*Spulni*', was killed in action on 12 October 1944 when he was shot down over Veszprém by the Mustangs while landing his aircraft. (Collection of László Dániel)

A photograph that was later colored, showing *hadnagy* Michna in the autumn of 1943 at the airfield at Székesfehérvár-Börgönd. (Collection of György Michna)

Zászlós Sándor Hautzinger in the Ukraine in the summer of 1943, at the wing of a Hungarian Ju 52/3m transport aircraft. (Collection of Balázs Jásdi)

During the heavy fighting in January, *százados* Pottyondy managed to increase the number of his air victories by three – two fighters and a bomber aircraft. On 3 January, he reported his first victory over a fighter aircraft at Csabdi; this was probably one of the Yak-9Ds of 659 th IAP that was lost in the area. On 14 January, he reported his third air victory over a Boston bomber: this aircraft, the A-20 G of the Soviet 453rd BAP (serial number 42-54166) flown by *starshiy leytenant* G.R. Voevodin, caught fire during the air combat north of Budapest, and two gunners were wounded in the fuselage. The aircraft crash-landed east of the Danube, 2.5km north of Rákospalota, where the bomber was wrecked. *Százados* Pottyondy achieved his third air victory of the month on 22 January over an La-5 at Ercsi; this was probably the La-5FN of 116th IAP that was lost on that day.[63]

Százados László Pottyondy with *Hauptmann* Helmut Lipfert (1916–1990) – at this time commander of 6./JG 52, who achieved 203 air victories by the end of the war – drinking some spirits to 'help their aid', sometime at the end of 1944. On the left side of the picture, *zászlós* Lajos Török can be seen, a passenger of the FW 58 flown by Ferenc Málnássy when it was shot down. (From the collection of Bernd Barbas)

One of Pottyondy's subordinated pilots (and his wingman on many occasions), *zászlós* Béla Sűrű, remembered shooting down a Soviet Boston in the area of Esztergom with *százados* Pottyondy. The crew of the aircraft bailed out beyond enemy lines and the radio transmission interception also confirmed this. Although he was not sure of the date – according to him, it possibly happened on 24 February – the aircraft was almost surely the Boston of 14 January that was credited only to Pottyondy, and not as a shared kill (as we have already discussed, the category of shared kills had been dissolved by then).[64]

Százados Pottyondy with a German war correspondent *Leutnant*. *Százados* Pottyondy wears the pin of JG 52 besides the '*Ricsi*' pin, which is also worn by the war correspondent. Unfortunately, the third badge between these two cannot be identified, because the photograph is blurred. (From the collection of Bernd Barbas)

During January 1945, Pottyondy's squadron and group was incorporated into 101 Fighter Wing as 101/III Group. The 102/2 Squadron was renamed 101/8 Squadron, but the command positions in the group were not changed: the group commander remained *őrnagy* József Kovács, the sister squadron was still

63 Horváth, *Bostonok a magyar égen és földben*, p. 89; Gábor Horváth on documents of TsAMO.
64 *HM HIM HL*, documents of 101 Fighter Wing, box nr. 110, Wing Order Nr. 1945/75; also based on the correspondence with Béla Sűrű, 16 April 2004.

led by *főhadnagy* László Máthé and 101/9 Squadron became the former fighter ferry squadron, led by *százados* István Békássy.

According to a surviving summary written by Pottyondy's group commander, by 29 January 1945 he achieved 11 air victories over 119 combat sorties.[65]

In February 1945, *százados* Pottyondy completed six combat sorties. During one of these, on the 20th, he also achieved his 12th air victory. He took off at 10:07, leading two flights on a free hunt; according to their report, they engaged a formation of four Il-2s and four Yak-9s flying at an altitude of 500 meters. *Százados* Pottyondy attacked one of the fighters, the port wing of which was blown up by bursts from Pottyondy's 3cm cannon. The witness to the victory was *hadnagy* Dániel Holéczy from 101/9 Squadron. This time, his victim was a prominent Soviet ace: *starshiy leytenant* Ivan Nikitovich Tabakov, born in 1922 and on front-line service since 1942, a pilot of 150th GIAP with 23 individual air victories and one shared kill (five of these victories achieved over Hungary) before his death on this day. His aircraft was a Yak-3 with serial number 2119.[66]

Százados Pottyondy achieved his final confirmed air victory (his 13th) on 8 March 1945, while leading a flight of four aircraft on a free hunt in the area of Székesfehérvár. The formation took off at 15:50 and engaged eight Il-2s and two escorting Yakovlev fighters in the Soponya area; *százados* Pottyondy reported shooting down an Il-2 at 16:34. Although the crash itself could not be seen, the victory was confirmed by *hadnagy* Géza Szenteleky and *zászlós* Sűrű. At the same time, a station of the German ground control and observer service, codenamed '*Holzauge 10*' (Holzauge is literally wooden eye, it was the nickname of the second element's wingman of a finger four formation since a wooden eye never tires)'witnessed the crash and attested to it. The fourth aircraft of the Hungarian flight crashed in the heavy enemy anti-aircraft fire, and the pilot, Győző Inkey, bailed out over enemy territory; he never returned, and was presumably killed. One other aircraft of the flight, which could not be identified – maybe Pottyondy's – was hit twice on its port wing, probably also due to anti-aircraft fire.

Pottyondy's last victim was probably the aircraft flown by *mladshiy leytenant* I.K. Burakovsky of 989th SAP (serial number 11560), which crash-landed northwest of Rácalmás, its crew unharmed. The damage inflicted was repaired later.[67]

The *százados*'s last combat sortie was flown on 21 April 1945, when he led an eight-aircraft flight on a free hunt between 16:35 and 18:25. This time, however, there was no air combat, because the spotted Soviet formation pulled up into the clouds.[68]

Pottyondy went into captivity with his unit in May 1945, and did not return to Hungary. After the war, he emigrated to the USA and settled in Little Rock, Arkansas. Here, with the help of another Hungarian immigrant, he obtained an American private pilot certificate on 30 April 1951, and started to work in agricultural aviation. As a crop duster, he flew a Boeing

65 *HM HIM HL*, documents of 101 Fighter Wing, box nr. 112, Royal Hungarian 102 Honvéd Fighter Group, summary of decorated officers and enlisted.

66 *HM HIM HL*, documents of 101 Fighter Wing, box nr. 113, after-action reports and mission logs of 101 Fighter Wing, 20 February 1945; Bikhov, *Sovetskie Asy 1941–1945*, p. 493 (where the date of Tabakov's death is incorrectly given as 12 March 1945); Horváth, *Bostonok a magyar égen és földben*, p. 127.

67 *HM HIM HL*, documents of 101 Fighter Wing, box nr. 113, mission log of 101 Fighter Wing, 8 March 1945; Horváth, *Bostonok a magyar égen és földben*, p. 152. Burakovsky and his gunner were killed 11 days later; details of the event can be found under Fábián's entry.

68 *HM HIM HL*, documents of 101 Fighter Wing, box nr. 113, mission log of 101 Fighter Wing, 21 April 1945.

This picture was taken on 25 January 1945 when Károly Beregfy visited Veszprém and inspected 101 Fighter Wing. In the picture he is presenting *Hauptmann* Helmut Lipfert with the *Magyar Érdemrend tisztikeresztje*. Between them stands *százados* Pottyondy, and in front of Lipfert, in the row, the short József Málik is very easily recognized. (From the collection of Sándor Sáth)

Stearman Model 75 Kaydet aircraft. This type was called the Stearman for short and was, during the war, the primary American training aircraft: a simple, easily handled, radial engine powered small double-seated biplane. It was available for a few hundred dollars after the war, and so were used in great numbers in agriculture. Pottyondy's American civil aviation career ended, however, on 29 July 1951, when he crashed a Stearman into the ground in Desha County, Arkansas. He was rushed to hospital in nearby Dumas, but died two days later due to internal injuries and severe burns, on 31 July 1951. It is said the cause of the accident was human error: according to someone who remembered the event, the aircraft crashed while performing aerobatics at a low altitude. According to another version, the aircraft collided with electrical wires while crop dusting. László Pottyondy was laid to rest in Little Rock.

FŐHADNAGY LÁSZLÓ MÁTHÉ

Number of aerial victories: 13
Successes against ground targets: n.d.a.
Number of flown combat sorties: 135
Number of hours flown in the air force: 594 hours 56 minutes
Nicknames: *Dazser*, *Laci*, *Mazsola*
Identification number: n.d.a.

Decorations

- *Magyar Koronás Ezüst Érdemérem hadiszalagon a kardokkal* (25 April 1945)
- *Magyar Koronás Bronz Érdemérem hadiszalagon a kardokkal* (25 January 1945)
- *Tűzkereszt I fokozata a kardokkal és koszorúval*
- *Felvidéki Emlékérem*
- *Erdélyi Emlékérem*
- *Délvidéki Emlékérem*
- German Iron Cross 1st Class (2 April 1945)
- German Iron Cross 2nd Class (16 November 1944)
- Gold *Frontflugspange* (17 February 1945)
- Bulgarian Observer Badge (summer of 1939)

Victories

Number	Date	Aircraft	Location
1	13 September 1944 at 15:30	Il-2	Sanok E 2km
2	14 September 1944 at 11:28	Il-2	Sanok SE 5km
3	14 September 1944 at 15:30	Il-2	Krosno S 10km
4	14 September 1944 at 15:33	Yak-9	Krosno S 15km
5	20 October 1944 at 14:30	La-5	Mezőtúr W 20km
6	21 December 1944 at 14:50	Yak-9	Székesfehérvár SW 4km
7	24 December 1944	La-5	
8	22 January 1945 at 12:28	Yak-9	Bugyi N 1km
9	1 March 1945 at 14:50	B-24	Kurd NW 2.5km (Sárvár SE 3km)
10	11 March 1945 at 17:32 (17:25)	La-5 (Yak-9)	Pusztaszabolcs NE 5km
11	13 March 1945 at 16:26	Yak-9	Baracska SE 6km
12	19 March 1945 at 11:51	Yak-9	Csór E 8km
13	19 March 1945 at 15:40	Yak-3	Ősi

Aircraft flown

Bf 109 G-6: V-388 (14–15 September 1944), V-392 (14 September 1944), V-390 (16 September 1944)

László Máthé was born on 28 August 1919 in Csíkszereda (today Miercurea Ciuc, Romania), Transylvania, to a *székely* noble family. Because Transylvania was ceded to Romania after the First World War, however, in 1920 the family moved within the new borders of Hungary, where they settled in Kaposvár. His father was a lawyer and worked as a chief prosecutor; the three children of the family – all boys, of whom László was the middle child – were therefore raised without the pretty frequent hardships and destitution of the refugee families from the lost territories. László Máthé graduated from high school (*Somssich Pál* [today the *Táncsics Mihály*] *Gimnázium*) in June 1937, with commendation.[69]

69 Record Office of the Táncsics Mihály Gimnázium (*Táncsics Mihály high school*), matriculation register from 1936/37, acc. nr. note 30.

László Máthé as an aviation cadet in the old-style leather flight suit called 'the devil's skin', in Nyíregyháza, 1938. (From the collection of László Máthé)

In parallel to his entrance exam to the Ludovika, the very talented young man also completed the entrance exam to the medical university and was admitted to both institutes. Because of his strong interest in aviation, however, he chose a career as a military pilot. In 1938, he received his primary flight training at the *Regvi* (pilot training group, *repülőgépvezető iskolaosztály*), but his class completed the last year at the *Kassai Repülőakadémia* that opened on 5 November 1939, and graduated as *hadnagy* on 4 July 1940, with rank as of 1 July 1940. Máthé did excellently at the *Akadémia* too; he graduated with rank number 1, the first in his class.[70] After graduation, he became a flight leader at 1/2 Fighter Squadron at Mátyásföld, and from here they were deployed to Kolozsvár-Szamosfalva in September 1940, where the Squadron received the new unit number '2/4' due to the renumbering of the group.

During the campaign against Yugoslavia, his squadron moved to Kecskemét and completed a few escort missions, of which he took part in one. The real baptism of fire came during the summer, during the war against the Soviet Union; 2/II Fighter Group was deployed to Bustyaháza and sent into combat at the end of June and at the beginning of July. Due to the disbandment of his squadron and the reorganization of the fighter forces at Kolozsvár, from 1 November he served with 2 Fighter Training Group. During 1942 and the first half of 1943, he was stationed in Kolozsvár; on 1 May 1943, he was promoted to *főhadnagy*. His retraining to Bf 109 was completed at Börgönd during June and July; in December 1943, he was reassigned to 2/1 Fighter Squadron at Ferihegy. On 23 February, he was reassigned to the independent 5/2 Fighter Squadron stationed at the front. From the end of March, he took the position of deputy commander of the squadron from László Molnár, who returned to Hungary.

Over the spring and the summer, the squadron was not as successful; most of the battle-hardened veterans returned home, and new pilots replaced them.

On 5 May 1944, east of Wlodzimierz, *főhadnagy* Máthé pulled his aircraft up from a dive too quickly during air combat and got a slight femoral hernia on his right side. This case is a typical example of an aspect of aviation that is very little researched: the effect of physically demanding maneuvers on the body during air combat. Because of the nature of the injury, *főhadnagy* Máthé did not receive his wound clasp for his *Tűzkereszt* immediately; he complained about it and, on 29 April 1945, he applied for it. Although he should have been eligible for the decoration and

70 *Honvédségi Közlöny* (*Személyes ügyek)*, nr. 1940/20 (4 July 1940), p. 154.

Three important officers of 2/4 Fighter Squadron in the spring of 1941 in the canteen of the airfield at Kolozsvár-Szamosfalva. From left to right: *százados* György Gulden (1905–1972), squadron commander; *hadnagy* László Máthé, flight leader; and squadron deputy commander *hadnagy* Pál Irányi. (From the collection of László Máthé)

Főhadnagy Máthé is helped by the chief mechanic of his aircraft, *őrmester* György Balázs, before going on a combat sortie. The nickname '*Eta*' can clearly be seen on the Messerschmitt behind the cockpit. (From the collection of László Máthé)

the medical officer of 101 Fighter Wing attested to this, the author has not been able to find any clues that the decoration was awarded to Máthé.[71]

Not long after his injury, on 30 May 1944, his unit (5/2 Fighter Squadron) was renamed 102 Independent Fighter Squadron. After the arrival of the second squadron to the front and before the founding of 102 Fighter Group, it was again renamed 102/1 Fighter Squadron.

Főhadnagy Máthé achieved his first air victories in the middle of September when he shot down four enemy aircraft, among them three Il-2s, in the area of Sanok and Krosno. For the first and last air victory, the witness was *főhadnagy* Dr Varga; *hadnagy* Galánfy witnessed the second Il-2; and *szakaszvezető* Varga witnessed the Yak-9. The events of his first air victory were recounted by a German war correspondent, Walter Serocks, in the *Magyar Szárnyak*, the contemporary aviation newspaper:

> I flew right into the middle of the smoke cloud, and suddenly noticed 16 aircraft in formation. One of the aircraft was flying right in front of me, but as I hesitated, unable to decide if it was friend or foe (because my comrades should have been around me somewhere), I approached him and noticed the red star on its wing. I took a big turn and I was behind him, but in the meantime I had also been spotted by the pilot of the enemy aircraft, for he pushed his aircraft downward with great speed. However, he was not able to escape

71 Logbook of László Máthé (full copy owned by the author); field medical examiner report of the injuries (copy owned by the author).

Főhadnagy Máthé sits into his aircraft in the 'crossfire' of German war correspondents, on the airfield at Munkács, in September 1944. (From the collection of László Máthé)

> my Messerschmitt. I went closer and closer and my bursts hit him on the fuselage and the wings; it began emitting smoke, and the aircraft nose-dived toward the ground. I was proud that I had managed to achieve my first air victory in the defense of my country.[72]

The next day proved the most successful in his air force career: on two free hunt sorties, he scored three kills altogether. The squadron log contains a much clearer story of the day's successes than what had previously been written by the war correspondent:

> 10km south of Sanok … I noticed huge fires with my wingman, *fhdgy.* Dr Varga, over which approximately eight Il-2 type ground-attack aircraft were attacking our ground troops. I attacked one of the Il-2s with long bursts until it caught fire and dived toward the ground, trailing thick smoke. Meanwhile, my wingman turned against the four Russian Yak-9s that were attacking us; I disengaged from the plummeting Il-2 and joined him with a climbing turn. Disengaging from the enemy, I interrupted the combat.[73]

Máthé's fifth air victory was achieved on 20 October 1944 against an La-5, west of Mezőtúr. The witnesses in this case were *főhadnagy* Dr Vajda and *szakaszvezető* Kiss. This kill was later confirmed by Air Force Order Nr. 1945/4.

72 'Német haditudósítók írják', *Magyar Szárnyak*, 15 October 1944, p. 5.
73 Excerpts from the logs of 102/1 Fighter Squadron, 14–16 September 1944 (copy owned by the author).

On 15 November, 102 Fighter Group was established. *Őrnagy* József Kovács, the former squadron commander of 102/1 Squadron, was appointed as group commander; *százados* Endre Nemes was meant to have been promoted to his place as squadron commander, but at the last minute Nemes was given another task. Thus *főhadnagy* Máthé, the former deputy commander, took over the role. He led the veteran squadron from this date until the end of the war.

Máthé's sixth kill was scored on 21 December 1944 when he shot a Yak-9 down 4km southwest of Székesfehérvár. In this case, a ground witness, the German 7/35 air defence observation point, attested to the success. Máthé's victim was most probably *mladshiy leytenant* A.D. Kaftanov from 611st IAP (Yak-9M, serial number: 2715322), who was killed during an air combat over Székesfehérvár.[74]

Főhadnagy Máthé socred another kill over an La-5 on 24 December 1944, but this was not included in his list of air victories because of an administrative error. The air victory was registered in his logbook, and it was also contained in the registry created by his group commander; in other words, the victory features in two different, independent official sources. Unfortunately, the location and time are unknown (295th IAD lost seven La-5s on this day in the presumed area of the frequent engagements).[75]

From 1 January 1944 to 31 December, Máthé's squadron completed 1,339 combat sorties, achieved 67 confirmed air victories (at least seven credited to Máthé) and brought down two observation balloons as well. It also destroyed 17 transport trucks, one oil truck and a reconnaissance armored car.[76]

The *főhadnagy* scored his first victory of 1945 at 12:28 on 22 January, during the day's extremely intense combat activity. His victim was a Yakovlev fighter 1km north of Bugyi, and the witness was *hadnagy* Szeverényi. In this case, the victim was again a pilot of 611st IAP, *mladshiy leytenant* N.A. Verbovitsky, who was killed when his Yak-9T (serial number 0815355) burned and crashed, according to Soviet reports, at 12:20, 6–8km east of Kiskunlacháza (that is, in the area of Bugyi) after a Bf 109 shot him down.[77]

According to the recommendation of his group commander, prior to 29 January 1945, *főhadnagy* Máthé had completed 101 combat sorties and achieved eight air victories (including his second mention of the kill of 24 December 1944).[78] In February, *főhadnagy* Máthé completed flew six further combat sorties, but he did not score another victory that month.

However, March 1945 was again a very productive month for him. On 1 March 1945, he and members of his squadron scrambled on a lonely Liberator at 14:30. During his first pass, he set the inner engine on the starboard side aflame over Tótvázsony, and huge parts were loosened and ripped off the aircraft. According to the report of the Hungarian fighters, four

74 Logbook of László Máthé, surviving documentation regarding the victories of László Máthé (copy owned by the author), and Gábor Horváth on documents of TsAMO.

75 Logbook of László Máthé; Gábor Horváth on documents of TsAMO.

76 *HM HIM HL*, documents of 101 Fighter Wing, box nr. 112, high command of the Royal Hungarian 102 Honvéd Fighter Group, summarized score report of 102 Fighter Group until 31 December 1944.

77 Surviving documentation regarding the victories of László Máthé (copy owned by the author); Horváth, *Bostonok a magyar égen és földben*, p. 119 (which incorrectly associates the victory with Hungarian ground-attack aircraft).

78 *HM HIM HL*, documents of 101 Fighter Wing, box nr. 112, Royal Hungarian 102 Honvéd Fighter Group, summary of decorated officers and enlisted.

crew members bailed out of the aircraft between Balatonszőlős and Balatonfüred. With his second pass, Máthé set the outer starboard engine of the heavy bomber aflame, after which the B-24 belly-landed at 15:40 on Soviet-held territory, 2.5km northwest of Kurd. The air victory was witnessed by *hadnagy* Kovács, *zászlós* Haraszthy and *szakaszvezető* Kiss. The victim was a B-24L (serial number 44-49936) of 484th BG's 827th Squadron flown by 1st Lieutenant William K. Sutton. In reality, five crew members bailed out of the aircraft and were captured on Hungarian territory; the other six crew members reached Soviet-occupied territory. The report of the Hungarian fighters incorrectly marked the location at which the aircraft belly-landed much further northward than Kurd; the air victory itself was thus confirmed with the location of Sárvár southeast in Wing Order Nr. 1945/62, while the American crew mistook the attacking Bf 109s for Fw 190s and even reported shooting one of them down.[79]

This was the last Liberator shot down by the Hungarians fighters during the Second World War. The shooting down of the last four-engined (a B-17) was reported two weeks later, confirmed to *zászlós* Ottó Fekete of the 101/5 Squadron on 15 March 1945.

In the late afternoon of 11 March, at 16:50, *főhadnagy* Máthé led a flight on a free hunt in the area of Adony–Káloz. His four Hungarian Messerschmitts met a lonely La-5, which was shot down by *főhadnagy* Máthé 5km northeast of Pusztaszabolcs; the witness was *főhadnagy* Vajda. This air victory was also confirmed in Wing Order Nr. 1945/62. The aircraft was listed in the unit's mission log, in the after-action report and in the confirming Air Force Order as an La-5; but the logbook mentions a Yak-9.[80]

Two days later, *főhadnagy* Máthé scored another air victory while leading another flight on a free hunt. The Hungarian formation took off at 15:49 and engaged four Il-2s and eight Yakovlev fighters in combat in the airspace south of Gárdony; *főhadnagy* Máthé shot down one of these south of Baracska at 16:26. The Soviet aircraft crashed to the ground and was wrecked. The witnesses were, in this case, *főhadnagy* Schmidt and *hadnagy* Bajza. This air victory was again confirmed by Wing Order Nr. 1945/62.[81]

Főhadnagy Máthé was successful in air combat for the last time on 19 March 1945, in this case on two sorties. At first, he led a flight of eight aircraft against Il-2s operating in the area of Csór at 11:12. Although they did not reach the Soviet ground-attack aircraft and two smaller fighter formations fled from them into the clouds, at 11:51 *főhadnagy* Máthé successfully shot down a Yak-9 east of Csór, which plummeted in flames into the clouds below. The witness, in this case, was not one of the pilots from his own flight, but a young ace from II./JG 52, *Leutnant* Peter Düttmann.[82]

79 NARA MACR 12508; *HM HIM HL*, documents of 101 Fighter Wing, box nr. 113, after-action reports and mission logs of 101 Fighter Wing, 1 March 1945; box nr. 110, Wing Order Nr. 1945/62; Zoltán Tálosi, *Háborús évek. Légiesemények és harcok Tolna megyében* (Szekszárd: privately published, 2002), p. 229.

80 *HM HIM HL*, documents of 101 Fighter Wing, box nr. 113, after-action reports and mission logs of 101 Fighter Wing, 11 March 1945; logbook of László Máthé.

81 *HM HIM HL*, documents of 101 Fighter Wing, box nr. 113, after-action reports and mission logs of 101 Fighter Wing, 13 March 1945; box nr. 110, Wing Order Nr. 1945/62.

82 *HM HIM HL*, documents of 101 Fighter Wing, box nr. 113, after-action reports and mission logs of 101 Fighter Wing, 19 March 1945. Düttmann, who was also decorated with the Knight's Cross of the Iron Cross, had 152 confirmed and a further 42 unconfirmed air victories prior to the end of the war. Among his April victories, there is a T-34/85 and an M4 Sherman tank each – for the German

On the same day, at 15:17, *főhadnagy* Máthé again took off leading eight aircraft. The two Hungarian flights this time went into combat with Boston bomber formations escorted by Yakovlev fighters. During this combat, at 15:40, Máthé reported shooting down a Yak-3 at Ősi – the aircraft was hit on the engine and thick smoke trailed behind as it disappeared into the clouds below. The mission log designates this aircraft as his 12th air victory – as the La-5 of 24 December had not been registered, this kill should actually be counted as his 13th – but it was not confirmed in any Wing Orders (similarly to a number of other air victories for 101/III Group). At 15:57, Máthé managed to hit a Boston on the fuselage. This aircraft appears in the combat report as having been 'fired upon effectively', but is counted as damaged among the pilot's results by the author and not as a kill, because it was not designated as such either in the mission log or in the combat report (and Máthé himself did not count it as a victory). During the air combat, the formations engaged the Yak-3s and the Yak-9Ds of 659th IAP and the Bostons of 244th BAD, but none of the enemy aircraft crashed.[83]

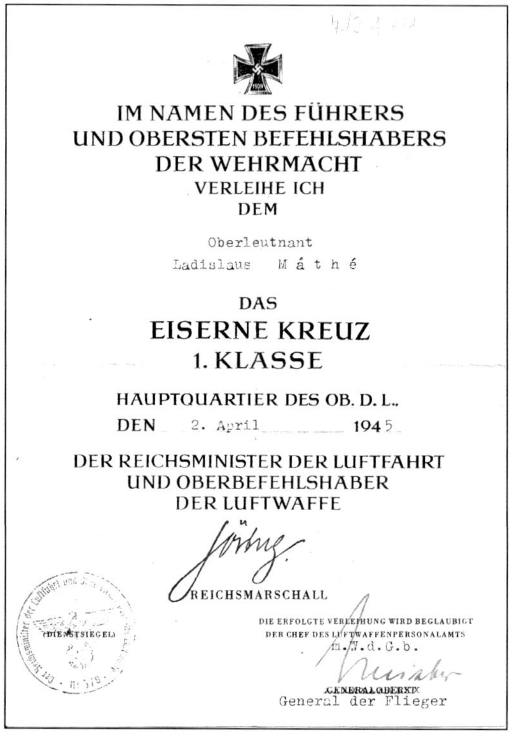
IM NAMEN DES FÜHRERS
UND OBERSTEN BEFEHLSHABERS
DER WEHRMACHT
VERLEIHE ICH
DEM
Oberleutnant
Ladislaus Máthé
DAS
EISERNE KREUZ
1. KLASSE
HAUPTQUARTIER DES OB. D. L.
DEN 2. April 1945
DER REICHSMINISTER DER LUFTFAHRT
UND OBERBEFEHLSHABER
DER LUFTWAFFE
REICHSMARSCHALL
(DIENSTSIEGEL)
DIE ERFOLGTE VERLEIHUNG WIRD BEGLAUBIGT
DER CHEF DES LUFTWAFFENPERSONALAMTS
m.W.d.G.b.
General der Flieger

Awarding document of the German Iron Cross 1st Class for László Máthé. (From the collection of László Máthé)

On 23 March 1945, around noon, Máthé led a flight on a free hunt from Kenyeri, but nothing in particular happened during this sortie. This was his last combat sortie from a Hungarian airfield, and the next to last combat mission of his military career. His very last sortie was completed (according to his logbook) on 10 April from Raffelding. According to a list the author has compiled based on the pilot's logbook, Máthé flew 135 combat sorties altogether: one against Yugoslavia, five air defense sorties and eight offensive sorties against the Soviets during the summer of 1941, and a further 121 combat sorties over the Eastern Front during 1944–1945. During these combat sorties, he took part in 32 air combats and achieved the air victories that have been detailed above.[84]

fighter pilots, these types of targets were listed among their victories at the very end of the war. For more on Düttmann (Gießen, 23 May 1923–Echterdingen, 9 January 2001), see Peter Düttmann, *Wir kämpften in einsamen Höhen* (Leipzig: Traditionsgemeinschaft JG 52, 2002), p. 256; Obermaier, *Die Ritterkreuzträger der Luftwaffe 1939–45*, p. 104.

83 *HM HIM HL*, documents of 101 Fighter Wing, box nr. 113, after-action reports and mission logs of 101 Fighter Wing, 19 March 1945; Horváth, *Bostonok a magyar égen és földben*, p. 185.

84 Logbook of László Máthé.

Főhadnagy László Máthé was captured with 101 Fighter Wing in May 1945. He never returned to Hungary while it was occupied by the Soviets. After the war, he worked in Munich as a civil servant in the US Armed Forces, then emigrated to Argentina in 1949. After his arrival, he would have worked for the Argentinean Civilian Aviation, but he did not speak Spanish, so he could not exploit this option. This meant he had to give up his hopes of flying again, which he could only do when his Argentinean friends took him into the air.

At the beginning of his civilian life in Argentina, he worked as an aide in a carpenter's shop, then for a precision mechanic company. In his later years, he continued to work in this field and became a supplier for a number of companies and car factories.

A portrait from the end of the war of an excellent squadron commander: László Máthé in 1945. On the left side of his chest, near the German Iron Cross 1st Class, the Bulgarian Observer Badge can be seen, because in the late summer of 1939 his class went to Bulgaria, where they received this badge. (From the collection of László Máthé)

László Máthé died on 11 July 2006 in Villa Carlos Paz, Córdoba. To his great pride, László Máthé Jr., his eldest son, became a military engineer colonel of the Argentinean air force (*Fuerza Aérea Argentina*), from which he retired on 28 February 2014. As Captain, he took part in the Falkland's War in 1982, commanding the radar station and the defence of the northern sector of the airfield at Comodoro Rivadavia (*Aeropuerto de Comodoro Rivadavia 'Gral. Enrique Mosconi'*) on the shore of the Atlantic Ocean. For his service, he received the following decorations: *Distinción Número 4 de la Fuerza Aérea Argentina 'Al combatiente de Malvinas'*, and the *Medalla del Congreso Nacional Argentino: 'Al combatiente de Malvinas'*.[85]

HADNAGY JÓZSEF MÁLIK

Number of aerial victories: 12 (+1)
Successes against ground targets: n.d.a.
Number of flown combat sorties: 60 (20 against Americans)
Number of hours flown in the air force: n.d.a.
Nicknames: *Jóska*, *Józsika*, *Félbefűrészelt Óriás*
Identification number: 3181-22-1218

85 Information about his civilian life has been collected based on documents preserved by the Máthé family, who were kind enough to provide them to the author.

Decorations

- *Magyar Érdemrend lovagkeresztje hadiszalagon a kardokkal* (25 January 1945)
- *Magyar Koronás Ezüst Érdemérem hadiszalagon a kardokkal* (29 January 1945)
- *Kormányzói dicsérő elismerés Magyar Koronás Bronz Érdemérme hadiszalagon a kardokkal* (1 November 1944)
- *Tűzkereszt I fokozata a kardokkal és koszorúval*, one wound clasp
- German Iron Cross 1st Class (April 1945)
- German Iron Cross 2nd Class (8 March 1945)

Victories

Number	Date	Aircraft	Location
1	14 June 1944	P-38	Pusztavám SE
2	27 June 1944	B-17	Budakeszi N
3	2 July 1944	B-24	Gyuró
4	7 August 1944	P-51	Ikervár (Meggyeskovácsi)
–	21 August 1944	B-24	Hajdúböszörmény
5	12 October 1944	P-51	near Lake Balaton (Nádasdladány)
6	5 November 1944	B-24	(*HSS*) Iharos N
7	3 January 1945	Yak-9	Gödöllő N
8	22 January 1945	La-5	Vál S
9	23 January 1945	La-5	Üllő W
10	2 February 1945	Pe-2	Ráckeresztúr S
11	9 March 1945 at 10:24	Boston III	Csór S (Várpalota SE)
12	16 March 1945 at 15:15	Yak-9	Bia

Aircraft flown

Bf 109 G-14/U4: W-171 (9 March 1945)

József Málik was born on 12 June 1922 in Kecskemét. His father of the same name was an infantry officer; at the time his son was born he was a *százados*, at the end of the war, an *ezredes*. According to the family tradition, József also chose a military career: he was also a *cőger* and graduated from the *Zrínyi Miklós Reáliskolai Nevelőintézet* in Pécs, where he was the classmate and inseparable friend of Lajos Tóth.

After graduation, he attended the *Repülőakadémia* with Tóth, and graduated as *hadnagy* on 6 December 1942, as of 1 December 1942, with rank number 5.[86]

After his graduation, and still alongside Tóth, he was assigned to 1 Fighter Training Group in Szolnok. During 1943, Málik served in Szolnok and was not deployed to the Eastern Front. Consequently, his first combat experiences were obtained in home defense in the spring of 1944.[87]

86 *Honvédségi Közlöny* (*Személyes ügyek)*, nr. 1942/50 (4 December 1942), p. 1265.
87 *HM HIM KI*, document folder nr. 65197.

József Málik as a student of the *Repülőkadémia* in 1942. (From the author's collection)

Meghívó.

A m. kir. „Horthy Miklós" honvéd repülőakadémia folyó évi december hó 6-án 11 óra 15 perckor rendezi

hadnagyavatási ünnepségét,

melyre tisztelettel meghívja

az akadémia parancsnokság.

Öltözet: polgári ruhában megjelenők részére sötét vagy magyaros, tisztek részére soron és renden kívüli dísz.

Invitation to the graduation ceremony of *hadnagys* on 6 December 1942. Three pilots from the class became aces: *hadnagys* Tóth, Málik and Szeverényi. Sadly, none of them lived to celebrate their 30th birthday. (From the author's collection)

On 13 April 1944, 1/2 Fighter Squadron scrambled to engage the American formations raiding Budapest. The squadron was still flying obsolete Re.2000 fighters manufactured by *MÁVAG*; one of the four aircraft was flown by *hadnagy* Málik, for whom this was the first combat sortie. The Hungarian *Héja*s were attacked east of Budapest by the P-47 Thunderbolts of 325th FG's 317th Squadron, and two were shot down. *Hadnagy* Málik and *hadnagy* Forró bailed out near Ócsa and survived without injury. The Hungarian aircraft were shot down by two experienced P-47 aces, although it is impossible to determine who shot down whom: one of the victories was reported by 1st Lieutenant Eugene H. Emmons (who identified his opponent's aircraft type incorrectly as a 'Re.2001'); the other aircraft was shot down by 1st Lieutenant George P. Novotny, although he only reported damaging a 'Re.2001'. Of Emmons's nine air victories, this was the sixth; Novotny had achieved eight confirmed air victories during the war, all of them before this particular air combat.[88]

As of May 1944, after the forming of 101 Fighter Group, *hadnagy* Málik was transferred to Veszprém to 101/2 Fighter Squadron, where he served again with his good friend, Lajos Tóth.

During the summer, intense combat activities began in home air defense, and Málik achieved his first air victory on 14 June over a Lightning of 14th FG's 49th Squadron.

One of the 1944 issues of *Magyar Szárnyak* published the following about his first victory, although it was probably a bit 'touched up' by the journalists:

88 NARA 325th FG Combat Claim Forms (the author wishes to express his gratitude to Frank Olynyk for his kind help in accessing the source); Pataky, Rozsos, and Sárhidai, *Légi háború Magyarország felett*, vol. 2, p. 191. For Emmons, see Olynyk, *Stars and Bars,* p. 257. For Novotny, see *ibid.*, p. 476. The author has also tried to contact George Novotny, but he was not able to provide any further usable information.

Graduation of *hadnagys* at Kassa, 6 December in 1942. József Málik is on the right end of the rear line. (From the author's collection)

1st Lieutenant George P. Novotny, an ace of 325th FG's 317th FS with eight confirmed air victories reported to 'have damaged' a 'Re.2001' on 13 April 1944. In reality both of the Hungarian *Héjas* whom they attacked crashed; the pilots, *hadnagys* Málik and Forró, bailed out near Ócsa (Dwayne Tabatt via Carl Molesworth)

On June 14, at last, I was able to engage the enemy fighters. Lightnings again! *So now I will repay you for the last time*, I thought, and attacked the formation of approximately 10 twin-boom aircraft from below. One of them immediately left the the formation and turned on me. A wild dogfight ensued; it was a serious air combat. Sometimes he was the one behind me and sometimes I got behind him, and his aircraft absorbed a good number of machine gun bursts, but it seemed like nothing to him! At last, I was able to get myself into an ideal position to attack, and I fired a long burst from all of my weapons into his port boom.

The port engine burst into flames, and the aircraft plummeted with a sharp dive toward the ground. The Lightning caught fire pretty quickly, and the pilot was unable to bail out [*hadnagy* Málik did not see the events correctly, assuming this narrative is told in his words and not those of journalists trying to make the story even more interesting: all of the pilots from the Lightnings shot down on this day were able to bail out]. It crashed with a big explosion.[89]

89 György Stirling, 'Magyar vadászok között', *Magyar Szárnyak*, 1 July 1944, p. 5.

The air victory is covered in Air Force Confidential Order Nr. 1944/63 as a shared kill with *őrmester* István Fábián (for the later discrepancies regarding this issue, see the biography for Fábián). According to the memories of his squadron mate, Pál Forró, American fighters shot Málik down on 16 June 1944; he was forced to bail out of the aircraft for the second time (according to the memories of his comrades, Málik bailed out at least five times from his aircraft over 1944–45).[90]

His first air victory against a four-engined B-17 was reported on 27 June 1944; not even a week later it was followed by a B-24, on 2 July. In Air Force Confidential Order Nr. 1944/63, the date of his air victory against the Liberator is mistyped and so it was also confirmed to 27 June. While 27 July would have been possible, even 27 June is definitely incorrect; what is more, even the name of the village is slightly mistyped in the order. Regarding his earlier air victory against the B-17, the aircraft type is also recorded incorrectly in Wing Order Nr. 1945/62 (as a Liberator), although B-17s had been attacking the capital that day. In Air Force Confidential Order Nr. 1944/63, the Liberator Málik shot down on 27 June 1944 features with the location of 'Gyuros'; the Wing Order for 27 June 1944 contains a Liberator with the location of Budakeszi north. This refers to two different victories and are full of typing errors. The victory registry of air victories against four-engines, compiled in the spring of 1945, only reaffirms that Málik scored three air victories against four-engines.[91]

1st Lieutenant Eugene H. Emmons, ace of 325th FG's 317th Fighter Squadron, with nine confirmed air victories, achieved his sixth kill against a Hungarian Re.2000 on 13 April 1944; the victim was reported to be a 'Re.2001' (Dwayne Tabatt via Carl Molesworth)

The Liberator that crashed at Gyuró on 2 July 1944 was a B-24H (serial number 42-52295) of 456th BG's 744th Squadron flown by 2nd Lieutenant Roy F. Huls. None of the 10 crew members survived the crash.[92]

Málik's air victory against US aircraft was scored during the tragic clash with 31st FG on 7 August 1944. During this mission, *hadnagy* Málik flew behind László Molnár; it was Málik who received the credit for shooting down the aircraft of 2nd Lieutenant Leoborn E. Richards (P-51D, serial number 4413454), the man who hit Molnár's aircraft first. The young pilot of 307th Fighter Squadron from Nebraska, was killed when his aircraft crashed near Balozsameggyes (today part of Meggyeskovácsi). Wing Order Nr. 1945/62 credited this air victory to Málik with the location of Ikervár.[93]

90 Manuscript recollections of Pál Forró (copy owned by the author).
91 *HM HIM HL*, documents of 101 Fighter Wing, box nr. 110, Air Force Confidential Order Nr. 1944/63, Wing Order Nr. 1945/62; also box nr. 113, record of victories against four-engines.
92 NARA MACR 6438.
93 NARA MACR 14418.

Two weeks later, during the air combat with the Americans raiding Hajdúböszörmény, Málik reported shooting down a B-24, but this claim was not confirmed and was later deleted in Wing Order Nr. 1945/27.

On the afternoon of 12 October 1944, the wing heavily supported the Hungarian 3rd Army in its combat actions along the Tisza River, using forced strafing runs. On returning from the mission without ammunition and fuel, the Hungarian aircraft were attacked by Mustangs near Veszprém. According to comrades, the engine of *hadnagy* Málik's aircraft – after he had reported shooting down a Mustang – stopped on running out of fuel, and he had to bail out of his Bf 109. This kill was confirmed in Air Force Order Nr. 1944/3, issued on 17 November 1944, with a location at the Balaton; Wing Order Nr. 1945/62, issued five months later, places the air victory in Nádasdladány (although this is referring to the same aircraft).

The air victory was probably confirmed a second time because of an administrative error, and the clerks collecting the documents for Wing Order Nr. 1945/62 did not notice the previous Air Force Order confirming that particular air victory (the pilot himself was dead by the time Wing Order Nr. 1945/62 was issued on 19 April 1945, and so was unable to inform them of this problem). Although two Mustangs were indeed destroyed on 12 October over Hungarian territory, according to the American combat loss reports they were shot down by anti-aircraft artillery. In the case of the aircraft from 332nd FG that crashed south of Lake Balaton at Somogybabod, the anti-aircraft artillery kill is certain, and the victory was confirmed to Hungarian 103/1 Anti-Aircraft Gun Battery.[94]

Hadnagy Málik reported his last air victory against four-engined heavy bombers on the final combat mission of Hungarian fighters in large formations against the Americans on 5 November 1944. This air victory was confirmed as '*Herausschuss*' by Wing Order Nr. 1945/62.

During 1944, József Málik had completed 20 combat sorties altogether against the Americans, and the six air victories he achieved during these sorties made him one of the most successful Hungarian fighter pilots against American aircraft – even though he was forced to leave his aircraft and bail out a number of times.

Hadnagy Málik reported shooting down his first Soviet opponent on 3 January 1945 north of Gödöllő; his victim was a Yakovlev fighter.

His next air victory was scored on 22 January over an La-5 south of Vál. This air victory appears with the date of 22 February in Wing Order Nr. 1945/62, but according to the information collected by the author, this is clearly a typing error. On 22 February, neither the mission log nor the combat report of 101 Fighter Wing mentions any enemy aircraft shot down by *hadnagy* Málik, nor is one included in the summary report at the end of the month; there is, however, a air victory claimed by Málik against an La-5 in the diary of Sándor Tábori on 22 January. The aircraft was probably the La-5F (serial number 39215251) of 164th IAP flown by *leytenant* V.S. Svistelnikov that crash-landed east of Pázmánd, southeast of Vál, due to damage inflicted during air combat.[95] In the second half of January, *hadnagy* Málik was reassigned from

94 *HM HIM HL*, documents of 101 Fighter Wing, box nr. 110, Air Force Order Nr. 1944/3 and Wing Order Nr. 1945/62; NARA MACR 9082 and 9084; recollections and letter of Walter McCreary (1918–2015) to the author, 4 May 2008. The pilot was taken into captivity at Somogybabod.

95 *HM HIM HL*, documents of 101 Fighter Wing, box nr. 110, Wing Order Nr. 1945/62; box nr. 113, after-action reports and mission logs of 101 Fighter Wing, 22 February 1945; Horváth, *Bostonok a magyar égen és földben*, p. 119.

Pilots of 101/2 Squadron in readiness in Veszprém, in the summer of 1944. The second from the left is *hadnagy* József Málik. (*HM HIM* Photographic Archives 97.601/397)

A 1943 picture of Roy F. Huls from 1943; the pilot of the Liberator from 456th BG that crashed at Gyuró on 2 July 1944 (serial number 42-52295). The shooting down of the heavy bomber was confirmed to *hadnagy* Málik. (From the collection of Don Brownlee)

101/2 Squadron to 101/1 Squadron and took over command, replacing *főhadnagy* Jenő Murányi. His promotion to squadron commander appeared in Wing Order Nr. 1945/18 on 23 January.[96]

Wing Order Nr. 1945/62 also confirmed another of his kills against the Soviets on 23 January, once more against an La-5. During his 44th combat sortie on 2 February 1945, *hadnagy* Málik reported shooting down a Pe-2; over 1944–45 over Hungary, only two Hungarian air victories against Pe-2s were reported, and this was the second (the first was *őrmester* Fábián's victory on 16 January 1945). If the type was correctly identified, this was again a victory against a long-range reconnaissance aircraft; however, according to Soviet sources, there were no Pe-2 losses on that day. If the issue was ascribable to a typing error, the date might also have been a mistake, but the month must be correct as the aircraft was included in the summary list of air victories during February. The Pe-2s that went missing in January were thus out of question, and there were a number of such aircraft. The only serious damage to a long-range reconnaissance aircraft reported by the Soviets during that month was two days after the day in question; the report regarded a Pe-2 of 39th ORAP, which suffered serious damage during air combat over Dunaföldvár. The observer was killed, but according to the report of the crew, their aircraft was attacked by mistake by three of their own La-5s, which inflicted extensive damage to the Pe-2.[97]

Altogether, Málik's squadron completed 72 individual combat sorties during February. The wing documents only mention *hadnagy* Málik's Pe-2 and *hadnagy* Michna's double kill over Yakovlev fighters (for which more details will follow); there is no trace of the La-5 that was mistakenly confirmed for 22 February.

96 *HM HIM HL*, documents of 101 Fighter Wing, box nr. 110, Wing Order Nr. 1945/18.
97 *HM HIM HL*, documents of 101 Fighter Wing, box nr. 112, summarized score report of 101 Fighter Wing from February [1945]; Horváth, *Bostonok a magyar égen és földben*, p. 263.

Two inseparable friends: *hadnagys* József Málik and Lajos Tóth at the end of January 1945 in Veszprém. (From the author's collection).

A picture of *starshiy leytenant* Vasily Ivanovich Tulsky from after the war. Tulsky served as a pilot of 452nd BAP in the war, and the Boston (serial number 42-54225) which was shot down by *hadnagy* Málik on 9 March 1945 was his aircraft (TsAMO via Horváth)

Hadnagy Málik's next successful sortie took place on 9 March 1945. He took off at 10:15 as a member of an eight-aircraft flight led by *főhadnagy* Máthé on a free hunt in the area of Várpalota–Székesfehérvár; three out of the eight aircraft returned to the airfield because of various problems, so only five actually took part in the mission. Soon after, the formation engaged a Boston formation flying with a fighter escort south of Öskü. According to the combat report and the combat mission log, the Hungarian fighters engaged two formations of nine Bostons each – altogether about 18 bomber aircraft – between 10:24 and 10:30. At 10:24, *hadnagy* Málik shot a bomber out of the formation that was turning eastward: according to his report, parts began falling off the aircraft, then it burst into flames. The witness was *zászlós* Asztalos, who also shot down an aircraft. Not long afterward, *hadnagy* Málik was also shot down in his Bf 109 G-14/U4 (WNr. 512644, manufactured in Wiener Neustadt). He bailed out around 10:30 southeast of Öskü, with only minor injuries. As this happened near Veszprém, the pilot was able to return to his unit by noon. *Hadnagy* Málik received a wound clasp for his *Tűzkereszt* because of the injuries inflicted while bailing out of his aircraft. According to the wing's mission log, Málik was shot down by the Soviet escort fighters. The mission log recorded that he plummeted into the clouds with a burning aircraft at 10:26 southeast of Várpalota because the clouds prevented his comrades seeing him bail out. Regarding *hadnagy* Málik's air victory, the Hungarian fighters had engaged the Bostons of 452nd BAP; one was destroyed and one seriously damaged during the air combat. József Málik's victim was in all probability the destroyed aircraft of 452nd BAP, the A-20G Boston (serial number 4254225) of *starshiy leytenant* V.I. Tulsky, which flew over the Danube and belly-landed 8km east of Solt and then burned out; one crew member was wounded.

Málik's aircraft was probably shot down by the squadron commander of 179th GIAP (the unit was equipped with La-7s and was tasked with escorting the bombers), *starshiy leytenant* Ivan Ivanovich Bezmeltsev, who reported shooting down a Bf 109 west of Székesfehérvár, an act witnessed by two members of his formation. This was Bezmeltsev's seventh victory; he ended the war with 10 confirmed air victories.[98]

Málik was, therefore, shot down both by an American and a Soviet ace. This was something of an extraordinary experience in the Second World War, and no other Hungarian ace could say the same.

Málik's last air victory occurred on 16 March 1945. He took off at 14:54 with his flight on a free hunt in the airspace of Magyaralmás. In the area of Lovasberény, according to the report, a larger Boston formation of about 20 aircraft was spotted escorted by two Yakovlev fighters. After an approximately 10-minute-long air combat with the fighters, *hadnagy* Málik shot down a Yakovlev at 15:15 over Bia; the aircraft blew up in mid-air because of the cannon hits, and the pilot – according to Málik's report – was killed. The witness to the air victory was *őrmester* Buday. This aircraft was probably a Yak-9D of 659th IAP, which went missing after a Boston escort mission. The pilot, *mladshiy leytenant* V.A. Korotkevich, was seriously wounded, but survived the destruction of his aircraft.

The last sorties of *hadnagy* Málik from Veszprém were not successful. He was retreating with the wing and was unable to achieve a confirmed victory in Austrian airspace. He completed his last sortie on the morning of 15 April 1945, leading a flight on a reconnaissance mission into the area of Vienna and Sankt Pölten. During this mission, they met a lone Boston at high altitude, and attacked it until it reached the clouds. One of Málik's wingmen was convinced it had already been hit, but probably the attack did not cause any significant damage.[99]

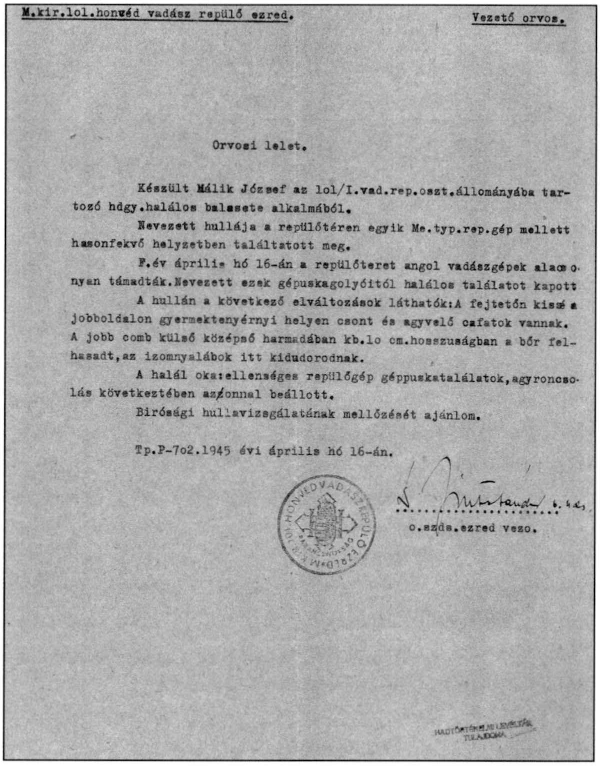

M.kir.lol.honvéd vadász repülő ezred. Vezető orvos.

Orvosi lelet.

Készült Málik József az lol/I.vad.rep.oszt.állományába tartozó hdgy.halálos balesete alkalmából.

Nevezett hullája a repülőtéren egyik Me.typ.rep.gép mellett hasonfekvő helyzetben találtatott meg.

F.év április hó 16-án a repülőteret angol vadászgépek alacsonyan támadták.Nevezett ezek gépuskagolyóitól halálos találatot kapott

A hullán a következő elváltozások láthatók:A fejtetőn kissé a jobboldalon gyermektenyérnyi helyen csont és agyvelő cafatok vannak. A jobb comb külső középső harmadában kb.lo cm.hosszuságban a bőr felhasadt,az izomnyalábok itt kidudorodnak.

A halál oka:ellenséges repülőgép géppuskatalálatok,agyroncsolás következtében azonnal beállott.

Birósági hullavizsgálatának mellőzését ajánlom.

Tp.P-7o2.1945 évi április hó 16-án.

o.szds.ezred vezo.

Medical report declaring the death of József Málik. (*HM HIM* Military Archives)

98 *HM HIM HL*, documents of 101 Fighter Wing, box nr. 113, after-action reports and mission logs of 101 Fighter Wing, 9 March 1945; Bikhov, *Sovetskie Asy 1941–1945*, pp. 52–53; Horváth, *Bostonok a magyar égen és földben*, pp. 134–137.

99 Tobak, *Pumák földön-égen*, pp. 256–257.

The grave of *hadnagy* József Málik in the Jaunitzfeld military cemetery near Freistadt, Austria. (From the author's collection)

On 16 April 1945, the fighter forces of 8th AAF performed particularly intensive strafing attacks on Austrian and other airfields. Raffelding was also targeted by several strafings, and one of them caused the death of *hadnagy* Málik. In the afternoon, a 0.50 caliber (12.7mm) round from a strafing Mustang hit *hadnagy* Málik in the head while he was lying near a Bf 109; he died instantly.

After Málik was killed, his wing commander recommended him posthumously to receive the *Magyar Érdemrend tisztikeresztje hadidíszítményekkel és kardokkal*, but he did not receive anything for this recommendation. His merits were appraised in it: 'He had a large number of air ictories and was one of the most successful Hungarian fighter pilots. During his sorties, he excelled due to his daring and brave and gallant manners.'[100]

Only 10 victories were mentioned in this hastily-prepared recommendation, which omitted his B-17 and one of the La-5s. All 12 of his air victories had been confirmed by various authorities: Air Force Confidential Order Nr. 1944/63 covered two of them; one was included in Air Force Order Nr. 1944/3; and 10 were included in Wing Order Nr. 1945/62. Of these, the latter included the second confirmation discussed above of the Mustang that had already been credited to Málik in Air Force Order Nr. 1944/3.

Hadnagy Málik was buried in the cemetery at Eferding on 17 April 1945 (19 April, according to Wing Order Nr. 1945/62). In the 1980s, the cemetery was abolished and Málik was reburied to the Jaunitzfeld military cemetery near Freistadt, and this is where József Málik is now at rest.

100 *HM HIM HL*, documents of 101 Fighter Wing, box nr. 113, recommendations for decorations.

HADNAGY FERENC MÁLNÁSSY

Number of aerial victories: 12
Successes against ground targets: one truck, one car (+?)
Number of flown combat sorties: 75+
Number of hours flown in the air force: n.d.a.
Nicknames: *Frici*, *Málna Franci*
Identification number: 1432-23-0144

Decorations

- *Magyar Koronás Bronz Érdemérem hadiszalagon a kardokkal* (3 February 1945)
- *Tűzkereszt I fokozata a kardokkal és koszorúval*, with one wound clasp
- German Iron Cross 1st Class (17 March 1945)
- German Iron Cross 2nd Class (8 March 1945)
- Silver *Frontflugspange* (1945)

Victories

Number	Date	Aircraft	Location
1	9 October 1944	La-5	Tuchla
2	1 November 1944	Boston III	Tiszakécske
3	13 November 1944	Il-2	Jászapáti
4	5 December 1944	Il-2	Hatvan
5	5 December 1944	La-5	Hatvan
6	14 December 1944	Il-2	Hatvan (Balatonkenese)
7	14 December 1944	Il-2	Hatvan (Balatonkenese)
8	14 January 1944	Boston III	Csepel
9	14 January 1944	La-5	Baracska
10	14 January 1944	La-5	Baracska
11	13 March 1945 at 10:05	Yak-9 (La-5?)	Káloz N, Seregélyes S–SW
12	20 March 1945 at 12:00	Il-2	Balatonkenese

Aircraft flown

Bf 109 G-10/U4: WNr. 610556 (13 March 1945); n.d.a. of markings

Ferenc Málnássy was born on 26 August in Balassagyarmat. He was the family's only son, although he had a younger sister. His father (of the same name) was a military field doctor, with a rank of *alezredes* at the end of the Second World War.[101] The easy-going '*Málna Franci*' ('*Málna*' means raspberry; *Franci* is a nickname for Ferenc) was a *cőger* from Sopron; he received his primary flight training at the Győr unit of the *HMNRA* in 1941. He graduated as *hadnagy* on 20 August 1943 at Kassa, as of 1 September, with rank number 32.[102]

101 *HM HIM HL*, AKVI 1896/1527.
102 *Honvédségi Közlöny* (*Személyes ügyek)*, nr. 1943/48 (1 December 1943), after correction, p. 1710.

Soldier father, soldier son. Ferenc Málnássy as a '*cőger*' with his father at Balassagyarmat at Christmas 1934. (From the collection of the Málnássy family)

Ferenc Málnássy as a student at the *Repülőkadémia* in 1943. (From the author's collection)

After graduation he was assigned to Kolozsvár, to 2/2 Fighter Squadron, led by László Pottyondy.

He arrived at the Eastern Front with his squadron on 7 June 1944, and from this date until his tragic death he served in the same squadron, although it was renamed twice: first as 102/2, then as 101/8 Fighter Squadron.

He achieved his first air victory on 9 October 1944, when he shot down an La-5 in the Carpathians northeast of the Uzhok Pass, in the area of Tuchla (Turka). During the course of November, he achieved another two air victories in Hungarian airspace. Of these, the first was reported on 1 November against a Boston of 452nd BAP. The kill was confirmed to Málnássy with a location of Újkécske (now part of Tiszakécske). The Hungarian fighters reported two victories over Bostons on that day; apart from Málnássy's own, the other was reported by *zászlós* Kálmán, and two aircraft of the Soviet Regiment also belly-landed that day. Of these, the A-20 G (serial number 42-53754) flown by *mladshiy leytenant* A.J. Polonsky was written off, although his crew managed to survive the crash-landing 6km west of Gyomaendrőd. Of the two Hungarian kills, Málnássy's victory was closer to where Polonsky crash-landed.

In November, *hadnagy* Málnássy reported another air victory, this time against an Il-2, on 13 April at Jászapáti. This kill is not corroborated by Soviet official documents; according to them, there were no Il-2 losses at the specific location on that day. *Hadnagy* Málnássy achieved two double air victories in December, which made his name and earned him ace status. His first double air victory was achieved on 5 December at Hatvan and consisted of a Soviet Il-2,

The humorous drawings of Ferenc Málnássy. He had a preliminary contract with the *Hunnia Filmstúdió* for graphic works, but this was not realized. (From the collection of the Málnássy family)

The Bf 109 G-6 ('Black 2') of 102/2 Fighter Squadron in the autumn of 1944. It is possible that this aircraft was also flown by *hadnagy* Ferenc Málnássy (*HM HIM* Photographic Archives 97.841/418)

probably from 90th GSAP, and an La-5. His second double kill was reported on 14 December against Il-2s. Air Force Order Nr. 1945/10 confirmed his four December victories and gave the location of the second double kill as Hatvan too; however, this was probably a mistype repeating the location of the 5 December double kill, as Hatvan had been captured by the Soviets three weeks earlier and there were no major military actions around the town during the period under discussion, with considerable air support. The situation at the eastern end of Lake Balaton, however, was very much like that described above, where extremely heavy air combat activity occurred on 14 December between the German–Hungarian and Soviet air forces. According to the author, these two air victories were achieved by *hadnagy* Málnássy in the area of Balatonakarattya–Balatonkenese against the aircraft of 715th SAP. The same Air Force Order confirmed three further air victories for his group in this area: two Il-2s for *zászlós* Kálmán and an La-5 for *hadnagy* György Horváth. The error was not corrected, probably because there was simply no time to correct an error that had already appeared in an order issued on 22 February. The last surviving Air Force Order is Nr. 1945/13 of 2 March 1945; the same confirming order, Nr. 1945/10, corrects a typing error regarding an air victory achieved on 16 June 1944 and confirmed on 18 July 1944 – in other words, correcting a mistake made during the summer of 1944, more than seven months previously.[103]

103 *HM HIM HL*, documents of 101 Fighter Wing, box nr. 110, Air Force Order Nr. 1945/10; Horváth, *Bostonok a magyar égen és földben*, pp. 49, 79–80.

Hadnagy Ferenc Málnássy in the winter of 1944–45. (From the author's collection)

Hadnagys Tibor Makó (on the left) and Ferenc Málnássy, pilots of 102/2 Fighter Squadron, on the Budaörs airfield in November 1944. Makó achieved three air victories in 1943 as a long-range reconnaissance pilot; he was killed at dawn on 23 December 1944, during a Soviet air raid near Várpalota, when fragments of a small calibre fragmentation bomb hit him in the head. (From the author's collection)

Hadnagy Málnássy's most successful day was 14 January 1945, when he reported shooting down three aircraft – one Boston and two La-5s. The bomber he reported shooting down was probably the A-20B (serial number 41-2802) of 449th BAP's 1st Squadron, flown by *mladshiy leytenant* N.F. Bakanev. After being seriously damaged by a Bf 109, as a result of which the navigator was killed, the aircraft belly-landed at Tököl, where an La-5 also crashed into it, wrecking it. The La-5s of the supporting 31st IAP and the other Lavochkin units of the 17th Air Army did not report any La-5 air combat damage during the day, and there is no specific data about the particular La-5 of 530th IAP that ran into the Boston while landing regarding whether it had already been damaged (probably in air combat).[104]

According to a recommendation from his group commander, *hadnagy* Málnássy had completed 64 combat sorties and achieved 10 air victories by 29 January 1945.[105] During February, he completed a further eight combat sorties, although he did not score any new kills. An interesting note remains regarding one of his successful strafing runs: on 22 February,

104 Horváth, *Bostonok a magyar égen és földben*, pp. 105–107.
105 *HM HIM HL*, documents of 101 Fighter Wing, box nr. 112, Royal Hungarian 102 Honvéd Fighter Group, summary of decorated officers and enlisted men.

around 16:00, he set fire to a Soviet truck and a (staff?) car on the road between Dinnyés and Gárdony.[106]

Hadnagy Málnássy achieved his 11th air victory after after nearly two months, on 13 March 1945. On this morning, at 09:37, his flight was deployed in combat following a scramble north-east of Székesfehérvár, against Il-2s appearing from beneath the cloud base. The Hungarians did not reach the Soviet ground-attack aircraft, but they engaged the enemy fighters, and *hadnagy* Málnássy shot down a Yak-9 at 10:05 north of Káloz, south-southwest of Seregélyes. The air victory was witnessed by *hadnagy* Galambos. At the same time however, he was himself hit by his own anti-aircraft defense, probably a German 2cm four-barreled anti-aircraft gun (*Flakvierling*). The shell exploded in the cockpit and Málnássy suffered a number of minor fragment injuries on the right side of his face; he therefore received the wound clasp for his *Tűzkereszt*. He belly-landed with his damaged aircraft southwest of Székesfehérvár, near the road to Veszprém. His Messerschmitt Bf 109 G-10/U4 (WNr. 610556, manufactured in Wiener Neustadt) suffered 30 percent damage.[107]

While the combat report mentions a Yak-9, Wing Order Nr. 1945/75 (which confirmed the air victory) notes an La-5 for Málnássy, but this was probably a typing error.

He shot down his last enemy aircraft on 20 March 1945, when he took off as part of an eight-aircraft flight at 11:37 for a free hunt and hit an Il-2 over Balatonkenese at 12:00. They lost sight of the seriously damaged aircraft, which was emitting great quantities of smoke, and were therefore unable to determine the exact location of the crash. The kill was witnessed by *zászlós* Bartos, but it was not credited in the Wing Orders issued toward the end of the war, similarly to many other air victories of 101/III Group.[108]

On 22 March 1945, during the evacuation of the Veszprém airfield, and following a tragically misunderstood verbal order (the origin of which cannot be determined), Málnássy took off with three comrades from Kenyeri to Veszprém on the Fw 58 courier aircraft of 101/8 Squadron the K.334, instead of using the much safer ground roads, to evacuate the operational aircraft that were still there. The Weihe took off not long after 12:00 and became an easy target at Kemenesmagasi for the Lightnings of 14th FG's 49th Fighter Squadron strafing ground targets in the area. The large, clumsy and unarmed courier aircraft was shot down by 1st Lieutenant Hochstetler in his P-38; he was in the best position to attack it, and reported shooting down a twin-engined, non-identified type courier aircraft. The first burst fired by the American hit Málnássy in the head; he was piloting the aircraft, and died instantly. The Weihe crash-landed southeast of Kemenesmagasi, engulfed in flames; the other three pilots in the aircraft were wounded. Of them, *hadnagy* László Benárd died of his wounds on 27 March, while *zászlós* Lajos Török and *őrmester* István Kárpáti survived, although seriously wounded.

Hadnagy Ferenc Málnássy was buried by his comrades on 23 March 1945 at Kenyeri, he rests there to this day.[109]

106 *HM HIM HL*, documents of 101 Fighter Wing, box nr. 113, after-action reports and mission logs of 101 Fighter Wing, 22 February 1945.

107 *HM HIM HL*, documents of 101 Fighter Wing, box nr. 110, Wing Order Nr. 1945/52; Bundesarchiv-Militärarchiv RL 2 III/1199/43.

108 *HM HIM HL*, documents of 101 Fighter Wing, box nr. 113, after-action reports and mission logs of 101 Fighter Wing, 20 March 1945.

109 Rábakecskéd, then an independent settlement, has since merged with Kenyeri and now forms part of this village. Kenyeri therefore now has two separate cemeteries. The old Kenyeri cemetery can be

Hadnagy Málnássy inspecting the marks of meeting the enemy in an aircraft in the winter of 1944–45 (it seems that it is a wing of a *Weihe*). Like István Fábián, he wore a red dotted scarf all the time. (From the author's collection)

Hadnagy Málnássy was the most successful pilot of those who graduated on 20 August 1943. The author would also like to emphasize the need to consider the problem of decorations connected with him: at the time of his death, he only had a *Tűzkereszt* and his German decoration. Although he was given a *Magyar Koronás Bronz Érdemérem hadiszalagon a kardokkal*, this decoration never physically reached him; and, although his squadron commander recommended him five times (!) for combat decoration, this had little practical effect. This daredevil fighter pilot never received any more decorations, not even posthumously. His posthumous recommendation was not granted, possibly due to the fact that Málnássy was blamed for the loss of the Weihe: while investigating the circumstances of the crash, 101/III Group, which was thought to have issued the takeoff order, turned out not to have done so.

George Edward Hochstetler, who shot down Málnássy's Weihe, was born in Woodburn, Oregon, on 13 March 1923. He graduated in Salem from the local high school in 1940. After graduation, he attended Willamette University for a short time before answering the call of the air force in 1942. He completed his flight training in February 1944 and at the same was promoted to 2nd Lieutenant. He arrived in Italy and was assigned to 14th FG in the autumn of 1944. He shot down the Weihe on his 43rd combat sortie; this was his only confirmed air victory during the war, although on 17 December 1944 he also damaged an Fw 190. Against ground targets, however, he was very successful, and he was especially good at locomotive busting. Prior to the end of the war, he ended his combat tour with 51 sorties. He remained in the air force after the war and served in the Korean War as an engineering officer and as a pilot. He retired from the air force in 1962 as a Lieutenant Colonel. He did not cut all ties with aviation as a civilian, but later trained commercial pilots. George Hochstetler died on 11 December 2005 in Medford, Oregon, and was laid to rest in the cemetery of Gold Beach Rogue River in Oregon.[110]

found in the middle of the village on Rákóczi Street; the old Rábakecskéd cemetery can be found along the northern perimeter of the village. Ferenc Málnássy is buried in the former cemetery.

110 The author was lucky to find George Hochstetler while he was still alive. According to the family, the letter sent to him by the author about the aircraft he had shot down greatly interested him. Unfortunately, he was not able to reply and died soon after. The biographical data and the photograph of him were given to the author by Hochstetler's family.

George E. Hochstetler as a young 2nd Lieutenant at the beginning of 1944. He was the one who shot down the *Weihe* flown by Ferenc Málnássy. (From the collection of the Hochstetler family)

The grave of *hadnagy* Ferenc Málnássy in the Kenyeri cemetery (photograph of the author, 23 October 2013)

HADNAGY VITÉZ SZAMOSÚJVÁRNÉMETI LÁSZLÓ DÁNIEL

Number of aerial victories: 11 (+1)
Successes against ground targets: n.d.a.
Number of flown combat sorties: 70 (19 against Americans)
Number of hours flown in the air force: 463 hours 40 minutes
Nicknames: *Dani*, *Laci*
Identification number: 3008-22-6584

Decorations

- *Magyar Koronás Ezüst Érdemérem hadiszalagon a kardokkal* (29 January 1945)
- *Magyar Koronás Ezüst Érdemérem hadiszalagon a kardokkal*, second award (25 April 1945)
- *Kormányzói dicsérő elismerés Magyar Koronás Bronz Érdemérme hadiszalagon a kardokkal* (1 November 1944)
- *Tűzkereszt I fokozata a kardokkal és koszorúval*
- German Iron Cross 2nd Class (8 March 1945)

Victories

Number	Date	Aircraft	Location
1	14 June 1944	P-38	Pusztavám SE, Lippa well
–	27 June 1944	P-38	
2	2 July 1944	P-38	Enying (Mezőkomárom NW)
3	30 July 1944	B-24	Nádasdladány
4	30 July 1944	B-24	Nádasdladány
5	22 August 1944	B-24	Csönge
6	8 January 1945, between 10:15 and 11:30	La-5	Székesfehérvár NE
7	9 March 1945 at 13:20	Yak-9	Between Igal and Tab, at Tab
8	11 March 1945 at 11:30	Il-2	Seregélyes–Adony, Sárosd NE
9	16 March 1945 at 15:07	Il-2	Székesfehérvár N 15km, Pátka S
10	20 March 1945 at 15:48	Yak-3	Bakonycsernye S
11	21 March 1945 at 07:45	Yak-9	Várpalota S

Aircraft flown

Bf 109 G-6: V.794 (13 April 1944), V.811 (early summer of 1944), Bf 109 G-6/U4: W-021 (second half of August–beginning of October 1944), W-016 (27 August 1944), Bf 109 G-14/U4: W-183 (27 March 1945), Bf 109 G-10/U4: 'Blue 9' (spring of 1945)

László Dániel was born on 22 November 1922 in Budapest, an only child. The title of *vitéz* was originally awarded to his father, who bore the same name as his son. He was at first a landholder, then a bank clerk; as a reserve officer of 1st Honvéd Hussar Regiment in the First World War on the Eastern Front, he was admitted into the order based on the decorations he had earned through his wartime service and bravery. His son inherited the title from him. The

László Dániel as *HMNRA* student in the summer of 1941, performing a punishment: he is going round the sports airfield at Ferihegy crawling. (From the collection of László Dániel)

family received a title of nobility from Charles III in 1725; the family name was written both as Daniel and Dániel (Daniel was the older spelling). The nobility denomination was not used by the family.[111] László Dániel graduated from high school (*Budapesti Piarista Gimnázium*) in 1941, with good grades. His primary flight training was completed at the *HMNRA BSZKRT* (*Budapest Székesfőváros Közlekedési Részvénytársaság*, Budapest Public Transport Plc.) in the summer of 1941 at Ferihegy.

He was a classmate of István Kálmán and was graduated as *hadnagy* on 6 December 1943, as of 1 September 1943, with rank number 62.[112] Aviation was his childhood dream, and the impulse to choose a professional military career came from the family: many of his ancestors had been military officers (on his mother's side, he was even related to one of the martyr generals of the Hungarian Revolution of 1848 Arisztid Dessewfy, who was executed by the Habsburgs in 1849). In the long term, he had plans to serve as a staff officer, but he was not able to fulfill these kinds of ambitions after the war. The skilled young officer was very interested in technical questions, so he requested to work for the *Repülő Kísérleti Intézet* (*RKI*, Aviation Experimental Institute) and was assigned there to complete a

Karpaszományos őrvezető László Dániel in the spring of 1942 on Szombathely with an aircraft model. (From the collection of László Dániel)

111 Based on Ministry of Interior Certificate Nr. 29045/1932 (copy owned by the author). Today the family, which lives in Chile, uses the spelling Daniel.
112 *Honvédségi Közlöny* (*Személyes ügyek)*, nr. 1943/48 (1 December 1943), p. 1707.

test pilot training course. He had excellent qualifications, and served there from December 1943 to May 1944. His first combat sortie was flown while he was still serving at the *RKI* on 13 April 1944, during which he damaged a B-24.[113]

Hadnagy Dániel was reassigned to Veszprém in 1944 May following the formation of 101 Fighter Group, of which he became the engineering officer of 101/3 Squadron. He achieved his first victory in air combat on 14 June 1944, when he shot down a Lightning of 14th FG's 49th Squadron, credited to him as a shared air victory with *hadnagy* Pál Forró in Air Force Confidential Order Nr. 1944/63. This was the victory for which he received his first *Signum Laudis*.

László Dániel as a student at the *Repülőkadémia*, in 1943. (From the author's collection)

Over the next three weeks, *hadnagy* Dániel reported shooting down two more P-38s: one on 27 June and one on 2 July. In reality, no P-38s were lost on Hungarian territory on those days. His first claim was deleted by Wing Order Nr. 1945/27, but the second Lightning was credited to him at the end of the war by Wing Order Nr. 1945/62, which also confirmed his six air victories against the Soviets in 1945. The endurance of the Lightnings has already been discussed a number of times; often they were able to return to home base with only one operating engine, or having been hit dozens of times.

On 30 July, Dániel was the second element leader in the flight of *hadnagy* Molnár that reported shooting two four-engined aircraft out of formation over Nádasdladány. Some sources only credit one of these victories to his individual record, while others credit him with both. Consequently, some documents of the fighter wing credit Dániel with fewer air victories than are indicated in this work by the author. For more, see the chapter on the description and identification of air victories and the confirmation system in place for them.

On 22 August 1944, *hadnagy* Dániel shot down his 'very own' Liberator: a B-24J (serial number 42-51300) of 451st BG's 726th Squadron flown by 2nd Lieutenant Valerian E. Klein. The four-engined crashed near Csönge, exploding in the air before impact, and three of the crew were killed; another five were captured. The pilot, Valerian Klein, was also killed in the crash; he had already shown outstanding bravery and defiance by bringing back a seriously damaged aircraft and a badly wounded comrade to base following heavy anti-aircraft fire, even though one of his engines in the war over Hungary was not functioning. On this occasion, Klein one of the greatest examples of self-sacrifice that went far beyond personal bravery. After his B-24 had caught fire, he ordered his comrades to leave the aircraft and bail out. After issuing orders, the flight engineer said he could not bail out because his parachute was damaged. Klein then sat back down and tried to crash-land to rescue the comrade he had already saved once before.

113 *HM HIM KI*, document folder nr. 13908; logbook of László Dániel (original owned by the author); recollections of László Dániel in manuscript, entitled *Így kezdődött…*; also based on a letter from László Dániel to the author, 4 May 2004.

Klein paid for this bravery with his life when the aircraft exploded; he and his flight engineer were still on board at the time of the explosion. The third casualty was one of the gunners, who had bailed out but his parachute did not deploy. In a similar case, 1st Lieutenant Donald Dale Pucket of 98th BG was decorated posthumously with the Medal of Honor after he was killed on 9 July 1944 at Ploesti. However, Klein did not receive this decoration.[114]

In October 1944, *hadnagy* Dániel was recommended for his second *Signum Laudis*. The victory of 22 August was included in the recommendation, but the decoration was not granted.

Dániel took part in the last mission in large formations against Americans on 5 November 1944, during which the Mustangs chased him; however because he was the engineering officer in the squadron, his aircraft was the first to have a methanol water injection performance enhancer built in, so he managed to escape and land his damaged aircraft at Tapolca.

Hadnagy Dániel completed 19 combat sorties altogether in 1944 against the Americans; he especially emphasized to the author that combat missions flown against the Americans in vastly superior numbers could not be compared to the later air combats against the Soviets.[115]

Dániel reported his first air victory against the Soviets of 1945 on the morning of 8 January, northeast of Székesfehérvár; the witness was his wingman, *karpaszományos szakaszvezető* Ferenc Szűcs. The formation was on a free hunt and had been in the air between 10:15 and 10:30. As has also been mentioned in Szentgyörgyi's biography, no La-5s crashed that day in air combat over Hungary according to Soviet sources, so the victim of *hadnagy* Dániel must only have been damaged. *Hadnagy* Dániel flew his 50th combat mission at the end of January.[116]

At the beginning of March, *hadnagy* Tibor Tobak, who was wounded on 22 December 1944, returned to service, and the second flight of 101/3 Squadron was formed with *hadnagy* László Dániel as flight leader (with *karpaszományos szakaszvezető* Ferenc Szűcs as his wingman) and *hadnagy* Tibor Tobak as second element leader (with *hadnagy* Gyula Pintér as his wingman). The flight, led by *hadnagy* Dániel, was very successful in the middle of the month; between 9 and 21 March they reported 12

Pilot of the Liberator that was confirmed to *hadnagy* Dániel on 22 August 1944 at Csönge: 2nd Lieutenant Valerian E. Klein, who sacrificed himself for his comrade. (From the collection of the Klein family)

114 NARAMACR 8002; also based on the letter of Morris Barker to the author, 2 February 2005; Barrett Tillman, *Above and Beyond. The Aviation Medals of Honor* (Washington DC: Smithsonian, 2002), pp. 111–114.

115 Letter from László Dániel to the author, 14 November 2002.

116 *HM HIM HL*, box 1122. microfilm, logs of 101/3 Fighter Squadron, logbook of László Dániel.

kills against Soviet aircraft without any losses. Of this number, *hadnagy* Dániel, flying with the 'Blue 9', achieved five confirmed air victories.

Dániel achieved his first air victory of this period on 9 March. He led eight aircraft in combat readiness, which took off at the given rocket signal with a scramble at 13:10 against the Boston formation that had appeared in the area of Berhida with heavy fighter protection. The Soviet formation turned south, but the Hungarian fighters reached them south of Lake Balaton and reported shooting down three aircraft. *Hadnagy* Dániel reported a victory over a Yak-9 at Tab at 13:20; the witness was his wingman, *szakaszvezető* Szűcs; but according to the sources of 288th IAD, which was escorting the Bostons, no total losses were suffered this day.[117]

Two days later, on 11 March, at 10:58, *hadnagy* Dániel led two flights from scramble against a Soviet bomber formation with a heavy fighter escort that was approaching the Veszprém airfield, but the bombers turned away from the town. On seeing this, the Hungarian fighters turned to a free hunt, during which they met six Il-2s between Seregélyes and Adony. In the ensuing air combat, the Hungarian flight shot down two aircraft: one was shot down at 11:30 northeast of Sárosd by *hadnagy* Dániel; the witness to his success was *hadnagy* Gyula Pintér. The other aircraft was shot down by *zászlós* Huszár, who reported his kill at 11:29 southwest of Adony; his witness was *hadnagy* Dániel. The aircraft shot down were probably Sturmoviks of 210th SAP, two of which crash-landed northeast of Szabadegyháza: *mladshiy leytenant* B.M. Pesterov (serial number 10361) and *mladshiy leytenant* V.V. Nikitin (serial number 12010). Both crews were unharmed.[118]

The tail gunner of the Liberator which was confirmed to *hadnagy* Dániel on 22 August 1944 at Csönge, Morris Barker (in the middle), between his two cousins (the first of whom served as a bomber pilot, the other as a fighter pilot in England). This was Barker's sixth combat sortie. (From the collection of Morris Barker)

Hadnagy Dániel reported his fourth air victory against Soviet aircraft on 16 March when he led his flight on a free hunt mission in the airspace north of Székesfehérvár. The four Messerschmitts took off at 14:24 and shot down three Il-2s approximately 15km northeast of Székesfehérvár, near Pátka. *Hadnagy* Dániel's victim was hit at 15:07 in the fuselage by the rounds of the 3cm cannon and blew up in mid-air. The burning wreck crashed south of Pátka, burying the

117 *HM HIM HL*, documents of 101 Fighter Wing, box nr. 113, after-action reports and mission logs of 101 Fighter Wing, 9 March 1945; Horváth, *Bostonok a magyar égen és földben*, p. 155.
118 *HM HIM HL*, documents of 101 Fighter Wing, box nr. 113, after-action reports and mission logs of 101 Fighter Wing, 11 March 1945; Horváth, *Bostonok a magyar égen és földben*, pp. 156–157.

two crew members. The witnesses were *hadnagy* Pintér and *hadnagy* Tobak. The shot-down aircraft was certainly an Il-2 of 951st SAP, possibly the aircraft of 2nd *leytenant* V.I. Gladkiy (two of their Il-2s were destroyed in air combat, and Gladkiy's crashed east of Sárkeresztes).[119]

Hadnagy Gyula Pintér wrote the following about this air combat and Dániel's and his own's kills in his diary:

> The flight took off. Free hunt at Székesfehérvár. The visibility was extremely bad. The sun was blinding in the vapor and the sunshine was piercing as if it had steel tips. We could not see the ground from 6,000 meters, even though there was no cloud, only a 6,000 meter thick vapor blanket. … Remaining together was a huge problem, so I did not know for sure where we were. … We descended slowly. We were at 1,500 meters when at last we noticed, or rather, we sensed the reported Il-2s on a strafing run. Down on the ground, huge billowing pillars of smoke were detected up to approximately 100 meters. The sluggish birds were crawling among these like thieves on the streets of a big city. We dived upon them in an extended echelon. We heard Dani's voice: 'Are you coming after me?' and the two replies: 'Coming after you!' 'Coming after you!' [*karpaszományos szakaszvezető* Ferenc Szűcs, the wingman of *hadnagy* Dániel, had already left the formation, so the fourth aircraft was not present in the air combat.] Among the greyish clouds of smoke, angry little puffs flew past us. Dani's Messer flickered in front of the dim background of the smoke when he opened fire. I saw an Il-2's wing root completely engulfed in flames, the smoke almost glowing red. I said, *Nah, this is completely Dani's style.* … Then we ran into a large billowing smoke screen, and for a few seconds we could not see anything; then, all of a sudden, the smoke ripped apart and an Il was in front of me. I couldn't see Dani or *Cica* [the nickname of *hadnagy* Tibor Tobak; it means 'Kitty']. I could barely see the Il itself, which was trying to hide in the clouds. The armored glass had oil splashed on it, so one needed to fly in traverse mode and to peek sideways to see the Il if it was still there. Actually, it was now in the *Revi*'s crosshair [the short name for the *Reflexvisier*, the gunsight]. Just a small push forward, very fine movements of the hands, and then a short burst. A huge flash in front of me; I pulled up the nose of the aircraft and looked back. Meanwhile, I pushed the button of the cannon repeatedly, because the sound seemed suspiciously short to me. The Il drew thick black lines among the smoke and crashed into the ground with a huge explosion. As it turned out later, only one cannon shell was shot, and the cannon had stuck after that. But that single shell was a hit.[120]

On 20 March, Dániel took off with his flight at 15:29 for a free hunt and engaged Soviet Yak-3s at an altitude of 5,000 meters. *Hadnagy* Dániel reported shooting down an aircraft at 15:48; according to his report, the Soviet Yak had been hit on the fuselage and cockpit by cannon and machine gun rounds. Trailing thick black smoke, it crashed into the ground south of Bakonycsernye; the pilot was not able to bail out (although Soviet sources do not mention any Yak-3 total losses for the day in that particular area). The witness was again *hadnagy* Pintér.[121]

119 *HM HIM HL*, documents of 101 Fighter Wing, box nr. 113, after-action reports and mission logs of 101 Fighter Wing, 16 March 1945; Horváth, *Bostonok a magyar égen és földben*, p. 189.
120 Diary of Gyula Pintér (copy owned by the author).
121 *HM HIM HL*, documents of 101 Fighter Wing, box nr. 113, mission logs of 101 Fighter Wing, 20 March 1945; Horváth, *Bostonok a magyar égen és földben*, p. 188.

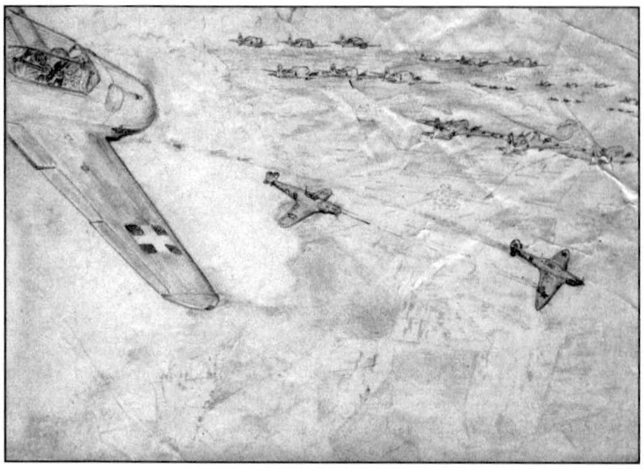

A drawing depicting *hadnagy* Dániel's victory on 9 March 1945, made by one of their comrades in the squadron (drawing by Gyula Pintér)

On 21 March 1945, the Dániel flight, according to their report, shot down three Yak-9s; two pilots bailed out. On this humorous drawing, *hadnagy* Dániel characteristically defends the enemy pilots from the 'bloodthirsty' Messerschmitts and says: 'Don't harm them if they are already hanging [on the parachutes]!' (drawing by Gyula Pintér)

The witness has drawn the air victory of *hadnagy* Dániel against an Il-2 on 16 March 1945. The drawing was made probably on the same day (drawing by Gyula Pintér)

Hadnagy Dániel's last confirmed air victory was achieved in the morning of 21 March 1945, when he was leading an eight-aircraft formation on a free hunt in the area east of Veszprém. The formation took off at 07:20; the flight of *hadnagy* Dániel was the striking flight, and the other four aircraft were flying above and behind to cover them. The Hungarian fighters met three Yak-9s south of Várpalota at an altitude of 5,500 meters, but according to the report they were shot down in seconds by *hadnagy* Dániel's flight at 07:45. One of the air victories was claimed by *hadnagy* Dániel, and the pilot was able to bail out of the plummeting aircraft. The witnesses were *hadnagy* Tobak and *szakaszvezető* Szűcs. Their opponents are not identifiable based on Soviet sources, because there is no sign in available Soviet documents that three aircraft were lost on this date and in this area.[122]

László Dániel flew his last combat sortie in the late afternoon of 3 April 1945 as a formation leader, leading two flights on a strafing run. They destroyed six to eight vehicles and the same number of carts; they also strafed the marching cavalry, although one of the pilots in the formation, *hadnagy* József Gáspárfalvi, was shot down by Soviet anti-aircraft defense. The young pilot crash-landed and was captured.[123]

122 *HM HIM HL*, documents of 101 Fighter Wing, box nr. 113, after-action reports and mission logs of 101 Fighter Wing, 21 March 1945.

123 *HM HIM HL*, documents of 101 Fighter Wing, box nr. 113, after-action reports and mission logs of 101 Fighter Wing, 3 April 1945.

Hadnagy Dániel was reassigned to Pocking on 9 April 1945, to the huge camp of the Hungarian Air Force; he flew no more in combat environment.

His last recommendation for decoration was written in April, for the *Magyar Érdemrend lovagkeresztje hadiszalagon a kardokkal*. Instead of this, he later received the second silver *Signum*. The recommendation describes him as follows: 'With his high number of air victories, he is among the most successful Hungarian fighter pilots. During each and every mission he has stood out with his clever combat tactics, his bold bravery and his heroism.'[124]

The author would like to add something to the clever combat tactics mentioned in the recommendation. *Hadnagy* Gyula Pintér, who was part of Dániel's flight, mentioned to the author a number of times that he felt safe when flying with *hadnagy* Dániel, because the highly intelligent flight leader led his unit very cleverly. Dániel himself mentioned to the author that he was proud of bringing his wingmen and flight members home every single time; he never lost anybody in air combat, neither as element or flight leader. The only time he lost somebody was due to anti-aircraft fire on 3 April 1945, during the above-mentioned event involving *hadnagy* Gáspárfalvi.[125]

László Dániel went into American captivity in Pocking and returned home at the end of September 1945. After the war, from January 1946 to March 1949, he worked as a bank clerk in the National Bank of Hungary. Urged by the ever-worsening political situation, he left the country in March 1949 across the Austrian green borders with the help of a human trafficker.

Dániel arrived in Chile in October 1949 with István Kálmán, and this country became his second, chosen homeland. At first, he worked in electronics, but after managing to enter the Santiago Aviation Club, he became an instructor and then an agricultural pilot. From 1968, he also flew to suppress wildfires; he was the first in Chile to carry out this task regularly. He flew for more than 40 years in his chosen home as an instructor and agricultural pilot. The aircraft type he used most often was a Cessna A188B-300 AGtruck, and he was even able to purchase an older, used, but excellent Cessna 188 for himself (registration code CC-CEQ). As he was flying a lot for the Santiago Aviation Club, he was also able to rent their aircraft at a reduced price, so he was also able to fly his favourite plane, the Beechcraft Bonanza, at weekends.

László Dániel flew 16,422 flight hours altogether in Chile, all with light aircraft, mainly at a low altitude and in very difficult conditions. His last takeoff was in February 2003, three months after his 80th birthday. The veteran pilot concluded his aviation career with around 17,000 flight hours; he had flown the most flight hours among the Hungarian aces if we take into account his whole aviation career. László Dániel currently lives in Chile, and his oldest son is an aviation engineer.

124 *HM HIM HL*, documents of 101 Fighter Wing, box nr. 113, recommendations for decorations.
125 According to the interview with Gyula Pintér, 20 October 2002; letter from László Dániel to the author, 6 May 2002.

Fighter Aces With 5–9 Air Victories

TISZTJELÖLT ŐRMESTER LAJOS BUDAY

Number of aerial victories: 9 (+1)
Successes against ground targets: n.d.a.
Number of flown combat sorties: 40+ (18 against Americans)
Number of hours flown in the air force: n.d.a.
Nicknames: *Lali*, *Lojás*
Identification number: 3001-22-0356

Decorations

- *Magyar Nagy Ezüst Vitézségi Érem* (25 January 1945)
- *Magyar Nagy Ezüst Vitézségi Érem* for the second time (25 April 1945; posthumous)
- *Magyar Kis Ezüst Vitézségi Érem* (13 February 1945)
- *Tűzkereszt I fokozata a kardokkal és koszorúval*
- German Iron Cross 1st Class (April 1945; posthumous)
- German Iron Cross 2nd Class (8 March 1945)

Victories

Number	Date	Aircraft	Location
1	26 June 1944, between 08:30 and 09:45	B-24	Meggyeskovácsi
–	7 August 1944	P-51	Sárvár
2	22 August 1944	B-24	Kemeneshőgyész
3	5 November 1944	B-24	Pusztamagyaród NW
4	17 November 1944	Boston	Solt NE 5km
5	3 January 1945	La-5	Pázmánd (GS 8-9)
6	16 January 1945, between 14:45 and 15:40	Yak-9	Seregélyes (HS-4)
7	19 January 1945	Yak-9	Tolna NW (KS-5)
8	11 March 1945 at 17:32	Il-2	Sárkeresztúr NE
9	11 March 1945 at 17:36	La-5	Sárkeresztúr NE (Adony W)

Aircraft flown

n.d.a.

HMNRA-pupils at Ferihegy, in the summer of 1941. Two of them later became aces: the one on the left, without a helmet, laughing straight at the camera, is András Huszár; on the right is Lajos Buday, with his helmet drawn back on his forehead. (From the author's collection)

Lajos Buday as a fighter school instructor in the summer of 1943, in Kecskemét, with his students who belonged to the officer class to be graduated on 6 December 1943. At the back, from the left to the right: Pál Balogh R., Lajos Buday, Alajos Egry and András Huszár. Pál Bélavári and György Birkhoffer are sitting in the foreground. (From the author's collection)

Lajos Buday – third from right – on the Tapolca airfield with his students belonging to the officer class due to graduate on 6 December 1943. The third from the left is Mihály Karátsonyi, the fourth is Imre Varga (later an acclaimed sculptor, awarded with the Kossuth Prize) and the sixth is László Dániel. In the middle of the squatting row is András Huszár. (From the collection of László Dániel)

Lajos Buday was born on 19 March 1922 in Budapest, the younger boy in a family of working class. As far as the author knows, he attended high school for two years but left school before graduating, probably for financial reasons. His original job was as a mechanic; he started gliding in 1939 and achieved outstanding results, receiving the 56th Hungarian Silver Badge with the international (*ISTUS*) badge nr. 1909. He completed the requirements for the 'D' badge as follows: a flight with a duration of 5 hours and 35 minutes on 19 March 1941; a distance flight of 71km on 5 August 1941; and a flight gain of height 1,385 meters on 22 June 1941.[1]

As a member of the primary flight training enlisted class of 1941, he received his primary flight training at Ferihegy in 1941 at the *HMNRA* and entered service at the *Regvi* at the end of the year. He was promoted to military pilot at the end of 1942. His skills were exceptionally outstanding; by the spring of 1943, he was already an instructor at the Tapolca airfield of the Fighter Combat Training Group. From here, he was later reassigned to Kolozsvár.

According to family data, he was at the front from 1 November to 31 December 1943 (although he was not sent into combat), before being redeployed to his original unit. He arrived at Veszprém in the early summer of 1944 and officially transferred to 101/1 Fighter Squadron as of 10 June 1944; he served with this unit until he was killed. Throughout all the reassignments and redeployments, his friend and classmate, Pál László Szikora, remained with him.

According to his fragmentary notes, he probably completed his first training takeoffs on 17 June 1944 at the group with a Bf 109 G, and his first combat sortie was completed on 26 June 1944 between 08:30 and 09:45. During this mission, he scored his first confirmed air victory over the northwestern part of the Transdanubia, picking a four-engined out of a big Liberator formation. The victory was confirmed to him with the location of Balozsameggyes (Air Force Confidential Order Nr. 1944/63 mentions the same village, which is today part of Meggyeskovácsi). According to the report of the *Magyar Királyi Államéptészeti Hivatal* (Royal Hungarian Bureau of Architecture) on 26 June, 'An enemy English [sic!] four-engined aircraft crashed near the village of Balozsameggyes. Of the 11 member crew, one was killed, nine were captured, and one is in hiding.'[2] This aircraft was a B-24J (serial number 42-99762) from 98th BG's 343rd Squadron flown by 1st Lieutenant David A. Himes. Of the 11 crew members, two were killed, one being the nose gunner who died in the crash – Staff Sergeant Nicholas Z. Kish, who was of Hungarian descent.[3]

On 7 August, Buday took part in the mission that ended tragically for the Hungarian fighters. He was not shot down, however, but reported shooting down a Mustang. This claim was nevertheless not confirmed; half a year later, Wing Order Nr. 1945/27 deleted it entirely, probably as he had targeted the same aircraft as *hadnagy* Málik.

1 *Magyar Szárnyak*, 15 March 1942, p. 28; see also Imre Mitter (ed.), *A Magyar vitorlázórepülés képes története 1929–1999* (Budapest: 3,14 L Kft., 1999), p. 231. According to Mitter, Buday was not the 56th but the 58th Hungarian holder of the Silver Badge. Buday has a personal document folder in the HM HIM Central Record Office (nr. 516/616), but this was created after the war and contains nothing apart from a request from his late widow.

2 *MNL Vas Megye Levéltára* (National Archives, Vas County Archives), M. *Kir. Államéptészeti Hivatal*, Szombathely. *Ellenséges berepülés alkalmával történt eseményekről jelentés. Jelentés az 1944 június 26-ai berepülésről*, Point 2; also based on the notes of Lajos Buday (copy owned by the author).

3 NARA MACR 6446, also based on the documents preserved by the cousin of Kish (Frederick M. Clepper). The parents of Kish emigrated from Gáva (today part of Gávavencsellő) to the United States.

On 22 August 1944, he managed to shoot down another Liberator: this was the 100th claimed air victory of the 'Puma' Group against the Americans. According to the victory registry of four-engines, one of his Liberators was a shared kill with a German pilot; in the author's opinion, the 22 August 1944 victory was it – perhaps an Fw 190 pilot from II./JG 300 or IV./JG 3 was the other attacker. The location of this kill was recorded in his personal notes; as mentioned earlier, the order confirming this day's air victories was lost and the content is only known in part. Buday's victim was the Liberator (B-24G, serial number 42-78445) flown by 2nd Lieutenant Alfred M. Donelson from 451st BG's 724th Squadron; the aircraft exploded in mid-air and crashed west of Kemeneshőgyész, 2km southwest of Magyargencs. Of the 11-member crew, only the bombardier survived. On the same day, another Liberator crashed near Magyargencs; altogether 17 crew members were killed from the two aircraft and registered and buried in the village.

The burning wreck of the B-24J (serial number 42-99762) belonging to 98th BG's 343rd Squadron crashed east of Balozsameggyes on 26 June 1944. The kill was confirmed to Lajos Buday (Photographic Archives of the *Nádasdy Ferenc Múzeum*)

Buday's comrades presented him with an engraved silver cigarette case on the occasion of the jubilee. Six days later, on 28 August, Sándor Budinszky, a reporter for the Hungarian radio, interviewed Lajos Buday on the occasion of this 100th air victory.

Buday's third (and last) four-engined kill was reported on 5 November 1944 in the airspace of Zala county. Wing Order Nr. 1945/62 confirmed the victory to him with a location northwest of Pusztamagyaród. The same Wing Order also confirmed his six air victories against Soviet aircraft.

Szakaszvezető Buday completed 18 combat sorties altogether against the Americans in 1944; because of his three confirmed air victories against Liberators, he became the most successful enlisted '*Viermot-töter*', or 'four-engined killer', among the Pumas.

He reported shooting down his first Soviet aircraft on 17 November 1944 when he claimed a Boston bomber 5km northeast of Solt. The witness was *zászlós* Lajos Buzogány. However, apart from the Boston described in detail in the biography of Pottyondy, there were no other total Boston losses in air combat on the Soviet side that day. Buday ended 1944 with four confirmed air victories.

Buday was very successful in January 1945: he shot down three confirmed Soviet aircraft. On 16 January, he reported a victory over a Yak-9 in the afternoon, probably the Yak-3 with serial number 3918 belonging to 659th IAP and flown by *starshiy leytenant* M.A. Fisenko, who was killed. The Soviet aircraft crashed in the area of Perkáta, approximately 15km southeast of the reported Seregélyes area. The 24-year-old *starshiy leytenant* Mikhail Alexandrovich Fisenko was a flight leader and a successful pilot who achieved four individual and three shared air victories prior to his death. The witnesses to Buday's kill were his wingman *szakaszvezető* Nagy, furthermore, *hadnagy* Szőcs and *őrmester* Domján from 101/3 Squadron, as the two squadrons

'Toddlin Trollop' was the nickname of the Liberator (451st BG, B-24G, serial number 42-78445), which became the 100th registered air victory of 101 Fighter Group against Americans. The victory was confirmed to Lajos Buday, the four-engined crashed west of Kemeneshőgyész. (From the collection of Damon Notestone)

Szakaszvezető Lajos Buday in the autumn of 1944 at Veszprém-Jutas. He was greatly skilled but humble; he was a man loved by his comrades and all who knew him. (From the author's collection)

deployed one element each on a free hunt between 14:45 and 15:40 on that day. In the Soviet loss report, six Yak-3s were reported as having been engaged in air combat with eight Bf 109s at 14:10 Hungarian time, of which they shot down three; they themselves lost Fisenko. However, there were no German–Hungarian Bf 109 losses in the area, and no other kill against Yakovlevs was reported, either by Hungarian or German pilots. The time of the air combat was probably mistyped in the Soviet report, and it was probably 15:10.[4]

Buday's next air victory over Tolna county on 19 January was witnessed by *hadnagy*s Michna, Cserny and Benkő from his squadron, with whom he was flying on the mission (*hadnagy* Michna also reported shooting down a Yak). These two Yak kills were probably over the Yak-9 of *kapitan* M.J. Zhivayev from the staff of 288th IAD, who was captured on a mission in the area of Sárbogárd; and the reconnaissance Yak-9D with serial number 17166088 of 39th ORAP, whose pilot reported that four Bf 109s attacked him during his return from a reconnaissance mission to Őcsény. The aircraft was flown by 2nd *leytenant* N.N. Ribakov; it was hit 35 times and severely damaged, and thus written off after landing (the pilot was unharmed). As a four-aircraft flight was deployed here and because no other air victories were claimed in the area (north of Őcsény), these two Soviet aircraft must have been the victims of the Hungarian fighters.[5]

Following his successes in air combat, Buday became a flight leader as early as the spring of 1945. In most cases, however, he flew as second element leader in the flight of *hadnagy* Miklós Cserny, and his wingman was always his classmate, *szakaszvezető* József Nagy.

4 *HM HIM HL*, box 1122 microfilm, logs of 101/3 Fighter Squadron; Bikhov, *Sovetskie Asy 1941–1945*, p. 601; Horváth, *Bostonok a magyar égen és földben*, p. 83; Gábor Horváth on documents of TsAMO.

5 Based on the original notes of Lajos Buday (copies owned by the author); Horváth, *Bostonok a magyar égen és földben*, p. 263; Gábor Horváth on documents of TsAMO.

The victim of Lajos Buday on 16 January 1945 was *starshiy leytenant* Mikhail Alexandrovich Fisenko, flight leader of 659th IAP, third from right in this group photograph (Holostyak via Horváth)

As of 1 March 1945, Buday was promoted to *őrmester* out of turn im recognition of his outstanding combat achievements. On 12 March, his request to join the officer training course was granted; like István Fábián, therefore, he was also entitled to wear the officer candidate badge.[6]

Buday's last confirmed air victories were achieved on 11 March, late in the afternoon, when four aircraft led by *hadnagy* Miklós Cserny took off at 16:50 on a free hunt over the area south of Lake Velence. The flight engaged six Yak-9s, two La-5s and four Il-2s northeast of Sárkeresztúr. As the second element leader, Buday shot down a ground-attack aircraft at 17:32, then a Lavochkin four minutes later, which wanted to enter the combat. In both cases, the witness to the air victories was *szakaszvezető* József Nagy.[7]

Lajos Buday's fate was sealed on 17 March 1945. In the afternoon of this day, at 15:43, the flight of *hadnagy* Miklós

in Veszprém, when he received his first Hungarian Great Silver Medal for Bravery. (From the collection of Sándor Sáth)

6 *HM HIM HL*, documents of 101 Fighter Wing, box nr. 112, Wing Order Nr. 1945/47.

7 *HM HIM HL*, documents of 101 Fighter Wing, box nr. 113, mission logs of 101 Fighter Wing, 11 March 1945.

Cserny took off on a free hunt to engage some Il-2s reported east of Veszprém. Buday was flying with a reserve aircraft on this mission, and perhaps not everything was in proper condition on the aircraft. According to both the mission log and the combat report, 10 minutes after takeoff the flight was climbing between Csór and Iszkaszentgyörgy when eight La-7s attacked them from the direction of the sun with great altitude advantage. Cserny was late in taking off and reached his flight later; he was also shot down, but able to bail out. He was, however, so badly wounded that he lost one of his legs. The fourth aircraft in the flight under *szakaszvezető* Faludi was also damaged when it returned to Veszprém. The aircraft ('Red 2') of Buday's wingman, *szakaszvezető* József Nagy, was severely damaged by 14 hits, although he was able to fly back to Veszprém; the Soviet aircraft then targeted Buday. Buday's aircraft was severely damaged; he bailed out at Úrhida, but the Soviet fighter behind him continued firing and Buday was hit in the neck and died instantly, fell to the ground at high speed. According to one recollection, he managed to open his parachute, but it was shot to pieces by the attacking fighter. It is nevertheless certain that he died in mid-air due to the neck wound. Although the reports mention La-7s (precisely eight of them, which suggests they had been counted), the memories of the survivors are ambivalent. The Hungarian pilots were not merely unable to count their opponents, but were also unsure about their type. On the Soviet side, only one victory claim was made by a Lavochkin, although unfortunately the date and time did not survive. This sole claim was reported by *starshiy leytenant* Viktor Fedorovich Bersenev in an La-5 from 848th IAP, who was leading a six-aircraft flight on the day and reported shooting down a Bf 109 northwest of Székesfehérvár (1km south of Moha).

This was *starshiy leytenant* Bersenev's third (and last) confirmed air victory during the Second World War; all three of his victims were Bf 109s. However, because not a loan aircraft was attacked on this occasion and some air victory claims on the Soviet side were exact matches in terms of date and location, it seems certain that the Hungarian flight was attacked by Yak-3s of 866th IAP, which reported shooting down five Bf 109s southwest of Székesfehérvár. Of these, four were shot down around 15:30; three were hit by *kapitan* Koldunov, and one by *leytenant* Bogdanov. The fifth was shot down at 15:55, reported by *kapitan* Panin – this may have been the aircraft of *hadnagy* Cserny.

Based on this, Buday was probably the victim of Alexander Ivanovich Koldunov, who was one of the most outstanding fighter pilots of the Soviet Air Force during the Second World War.

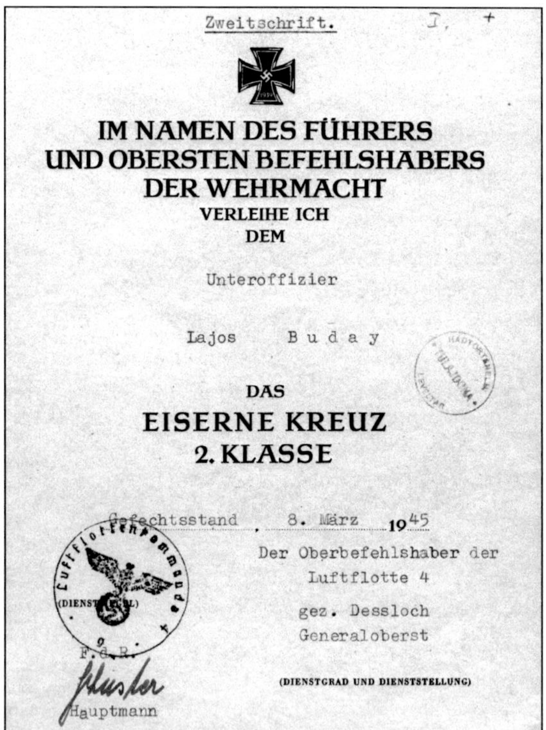

Zweitschrift.

IM NAMEN DES FÜHRERS
UND OBERSTEN BEFEHLSHABERS
DER WEHRMACHT
VERLEIHE ICH
DEM

Unteroffizier

Lajos Buday

DAS
EISERNE KREUZ
2. KLASSE

Gefechtsstand, 8. März 1945

Der Oberbefehlshaber der
Luftflotte 4

gez. Dessloch
Generaloberst

(DIENSTGRAD UND DIENSTSTELLUNG)

F.d.R.
Hauptmann

Awarding document of Lajos Buday's German Iron Cross 2nd Class (*HM HIM* Military Archives)

He was born on 20 September 1923 in Moshchinovo in the Smolensk area. He finished his pilot training in the summer of 1943; as of June the same year, he was already a pilot in 866th IAP, and remained there until the end of the war. He completed 412 combat sorties, during which he was engaged in 95 air combats, achieving 46 individual and one shared air victories. He was decorated twice with the Golden Star of the Hero of the Soviet Union, three Lenin Orders, six Orders of the Red Star, one Alexander Nevsky Order, two 1st Classes of the Order of the Patriotic War and one Order of the Red Banner. He achieved the largest number of air victories on the Soviet side over Hungary in 1944–45 (24), considering the contemporary borders. He remained in service after the war and had an exceptionally bright career; at its height he was commander in chief of the Soviet Air Force from 1978 to 1987, as an air marshal. He retired from this position after the memorable event when Mathias Rust landed in Moscow with a Cessna-172. Koldunov died in Moscow on 7 June 1992.

Lajos Buday probably became the victim of Alexander Ivanovich Koldunov, the most successful Soviet fighter pilot in the air war over Hungary in 1944-45. Koldunov received two Hero of the Soviet Union titles and led an outstanding career after the war. This is a photo of him as *general mayor*. (From the collection of Dmitry Hazanov)

One other Soviet pilot who also reported a victory against a Bf 109 during the air combat of 17 March was *kapitan* Ivan Fedorovich Panin, another ace: he achieved 12 air victories during the war, and this was his ninth. In 1945, he scored six kills over Hungary.[8]

Lajos Buday was the last 'Puma' pilot to be buried in Veszprém, on 21 March 1945. His funeral, however, led to another tragedy. During the funeral service, the area of the cemetery was bombed by soviet aircraft, and one of the ground crew of the wing in attendance, *tizedes* Lajos Kabai, was killed when he was struck by a bomb fragment.[9] Buday's coffin was hit directly by a bomb and was practically eliminated; there was nothing left of him to bury, so in reality he did not have a registered grave.

His second, posthumous recommendation for the *Magyar Nagy Ezüst Vitézségi Érem* described him as follows: '*Őrm.* Lajos Budai stood out among his comrades in all of his combat sorties with his boldness and bravery.'[10]

Although in this and a few other documents his name is spelled with an 'i', in reality, he always spelled his name with a 'y' – that is, as *Buday*.

8 *HM HIM HL*, documents of 101 Fighter Wing, box nr. 113, after-action reports and mission logs of 101 Fighter Wing, 17 March 1945; notes of József Nagy and Károly Faludi in manuscript (original and copies owned by the author); the interview of Miklós Cserny (1921–2007) by the author, 6 February 2004. For the Soviet pilots, see also Bikhov, *Sovetskie Asy 1941–1945*, p. 244 (Koldunov), p. 389 (Panin); Nikita Yegorov on documents of TsAMO.

9 *HM HIM HL*, documents of 101 Fighter Wing, box nr. 113, list of personnel killed in action.

10 *HM HIM HL*, documents of 101 Fighter Wing, box nr. 113, recommendations for decoration.

He was a humble, quiet and valued man who was well loved by all his comrades. He was the most successful pilot in the Second World War among the enlisted pilots, having completed their primary flight training in 1941. Apart from the air victories mentioned above, the brother of his widow remembers that Buday still had one or two air victory claims, but no details of them have survived. Allegedly, he also shot down a Soviet pilot during his last air combat, but there were no witnesses and the claim was not even submitted.[11]

Lajos Buday had married shortly before his tragic death, on 20 November 1944, but he and his wife did not have much time together. His widow died in 2004; as a heart-warming example of love beyond the grave, she requested that photographs of Lajos Buday be placed in the coffin with her.

ŐRMESTER VITÉZ PÁL KOVÁCS

Number of aerial victories: 8 (+1)
Successes against ground targets: n.d.a.
Number of flown combat sorties: approximately 115
Number of hours flown in the air force: n.d.a.
Nickname: *Paja*
Identification number: 0338-19-0208

Decorations

- *Magyar Nagy Ezüst Vitézségi Érem* (16 September 1943)
- *Magyar Nagy Ezüst Vitézségi Érem* for the second time (18 December 1944; posthumous)
- *Magyar Bronz Vitézségi Érem* (18 November 1943)
- *Magyar Bronz Vitézségi Érem* for the second time (13 February 1945; posthumous)
- *Tűzkereszt I fokozata a kardokkal és koszorúval*
- *Erdélyi Emlékérem*
- *Délvidéki Emlékérem*
- German Iron Cross 2nd Class (1943)
- Italian Pilot Badge (1939)

Victories

Number	Date	Aircraft	Location
1	5 July 1943	Soviet single-engine (La-5/Il-2)	Kharkiv
2	5 July 1943	Soviet single-engine (La-5/Il-2)	Kharkiv
3	Summer 1943	Soviet aircraft (Yak-1?)	
4	Summer 1943	Soviet aircraft	
5	1943–44	Soviet aircraft	
6	16 June 1944	P-38	Kereki NE, Gyugypuszta
–	30 June 1944	P-38	
7	30 July 1944	B-24	Nádasdladány
8	30 July 1944	B-24	Nádasdladány

11 As far as the author knows, the family of Lajos Buday has died out. The brother of his widow was of great help to the author during his research into Buday's life.

Aircraft flown

Re.2000: V.435 (5 January, 14 January 1943), Bf 109 F-4: V.041 (5 July 1943), Bf 109 G-6/U4: W-030 (22 August 1944)

Pál Kovács was born on 22 June 1919 in Gyula to a farmer family, the last, ninth child and fifth son of his aging parents.[12] With his height of 159cm, he was one of the shortest Hungarian aces. After his family exchanged their lands for a property that was (unknown to them) mortgaged, they lost everything and moved to Budapest in 1937. Although aviation was always a childhood dream for Pál Kovács, after attending elementary and state civic schools in Gyula, he attended a commercial school. The possibility of leaving this circle of life came with the announcement of the DRT, to which he applied as a Budapest resident, and he received his pilot training in Italy between October 1938 and the late autumn of 1939. After he returned from Italy as one of the first – and best – students, he was promoted to *őrvezető* as of 1 December 1939.[13]

Following this, he was assigned to 2/1 Fighter Squadron and stationed in Nyíregyháza. He was promoted to *tizedes* as of 1 May 1940, then to *szakaszvezető* as of 1 December. In May 1941, he was assigned to *Héja* retraining in Veszprém. Due to the reorganization of the Royal Hungarian Air Force and the disbandment of the Fighter Group in Nyíregyháza, Kovács was assigned to Mátyásföld and 5/2 Fighter Squadron as of 31 October 1941.[14] He was deployed to the Eastern Front in December 1942 with the squadron.

In January 1943, he flew two *Héja* combat sorties with the V.435 aircraft. The first was on 5 January in the morning between 07:30 and 08:30 – a late order and thus an unsuccessful scramble to counter a four-engined Soviet TB-3. As the aircraft could no longer be found, he and his element leader, *hadnagy* Szalay, went on an uneventful free hunt. His second sortie, on 14 January between 13:05 and 13:50 in the area of Ostrogozhsk, was a protective and reconnaissance mission with *százados* Gyula Horváth and *szakaszvezető* János Mátyás.[15]

In the spring of 1943, he and his squadron were retrained to Bf 109 in Uman, and he completed his first Messerschmitt combat sortie at the end of April 1943. Kovács flew most of his missions on the Eastern Front as a wingman to György Debrődy.

He scored his first two confirmed air victories at the beginning of the battle of Kursk, at dawn on 5 July near Kharkhiv. There are no surviving documents or notes from which we might gain information regarding the types of the two aircraft he shot down; they are usually referred to as Il-2s, but there is no evidence to confirm this. His victims could equally have been La-5s from the 295th IAD, with whom his element leader, *hadnagy* Debrődy, was also engaged in combat.

12 His father was 47 and his mother was 41 when he was born. In the military records and registers (personal document folder nr. 140105, other documents), the date of birth of Pál Kovács is incorrect (20 June 1919), and his mother's name is stated as Julianna Csőke. In the state birth certificate, his mother's name is Julianna Szabó. For this, see also *MNL Békés Megye Levéltára* (National Archives, Békés County Archives), XXXIII/1, state birth registry of the town of Gyula for 1919, counterpart, acc. nr. note 208. The mystery around the name of his mother was cleared up with the help of the family: Csőke was the name of his mother's stepfather, and he asked her to use the name, although this was unofficial.

13 *HM HIM KI*, document folder nr. 140105.

14 *HM HIM KI*, document folder nr. 140105.

15 *HM HIM HL*, documents of the 2nd Army, box nr. 17, after-action report of 5/I Fighter Group, attachments 10 and 26 (mission reports).

A group of pilots in front of the V-12 Messerschmitt Bf 109 F-4 at the beginning of 1943. The first on the right is Pál Kovács; the fourth is János Mátyás. (From the collection of János Mátyás)

This unit lost a number of aircraft during the morning mission, and there were no German air victory claims for such types from the given area and in the given time frame.

Kovács achieved two more kills before the end of September, by which time he had four confirmed air victories. He may even have scored another victory or two on 6 July, because there were a few air victories for 5/2 Squadron for this day scored by an unknown pilot. Given the processing time already for decorations, this would explain why Kovács received the *Magyar Nagy Ezüst Vitézségi Érem* on 16 September.

Kovács was promoted to *őrmester* at the end of summer or early autumn; sometime during the winter, he managed to shoot down another Soviet aircraft, although on 29 October he was still registered as having four confirmed air victories.[16]

He returned home from the front at the beginning of 1944, having completed 98 combat sorties and achieved five confirmed air victories.[17]

In May 1944, he was transferred with his squadron from Mátyásföld to Veszprém; from this time on he flew in the 101/3 Fighter Squadron, led by *főhadnagy* József Bejczy.

His first American air victory was scored during the large air combat of 16 June 1944, when he shot down a Lightning of 1st FG over Gyugypuszta near Balatonkereki (Kereki). *Őrmester* Kovács reported shooting down another P-38 on 30 June, but this aircraft was not credited to him; eight months later, Wing Order Nr. 1945/27 deleted the claim.[18]

On 30 July, he was with László Molnár when the flight attacked the American Liberators head on and reported shooting two aircraft out of formation. These were his last successes. It is interesting to note that one of the unit documents credits him with nine air victories; in at least one case, therefore, Kovács's 30 June claim of the Lightning was added to his number of confirmed air victories.

He took off on his last mission on 22 August 1944. During the engagement with the Americans, his aircraft was hit. The brand new Bf 109 G-6/U4 of *őrmester* Pál Kovács, manufactured in Győr, with the markings W-030, crashed to the ground at 13:15 near Kiskomárom

16 *Üvölt a Puma*, 3 November 1943, p. 1.
17 *HM HIM HL*, documents of 101 Fighter Wing, box nr. 112, Royal Hungarian 102 Honvéd Fighter Group, summary of decorated officers and enlisted.
18 *HM HIM HL*, documents of 101 Fighter Wing, box nr. 110, Air Force Confidential Order Nr. 1944/63 and Wing Order Nr. 1945/27.

Altábornagy Sándor Magyarosy (1891–1972), commander of the Royal Hungarian Air Force, congratulates *őrmester* Pál Kovács on the Eastern Front, probably in the second half of August 1943. In the picture there are successful fighter pilots: in the row from left to right: *főhadnagy* Elemér Kálmán (after achieving four air victories he was killed after an anti-aircraft artillery hit on 4 December 1943), *hadnagy* György Pávay-Vajna (three air victories), *hadnagy* György Debrődy, *zászlós* Sándor Hautzinger, *őrmester* Pál Kovács and *törzsőrmester* Dezső Szentgyörgyi. (From the author's collection)

The funeral of Pál Kovács in the New Public Cemetery of Budapest (Rákoskeresztúr). (From the collection of the Kovács family)

Őrmester Pál Kovács in the early summer of 1944. (From the collection of the Kovács family)

(today part of Zalakomár); the *őrmester* was killed. According to the recollection of one of his squadron comrades decades after the war, Pál Kovács was shot down by the gunners of the Liberators he had attacked and crashed while still in his aircraft, but this memory is certainly inaccurate. According to the squadron log, Kovács was shot down by Mustangs; according to his relatives, he bailed out, but his opponents shot him while descending on his parachute. According to family memories, civilians on the ground rushed toward the pilot as he came down; when they reached him, he lifted one of his hands for a few seconds, but died almost instantly from his grave injuries.[19]

Unfortunately, no information can be found about the crash, either in the *MNL Zala Megyei Levéltára* (National Archives, Zala County Archives) or in the *Historia Domus* (the history of the local parish at Kiskomárom). The author was therefore unable to uncover any further data to explain the circumstances of the shooting down of the aircraft more accurately, or to add any more details to the event. Pál Kovács almost certainly became the victim of one of the pilots of 325th FG's 317th Fighter Squadron, which reported shooting down four Bf 109s around 13:30 to 13:45 in the Balaton area and to the south-southwest from it. Of these pilots, the claim of 2nd Lieutenant Elvador E. Ritter is the only one that reports that the pilot of the shot-down Messerschmitt did not bail out. The other three pilots (1st Lieutenant Barrie S. Davis, 1st Lieutenant Walter R. Hinton and Flight Officer Richard A. Troutt) mention the pilot of the aircraft they shot down bailing out and leaving the aircraft in their combat claim forms.[20] It is today impossible to determine which of these successful pilots – or even which of their wingmen – shot down Pál Kovács.

Kovács had already requested his admission into the *Vitézi Rend* Order in 1944 based on his own merits; his actual admission must have happened shortly before his death.

In autumn, the 11 members of the German liaison staff working at 101 Fighter Wing collected 1,100 *pengő*s (Hungarian money between 1 January 1927 and 31 July 1946) as an expression of comradeship and solidarity, and sent it to the wing commander to distribute among the most deserving relatives and families of the fallen pilots. The money was halved, and 550 *pengő*s were given to the family of Pál Kovács. The other half of the money was given to the relatives of *szakaszvezető* Ernő Horváth, who was killed on 1 November 1944.[21]

Pál Kovács was buried in Budapest, in the *Új Köztemető*, on 27 August 1944 (grave nr. 32/I-10-24). This was not a military grave, but the next plot in line. The plot was made available for repurchase in 1981; unfortunately, no action was taken, although there was no exhumation until 1984. After this, the plot was sold to bury a newly deceased person.[22]

19 *HM HIM HL*, 638.052/22 v. 1944, box 1122 microfilm, logs of 101/3 Fighter Squadron; Tobak, *Pumák földön-égen*, p. 137.

20 Davis was an ace with six air victories, who achieved his fifth and sixth victories on this day; of his kills, four were achieved in Hungarian airspace. For Barrie Davis (Lenoir County, 22 December 1923–Zebulon, 19 August 2014), see Olynyk, *Stars and Bars*, p. 223. I have also asked Barrie Davies while he was still with us about his memories regarding this dogfight, but he was not able to provide any further details or information in connection with that day. The detailed circumstances of the death of Pál Kovács were only disclosed to the author after the death of Barrie Davis, so he did not ask the pilot about this; but the author does not think it impossible, based on the personality of Davis, that he was the one who shot down Kovács while he was descending on his parachute.

21 *HM HIM HL*, documents of 101 Fighter Wing, box nr. 110, Wing Order Nr. 1944/45.

22 The author wishes to express his gratitude to the *Budapesti Temetkezési Intézet Zrt.* (Budapest Funeral Company) for their kind help in clarifying the data regarding the grave.

ALEZREDES NEMES BELÉNYESI ALADÁR HEPPES

Number of aerial victories: 8
Successes against ground targets: a locomotive + ?
Number of flown combat sorties: 33 (9 against Americans)
Number of hours flown in the air force: 1,364
Nicknames: *Ali*, *Öreg Puma*
Identification number: n.d.a.

Decorations

- *Magyar Érdemrend tisztikeresztje hadidíszítménnyel és kardokkal* (1 November 1944)
- *Magyar Érdemrend lovagkeresztje hadiszalagon a kardokkal* (20 September 1943)
- *Kormányzói dicsérő elismerés Magyar Koronás Bronz Érdemérme hadiszalagon a kardokkal* (20 May 1943)
- *Kormányzói dicsérő elismerés Magyar Koronás Bronz Érdemérme* (2 July 1939)
- *Tűzkereszt I fokozata a kardokkal és koszorúval*
- *Felvidéki Emlékérem*
- *Erdélyi Emlékérem*
- *Délvidéki Emlékérem*
- German Iron Cross 1st Class (3 September 1944)
- German Iron Cross 2nd Class (5 February 1943)
- Bronze *Frontflugspange* (20 April 1945)
- Croatian Pilot Badge (1942)

Victories

Number	Date	Aircraft	Location
1	30 May 1943	Yak-1	Kupiansk N
2	30 May 1943	Yak-1	Kupiansk N
3	6 July 1943	Il-2	Between Volchansk and Belgorod
4	3 August 1943	Yak-1	Belgorod NW
5	26 June 1944 at 09:25	B-24	Nagyacsád
6	26 June 1944	B-24	Mosonszolnok
7	2 July 1944	B-24	Pusztaszabolcs W
8	7 July 1944	B-24	Hajmáskér

Aircraft flown

Re.2000: V.435 (15 January 1943), Bf 109 F-4: V.039 (30 May 1943)

Aladár Heppes was born in Arad on 20 November 1904. His father (of the same name) was a county chief notary. The nobility and the 'Belényesi' forename was granted in 1911 from Franz Joseph I to the paternal grandfather, Miklós Heppes, upon his retirement as council chairman of the court of appeal; the Heppes family actively used their noble forename.[23] During the First World War, the father of Aladár Heppes was a reserve *főhadnagy* of the 2nd Hussar Regiment, and was killed in Galicia near Zavonie on 26 July 1915 in Russian artillery fire. Thereafter, the 12-year-old Aladár and his brother, Miklós, who was three years older[24] (and who also became a pilot), went to military school as war orphans. As he could only start in the first year, Aladár lost two years of school and graduated at the *Akadémia* at the age of 24.

Aladár Heppes in 1917, as a student at the military cadet school. (From the collection of the Heppes family)

His high school studies were completed at various elementary- and secondary-level cadet schools (*al–és főreáliskola*). He was always the best in his class, and he was also the best in his class at the Ludovika between 1924 and 1928. In the final two years, he was also the chairman of the *LASE* (*Ludovika Akadémia Sport Egylet*, Ludovika Academy Sports Club). He was a successful athlete, especially in the high jump and 400m hurdles, and he won a national college championship in the high jump.[25] On 20 August 1928, he was the first in his class to graduate as *tüzér* (artillery) *főhadnagy* in Budapest. István Fejes, one of the most successful Hungarian figher aces of the First World War, took him first to fly with a Hansa-Brandenburg C.I at Székesfehérvár.

He completed his primary, basic and advanced flight training at the *Regvi* in 1928–29, and received the golden eagle in 1929. After this, he served in Budapest for a year as the commander of the engineer training squadron of the air force. As of 1 November 1931, he was assigned to Kaposvár as deputy commander of III Short-Range Reconnaissance Squadron, which was formed there and equipped with Fokker C.V.Ds. He was also briefly occupied with glider aircraft from 1930, first at the Farkashegy in the *Movero* association, then at Kaposvár in the *Sacero* sports aviation club. In August 1935, he took part in the fighter training at Szombathely with CR.20s; soon after, as of 1 October, he was reassigned from Kaposvár to Székesfehérvár and to 1/3 Fighter Squadron, which had just been formed. He was retrained to CR.32 in 1936 with the arrival of the new aircraft. Heppes designed and drew the 'Puma' badge of 1/3 Fighter Squadron; the motto of the squadron, – '*Vezérünk a bátorság, kísérőnk a szerencse*' ('Courage is our leader, luck our escort') – originated from the squadron commander, Mihály Nagy. The squadron was transferred from Székesfehérvár to Veszprém in 1937; from

23 *Budapesti Közlöny*, 10 February 1911, p. 1.
24 For Miklós Heppes (Arad, 4 December 1901–Wilderswil, 27 April 1962), see Csaba B. Stenge, 'Vitéz nemes belényesi Heppes Miklós repülő-alezredes', *Magyar Repüléstörténeti Társaság Évkönyve*, 2012, pp. 79–84.
25 Árpád Platthy, 'Repülő sportolók', *Magyar Szárnyak Évkönyv*, 1981, p. 77.

the end of 1938, *főhadnagy* Aladár Heppes took over the position of squadron commander from *százados* Mihály Nagy, who left the unit.[26] In March 1939, during the retaking of *Kárpátalja* (the traditional Hungarian name for the region of Zakarpattia Oblast), he has relocated with the squadron to Ungvár (today Uzhhorod, Ukraine), and then to the auxiliary airfield of Csap (today Chop, Ukraine); but here, as the airfield was in the floodplain of the Latorca and Tisza Rivers, his aircraft got bogged down in the mud and the glory of the victory over the Slovak aircraft on 24 March went to 1/1 *'Íjász'* Squadron led by *főhadnagy* Béla Csekme. The time of the Pumas had not yet come.

Because of the leadership skills he had shown during the deployment, he was awarded the first *Signum*, but this was not yet given to him on war ribbons (*'hadiszalag'*).[27] Heppes was promoted to *százados* as of 1 May 1939; thereafter, he was also the adjutant of the 1/I Fighter Group, then worked as an organization and mobilization officer for the air force command. As a result of another reorganization and renumbering, his squadron received the number 2/2 and was transferred to Nyíregyháza in 1939, where they were stationed until the early autumn of 1941. In April 1941, during the short campaign against Yugoslavia, 2/I Fighter Group was also in readiness, even though it was equipped with the old CR.32s; however, they were not called into combat. *Százados* Heppes then received a certificate of commendation from the Chief of Staff of the Royal Hungarian Armed Forces.

Százados Aladár Heppes in the dark times after the Soviet breakthrough at the Don. The picture was probably taken at the beginning of February 1943 in Kharkhiv. Aladár Heppes has an MP35 Bergmann submachine gun on his shoulder. (From the author's collection)

From June 1941, *százados* Heppes took over the command of 2/I Fighter Group. In the autumn, he was reassigned as the commander of 5/I Fighter Group, which had been formed in November at Mátyásföld. He also served as the commander of the airfield. He remained here until the end of 1942, when he was deployed to the front.

In January 1943, he flew one combat sortie with one of the old *Héja*s, the V.435, after the Soviet breakthrough: it was a reconnaissance mission on the morning of 15 January to assess the situation on the ground. He carried out his mission with over-spinning propeller due to a fault in the propeller adjuster.[28]

The majority of the units of the brigade were encircled a few days later at Ilovskoye, where the energetic *százados* Heppes again showed exceptional skill and fortitude in organizing and leading the defense and the breakout.

In February, after he was relocated back to Uman (and without neglecting his other duties), he could finally begin retraining for the long-anticipated

26 *HM HIM KI*, document folder nr. 41825; recollections of Aladár Heppes.
27 *Honvédségi Közlöny* (*Személyes ügyek*), nr. 1939/3 (19 July 1939), p. 19.
28 *HM HIM HL*, documents of the 2nd Army, box nr. 17, after-action report of 5/I Fighter Group, attachment 28 (mission report).

Messerschmitt Bf 109. He completed his first flight with a Bf 109 on 10 March. The retraining of the new pilots lasted until the end of April, during which time Heppes traveled continuously between 1/1 Fighter Squadron (deployed from Kharkhiv to fly combat missions) and the retraining group in Uman, mainly 5/2 Squadron and the group staff.

He flew his first Messerschmitt combat sortie from Kharkhiv on 5 April 1943; thereafter, he completed a further four combat sorties before the end of the month. All were fighter-bomber missions.[29]

Heppes was promoted to *őrnagy* as of 1 May 1943 and completed a further five combat sorties during the month, finally achieving his first air victories. On 29 May, after a bomber escort mission in the area of Kupiansk, he strafed and knocked out the locomotive of a Soviet train. Next morning, after escorting the Hungarian Ju 88 bombers attacking the train station at Valuyki, he achieved a double kill during a free hunt. *Őrnagy* Heppes told the following story about the air combat to war correspondents:

> After a short while, we saw black dots emerging. Without any thought, we were upon them, and after a few seconds, we were already surrounded by seven to eight enemy aircraft looking for the easiest prey. In the ensuing dogfight, I suddenly saw that one Russian fighter would be an excellent target for me; the next moment, another aircraft came rushing toward me with exceptional speed. There was no time to consider my options; I turned my aircraft to face him and, pushing down a bit, I engaged the enemy with cannon and machine gun fire. For several seconds, our aircraft rushed at each other in a hail of bullets. The bursts of the Soviet pilot were sweeping away over my head, but mines hit right on the cooler on the belly of the Russian aircraft. After a quick pause, the enemy fighter flew past me and plummeted to its fate.
>
> I could not really recover from this unexpected and quick turn of events before I was fired upon by a phosphor burst from one of the Russian aircraft swarming below like ants. Thank God none was a hit. My wingman, *hadnagy* L. [*hadnagy* György Lipták] came onto the radio and told me I could go on fine because he would secure my back. I rushed out of the swarm and was considering the uneven balance of forces but, upon seeing the excitement of the good *hadnagy*, I decided to attack again. Like an arrow, I went right at the swarm of Russian fighters. I had picked out an enemy aircraft as my target when a Russian fighter just fell in front of me from right above and placed himself approximately 1,000 meters from me in such a position that I could not have wished for any better; so I must assume he did not see me at all. As I rushed toward him, I wondered if he would notice me. At 100 meters, then at 50 meters, I opened fire and sprayed bullets at him at the fastest rate. The Russian realized the situation at once and tried to avoid me with a desperate turn, but this only made things worse for him because he exposed his cockpit to my fire. I fired one more accurate burst and the enemy aircraft slipped downward on his back.[30]

One of the pilots of 5/2 Squadron, *törzsőrmester* Zoltán Tóth (for a long time a Heppes's subordinate in the 'Puma' Squadron), heard the dogfight on the radio and immediately returned

29 Based on the logbook of Aladár Heppes.

30 Gyula Kádár, 'A magyar vadászrepülők harca a szovjet túlerő ellen', *Magyar Szárnyak*, 15 July 1943, p. 15; Kádár, *Sasok harca*, pp. 121–122.

Őrnagy Aladár Heppes in Kharkhiv, in May 1943 in front of his first Messerschmitt, the Bf 109 F-4 marked V039. (From the author's collection)

Őrnagy Heppes in the cockpit of his first Messerschmitt. The frontal armored glass is visibly missing. (From the author's collection)

from the bomber escort to the fight. However he only saw two pillars of smoke on the ground, which he identified as shot down aircraft; thus the reported air victories were confirmed in Air Force Confidential Order Nr. 1943/30. The dogfight was probably fought with the Yak-1s of 814th IAP, of which the aircraft of 2nd *leytenant* V.V. Bobkov was damaged in a fight with two Messerschmitts, but was able to return to base (the Soviet formation was in the air between 04:36 and 05:45 Hungarian time). Valentin Vasilievich Bobkov was a *mayor* at the end of the war, having completed 300 combat sorties, during which he achieved 13 individual and four shared victories. For his military achievements, he was decorated with the title of the Hero of the Soviet Union in the summer of 1945.[31]

Heppes achieved his next aerial victory in the midst of the raging battle of Kursk, on the morning of 6 July 1943. His victim was an Il-2 ground-attack aircraft in the Volchansk area, which crashed beyond the Russian lines after the oil cooler was set aflame by the Hungarian pilot. The witness was his wingman, the group adjutant, *főhadnagy* Bejczy – who also shot down a Soviet aircraft from behind the *őrnagy* – and the German troops on the front line. The air victory was confirmed in Air Force Confidential Order Nr. 1943/42.

Major Heppes flew his first combat sortie with a Bf 109 G-2 on 22 July (prior to this, he had flown with an old Bf 109 F-4).[32]

He shot down his last Soviet aircraft on 3 August 1943. On this day, he completed three free hunt missions combined with a bomber escort with his wingman, *főhadnagy* Bejczy. During the second mission, he shot down a Yak-1. In his handwritten memories, he recalled the events as follows:

31 Recollections of Aladár Heppes in manuscript, also based on his logbook. For Bobkov, see also Bikhov, *Sovetskie Asy 1941–1945,* p. 62. For the data on the Soviet fighters, the author owes gratitude to Nikita Yegorov on documents of TsAMO.

32 Recollections of Aladár Heppes in manuscript, also based on his logbook.

After we had flown a free hunt, my wingman, Bejczy, and I landed on a German provisional airstrip to fill up the fuel south of Belgorod, then we flew to the northwestern area of Belgorod at an altitude of 3,000 meters to search for bombers who lacked fighter escort. Soon after, we found one, flying southwest to northeast, a few hundred meters above us. We wanted to join the bomber when I noticed a Russian aircraft pair right below, echeloned to the left side; they were emerging toward the bombers. In a dive, I turned on the wingman, who must have been watching his element leader closely or was preoccupied with the attack, because I was able to approach him up to 75 meters without him changing his flight path. My burst hit him from the nose to the cockpit; fire and smoke gushed out of the aircraft, and it went down below me. But now the element leader was approximately 200 meters in front of me. Before I could approach him, with a steep right dive he turned away from the bombers and pushed his aircraft eastward to escape me. He managed to gain some space between us and this space was not lessening.

I was hoping for him to slow down a bit before landing, so I followed him, but I needed to pay attention to the growing traffic, which still hadn't detected me. Approaching the ground faster and faster, it became evident that he was trying to reach his airfield, which was proven even more conclusively by the fact that the traffic was considerably greater here. I was short on fuel; I only knew vaguely where I was; I therefore turned back toward the west. The constant watching of the air and the low altitude did not help me much to know where I am, but I was hoping to return very soon somewhere beyond our lines. The Donets was just not turning up; I was almost out of fuel, so, warmly hoping I was already beyond our own lines, I tried to look for a landing area. I soon found one in the shape of a long meadow. Landing gear out; '*Klappe*' out [flap, in Hungarian '*fékszárny*']; and I had almost landed when Russian soldiers came out of the bushes, running and shouting. Speed, landing gear in, '*Klappe*' in, and I continued my low altitude flight toward the west, now only hoping to be able to belly-land the aircraft when the fuel ran out. Only one or two minutes could have gone by when I saw a pair of train tracks, and a watchman's house and a swastika flowerbed near that; then a slope, and a longish meadow. Landing gear out, '*Klappe*' out, and after a relatively small amount of hopping about, I ran the last part of the rolling out with the engine stopped.

I got out and looked around; dead silence – a flock of sheep was grazing in the distance. An hour later the herdsman came, driven by curiosity, and because we did not have a common language, I only learned '*Russky nyet, German da*', which filled me with satisfaction. Around noon, a German infantry patrol came, whom I asked to notify the closest German airfield when they got back to their station where I was and that I needed fuel, and if possible to notify the Kharkhiv airfield that I had emergency landed fine and that everything was in order. The waiting came again; for hours, nothing happened. Then, a German *Kf.* [short-range reconnaissance] aircraft flew past me and noticed me. I signaled to them that I needed fuel. They acknowledged this by waggling their wings and disappeared; in half an hour, a Storch came with fuel, tools and the information that I was somewhere near the Sumy–Kharkhiv train route, much further north than I had planned.[33]

33 Recollections of Aladár Heppes.

Based on the witness report of *főhadnagy* Bejczy and the sought-out German He 111 bombers, the shot-down wingman Yak-1 was confirmed to the *őrnagy*.[34]

The three missions Heppes completed on this day, 3 August 1943, were the last combat sorties he flew on the Eastern Front. From the second half of August, the pilots of 1/1 Fighter Squadron gradually returned home; only 5/2 Squadron remained at the front as an independent squadron. The group staff had also been drawn back to Mátyásföld during the autumn.

Őrnagy Heppes takes off from Veszprém to a mission in a Bf 109 G-6 (manufactured in Győr) in the early summer of 1944. (From the collection of László Hemmert)

In 1943, Heppes completed 24 combat sorties in the front area. One was completed with *Héja*, the others with Messerschmitt (of these, seven were fighter-bomber missions), and he scored four air victories.[35]

Őrnagy Heppes was entitled to develop the new fighter tactical guide, and officially took command of the Fighter Combat Training Group at Tapolca from 1 October 1943.[36]

Aladár Heppes with German and Hungarian pilots in Veszprém, in the summer of 1944. *Őrnagy* Heppes can be seen facing the camera on the left, *hadnagy* László Molnár sits in the foreground to the left (with his back to the camera), *hadnagy* György Debrődy can be seen on the right. (From the author's collection)

To be able to act more effectively against the American air raids from the beginning of April 1944, the command of the Royal Hungarian Air Force decided to establish a new fighter group in Veszprém. Based on his experience, qualities and achievements, *őrnagy* Heppes was promoted to the command of 101 Fighter Group as of 28 April 1944. Naturally, the 'Puma' badge and the spirit of the group were also brought over.

34 Recollections of Aladár Heppes in manuscript, also based on his logbook.
35 Based on the logbook of Aladár Heppes.
36 *HM HIM KI*, document folder nr. 41825.

Őrnagy Heppes first led the group in air combat on 30 May 1944, but, due to the inexperienced ground control crew, they were deployed late and unable to reach the American formations. The mission report of this event was written by the group commander as follows:

> I report, that the mission report pertaining to 30 May 1944 occurred as follows.
> a) The formation took off from 'combat readiness' at 10:43.
> b) Number of deployed aircraft: group staff: 4.
> 1 Sqdr.: 8.
> 2 Sqdr.: 8.
> 3 Sqdr.: 12.
> Total: 32.
> c) There was no contact with the enemy.
> I received deployment orders at 10:39.
> I took off at 10:43.
> Over Veszprém, at 2,500 meters, I received an attack order to Alsólendva (today Lendava, Slovenia) at 10:57.
> At 11:05, I was over Tihany at 4,000 meters.
> At 11:10, over Nagykanizsa at 7,000 meters, I reported my position.
> At 11:23, upon multiple requests, I was given a location between Szombathely and Nagykanizsa where enemy formations were detected, heading south. I have not received any time indication of when the formation was detected. In reality, the said formation had already been left in a southern direction from the airspace of the country.
> At 11:28, I reported over Szombathely at 7,500 meters. I received the return order at 11:30.
> Gathering over Tihany, I received orders to land without regrouping and refueling. At 12:05, the 32 aircraft landed. I reported that I heard the radio of '*Vércse*' ('*Kestrel*', the ground control centre in Budapest) faintly and only occasionally; this could not be deemed proper control. Our own '*Erdő*' station ['*Forest*', the ground control station at Veszprém] was heard clearly, but '*Vércse*' bothered me a number of times and it worked with a considerable lag. It would be useful for the formation if, when they report their own position, a report on the enemy position should be reported to them, or at least the words 'no new observance', because lacking this information leaves the group in an insecure position, and it is essential to include the time of observation in the position report, because it is not possible to lead properly under these circumstances.
> The formations were moving properly, and there were no problems with the aircraft either. One aircraft safely emergency landed because of vibrating engine.[37]

The notifications, reports and commands from ground control, which were arriving late, caused many problems afterwards as well.

A number of large-scale combat missions took place over the summer; of these, *őrnagy* Heppes led the ones on 16, 26 and 30 June, and the ones on 2 and 7 July. On 16 June, the gunners of

37 The copy of the original mission report is owned by the author.

Őrnagy Aladár Heppes with *százados* Miklós Scholtz on his left, who achieved two aerial victories against Americans and finished the war as the commander of 101/I Fighter Group. (From the collection of László Hemmert)

the American Liberators hit the fuselage of his aircraft; the canopy was also torn off, but the pilot was luckily unharmed and managed to bring the aircraft back to Veszprém. Ten days later, on the morning of 26 June, he managed to exact revenge on the Liberators by shooting down two of them, one of which was shot out of a large formation (the other was a lone aircraft). One of his confirmed aerial victories of the day was the B-24H of 456th BG's 744th Bomber Squadron (serial number 4252233) flown by 2nd Lieutenant Dudley B. Field, which crashed at Nagyacsád. The 10-member crew was captured.

During the large-scale mission of 2 July, he also managed to shoot down a B-24, this time again from the 456th BG. The Hungarian group commander was credited with the aircraft that crashed near Pusztaszabolcs (serial number 42-51077) from the 744th Bomber Squadron, flown by 1st Lieutenant Edward C. Jones. Of the 11-member crew, six were taken captive; five crew members, including the pilot, were killed.[38]

Őrnagy Heppes flew his last two combat missions on 7 July. During the first mission, he led a 10-aircraft formation and scored his last air victory near Hajmáskér against the B-24G of 454th BG's 737th Bomber Squadron (serial number 42-78297) flown by 1st Lieutenant Edward W. Rodgers; apart from the navigator, everybody survived the crash and was taken captive. The victory was credited as a shared one with *hadnagy* Gellért Barsi, although Air Force Confidential Order Nr. 1944/63 records them as separate.[39] On this day, after the large-scale formation mission had concluded, Heppes also took off with another aircraft as an element leader at 13:05 with scramble to chase a lonely Liberator.

Of this unsuccessful mission, the last combat sortie of his life, he wrote the following record in the combat report he submitted:

38 NARA MACR 6435, 6439.
39 NARA MACR 6570.

> I noticed a lonely Liberator flying over the airfield, and at once we took off with my wingman. At JP.8 and LP.4 [the first is a map section north of Lake Balaton; the second is an area southwest of the lake], we have carried out a number of passes, but we did not notice any results, even though my bursts were well-placed. We did not see the aircraft leaving Hungarian airspace.[40]

The pilot of the Liberator that crashed at Pusztaszabolcs on 2 July 1944 (456th BG, serial number 4251077), 1st Lieutenant Edward C. Jones, who was killed. The shooting down of the aircraft was credited to *őrnagy* Heppes (Jones via Deller)

After the unsuccessful chase, he landed at 14:20 in Veszprém. It was not mentioned in the report but his ammunition was expended quickly, presumably the ground crew could not possibly have had enough time to replenish the ammunition after the first mission.

It was soon decided that 101 Fighter Group would be upgraded to a wing-size force, and *őrnagy* Heppes – who was close to his 40th birthday at the time, and who was the oldest active Hungarian fighter pilot – was officially forbidden to go on missions from this time.

Aladár Heppes flew 33 combat sorties altogether, during which he was engaged in 13 air combats. During the period spent in home defense, he completed nine sorties against the Americans and achieved four confirmed aerial victories, all against four-engined heavy bombers.[41] His unit was extended to wing size during September 1944 with the establishment of the second group, and the command remained with Heppes until the end of the war.

On 28 January 1945, the commander of the air force promoted Heppes to *alezredes* out of turn. The recommendation stated the following:

> From 12 December 1942 to the beginning of December 1943, *őrgy.* Aladár Heppes was the cmdr. of 5/I Fig. Gr. as *százados* during the combat activity period against the Soviets. From 1 May 1944 to 25 August 1944, he was the cmdr. of the independent 101 Fighter Group and took part in several missions to fight off the American air raids. From 15 August 1944 up to this day, as the cmdr. of 101 Fighter Wing, he has been leading his unit into air combat [as mentioned earlier, *őrnagy* Heppes was excluded from flying combat missions since the end of the summer of 1944, so after that time he was not able to lead the unit from the air]. … As a fighter wing commander, he is exceptional in his leadership and duties.[42]

40 The copy of the original mission report is owned by the author.
41 Based on the logbook of Aladár Heppes.
42 *HM HIM HL*, recommendations for decorations, box nr. 13, group 510.a.

Alezredes Aladár Heppes as the commander of 101 Fighter Wing in Veszprém, in February 1945 (*HM HIM* Photographic Archives 97031)

Original surrender document of 101 Fighter Wing, preserved by Aladár Heppes. (From the collection of the Heppes family)

The recommendation met with a positive response, and Heppes was promoted to *alezredes* out of turn on 1 February 1945.[43]

Heppes was taken captive with his wing in May 1945, and never returned home again. Heppes settled in the US at the beginning of the 1950s in Connecticut and worked for Consolidated Diesel Inc. as the manager of the technical information department until his retirement. He worked to introduce the Hungarian fighter pilots and their activity during the Second World War to as wide an audience as possible, and was collecting and organizing material and documents in connection with this effort. The excellent commander of 101 'Puma' Fighter Wing died on 15 August 1988 in Ridgefield, Connecticut; his ashes were buried in the garden of his family home.[44]

43 *HM HIM HL*, documents of 101 Fighter Wing, box nr. 110, Wing Order Nr. 1945/44.
44 After the plot was sold, it was sadly built over; the exhumation and reburial of Aladár Heppes is thus no longer possible.

SZÁZADOS GYÖRGY UJSZÁSZY

Number of aerial victories: 7 (+9)
Successes against ground targets: n.d.a.
Number of flown combat sorties: 120+
Number of hours flown in the air force: 1,050
Nicknames: *Apuka*, *Gyurka*
Identification number: 2594-12-0187

Decorations

- *Magyar Érdemrend lovagkeresztje hadiszalagon a kardokkal* (20 September 1943)
- *Újólagos Kormányzói dicsérő elismerés Magyar Koronás Ezüst Érdemérme hadiszalagon a kardokkal* (12 May 1942)
- *Újólagos Kormányzói dicsérő elismerés Magyar Koronás Ezüst Érdemérme hadiszalagon a kardokkal*, for the second time (1 November 1944)
- *Kormányzói dicsérő elismerés Magyar Koronás Bronz Érdemérme hadiszalagon a kardokkal* (2 July 1939)
- *Tűzkereszt I fokozata a kardokkal és koszorúval*
- *Felvidéki Emlékérem*
- *Erdélyi Emlékérem*
- *Délvidéki Emlékérem*
- German Iron Cross 2nd Class (spring 1944)
- Silver *Frontflugspange* (20 April 1945)

Victories

Number	Date	Aircraft	Location
1	27 August 1941	'I-17' (MiG-3/LaGG-3)	Ulyanovka (Dnepropetrovsk)
2	27 August 1941	'I-17' (MiG-3/LaGG-3)	Ulyanovka (Dnepropetrovsk)
3	27 April 1943	Il-2	
4	28 April 1943	La-5	
–	7 July 1943	La-5	
5	13 July 1943	Il-2	Belgorod N
6	13 July 1943	Il-2	Belgorod N
7	1 August 1943	Boston	
–	3 August 1943	La-5	
–	3 August 1943	Soviet aircraft	
–	3 August 1943	Soviet aircraft	
–	3 August 1943	Soviet aircraft	
–	4 August 1943	Soviet aircraft	
–	4 August 1943	Soviet aircraft	
–	7 August 1943	Soviet aircraft	
–	7 August 1943	Soviet aircraft	

Aircraft flown
CR.42: V.210 (summer of 1941), Bf 109 G-2: V312 (summer of 1943)

György Ujszászy was born in Veszprém on 30 May 1912 to an intellectual family with two children (he had an older sister). His father was a roadworks engineer, and later an engineering councilor.[45] He started attending high school in Veszprém (*Veszprémi Piarista Gimnázium*), but after two years, because his family moved to Esztergom, he went to high school in Tata (*piarista Gróf Esterházy Miklós Reálgimnázium,* today called *Eötvös József Gimnázium*); he graduated from here in 1932.[46] Thereafter, he was admitted to the *Ludovika Akadémia* (2nd Department), where he graduated as *hadnagy* on 20 August 1936. He was the fourth in his class. Ujszászy was also preoccupied with gliders during his powered flight training. In August 1936, he completed the 'B' level at Strázsa Hill at the *Movero* (*Esztergomi Sportrepülő Egyesület*, Esztergom Sport Aviation Club).[47]

Before graduating, their 16-member class had not yet fully completed their combat pilot training – they had only done so to the basic level. All the class members were thus graduated as observers and were deployed to the bombers and the reconnaissance units. Later, when the advanced level of the training ended, only two were taken on by the fighters: Ujszászy and the first in class, Zoltán Gáspárdy, but he died on 15 February 1939 in a CR.32 crash.[48]

György Ujszászy as the young *hadnagy* observer of 3/4 '*Bomba Matyi*' Squadron in 1937. On his chest the golden eagle is the badge of the Hungarian observers, which was distinguished from the pilots' golden eagle badge by the lack of the crown. (From the author's collection)

Ujszászy was assigned to Szombathely after the graduation, where he served as a recruit instructor from December 1936 to February 1937. Afterward, he was assigned to the newly-founded 3/II Bomber Group; he was placed as an observer in 3/4 '*Bomba Matyi*' Bomber Squadron led by *százados* Gyula Vághegyi. In May 1937, the squadron was relocated to Pápa. During the summer of 1938, Ujszászy completed his advanced level pilot training in Nyíregyháza, but he still remained with the bombers. On their first alert in October 1938, they relocated to the military airstrip at Kisbér.

Ujszászy experienced his first combat during the return of *Kárpátalja*, when his squadron was relocated to Debrecen and sent into combat on 17 March 1939. On this day two Ju 86's were deployed to support the Hungarian land forces thrusting forward in the Ung

45 National Archives, Veszprém County Archives (*MNL Veszprém Megye Levéltára*), XXXIII/1, Veszprém state birth registry from 1912, counterpart, note nr. 187. fsz.
46 Record Office of the *Eötvös József Gimnázium és Kollégium* (Eötvös József High School), matriculation register for 1932, register note nr. 36.
47 *Movero Esztergomi Sportrepülő Egyesület Közlönye*, 1936:1, p. 10.
48 For Gáspárdy and his fatal accident, see Becze, '*Kőr Ász*', pp. 7–9.

valley. At 17:00, from an altitude of 3,400 meters between Nagyberezna (today Veliky Berezny, Ukraine) and Sóslak (today Sil', Ukraine), they bombed the positions of the Czechoslovakian 36/III Battalion, covering the retreat of their comrades and the evacuation of public services.[49] As the observer of the aircraft flown by *főhadnagy* László Bene, Ujszászy performed an accurate bombing despite the unfavorable weather, upon which the resistance of the enemy battalion was immediately collapsed in the area. This was the first live bombing mission of the Royal Hungarian Air Force and Ujszászy received his first military decoration for it (his first *Signum*), the recommendation for which said the following about him:

> Despite the snowstorms along the whole length of the route, his navigational calculations were exact, whether above cloud level or within the clouds. He navigated the incomplete flight toward the target with full confidence. The bombs were released accurately, despite heavy anti-aircraft fire. As a result of the bombing, the enemy resistance in the Ung valley has been broken and our troops have been able to occupy the valley quickly.[50]

According to the author's opinion, however, 'heavy anti-aircraft fire' has been mistranscribed, because no anti-aircraft artillery pieces were stationed in the Ung valley that could have been powerful enough to reach the aircraft – there was only a battery of field artillery. Nor had any artillery on the Hungarian side been drawn that far forward that might have been responsible for friendly fire.

During the mission, Ujszászy suffered frostbite wounds on his fingers on both hands, and was therefore unable to take part in the bombing mission at Spišská Nová Ves a week later (although it is possible he could not have gone anyway, so as to avoid undertaking more missions than his peers, as there was serious rivalry among the crew members in this respect). In the summer of 1939, Ujszászy completed bomber school at Szombathely; on 20 October, at Pápa, he completed instrument rating school; and on 10 December 1939, he completed a wireless operator course.

Ujszászy was promoted to *főhadnagy* on 1 May 1940. From December 1940 to February 1941, he was a recruit instructor at Nagyvárad (today Oradea, Romania); by this time he had been reassigned to 1/3 Fighter Squadron at Mátyásföld as deputy commander. From here, he was sent to recruit training, where he served along with two prospective aces who had been relocated from 1/4 Fighter Squadron: *hadnagy* József Bejczy and *szakaszvezető* János Mátyás.

From March to June 1941, *főhadnagy* Ujszászy was reassigned to the fighter school at Vát. He returned to his own unit in April 1941, at the time of the campaign against Yugoslavia. The chief of staff of the Royal Hungarian Army presented him with a commendatory certificate for his achievements during this period, but his main challenge as a fighter pilot was still ahead of him, in the summer and autumn of 1941, with the deployment of 1/3 Fighter Squadron to the Eastern Front.

Upon the relocation of the squadron in July 1941, *főhadnagy* Ujszászy led the ground crew of the unit and so arrived a few days later than his flying comrades. His first combat sortie against the Soviets was completed on 17 July 1941 – a particularly calm mission without enemy contact, the task being a short-range reconnaissance escort.

49 Stenge, *Baptism of Fire*, pp. 20–22.
50 *HM HIM HL*, recommendations for decorations, box nr. 1, nr. 844.

Hadnagy György Ujszászy (on the right) and *főhadnagy* László Bene in a crater caused by the impact of a bomb they dropped near the road between Uzsok (Uzhok) and Ungvár, end March 1939 (*HM HIM* Photographic Archives 97.601/065)

He engaged the enemy only once during this period while flying CR.42: on 27 August 1941, in the morning, on his 23rd combat sortie against the Soviet Union. He led his own flight east of Dnepropetrovsk, and engaged the enemy fighters in the area of Ulyanovka over a Soviet field airstrip. He reported shooting down two 'I-17's, as he did not recognise the shape of the modern Soviet monoplanes. The Soviet unit engaged on this occasion by the Hungarian fighters has not yet been positively identified: probably they were MiG-3s or aircraft of a fighter regiment equipped with early LaGG-3s. In the squadron log, the location is identified as Ulyanovka; in a regulation, the location of the double victory is pinpointed as Dnepropetrovsk.

Ujszászy's squadron returned to Mátyásföld on 26 November 1941. With his unit, *főhadnagy* Ujszászy completed 45 combat sorties; besides his two air victories, he also completed a number of strafing runs against various targets over the course of 1941 in Ukraine.

Due to reorganisations, the former 1/II Fighter Group at Mátyásföld was renamed as 5/1 Fighter Group, while the former 1/3 Fighter Squadron became 5/1 Fighter

Hadnagy György Ujszászy (on the left) and *főhadnagy* László Bene. Ujszászy is showing his bandaged fingers frozen on the mission on 17 March 1939. László Bene (1910–1941) remained at Pápa within the parachute transport squadron, after the relocation of the bomber group. He was killed as the co-pilot of the leading SM 75 when it crashed in Veszprém, on 12 April 1941, during the parachute drop mission against Yugoslavia (*HM HIM* Photographic Archives 97.601/068)

The aircraft (marked V-210) of 1/3 Fighter Squadron in Miskolc on 3 November 1939. Two days later the *Repülőakadémia* was opened at Kassa, and the aircraft had flown from Miskolc for the opening ceremony. Later, the V-210 became Ujszászy's personal aircraft. (From the author's collection).

Painting the first victory markings on the vertical stabilizer of the aircraft of *főhadnagy* Ujszászy. (From the collection of the Ujszászy family)

Főhadnagy Ujszászy photographed at the end of August 1941, after his double victory. The difference between the number V.210 painted on this aircraft fuselage and the earlier version is clearly visible. (From the collection of the Ujszászy family)

Squadron; Ujszászy took over the command of this squadron from the beginning of 1942, and was promoted to *százados* as of 1 April 1942.

He was deployed to the front again in December 1942 to take command of 1/1 Fighter Squadron. However, in the combats that took place during the winter breakthrough, the squadron was still led by it former deputy commander (who was now interim commander), *főhadnagy* György Bánlaky. *Százados* Ujszászy was retrained to Bf 109 together with the group staff in Uman at the beginning of 1943.

After Ujszászy completed his retraining and relocated to Kharkhiv, he took command of his squadron. On 16 April 1943, he completed his first Messerschmitt combat sortie. *Oberleutnant* Joachim Kirschner,[51] commander of 5./JG 3, took Ujszászy on a little familiarisation flight deep beyond the enemy lines, during which Kirschner engaged and shot down a Soviet aircraft that wanted to land on its own airfield. The mission was repeated the next day and the day after that, the only change being that this time *százados* Ujszászy was flying as a leader and shot down an Il-2 on the first day (and an La-5 on the second). These aerial victories were not recorded in the personal record of the pilot, probably because of an administrative error, even though Kirschner witnessed both.[52]

51 Joachim Kirschner achieved 188 aerial victories. As a *Hauptmann* and the commander of IV./JG 27, he was shot down by a P-47 of 57th FG on 17 December 1943 and was forced to bail out of his aircraft south of Mostar, where he landed in the vicinity of Donje Hrasno. He was captured by Yugoslav Partisans, who probably tortured him before he was killed by them. For Joachim Kirschner (Niederlössnitz, 7 June 1920–Donje Hrasno, 17 December 1943), see Obermaier, *Die Ritterkreuzträger der Luftwaffe 1939–45*, p. 58.

52 Excerpts from the logs of 1/1 Fighter Squadron. This abridged log was prepared by Ujszászy, and it contained the combat sorties and victories of some of the pilots from the squadron log. It is considered to be valid and authentic based on comparisons with other sources – personal logbooks

Like his subordinate pilots, *százados* Ujszászy met a multitude of enemy aircraft during the battle of Kursk. Between 7 July and 7 August, he reported shooting down 12 enemy aircraft, although only three were credited to him, even though some of the other claims were witnessed. Apart from these recorded and claimed aircraft, Ujszászy badly damaged an La-5 on 8 July, but did not report it as a kill.[53]

Of the three confirmed aerial victories he scored during this period, two were achieved on 13 July north of Belgorod. During the combat mission with *szakaszvezető* István Fábián, he shot down two aircraft from a formation of five Il-2s next to a German 8.8cm anti-aircraft gun position used for anti-tank purposes, which was attacked by the Soviet aircraft by strafing. His first victim was the aircraft on the far right of the formation, which, upon being hit, almost crashed into the German 8.8cm gun and hit the ground next to it. The other aircraft then ceased their attack and tried to reach the nearby cloud layer; however, Ujszászy still reached one of them and sent a long burst after it from a distance of approximately 30 meters before the Ilyushin went into the clouds. *Százados* Ujszászy pushed his aircraft under the clouds and spotted his second victim instantly as it was plummeting down in flames. Both kills were confirmed by his wingman and also by the crew members of the German anti-aircraft gun.

His last confirmed air victory was achieved on 1 August 1943, when he shot down a Boston bomber (his wingman, *főhadnagy* Bejczy, was also successful). *Százados* Ujszászy remembered the mission as follows:

> We were going on free hunts, rotating each other in these days from early at dawn until evening. The German ground radio stations controlling the aircraft signaled to us on the radio that there were enemy bombers over Belgorod. We were flying in that direction, and we noticed heavy anti-aircraft fire. Bejczy told me via radio that he saw many Soviet bombers. The anti-aircraft shells of the Germans started to whizz around me, so I did a large loop and flew farther. Then I hear my wingman's voice again: 'The bombers are under us!' It was because the German anti-aircraft fire effectively made the enemy aircraft dispersed in every direction. So now I saw one of the Soviet bombers before me at a relatively large distance. I immediately opened fire, at that moment the anti-aircraft guns stopped firing and let us take care of the enemy. I approached the Soviet with the Messerschmitt and at first I aimed my fire accurately with the machine gun. The rear gunner was keen on returning the fire. Now I was only aiming at the gunner, and after a few seconds there came no sign of life from him. Now I could aim at the big fat fuselage of the bomber with the concentrated fire from my two machine guns and the cannon. It had such heavy armor it did not seem to want to go down. … We were already way beyond enemy lines at an altitude of approximately 600 meters. The enemy bomber in front of me was fast approaching the ground, so in the end, we were flying pretty low. I reached him and almost crashed into him; I suddenly pulled up. … After completing a huge loop upward I looked around at approximately 1,000 meters and sought the bomber but I saw nothing. … The two Messerschmitts replacing us were greeting us in the air. From one of

and the squadron-related documents that survive from January and February 1943. One should therefore not assume of course that he would have 'created' the data relating to his own kills.

53 Excerpts from the logs of 1/1 Fighter Squadron.

Százados Ujszászy in the spring of 1942 in Mátyásföld, with some of the pilots of the reorganized and renumbered former 1/3 Fighter Squadron. Ujszászy is the second from the left. On the left is *százados* László Tomor; on the right, next to Ujszászy, is *zászlós* Miklós Kun, both of whom achieved one air victory in 1941. On the right of the picture stands *törzsőrmester* Sándor Szobránczi. (From the author's collection)

The Bf 109 G-2 marked V312 near Kharkhiv on a frontline airfield in the summer of 1943. The aircraft was flown by *százados* Ujszászy (*HM HIM* Photographic Archives 97.601/386)

Százados Ujszászy compliments his Bf 109 after he has shot down an Il-2 ground-attack aircraft with it. Kharkhiv, summer 1943 (*HM HIM* Photographic Archives 97.601/291)

them, *hadnagy* Debrődy said he had seen the bomber I was chasing falling vertically into the forest. One of the radio stations immediately broadcast the news that a German assault battery commander had reported the shooting down of the aircraft. These were the 25th and 26th aerial victories of our squadron.[54]

54 Gyula Kádár, 'Beszélgetés Ujszászy György magyar lovagkeresztes vadászrepülő századossal', *Magyarság*, 14 November 1943, p. 5.

On his most intensive combat day, 3 August, Ujszászy flew 10 combat sorties and reported shooting down four enemy aircraft, but all remained unconfirmed. One of these victories was against an La-5 during an escort mission of He 111 bombers, with *törzsőrmester* Szentgyörgyi as his wingman. During the air combat, both Hungarian pilots reported shooting down an enemy fighter each, but neither saw the other's kills while fighting the enemy in superior numbers. Both victories, therefore, remained unconfirmed, as they lacked witnesses, and the author has not found any data regarding German bombers witnessing the kills. Nor have I found any details about Ujszászy's other three claims from that day.[55]

Százados Ujszászy completed his last mission over Ukraine on 18 August 1943. Since April, he had flown 72 combat sorties, and the experienced pilot had not even been hit once. Soon afterward, he returned home with some members of the squadron – not to Mátyásföld, but to the base of 1/1 Squadron in Szolnok, as he had retained his rank as squadron commander (the staff of 5/I Group and 1/1 Squadron arrived in Mátyásföld on 25 September 1943, from where 1/1 Squadron relocated to its home base in Szolnok).

Ujszászy's first mission against the Americans was completed on 13 April 1944 from Szolnok, during which he scored an aerial victory over a Liberator together with his wingman, *őrmester* Károly Kereki. However, the rear gunner hit Kereki's engine; the pilot bailed out, but his parachute became entangled in the tail of his Messerchmitt and both crashed into the ground, killing the pilot. *Százados* Ujszászy tried to get the victory credited to *őrmester* Kereki, but it remained unconfirmed.

Ujszászy's squadron was the second squadron – with a call sign of '*Retek*' – of 101 Fighter Group, formed in Veszprém. From May until the end of September, therefore, he led his unit in Veszprém, although he was now going on missions less and less frequently due to his other service obligations. When the group was reorganized as a wing following an order of 19 September 1944, he became the deputy commander of 101/I Fighter Group, under group commander *százados* Miklós Scholtz, the former commander of 101/1 Squadron. *Százados* Ujszászy served in this position until the end of the year, at which point, following an order issued on 23 December 1944, he was reassigned as second adjutant of the wing command. He served in this position until 3 April 1945; he then took over from *őrnagy* Gyula Csathó as first adjutant of the wing. Ujszászy witnessed the end of the war in this position and went into American captivity with 101 Fighter Wing in May 1945.[56]

Some administrative errors definitely took place, not only regarding the number of his air victories and wartime achievements, but also regarding the number of Ujszászy's combat sorties. A summarized report from the end of the war only credited 88 combat sorties to him; he therefore only received a silver and not a golden *Frontflugspange* from the Germans, even though he had earned the golden badge, as the logs of 1/3 and 1/1 company together credit him with 117 combat sorties on the Eastern Front between 1941 and 1943.[57]

At the end of the war, during the retreat to Austria, *százados* Ujszászy experienced a telling example of the increasingly violent behavior of the German troops against the Hungarians

55 Excerpts from the logs of 1/1 Fighter Squadron.
56 *HM HIM HL*, documents of 101 Fighter Wing, box nr. 110, Wing Orders Nr.1945/11 and 1945/51.
57 Excerpts from the logs of 1/1 Fighter Squadron prepared by *százados* Ujszászy (owned by the author); Becze, '*Kőr Ász*', pp. 21–77.

when his own DKW F8 Cabriolet car, with the registration number AN 639, was stolen from him, together with all the valuables inside it.[58]

After he was captured with his unit, he did not return to Hungary. Besides his uncertain future there, he was also influenced by the fate of his paternal uncle. *Vezérőrnagy* István Ujszászy had been commander of the Army Staff 2nd Department (intelligence and counterespionage), then commander of the *Államvédelmi Központ* (Center of State Security); he was promptly arrested in 1945 by the NKVD and later died in captivity under unknown circumstances.

Ujszászy wanted at first to join the Polish Air Force with a group of Hungarian pilots, but after the collapse of this plan, he worked for the British Army in Innsbruck from 1947. He arrived at his new chosen country, the United States, in November 1950. Before moving to the US, according to his son, he might have had some connections with the CIA, which employed individuals from the other side of the Iron Curtain for different tasks, and this helped him. He settled in Pennsylvania, where he worked in the construction industry, on the engineering board of the Bethlehem Steel Corporation. He obtained a pilot's license in the US and managed to fly here and there with smaller aircraft, but not too frequently. Like the wing commander, Aladár Heppes, Ujszászy also helped collect and organize the documents of the Royal Hungarian Air Force; he himself saved invaluable photographs and documents, for example the full log of 1/3 Squadron from the time of the campaign against the Soviet Union in 1941, as well as an invaluable excerpt from the wartime log of 1/1 Fighter Squadron for the period between 1942 and 1943.

György Ujszászy died on 2 October 1981 in Pottstown, Pennsylvania, and was laid to rest there.

FŐHADNAGY PÁL IRÁNYI

Number of aerial victories: 7
Successes against ground targets: two transport trucks + ?
Number of flown combat sorties: 101
Number of hours flown in the air force: n.d.a.
Nicknames: *Cuni*, *Pali*
Identification number: 5485-18-0453

Decorations

- *Magyar Érdemrend lovagkeresztje hadiszalagon a kardokkal* (1 November 1944)
- *Újólagos Kormányzói dicsérő elismerés Magyar Koronás Ezüst Érdemérme hadiszalagon a kardokkal* (11 March 1943)

58 *HM HIM HL*, documents of 101 Fighter Wing, box nr. 112, registry of personnel on the wing staff and the personal belongings carried away by the Germans. *Százados* Ujszászy's personal car was stolen with a full set of tools, five outer and six inner tires for the wheels, one spare battery, 100kg of almonds, one pair of rubber boots, one pair of skiing shoes, a camelhair blanket and 1,600 *pengő* in cash. This list contains records of the personal loss of seven people from the wing staff. As such a document has not survived in relation to the full wing, neither the personal nor the unit losses can be assessed.

- *Kormányzói dicsérő elismerés Magyar Koronás Bronz Érdemérme hadiszalagon a kardokkal* (12 August 1941)
- *Tűzkereszt I fokozata a kardokkal és koszorúval*, with two wound clasps
- *Felvidéki Emlékérem*
- *Erdélyi Emlékérem*
- *Délvidéki Emlékérem*
- German Iron Cross 1st Class (17 March 1945)
- German Iron Cross 2nd Class (8 March 1945)
- Bulgarian Pilot Badge (summer of 1939)

Victories

Number	Date	Aircraft	Location
1	10 August 1942 at 13:00	LaGG-3	Davidovka
2	2 September 1942 at 06:00	Il-2	Korotoyak
3	13 April 1944	B-24	Ferihegy N
4	16 June 1944	B-24	
5	26 June 1944	P-38	Tét N/Pápa N 18km
6	2 July 1944	B-24	Pettendpuszta (Kápolnásnyék)
7	2 July 1944	B-24	Near Veszprém

Aircraft flown
CR.42: V.254 (8 July 1941), Bf 109 G-6/U4: W-070 (6 December 1944)

Pál Irányi was born on 6 October 1918 in Szatmárnémeti (today Satu Mare, Romania). His father was an evangelical pastor; after the town was ceded to Romania by the Treaty of Trianon, he was arrested on 12 February 1921 by the Romanian police and charged with irredentism, spying and conspiracy. The Romanian Military Court sentenced him to five years of forced labor. After his arrest, his wife and two children (Pali and his older sister) escaped to Hungary via the green borders. Kamill Irányi served his sentence in Romanian state prisons (including the infamous Jilava prison) for three years before being freed on 17 November 1923 as part of the first official Romanian–Hungarian prisoner exchange program. At first, he worked in Budapest, but the family later settled in Székesfehérvár.[59]

Pál Irányi also became a *cőger*. He graduated from the *Zrínyi Miklós Reáliskolai Nevelőintézet* in Pécs as first in his class. He did not only have exceptional intellectual abilities; he was also a good sportsman, and he was especially good at fencing. His primary flight training was completed at Nyíregyháza in 1936; he graduated as *hadnagy* from the 2nd Department of the Ludovika *Akadémia* on 20 August 1939, as of 1 September 1939, with rank number 2 (altogether 20th).[60] After he completed the fighter school at Börgönd, from December 1939 he served in Budapest-Mátyásföld with 1/1 Fighter Squadron led by *százados* Aladár Szobránczy. He also served as the

59 *Evangélikusok Lapja*, 25 November 1923, p. 5; contemporary documents and notes preserved by the Irányi family.
60 *Honvédségi Közlöny* (*Személyes ügyek)*, nr. 1939/6 (19 August 1939), p. 31.

engineering officer of the squadron (his deputy was Béla Lipcsey). In September 1940, the squadron relocated to Kolozsvár-Szamosfalva, where he was soon reassigned as deputy commander to the twin squadron (2/4 Squadron) led by *százados* György Gulden, where he served with László Máthé.

During the campaign against Yugoslavia, the squadron was relocated to Kecskemét, but it was not given important roles. His first missions against the Soviet Union were completed at the end of June and at the beginning of July in 1941 from Bustyaháza (today Bustino, Ukraine).

Hadnagy Irányi completed eight combat sorties with 2/4 Fighter Squadron against the Soviet Union in the summer of 1941, but the eighth almost cost him his life. On 8 July 1941, he and his flight were on a forced mission in extremely bad weather, and all three CR.42s crashed in the northeastern Carpathians near the village of Dora. One of his wingmen, *szakaszvezető* Antal Nébli, was killed; the other, *szakaszvezető* Endre Bajcsi, was seriously injured. *Hadnagy* Irányi himself suffered a concussion and minor facial injuries when his CR.42 (the V.254) crashed into the trees on a mountainside (his aircraft was completely destroyed). He received his first *Signum* for this mission and his first wound clasp for the *Tűzkereszt* (which he received later). His theoretical interests are shown by the fact that he wrote an article for the leading contemporary military journal on the question of choosing candidates for becoming airmen.[61]

The young Pál Irányi as *cőger*: he was one of the most talented students of the *Zrínyi Miklós Reáliskolai Nevelőintézet* in Pécs. (From the collection of the Irányi family)

After the dissolution of the squadron on 1 November 1941, he remained at Kolozsvár in the 2 Fighter Training Group (2/1 Fighter Squadron). In April 1942, when it was decided that 2/1 Squadron, led by *százados* Béla Keresztes, was being deployed to the front, he received retraining to fly Re.2000 in Szolnok. Meanwhile, he was promoted to *főhadnagy* as of 1 April 1942.

On 1 July 1942, while landing in Kolomea during his deployment to the Eastern Front, Irányi overturned with his *Héja* aircraft and suffered another small facial injury – two parallel 3cm slits on his right cheek – for which he received his second wound clasp for his *Tűzkereszt*.[62] On the Eastern Front during the summer of 1942, Irányi was one of the few successful *Héja* pilots. He scored his first air victory on 10 August in the early afternoon behind Soviet lines in the airspace over Davidovka, during a dogfight with LaGG-3 fighters. His opponent was one of the aircraft of 737th IAP; the Soviet unit did not report a total loss for the day, but they did report

61 *HM HIM HL*, Vkf. 1941. 1. oszt. 5813/eln; *hadnagy* Pál Irányi, 'Kiválasztás a repülőfegyvernemhez lélektani alapon', *Magyar Katonai Szemle*, 1941:10, pp. 128–132.

62 *HM HIM HL*, HM 740469/22.-1943.

shooting down a 'Macchi C.200' in air combat (the Hungarian unit lost no aircraft either). Irányi's reported kill was confirmed as there were ground witnesses (artillery observers).[63]

His second aerial victory was achieved on 2 September 1942 against a heavily armored Il-2 over Korotoyak, overhead of the German 336 *Infanteriedivision* and in a combat to eliminate the bridgehead. He remembered the successful air combat as follows:

Főhadnagy Pál Irányi and *karpaszományos őrvezető* László Kovács-Nagy (later *zászlós*, with two kills), pilots of the 2/1. Fighter Squadron of Kolozsvár, in front of an Italian '*Héja*' in the spring of 1942. (From the author's collection)

> Our position is advantageous because the Russians are northwest of us and the sun shines from our back. And they are not more numerous than us up here! At last, for once in our lives we are not up against vastly superior numbers. … The four small black dots approach with dazzling speed. We can already make out their narrow fuselage and their wings attached on the lower side. Il-2s, heavily armored types that attack at low altitudes. With machine guns, their only soft spot is the frontal upper part of the engine. I am attacking at a 45 percent angle, so, unfortunately, I cannot fire at the engine compartment – for this, I would have to attack from closer and from more of a perch position. I am already too level with him from behind. I open fire and hope his reaction will be to turn and show me a more vulnerable part of his aircraft. … The Russian turns onto its back and starts diving. We already know this trick, and as per the best technique I do not go after him, but increase my altitude and look down on him from a perch position. I don't need to wait for him too long; he ends his dive and tries to escape eastward in panic. Now is the time for me to go after him; I start diving too and open fire from my machine guns. The Russian suddenly turns his aircraft left and starts to turn. He wants to get into my rear! I anxiously check my gunsight and force my aircraft into even narrower turn. My guns fire wildly. Now I can clearly see the hits on the upper side of the nose. Suddenly a huge flame erupts out of the engine compartment, the aircraft lurching and starts to plummet right down toward the ground! His path is marked by a brownish black trail of smoke. He crashes into the ground and huge pillars of smoke and black dust rising. I have made it … he flew into my burst with his turn.[64]

63 Árpád Járomy, *Csatarepülők* (Budapest: Stádium, 1943), p. 216.
64 Járomy, *Csatarepülők*, pp. 236–237.

Főhadnagy Pál Irányi –third from the left – as the deputy commander of 101/1 Fighter Squadron in the late spring of 1944 in Veszprém. Fourth from left is *hadnagy* László Hemmert; the fifth is *őrmester* Zoltán Raposa, and the sixth is *szakaszvezető* Lajos Buday. (From the collection of László Hemmert)

The witness to this aerial victory was *hadnagy* Count Nándor Orssich.

That autumn, *főhadnagy* Irányi did not succeed in scoring more kills. The number of his combat sorties with *Héja* on the front in 1942 amounted to 40, with two confirmed air victories. The majority of his squadron returned home during the autumn, and the replacing unit started to arrive as well, but Irányi remained on the Eastern Front with some non-commissioned officer pilots until 5 January 1943, when they were put on a train at Stary Oskol and began the journey home. He therefore avoided the combats of the winter retreat. After his return, *főhadnagy* Irányi was assigned to Mátyásföld. He received Bf 109 retraining in the spring, even though there were still *MÁVAG*-manufactured *Héja*s serving in home defense. From September, he was stationed at Ferihegy, and he became the deputy commander of 2/1 Fighter Squadron, now led by *százados* Miklós Scholtz. The squadron only received Messerschmitts at the beginning of February 1944 and engaged in combat with the Americans for the first time on 17 March 1944, before the Allied bombing raids began in April against Hungary.

Főhadnagy Irányi shot down his first American aircraft on 13 April 1944, during the second large-scale raid on Budapest. On this day, he attacked one of the Liberators of the American formation bombing the base of the squadron at Ferihegy. The aircraft (B-24H, serial number 41-28833), which belonged to 449th BG's 719th BS and was flown by 2nd Lieutenant Warren N. Rustad, exploded in mid-air and the whole 10-member crew was killed. According to the American report, another Liberator of 376th BG accidentally dropped a 20-pound (approximately 9kg) fragmentation bomb on the starboard wing of Rustad's aircraft, adding to its destruction. The aircraft was credited to Irányi with two points, as a shared victory with the anti-aircraft artillery, even though the anti-aircraft artillery had little to do with the aircraft's destruction.[65] Irányi remembered the aerial victory as follows:

65 NARA MACR 4096.

We received orders to land, refuel and replenish our ammunition to be ready for a new mission. I was the leader of the second flight, and the aircraft of the first flight were already running on the ground before me when I heard on the radio: 'Bombers over Budapest!'

At the same time, I saw huge blasts going off right in front of my eyes. … Obviously, we hadn't landed on the bombed airfield, but we remained in the air. After I got through the smoke screen and looked around, I noticed an enormous enemy formation above our heads! … I ordered my wingman via the radio to close up. I decided to attack these bombers!

The little red light indicating a shortage of fuel was flashing wildly, but I did not heed anything but the bombers and the destruction they inflicted on the ground. They must pay for this! … I started to climb at the steepest possible angle! … Soon I got overhead of the American formation. I chose the very last bomber, a Liberator, which was lagging behind the others. I knew I had no fuel for a second attack – I opened fire from far away! I wanted to put everything I had into this single attack! I saw my rounds hitting the huge fuselage of the aircraft! I was very close now, I almost ran over it, and he was firing wildly at me from his guns [sic] and machine guns. I could barely be further than 25–30 meters from him when I suddenly needed to nosedive my aircraft so as not to run into the huge aircraft at a speed of 600km/h. At the same time, yellowish fire spurted out of its fuselage. …

As soon as I finished my dive and could at last look back, I saw that my victim had been blown to pieces, its parts plummeting down in flames, and nobody had bailed out. …

But I did not have more time to watch the results of my aerial victory further, because my engine started coughing. I turned back toward the airfield and was annoyed to see that my fuel gauge was showing zero; the little red light was not flashing anymore but was lit up continuously …

After all this, I could not do anything else but try to reach the airfield safely. With a clogging engine, I used my last drops of my fuel to put my aircraft down on the familiar ground.[66]

Főhadnagy Pál Irányi with *főhadnagy* György Pávay-Vajna (on the right) in Veszprém, in the summer of 1944. György Pávay-Vajna (1920–1999) ended the war as the commander of 101/5 Fighter Squadron. (From the collection of László Hemmert)

With the formation of 101 Fighter Group, the former 2/1 Fighter Squadron became the first squadron of the group, with a call sign of '*Zongora*'. Its experienced deputy commander

66 'Őszinte beszéd a rádióban a magyar vadászrepülők Budapest feletti harcairól', *Egyedül vagyunk*, 5 May 1944, pp. 4–5.

had not only led his squadron, but also in many cases the group itself, against the Americans during the summer missions.

During the mission on 24 May 1944, American fighters surprised Irányi and shot him down from behind. He was able to belly-land his damaged aircraft with its smoking engine in Vas County, probably near Rózsamajor. This was the only occasion during the war that enemy aircraft were able to shoot him down.

His next four-engined was probably shot down on 16 June 1944, together with *hadnagy* Karátsonyi. Unfortunately, the time and the exact date are also missing in this case; only the record of the shared victory against the heavy bomber are known about this event.

On 26 June 1944, Irányi again reported shooting down a Lightning, but this claim was for a long time left unconfirmed, mainly because there was no P-38 wreck known in the area at the time. At last, Wing Order Nr. 1945/20, issued 26 January 1945, ordered the claim report to be re-edited and sent to Air Force Command for re-evaluation, because the original claim report had probably been lost and because witness reports had been added to the victory claim report from *hadnagy* Benkő, *szakaszvezető* Faludi and *szakaszvezető* Nagy. This meant the confirmation of the aerial victory in practical terms, but this particular kill was not officially confirmed in the Wing Orders at the end of the war, perhaps because of the conflict between Irányi and Heppes.[67] During the mission, Irányi attacked a Lightning at 7,000 meters with altitude advantage, firing at him directly at very close range until 30–10 meters, hitting the target multiple times. The P-38 immediately began to plummet uncontrollably (the eyewitnesses thought the pilot himself had been hit). *Főhadnagy* Irányi did not follow the falling aircraft because more Lightnings were arriving at the scene, and the experienced pilot led his flight into a climb and left the American fighters behind.

According to data collected by the author, one of the main problems with the confirmation of the aerial victory was that a typing error occurred in the report: it gave Tés north as the location, not Tét north, which was the actual scene of the air combat. Tés north is much more eastward; the fighting took place in the area of Győr, which was confirmed not only by the general witness reports but also by the notes of Lajos Benkő, who noted a 'half' Lightning had been shot down with a location of Pápa 18km north. In the author's opinion, this shared kill, which was not officially claimed by Benkő, clearly shows that he was also firing at the same Lightning that was being attacked by Irányi, and which he felt he had also hit.[68]

The engagement certainly happened against the P-38s of 82nd FG. The 95th Fighter Squadron lost a killed pilot, 2nd Lieutenant Ray W. Allen (P-38J, serial number 42-104393), who crashed to the ground on Slovak territory northeast of Bratislava, near near Szentgyörgy (Svät. Jur.).[69] From an altitude of 7,000 meters in the Győr area, even a seriously wounded pilot might bring his aircraft to this area at any time; however, it is also possible that this Lightning was shot down by a gunner of a German twin-engined destroyer from ZG 76 that later also crashed and did not report the air victory. Apart from Irányi's claim, only one other aerial victory claim was made in the area against P-38s, and another P-38 was indeed shot down by the German destroyers, the American pilot of which was taken captive.

67 *HM HIM HL*, documents of 101 Fighter Wing, box nr. 110, Wing Order Nr. 1945/20; for the records, see Pataky, Rozsos, and Sárhidai, *Légi háború Magyarország felett*, vol. 2, p. 71.
68 Notes of Lajos Benkő and József Nagy (copies owned by the author).
69 Kaššák and Hrodegh, *Konečná Zastávka*, pp. 38–40.

Crew of the Liberator shot down by *főhadnagy* Irányi and *hadnagy* Lajos Benkő on 2 July 1944 at Pettendpuszta. The pilot, 2nd Lieutenant Lawrence D. Whittaker, is third from left in the back row (Riley via Mohos)

The attacked P-38 could also possibly have been the aircraft of 2nd Lieutenant Roy I. Harman from the same squadron. Harman's cockpit was pierced by two 2cm cannon shells, lightly wounding the pilot (who was extremely lucky to survive it); the aircraft itself was hit three times by 13mm heavy machine guns in the middle of its wings as well. In total, two Lightnings were lost during the air combat; a further five were damaged.[70]

Irányi achieved another two aerial victories in July 1944, both against American Liberators. Of these, the first was reported during the large-scale air battle over Budapest on 2 July 1944; the kill was confirmed with a location of Pettendpuszta. This Pettendpuszta aircraft was attacked by Irányi and *hadnagy* Lajos Benkő, along with the two wingmen of the four-aircraft flight. The aircraft flown by 2nd Lieutenant Lawrence D. Whittaker was blown up and fell to pieces in mid-air; of the crew, only two survived, and eight were killed (456th BG, B-24J, serial number 42-99799).[71]

Interestingly, the aircraft at Pettendpuszta was also claimed by the German anti-aircraft artillery group at Budapest (*17 Flakbrigade*), for whom it was confirmed, even though the aircraft was shot down by fighters not only according to the reports of the fighters themselves, but also according to the report of other aircraft in the formation and the survivors. In contrast,

70 82nd Fighter Group Mission No. 714, Narrative Report (copy owned by the author).
71 NARA MACR 6440.

the German anti-aircraft artillery crew stated that there had been no German or Hungarian fighters in the area at the moment of their success.[72]

The other aircraft was shot down by Irányi on 7 July; this was confirmed in Wing Confidential Order Nr. 1944/63 of 2 July, with the location of Felsőörs. In this case, the date is an error, and the location is also incorrect, as the B-24 that crashed at Felsőörs on 7 July (from the 459th BG) was credited to *hadnagy* Benkő and was not a shared victory. Because the sources are extremely scarce, and because of the mistaken location, it is not possible to pinpoint the location of the aircraft shot down by *főhadnagy* Irányi; as such, it can only be presumed, and on that day Hungarian fighters shot down a number of four-engines in the area of Veszprém. A surviving letter from *hadnagy* Molnár also mentions that *főhadnagy* Irányi shot down an enemy Liberator near Veszprém on this date. This same four-engined was also credited to *főhadnagy* Irányi as a shared victory with the anti-aircraft artillery, with two points (practically all his Liberators were confirmed as shared aerial victories – two with the anti-aircraft artillery, one with *hadnagy* Karátsonyi and one with *hadnagy* Benkő).[73]

The recommendation to award him with the *Magyar Érdemrend lovagkeresztje hadiszalagon a kardokkal*, issued on 9 September 1944, commends *főhadnagy* Irányi: 'The said person, with his high number of air victories and his numerous combat sorties, is one of the most successful fighter pilots of the group. On a number of missions, while flying as squadron commander and then as group commander, he has ensured the success of the group through his skilled leadership.'[74]

When the Fighter Group was reorganised to a wing at the beginning of September 1944, *százados* Scholtz left his position as squadron commander and took the leadership of 101/I Group. *Főhadnagy* Irányi became squadron commander of 101/1 Squadron. He kept this position until the beginning of November, when he was reassigned to the group staff as deputy group commander.[75]

Among *főhadnagy* Irányi's missions against the Soviets was the notable one completed on 4 December, when he led the formation of 101/1 Fighter Squadron on an extremely effective strafing attack in Somogy County against the marching troops of the 3rd Ukrainian Front. During this attack, they destroyed three armored vehicles (probably two armored reconnaissance cars, which are featured in the summary report compiled of the results of the German-Hungarian aircraft, and an SU-76M type self-propelled assault gun), two anti-aircraft guns and one field artillery battery, along with a number of transport trucks and other vehicles. They also strafed the marching columns effectively, mainly on the roads between Kaposvár and Siófok. At least two transport trucks – south of Siófok – were destroyed by Irányi personally. The Soviet 7th Guards Airborne Division and the 80th Guards Rifle Division, which made up the majority of the forces in the area, also suffered extensive losses from the strafing attacks of the Hungarian

72 Bundesarchiv-Militärarchiv RL 5/5; see also Csaba Becze, 'Benkő Lajos – egy veszprémi vadászpilóta a második világháborúban', *Veszprémi Szemle*, 2010:1–2, pp. 13–31.

73 *HM HIM HL*, documents of 101 Fighter Wing, box nr. 110, Air Force Confidential Order Nr. 1944/63; box nr. 113, record of victories against four-engines; letter of 2nd Lieutenant László Molnár to his parents, 9 July 1944 (copy owned by the author, the original in possession of Krisztián Tóth).

74 *HM HIM HL*, documents of 101 Fighter Wing, box nr. 113, telegram, 1st Air Division high command.

75 *HM HIM HL*, documents of 101 Fighter Wing, box nr. 110, Wing Order Nr. 1944/35.

The wreck of the Liberator nicknamed 'Salvo Susie' (456th BG. B-24J serial number 4299799) crashed at Pettendpuszta on 2 July 1944 (*HM HIM* Photographic Archives 105060)

fighters. The 85th Independent Guards Self-Propelled Artillery Division supporting the 80th Guards Rifle Division also lost a loader on this day near Szántód (probably due to the hits suffered by the open combat compartment of his SU-76), and he might also have been the victim of the Hungarian strafing runs.[76]

The following article was published in a contemporary newspaper about the successful strike, in which Pál Irányi and Lajos Tóth were also interviewed:

> The aircraft circled the Lake Balaton and attacked the Soviets from the rear at Kaposvár. Motorized infantry, cavalry and Soviet infantry were marching on the uneven road toward Balatonföldvár. At Somogyecse [Somogyacsa], Andacs [Andocs] and Kaposfüred, the columns were attacked; they then turned away toward Igal. The fighter pilot has a hard task: he searches for the target, and attacks the road with an overwhelming force. His propeller roars over the road in a low-altitude flight, and while controlling the aircraft at this breakneck speed, his weapons also need to be controlled – the machine guns and the 3cm automatic cannon from which there is no escape for the enemy, not even underground.
>
> 'We have been pounding them at Igal,' *főhadnagy* Irányi tells us, then adds: 'A sea of ammunition-loaded carts and transport vehicles were standing crammed into the main square of Igal when the Pumas went into full attack.'
>
> 'We were left with smoke and fire from Igal,' adds Tóth, who was leading the second squadron after the first strafing run: 'An armored fighting vehicle was burning like a torch before Igal – so the Pumas were aiming well.' *Főhadnagy* Irányi and his squadron also knocked out two armored fighting vehicles at Som[ogy]acsa. It was a nerve-wrenching, deadly competition of the two best weapons in this modern war: the aircraft attacked like a hawk, at a speed of 400–500km/h, flying past the armored fighting vehicle a meter away and firing its 3cm automatic cannon with a steady hand. The blue shell melted and penetrated the armor and exploded within the armored fighting vehicle, tearing the steel monster apart. Two anti-aircraft guns and a whole battery were destroyed by the

76 'Puma vadászrepülők pusztítják az orosz erőket Siófok és Kaposvár között', *Lármafa*, December 1944 (unknown issue), p. 3; Norbert Számvéber, *Páncélos-hadviselés a budapesti csatában 1944 október 29–1945 február 13* (Nagykovácsi: Puedlo, 2011), p. 120. The author wishes to express his gratitude to Gábor Horváth and Dr Norbert Számvéber for their kind help.

> Hungarians. Then, they turned toward Siófok. The ships had just left the harbor when the town was approached by the Russians. At the back of the armored fighting vehicles came the motorized infantry.
>
> 'Siófok was burning with big flames,' adds *főhadnagy* Irányi, who knocked out two fully loaded transport vehicles on the road. 'Even the most beautiful trees on the promenade on the shore caught fire.'[77]

During 1944, *főhadnagy* Irányi completed 36 combat sorties altogether against Americans. This exceptionally large number (compared to the other pilots) was mainly due to the fact that, as the deputy commander of 2/1 Squadron, he also took part in the home air defense as early as the beginning of 1944, during which they had not even engaged the enemy. This veteran commander therefore had the highest number of combat sorties against the Americans among the Hungarian fighter pilots.

Irányi completed his last (101st) combat sortie on 23 January 1945. Taking off at 10:15, he led a flight into the area of Székesfehérvár on a free hunt, during which they engaged the enemy, but without any apparent results.

Following this, his wing commander, Aladár Heppes, forbade him to fly missions in future. He made up an excuse and proposed relocating him as an officer who was not eligible for commander roles. Their disagreement was of a personal nature (the author will not go into the details of it here), and its escalation was the fault of both officers – but the final word was Heppes's. With Irányi's prohibition, the unit was thus deprived of one of its best formation leaders.

Irányi did not want to accept the situation, and with six of his formes squadron mates, among them few pilots from 101/1 Squadron, reported *alezredes* Heppes to the Arrow Cross authorities – probably to the military investigation sub-department of the *Nemzeti Számonkérés Szervezete* ('National Impeachment Organization', operating against the enemies of the Hungarist State). The reason was that 'he [Heppes] does not command the wing in a true "Hungarist" manner'. This attempt was unsuccessful; Irányi was even detained for some time, and eventually needed to resign himself over the issue. He afterward went to Pocking, to the assembly airfield of the Hungarian air force, and this is where he was taken POW by US forces in May 1945.

Pál Irányi did not come home from American captivity, but remained in Germany. From 1946, he was employed by the French army – probably as a member of the GAE (*Groupe d'Auxiliaires Etrangers*), an organization established for auxiliary military tasks and made up of non-French nationals. In 1949, he became a manager of the IRO (International Refugee Organization), which dealt with international refugee issues. He and his family moved from Germany to Venezuela in August 1950. Here, he worked as an aviation instructor, a topographer, a drinks seller, a sports teacher and finally as a fencing master. From 1955, he led the sports department of the officer trainer school of the Venezuelan Air Force in Maracay. From Venezuela, he moved back to Germany in 1961 August, and he mainly worked as a fencing master in schools and universities (Mainz, Heidelberg, Karlsruhe and Wennheim) until his retirement.

Pál Irányi died on 23 August 1996 in Müllheim, and was laid to rest in Mannheim cemetery.

77 'Puma vadászrepülők pusztítják az orosz erőket Siófok és Kaposvár között,' p. 3.

HADNAGY KÁLMÁN SZEVERÉNYI

Number of aerial victories: 7
Successes against ground targets: n.d.a.
Number of flown combat sorties: 159
Number of hours flown in the air force: n.d.a.
Nickname: *Szever*
Identification number: 3181-20-0605

Decorations

- *Újólagos Kormányzói dicsérő elismerés Magyar Koronás Ezüst Érdemérme hadiszalagon a kardokkal* (5 June 1944)
- *Kormányzói dicsérő elismerés Magyar Koronás Bronz Érdemérme hadiszalagon a kardokkal* (24 March 1944)
- *Tűzkereszt I fokozata a kardokkal és koszorúval*
- *Erdélyi Emlékérem*
- German Iron Cross 2nd Class (1944)
- Gold *Frontflugspange* (1944)

Victories

Number	Date	Aircraft	Location
1	7 October 1943	La-5	Along the Dnieper
2	August 1944	Soviet fighter	Mielec SE?
3	28 October 1944	Boston III	Tiszavasvári
4	11 November 1944	Il-2	Kecskemét
5	13 November 1944	Il-2	Jászberény
6	1944–45	Soviet aircraft	
7	21 February 1945 at 13:50	B-17	Soponya SW

Aircraft flown

Bf 109 G-6: V-387 (14 September 1944), V-391 (15–16 September 1944)

Kálmán Szeverényi was born on 25 February 1920 in Kecskemét into a family of nine children. His father was a forester. His family name is particularly interesting because, when he was registered as a newborn, his father's name was mistakenly recorded as 'Szeveréni'. Kálmán thus received his school certificates under this name and was also graduated into the air force with it; he is therefore featured in all official military documents with this name, despite the fact that the birth registry was officially corrected on 27 January 1941. He himself was not bothered with the error and used both versions of his name, as we have a number of letters and other documents from him after 1941 signed as 'Szeveréni'. Despite this, the official version remains 'Szeverényi'; the family used this spelling in the past and uses it still, so this is the spelling used in this work.[78]

78 *MNL Bács-Kiskun Megye Levéltára* (National Archives, Bács-Kiskun County Archives), XXXIII/1, birth registry of the town Kecskemét for 1920, counterpart, note 1920/606 fsz. The correction of the

Hadnagy Kálmán Szeverényi immediately after his graduation. (From the collection of the Szeverényi family)

Kálmán Szeverényi is sitting on the port main undercarriage of his white-painted Messerschmitt Bf 109 G-2 in Ukraine, in 1943. (From the collection of Emil Terray)

Kálmán Szeverényi graduated from his hometown (in the *Piarista Általános Iskola, Gimnázium és Kollégium*) in 1938, with excellent grades. At high school, he was classmate of Ervin Flóznik, who later also became a fighter ace. They probably urged and motivated each other in their decisions related to military flying; in the long run, Szeverényi wanted to be a staff officer. Szeverényi received his primary flight training in Szeged in the summer of 1939, at the *HMNRA* Algyő department, financed by the *Délvidéki Aero Club* (Southern Hungarian Aero Club).

He spent the following year in an air force unit service and enrolled at the *Repülőakadémia* at Kassa in the autumn of 1940, where he graduated as *repülő hadnagy* on 6 December 1942, member of the class of Lajos Tóth and József Málik. Compared to his classmates, however, who were admitted to the academy right after high school, Szeverényi had already spent a year in troop service and was therefore graduated as a *hadnagy* as of 1 July 1942, with rank number 26.[79] After his graduation, *hadnagy* Szeverényi was assigned to 5/I Fighter Group, stationed at Mátyásföld.

The young *hadnagy* was deployed to the Eastern Front on 17 July 1943, while the battle of Kursk was raging, and was assigned to 5/2 Squadron of his group.

Szeverényi achieved his first confirmed aerial victory on 7 October 1943 under extraordinary circumstances. He attacked a Soviet La-5 in the Dnieper area, but before he could open fire, the Soviet pilot panicked and bailed out. The field magazine of the Hungarian fighters, *Üvölt a Puma*, commemorated the incident with these funny lines:

misspelled name was based on Decree Nr. 1173/1941.

79 *Honvédségi Közlöny* (*Személyes ügyek*), 1942/50, 4 December 1942, p. 1263.

A trio of aces in January 1944 at Vinnytsia: *hadnagys* György Debrődy, László Molnár and Kálmán Szeverényi. (From the collection of the Szeverényi family)

Hadnagys Szeverényi, Molnár and Debrődy in front of the aircraft of *hadnagy* Molnár (marked 66) at the beginning of 1944 (*HM HIM* Photographic Archives 106.719/119)

> *Hadnagy* Szeverényi achieved a kill in an absolutely extraordinary way. He placed himself behind a Lagg 5; the Russian started to turn – excellent firing position; Szeverényi wanted to open fire at once, but the Russian looked back and, in the next second, before any bursts had time to be fired, he just bailed out of his aircraft! His parachute was still descending when his aircraft crashed to the ground and exploded. This is what I call ammunition saving! However, some say that *hdgy*. Szeverényi switched to the Russian radio frequency and sent the pilot spine-chilling messages, which terrified his enemy.[80]

For the opponents of the Hungarian fighters on 7 October 1944, please see more details described in the biography of László Molnár.

The cheerful, well-balanced and popular Szeverényi according to the available data closed 1943 with this sole aerial victory.

In March 1944, Szeverényi faced a serious health issue: he developed acute appendicitis, upon which he was immediately admitted to the Proskurov military hospital on 8 March 1944. There it turned out that the perforation of his appendix had caused peritonitis. After an operation was performed, he was sent to the military hospital at Stanislau and then transported back to Hungary.[81] *Hadnagy* Szeverényi spent his convalescence and a short break to recover his health at home. He probably went back to his unit in the late spring or early summer of 1944; his unit

80 *Üvölt a Puma*, 3 November 1943, p. 4.
81 *HM HIM HL*, HM 620 959/22.v.-1944.

Kálmán Szeverényi's Bf 109 G-6 (V-391) in the late summer of 1944 (WNr. 166488). *Hadnagy* Szeverényi was killed on 22 February 1945 in this aircraft; it was already quite old by then. (From the collection of the Szeverényi family)

had, in the meantime, been renumbered from 5/2 to 102 Independent Fighter Squadron, before subsequently becoming 102/1 Squadron. Szeverényi probably received his last Messerschmitt Bf 109 G-6 (the V.391) in July 1944, which he flew until his death.

Hadnagy Szeverényi achieved his next air victory, probably at the beginning of August 1944. During the mission, six aircraft of his squadron were escorting German and Hungarian Junkers Ju 87 dive bombers against targets southeast of Mielec. Over the target area, Soviet fighters attacked the formation, and in the ensuing dogfight Szeverényi managed to shoot down a Soviet aircraft, although his own aircraft was also damaged.[82]

Szeverényi has reported his next (known) air victory during the home defense period, over Hungary on 28 October 1944. The victim this time was a Soviet Boston bomber, from 453rd BAP's 2nd Squadron. The aircraft was flown by *leytenant* L.Y. Sedov (an A-20 G, serial number 42-54244); its four-member crew, including a female gunner, was killed. The kill was credited to Szeverényi with a location of Büdszentmihály (now part of the town of Tiszavasvári). The particularly interesting thing about this event is that the same aircraft was reported as having been shot down by *Leutnant* Heinz Ewald, one of the young and successful pilots of II./JG 52. Ewald took off at 14:20 for his 255th combat sortie from his unit's airfield at Taktakenéz, after a scramble was ordered to counter the bomber; at 14:28, he was again on the ground. Unfortunately, we lack both German and Hungarian sources to tell us exactly what happened, but it seems certain that both men claiming the aircraft had been attacking it, although *hadnagy* Szeverényi may have been the first to make a succesful pass. It seems plausible, however, that the German pilot renounced his attempts and let his Hungarian comrade have a go. He did not officially claim the aircraft, but only noted it down in his diary; Ewald only wrote of the events in his *Flugbuch* that the aerial victory was 'confirmed for the Hungarians'.[83]

82 György Punka, *A Messzer. Bf 109-ek a Magyar Királyi Honvéd Légierőben* (Budapest: OMIKK, 1995), p. 97. The author has not found any details or any information regarding this victory.

83 For the Boston, see Horváth, *Bostonok a magyar égen és földben*, pp. 41–42; see also the relevant note in Heinz Ewald's *Flugbuch*. The author wishes to express his gratitude to Bernd Barbas

Heinz Ewald had 30 confirmed aerial victories by this time, a number that had grown to 84 by the end of the war (he had a further 15 unconfirmed victories). He was decorated with the Knights Cross of the Iron Cross on 20 April 1945.[84]

Kálmán Szeverényi achieved his next kill in the airspace over his hometown, Kecskemét, on 15 November by shooting down an Il-2; the aircraft probably served in the 90th or 91st GSAP. Two days later, he destroyed another Soviet ground-attack aircraft, this time in the Jászberény area. This aircraft was the Il-2 of 235th SAP (serial number 10454) flown by *mladshiy leytenant* N.F. Burkanov, which crashed into a house in Jászberény and was destroyed with its full crew. The Soviet report mentioned an anti-aircraft hit, but this could have come from an unnoticed, low-flying Bf 109 attacking from a dead spot. The three aerial victories achieved by Szeverényi in October and November 1944 were confirmed by Air Force Order Nr. 1945/4.[85]

According to the summary of his group commander, *őrnagy* József Kovács, Szeverényi had, until 29 January 1945, flown 151 combat sorties in his squadron (5/2, then 102 Independent, then 102/1 Squadron; from the end of January 1945, the unit was called 101/7 Squadron), scoring six aerial victories. This means another confirmed air victory, but the details are not known. This kill against a Soviet aircraft could have happened any time between November 1943 and January 1945. The latest possible date is January 1945, because many details regarding his sixth aerial victory in January 1945 were lost following the destruction of the documents of the unit on being reformed from 102 Group to 101/III Group. Some place his sixth aerial victory to 13 February 1945 and provide a B-17 as a victim, but this cannot be valid, as the partially-surviving documents of 101 Fighter Wing from February 1945 do not support this theory. The B-17 that crashed on the appointed day over Hungary was not destroyed due to fighter attack, as stated by American sources.[86] Considering the intensity of the combat actions the squadron was involved in, and by investigating the surviving documents, it is highly probable that Szeverényi achieved this victory in January or February 1944 – or perhaps December 1944, or January 1945.

One of the pilots of 453rd BAP, *mladshiy leytenant* Leonid Yefimovich Sedov (1923–1944) – from the left – rolling bad quality cigarettes with one of his comrades in the pause between missions. The Boston of *mladshiy leytenant* Sedov (serial number 42-54244) was shot down by Kálmán Szeverényi on 28 October 1944, and the four crew members were killed (Sedov via Horváth)

(*Traditionsgemeinschaft JG 52*) for the German data originating in the legacy of Heinz Ewald (Sopot, 1 September 1922–Coburg, 14 March 2002), and for the copy of the relevant part of the *Flugbuch*. Unfortunately, the privately published recollections of Heinz Ewald, who was awarded the *Magyar Érdemrend tisztikeresztje* in February 1945 for his achievements over Hungary, contain mostly anecdotes and stories, and he has not written anything about this particular event: see *Esau – Heinz Ewald als Jagdflieger im erfolgreichsten Jagdgeschwader 1943–1945* (Coburg: Eigenverlag, 1980), p. 182.

84 For Heinz Ewald, see Obermaier, *Die Ritterkreuzträger der Luftwaffe 1939–45*, p. 108.

85 *HM HIM HL*, documents of 101 Fighter Wing, box nr. 110, Air Force Order Nr. 1945/4; Gábor Horváth on documents of TsAMO.

86 For the incorrect data, see Punka, *A Messzer. Bf 109-ek a Magyar Királyi Honvéd Légierőben*, pp. 76, 110.

Szeverényi flew his last seven combat sorties in February 1945, during which he scored another confirmed aerial victory, shooting down a B-17. On 21 February, six aircraft of his squadron received start orders from airfield-defense combat-readiness at 12:45. The patrolling Hungarian fighters met a lone B-17 over Szabadbattyán at 13:42 (B-17G from 2nd BG's 429th BS, serial number 446689). They attacked the aircraft and set both starboard engines aflame; of the 10-member crew, four bailed out over Soviet-occupied territory (the pilot, 1st Lieutenant Eugene F. Bull, as well as the co-pilot, the navigator and the bombardier, but the other six bailed out over Hungarian territory and were captured. Of the latter, the tail gunner, Technical Sergeant Ted J. Bunnell, had already been wounded in the aircraft; according to the recollections of his comrades, he was again seriously wounded in the leg when one of the Messerschmitts attacked him while descending on parachute. On 9 March, he died of his wounds. The bomber crashed into the ground at 13:51 southwest of Soponya – 3km northeast of Dég, as it was reported not very precisely by the Hungarian fighters. The kill was reported by *hadnagy* Szeverényi, with *főhadnagy* Szénási and *szakaszvezető* Kiss as witnesses.[87]

The author was not able to trace exactly which of the four Hungarian aircraft shot at the American while he was descending on his parachute; maybe this was revenge for László Molnár, who had flown with many of the fighters in the squadron over the winter of 1943–44. However, as the Americans bailed out over fronts that were hard to determine precisely from the air, the act might have been an attempt to liquidate the American, who otherwise might have escaped without harm over the Soviet lines. According to my knowledge, this is the only instance during the war that Hungarian pilots targeted an enemy crewmember on parachute, but this again shows that such cases happened everywhere.

This was the seventh – and last – confirmed air victory for Szeverényi. The pilot only survived for one more day. On 22 February 1945, eight aircraft of 101/III Fighter Group took off at 16:10 for a free hunt led by *százados* Pottyondy. Szeverényi was among them; his flight flew behind *százados* Pottyondy's flight. At 16:30, at 6,000 meters and approaching Tata, Szeverényi noticed a squadron-strength Yakovlev formation below them to the south. He reported this to Pottyondy via radio, but the response was that they should keep to their instructions and fly along. However, the Soviet formation had also noticed the Hungarian Messerschmitts; the last pilot pushed up the nose of his aircraft and fired a long burst from his cannon on the Hungarians from a great distance. The aircraft of *hadnagy* Szeverényi was hit, and he suffered some minor splinter injuries. The water cooler of the engine was also damaged. (There was no Soviet aerial victory claim in the area on that day; the Soviet pilot was probably unaware that he had hit the Hungarian.) The cooling water quickly leaked out of Szeverényi's aircraft. He had two options to choose from before the engine seized: he could either bail out, or he could try to belly-land the aircraft. His wingman, *hadnagy* Lajos Galánfy, encouraged him to take the first option, but *hadnagy* Szeverényi did not want to destroy his aircraft because he liked it so much, as he had been flying it for more than six months; he therefore chose to belly-land. The aircraft slid into an artificial fish-farming lake (nr. 19.) directly north of Tata near the road to Naszály.

The mechanic of his aircraft, *szakaszvezető* János Domonkos, remembered the event as follows:

87 NARA MACR 12099, *HM HIM HL*, documents of 101 Fighter Wing, box nr. 113, after-action reports and mission logs of 101 Fighter Wing, 21 February 1945.

> He tried to crash-land into a ditch in the southern part of Tatatóváros [Tata and Tóváros were united in 1938, and were only briefly called Tatatóváros; the name was officially changed to Tata in 1939], on an approximately 350-meter long strip of land, which was cut through the middle by an approximately 1.5 meter high ridge; on the other side were the reed and the deep lake. According to the visible clues and according to the description by *hdgy*. Galánfy, the aircraft landed on the edge of the hollow area, which required great skill, but on the frozen ground it would have needed more distance to dampen the speed with which the aircraft crashed into the bank in front of it. Thus the aircraft tumbled over the bank, and for approximately 30 meters it slid into the frozen lake, half submerged in the icy water. Galánfy circled overhead for five to seven minutes but he did not see Szeverényi climbing out of the aircraft, although the aircraft itself was visibly badly damaged.
>
> Upon returning to Veszprém, the Red Cross vehicle was ready in a minute, and Galánfy and I sped with it toward the lake. We arrived at around 10:00 pm at night. The ice was shattered completely so we were not able to approach the aircraft. We called him but received no answer. I constructed a rope from belts and I climbed from ice table to ice table to reach the aircraft, but the pilot was not there. The harness was cut; I found some remains from his airman's coat and blood marks on the seat, and the control panel had been pushed back by the impact of the crash.
>
> We went to the gardener's underground hut nearby and asked around. The gardener told us that, approximately half an hour after the crash, Szeverényi had been rescued by the Germans. We then rushed to the military command post in Tatatóváros, where we were told that the airman was being cared for in the hospital converted from the building of the local civilian school [this was the Field Hospital Nr. 7, now an elementary school, *Vaszary János Általános Iskola*]. Here the attending doctor told us that the airman had been immediately operated on to remove fragments of the cannon shell splinters. Otherwise, it is all good and the pilot had just told everyone the story of his crash-landing. The doctor allowed us to visit him and came along. In the corridor, a nurse rushed toward us and reported that the *hadnagy* had suddenly felt very indisposed. When we entered the room, he recognized us. He said to me: 'Domi, could you write to my parents?' Ten minutes later the doctor declared him dead.[88]

Hadnagy Szeverényi had not suffered serious shrapnel injuries, but crash-landing on particularly rough terrain had caused serious internal injuries, and the internal bleeding from these caused his death. He died a short time before midnight. The direct cause of his death was probably liver rupture, and his serious internal injuries were caused by him loosening his harness after taking off to allow himself a bit more movement and to see better during the mission; he had forgotten to tighten them again before crash-landing. The most probable cause of Kálmán Szeverényi's death was therefore internal bleeding due to blunt abdominal trauma.[89]

Szeverényi's old aircraft was the abovementioned Bf 109 G-6 (WNr. 166488), originally numbered V391, manufactured in Regensburg and equipped with an Erla canopy. The aircraft

88 Recollections of János Domonkos, 26 January 1976 (copy owned by the author).
89 Based on the kind communication of Tibor Tobak, 16 November 1993; letter of senior consultant orthopedic surgeon Professor György Szabó, 24 May 2013.

suffered 80 percent damage according to the Hungarian reports, but only 60 percent according to the German statistics.[90] Szeverényi had previously been recommended for the *Magyar Érdemrend lovagkeresztje*; he was also posthumously recommended for the *Magyar Érdemrend tisztikeresztje*. However, neither decoration was awarded to him.

The body of *hadnagy* Kálmán Szeverényi was brought back by the comrades to Veszprém, where he was buried on 24 February 1945. His body was exhumed after the war at the request of his parents, who had been visited by *szakaszvezető* János Domonkos, who told them the story of their son's death. Szeverényi was reinterred on 14 March 1946 in Kecskemét, in the Szentháromság Cemetery. Kálmán Szeverényi was buried with his brother, three years his senior, who had served in the armored forces as *törzsőrmester* and who was wounded on 24 October 1944 south of Kiskunfélegyháza, when his tank was knocked out; he died on 26 December 1944 in Pápa as a result of the serious injuries he suffered. Kálmán Szeverényi, and his brother, were again removed at the beginning of the 1960s to the family vault in the newly opened Communal Cemetery of Kecskemét (HB lot, row I, grave 3).[91]

HADNAGY KÁLMÁN NÁNÁSI

Number of aerial victories: 6 (+5)
Successes against ground targets: 1 locomotive, 3 railway cars, 2 trucks (+?)
Number of flown combat sorties: 39 (11 against Americans)
Number of hours flown in the air force: n.d.a.
Nickname: *Nána*
Identification number: 1682-20-0130

Decorations

- *Magyar Koronás Ezüst Érdemérem hadiszalagon a kardokkal* (25 April 1945; posthumous)
- *Magyar Koronás Bronz Érdemérem hadiszalagon a kardokkal* (22 February 1945)
- *Tűzkereszt I fokozata a kardokkal és koszorúval*
- *Délvidéki Emlékérem*
- German Iron Cross 2nd Class (8 March 1945)

Victories

Number	Date	Aircraft	Location
–	21 August 1944	B-24	
–	5 November 1944	B-24	
1	24 December 1944 at 14:00	La-5	Esztergom N (Bicske SE)
2	3 January 1945 at 13:15	Yak-9	Velence N (Bicske)

90 *HM HIM HL*, documents of 101 Fighter Wing, box nr. 112, summarized score report of February 1945; Bundesarchiv-Militärarchiv RL 2 III/1197/114.

91 For Kálmán Szeverényi, see Csaba B. Stenge, 'Egy kecskeméti repülő ász, Szeverényi Kálmán életútja', *Hadtudományi Szemle*, 2013:4, pp. 68–77.

Number	Date	Aircraft	Location
3	22 January 1945 at 11:00	Il-2	Szigetszentmiklós SW 2km (Székesfehérvár)
–	22 January 1945	Il-2	
–	22 January 1945	Yak-9	
4	4 February 1945	La-5	Ladánybene NW (Budapest)
–	4 February 1945	La-5	
5	21 March 1945 at 15:30	Yak-9	Tata SE
6	23 March 1945 at 11:42	Yak-9	Siófok SW

A landing completed by Kálmán Nánási on a treetop in 1938 near Budaörs. The glider aircraft is a Hol's der Teufel (registration number B-0104). (From the author's collection)

Kálmán Nánási as a student at the *Repülőkadémia*, shortly before his graduation as *hadnagy* in 1943. (From the author's collection)

Aircraft flown

Bf 109 G-6: V.853 (7 August 1944), Bf 109 G-6/U4: W-049 (12 October 1944), Bf 109 G-14/U4: W-154 (before 12 February 1945)

Kálmán Nánási was born in Rákospalota on 11 February 1920; his father was a locomotive driver.[92] He started to fly with glider aircraft from his early childhood, and became the 104th Hungarian person to receive the C badge; he completed his 15.5 minutes exam flight on 24 October 1937 at Farkashegy as a member of the *MOVERO* (*Magyar Országos Véderő Egylet Repülő Osztály*, Hungarian Defense Association Aviation Department).[93] After he graduated from high school in Budapest, he received his primary flight training at *BSZKRT* Budaörs in the summer of 1939.[94] He entered the *Regvi* from here as a reserve officer candidate, which he completed in 1941; in the same year, he was appointed as a pilot.

92 *Budapest Főváros Levéltára* (Budapest City Archives), XXXIII/1, state birth registry of the town of Rákospalota for 1920, counterpart, acc, nr. note 130.
93 Mitter (ed.), *A magyar vitorlázórepülés képes története*, p. 229.
94 Pál Csonka, 'Kezdő szárnypróbálgatások', *Magyar Szárnyak Évkönyv,* 1989, pp. 102–103.

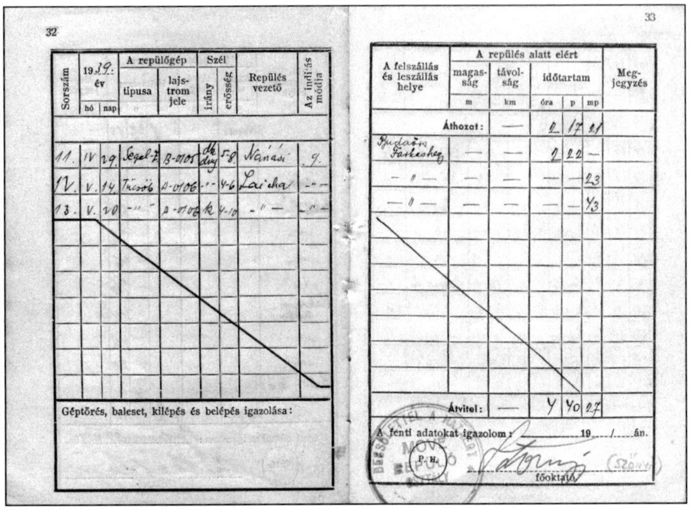

Two pages from András Huszár's *Repülési napló motor nélküli sportrepülők számára* (Flight log for sport aviators of non-powered aircraft) from Farkashegy, 29 April 1939. Flight supervisor: Kálmán Nánási. (From the author's collection)

The *hadapród őrmester* was highly skilled, so he was kept on at the *Regvi* as an instructor from the winter of 1941–42. After he was taken in for the commissioned officer's training, he entered the Academy at Kassa in the autumn of 1942 and graduated as a *hadnagy* on 20 August 1943, as of 1 September 1943, with rank number 45.[95] After his graduation, he returned to the *Regvi* in Szombathely as an instructor during the autumn of 1943.

He volunteered to the 101 Fighter Group after receiving his Bf 109 type training during June and July 1944. Nánási was assigned to 101/3 Fighter Squadron led by *főhadnagy* József Bejczy; he entered the squadron on 27 July 1944.[96]

Nánási flew his first combat sortie on 7 August 1944, during which his auxiliary fuel tank was not feeding properly; he therefore belly landed his aircraft because of fuel starvation west of Zalaszentgrót (Bf 109 G-6, V.853, serial number 95435 – he was not hit by the Mustangs).

His first aerial victory was reported on 21 August 1944 over one of the four-engines of the American formation raiding the airfield at Hajdúböszörmény. This claim was not confirmed, and half a year later it was deleted by Wing Order Nr. 1945/27.[97]

On 12 October 1944, *hadnagy* Kálmán Nánási was shot down by Mustangs while returning to Veszprém from a strafing run south of Szeged. The Hungarian pilot belly-landed at Csopak, in the reeds of Kerekedi Bay. His Bf 109 (marked W-049) was probably shot down by 1st Lieutenant Lee Archer of 332nd FG, who reported shooting down three Messerschmitts in the area. He was the most successful member of his unit with four confirmed aerial victories; the 332nd FG was famous for employing exclusively colored pilots and ground crew.[98]

On 26 October 1944, Nánási was reassigned to 101/5 Fighter Squadron, which was stationed at Kenyeri airfield.

95 *Honvédségi Közlöny (Személyes ügyek)*, nr. 1943/48 (1 December 1943), after correction, p. 1710.
96 Tobak, *Pumák földön-égen*, pp. 110–117.
97 *HM HIM HL*, documents of 101 Fighter Wing, box nr. 110, Wing Order Nr. 1945/27.
98 For Archer's memories regarding the dogfight see Charles E. Francis, *The Tuskegee Airmen: The Men Who Changed A Nation* (Boston: Branden Publishing, 1997), pp. 180–181.

Hadapród őrmester Kálmán Nánási, instructor at the *Regvi*, on B airfield at Szombathely, with a CR.32 aircraft, spring 1942. (From the author's collection).

He was already with his new squadron on 5 November 1944, when the 101 'Puma' Fighter Wing flew their last mission against the Americans. He reported shooting down a Liberator, but we do not possess any evidence that this claim was ever confirmed. The kill was not among the claims deleted in 1945, but Nánási's name is not in the aerial victory register compiled in the spring of 1945 either, consisting of individuals who had shot down four-engines.

Nánási flew 11 combat sorties altogether against the Americans in 1944, and reported shooting down two four-engines (neither confirmed). His first Soviet aircraft – an La-5 fighter – was shot down on 24 December 1944 as his first confirmed air victory (the Soviet 295th IAD lost seven La-5s on this day). This air victory was followed by two more confirmed (and a number of unconfirmed) aerial victories in January. His first confirmed kill in January was over a Yakovlev fighter on 3 January; the event featured in the wing's documents with two different locations. The opponent of the Hungarian pilot was probably a Yak-9 of 659th IAP. The next victory he achieved was against an Il-2 during the extremely intense combat activities on 22 January.[99]

On 4 February, Nánási completed his 20th combat sortie and shot down an La-5. A recommendation putting him forward for a decoration mentions Budapest as a location for this aerial victory, while Wing Order Nr. 1945/62 mentions 'Ladánybeséd'; as no village has ever existed with this name, however, the author of the document was probably thinking of Ladánybene.

In March, Nánási completed five combat sorties. During the second half of the month, he achieved a further two confirmed air victories for which we know the details.[100] On 21 March, *hadnagy* Nánási was leading two flights on a free hunt in the area of Tata–Kocs. The flights took off at 15:05 from Kenyeri, and soon met 12 Il-2s and their escorting 20 Yak-9s over the target area. In the ensuing air combat at 15:30, Nánási shot down a Yak-9 southeast of Tata, which crashed into the ground in flames with its pilots; the witness was *hadnagy* Nyári. After

99 The Soviet data was provided by Gábor Horváth, based on the documents of TsAMO.
100 *HM HIM HL*, documents of 101 Fighter Wing, box nr. 113, personal situational report, March 1945.

Hadnagys Kálmán Nánási (on the left) and Tibor Tobak in July 1944 in Veszprém, on an aircraft of 101/3 Fighter Squadron. (From the collection of Tibor Tobak)

The Hungarian Messerschmitt Bf 109 G-6 (V.853, serial number 95435) belly-landed after the large air battle on 7 August 1944. The aircraft was flown by *hadnagy* Kálmán Nánási and the emergency landing was due to fuel shortage near Zalaszentgrót. (From the collection of János Pocskai)

the successful dogfight, Nánási led his flights over the Vértessomló–Dad road, strafing and destroying nine trucks and one heavy artillery tractor. During the reported time (15:30), 179th IAP lost a 7-kill ace, the 23-year-old *leytenant* Viktor Yakovlevich Ragulin, who was flying a Yak-9M. Although the Soviet formation reported an air combat with Fw 190s at Ács (victory over one of these had already been confirmed to Ragulin, his last kill), it was fought mainly against Bf 109s. The picture is further complicated by the fact that an outstanding German ace, *Hauptmann* Helmut Lipfert,[101] who achieved the highest number of air victories over Hungary in 1944–45 (almost 50), also reported shooting down a Yak at 15:30 in the area of Felsőgalla; the victim may therefore have been his and not Nánási's, although Nánási's reported area is closer to Ács.[102]

Hadnagy Nánási achieved his last confirmed aerial victory on 23 March. On this day, eight aircraft from the squadron took off from Kenyeri on a free hunt. The aircraft met a strong Boston formation escorted by Yak-9s (the Hungarian fighters reported two Yakovlevs, although in reality there were five, and these could only join the air combat after a delay because they were flying partly in front of the bombers). *Hadnagy* Nánási attacked one of the escort fighters and at 11:42, he reported its destruction. According to him, the aircraft crashed into the ground near Siófok with its pilot (one of the sources states that the crash was south of the town, while others say it was west of Siófok). The witnesses were *hadnagys* Báthy and Nyári. The mixed Yakovlev formation (from 659th and 897th IAPs) escorting the Bostons of 861st BAP did not lose any aircraft during the air combat.[103]

101 For Helmut Lipfert (Lippelsdorf, 6 August 1916–Einbeck, 10 August 1990), see Obermaier, *Die Ritterkreuzträger der Luftwaffe 1939–45*, p. 76.

102 Bikhov, *Sovetskie Asy 1941-1945*, p. 421; Helmut Lipfert, *Das Tagebuch des Hauptmann Lipfert* (Stuttgart: Motorbuch Verlag, 1973), p. 279.

103 *HM HIM HL*, documents of 101 Fighter Wing, box nr. 113, after-action reports and mission logs of 101 Fighter Wing, 23 March 1945; Horváth, *Bostonok a magyar égen és földben*, pp. 193–200.

Hadnagy Nánási took off at 16:05 on 4 April 1945 for his last combat mission from Tulln, as the second element leader in the flight led by *hadnagy* Gellért Barsi. The 101/II Group completed 15 aircraft sorties altogether on this day during four missions against the advancing Soviet troops from Tulln airfield, tasked with strafing and reconnoitering. Of these, 14 sorties were successful, as one aircraft of the first flight was unable to retract his undercarriage and thus returned immediately. The flights of 101/II Group suffered extensive losses on this day, and three of their pilots – *szakaszvezető* Fülöp, *hadnagy* Nánási and *főhadnagy* Füleky – never returned. The flight led by Barsi *hadnagy* was the third formation thrown into combat from the group; their task was to carry out strafing runs in the area northwest and northeast of Wiener Neustadt, while conducting reconnaissance of Soviet movements. The flight encountered heavy anti-aircraft fire but destroyed four trucks and a number of horse-drawn vehicles, besides setting an airfield fuel storage facility on fire; however, according to their report south of Kottingbrunn at 16:40, *hadnagy* Nánási's aircraft was hit by an anti-aircraft projectile and plummeted in flames, crashing into a railway embankment. Nánási did not have a chance to bail out – perhaps he had already been fatally wounded in mid-air – and was killed.[104]

Lee A. Archer (1919–2010), who was the most successful pilot of 332nd FG with four confirmed victories, and who probably shot down the aircraft of Kálmán Nánási on 12 October 1944 (US Air Force Photo)

Nánási's wingman, *hadnagy* György Endrői, remembered the death of his element leader decades later:

> '*Nána*' began to dive at full speed. I tried to fly closer to him. This was the first time in my life when I saw a fire curtain, and it truly did resemble a curtain. There were many weapons positioned on the edge of the airfield; all the crew were firing at us without a pause, waiting for us to get there. We arrived over them at high speed, and a grassy hill came before Nánásy's [*sic*] aircraft. He opened fire at it with his cannon and, as it happened to be a fuel storage, it immediately blew up. A towing vehicle crept into my scope … and we had to fly through a curtain of phosphorous trails. I admit I even closed my eyes! We almost brushed the grass of the airfield with our propellers when I again opened my eyes and saw that a blazing projectile was sweeping toward us from the rear, after Nánásy's

104 *HM HIM HL*, documents of 101 Fighter Wing, box nr. 113, mission log of 101 Fighter Wing, 4 April 1945.

> aircraft. I thought I still had time to shout into the radio: '*Nána*, up! Pull up!' But before I could say anything, the blazing ball just disappeared into the fuselage. Fuel was leaking from it, slowly emerging, its starboard wing tipped downward … if he goes down on me, there's no way out. He was surely hit too, the port wing was more upward now, and the aircraft was still moving in a slow spin. An airfield building came before me – passing over it, I saw that *Nána* was already flying on his back. … A steep railway embankment was before us. … I sped up and looked back. The aircraft, flying on its back, probably with *hadnagy* Kálmán Nánásy already dead, flew right into the embankment and was blown up immediately.[105]

The airfield they had been attacking was certainly Bad Vöslau, east of the town itself and northeast of Kottingbrunn. Four aircraft wrecks were found in Leobersdorf, directly south of Kottingbrunn; one of them was probably the Ju 52 that crashed on 25 October 1944, and the other three were combat losses from the end of the war. One of the wrecks was found on the Alleegasse, running parallel to an east–west railway sideline – this was a Hungarian wreck, but not Nánási's Messerschmitt (the pilot of the former aircraft bailed out and it crashed before the end of March, as one of the local witnesses left Leobersdorf on 31 March 1945). In Sollenau, directly south of Kottingbrunn, an aged witness said a single-engine aircraft crashed near the embankment, and its pilot died – this was Nánási's aircraft, but so far the author has not been able to obtain more accurate details. It is perhaps important to note that there are a number of railway embankments in the area and a 19th century water conduit drawing toward Vienna with a high embankment that emerges overground in some places. This might also be the location where Nánási's aircraft crashed, mistakenly reported as a railway embankment.[106]

Zweitschrift.

IM NAMEN DES FÜHRERS
UND OBERSTEN BEFEHLSHABERS
DER WEHRMACHT
VERLEIHE ICH
DEM

Leutnant

Kálmán Nánási

DAS

EISERNE KREUZ
2. KLASSE

…chtsstand, 8. März 1945

Der Oberbefehlshaber der
Luftflotte 4

gez. Dessloch
Generaloberst

(DIENSTGRAD UND DIENSTSTELLUNG)

F.d.R.

Hauptmann

Award certificate of the German Iron Cross 2nd Class belonging to *hadnagy* Kálmán Nánási (*HM HIM* Military Archives)

105 György Endrői, 'Velem történt 1944–45-ben', *Magyar Szárnyak Évkönyv*, 1996, pp. 204–205.
106 Alois Schabes, *Der Markt Leobersdorf. Von der ältesten Zeit bis zur Gegenwart* (Leobensdorf: Marktgemeinde Leobensdorf, 1976), p. 230. The author wishes to express his gratitude to Austrian researcher Kurt Rieder for his help.

According to the last, posthumous recommendation for decorating Kálmán Nánási, aside from his six confirmed aerial victories he had also destroyed a locomotive, three freight cars and two trucks during his four strafing runs. According to the documents of the wing, however, his strafing successes were on a far greater scale.[107]

SZAKASZVEZETŐ LAJOS KRASCSENICS

Number of aerial victories: 6 (+5)
Successes against ground targets: n.d.a.
Number of flown combat sorties: about 50 (8 against Americans)
Number of hours flown in the air force: 730
Nickname: *Tülök*
Identification number: 1390-21-0112

Decorations

- *Magyar Nagy Ezüst Vitézségi Érem* (25 January 1945)
- *Magyar Bronz Vitézségi Érem* (20 December 1944)
- *Tűzkereszt I fokozata a kardokkal és koszorúval*
- German Iron Cross 2nd Class (8 March 1945)
- Bronze *Frontflugspange* (20 April 1945)

Victories

Number	Date	Aircraft	Location
1	21 August 1944	B-17 (B-24)	Hajdúböszörmény
2	1 November 1944	B-24	Over Croatian territory
–	November 1944	Yak-9	
3	13 November 1944 at 14:48	Yak-9	Tápiószele S
4	21 December 1944	La-5	Székesfehérvár
–	January 1945	Yak-9	
5	16 January 1945	La-5	Sárosd W
6	18 January 1945	Il-2	Polgárdi E
–	March 1945	Yak-9	
–	March 1945	Il-2	
–	March 1945	La-5	

Aircraft flown

Bf 109 G-14/U4: W-178 (23 January 1945), W-114 (2 February 1945), Bf 109 G-10/U4: 'Yellow 9' (27 March 1945), 'White 3' (14 April 1945)

107 *HM HIM HL*, documents of 101 Fighter Wing, box nr. 113, recommendations for decoration.

Lajos Krascsenics was born in Vizslás in Nógrád County on 12 September 1921 to a family of two children (he had a younger sister). His father's original occupation was as a gardener; he was later employed as a bartender at a pub.[108] The family later moved to Budapest, where Lajos Krascsenics trained to be a merchant assistant. His interest in aviation was sparked in 1931 by the flight of the Graf Zeppelin airship over Hungary; he began flying gliders in Budapest. From 1940, every Sunday he went to Hármashatárhegy, sometimes to Strázsa Hill near Esztergom, to practice gliding with the Budapest boy scouts. He completed his B badge flight on 28 August 1940.[109]

Lajos Krascsenics in August 1941 on the Debrecen-Nyulas airfield, in front of a Bü 131 primary training aircraft of the *HMNRA*. (From the author's collection)

Krascsenics received his primary flight training in the summer of 1941 at Debrecen-Nyulas airfield from the *HMNRA*, together with János Róza. At the end of the year, he was assigned to the *Regvi* in Szombathely, then in 1942 he was reassigned to the combat training group in Börgönd, where he also received short-range reconnaissance combat training.

From 1943 the skilled young pilot was employed as a fighter instructor at the group.

In March 1944, after the German occupation of Hungary, his unit moved to Pápa. From here, in late spring, he asked to be reassigned to Mátyásföld, where he flew with a *Héja* as target simulation aircraft for the anti-aircraft artillery. He then applied to the 'Puma' Group in Veszprém, and he was assigned to 101/2 Squadron. He arrived at this unit on 14 July 1944, and his first combat sortie was completed on 30 July 1944.

The fun jazz band of the Debrecen-Nyulas *HMNRA* class of summer 1941. The second from the left is János Róza; the fourth is Lajos Krascsenics, the two prospective aces of the unit. (From the author's collection)

Krascsenics reported his first air victory on 21 August 1944 against a B-17 from the bomber unit raiding the field airfield of Hajdúböszörmény. The claim was at first deleted by Wing Order Nr. 1945/27, and it

108 MNL Nógrád Megye Levéltára (*National Archives, Nógrád County Archives*), XXXIII/1, state birth registry of the village of Kazár for 1921, counterpart, note 112. fsz.

109 'A Magyar Aero Szövetség Közleményei: üzemi jelentések [1940] július-augusztus hóról', *Magyar Szárnyak*, 1 October 1940, p. 28.

Lajos Krascsenics on the airfield at Székesfehérvár-Börgönd in the summer of 1942, in front of a WM-21 '*Sólyom*' as a short-range reconnaissance pilot. Krascsenics is the second from the left, the fourth is Mátyás Lőrincz, the second prospective ace from the group. Between them is Sándor Nagy (1922-1990), who was later a journalist and author and who won the Stalin Prize in 1952. (From the author's collection)

also appears in the registry of aerial victories against four-engines as a deleted kill, but it was eventually added to his individual successes. No four-engines crashed in the area on this the day, although several claims were confirmed for German fighters, and the uncertainty of this Hungarian claim adds to the confusion. It also needs to be noted that the airfield was attacked by B-24s on that day, not B-17s.

Krascsenics reported his second air victory against a four-engined on 1 November against a lone Liberator over Croatian territory. He remembered the events as follows:

> *Now you won't be coming over here again*, I said to myself, while I was climbing at full speed and rushing after the innocent little sheep straying from the herd. It seemed to be time to repay something of the great humiliation we many times suffered due to their superior numbers. I thought: *This is the real equal fight – one on one! Although the belly of that aircraft hides 10 gunners waiting to empty their clips into me, now they will swallow their chewing gum. Then you can smile if you are able to!* – I was encouraging myself in this way because I had plenty of time while chasing the four-engined flying at an altitude of 6,000 meters. We had already left Nagykanizsa when I managed to place myself in firing position. Climbing from right astern, I attacked him from the side because he offered a much bigger target that way. I hadn't even opened fire when I already saw a parachute opening behind the aircraft, but only from the corner of my eye, because I was watching the aircraft itself getting bigger and bigger and taking all the bursts I fired into it. In a split second, I swept past, switched to the other side and fired at it from that direction too. It seems the guys suddenly felt too hot

> inside, because they were just jumped out of the aircraft one by one, avoiding the fire of the fuel ignited by one of my phosphorous hits! I felt I'd done good work.[110]

In the absence of witnesses, Wing Order Nr. 1945/31 did not confirm this kill, which also appeared as a deleted claim in 101 Fighter Wing's registry of aerial victories against four-engines. It was, however, later added to Krascsenics's results: a document from 30 January 1945 and a March 1945 record also credit him with six aerial victories.[111]

During 1944, Lajos Krascsenics completed eight combat sorties altogether against the Americans; he also reported the two air victories discussed above against the two four-engines. He achieved his first kill against a Soviet aircraft on 13 November 1944, when his squadron overcome and defeated a Yakovlev formation in superior numbers in a dogfight south-southeast of Jászberény. The aerial victory was confirmed in Air Force Order Nr. 1945/1. Krascsenics concluded his string of successes for 1944 with a kill on 21 December 1944, when he shot down an La-5 in the area of Székesfehérvár. Air Force Order Nr. 1945/13 confirmed this success. According to him, he also achieved another victory at the beginning of November, although it was without a witness.

Krascsenics's most successful month was January 1945, when he achieved two confirmed kills and one unconfirmed victory against the Soviets. Both confirmed aerial victories – an La-5 fighter on 16 January and an Il-2 ground-attack aircraft on 18 January, which might have belonged to 751st SAP – were confirmed in Wing Order Nr. 1945/62; the witness in both cases was *zászlós* Géza Bartos, flying as Krascsenics's wingman. *Zászlós* Bartos recalled Krascsenics's air victory on 16 January against the Lavochkin:

> Left ahead of us, we noticed two Ju 52s at the same time with Krascsenics. They were going in the same direction as us. With a little bit of extra speed, we approached them and realized that four La-5 fighters were following them and attacking intensely at the two slow transport planes. My element leader, Krascsenics, attacked immediately, but we did not yet have the necessary firing range when the La-5s sensed the danger, dived and fled eastward.
>
> After a short chase, during which I tried to 'stick' as much as possible to my element leader, I saw a long burst from Krascsenics hitting the back of one of the La-5s. A large part of the aircraft skin flew off the fighter; a few seconds later, it crashed into a wooded area.[112]

Szakaszvezető Krascsenics received his *Magyar Nagy Ezüst Vitézségi Érem* on 25 January 1945 from the Minister of Defense himself, who came to visit 101 Fighter Wing. According to Krascsenics, he achieved three more victories in March 1945 in the area of Dég during a single sortie, albeit these were without witnesses; he also belly-landed twice at the beginning of 1945 due to extensive damage to his aircraft. The partially surviving documents of 101 Fighter Wing contain the unit's register-book, so we have references to other records that have since

110 Krascsenics, *Egy magyar királyi vadászrepülő visszaemlékezései*, p. 53.

111 *HM HIM HL*, documents of 101 Fighter Wing, box nr. 112, various records and registers connected with achievements.

112 Recollections of *zászlós* Géza Bartos, in manuscript (copy owned by the author).

been lost. These sources mentioned two damaged aircraft related to him: under item nr. 697, the Bf 109 W-178, on 23 January 1945; and Bf 109 W-114 under item nr. 696, on 2 February.[113]

Krascsenics destroyed a number of enemy vehicles during his strafing runs, but we do not have any exact data for this. A summary created at the end of the war mentions that Krascsenics accomplished 43 combat sorties, but this must be an error, as he flew his 36th combat sortie on 12 February 1945 and completed many more during March and April, flying his last combat sortie in the middle of April.

He went into American captivity in May 1945 with his wing, and returned to Hungary as early as October the same year. After this, he was a farmer in Lébény for a time. In 1949–50, he was an instructor for *OMRE* in Győr and Szentes. In the latter place, he served with György Michna, who is also featured in this work. Krascsenics commanded the Szentes aviation training school from the summer of 1949 and he received the bronze class of *Népi Repülésért Érdemjelvény* (Medal of Merit for the People's Aviation) on 4 September 1949 for his work there.[114] From January to the beginning of June 1950, Krascsenics worked as the commander for the aviation training school in Győr, but was then removed from *OMRE* and forbidden to fly again (no reason was given for this prohibition). As a civilian, he later worked in the factory catering field; from 1957, he was an accountant in the Lébény *téesz* (*termelőszövetkezet,* collective farm), subsequently serving as chief accountant until his retirement in 1981. No documents or data remains regarding possible monitoring on Krascsenics carried out by the home interior authorities in the *Állambiztonsági Szolgálatok Történeti Levéltára* (Historical Archives of the Hungarian State Security). After the democratic transformation, the Minister of Defense promoted Krascsenics to *hadnagy* (retired) on 30 June 1994 in Order Nr. 307/1994.[115]

Krascsenics was one of the few Hungarian pilots who wrote and published memoirs after the war. His memoir of the Second World War was published in 1990.[116] A few years later, in 1999, he published another book, although this was more a work of literature rather than a memoir. This touched on his time at the *OMRE* school at Szentes.[117]

Lajos Krascsenics died on 5 August 2001 in Győr. He was laid to rest in Lébény.

113 *HM HIM HL*, documents of 101 Fighter Wing, box nr. 111, based on the registry book of 101 Fighter Wing.

114 *Magyar Repülés*, 10 October 1949, p. 359.

115 *HM HIM KI*, document folder nr. 507/1660. The personal document folder of Lajos Krascsenics does not contain any documents in connection with his military service during the war; it only contains a few documents related to his promotion after the democratic transformation.

116 Krascsenics, *Egy magyar királyi vadászrepülő visszaemlékezései*, p. 215.

117 Lajos Krascsenics, *Repülő hétköznapok, avagy a reptéren mindig történik valami – Egy repülőiskola életéből 1949* (Győr: privately published, 1999), p. 197. In this work, Krascsenics speaks of himself in the third person singular, and calls himself 'Péter Kaszás' throughout. The school in Szentes is called 'the school at Szengecs'. György Michna, who was also an instructor there, features in the book as 'Mihályfi György'.

HADNAGY VITÉZ SZOMOLNOKI IMRE PÁNCZÉL

Hadnagy Imre Pánczél, shortly after his graduation in 1941. (From the author's collection)

Number of aerial victories: 6 (+1)
Successes against ground targets: 3 locomotives, 17 vehicles +?
Number of flown combat sorties: 50+
Number of hours flown in the air force: n.d.a.
Nickname: *Pufi*
Identification number: 3242-20-0569

Decorations

- *Magyar Érdemrend lovagkeresztje hadiszalagon a kardokkal* (18 March 1943; posthumous)
- *Kormányzói dicsérő elismerés Magyar Koronás Bronz Érdemérme hadiszalagon a kardokkal* (1 October 1942)
- *Tűzkereszt I fokozata a kardokkal és koszorúval*
- *Felvidéki Emlékérem*
- *Délvidéki Emlékérem*
- German Iron Cross 2nd Class (21 December 1942)

Victories

Number	Date	Aircraft	Location
1	6 August 1942	Soviet fighter (LaGG-3/P-39)	Uriv?
2	30 October 1942	Il-2	Ostrogozhsk N
–	31 October 1942	Il-2	
3	31 October 1942	Il-2	Alexeyevka E, Soldatskoye
4	31 October 1942	Il-2	Alexeyevka E, Soldatskoye
5	16 December 1942	Il-2	Pavlovsk S
6	16 December 1942	Il-2	Pavlovsk S

Aircraft flown

Bf 109 F-4: V-04 (11 January 1943)

Imre Pánczél was born on 13 June 1920 in Pécs, the fifth child of his aging father, who was working as a state chief forestry councilor.[118] Nobility was bestowed on the family in 1913, but

118 *MNL Baranya Megye Levéltára* (National Archives, Baranya County Archives), XXXIII/1, state birth registry of the city of Pécs for 1920, counterpart, acc. nr. note 569. In the commissioned officers' registry for 1942, Pánczél's birth date features incorrectly as 13 April 1920 (probably because of the classic error of mixing up months VI and IV). In the authoritative state birth registry, the correct date is given (13 June 1920), with the date of announcement given as 14 June 1920. Imre Pánczél's name is also written incorrectly in a number of military documents as 'Páncél'. Although he was a

A group of pilots of 1/1 Fighter Squadron at the beginning of August 1942. From left to right: *főhadnagy* István Horthy, Deputy Regent (one air victory), *hadnagy* László Kázár (three air victories), *hadnagy* Imre Pánczél, *zászlós* József Rőmer, *hadapród őrmester* Zoltán Molnár, *őrmester* Dezső Szentgyörgyi, *őrmester* Zoltán Raposa and *szakaszvezető* Zoltán Nemeslaki (*HM HIM* Photographic Archives 19.021)

Imre Pánczél did not use his noble forename.[119] He graduated with good grades from high school in his hometown (*ciszterci rend Nagy Lajos Gimnáziuma*) in 1938.

Aviation was his childhood dream, and he succeeded in entering the *Repülőakadémia* right after graduation; he started his studies there in the autumn of 1938, in Budapest (Ludovika 2nd Department), before graduating as *hadnagy* on 20 August 1941 in Kassa, as of 1 September, with rank number 16. He was a classmate of Béla Füleky.[120] After graduation, he was assigned to Szolnok, to 1/I Fighter Group.

Hadnagy Pánczél took off from Szolnok as part of 1/1 Fighter Squadron for the Eastern Front on 1 July 1942. His first combat sortie was probably completed on 6 July; two days later, returning from a bomber escort task, he had to belly-land his aircraft near the airfield because of engine failure (the Piaggio P.IX RC 40 radial engines of the Re.2000s caused a particularly great number of problems).[121] On 18 July, he was sent into combat as an element leader over the Hungarian troops eliminating the Uriv–Storozhevoye bridgehead. After the successful battle – with Dezső Szentgyörgyi, who also took part – he received a commendation certificate from the commander of the 1st Field Armored Division.

On 6 August, however, the Soviet troops again created a bridgehead at Uriv (and other areas). During that day's increased combat activity, Pánczél scored his first aerial victory by shooting down a Soviet fighter aircraft. He has told the story in a letter to his parents:

commissioned officer, his personal document folder has not survived in the Central Record Office of the HM HIM.

119 Béla Kempelen, *Magyar nemes családok*, vol. 8 (Budapest: Grill Károly Könyvkiadóvállalata, 1914), pp. 117, 506. The title of nobility was granted to the grandfather, János Pachmajer, chief treasurer of the Selmecbánya (today Banská Štiavnica, Slovakia) mining district, on 31 May 1913. His son Ottó's name was Hungarianized from Pachmajer to Pánczél in 1883, while the grandfather, called either Pachmajer or Pachmayer, died in Pécs in 1924 with his original name, without it being Hungarianized.

120 *Honvédségi Közlöny* (*Személyes ügyek)*, nr. 1941/37 (19 August 1941), p. 479.

121 György Farkas, *Horthy István repülő főhadnagy tragikus halála* (Budapest: Auktor, 1992), p. 44.

> The first [victory] was scored by the Deputy Regent, and I also succeeded in shooting down my first Rata. The fighting was quite hard, but the Hungarian bravery and better training won over the superior numbers of the enemy and their better aircraft. Our aircraft were hit quite a few times, but no important damage was done, either to aircraft or to men.[122]

In the newspaper article reprinting this letter, the date of the victory is stated as 5 August, but this is clearly an error, as there was no combat activity on that day between Hungarian and Soviet aircraft. On the following day, the Soviet units began large-scale crossings at the Don in the front-line section of the Hungarian 2nd Army with the intention of creating bridgeheads. The Soviet air force was also thrown intensively into combat from that day onward, clashing a number of times with Hungarian fighters (the latter also met LaGG-3 and P-39 Airacobra types that day). István Horthy also reported successfully attacked a Soviet fighter aircraft; this was later confirmed to him as a victory. Over the next four days, there were a number of engagements between Soviet and Hungarian fighters over the sections of the Hungarian 2nd Army, so the note could possibly relate to this period – although, from 6 to 10 August 1942, Soviet sources do not mention any loss of a fighter aircraft to Hungarian Re.2000s (which were always referred to by the Soviets as 'Macchi C.200', mistaking them with the Italian Macchi fighters stationed further south). Unfortunately, due to the widespread destruction of sources, it is almost impossible to pinpoint the correct succession of events. Even though the documents of the Hungarian 2nd Army from 1942 are relatively well preserved, this is not the case for the daily documents of the air force, as in most cases the detailed combat mission reports, as well as the names of the pilots sent into combat, are completely lost. According to the author, however, the letter refers to 6 August.[123]

By the end of August, *hadnagy* Pánczél had completed his 25th combat sortie and received two weeks off to return to Hungary. He returned to the front in the second half of September.

At the beginning of October 1942, the majority of the pilots of 1/1 Fighter Squadron was assigned to Messerschmitt Bf 109 retraining at Stary Oskol, and the command of the section remaining at Ilovskoye was granted to *hadnagy* Pánczél.

While leading his flight at the end of October, *hadnagy* Pánczél achieved excellent results in combat activity against the Soviet aircraft on 29, 30 and 31 October (mostly repelling the formations of Il-2s attacking railway targets). A contemporary combat report (Combat Report Nr. 28 of the commander of the *Honvéd* Army Staff) also mentions that our fighters succeeded in shooting down five enemy aircraft in two days.[124]

Unfortunately, the surviving documents are fragmented and contradictory. In terms of 29 October, the author has not found clear evidence that *hadnagy* Pánczél achieved an aerial victory on this day. A combat mission was also considered successful if the attackers were prevented from carrying out their tasks; this was probably what happened on this occasion, because the

122 Béla Nagy, 'Szomolnoki Pánczél Imre m. kir. repülőhadnagy', *Magyar Szárnyak*, 15 November 1943, p. 11.

123 For the bridgehead battles of the Hungarian 2nd Army around the beginning of August 1942, see Csaba Becze, *'A pokol tornácán…' A magyar királyi 2 honvéd hadsereg hídfőcsatái a Donnál (1942 július–szeptember)* (Budapest: Paktum, 2006), pp. 31–45.

124 'Hadijelentések, csaták és új fordulatok', *Magyar Futár*, 12 August 1942, p. 16.

Hadnagy Imre Pánczél in his *Héja* during the summer of 1942. The markings of the aircraft are not visible, but this one is certainly not the Re.2000, V.470, which he flew during a few missions in October. (From the author's collection)

evening report issued in German states that, during the day, anti-aircraft artillery shot down four enemy aircraft, but there is no mention of a kill achieved by fighters. The report also notes that Ostrogozhsk was hit 13 times by airstrikes during the day. This probably included formations that were successfully prevented from attacking by the *Héja*s.[125] On 31 October, the Hungarian 2nd Army issued a summary daily report that also mentioned an enemy aircraft that was shot down by a fighter and had to crash-land. This was Pánczél's victim; he was covering the train station of Ostrogozhsk during the day with his flight when he noticed anti-aircraft fire northeast of the city. He turned toward the area and saw three Il-2s, forced them to drop their bombs over an uninhabited area and shot one down as the aircraft tried to escape northward; the Shturmovik crash-landed. The Iljusin was one of the aircraft of 567th SAP, its pilot the 26-year-old *mladshiy leytenant* A.A. Kalinin, who was registered as missing in action (in fact, he was captured and survived the war).[126]

In the afternoon of 31 October, Pánczél and his four *Héja*s attacked a formation of 12 Il-2s from 227th SAD and their four escorting Hurricane Mk IIs from 438th IAP, which were attacking the Alexeyevka railway station. During the ensuing heavy air combat, '*Pufi*' – who was sticking to the ground-attack aircraft like a bulldog – shot down three Il-2s. Two crashed beyond the Hungarian lines and one crash-landed beyond their own lines; only the first two of these aerial victories were confirmed. Pánczél's victims again belonged to 567th SAP; they were 26-year-old *starshina* A.A. Savin, who was reported killed, and the 23-year-old *starshiy serzhant* P.M. Chernov, who was reported as missing. In the contemporary documents, the location of the wrecks was reported as Soldatskoye.[127]

125 *HM HIM HL*, documents of the 2nd Army, box 4, various documents in German.
126 *HM HIM HL*, documents of the 2nd Army, box 7, log appendix nr. 1249; box nr. 31, diary of *zászlós* Miklós Nemeskéri-Kiss, 30 October 1942; Tivadar Genersich, 'Vadászrepülő feladatok', *Magyar Katonai Szemle*, 1943:9, p. 549; Centralni Arhiv Ministarstva Oboroni Rossijskij Federaciji, fond 58, *opis* 818883, *delo* 1798; Gábor Horváth on documents of TsAMO.
127 Centralni Arhiv Ministarstva Oboroni Rossijskij Federaciji, fond 58, *opis* 818883, *delo* 1798; Genersich, 'Vadászrepülő feladatok', pp. 549–550.

Pánczél recounted the events in a letter to his parents:

> Only two aerial victories were credited to me, because the third aircraft was just damaged and crash-landed close to the Hungarian lines. The powerless aircraft was then destroyed by the Hungarian artillery, and the victory was credited to them. The air combat during the first two days was relatively easy, but on the third day I had a fierce engagement against an enemy formation of 16 aircraft, partly fighters, partly destroyers; the combat lasted 22 minutes and, for me, resulted in shooting down three aircraft and losing just one. I barely escaped unscathed.[128]

According to the memories of *leytenant* Anatoly Leonidovich Kozhevnikov, who was leading the Hurricane formation between 13:15 and 14:25[129] on his 158th combat sortie, his flight was attacked by four 'fascist Macchi C.200s', two of which were shot down by the Hurricanes in the area of Prokopets, without any own fighter losses. One of these was reported by him as his own second aerial victory. Kozhevnikov achieved 25 air victories before the end of the war; for his performance and successes he was awarded the title of Hero of the Soviet Union in the summer of 1945.[130]

In reality, the Hungarian fighters lost one aircraft. The fuselage of the aircraft of *őrmester* István Takács was hit by multiple 20mm cannon shells, and the seriously wounded pilot died of his wounds after crash-landing. *Hadapród őrmester* László Kovács-Nagy reported having shot down a 'LaGG-3', but the Soviet fighters did not report any losses.

The fact that one of Pánczél's victories was given to the field artillery needs no commentary. Nevertheless, the skilled pilot, with his summer and autumn aerial victories, became the most successful pilot flying the Reggiane Re.2000 aircraft type. A contemporary source credit *hadnagy* Pánczél with seven victories; it could therefore be that the kill that had been credited to the artillery was later restored to Pánczél, so the lack of confirmation for this aerial victory to him is uncertain. If it was later credited to Pánczél, it was the right thing to do, and it must be noted; however, the author has not found any clear evidence for either scenario.

At the beginning of November, Pánczél was redeployed to Stary Oskol, where he retrained to Bf 109 F-4 and started to go on missions, mainly fighter-bomber type tasks.

On 6 December, the Hungarian fighter-bomber squadron moved to Rossosh, behind the lines of the Italian 8th Army, so as to support them more intensively. In the heavy fighting over the four days following their arrival, *hadnagy* Pánczél destroyed three locomotives, 17 vehicles, 30 horses and a large number of Soviet soldiers during his strafing runs and bombings. The Hungarian squadron also managed to destroy an important field artillery battery, which considerably contributed to the success of the Italian counterattack in the area.[131]

128 Nagy, 'Szomolnoki Pánczél Imre m. kir. repülőhadnagy,' p. 11.

129 In the text, the author always uses the Hungarian and Central European times, as this was used by the aviators deep in the Soviet Union and on the Don. In contrast, the Soviets have always used Moscow times, both within the Soviet Union and in Hungary. To avoid misunderstandings, the author has used Hungarian and Central European times for both Soviet and Hungarian aviators. Moscow time is +2 hours ahead of Hungarian time.

130 Recollections of Anatoly Leonidovich Kozhevnikov (in manuscript) of his 158th combat sortie (copy owned by the author); Bikhov, *Sovetskie Asy 1941–1945. Pobedy Stalinskich sokolov*, p. 240.

131 Nagy, 'Szomolnoki Pánczél Imre m. kir. repülőhadnagy', p. 12.

On 16 December, the Soviet troops launched their 'Small Saturn' offensive on the Italian 8th Army's sector. During the day, the air activity on both sides became intense, and the Hungarian fighters succeeded in shooting down four Il-2s, two of them by Pánczél. The other successful pilot, *főhadnagy* György Bánlaky, remembered the combat as follows:

> During the morning I went with *hadnagy* Pánczél, my wingman, on a fighter-bomber mission against enemy troop concentrations. Over the Don, I noticed two Il-2s. They were heading toward our areas but, when they noticed us, they turned away and fled. We turned after them, and dropped our bombs when we reached enemy territory; as we approached them at 30–40 meters, we opened fire at them. I attacked one and *hadnagy* Pánczél went after the other. Upon receiving our short cannon bursts, the two aircraft crashed next to each other and burned out. On the same day, in the afternoon, and under very similar circumstances, I shot down two more Il-2s with *hadnagy* Pánczél.[132]

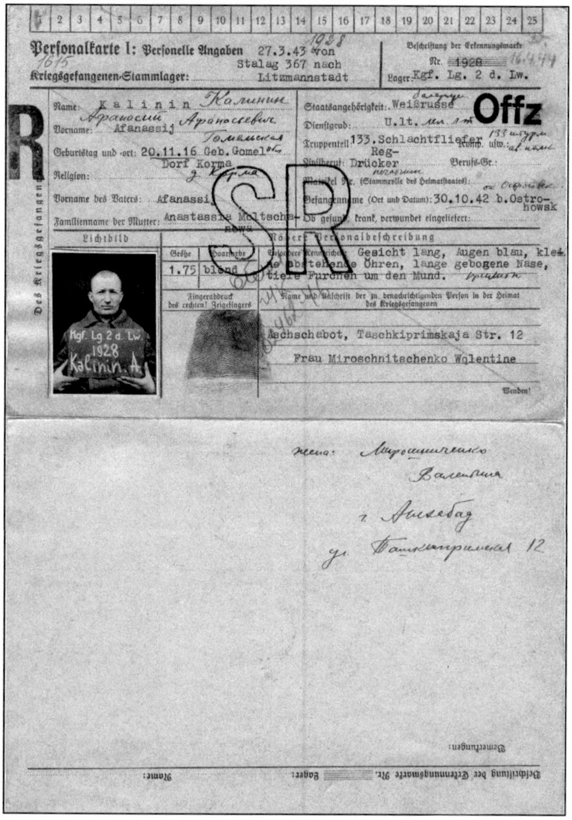

German POW card of *mladshiy leytenant* Afanasiy Afanasyevich Kalinin which was taken by the Soviets; the pilot was shot down by Imre Pánczél on 30 October 1942. (TsAMO)

A contemporary scientific journal published a slightly different and partly supplemental description. It explains that the Hungarian Bf 109s had completed their bombing run against the intended target when they received the report of a radio observer station that two Il-2s were heading toward the Italian lines; with this, they succeeded in intercepting and destroying these aircraft.[133] These were the first confirmed Hungarian Messerschmitt Bf 109 aerial victories, and with his successes of this day, Pánczél became the first official Hungarian fighter ace of the Second World War. From the many Soviet losses on that day (due to a lack of details), it is not possible to identify the Soviet aircraft. The shot-down Il-2s probably belonged to Soviet 17th Air Army, and were probably aircraft of 267th SAD.

132 Nagy, 'Szomolnoki Pánczél Imre m. kir. repülőhadnagy', p. 12.
133 Genersich, 'Vadászrepülő feladatok', pp. 551–552.

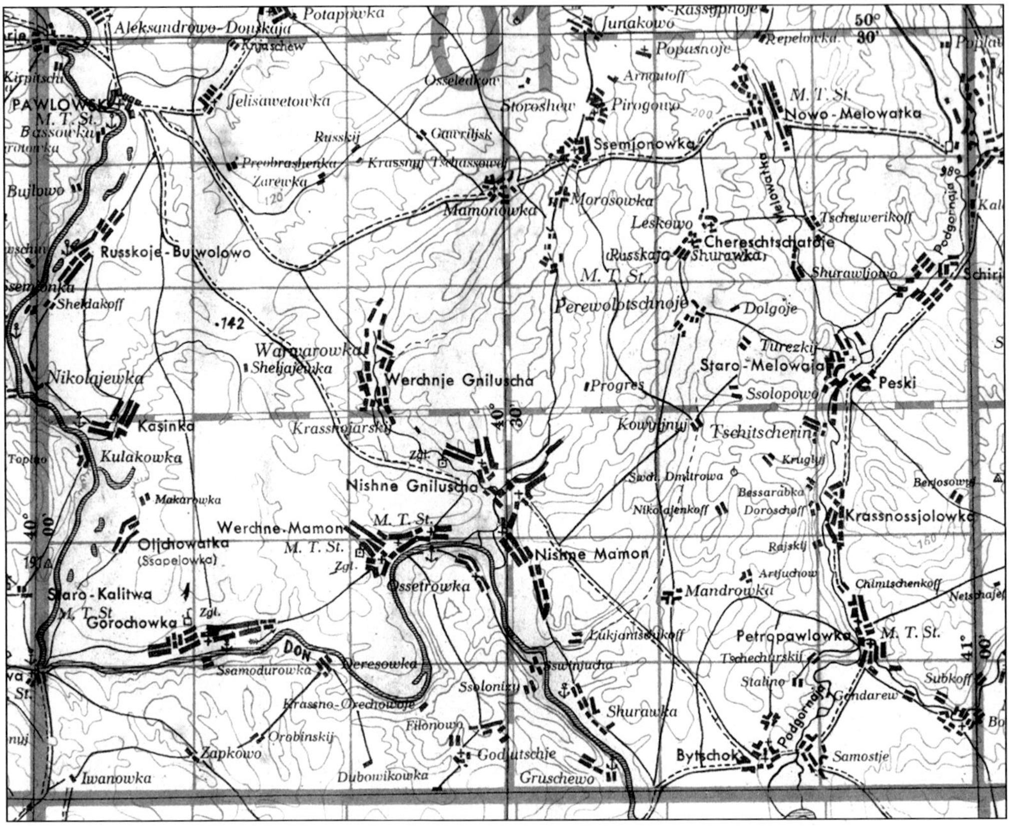

1:500,000 scale Luftwaffe code-map of the Soviet bridgehead at Verhniy Mamon in the section of the Italian 8th Army (on this map, the village names are Germanized). Somewhere in this area, the Bánlaky–Pánczél duo achieved their two double kills on 16 December 1942; this was marked as 'Pavlovsk S' by the author. (From the author's collection)

The fateful year of 1943 arrived with bad weather. Pánczél could only fly his first combat sorties of the year on 11 January; they were his last. First, between 09:30 and 10:30, he completed a fighter-bomber mission with *őrmester* Zoltán Raposa against Soviet forces in the area of Posyukov. The bombs exploded among the houses of the village and on the local road, and there was no anti-aircraft activity. At 11:30, he took off on another mission, a free hunt in the airspace around Svoboda, Davidovka and Korotoyak. After an uneventful hour's flight, he turned back with his wingman, *zászlós* Szabó. The pair flew over the front at an altitude of approximately 300 meters near Svoboda. At the first line, they were greeted with heavy fire from infantry weapons; according to his wingman, *hadnagy* Pánczél's aircraft (Bf 109 F-4, V-04) began to turn leftward after a minute or two, and at the same time, two small licks of fire appeared on the underside of the fuselage, which grew in a matter of seconds and engulfed the aircraft. *Hadnagy* Pánczél managed to jettison the canopy, but, because of the low altitude and his likely wounds, he did not have time to bail out. The aircraft crashed, covered in flames, east of Ostrogozhsk, near the village of Kodubets.[134]

Based on a thorough investigation of the case, the surviving official documents and the memories of the witnesses, *hadnagy* Imre Pánczél had probably become a victim of his own anti-aircraft fire. The visibility was not ideal, and the troops did not recognise the approaching aircraft at a low altitude in time; the Hungarian anti-aircraft defense opened fire at them. During the day, the anti-aircraft units of the Hungarian IV Corps reported shooting down two enemy aircraft. To my knowledge, one was claimed in the Uriv-Storozhevoye area by the section of the 20 and 7 Light Divisions, but the other was probably the aircraft of *hadnagy* Pánczél. His body was interred on 14 January 1943 by his comrades in the Alexeyevka cemetery. His father, Ottó Pánczél, requested that his son be admitted into the *Vitézi Rend*, which was granted. The *Magyar Érdemrend lovagkeresztje hadiszalagon a kardokkal* was also presented posthumously to Imre Pánczél. With his death, Ottó Pánczél lost his second son, the youngest of three. His oldest son, Miklós Pánczél, was born to his first wife in Besztercebánya (today Banská Bystrica, Slovakia) in 1896, and graduated from high school in Pécs in 1914 (*ciszterci rend Nagy Lajos Gimnázium*). During the First World War, he had served on the Russian and Italian fronts as a reserve *főhadnagy* in the k.u.k. 69th Infantry Regiment. The young officer was seriously wounded twice and died in 1921 as a result of these injuries.

Granite grave marker with the name of Imre Pánczél in the *II Magyar Központi Katonai Temető* (2nd Central Hungarian Military Cemetery) at Rudkino, Russia. His name is the 15th from the bottom. Unfortunately, both the family name and the birth date are incorrect on the memorial (photographed by the author, 15 May 2014.)

134 *HM HIM HL*, documents of the 2nd Army, box nr. 17, after-action report of 1/1 Fighter Squadron, note on 11 January 1943; Nagy, 'Szomolnoki Pánczél Imre m. kir. repülőhadnagy', p. 12.

HADNAGY GYÖRGY MICHNA

György Michna as a glider pilot on the Szanda field near Szolnok in 1938, with an R07a '*Tücsök*' primary glider. (From the author's collection)

Number of aerial victories: 6 (+1)
Successes against ground targets: n.d.a.
Number of flown combat sorties: 61
Number of hours flown in the air force: 620
Nickname: *Gyuri*
Identification number: 3221-21-1476

Decorations

- *Magyar Koronás Ezüst Érdemérem hadiszalagon a kardokkal* (25 April 1945)
- *Magyar Koronás Bronz Érdemérem hadiszalagon a kardokkal* (4 March 1945)
- *Tűzkereszt I fokozata a kardokkal és koszorúval*, with one wound clasp
- *Délvidéki Emlékérem*
- German Iron Cross 2nd Class (8 March 1945)
- German Silver *Frontflugspange* (20 April 1945)

Victories

Number	Date	Aircraft	Location
1	5 November 1944	B-24	(*Herausschuss*) Felsősegesd W
2	8 December 1944	La-5	Székesfehérvár E (HS-8)
3	8 December 1944	Yak-9	Kápolnásnyék E
4	19 January 1945	Yak-9	Tolna NW
5	12 February 1945	Yak-9	Nagykáta S
6	12 February 1945	Yak-9	Dunaharaszti N
–	20 March 1945 at 14:15	Yak-9	Tata, Lake Öreg S

Aircraft flown

Bf 109 G-6/U4: W-044 (25 January 1945), Bf 109 G-14/U4: W-144 (3 January 1945)

György Michna was born on 19 December 1921 in Miskolc; he had a younger sister and their father was a pharmacist. The family originated from Upper Hungary (*Felvidék*) and had received nobility in 1655 from King Ferdinand III.[135]

The family originally lived in Sajószentpéter, then moved to Pápa in 1927. Michna graduated from high school there (*Pápai Református Kollégium*), and stood out through his sporting, rather than his academic, abilities. He was very successful in swimming, sport shooting, tennis, fencing, boxing and gymnastics; in 1940 – the year his team won second place in a national

135 Mihály Forgon, *Gömör-Kishont vármegye nemes családai* (Somorja: Méry Ratio, 2001), pp. 462–463; Béla Kempelen, *Magyar nemes családok*, vol. 7 (Budapest: Grill Károly Könyvkiadóvállalata, 1913), p. 189.

György Michna as a student at *HMNRA* shakes hands with *ezredes* Dezső Laborczfy, deputy chair of the Managing Committee of the *HMNRA* in the summer of 1940. Behind Laborczfy stands the bareheaded László Almásy, the famous Africa-explorer, who also had a very important role in managing the *HMNRA*. (From the collection of György Michna)

gymnastics championship – he became school champion.[136] His interest in aviation was sparked by the opening of the military airfield at Pápa, where 3/II Bomber Group was formed in 1937, and where György Ujszászy was in service.

Michna started his career in aviation during his high school years with glider planes. During two summer camps at the field of Szanda at Szolnok, he completed the B level.

Michna received his primary flight training in the summer of 1940 at the *HMNRA* at Győr, as part of the first class trained there. According to memories, he would have continued training in the commissioned officer group, but his superiors read one of his public postcards that contained some critical comments, and he was put into the reserve officers group instead, entering the *Regvi* at Szombathely.[137] After completing his course at *Regvi* and the fighter course, *karpaszományos őrmester* Michna was assigned to 5/I Fighter Group at Mátyásföld in June 1942.

He was sent to the *Repülőakadémia* in Kassa in October 1942, along with a group of reserve officer candidates. They completed their last year here and graduated as *hadnagy* on 20 August 1943, together with the academy class, which included Ferenc Málnássy. This group of reserve aviators sent to the academy holding the rank of *hadapród őrmester* also included Kálmán Nánási and Lajos Benkő, who are also featured in this work. Michna – and others in his reservist group

136 School year bulletin for 1939–41, *Dunántúli Református Egyházkerület Pápai Főiskolája* (College of the Reformed Church at Pápa), 1940, pp. 60–63.
137 Tobak, *Pumák földön-égen*, pp. 68–69.

who became officers – thus received the same qualification as those who had been learning at the *Akadémia* the whole time, but he had more practical experience and more hours spent in the air, which was much more important on the front than long hours spent acquiring theoretical knowledge. He was therefore the one instructing his classmates (who had flown significantly fewer hours) with an Ar 96 at Miskolc during the summer of 1943, so that they could also receive their golden eagle, the Royal Hungarian Air Force pilot badge, at the time of their graduation.

Michna graduated as *hadnagy* on 20 August 1943 in Kassa as of 1 September 1943, with rank number 56.[138] After the graduation, he was reassigned to Mátyásföld, to 5/I Fighter Group. He retrained to Messerschmitts at Börgönd in the autumn of 1943, before returning to Mátyásföld. In the spring of 1944, he was assigned to the newly created 1 Squadron of 101 Fighter Group in Veszprém, where the deputy commander of the squadron, Pál Irányi, became his mentor. Their fathers had also been classmates at Igló (today Spišská Nová Ves, Slovakia) from elementary school onward, so their two families enjoyed a very close relationship.

According to his memories, Michna's first sortie was completed on 24 May 1944. The first aircraft he took off with had engine problems and he needed to turn back, but he did not want to be left out of the mission and so took off again with an aircraft in reserve. He did not reach the Hungarian formation, so he joined German fighters and attacked a formation of Liberators over Vienna. Over the summer, he achieved hits to a number of American aircraft, but did not shoot any down; nor, however, did the Americans succeed in shooting him down.

Michna has achieved his first confirmed aerial victory on 5 November 1944 against a Liberator during the last large-scale combat mission of the wing against the Americans. After this, however, the escorting Mustangs also shot him down; *hadnagy* Michna bailed out of his aircraft near Litér from an altitude of 150 meters. The Hungarian pilot suffered major bruises when his tangled parachute only half-opened; this was why he received the wound clasp for his *Tűzkereszt*. Michna only stayed in Veszprém hospital for a short time and soon returned to his squadron. The documents of 101 Fighter Wing mention him being wounded on 7 November, but this is a typing error. A surviving report from the Ministry of Defense gives the correct date of 5 November and the time of the crash as 13:00, and lists Michna's injuries as leg and abdominal muscle strains.[139] *Hadnagy* Michna's aircraft was shot down by 1st Lieutenant Oscar Rau, a pilot of 325th FG's 318th Fighter Squadron. Rau achieved four aerial victories against Bf 109s on this mission, and received the second-highest American military award for valour (Distinguished Service Cross). At 13:40, Rau reported shooting down his third aircraft of the day in the area around Balaton: he attacked and downed a lone Messerschmitt flying at a low altitude, the pilot of which climbed his aircraft and (according to Rau's estimation) bailed out at an altitude of 800 feet (240 meters). According to the author, this must refer to Michna's Messerschmitt.[140]

Michna had his victory claim against the B-24 confirmed as 'shot out' in April 1945, with a location west of Felsősegesd.[141]

138 *Honvédségi Közlöny (Személyes ügyek)*, nr. 1943/48 (1 December 1943), after correction, p. 1710.
139 *HM HIM HL*, HM 9105/8 nyv. o.-1945.
140 NARA 325th FG Combat Claim Forms.
141 *HM HIM HL*, documents of 101 Fighter Wing, box nr. 110, Wing Order Nr. 1945/62.

Karpaszományos őrvezető György Michna at the *Regvi* in Szombathely, in the autumn of 1940. (From the collection of György Michna).

György Michna practices in the radio classroom at the *Repülőakadémia* in the late autumn of 1942. (From the author's collection)

György Michna in the cockpit of an Ar 96, while instructing his classmates at the airfield at Miskolc, spring 1943. (From the collection of György Michna)

György Michna as a student at the *Repülőakadémia*, shortly before his graduation as *hadnagy*, in the summer of 1943. (From the author's collection)

During combat against the Soviets, it became quickly apparent that Michna had more knowledge and experience than the average Soviet fighter pilot, and the Hungarian pilot soon reported shooting down half a dozen Soviet fighter aircraft.

His first two kills against the Soviets were scored on 8 December 1944; the La-5 was confirmed by Air Force Order Nr. 1945/13, with a map code location of HS-8. He also reported shooting down a Yak-9, although the latter loss is not confirmed by Soviet sources.

The diary of Sándor Tábori mentions a possible victory of Michna on 11 January against an Il-2 during a free hunt, but he was not a witness and Michna himself did not remember it; the report probably arose due to Tábori hearing incorrect news. Eight days later, on 19 January, Michna reported shooting down a Yak-9, achieving his fourth confirmed aerial victory.

The combat mission on 12 February was especially important to him: Michna reported shooting down both members of a Yak-9 pair who were trying to attack a German Fw 190. According to Soviet sources, a Yakovlev fighter was shot down and crash-landed on that afternoon (the aircraft took off at 14:20); this was the Yak-3 of *leytenant* Krasyukov of 866th IAP, which was damaged over Enying by a Bf 109 and was forced to crash-land at Dunavecse (the aircraft was later repaired).[142]

Michna achieved a victory without witnesses on 20 March 1945. He led eight aircraft on a free hunt at 13:40 in the area of Tata–Nagyigmánd. During the mission, they engaged seven Yakovlev fighters in combat over Tata; *hadnagy* Michna shot down one of them, which crashed to the ground at 14:15 south of Lake Öreg in Tata. According to his Hungarian opponent, the Soviet pilot died because he did not bail out. As this victory was not witnessed by anybody else, this claim was not confirmed.[143]

Michna took off for the last time as a formation leader in the early afternoon of 5 April 1945 (the formation only consisted of an element) on a reconnaissance task south of Tulln. He probably completed his last missions in the middle of April.

Michna was taken captive by the Americans with his wing in May 1945 and returned home as early as December 1945. However, he encountered unforeseen hardships at home. His parents were immediately interned by Dezső Sulyok[144] at Pápa, although they were later both freed due to a lack of evidence against them. (Sulyok thus practically 'paid off' the debt of a personal disagreement with Michna's father.) Michna spent the next year and a half as a milkman in Marcali at a relative's house so as to avoid being in the spotlight. On 6 March 1946, his wartime activity was verified; on 10 October 1946, he was put on the 'B' list and discharged from active military service. Following this, he was a car escort in Budapest for a short period, and then (from 1948) he became an instructor at *OMRE*, first in Balatonkiliti and then in Szentes. In Szentes, he served with one of his former comrades in the wing, Lajos Krascsenics, as his subordinate. (Former officers were less trusted by the new regime than the NCO pilots; thus Krascsenics became the commander, and the former officers were his subordinates). For his work

142 For the data about the Soviet fighters, the author wishes to express his gratitude to Nikita Yegorov on documents of TsAMO.

143 *HM HIM HL*, documents of 101 Fighter Wing, box nr. 113, mission log of 101 Fighter Wing, 20 March 1945.

144 Dezső Sulyok (Simaházapuszta-Adásztevel, 28 March 1897–New York, 18 May 1965), politician, Member of Parliament and (from 1 April to 1 September 1945) mayor and city chief constable of Pápa.

at *OMRE*, Michna was awarded the Bronze Class of the *Népi Repülésért Érdemjelvény* on 4 September 1949,[145] but he was removed from *OMRE* on 1 May 1950 and was not allowed to fly again.

After this, Michna worked for a long time as a driver. In 1950, he was a truck driver at *Aszfaltozó és Kövező Vállalat* (an asphalt and gravel works company); he then went to work for *Mélyépítő Teherfuvarozó Vállalat* (an civil engineering construction and transport company). After the oppression of the revolution of 1956, when the trials and the accusations began, Michna was also harassed. The following was written on his supervision papers on 20 December 1957 by the military committee: 'He was a professional Horthy aviation officer. Owner of two *Signum Laudis* decorations and a German Iron Cross 2nd Class. He completed the *Repülőakadémia*. His parents were interned in 1945. He is not reliable. Recommendation: demotion.'[146] As a consequence of this, Michna was degraded to the rank of reserve private by the Ministry of Defense Order Nr. HM 0269/58.

The pilot who shot down the aircraft of György Michna on 5 November 1944: Oscar Rau with a P-40F Warhawk (serial number 41-14158) fighter aircraft in 1943. (From the collection of the Rau family)

In 1958, he managed to get a new job, one that almost seemed like winning the jackpot: he became personal chauffeur to the Indian Ambassador in Hungary. Because of this high-profile job, the state security authorities tried to arrange for him to work for them and spy on the Indians, but he refused. This was not forgotten; according to the surviving documents of *Állambiztonsági Szolgálatok Történeti Levéltára*, from 1967 he was closely watched by an agent under the pseudonym 'János Rácz', who continuously compiled reports on him until 16 July 1974, when Michna was arrested for smuggling (of which he was indeed guilty, using the official embassy car). However, it should also be noted that, at this time, many products deemed everyday items in the West were absolutely unavailable in the Eastern bloc, so those who traveled to the West were frequently caught up in the smuggling trade (especially people working in embassies, or as MALÉV pilots.) For most of them there were no consequences, but the authorities were only waiting for a reason to get Michna arrested after he had refused to work for them. The agent himself constantly teased him, asking for more smuggled products. Officially, Michna was charged with 'breaching the foreign exchange economy and custom crimes' and was sentenced to three years and 10 months in a high-security prison (the sentence was issued on 17 December 1975 in Sentence Nr. 16.B.6028/974/7 of the Budapest Jury). The agent was still sending reports on him, so altogether he followed and spied on Michna for nine years.

145 *Magyar Repülés*, 10 October 1949, p. 359.
146 *HM HIM KI*, document folder nr. 66106.

Hadnagy Michna in the autumn of 1943, at the airfield at Székesfehérvár-Börgönd, with the MÁVAG-*Héja* V.533. (From the collection of György Michna)

This observation was extended to Michna's friends, and thus to many other Hungarian and German pilots. For example, Rudi Rothenfelder was also spied on from 1968; he had earlier served in Hungary as a fighter-instructor and continued to visit the country relatively frequently after the war.[147]

After his release, Michna – an exceptionally strong and life-loving man – rebuilt his life and started working as a driver. He also worked on conserving and restoring paintings, which he continued to do after his retirement. After the democratic transformation of 1989, on 30 June 1992, Minister of Defense Order Nr. 55/1992 restored Michna's rank as reserve *hadnagy* and promoted him to reserve *főhadnagy*. Five years later, Minister of Defense Order Nr. 926/1997 promoted Michna to *őrnagy* as of 20 August 1997.

György Michna died on 26 August 2012 in Budakeszi. His ashes were laid to rest with a military honour on 24 September in the cemetery of Budakeszi.[148]

FŐHADNAGY ERVIN FLÓZNIK

Number of aerial victories: 6
Successes against ground targets: n.d.a.
Number of flown combat sorties: 90
Number of hours flown in the air force: n.d.a.
Nickname: *Pierre*
Identification number: 3004-20-2786

147 *Állambiztonsági Szolgálatok Történeti Levéltára*, 2.2.1.II/6.3, 3.1.2.M-37766; also the interview of György Michna, 7 March 2001.

148 For details of the civilian life of György Michna, see Csaba B. Stenge, '*In memoriam* Michna György', *Magyar Repüléstörténeti Társaság Évkönyve*, 2012, pp. 65–68.

Decorations

- *Magyar Koronás Ezüst Érdemérem hadiszalagon a kardokkal* (25 April 1945; posthumous)
- *Tűzkereszt I fokozata a kardokkal és koszorúval*
- *Erdélyi Emlékérem*
- *Délvidéki Emlékérem*
- German Iron Cross 2nd Class (8 March 1945; posthumous)

Victories

Number	Date	Aircraft	Location
1	15 September 1944, between 10:05 and 11:25	Yak-9	Krosno S 8km
2	17 November 1944	Il-2	Gyöngyös NW 3km
3	17 November 1944	Il-2	Gyöngyös
4	22 December 1944	Yak-9	Sárszentmihály N 3km
5	6 January 1945	Il-2	Székesfehérvár SE 3km
6	8 January 1945	La-5	Budapest SW, area of Székesfehérvár (?)

Aircraft flown

Bf 109 G-6: V391 (15 September 1944), V-388 (16 September 1944)

Ervin Flóznik was born on 8 September 1920 in Abrudbánya (today Abrud, Romania), the only boy of two children. The Flóznik family moved from the area of Transylvania that was ceded to Romania after the Trianon Treaty to Budapest in 1925, then to Kecskemét, where the father, Dr Lajos Flóznik (who was a legal practitioner), had a financial secretary job. Ervin Flóznik – for whom aviation was a childhood dream – graduated from high school (*Kecskeméti Piarista Gimnázium*), where Kálmán Szeverényi was among his classmates.[149] After graduation in May 1938, he enlisted at Nyíregyháza, where he received his primary flight training. In 1939, he completed the reserve officer course and completed his pilot course in 1940. The young *hadapród őrmester* was promoted to reserve *zászlós* in 1941. During the early months of his military service, he was a pilot instructor at Börgönd, where he served with the combat training group. He was commissioned on 1 November 1942, at the same time as he was promoted to *hadnagy* (as of 1 September 1941).[150]

Ervin Flóznik in March 1944 on the Eastern Front. (From the author's collection)

149 Record Office of the Piarist school in Kecskemét, matriculation register of 1938; also based on the correspondence with the Szeverényi family.

150 *HM HIM KI*, document folder nr. 20344.

He commenced his military service on the front on 22 January 1944 as a pilot of 5/2 Fighter Squadron. Like every newcomer, at first he flew as a wingman, but by the summer he was already a flight leader. His first noted achievement in air combat came on 30 April 1944 in the area of Kissielin, where he chased away superior numbers of Soviet fighters and succeeded in defending the German ground-attack aircraft.[151]

Flóznik was promoted to *főhadnagy* as of 1 July 1944. Between 10 and 20 July, he executed five scrambles on enemy aircraft appearing over the detached outpost airfield of Włodzimierz (today Volodymyr-Volynsykiy in Ukraine), thus preventing the bombing of the city. On 21 July, as a ground commander during the relocation from Zamość to Pulawi, he volunteered to go back with repair materials to trucks that became encircled by the Soviet armored wedges; he repaired the trucks and led them back with their supplies to Lublin amid continuous fighting at the rear. Lublin was encircled by the Soviet armored units, but he managed to break out of the encirclement in close quarter combat with two Pz. VI Tigers.[152]

His first recommendation for a bronze *Signum* was issued in September 1944; 62 combat sorties and five air combats were listed, with the earlier detailed events. The recommendation reached the command of the Air Brigade and was supported, and the chief of the Army Staff (*Honvéd Vezérkar főnöke*) also suggested that the decoration be granted, but for unknown reasons it never was.[153]

Főhadnagy Ervin Flóznik achieved his first aerial victory (like many of his comrades in the squadron) in the middle of September 1944. On 15 September, he shot down a Yak-9 south of Krosno. Flóznik took off at 10:05 as a flight leader for a free hunt in the area of Sanok and Dukla. The squadron diary details his victory and that of his wingman, *hadnagy* Galánfi:

> Upon arriving in the area, *fhdgy*. Flóznik and his wingman noticed six to eight Yak-9s over the smokescreen. At a low altitude, the Il-2 aircraft attacked the ground troops. *Fhdgy*. Flóznik and his wingman immediately engaged the Soviet fighters in a dogfight, which lasted six to eight minutes and resulted in shooting down a Yak-9 for both airmen.[154]

Főhadnagy Flóznik was given the task of securing the roads for the German armored counterattack in the area of Mezőtúr on 20 October. While executing this task, he was hit by Soviet anti-aircraft artillery, but he managed to crash-land his burning aircraft next to the *24 Panzer-Division* that was thrusting forward. He took part in armored combat with the division for three days before returning to his unit.[155]

Flóznik achieved his next confirmed air victory on 17 November 1944 in the area of Gyöngyös, against Il-2s. A decoration recommendation lists one kill for him on this day, but Air Force Order Nr. 1945/4 confirms two victories in the area on the specified date. Although Air Force Order Nr. 1945/4 contains a number of typing errors, the two victories are listed with numbers also written out in letters, so it is most probably not an error (although the few surviving

151 *HM HIM HL*, recommendations for decorations, box nr. 13, group 398/a.
152 *HM HIM HL*, recommendations for decorations, box nr. 13, group 398/a.
153 *HM HIM HL*, recommendations for decorations, box nr. 13, group 398/a.
154 Excerpts from the logs of 102/1 Fighter Squadron, 14–16 September 1944 (copy owned by the author).
155 *HM HIM HL*, recommendations for decorations, box nr. 13, group 531/a.

Table of the 1943 class of the senior officer course at Kassa. Ervin Flóznik is second from the right in the lowest row. (From the author's collection)

Bf 109 G-6 (V-384) of 102/1 Fighter Squadron in the summer of 1944; Ervin Flóznik probably also flew this aircraft a number of times. The aircraft crash-landed with its engine still running; this photograph was taken at the beginning of July 1944, near Sokal (Lemberg NE 75km), and the mechanics of the squadron are working on the engine. (From the author's collection)

Briefing of an escort mission with the German dive bombers on the Zamość airfield at 102 Independent Fighter Squadron on 16 June 1944. (From the collection of László Máthé)

documents of his squadron credit Flóznik with five victories, this could also have been a typing error). Soviet forces also confirm the loss of an Il-2 from 188th GSAP near Gyöngyös, and this aircraft was almost certainly Flóznik's victim. According to this report, during the afternoon, 11 Il-2s with four La-5s were attacking targets on the western-northwestern perimeter of Gyöngyös. The fighter escort was engaged in combat with two Bf 109s, while (according to the report) two 'Fw 190s' surprised the ground-attack aircraft formation from the rear and below and shot down the aircraft of *mladshiy leytenant* G.S. Tyurikov, which crashed and exploded with its crew 8km west of Gyöngyös. In the area and on this particular day, no victories were claimed by Fw 190s; nor were any victories against Il-2s reported by German Bf 109s during the afternoon – this aircraft was therefore definitely Flóznik's victim. Mixing up Fw 190s and Bf 109s was common among the Soviets.[156]

At the end of December and at the beginning of January, *főhadnagy* Flóznik shot down two fighter aircraft and an Il-2; his comrades were very much impressed by his deeds. On 22 December 1944, west of Székesfehérvár and 3km north of Sárszentmihály, he reported shooting down a Yak-9. His victim was probably the aircraft of *mladshiy leytenant* N.I. Hlebantsov (Yak-9D, serial number 16166099) from 897th IAP; the pilot was killed (according to the Soviet report, Hlebantsov did not return after being engaged in combat with six Bf 109s in the area

156 *HM HIM HL*, recommendations for decorations, box nr. 13, group 531/a; documents of 101 Fighter Wing, box nr. 110, Air Force Order Nr. 1945/4; Gábor Horváth on documents of TsAMO.

of Zámoly). His Il-2 victim of 6 January, 3km southeast of Székesfehérvár, was probably the aircraft (serial number 11377) flown by *mladshiy leytenant* G.N. Shumeyev of 707th SAP. According to Soviet reports, the 10-plane formation was attacked by four Bf 109s while taking off and forming up; Shumeyev's aircraft was shot down at this point. The crew survived the destruction of the Il-2.

Unfortunately, we do not know the details of the location of Flóznik's last aerial victory; it was presumably achieved in the area southwest of Budapest (probably around Székesfehérvár), but there were no lost Lavochkins on this day among the combat losses in the Soviet reports. Two of Flóznik's kills are included in surviving Air Force Orders, and a further four on his recommendations for decorations.[157]

Főhadnagy Ervin Flóznik was killed on 14 January 1945 when he crashed to the ground in extremely bad weather conditions while on a return flight from a combat mission. His fellow squadron member, István Kálmán, remembered that Flóznik crashed into the side of Papod Hill somewhere around Lókút, and the local people buried him near the wreck of his aircraft in the spring of 1945.[158] This recollection, however – which was not a witness account, but which was put together with information from other sources – is not exactly correct. According to the author's investigations, the locals around Lókút did not know of any crashed Hungarian aircraft, although the locals buried the crew members of a Soviet Il-2 at the end of 1944. It can therefore be assumed that the aircraft crashed a little further eastward, that is, northeast of Papod, where we actually know of a Bf 109 wreck site.

Flóznik was posthumously recommended for the *Magyar Érdemrend lovagkeresztje hadiszalagon a kardokkal* on 24 April 1945. Next day, he received the *Magyar Koronás Ezüst Érdemérem hadiszalagon a kardokkal. Főhadnagy* Flóznik also had two other earlier recommendations that were pending: the *Magyar Koronás Ezüst Érdemérem* and the *Magyar Koronás Bronz Érdemérem*. In the case of the unsorted award, there were no apparent reasons why it had been ignored. In the case of the last recommendation, in connection with the reason why the lower-rank decoration was awarded, the following can be added: as has already been discussed in the chapter of decorations, these recommendations were dealt with by the command of the air force, and the last commander of the Royal Hungarian Air Force (*vezérezredes* Kálmán Ternegg) only had authority to grant the *Magyar Koronás Érdemérem* – and just, the Bronze Class – and the anomalies in connection with the Silver Class were detailed in the chapter on decorations and medals. It was thus not within his scope of authority to grant the classes of *Magyar Érdemrend*, which remained the sole authority of the 'Leader of the Nation'.

157 *HM HIM HL*, recommendations for decorations, box nr. 13, group 531/a; documents of 101 Fighter Wing, box nr. 110, Air Force Order Nr. 1945/4; Horváth, *Bostonok a magyar égen és földben*, p. 73; Nikita Yegorov on documents of TsAMO.

158 Gyula Gaál, 'Szabadvadászat', *Magyar Szárnyak Évkönyv*, 1992, p. 53.

HADNAGY MIHÁLY KARÁTSONYI

Number of aerial victories: 6
Successes against ground targets: –
Number of flown combat sorties: 25 (14 against Americans)
Number of hours flown in the air force: 650
Nicknames: *Miska*, *Misu*
Identification number: 1678-22-0713

Decorations

- *Magyar Érdemrend lovagkeresztje hadiszalagon a kardokkal* (29 January 1945)
- *Kormányzói dicsérő elismerés Magyar Koronás Bronz Érdemérme hadiszalagon a kardokkal* (1 November 1944)
- *Tűzkereszt I fokozata a kardokkal és koszorúval*, one wound clasp
- German Iron Cross 1st Class (17 March 1945)
- German Iron Cross 2nd Class (8 March 1945)
- Bronze *Frontflugspange* (20 April 1945)

Victories

Number	Date	Aircraft	Location
1	16 June 1944	P-38	Iszkaszentgyörgy, fisherman's lake
2	16 June 1944	B-24	Area of Lake Balaton (?)
3	14 July 1944	P-38	Környe W
4	14 July 1944	P-38	Környe W
5	27 July 1944	B-24	Szabadbattyán
6	Summer 1944	B-17	

Aircraft flown
Bf 109 G-6: V.805 (summer of 1944)

Mihály Karátsonyi was born on 27 November 1922 in Nagykőrös, the eldest son of five children. His father (who had the same name) owned a steam mill. The family later moved to Jászapáti and then to Kaposvár, but Mihály finished high school in Jászapáti (*magyar királyi katolikus Gróf Széchenyi István Reálgimnázium*).[159] He then chose a career as a military pilot and attended the *Repülőakadémia* at Kassa.

He completed his primary flight training in the summer of 1941 at *HMNRA* in Pécs. Karátsonyi graduated as a *hadnagy* on 6 December 1943 as of 1 September 1943, with rank number 96; he was in the same class as István Kálmán and László Dániel.[160] At the academy, Karátsonyi excelled in sports, especially the pentathlon.

159 Record Office of the *Gróf Széchenyi István Katolikus Gimnázium* (Gróf Széchenyi István Catholic High School) in Jászapáti, matriculation register for 1941, certificate number 13.
160 *Honvédségi Közlöny* (*Személyes ügyek*), 1943/48 (1 December 1943), p. 1708.

After his graduation, at the beginning of May 1944, he was sent to Mátyásföld as part of 5/3 Fighter Squadron, led by *főhadnagy* József Bejczy (which turned out to be 101/3 Fighter Squadron); the unit was subsequently relocated to Veszprém.

Mihály Karátsonyi as a student at the *Repülőakadémia*, shortly before his graduation. (From the author's collection)

His first combat mission took place on 16 June 1944, and he was immediately successful: he shot down a Lightning and a four-engined bomber, the latter alongside *főhadnagy* Irányi. His Lightning claim was confirmed by Anti-Aircraft Forces Command Order Nr. 1944/9 of 18 July, at first mistakenly as a shared kill with *főhadnagy* Irányi (their shared victory of that day was over the four-engined bomber). This error was corrected more than half a year later in Point 4 of Air Force Order Nr. 1945/10 of February 1945. In the case of the four-engined he and Irányi shot down, the location is unfortunately unknown; this was probably included in Anti-Aircraft Forces Command Order Nr. 1944/9, which has not survived. The later Air Force Confidential Order Nr. 1944/63 served as a 'collection of orders', but it does not include all victories confirmed on 16 June, and this one is excluded. The log of 101/3 Squadron contains a B-17 credited to Karátsonyi as a victory on that day, but this was probably an error (what remains of the squadron log contains a few similar errors of this kind).[161]

The P-38 confirmation was again incorrect in terms of location, as the aircraft was mixed up with another: the aircraft that crashed at Iszkaszentgyörgy was definitely not a Lightning, but a Mustang – the only one lost on that day, from the 52nd FG. This aircraft was shot down in error by the Lightnings of 1st FG, and not by Hungarian pilots. Although a former pilot of 1st FG wrote to the author many years ago to claim that this was 'impossible', the probability is increased by the combat loss report; the likelihood becomes a certainty when considering the account of the surviving Mustang pilot, who recounted that he was shot down by Lightnings and the aircraft crashed near a smaller lake, probably the fishing lake at Iszkaszentgyörgy. It should also be mentioned that another Mustang was shot down at the end of July by Lightnings over Hungary.[162]

Karátsonyi's next (double) kill took place on 14 July 1944, when two Lightnings of 14th FG's 49th FS collided into each other while attacked by him and crashed between Környe and Kömlőd. The pilots (1st Lieutenant John G. Schill, P-38J serial number 42-104148, and 2nd Lieutenant Clyde E. Durbin, serial number 43-28814) were killed. Karátsonyi recalled the air combat as follows:

161 *HM HIM HL*, documents of 101 Fighter Wing, box nr. 110, Air Force Order Nr. 10, 22 February 1945; box nr. 113, record of victories against four-engines; box nr. 1122, logs of 101/3 Fighter Squadron.

162 NARA MACR 5816; Crawford, *Three Crawford Brothers*, pp. 414–423.

> My two Lightnings were shot down in extremely lucky circumstances on 14 July. Three comrades and I were attacking a formation of 20–30 twin-boom aircraft and were engaged in a heavy dogfight with them. After a short fight, I managed to hit one of the Americans, which luckily crashed into the other aircraft flying next to it, taking it with himself into the depths. Both pilots saved their lives with parachutes [in reality, both died]. The other half of the day was not that successful, because 60 more Lightnings came after us in aid of their comrades, and we decided it would be best not to engage with them as the combat seemed beyond hope. We dived at once and plummeted toward the grounds in three different directions, but they came after us even at that low altitude. I managed to escape literally by a hair's breadth, flying from the northwestern edge of western Hungary (*Dunántúl*) to Szolnok, where they did not follow me.[163]

Hadnagy Mihály Karátsonyi in 1944. (From the collection of Mihály Karátsonyi)

The heavy fighting with the Lignthings was confirmed in a letter written on 18 July 1944 by *hadnagy* László Molnár. Due to bad visibility, he had been driven out of the group formation with his flight, three of which became engaged in combat with the Americans 25–30km south of Komárom – first against 40, then against a total of 60 Lightnings. The three pilots were also driven away from each other, although none of them was shot down. In his letter, Molnár did not mention the two colliding Lightnings claimed by Karátsonyi, probably because he did not see it through the thick clouds surrounding them.[164]

Interestingly, the official recording of the double kill which is also confirmed by American sources. No trace of either the official confirmation or of the deletion of the claim survives in the fragmentary documents that remain. A recommendation for the Germans in December 1944 suggests that some official form of registering these kills must have existed. Although this document credited Karátsonyi with three four-engines and one Lightning (the one from 16 June), he was recommended for a 1st Class of the German Iron Cross (which he received). In contrast, for example, Lajos Benkő's four confirmed four-engines only earned him a 2nd Class of the German Iron Cross. Although one of his four-engines was later deleted from his list of aerial victories, this was not known at the time he received the decoration.[165]

163 'A Pumák egy napja II rész,' *Magyar Szárnyak*, 1 September 1944, p. 5.

164 Letter of *hadnagy* László Molnár, 18 July 1944 (copy owned by the author; original in possession of Krisztián Tóth).

165 *HM HIM HL*, documents of 101 Fighter Wing, box nr. 113, names those recommended for the German pilot badge, 17 December 1944. The 'Puma' pilots did not receive this badge, but following the recommendation, the mass awarding of Iron Crosses to the respective pilots began in the spring of 1945.

Hadnagy Karátsonyi in his Messerschmitt (V.805) in the early summer of 1944. (From the collection of Mihály Karátsonyi)

On 27 July, *hadnagy* Karátsonyi managed to shoot down another Liberator, which he remembered as follows:

> 27 July – we were on a mission with six aircraft. Molnár, Debrődy, Pál Kováts [*hadnagy* Pál Kovács, also spelled Kovách, Kováts, a pilot of 101/3 Squadron who graduated in the same class as Karátsonyi; not *őrmester* Pál Kovács, the ace, who flew in the same squadron], Szentgyörgyi, Skulka and myself. Southwest of Budapest we found the bombers. We attacked head-on, and it was a great success; we shot down four bombers with no losses on our side. I got my Liberator too.[166]

Hadnagy Karátsonyi's four-engined kill was mentioned in Air Force Confidential Order Nr. 1944/63 with a location of Szabadbattyán; the aircraft was a B-24H serving in 455th BG's 743'rd Bomber Squadron, piloted by 2nd Lieutenant R.A. Gulbranson. None of the nine-person crew survived the destruction of the aircraft (serial number 4252294).[167]

According to the registry of victories against four-engines, and also according to a later issued recommendation, *hadnagy* Karátsonyi had three aerial victories against four-engines (two B-24s and a B-17: one was an individual victory, one was shared with *főhadnagy* Irányi and one was shared with a German pilot). Because of the extremely scarce documents, however, the author did not manage to pinpoint the exact date of the third air victory.[168]

166 Mihály Karátsonyi, 'Lőttem… lőttünk… lőttek…', *Magyar Szárnyak Évkönyv*, 1981, p. 47.
167 NARA MACR 7031.
168 *HM HIM HL*, documents of 101 Fighter Wing, box nr. 113, record of victories against four-engines.

One of the Lightnings (serial number 42-104148) of 14th FG's 49th Fighter Squadron that crashed west of Környe on 14 July 1944, surrounded by Hungarian soldiers, police officers and civilians. The pilot of the aircraft, 1st Lieutenant John G. Schill, was killed, as well as the other pilot, 2nd Lieutenant Clyde E. Durbin, who collided with Schill's aircraft. The two crashed aircraft were claimed by *hadnagy* Karátsonyi. (From the collection of Péter Tarr)

Hadnagy Karátsonyi's last (14th) combat sortie against the Americans was completed on 7 August 1944. He was shot down by the Mustangs of 31st FG and bailed out of his aircraft with severe burns southeast of Rum. In one of the letters he wrote to the author, he mentioned that the Mustang that shot down his aircraft also strafed him on the ground, but luckily he missed.[169] After this, he was taken to the hospital in Szombathely. He remembered the events of his last summer combat sortie as follows:

> The loudspeaker called: 'Took off! Go!' The strong squadron-strength formation of 18 aircraft, taken from all three squadrons, was led by Laci Molnár. Gyurka Debrődy led the aircraft from 1 Squadron, *Drumi* Tóth those from 2 Squadron, and I myself those from 3 Squadron. In my flight, two were first-timers. I also remember Jóska Málik and *zászlós* Nyemecz; they were there too. As usual, after we took off, we climbed northwest. We were assigned to protect German heavy fighters. We were now close to Győr at an altitude of 7,000 meters when we spotted the German Messerschmitts. Their climbing ability and speed was lower than ours due to their heavy armament. The *Szikla* now ordered us to take up the task of escort. As the Germans were tuned in to another wavelength, we could only communicate with them via the *Szikla*. We took up the task of escorting this formation of approximately 20 aircraft 500 meters above and in the rear. When we were approximately over Székesfehérvár, we noticed the American bombers flying toward Budapest below us. When we were almost exactly over their heads, Molnár ordered on the radio: 'Jettison the

169 Letter of Mihály Karátsonyi to the author, 28 May 2004.

drop tank, *Revi*, armament on.' To our great surprise, the Germans did not release their drop tanks, but flew forward with a right turn toward the south and then toward the west. We were over the River Rába now; Molnár was constantly on the radio with the *Szikla*, but the orders were always that we should remain by the side of the Germans. Then, a voice came over the radio: 'Four Mustangs over us in the sun!' Another: 'There are at least 12 of them!' and their number was just growing. Molnár asked the *Szikla* to order the Germans to do something and not to continue circling around, because this was going to be a massacre. The answer was always: 'Escort the Germans!' A voice came over the radio: 'I've got engine problems; I'm disengaging!' Molnár: 'Don't disengage, you fool, you'll get shot down immediately!' Response: 'I won't disengage.' As this went on, we feared our fuel would not be sufficient to return home, let alone have a dogfight. Then, in an instant, the Mustang attack was upon us. Molnár rushed forward to warn the Germans, and I saw the Mustangs start up on Laci. With a right climbing turn I opened fire, without any hope of a hit, because there was no way to aim, I was just trying to deter their attention. When I looked back at my wingman, I saw nobody. I went into a dive, as I had done so many times before, and I managed to get out of the way of the direct attack. When I pulled up my aircraft at an altitude of 2,000 meters, I noticed a Messer with two Mustangs behind him. I turned toward them and, using my superior speed from my dive, I reached them in no time. I was in a good position, so I opened fire and hit him [one of the Mustangs] a good number of times. At that moment, I saw a bright trail, heard a large explosion and my aircraft shuddered as if hit by a bomb. Fire licks into the cockpit by my left foot. I looked back and saw Mustangs pouring fire on me. My first thought: *Get out of here*! I pushed my aircraft to dive – *maybe they'll overshoot* – and I released the canopy. Okay, but I had loosened the harnesses after taking off to let me move more freely in air combat, and they hadn't yet opened, and now, due to the centrifugal force and the huge air draft, half of my body was hanging out of the aircraft, which was plummeting vertically toward the ground (later eyewitnesses told me I was trailing a flame the length of a football pitch) without my being able to reach the control column. I saw myself crashing to the ground in the burning aircraft; my mother came into my mind; so, with an unbearable force, I pressed my thumb under the harness and I moved my hand down toward my belly to unlock it. Dead silence – I was out of the aircraft! I fell toward the ground on my back, and when I wanted to open the parachute, I couldn't find the release handle in its pocket. I opened my eyes and it was flickering right before me, so I grabbed it and pulled. The parachute opened like a big white sausage, and I made a somersault to avoid it yanking me too strongly. I succeeded because when it opened at last it stopped my fall with only a small lift. And then I hit the ground. ... Half of my body suffered third-degree burns. My eyelids were burnt; I could not open my eyes for three weeks and the doctors couldn't tell if I would ever see again. My lips, my gums were burnt, also the inside of my nose, which happened when the flames burst upward. From my neck to my feet, there was no skin left on me; my face swelled to double its normal size. In two weeks I lost half of my weight, and for three weeks I hung between life and death.[170]

170 Karátsonyi, 'Lőttem... lőttünk... lőttek...', pp. 48–49.

Hadnagy Karátsonyi was probably the most severely burnt Hungarian pilot to actually survive. He could thank his survival to his strong body, his willpower and the excellent care he received. The Mustang he attacked on this mission was not shot down; although it has occasionally been added to his individual tally, there are no traces in the contemporary sources of a full-value aerial victory claim, and no confirmation of one.

1st Lieutenant John G. Schill, pilot of one of the Lightnings crashed west of Környe. He was killed. This was his 60th combat sortie, and he had already achieved one confirmed aerial victory. (From the collection of the Schill family)

After his serious injuries were healed, Karátsonyi joined 101 Fighter Wing on 12 December 1944. At first, he was placed back in 101/3 Squadron, but he was not yet combat-ready; on 22 January, therefore, he was assigned to a ground position in wing command to help *százados* Ujszászy deal with the administrative issues surrounding the establishment of the new 101/III Fighter Group. On 12 February 1945, he was assigned to the staff of 101/III Group as command post officer.[171]

Karátsonyi was briefly assigned to 101/6 Squadron in the middle of March to fly introduction test flights; he was then reassigned to his squadron and, at the end of the war, he again went on missions until the middle of April.[172]

Karátsonyi was captured by the Americans with his unit. He also chose emigration, and in 1949 moved to the United States with his two younger brothers, where he obtained a degree in engineering and purchased a glass technique factory, which he developed very successfully. He became a supplier to NASA and to the aviation industry. He had a number of hobbies, including water skiing, but he was only truly happy when he was able to fly. At the beginning of the 1980s, he purchased a Mooney M20E aircraft (registration number N7424V) and painted the 'Puma' head on its vertical stabilizer. He flew this until his death. Karátsonyi became friends with many of his former adversaries, the former US fighter pilots.

Mihály Karátsonyi died in Los Angeles on 29 May 2005. As per his last wish, his ashes were brought back to Hungary and, on 12 September 2005, buried in Farkasréti Cemetery with full military honors.

ŐRMESTER JÁNOS MÁTYÁS

Number of aerial victories: 6
Successes against ground targets: n.d.a.
Number of flown combat sorties: around 110
Number of hours flown in the air force: n.d.a.

171 *HM HIM HL*, documents of 101 Fighter Wing, box nr. 110, Wing Orders Nrs. 1945/17, 32.
172 HM HIM HL, documents of 101 Fighter Wing, box nr. 110, Wing Order Nr. 1945/49.

Nickname: –
Identification number: 3004-17-0729

Decorations

- *Magyar Nagy Ezüst Vitézségi Érem* (10 July 1944)
- *Magyar Kis Ezüst Vitézségi Érem* (20 March 1944)
- *Magyar Bronz Érdemérem hadiszalagon* (25 April 1945)
- *Magyar Bronz Vitézségi Érem* (18 November 1943)
- *Magyar Bronz Vitézségi Érem*, for the second time (13 February 1945)
- *Tűzkereszt I fokozata a kardokkal és koszorúval*
- *Erdélyi Emlékérem*
- *Délvidéki Emlékérem*
- German Iron Cross 2nd Class (8 March 1945)
- Italian Pilot Badge (1939)

Victories

Number	Date	Aircraft	Location
1	3 August 1943	Il-2	Belgorod N
2	Before the end of October 1943	Soviet single-engine	
3	Winter 1943–44	Soviet single-engine	
4	Beginning of 1944	Soviet single-engine	
5	3 February 1944 at 09:45	La-5	Cherkasy W
6	16 June 1944	P-38	Értény NW

Aircraft flown

Re.2000: V.412 (14 January 1943), Bf 109 G-6/U4: W-028 (25 August 1944)

János Mátyás was born on 2 March 1917 in Transylvania, Vajdahunyad (today Hunedoara, Romania), to a family of five children (his father was a rail loader). The family fled their hometown from the Romanians and went to Budapest in 1920, where they began their new life in a railroad wagon. Because of the family's extremely difficult financial situation, János Mátyás did not have a chance to go to high school; after four years at elementary school, he learned a profession and became a typographer. He was only able to graduate from high school after the war, just like Dezső Szentgyörgyi.

Mátyás came to the Royal Hungarian Air Force without having any previous motivation. He entered service on 9 September 1938 following the call of the *DRT* because of the prospective safe salary, and he received his fighter training in Italy in 1938–39. According to his memories, just as had been the case with the typographer job, he grew to love flying and the military way of life.[173] Mátyás graduated among the first of the class, so he returned to Hungary from Grottaglie as early as the autumn of 1939. At home, after completing the fighter combat training at Börgönd, he was assigned to Mátyásföld to 1/4 '*Szent György*' Fighter Squadron.

173 Based on the interview of János Mátyás, 6 June 2002.

From December 1940 to January 1941, he was reassigned to Nagyvárad, and worked as instructor of air force recruits (he served with *hadnagy* József Bejczy from his own squadron and *főhadnagy* György Ujszászy from 1/3 Squadron).

Mátyás experienced his first combat in April 1941, during the campaign against Yugoslavia. His squadron completed a few missions to protect ground troops, and the Chief of Staff of the Army presented him a commendatory certificate.

János Mátyás in front of the Duce on the Grottaglie airfield. Next to the portrait of Mussolini, a part of a known fascist motto can be seen: *Credere, Obbedire, Combattere* – To believe, to obey, to fight. (From the author's collection)

At the end of October 1941, he was briefly sent to the sister unit on the Eastern Front – 1/3 *'Kör Ász'* Squadron, led by *százados* László Tomor – partly to obtain combat experience, and partly to fly one of two reserve aircraft to the front as a replacement for two worn out aircraft. The other aircraft was flown by *zászlós* György Pávay-Vajna. This time, Mátyás did not flew any combat sorties, partly because of the bad weather, and partly because of the low-intensity usage of the squadron in combat situations.[174] In November 1941, with the dissolution of 1/II Fighter Group and the formation of 5/I Fighter Group, he remained at Mátyásföld and was automatically reassigned to the new group (5/2 Squadron).

At the end of November 1942, he and part of his group were sent to the Eastern Front, where he acted as a replacement pilot. *Szakaszvezető* Mátyás was sent on a mission with the old *Héja*s only once before these aircraft were lost. On 14 January 1943, he was flying a reconnaissance and protecting mission with a V.412 as wingman to his squadron commander, *százados* Gyula Horváth; this was his first combat sortie on the Eastern Front.[175] He retrained to Messerschmitts in Uman, and flew his first combat sortie with the Bf 109 type in (presumably) May. Mátyás flew most of his combat sorties over the Eastern Front as wingman to *hadnagy* Miklós Kenyeres.

Mátyás achieved his first confirmed aerial victory on 3 August 1943: he was flying as the wingman of *hadnagy* György Debrődy and shot down an Il-2 north of Belgorod. He told the story of his first (and Debrődy's third) kill in the field magazine of 5/I Fighter Group:

> I was the wingman of *hdgy.* Debrődy and I protected him as we attacked the Russians. The *hdgy.* was firing; he then turned away, and there it was in front of me, the Il-7 [Il-2m3]. I began to shoot; some skin parts were torn off, then the aircraft caught fire and plummeted. I fired 20 cannon shells into him (he says, proudly) until it erupted in flames. In the

174 Becze, *'Kőr Ász'*, pp. 70–71.
175 *HM HIM HL*, documents of the 2nd Army, box nr. 17, after-action report of 5/I Fighter Group, from 1 January to 28 February 1943, appendix nr. 26 (mission report).

János Mátyás in an Italian Romeo Ro.41 two-seat trainer aircraft on the airfield at Grottaglie in 1939. The Royal Hungarian Air Force also had a few Romeos in service. (From the author's collection)

János Mátyás near a Fiat CR.32 on the airfield at Grottaglie in 1939. In the background, in front of the large airship hangar, Caproni Ca.310 Libecchio light bombers can be seen; this type had a short and disgraceful career in the Royal Hungarian Air Force. (From the author's collection)

Szakaszvezető János Mátyás in front of an aircraft of 1/3 Fighter Squadron in Ukraine, autumn 1941. (From the collection of János Mátyás)

János Mátyás climbs into his CR.42; the insignia of 1/4 '*Szent György*' Fighter Squadron can clearly be seen on the fuselage of the aircraft. (From the collection of János Mátyás)

> meantime, I nearly collided with another aircraft; then I followed the *hdgy.*, who was pushing the escaping Russian more and more toward the ground. I saw it crash, so we turned back.[176]

János Mátyás achieved another aerial victory before the end of October 1943, probably still in August or September, because on 29 October 1943 he was credited with two confirmed air victories by his squadron.[177]

176 *Üvölt a Puma*, 3 August 1943, p. 1.
177 *Üvölt a Puma*, 3 November 1943, p. 1.

Around 10 October, Soviet anti-aircraft artillery shot him down during a strafing run. He belly-landed behind the German lines and hit his head on the gunsight (he did not receive a wound clasp for his *Tűzkereszt* on this occasion). This was the only time during the war that Mátyás was shot down.[178]

As of 12 October 1943, he was taken into regular service and promoted to *őrmester*.

Over the winter of 1943–44, he shot down three further Soviet aircraft. One victory was probably scored in December, and two at the beginning of 1944. His last Soviet aircraft – an La-5 – was shot down on 3 February 1944 during the combat mission when *hadnagy* Miklós Kenyeres was shot down by the Soviet anti-aircraft artillery. At the end of the mission, *őrmester* Mátyás belly-landed near Novo Arkhangelsk due to a lack of fuel (for the details of the mission, see the biography of Miklós Kenyeres).

Őrmester Mátyás returned home from the Eastern Front to Mátyásföld at the end of February 1944. According to the summary of his squadron commander, he had completed 88 combat sorties and achieved five confirmed aerial victories. All his victims were single-engine aircraft.[179]

Mátyás was reassigned to Veszprém as of 1 May 1944 to 101/3 Fighter Squadron, which was formed there. His first combat mission against the Americans was flown on 14 June 1944, but he needed to disengage from the combat because his coolant boiled over. Two days later, he shot down a Lightning: Air Force Confidential Order Nr. 1944/63 features this as a shared kill with his squadron commander, *főhadnagy* József Bejczy. The P-38J aircraft crashed northwest of Értény, belonging to 82nd FG's 95th Fighter Squadron (serial number 43-28803); the pilot, 2nd Lieutenant Francis P. Hanlon, was killed.[180]

Over the summer, Mátyás did not succeed in achieving any more victories, although he hit at least one four-engined bomber and inflicted serious damage to it.

In November 1944, the pilot – who was a few years older than his comrades – was restricted from flying combat missions in consideration of his long combat service and his pregnant wife. From this point until the end of the war, he flew as a courier pilot on the wing staff, and also acted as a clerk at the wing's command post. His reassignment was announced in Wing Order Nr. 1944/44, issued on 18 November, but it had already been decided, presumably at the end of October. The original document – according to Mátyás's recollections – was also signed by his squadron commander, József Bejczy, who was killed on 4 November.[181]

Mátyás was taken POW by the Americans in May 1945 with his unit, and returned to Hungary in November 1945, when he at first settled with his family in Gyál. In August 1947, he was 'B-listed', discharged from military service and not allowed to fly again. From 1945 to 1952, Mátyás was constantly under police observation in Gyál; afterward, he moved back to Budapest. For the period following this, no observation documents survive in connection with János Mátyás at the *Állambiztonsági Szolgálatok Történeti Levéltára*.

178 Based on the interview of János Mátyás, 4 October 2003.

179 *HM HIM HL*, documents of 101 Fighter Wing, box nr. 112, Royal Hungarian 102 Honvéd Fighter Group, summary of decorated officers and enlisted; also based on the interview of János Mátyás, 4 October 2003.

180 *HM HIM HL*, documents of 101 Fighter Wing, box nr. 110, Air Force Confidential Order Nr. 1944/63; NARA MACR 6132.

181 *HM HIM HL*, documents of 101 Fighter Wing, box nr. 110, Wing Order Nr. 1944/44; also based on the interview of János Mátyás, 7 September 2004.

Mátyás worked in his original profession as a civilian (as a typographer). From 1952 until his retirement in 1977, he was a typesetter and typographer at the Athenaeum Printing House. After the democratic transformation of 1989, the Minister of Defense promoted Mátyás to *hadnagy* in Order Nr. 97/1994, as of 24 March 1994.[182]

János Mátyás died on 2 October 2010 in Budakeszi. His ashes were laid to rest in the columbarium of the Fasori Reformed Church.[183]

Őrmester János Mátyás in March 1944, after returning home from the Eastern Front. (From the collection of János Mátyás)

ŐRMESTER MÁTYÁS LŐRINCZ

Number of aerial victories: 6
Successes against ground targets: n.d.a.
Number of flown combat sorties: around 20
Number of hours flown in the air force: n.d.a.
Nickname: *Matyi*
Identification number: 5284-21-0044

Decorations

- *Magyar Nagy Ezüst Vitézségi Érem* (25 December 1944; posthumous)
- *Magyar Nagy Ezüst Vitézségi Érem*, for the second time (13 February 1945; posthumous)
- *Magyar Kis Ezüst Vitézségi Érem* (17 December 1944; posthumous)
- *Tűzkereszt I fokozata a kardokkal és koszorúval*

Victories

Number	Date	Aircraft	Location
1	16 June 1944, between 09:40 and 09:45	P-38	Balatonszántód
2	16 June 1944, between 09:40 and 09:45	P-38	Balatonendréd
3	16 June 1944, between 09:40 and 09:45	P-38	Balaton S
4	2 July 1944 at 10:28	B-24	Budapest SW
5	7 July 1944	B-24	Győrszentmárton (Pannonhalma)
6	12 October 1944	P-51	Aszófő (Veszprém)

182 *HM HIM KI*, document folder nr. 441/2280.
183 For János Mátyás, see more details in Csaba B. Stenge, 'A legidősebb még élő magyar vadászrepülő ász volt: *in memoriam* Mátyás János', *Katonaújság*, 2011/1, pp. 2–7.

Aircraft flown

Bf 109 G-6/U4: W-020 (early autumn of 1944)

Mátyás Lőrincz was born on 4 January 1921 in Nagyvárad, as the second child and only boy in his family. His father was an engineering councilor (a cadaster engineer).[184] The family remained in the area, which was given to the Romanians, and the young Mátyás Lőrincz spent his early life in several Transylvanian cities. Although he completed a few years of high school, he very much disliked mathematics and so left school to apprentice as a woodcarver and sculptor. His artistic ambitions were inherited from his mother, Magdolna Füzesséry (1894–1975), who received a diploma as a painter and sculptor in 1917 from the *Magyar Képzőművészeti Akadémia* (Hungarian Academy of Fine Arts), and who later had a successful painting career. Lőrincz already wanted to be a pilot, again inspired by a relative from his mother's side, István Füzesséry, who had served as a reconnaissance pilot during the First World War. His chance came after the summer of 1940, when, following the Second Vienna Award, he at last became a Hungarian citizen, and the *HMNRA* formed a primary flight training base in Marosvásárhely. Lőrincz was among the pupils of the first class here in 1941 (with another future ace, Ernő Kiss). After completing his primary flight training, Lőrincz was sent to the *Regvi* in Szombathely, and then to Börgönd as part of the combat training group in 1942, where he first received short-range reconnaissance combat training and (after that) fighter combat training.

At Börgönd – where he also got a type-training to the Messerschmitt – he was involved in a serious accident in 1943. While landing with a WM-21 Sólyom, an ill-disciplined German *Oberleutnant* glided in front of him against the regulations with his Messerschmitt, which he was unable to see because of the large radial engine of his Sólyom. They collided, and his propeller cut into the cockpit of the Bf 109 E and seriously wounded the German pilot in the head. Fortunately, Lőrincz was not injured; as the accident was purely the German pilot's fault, it did not hinder in the Hungarian pilot's career. He was reassigned from Börgönd to Szolnok as part of 1 Fighter Training Group, where he served until the spring of 1944. After this, he was reassigned to Veszprém as part of 101/2 Fighter Squadron, at the same time as the creation of 101 Fighter Group. His first combat mission was completed on 30 May 1944, although there was no enemy engagement involved. On his second mission, on 2 June, the Hungarian formation also missed the Americans, who attacked railway stations in Eastern Hungary instead of anticipated targets in Western Hungary on the first shuttle mission of Operation Frantic.

On 14 June, Lőrincz landed from the wrong direction on the airfield after a test flight with an aircraft that had a faulty undercarriage and was pouring oil all over the place (as a result of which he could see nothing from the cockpit). He was therefore forbidden to go on missions for a week. Lőrincz was a true daredevil, and he got the highest number of punisments at the 101 Fighter Group from his enlisted pilot class.

Two days later, on 16 June, the group was again preparing for a mission. Just before taking off, Lőrincz pleaded with *főhadnagy* János Kőhalmy to let him come too. This was his third combat mission and the first one which he actually met the enemy. He came back having achieved something extraordinary: three aerial victories – the only instance in the group that three kills in a single sortie were scored against the Americans.

184 The majority of the details of the life of Mátyás Lőrincz were provided by the family from documents preserved by them. He does not have a personal document folder in the Central Record Office of the *HM HIM*.

Mátyás Lőrincz in the WM-21 '*Sólyom*', the F.257, that collided with the 'Red 5' Bf 109 E that glided beneath him; the German pilot was seriously wounded. (From the collection of the Lőrincz family)

The pilot's handwritten draft of his combat report has survived. The document itself is very hard to decipher, but is nevertheless very important:

> On 16 June 1944, I took off on a mission as the fourth member of the third flight of 101/2 Fighter Squadron, our task was to provide fighter cover. The enemy formation was noticed at approx. 10:35 [sic – in reality, it was 09:35; the time was clearly mistyped, and not corrected in the handwritten version]. I released my drop tank, and the squadron turned to attack. A little while later, we were attacking the enemy bomber formation from above and the flank. I was diving on the middle bomber wave when I heard in the radio halfway through that somebody was asking for help because Lightnings were after him. Hearing this, I pulled up my aircraft from diving. Left of me, I noticed an Me 109 surrounded by four Lightnings in a left circle; I climbed above them with the speed I had gained from my dive, and dived upon the last twin-boom aircraft straight from the sun. The Lightning took a short burst from my cannon and exploded before my eyes. Seeing this, I rushed over him to engage the second Lightning with my cannon; the fuselage and both engines caught fire quickly, and it plummeted after the first. Trying my luck further, I flew past the second Lightning and opened fire with a long machinegun burst on the third; I managed to set its starboard engine and fuselage on fire. This third aircraft took a sharp right turn and disappeared below me, trailing a long blazing trail behind him.
>
> But before I could be able to attack the fourth remaining Lightning, I felt my aircraft shuddering by hits. Looking out to my wings, I saw the hit marks. I then thought, *Maybe this is my last flight.* I reported my three victories over the radio to my flight leader, along with the fact that I had been hit. After this, my concern was to free myself from any enemy by climbing to the sun and to bring my aircraft home in a relatively repairable state, which I succeeded in doing at 10:30 on the local airfield.
>
> The three Lightnings were shot out of a four-part left ring, one after the other, from a distance of approximately 50 to 30 meters in only one pass, over the area of Balatonföldvár–Ságvár–Tab–Gamás–Fonyód, between 09:40 and 09:45. I was not able to witness the actual impacts because of the intensity of the air combat.[185]

185 Copy of the original records, owned by the author.

Although it is very difficult to reconstruct the events and individual actions in an air combat of this scale, the American reports compiled from the pilots of a Lightning squadron exactly matched Lőrincz's description. The log of 1st Fighter Group's 71st Fighter Squadron mentions a lone Bf 109 attacking from dead astern directly south of the Lake Balaton at around 09:40, which first shot down the aircraft of 1st Lieutenant Shepard, then seriously damaged the aircraft of Captain Advey and the aircraft of 2nd Lieutenant Herbert Hatch (an ace with five aerial victories to his credit). Besides other damage, these aircraft also lost one of their engines each, and Captain Advey, the flight leader, suffered minor facial injuries due to shrapnel from a cannon round. 2nd Lieutenant Gerald Osgood, who escorted the damaged fighters back home with another aircraft, reported that the attacker had probably been shot down by him.[186]

On 16 June 1944, Mátyás Lőrincz also seriously damaged the P-38 of 2nd Lieutenant Herbert Brooks Hatch from 1st FG (he had five kills). In the picture he is showing off his aerial victory markings, which were reported on 10 June 1944, in combat with Romanian IAR-80 fighters. (From the collection of the Hatch family)

Szakaszvezető Lőrincz was promoted *őrmester* out of turn for his three kills, as of 1 July. The three aerial victories also featured in many contemporary sources; two were included in Air Force Confidential Order Nr. 1944/63, but these three victories were probably originally confirmed in Anti-Aircraft Force Command Order Nr. 9, issued on 18 July 1944. For unknown reasons, only two of them were included in Air Force Confidential Order Nr. 1944/63.

Lőrincz shot down his first four-engined heavy bomber on 2 July 1944. Although this victory was deleted seven months later (three months after the pilot had died) in Wing Order Nr. 1945/27, it was added to Lőrincz's victory tally, both at the time and later. Unfortunately, no exact description has survived to explain why the aerial victory's confirmation was uncertain, although the location given was not very exact. On this day, the German pilots significantly overclaimed against four-engined heavy bombers over Hungary, especially B-17s, not the Hungarians. The original victory report was as follows:

> At 09:35 on 2 July 1944, I took off with the 101 Fighter Group. The enemy was spotted south of Budapest, after coming from Komárom, where we joined the German fighter formations. With the lead of my element leader, I attacked a Liberator formation from above and behind. When I saw that the right engine of the Liberator (the one my commander was attacking) was emitting smoke and was engulfed in flames, I attacked the next bomber and I fired a long cannon and machine gun burst from 70 to 30 meters into its starboard

186 The logs of 1st FG's 71st FS, 16 June 1944 (copy owned by the author); recollections of 2nd Lieutenant Hatch in Herbert Hatch, *"Stub": An Ace and his Angel. Memoirs of a World War II Fighter Pilot* (Paducah, KY: Turner, 2000), pp. 53–54.

2nd Lieutenant Hatch returned to the airfield in his P-38 with one engine knocked out following the air combat of 16 June 1944. Damage can be seen here the shot-down port wingtip and a hit from a 2cm cannon on the port aileron. (From the collection of the Hatch family)

wing and engines. The outer starboard engine was instantly in flames and, as I was disengaging to the right to attack again, I saw the enemy aircraft leaving the formation with a sharp right turn. At this point, both starboard engines were already burning viciously. I could not notice anything else because a Mustang fighter aircraft attacked me; after a short dogfight, I had to escape, because I received three hits when I was disengaging from the Liberator, so I was unable to fight effectively and was forced to fly back home after a dive. I have announced my aerial victories via the radio, which was acknowledged by my group commander. The location of the impact was in the area of 14N-GS 3-6 [the map area directly southwest of Budapest], and the time was 10:28.[187]

It was most probably 2nd Lieutenant Gerald Osgood who damaged the aircraft of Mátyás Lőrincz in air combat on 16 June 1944; he reported a probable kill against the Bf 109 that wrought havoc among his Squadron members. (From the collection of Jack Cook)

187 Copy of the original records, owned by the author.

Őrmester Mátyás Lőrincz poses on the nose of his Messerschmitt Bf 109 in July 1944 at Veszprém-Jutas. (From the author's collection)

It's worth mentioning that the 456th BG's 744th Squadron lost six Liberators SW from Budapest around this time by the attack of Hungarian and German fighters. Lőrincz shot down his second Liberator five days later, on a mission on 7 July. This was included in Air Force Confidential Order Nr. 1944/63, with a location of Győrszentmárton (modern-day Pannonhalma).[188] His victim was most probably the B-24G (serial number 42-78350) flown by 1st Lieutenant Scott S. Murphy from 464th BG's 779th BS; the 10-member crew bailed out of the aircraft over Győr and was taken prisioner of war. According to the notes and memories of the American pilot, they were shot down over Győr by a lone Bf 109 after leaving the formation when their aircraft was damaged in anti-aircraft artillery fire over Blechhammer (their original target). These notes and a contemporary report by Lőrincz show significant similarities, and the location is the same.[189]

According to the recollection of one of his comrades, Lőrincz was shot down on 27 July 1944 by the Mustangs; he belly-landed near the Balaton.[190] If this memory is correct, the attackers must have come from either 325th FG or 332nd FG.

According to the documents of 101 Fighter Wing, Lőrincz flew 14 combat sorties altogether against the Americans (before the end of August), during which he scored five aerial victories.

Lőrincz's recommendation for the *Magyar Nagy Ezüst Vitézségi Érem*, issued on 9 September, stated: 'During his missions, his daring combat spirit and self-sacrificing comradeship were always apparent.'[191]

Lőrincz achieved his last confirmed victory on 12 October 1944 while returning from a strafing attack in the area of Veszprém, in an air combat with Mustangs attacking the landing Hungarian Messerschmitts. As has already been mentioned in the biography of *hadnagy* Málik, both the Mustangs that crashed that day over Hungarian territory were credited by American reports to anti-aircraft artillery fire, and one can certainly be credited to the anti-artillery units; the other, a Mustang of 325th FG's 319th FS (P-51B, serial number 43-24852 with 1st Lieutenant Richard H. Videto at the controls), crashed with its pilot, probably in the Vértes Mountains NE from Veszprém (an American eyewitness reported the cause of the crash as a damage suffered by a strafed locomotive's boiler explosion). This victory was confirmed with a location of Aszófő in Air Force Order Nr. 1944/3, while the later Wing Order Nr. 1945/62

188 NARA MACR 6572.

189 György Stirling, 'Repülőink hősi harcai', *Magyar Szárnyak*, 1 October 1944, p. 4; also based on the notes of 1st Lieutenant Murphy (now in the possession of his son).

190 Krascsenics, *Egy magyar királyi vadászrepülő visszaemlékezései*, p. 25.

191 *HM HIM HL*, documents of 101 Fighter Wing, box nr. 113, telegram, high command of 1 Air Division.

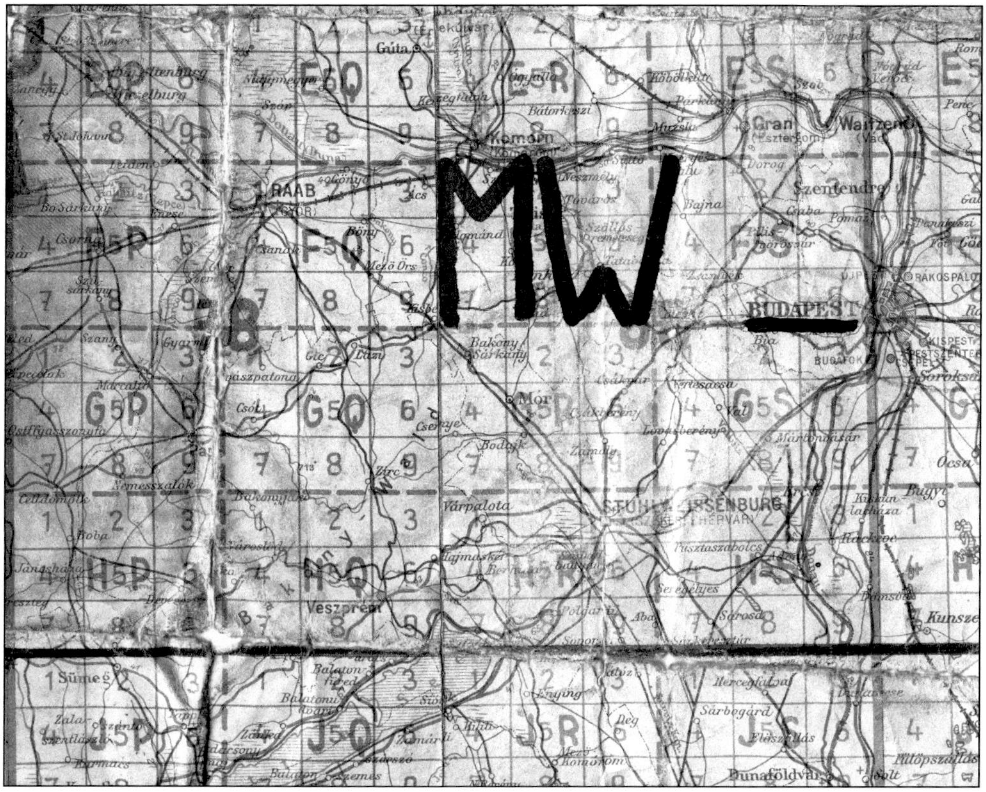

German code-map scaled to 1:1,000,000, also used by the Hungarian fighters, and the GS map strip on it, where Mátyás Lőrincz reported his aerial victory on 2 July 1944. (From the author's collection)

confirmed the same kill with a location of Veszprém. As happened for Málik, these confirmations referred to the same aircraft; the duplication probably occurred because Air Force Order Nr. 1944/3 was not at hand at the time of writing the Wing Order Nr. 1945/62, so the clerks while preparing it believed the victory of 12 October 1944 had not yet been confirmed.[192]

Lőrincz described this victory and the strafing runs against the Soviets in a letter to his father from the second half of October: 'As a matter of fact, I ended the career of another American pilot 10 days ago. I shot the chap down over this airfield at an altitude of 40 meters so he could not even bail out. I am also regularly out strafing the red columns, day by day.'[193]

Lőrincz took off for his last mission on 5 November 1944, the last large-scale formation mission of 101 Fighter Wing against the Americans. After attacking the bombers, he was engaged in combat with the arriving Mustangs when he received the fatal hit; he tried an emergency-landing northwest of Ságvár, at Gámpuszta, with his landing gears released. According

192 *HM HIM HL*, documents of 101 Fighter Wing, box nr. 110, Air Force Order Nr. 1944/3 and Wing Order Nr. 1945/62.

193 Letter of Mátyás Lőrincz to his father, 23 October 1944 (in the possession of the Lőrincz family; a copy is owned by the author).

to eyewitnesses, his wing hit a tree during landing and overturned the aircraft, which caught fire instantly. The pilot – who was already gravely injured in the air from a shot in his lungs – burned to death in the cockpit.

The family was notified by *hadnagy* János Karcsai[194] from 101/2 Fighter Squadron in a letter written in the absence of the squadron commander. The letter gave the exact circumstances in which the pilot was killed:

Mátyás Lőrincz bathes in Lake Balaton in a quite extraordinary trophy: he is passing time in a boat modified from a droppable 75 gal. (284 liter) aluminum extra fuel tank of a P-51 Mustang. (From the collection of the Lőrincz family)

> Mátyás was killed close to Ságvár. After the attack on the American bomber formation, Mustangs attacked and dispersed the Hungarian formation. Mátyás took action and fought back, but his experience, knowledge and personal bravery were of no use against the Mustangs, which were superior in numbers. His aircraft was hit several times and the engine started to emit smoke. He tried to save his aircraft. As the *levente* commander at Ságvár told us: an aircraft with a smoking engine and its landing gears out approached a meadow in the vicinity of the village. It later turned out that Mátyás himself had also been hit, as was shown by the wounds on his body. He must have fainted, because the aircraft, that had been gliding smoothly, began to waggle. It collided with a tree standing at the edge of the meadow and sheared it in half; the wings and the landing gear broke off. The aircraft then hit the ground and exploded. It somersaulted once or twice and then stopped. By the time those in the vicinity could get near, they could only state the death of the pilot.[195]

The pilot who shot Lőrincz down was from 325th FG's 318th Fighter Squadron. He was almost surely 1st Lieutenant Oscar Rau, who reported four victories in the area against Hungarian Bf 109s (these were his four kills of the war). Of these aerial victories, after examining the details contained in the victory reports, Lőrincz's aircraft was probably Rau's second.[196]

Mátyás Lőrincz was buried on 13 November 1944 in the 'Szent Antal' cemetery in Csorna, where his father resided at the time. In 1962, he was reburied in Budapest, next to his father, in the family vault at the cemetery of Rákospalota. His remains, and those of his father, were reinterred in May 1998 to Kispest to the columbarium of the 'Szent József' church in the Wekerle estate. The remains of Mátyás Lőrincz still rests there. Interestingly, Lőrincz's gravesite still exists at Csorna, probably due to problems surrounding the reburial, which was not recorded

194 Karcsai went missing on 28 January 1945 after Soviet heavy machineguns shot his plane down; he was taken into Soviet captivity and died there under unknown circumstances.
195 The copy of the letter is owned by the author.
196 NARA 325th FG Combat Claim Forms.

in the funeral records at Csorna. The gravesite remains in good condition, with the following inscription:

LŐRINCZ MÁTYÁS VADÁSZPILÓTA
ŐRMESTER
1921 ERDÉLY – DUNÁNTÚL 1944
ÉRTED SZENT MAGYAR HAZÁM!

(*Őrmester* Mátyás Lőrincz, fighter pilot, 1921 Transylvania – 1944 Western Hungary. For you, my holy Hungarian homeland!)

Mátyás Lőrincz poses with a Vizsla puppy on his aircraft in the late summer of 1944. (From the collection of the Lőrincz family)

1st Lieutenant Scott S. Murphy's drawing of his seriously damaged B-24 before the crew left it; the aircraft was called 'Princess Pat', named after Murphy's eldest daughter, and it crashed on 7 July 1944 at Győrszentmárton; it was shot down by Mátyás Lőrincz. (From the collection of the Murphy family)

1st Lieutenant Oscar Rau, an exceptionally talented pilot of 325th FG's 318th Fighter Squadron, poses in front of his Mustang. As 'Ockie' Rau missed the large-scale air battles during the summer, he did not score any more aerial victories beyond the four he achieved on 5 November 1944. (From the collection of the Rau family)

1st Lieutenant Oscar Rau's P-51B (serial number 43-6861, number 68), nicknamed 'Funnyface' after his first wife, after the air combat on 5 November 1944. The aerial victory markings are already painted on. (From the collection of the Rau family)

On 8 November 2008, at the location of the death of Mátyás Lőrincz, at Gámpuszta near Ságvár, a memorial was erected (author's own photograph, 16 November 2013)

Oscar 'Ockie' Rau Jr., who shot down both Mátyás Lőrincz and György Michna, was born in Newburgh, New York, on 24 May 1920. He graduated in Dover Plains and entered service in April 1941 at the USAF. He received his appointment as a pilot on 8 February 1944. After his arrival in Italy, he started to fly combat missions on 10 August 1944, and so he missed the large air battles in the summer, giving him much less of a chance to score victories. On 5 November, he flew his 29th combat sortie, during which he achieved four victories in a row, all against Bf 109s in the area of the eastern end of Lake Balaton (partly south, partly north of the lake). As a result of his exceptional performance during this mission (as we have already mentioned in the biography of György Michna), Rau was awarded the Distinguished Service Cross, which (after the Medal of Honor) is the second highest value military decoration of the United States armed forces.

A contemporary article mentions a letter he wrote to his mother speaking of a fifth victory, but there is no evidence in the combat claim forms of 325th FG to support an additional aerial victory, and his family also does not have any related documents. This statement in the article must have arisen from a misunderstanding, because another source mentions – most probably correctly – that Rau destroyed his fifth aircraft on the ground during a strafing run. Rau ended his combat tour with 70 sorties according to surviving documents, the combat sortie on 5 November was the only case in which he was engaged in air combat.

After the war, Rau was an Operating Engineer and employed as a crane operator and later as a business agent for the International Union of Operating Engineers Local 137. (Being a crane operator is some sort of a family tradition for them, since his father also worked as a crane operator, his son too became one and his grandson also wishes to work in this field.) Additionally worth a mention, that at one time the union owned a helicopter which he piloted. Rau died in Fishkill, New York, on 11 June 2004.[197]

According to the author, Rau might be the only opponent pilot to shoot down two Hungarian aces and achieved it in one single mission (György Michna was not an ace at the time when he was shot down, but later became one). The only other time this might have happened was during the air combat of 7 August, for which see the biography of László Molnár.

197 The author managed to find Rau's family in the United States; the details regarding his life were taken from documents preserved by them.

The final resting place of the remains of Mátyás Lőrincz in the columbarium of the *Szent József* church. (photograph of the author, 29 May 2014.)

The grave of Mátyás Lőrincz in the Szent Antal Cemetery of Csorna (photograph of the author, 2 October 2014)

SZAKASZVEZETŐ PÁL LÁSZLÓ SZIKORA

Number of aerial victories: 6
Successes against ground targets: n.d.a.
Number of flown combat sorties: 40 (17 against Americans)
Number of hours flown in the air force: n.d.a.
Nicknames: *Laci*, *Sziporka*
Identification number: 0336-22-0056

Decorations

- *Magyar Nagy Ezüst Vitézségi Érem* (25 January 1945)
- *Magyar Kis Ezüst Vitézségi Érem* (13 February 1945)
- *Tűzkereszt I fokozata a kardokkal és koszorúval*
- German Iron Cross 2nd Class (8 March 1945)

Victories

Number	Date	Aircraft	Location
1	2 July 1944	P-51	Vereb (Gödöllő?)
2	2 July 1944	B-17 (B-24?)	Kajászószentpéter
3	7 August 1944	P-51	
4	6 November 1944	P-38 (F-5)	Bakonybél
5	3 January 1945	Yak-9	Fót NE
6	3 January 1945	Yak-9	Ráckeresztúr N (Rákoskeresztúr?)

Aircraft flown
n.d.a.

Pál László Szikora was born on 14 January 1922 in Békéscsaba, to a craftsman's family of eight children. His father was a tailor, and Pál had two brothers and five sisters.[198] At home in Hungary he usually used the name 'László', but after emigrating he mainly used 'Pál', as László has no foreign equivalent.

A group of enlisted trainees who received primary flight training at the airfield at Szeged-Algyő from the *HMNRA* in the summer of 1941 (the two young men in berets are mechanics-students, who might not have been found eligible for pilot training during the medical examinations and they chose to work as mechanics). The third from the right is Pál László Szikora. In the background, Bücker Bü 131 D-2 training aircraft can be seen. (From the author's collection)

After heeding the call of the *HMNRA*, he received his primary flight training in the summer of 1941 at *HMNRA*'s Szeged section (Szeged-Algyő). At the end of 1941, he entered service at the *Regvi* at Szombathely and received the golden eagle in 1942.

The extremely talented Szikora was a pilot instructor of the fighter training group at Tapolca in the spring of 1943. He was also briefly reassigned to instruct at the *Kassai Repülőakadémia*; until January 1944, he also flew at Veszprém as an instructor in tandem-controlled WM–21 *Sólyom* aircraft.[199]

Recollections are very different regarding the events on 13 April 1944, when three instructors took off from Tapolca in *Héja* aircraft and engaged the Americans. It is not clear who was flying next to Lajos Kass; according to some memories, Szikora was also present, along with *hadnagy* László Molnár.[200]

On 18 June 1944, *szakaszvezető* Szikora was finally transferred to 101/1 Fighter Squadron, probably at his own request.

This daring and fearless pilot first took part in a large-scale combat mission on 2 July 1944 during the battle over Budapest, when he shot down a P-51 and a four-engined heavy bomber. Air Force Confidential Order Nr. 1944/63 recorded his aerial victory over the four-engined as a B-17 kill with a location of Kajászószentpéter (today Kajászó); according to the registry of victories against four-engines, which does not include the aircraft type, this was a shared victory with a German pilot. That day, 15 AAF lost four B-17s, three of which crashed within Hungarian

198 Pál László Szikora also does not have a personal document folder in the Central Record Office of the *HM HIM*, the majority of the personal data regarding him were provided by his relatives.
199 Pál Gótzy, *Repülési napló motoros sportrepülők számára* (partial copy owned by the author).
200 Farkas, *A m. kir. vitéz nagybányai Horthy István Honvéd Repülő Akadémiai évfolyamom története*, p. 125, mentions Szikora and Molnár; according to Pataky, Rozsos, and Sárhidai, *Légi háború Magyarország felett*, vol. 2, p. 176, based on the recollections of Kass, the two other pilots were *őrmester* Tüske and *szakaszvezető* Szilágyi.

Table of the class of pilots and mechanics that graduated in 1941 at the *Délvidéki Aero Club* section of the *HMNRA*. In the top right corner we can see the future ace of the group, Pál László Szikora. (From the collection of the Tanács family)

Three of the enlisted pilots of 101/1 Fighter Squadron in readiness at the Veszprém-Jutas airfield, in the early summer of 1944. From left to right: Pál László Szikora, and *szakaszvezetős* Károly Faludi (three kills) and Zoltán Skulka. Skulka achieved one aerial victory and was killed in air combat on 21 August 1944. (From the author's collection)

Pál László Szikora on 16 April 1943 on Tapolca, posing on one of the Italian-built *Héjas* of the fighter school. (From the author's collection)

territory. Given this number, one possible Hungarian and 14 German victories were claimed against B-17s. The Hungarian claim was only 'possible' because the aircraft Szikora shot down may not have been a B-17, as this may have been a typing error because a B-24 did indeed crash near Kajászó that day. This was one of the six bombers of 456th BG lost on 2 July 1944 due to the attack of 101 Fighter Group and the fighters of the German I./JG 302: the crashed aircraft had been flown by 2nd Lieutenant Delmar T. Hutchins, and six of the 10-member crew were taken POW (the other four were killed, it was a B-24, H serial number 4264487).

Of the three B-17s that crashed in Hungarian territory, two were certainly shot down by German twin-engine destroyers at Bábolnapuszta and Megyercs. The third Flying Fortress shot down was a B-17G (serial number 42-32014) of 99th BG's 348th Squadron, flown by 2nd Lieutenant Harry O. Reuse, which crashed further to the south, near the Dráva at Zaláta; the 10-member crew bailed out (in the official casualty report, the time was given as 12:15). This aircraft was also attacked by Bf 109s, so Szikora's victory was either over this B-17 or the B-24 of 2nd Lieutenant Hutchins. The other German pilot who (according to the report) took part in the attack was from I./JG 302, which had an extremely high number of claims for Liberators. *Leutnant* Wilhelm Hallenberger from 4./JG 302, who had eight victories, also reported shooting down a B-17 at 12:15 in the map section north of Kaposvár. Szikora could only have shot down this aircraft with this German pilot if he had also taken part in the second combat mission of the day, which was flown by a small formation; the two victories would thus have been achieved during separate missions.[201]

The wing of the Mustang (with the spectacular invasion stripes) that crashed on 2 July 1944 at Gödöllő; the wing was torn off mid-air and was found farther from the wreck itself (*HM HIM* Photographic Archives 87495)

The Mustang was confirmed for Szikora as a shared victory with *őrmester* Zoltán Raposa according to Air Force Confidential Order Nr. 1944/63. The P-51B was from 4th FG; that day's heavy fighting was so complicated, and the fragmentary sources are so confusing, that it cannot be completely certainly determined which aircraft was shot down by Szikora and which was actually credited to him. What is certain is that a Mustang of 325th FG crashed at Vereb and this area is mentioned in the confirmation document; the aircraft was, however, not destroyed by enemy action. 1st Lieutenant Cecil O. Dean

The impact crater of the Mustang that crashed on 2 July 1944 near Gödöllő. The aircraft was probably shot down by *szakaszvezető* Szikora and *őrmester* Raposa (*HM HIM* Photographic Archives 87496)

201 NARA MACR 6441, 6518; Reschke, *Jagdgeschwader 301/302 'Wilde Sau'*, pp. 84–88.

was not able to jettison his port external drop tank and while trying to do it waggling his wings his wingman, 2nd Lieutenant John P. Conant, collided with him, and his port wing sheared off the tail of Dean's P-51D. The six kill ace Dean thus had to bail out and was taken prisoner of war. According to the author, the most plausible explanation is that Szikora and Raposa shot down the aircraft of 1st Lieutenant Thomas S. Sharp of 4th FG's 334th Fighter Squadron.

1st Lieutenant Thomas S. Sharp, from 4th FG's 334th FS, killed on 2 July 1944 at Gödöllő. (4th FG Association)

Thomas Sharp was born on 7 June 1920 in McArthur, Ohio. He had been serving in 4th FG since 1 May 1944, and this was his 26th combat sortie (he had already destroyed two German aircraft on the ground during strafing runs). According to the memories of his comrades, he was not able to jettison his drop tanks before the combat over Budapest, and Bf 109s shot down his aircraft at a high altitude; it was blown to pieces and crashed like a meteorite into the park of the Grassalkovich mansion, along with its pilot. There were no other Hungarian or German claims of P-51 victories in that area on that day.[202]

We also have no data regarding which aircraft was first shot down by Szikora. Unfortunately, the exact personal dates are missing in both cases, but possibly the victory against the Mustang may have happened earlier; if the four-engined was indeed a B-17 shot down during a second mission, this is definite. According to the combat report prepared at 16:00, *szakaszvezető* Szikora had not yet returned. The reason for this may lie in a police document, according to which a Hungarian fighter aircraft emergency landed near Kajászószentpéter and was slightly damaged; the pilot was unharmed. This probably referred to Szikora; it may be that he did not ermergency land as a result of hits inflicted on him by the four-engines, but simply because he ran out of fuel in the heat of combat and was not able to reach Veszprém.

On 7 August, *szakaszvezető* Szikora was present in the formation scattered by the Mustangs of 31st FG, although they were unable to shoot him down. On the contrary, he himself reported a victory over an enemy aircraft. It is possible that he also opened fire on the aircraft that attacked László Molnár at first. The kill was at first deleted by Wing Order Nr. 1945/27, but was added back later to the list of his individual achievements. Only one Mustang was shot down by Hungarian fighters on this day, but it became two victories: one for Málik, and one for Szikora. Lajos Buday also claimed a victory, but it was deleted; apart from these, *hadnagy* Karátsonyi also reported a damaged Mustang.

202 NARA MACR 5798, 6336.

On 1 October 1944, Szikora volunteered to continue service for another year, along with two of his classmates: Ernő Horváth (killed on 1 November) and József Nagy (also featured in this work).[203] The majority of their classmates had already requested the same.

On 6 November 1944, the weather was extremely unfavorable. Despite this, at 10:50, all four squadrons of 101 Fighter Wing received the order to go into combat against the American formations entering the airspace of the *Dunántúl.* Szikora reported shooting down a P-38 northwest of Veszprém, but this was deleted due to a lack of witnesses (his wingman was above the clouds and did not see the action) by Wing Order Nr. 1945/31, even though the aircraft really did crash. The victim was a Lightning modified for photographic reconnaissance (F-5B variant) from 5th PRG's 32nd Squadron, flown by 2nd Lieutenant Clarence J. Baker (serial number 42-68286), which crashed in the area of Kerteskő, southeast of Bakonybél; the pilot was killed.[204] The kill was later added to Szikora's individual achievements.

On 13 November, Szikora avoided a serious accident by a hair's breadth when a new pilot, *tizedes* Sándor Tábori (who later became his permanent wingman), got too excited on his first combat sortie and performed a wrong turn, as a result of which his propeller sheared off the vertical stabilizer of Szikora's aircraft. Szikora was nevertheless able to nurse back his damaged plane to the airfield at Veszprém.[205]

On 23 December 1944, Szikora did not return from a combat sortie; he was thus mistakenly deleted from the wing on 28 December 1944 by Wing Order Nr. 1944/69, even though he returned to Veszprém on that very day. This five-day disappearance was probably due to a crash-landing near Budapest, after which he only started returning to Veszprém on the 24th, very narrowly escaping the Soviet encirclement around the city.

Szikora flew 17 combat sorties altogether in 1944 against the Americans, achieving four aerial victories.

On 3 January 1945, he again showed extraordinary skills when he reported shooting down two Yakovlev fighters (probably in air combat with the aircraft of 288th IAD).

Szakaszvezető Szikora was presented with the *Magyar Nagy Ezüst Vitézségi Érem* on 25 January 1945 in Veszprém by the Minister of Defense, *vezérezredes* Beregfy. Two documents from the unit, one dated 30 January and the other dated mid-March 1945, state that Szikora had scored six aerial victories; this means the two kills that had not been initially confirmed must have later been added to his individual achievements.

Szakaszvezető Pál László Szikora on 22 November 1944 in Veszprém. (From the collection of the Szikora family)

Szikora flew his 40th combat sortie on 12 February 1945, but soon after his wing commander grounded him because of the Irányi issue. Szikora was loyal to his

203 *HM HIM HL*, documents of 101 Fighter Wing, box nr. 110, Wing Order Nr. 1944/26.

204 NARA MACR 9670, D. Csaba Veress, 'Veszprém Megye és a Szövetséges Hatalmak stratégiai légitámadásai a második világháborúban', *A Veszprém Megyei Múzeumok Közleményei*, 1980:15, p. 197.

205 Diary of Sándor Tábori (copy owned by the author).

squadron commander and was one of the most ardent supporters of *főhadnagy* Irányi during his conflict with *alezredes* Heppes. This was why the latter removed the young *szakaszvezető* from the list of active pilots.

Szakaszvezető Szikora left 101 Fighter Wing and was reassigned to Pocking on 23 April 1945.[206] With his comrades, he was taken prisoner of war by the Americans in May and never returned home. Szikora moved to Venezuela soon after the end of the war, where he flew with the local airline, the Viasa; he was employed by them until his retirement. In his later years, he lived alone, undeservedly destitute; he died on 26 September 1988 in Caracas, and was buried there.

ZÁSZLÓS SÁNDOR HAUTZINGER

Number of aerial victories: 5 (+6?)
Successes against ground targets: n.d.a.
Number of flown combat sorties: around 80 (?)
Number of hours flown in the air force: n.d.a.
Nickname: –
Identification number: 3009-21-0427

Decorations

- *Tűzkereszt I fokozata a kardokkal és koszorúval*
- *Erdélyi Emlékérem*
- *Délvidéki Emlékérem*
- German Iron Cross 2nd Class (autumn 1943)

Victories

Number	Date	Aircraft	Location
–	20 July 1943	Soviet aircraft	
–	3 August 1943	Soviet aircraft	
1	4 August 1943	Il-2	Belgorod
–	5 August 1943	Soviet aircraft	
–	7 August 1943	Soviet aircraft	
2	8 August 1943	Yak-1	Belgorod
–	9 August 1943	Soviet aircraft	
3	10 August 1943	Il-2	Kharkiv
4	17 August 1943	Soviet aircraft	
–	5 September 1943	Il-2 (?)	
–	November 1943	Soviet aircraft?	

Aircraft flown

n.d.a.

206 *HM HIM HL*, documents of 101 Fighter Wing, box nr. 110, Wing Order Nr. 1945/65.

Sándor Hautzinger was born on 24 February 1921 in Budapest. His father (who had the same name) was a high school teacher. He graduated from a high school (*Eötvös József Gimnázium*) in the capital in 1939; for some time, Tibor Tobak was among his classmates.

Karpaszományos őrvezető Sándor Hautzinger. (From the collection of Balázs Jásdi)

He started gliding during his high school years and because of this he joined the air force. He enlisted in October 1939 at the *Regvi* at Ungvár, and later moved with the *Regvi* to Szombathely.

He completed his pilot training by the beginning of 1941. After this, late in the spring, he was assigned to 1/3 Fighter Squadron at Mátyásföld. He experienced his first combat during the campaign against the Soviet Union in 1941, although the young and inexperienced *hadapród őrmester* had not flown many combat sorties and was not engaged by the enemy. His first combat mission was flown on 20 July 1941 at dawn; this was a short-range reconnaissance escort, and no particular events occurred during the flight. After this, he possibly returned for a while to Hungary, because his next combat sortie (as a bomber escort) was, according to the squadron log, only flown on 30 September. The squadron log also mentions another mission three days later in which he took part, covering a certain area.[207]

Hadapród Sándor Hautzinger posing in the CR.42 (the V.206) of his squadron commander, László Tomor, in 1941, on the airfield at Budapest-Mátyásföld. (From the collection of Balázs Jásdi)

207 Becze, *'Kőr Ász'*, pp. 28–68.

As of 1 October 1941, he was promoted to reserve *zászlós*. His squadron commander, *százados* László Tomor, wrote the following humorous lines about him in his book *Harcok az orosz égen*, when describing the residents of the officers' room: 'The "Benjamin" [youngest member] of the room is *hadapród* Hautzinger. He is eating. He is still growing so he eats all day, every day.'[208]

After returning from the front in December 1941, Hautzinger was discharged and worked as a logistician for *Weiss Manfréd Repülőgép-és Motorgyár* (Manfred Weiss Aircraft and Engine Factory). Later, he aspired to become a test pilot.

In 1942, as a result of the reorganization, he became a pilot of 5/1 Fighter Squadron. He was called up in November that year and sent to the front again. He retrained to Messerschmitts in Uman in the spring of 1943, following which he was reassigned to 1/1 Squadron, with which he flew his first combat sortie on 19 July 1943. The next day he reported his first kill, which nevertheless remained unconfirmed due to a lack of witnesses. In approximately one month (by 18 August), he flew 55 Messerschmitt combat sorties within the 1/1 Squadron; with the squadron's withdrawal from the front, he was reassigned to 5/2 Independent Fighter Squadron and continued his front-line service in that unit.

Hautzinger began to score kills in a row on 3 August 1943, after the Soviet counterattack had begun in the direction of Belgorod and the intensity of the air combat activity increased. He himself flew six combat sorties on 3 August and five the next day.[209]

He remembered his first aerial victory on 4 August (apparently his first confirmed kill) in the field magazine *Üvölt a Puma*:

> One of them was back in Warwarovka. We were out on a free hunt with *őrmester* Kereki. Hellish anti-aircraft fire over the Russian armored wedge; I was hit, but not seriously. We noticed Il-2s attacking with a fighter escort at Belgorod. I attacked the one on the left side. My wingman warned me that I was being attacked from behind by the Russians, but I fired at the Il-2 nevertheless, and ignored the phosphorous trails at my back. When I finally saw it bursting in flames, I pulled up my aircraft and fled into the German anti-aircraft fire. I happily waggled my wings back at home after my first victory.[210]

This was his version of his kill on 8 August, published in the same magazine:

> On 8 August, I was with *hdgy.* Debrődy on a free hunt. We noticed approximately 25 Yak-1s. We dived on them with the great advantage we had gained from our speed and scattered with a harassing fire. I was firing at the aircraft attacking the *hdgy.*, which showed me an excellent target; under the impact of my hits from the cannon, it was blown to pieces. The pieces had not even reached the ground when I heard the confirmation of *fhdgy.* Bejczy.[211]

On 10 August, following a scramble at dawn, Hautzinger again shot down a Soviet ground-attack aircraft; it seems this kill was confirmed based upon the witness account of German

208 Tomor, *Harcok az orosz égen*, pp. 126–127.
209 Excerpts from the logs of 1/1 Fighter Squadron.
210 *Üvölt a Puma*, 3 November 1943, p. 4.
211 *Üvölt a Puma*, 3 November 1943, p. 4.

ground observers, possibly reinforced by radio monitoring (as he had taken off alone, Hautzinger obviously had no witnesses in the air). During the air combat, the aircraft of *zászlós* Hautzinger was hit on the cooler by the gunner of a Soviet ground-attack aircraft, and he had to belly-land his aircraft immediately on reaching the first lines. The Hungarian pilot recalled the event:

> At four o'clock, at dawn, I noticed that the northern parts of Charkow were being bombed; my wingman wasn't able to start, so I took off alone. The Il-2s were fleeing at a low altitude, close to the ground, and I attacked the last one. I fired at him at close range but could only fire single shots with my cannon, so I wanted to disengage. At this moment I was hit by an Il-7 [Il-2m3]; my coolant was gone and my RPM dropped, but luckily I managed to reach our own territory, even though I was also being fired and hit from the ground. Our short-range reconnaissance unit found where I was, and their 'Storch' came for me [a Fi 156 courier aircraft of the Hungarian 3/1 Short-Range Reconnaissance Squadron]. I was happy to go home and waggle my wing with the old Storch for now.[212]

At the end of October or at the beginning of November, Hautzinger was shot down in air combat by Soviet fighters; he crash-landed for the second time, suffering injuries to his neck and head. Despite his injuries, he did not receive another wound clasp for his *Tűzkereszt*, because in November 1943 a 'bomb' was suddenly detonated: he was discovered to have Jewish origins. This had been kept so well hidden by the family that he himself did not know his mother is a baptised Jew. Nevertheless, as a pilot without confirmed Christian origins, he was swiftly and quietly removed from the front and, in December 1943, was discharged from military service. The Anti-Jewish Laws from 1940 had made it mandatory for everyone serving in military service to prove their Christian origins back to their grandparents; and apart from a few exceptional cases, personnel of Jewish origin were not allowed to serve in the armed military service, only in the unarmed labor service.[213]

Zászlós Sándor Hautzinger in front of his Messerschmitt Bf 109 G-2/R6 in the autumn of 1943. (From the collection of Balázs Jásdi)

Hautzinger's exact individual achievements are unfortunately unclear, partly because of fragmentary or lost documents, and partly because a number of his aerial victories were being examined when he was discharged from the Royal Hungarian Air Force, so these processes simply stopped – not because any necessary requirements were missing, but because the air force no longer pursued the cases after his removal from military service. The awarding process of his first *Signum* also stopped when his family background came to light a short time before the decoration could actually be awarded; his recommendation was deleted due to his being 'not confirmed parentage'.

212 *Üvölt a Puma*, 3 November 1943, p. 4.
213 See Elek Karsai (ed.), *'Fegyvertelen álltak az aknamezőkön…': Dokumentumok a munkaszolgálat történetéhez Magyarországon*, vol. 1 (Budapest: MIOK, 1962), p. 38.

Hautzinger's comrades usually referred to him as having five confirmed air victories, although an unfinalized source from the end of October 1943 mentioned four confirmed aerial victories.[214] According to the memories of his family, he was sure to have had at least seven certain kills, among which five were confirmed. The log of 1/1 Fighter Squadron credits him with nine claims in the period up to 18 August. A number of them were without witnesses, but there were no reliable sources for the rest of the period, and the author was not able to find any certain documents (the author has only highlighted the four kills that can certainly be confirmed to him according to sources known to be exact and reliable). According to the research of Ferenc Kovács – whose documents are now in the possession of György Punka – Hautzinger had two more air victories: on 5 September, he shot down an Il-2; and there was another victory at the beginning of November. The author has not yet found any data confirming this.

One of the aircraft shot down by Hautzinger, which is not described in detail in the squadron log, was (according to Hautzinger's recollection) an La-5, which crashed with its pilot; the other cases were probably also mostly fighter.[215]

At the end of 1943, following his discharge, Hautzinger went back to work at the *WM*. In October 1944, after the Arrow Cross party took over Hungary, his reserve *zászlós* rank was taken away and he was demoted to private. In November 1944, a labour service order was sent to him, but he received an exemption for working in military factories. According to his family, when the factory was being relocated, the German general in control of the operation offered him a car with a German registration plate, but he refused. At this time, he went everywhere illegally in his Hungarian officer pilot uniform, and he always wore his Iron Cross 2nd Class.

On 6 December 1944, members of the Arrow Cross party escorted him, his wife and her sister to the Arrow Cross House on Bem Square in Budapest. One of his wife's former colleagues managed to get them sent home, and the family was not harassed again by the Arrow Cross Party members. Luckily, they also survived the siege of Budapest.

Zászlós Sándor Hautzinger after he was shot down for the second time and was injured in the autumn of 1943, shortly before his discharge. (From the collection of Jásdi Balázs)

After the war, and as a civilian, Hautzinger again worked as a logistician, first at the *WM*, then (between 1946–50) at the *Ganz Villamossági Gyár* (the Ganz Electric Factory), and (from 1950) at the *Forgácsoló Szerszámok Gyára* (Metal Cutting Machinery Factory). He changed his family name to Jásdi in 1948. After having to give up one of his most beloved activities – aviation – he spent more and more time pursuing another: rowing. From 1936 to 1948, he rowed at competition level; after receiving his Physical Trainer degree, he worked as a full-time coach in Csepel. The highlight of his coaching career was

214 *Üvölt a Puma*, 3 November 1943, p. 1.
215 Based on data kindly provided by Sándor Hautzinger's family, and on his own recollections.

when he became trainer to the Olympic team, and his most outstanding success was when his team won a silver medal in the coxless four events at the Mexico Olympics in 1968. In 1970, he was awarded the title of 'Master Coach'. His love of rowing was a family tradition inherited from his father, who had impressive achievements during the 'heroic age' of the sport: he had achieved fifth place in the coxed eight events during the Summer Olympics of 1908 in London; with a bit more luck, had they not met the winning English boat in the quarterfinals, they might even have won a silver medal. After this, in 1910 and in 1922, Hautzinger's father won a bronze medal, and in 1921 he won a silver medal as part of the male coxed eight event in the European Championships; as a member of the European Championship's male coxed four events, he also won a bronze medal in 1923 and a silver medal in 1925. He also competed with the latter team in the Olympic Games in 1924 and in 1928 – was his third and final Olympics, at the age of 43.

In the *Forgácsoló Szerszámok Gyára*, the internal state security services persuaded Sándor Jásdi to work for them in their search for 'internal enemies' from 22 March 1960 onward, under the name 'Sándor Jakab'. According to his files, these duties were carried out from pure patriotism; of course, looking at this in the context of the age, it seems certain that he was either afraid, or was being blackmailed to accept this 'honor'. Two days after being recruited, however, Jásdi reported to his senior officer that he would not give in any written report, as he was not going to cooperate with anyone, nor would he give any information about any individual. Because of his unwillingness to cooperate, he was discharged on 7 September without having handed in any information about anybody. Luckily he did not experience any negative effects from this, and when the authorities were looking for agents in the delegation that was to travel to Mexico in 1968, his name was mentioned as one who should not be contacted since he is not willing to cooperate, incidentally he did not travel with the team to Mexico.[216]

After 1945, Sándor Jásdi received the equivalent of his lost *zászlós* rank, reserve *alhadnagy*, but this was taken away in 1958 during the investigations that followed the fall of the Hungarian Revolution of 1956, and he again became a private. This was partly because he came from a white collar worker family; it was also because his paternal uncle was *vezérezredes* Gusztáv Jány, commander of the Hungarian 2nd Army in 1942–43, who was sentenced to death and executed in 1947 following a show trial, and because of whom the family was deemed as a highly unreliable.[217]

Sándor Jásdi died on the evening of the day of the Chernobyl disaster, 26 April 1986, in Budapest; he was laid to rest in the Farkasréti Cemetery. Sándor Jásdi Memorial Competitions are organized in his memory on the Danube by the Csepel Rowing Club.

It is very important to add that Sándor Hautzinger was not the only individual of Jewish descent who served among the pilots of the Royal Hungarian Air Force during the Second World War. Imre Hennyey (born Hager) was born on 14 July 1913 in Cattaro and graduated as *hadnagy* on 20 August 1935. His mother was still Jewish when he was born and was only baptised later. Because of this, his origins were well known within the air force. Hennyey was an excellent fencing sportsman – he was a college world epée champion (also individual epée national champion three times, and seven times team epée national champion). He took part in the 1948

216 *Állambiztonsági Szolgálatok Történeti Levéltára*, 3.1.1. B-92545.

217 *Állambiztonsági Szolgálatok Történeti Levéltára*, a 3.1.1. B-92545. Sándor Jásdi does not have a personal document folder in the Central Record Office of the *HM HIM* (the author assumes one existed, but was taken out and not returned). The anomalies surrounding his rank are recorded in documents kept by the state security services.

and the 1952 Olympics, where he was a member of the Hungarian male epée team and won fifth place both times. According to the author's research, his sporting accomplishments allowed *százados* Hennyey to remain within the air force after the German occupation and after the takeover of the Arrow Cross party; he ended the war as the deputy commander of one of the truly elite Hungarian units of the Second World War: 1 Night Fighter Squadron. In 1941, Hennyey served in the same squadron as Lajos Cseh, also featured in this work, as a pilot of I Short-Range Reconnaissance Squadron. The Hungarian 1 Night Fighter Squadron, equipped with Bf 110 G-4 with FuG 220 Lichtenstein SN-2 type radars, was the first in the history of Hungarian military aviation to use aircraft with on-board radar in combat. The next radar equipped aircraft in Hungarian service was the MiG-17F, which first arrived in Hungary in 1955.[218]

Sándor Boskovits was born on 15 October 1909 in Pécs; he graduated as *hadnagy* on 20 August 1931. His father was of Jewish origins, and again this was a known fact within the air force, although many false stories circulated regarding his father (for example, suggesting that he was a rabbi). According to data collected by the author, both parents were already Catholic at the time of their son's birth, so Boskovits himself was baptized Catholic. Boskovits was a fighter pilot, and later one of the test pilots of the RKI. *Alezredes* Lóránd Dóczy, commander of the RKI, stood by him in all situations, so Boskovits retained his position even after the German occupation of Hungary on 19 March 1944. *Százados* Boskovits was killed on 13 April 1944 at Dömsöd in air combat with the 15th AF's Lightnings, while defending Budapest. He was posthumously awarded the *Magyar Érdemrend lovagkeresztje hadiszalagon a kardokkal.*

His final resting place is in the Farkasréti Cemetery.[219]

SZÁZADOS BEJCZI JÓZSEF BEJCZY

Number of aerial victories: 5 (+4?)
Successes against ground targets: one locomotive + ?
Number of flown combat sorties: 60+
Number of hours flown in the air force: n.d.a.
Nickname: *Dzsó*
Identification number: 2369-16-0084

Decorations

- *Magyar Érdemrend tisztikeresztje hadidíszítménnyel és kardokkal* (10 January 1945; posthumous)
- *Magyar Érdemrend lovagkeresztje hadiszalagon a kardokkal* (1 November 1944)
- *Újólagos Kormányzói dicsérő elismerés Magyar Koronás Ezüst Érdemérme hadiszalagon a kardokkal* (9 March 1944)
- *Kormányzói dicsérő elismerés Magyar Koronás Bronz Érdemérme hadiszalagon a kardokkal* (20 September 1943)

218 For Imre Hennyey, see Csaba B. Stenge, 'Egy igazi repülő sportember – Hennyey Imre', *Katonaújság*, 2012:4, pp. 42–46.

219 *MNL Baranya Megye Levéltára* (National Archives, Baranya County Archives), XXXIII/1, state birth registry of the city of Pécs from 1909, counterpart, acc. nr.note 935; Csaba Becze, '2 pilotes juifs dans les forces de l'Axe', *Aero Journal*, 2008:4, pp. 4–8.

- *Tűzkereszt I fokozata a kardokkal és koszorúval*
- *Felvidéki Emlékérem*
- *Erdélyi Emlékérem*
- *Délvidéki Emlékérem*
- German Iron Cross 2nd Class (1943)

Victories

Number	Date	Aircraft	Location
1	6 July 1943	Yak-1	Volchansk
–	9 July 1943	Il-2, Boston?	
2	19 July 1943	Boston	
3	1 August 1943	Boston	
4	16 June 1944	P-38	Érteny NW
–	30 June 1944	B-24	
–	30 June 1944	P-38	
–	16 July 1944	B-24	
5	16 July 1944	B-24	Kenyeri

Aircraft flown

CR.42: V-212 (end of 1939, beginning of 1940), Re.2000: V.440 (12 January 1943), Bf 109 G-6: V.794 (beginning of summer 1944)

József Bejczy was born on 9 October 1916 in Körmend to a prominent teacher family, the last of seven children and the second boy. His father, Gábor Bejczy, was the director of the industrial school in Körmend. The Bejczy family was an old noble family from Vas County.[220] The noble forename was hardly ever used by the family, and he himself never did.

Bejczy was a *cőger* from Kőszeg; he graduated from the *Hunyadi Mátyás Reáliskolai Nevelőintézet* (Mátyás Hunyadi Infantry Cadet School – this institution only later became an *alreáliskola*, or an elementary-level military school). He graduated as *hadnagy* on 15 January 1939 at the Ludovika in Budapest. This graduation was brought forward because the prospect of war; originally, the graduation would have taken place on 20 August.

After completing the fighter combat training, he was assigned to Mátyásföld and was the deputy commander of 1/3 Fighter Squadron from the autumn of 1939; this unit was the first to receive the new CR.42 fighter aircraft in Hungary.

In October 1940, he was reassigned to the sister squadron, 1/4 Fighter Squadron, also stationed at Mátyásföld. From December 1940 to February 1941, he was an instructor for the air force recruits at Nagyvárad, where he was serving along with *szakaszvezető* János Mátyás from his own squadron and *főhadnagy* György Ujszászy from the sister unit, 1/3 Fighter Squadron.

He experienced his first combat in April 1941 during the campaign against Yugoslavia, as the deputy commander of 1/4 '*Szent György*' Fighter Squadron led by *százados* György Mocsáry;

220 Béla Kempelen, *Magyar nemes családok*, vol. 2 (Budapest: Grill Károly Könyvkiadóvállalata, 1911), p. 23.

he flew several covering and escort missions, the first of which took place on 11 April.[221]

The sister squadron, 1/3 *'Kőr Ász'*, led by the ambitious *százados* László Tomor, was deployed to the Eastern Front in July 1941 during the war against the Soviet Union to support the Hungarian Ist Rapid Corps in its battles. On 23 August 1941, however, *hadnagy* Bejczy was also deployed to the sister unit with two other pilots from his squadron to gain battle experience. He flew his first combat mission on 26 August 1941 in the airspace of Dnepropetrovsk, with the task of covering the German *Panzergruppe 1*. He flew two other relatively uneventful combat sorties in the 1/3 Fighter Squadron on 30 August and on 13 September before returning home from the Eastern Front.[222] Bejczy was promoted to *főhadnagy* on 1 November 1941; during the reorganization of the fighter forces, he was reassigned from his disbanded unit to 5/1 Fighter Squadron, but his home station remained Mátyásföld.

József Bejczy as a *cőger* from Kőszeg in April 1931. (From the collection of Kálmán Komjáthy)

During his service at Mátyásföld, he spent some time in Berlin, where he and three instructors of the fighter training group at Tapolca were briefly retrained to Bf 109 at Werneuchen airfield's *Jagdfliegerschule 1*. At last, in the middle of December 1942, he was deployed to the Eastern Front as a replacement adjutant to the commander of 5/I Fighter Group, *őrnagy* Aladár Heppes.

In January 1943, he flew two combat sorties with the old *Héja*s before the aircraft were destroyed: the first on 5 January, and the second on the day the Soviet attack began at Uriv (12 January). The first sortie was uneventful (during which he might have flown a V.439), but the second one deserves to be detailed here.[223]

On this day, the task of his squadron was to protect the German bombers at work in the Storozhevoye–Staraja Sevrostan–Uriv area, during a free hunt. The mission was flown by *főhadnagy* Bejczy with the *Héja* V.440, with *őrmester* Pál Domján, who flew the V.439. According to the mission report written by *főhadnagy* Bejczy:

> I took off at 12:00. We arrived at the target area at 12:10, where we partly flew above the system of trenches and partly tried to escort the German bombers. Aircraft appeared in the air: Ju 87, Ju 88, He 111 and Henschel 126. The majority of the diver bomber aircraft evaded us by going into a dive, and others turned back abruptly and fled into the clouds. We were directly under the cloud base, approximately at an altitude of 800-1,100m. In the 15th or 20th minute of being in the area, two MiG or LaGG fighters attacked me through a

221 Becze, *'Kőr Ász'*.
222 Becze, *'Kőr Ász'*, pp. 49–63.
223 During Bejczy's 5 January 1943 mission, the report contains a Re.2000 '4-129' because of a typing error. The aircraft probably was V.439 and was one of the Re.2000s in the best possible condition on the Eastern Front in January 1943.

The *'Kopfstand'* of the fine-handed József Bejczy, with the CR.42 (V-212) of 1/3 *'Kőr Ász'* Fighter Squadron at Budapest-Mátyásföld, after 5 November 1939, while returning from the honor flight at the opening ceremony of the *Repülőakadémia* at Kassa. The 1/3 Fighter Squadron was the first unit to receive Fiat CR.42s in the Royal Hungarian Air Force (*HM HIM* Photographic Archives 97.196.149)

Hadnagy József Bejczy at the airfield at Budapest-Mátyásföld in 1940. (From the author's collection)

hole in the clouds, from dead astern so I was not able to see them. *Őrmester* Domján noticed them instantly and he turned upon them immediately, upon which the aircraft, without opening fire at me, jumped back into the clouds and fled eastward. No other enemy air activity was detected. The number of the German aircraft in the area was about 18–25. … I left the area at 13:20 because my engine was knocking heavily and smoke and fire appeared in the cockpit. After 40 minutes of flight, I landed easily. During the landing, the engine stopped completely. The cause of all this is under investigation. Probably a connecting rod was broken.[224]

224 *HM HIM HL*, documents of the Hungarian 2nd Army, box 17, after-action report of 5/I Fighter Group, 1 January to 28 February 1943, appendix nr. 22 (mission log).

The author has deemed it important to quote more lengthily than usual from the above mission report for two reasons. The first is that this text shows the Hungarian *Héja*s had been present in the combat area for more than half a year to no avail, as the Germans still did not recognize the type and instantly believed it as a Russian fighter. The second is that the report clearly shows the very problematic mechanical condition these *Héja*s were in.

The group staff and 5/2 Squadron retreated to Uman. During the spring, they retrained to Messerschmitt Bf 109s. *Főhadnagy* Bejczy, although he was already qualified for the type, was not sent to 1/1 Squadron, but remained in Uman with the group staff, and was only deployed to Kharkhiv with the other pilots at the end of April. He flew his first Messerschmitt combat sortie on 26 April 1943.

Three days later, he was engaged in his first air battle with Soviet aircraft. On the morning of 29 April, he was in a state of airfield security readiness with his wingman, *szakaszvezető* István Fábián, when they received the news on the radio a few minutes before seven that six Soviet bomber aircraft were approaching Kharkhiv. They took off immediately with the other Hungarian aircraft pair on readiness, and *főhadnagy* Bejczy started to look for the Soviet aircraft to the east. Because they saw nothing, they turned back; in that instant, Bejczy saw the impacts from the Soviet bombers on the ground – they were coming from the north. Anti-aircraft artillery fire led him to a bomber flying at 3,000 meters. He remembered what happened as follows:

> I climbed above the Russian aircraft and ... fired at him with all my weapons, but a few seconds later I realized the ammo belt of my cannon had been torn. The heavy machine gun of the Soviet bomber below me was constantly firing at me. I was stubborn and remained behind it, and I tried to return fire with my machine guns. For a minute or two, my rounds hit the enemy aircraft beautifully, and I was happy when the port engine of the Russian started billowing smoke. Then the large bomber nose dived, and fled with the speed he thus gained. My wingman, *szakaszvezető* F[ábián], now arrived on the scene and hit the aircraft a few times with his cannon. I am sure this Ivan will not take part again in air activity any time soon.
>
> We were coming home at about 1,500 meters, and, for a certain amount of time, we were sad because we were unable to report a kill to the squadron commander after all. Suddenly, we met with two modern enemy fighters armed with eight machine guns. This was no joke; we tried to get behind them by turning over – and we, Hungarian fighters, are pretty good in a dogfight. So the two aircraft flew away in a dive toward the Soviet lines. A few minutes before 08:00 ... we landed.[225]

Főhadnagy Bejczy flew 14 combat sorties altogether over April and May; two of these were fighter-bomber missions.

The author has found interesting data in one of Bejczy's decoration recommendations. In the summer of 1943, he destroyed an important Soviet train's locomotive.[226] No other data survives of ground targets destroyed by him.

225 Kádár, *Sasok harca*, pp. 68–69.
226 *HM HIM HL*, recommendations for decorations, group 193.a, acc. nr. 11.

Főhadnagy József Bejczy in Berlin with two German pilots in 1942. (From the collection of Károly Zajtai)

Hungarian air force officers having fun in the winter of 1942–43. Releasing the pressure and stress was very important, and many times this was achieved with alcohol, but of course it could also happen without an aid. In the picture, *főhadnagy* Bejczy is dancing on the top of the table. (*HM HIM* Photographic Archives 97.601/251)

It is important to note that Bejczy was extremely popular with his subordinates. In the summer of 1943, *tizedes* József Tóth, one of the mechanics of 5/I Fighter Group, wrote the following in his diary about Bejczy, whom he had already known for some time as Bejczy had been his recruit instructor following his enlistment in 1940: 'He was the most humane among all the officers.'[227]

Bejczy scored his first confirmed aerial victory during the battle of Kursk, on the morning of 6 July 1943, when he shot down a Yak-1 fighter that was trying to attack his commander. The Yakovlev crashed in flames behind German lines near Volchansk. Aladár Heppes mentioned *főhadnagy* Bejczy's first kill (together with his own third victory) in a handwritten memoir:

> On 6 July, in the morning, we took off on a free hunt with my adjutant, *főhadnagy* József Bejczy, between Kharkhiv and Belgorod. … We flew over the front at an altitude of 1,500 meters for 45 minutes without seeing any enemy aircraft. Upon returning from Belgorod, halfway home, in the airspace of Volchansk, I noticed motion in our altitude that resembled air combat, deep beyond enemy lines. Upon turning toward it, I also noticed a number of Il-2s flying far from each other but making towards the Russian airspace, hundreds of meters below me. With a sharp left turn, I chose an aircraft that was already close to the front; I came out of the dive approximately 200 meters behind him and slightly above him. I fired a burst and the gunner fell silent at his machine gun. I pushed my aircraft under the descending shturmovik to get the oil cooler, the only truly vulnerable spot on that aircraft, and I fired a burst from approximately 100 meters. Smoke immediately began emitting out of the cooler, and at the same time I heard Bejczy's excited voice on the radio: 'Russian fighter behind Puma!' I pulled my aircraft up into a steep right turn, so I was not able to follow the Il-2 with my eyes. At the top of my climb, Bejczy stated on the radio that he had shot down the fighter sitting behind me. Bejczy closed up to me; we flew a circle over our own territory at an altitude of 2,000 meters and I noticed a huge pillar of smoke and fire on

227 *HM HIM HL*, research paper collection, nr. 3181, diary of *tizedes* József Tóth.

Főhadnagy Bejczy in his Messerschmitt Bf 109 F-4 at the airfield at Kharkhiv in the spring of 1943. The front armored glass is not mounted on this aircraft, which was probably the V035. (From the author's collection)

> the ground near the front. I congratulated Bejczy, then we flew back home, because our fuel was running out. After we landed, we immediately contacted the Volchansk front section via the German radio station at the airfield, and they confirmed both Bejczy's kill and my own Il-2 that crashed in Soviet territory.[228]

This aerial victory was followed by shooting down two twin-engine Boston bombers on 19 July and 1 August. A few works also mention another victory on 9 July, but this is either invalid or, possibly, a mistyping of 19 July; it may also be an unconfirmed and unreported victory. Meanwhile, Bejczy's most probably Messerschmitt was hit and destroyed in a Soviet air raid of Kharkhiv airfield in July.

After the group staff and one of the squadrons were withdrawn in the second half of August, Bejczy did not fly any more missions (like *őrnagy* Heppes). He returned home from the Eastern Front to Mátyásföld late in the autumn with three confirmed air victories, where he took command of 5/3 Fighter Squadron, which was formed at that time. In the spring of 1944, the third squadron of 101 Fighter Group was formed at Veszprém (its callsign was '*Drótkefe*') from 5/3 Squadron from Mátyásföld, which was under replenishment and which was led by *főhadnagy* József Bejczy. This is why he was reassigned to Veszprém as of 28 April 1944.

While leading 101/3 Fighter Squadron, Bejczy was engaged in air combat with the Americans for the first time on 14 June 1944. On this day, the squadron took off at 10:25 and reported shooting down seven Lightnings without any own loss. Of the seven kills, two (claimed

228 Recollections of Aladár Heppes.

by *szakaszvezető* Podoba and *szakaszvezető* Takács) were unconfirmed, while *hadnagy* Bélavári's kill was confirmed as a shared victory with *zászlós* Szentgyörgyi, and *hadnagy* Dániel's kill was confirmed as a shared victory with *hadnagy* Pál Forró. The weapons of *főhadnagy* Bejczy's aircraft were not functioning during the mission; he was hit on the port wing by a single machine gun round. Two days later, on 16 June, he led 11 aircraft of the squadron; in the ensuing heavy air combat, he reported shooting down a Lightning, which was confirmed as a shared kill with *őrmester* János Mátyás in Air Force Confidential Order Nr. 1944/63.

The grave of *százados* József Bejczy, in bad condition, in the Common Cemetery at Körmend (photographed by the author, 23 October 2013)

On the last mission of the month, on 30 June, *főhadnagy* Bejczy reported shooting down a B-24 and a P-38. These kills, however, were not confirmed, and both were deleted by Wing Order Nr. 1945/27, issued four months after the death of the pilot.[229] Over June, 101/3 Squadron was very successful in its air combats with the Americans; for a long time, it was the most successful squadron of 101 Fighter Group (later Wing), until 101/2 Squadron overtook these results at the end of the war.

Főhadnagy Bejczy was awarded the *Magyar Érdemrend lovagkeresztje hadiszalagon a kardokkal* in late autumn to honor his leadership of the squadron during June 1944, as well as the results his squadron had achieved.

The squadron commander succeeded in shooting down a Liberator in the airspace of Kenyeri on 16 July 1944, which crashed in flames. Bejczy remembered the combat mission as follows:

> The first four-engined heavy bomber was shot out by me out of formation relatively easily, while I met the other on my way home. He was also going home, only a bit further south than me. The sky was cloudy and he tried to escape me by jumping from one cloud to another. He did not succeed! I was resilient and flew above it; whenever he came out of the clouds, I hit him from the left or from the right with a burst. It was a hard case, but we played hide-and-seek until I finally managed to get him down. Two of his two engines burst into flames and he went down. I had hardly finished him before a larger Mustang formation attacked me; with their crushing superior numbers, they forced me toward the ground. It was a very hard air combat because the Mustang is a very good aircraft, and I

229 *HM HIM HL*, documents of 101 Fighter Wing, box nr. 110, Wing Order Nr. 1945/27.

> was not able to break free from their encirclement. In the end, my aircraft was hit so many times I was not able to control it and I had to crash-land. I managed to land without any major issues; as a closing point, I just want to say that the medevac Storch that was sent for me was actually flown by me back home, and over the airfield, I waggled the wings of the Storch to signal my double victory.[230]

The claim he made that he shot a heavy bomber out from a formation cannot be found in the surviving sources; nor is it among the confirmed or deleted victories.

At the beginning of August, Bejczy was briefly reassigned to the group staff, but shortly after he returned to lead his squadron. Bejczy was promoted to *százados* on 1 November 1944.

The life of this extremely popular pilot, who was loved and respected by all, came to an end on 4 November 1944. On this day he took off at 09:00, leading a flight of four aircraft on a weather-reconnaissance mission and free hunt in the area between the Tisza and the Duna Rivers. The aircraft were flying at an approximate altitude of 1,500 meters when they encountered extremely heavy anti-aircraft artillery fire over a Soviet armored grouping, south-southeast of Abony; one anti-aircraft shell made a direct hit on the aircraft of *százados* Bejczy. The Messerschmitt Bf 109 G-6/U4 (WNr. 126724, manufactured in Győr) burst into flame and crashed southwest of Abony; the pilot was killed. His body was buried by local townsfolk near his aircraft – since the area was already occupied by the Soviets, it was impossible to give him a decent burial. The grave fell into oblivion on the crop-growing land until October 2005, when Károly Magó found the wreck of the aircraft and Bejczy's grave nearby.[231]

The remains of József Bejczy were interred in the family grave in the Common Cemetery at Körmend on 2 March 2006 with full military honors (plot B-2, row 14, grave 15).

FŐHADNAGY BÉLA FÜLEKY

Number of aerial victories: 5 (+2)
Successes against ground targets: 5 trucks, 1 anti-aircraft machine gun post, 4 railway transport wagons
Number of flown combat sorties: 44
Number of hours flown in the air force: n.d.a.
Nicknames: *Béci*, *Fülcsi*
Identification number: 3004-19-3892

Decorations

- *Magyar Koronás Ezüst Érdemérem hadiszalagon a kardokkal* (25 April 1945; posthumous)
- *Magyar Koronás Bronz Érdemérem hadiszalagon a kardokkal* (17 January 1945)
- *Tűzkereszt I fokozata a kardokkal és koszorúval*, two wound clasps
- *Felvidéki Emlékérem*
- *Délvidéki Emlékérem*
- German Iron Cross 2nd Class (8 March 1945)

230 'A Pumák egy napja', *Magyar Szárnyak*, 15 August 1944, p. 5.
231 Károly Magó, 'Pilótasírok', in Zsolt Tóth (ed.), *Hőseink nyomában. Tanulmánykötet a hadisírok kutatásáról* (Budapest: Zrínyi Kiadó, 2013), pp. 266–267.

Victories

Number	Date	Aircraft	Location
1	3 November 1944	Il-2	Tiszasüly S–SW, Zana farm
2	17 December 1944 at 14:20	B-24	Dunaföldvár SW (Adony?)
3	5 January 1945	La-5	Bicske
–	18 January 1945	Boston	
–	19 January 1945	P-51	
4	20 January 1945 at 14:10 (12:10?)	Il-2	Lake Velence N (Csepel-sziget SE); Ráckeve–Szigetszentmárton–Kiskunlacháza
5	23 January 1945 at 10:48	Yak-9	Budapest SW

Aircraft flown
Bf 109 G-14/U4: W-128 (19 January 1945)

Béla Füleky was born on 18 September 1919 in Késmárk (today Kežmarok, Slovakia), the fourth and last child of a local teacher. He was the only boy in the family. His hometown was given to Czechoslovakia as a result of the Treaty of Trianon, following which his father was fired because of his Hungarian nationality. The family then relocated from the Felvidék to Hungary, and for five years they lived in Szombathely before settling in Veszprém, where his father (who had the same name) had a job in a local school (*Kerkápoly Károly Felsőkereskedelmi Iskola*). Béla Füleky graduated from high school (*Veszprémi Piarista Gimnázium*) in 1938 with good grades (he was one year above Debrődy).[232] Besides his good learning skills, he was a successful sportsman, especially in horse riding and pentathlon. After graduation, he immediately applied for the official air force officer training, which he began in Budapest (Ludovika2nd Department), but he graduated as *hadnagy* on 20 August 1941 with rank number 8 at the *Repülőakadémia* in Kassa, as a classmate of Imre Pánczél.[233] From 1 September 1941, he served with 1/I Fighter Group at Szolnok; after the reorganization of the air force, he was reassigned to 3 Bomber Group at Debrecen. He was probably unhappy to be removed from the fighters, but no documents survive to suggest the reason for this decision.

While the reckless Füleky was stationed in Debrecen, he caused a fatal accident as a result of personal disobedience. On 20 April 1942, while practicing maneuvers in coordination with the ground forces, he flew into an electricity wire near the small Nyulas sports airfield with his Bücker Bü 131 (registration number I.447) and tore it down; a ceramic insulator broke off and caused a death on the ground. The victim was the 30-year-old reserve *tizedes*, Gábor Galambos. During the landing, the aircraft overturned and suffered 70 percent damage. As a result of this accident, because of insubordination, Füleky was sentenced to three months in prison.[234]

232 *MNL Veszprém Megye Levéltára* (National Archives, Veszprém County Archives), VIII/52/5, Matriculation register of the Piarist High School in Veszprém, certificate nr. 1938/5.
233 *Honvédségi Közlöny* (*Személyes ügyek*), nr. 1941:37 (19 August 1941), p. 479.
234 *HM HIM HL*, HM 1942 13 p. 33140/eln; *HM HIM KI*, document folder nr. 21153; *MNL Hajdú-Bihar Megye Levéltára* (National Archives, Hajdú-Bihar County Archives), XXXIII/1, state death registry of the city of Debrecen for 1942, counterpart, acc nr. note 772.

Füleky was reassigned to 1 Fighter Training Group in Szolnok as of 1 January 1943, where he spent the next year and a half. On 1 January 1944, he was promoted to *főhadnagy*.[235]

His 1/2 Fighter Squadron was officially included in 101 Fighter Group, which was reformed as a wing from 4 September 1944 as the first squadron of II Group, with the name 101/4 Fighter Squadron. The unit was led by the veteran György Bánlaky, and *főhadnagy* Füleky became his deputy commander. The new squadron completed its first combat missions in October 1944.

Hadnagy Béla Füleky's portrait. (From the collection of the Füleky family)

Főhadnagy Füleky achieved his first aerial victory on 3 November 1944 when, during a free hunt mission, he shot down an Il-2 ground-attack aircraft in the airspace of Zana farm south of Tiszasüly. The witness was *zászlós* Mihály Sziráky, who himself shot down another Il-2; the claims were confirmed by Wing Order Nr. 1945/62. Their victims were an Il-2 pair from 235th SAP, led by *starshiy leytenant* N.T. Tarasov (aircraft with serial numbers 10299 and 11003). Tarasov and his gunner were taken POW; the other two airmen were able to hide and wait for the Soviet troops to arrive.[236]

Three days later, on 6 November 1944, the commander of 101/4 Fighter Squadron, *százados* György Bánlaky, crashed at Gyirmót (probably due to the failure of his aircraft's oxygen system) and was killed. The command of the squadron was taken over by *főhadnagy* Füleky; his appointment was issued in Wing Order Nr. 1944/34, on 7 November.[237]

The recommendation for Füleky's first decoration, issued on 24 November, describes him as follows: 'His dedication and capability to lead has been well proven in the past. His dauntless bravery and comradeship, ready for any and all sacrifices, make him an example to his subordinates and his comrades alike.'[238]

Főhadnagy Füleky's second air victory occurred on 17 December 1944 against a Liberator. His wingman, *őrmester* Zoltán Nemeslaki, remembered the event as follows:

> On 17 December 1944, we were in a state of readiness when we were alerted that there was a strafing attack on the southern side of Budapest. We went to the spot with squadron commander *főhadnagy* Füleky. By the time we got there, there was no activity in the air. We asked for directions via radio and received a free hunt order for the remaining time. We flew over the first lines

235 *HM HIM KI*, document folder nr. 21153.

236 *HM HIM HL*, documents of 101 Fighter Wing, box nr. 110, Wing Order Nr. 1945/62; Horváth, *Bostonok a magyar égen és földben*, p. 51; 588 *HM HIM HL*, documents of 101 Fighter Wing, box nr. 110, Wing Order Nr. 1944/34.

237 *HM HIM HL*, documents of 101 Fighter Wing, box nr. 110, Wing Order Nr. 1944/34.

238 *HM HIM HL*, recommendations for decorations, box nr. 13, group 510.a.

> and waited for something to engage with. More than half an hour passed; while flying south, I noticed a very small dot. I told my boss and we went after it at full speed. As we approached, we recognized it as a Liberator. My boss went first when we were in range. The tail gunner was constantly firing until the boss opened fire with his 3cm cannon. I also opened fire and aimed at the inner starboard engine, because supposedly that controlled the hydraulics. By this time, the crew members were bailing out one by one, and the guys were descending on four or five parachutes. As I was looking to the left, beyond the aircraft, I noticed that, at approximately 300 meters, some seven or eight La-5s are rushing toward us like a herd. The boss saw it too, because he dived at full speed, and we disengaged from the fight.[239]

Order Nr. 1945/62 confirmed the victory as a shared kill with *őrmester* Zoltán Nemeslaki; this was the last shared Hungarian aerial victory mentioned earlier. The aircraft shot down was probably either from the 455th BG (B-24H serial number 41-28982, 1st Lieutenant William V. Richards' crew), which crashed near Adony following a Messerschmitt attack, or another Liberator of 461st BG (B-24J serial number 42-51322, 1st Lieutenant Charles V. Lang's crew). Although Adony is north of Dunaföldvár, it was not uncommon to report erroneous locations, and besides the details of the air combat were very similar on both sides.[240]

Four days later, on 21 December, *főhadnagy* Füleky was lightly wounded during air combat – according to one comrade, he was shot down over his own airfield. He thus received the wound clasp for his *Tűzkereszt*.

His squadron completed 129 individual combat sorties over the course of 1944 (from 3 October to 31 December), during 22 formation missions, and achieved nine aerial victories, two of which were scored by Füleky. The squadron lost three pilots, two of them by accident.[241]

Füleky's most successful month was January 1945, when he achieved three confirmed aerial victories. He shot down an La-5 for the first time on 5 January, and this victory is included in a number of sources either as a probable kill or as one without witnesses; other sources, however, claim the kill was confirmed, and the witness, *főhadnagy* Géza Lója, also left recollections about the victory (which features in a decoration recommendation, dated 9 January due to a typing error). According to Lója, *őrnagy* István Fülöp (the group commander), *főhadnagy* Füleky, Géza Lója and *szakaszvezető* László Lehoczky were out on an airspace securing mission east of the Mór-ditch. Füleky and Lója's element noticed a group of La-5s approximately 500–1,000 meters beneath them. Füleky went into action at once, but Lója noticed three Yak-9s overhead that started attacking them. Lója managed to shoot down one of the Yak-9s from behind the commander, and Füleky also finished off one of the La-5s. Lója's kill was confirmed in Air Force Order Nr. 1945/4 with a location of Bajna. Füleky's opponent on this mission might have been one of the aircraft of 116th IAP, probably *mladshiy leytenant* I.Y. Kochetkov's La-5FN, serial number 39211446.[242]

239 Tálosi, *Háborús évek*, p. 193. Zoltán Nemeslaki said no more to the author about the shooting down of the aircraft, other than what is contained in this work, before dying on 25 January 2005; nor has any further information or data been preserved by Béla Füleky's relatives about this or any other of his kills.

240 NARA MACR 10495, 10742.

241 *HM HIM HL*, documents of 101 Fighter Wing, box nr. 113, registry of the activity of 101/II Fighter Group in 1944.

242 Gyula Gaál, 'Hadszíntér a felhők felett', *Magyar Szárnyak Évkönyv*, 1984, p. 35; Gábor Horváth on documents of TsAMO.

In the afternoon of 18 January, while flying with his squadron, Füleky met a Soviet Boston bomber and silenced the rear gunner. After this, he pulled his aircraft up and practically offered the Boston to anyone who was behind him. The aircraft was shot down at last by *főhadnagy* Lója; the kill was confirmed for him with a location of Sárkeresztúr west, although Füleky had made the first successful pass. The Boston was almost certainly the A-20G (serial number 43-9812) of 260th BAP's 1st Squadron, flown by *starshiy leytenant* V.T. Hohlov and his crew. The lonely Boston was on a reconnaissance flight; due to the damage inflicted on it during the air combat, it crash-landed southwest of the village of Som. All four members of the crew were wounded.[243]

Three pilots of 325th FG's 317th Fighter Squadron living in the same tent (from left to right): 2nd Lieutenants George D. Aiken, Frank M. Bolek and Robert W. Bean in the winter of 1944–45. Bean shot down Füleky's aircraft on 19 January 1945, and Aiken was the pilot of the Mustang that was lost over Croatian territory on that day. (From the collection of the Bolek family)

On the morning of 19 January 1945, Füleky was involved in a very interesting incident. During a free hunt mission, he and his wingman noticed a pair of Mustangs from 325th FG's 317th Fighter Squadron, which they attacked. *Főhadnagy* Füleky hit the element leader on the port wing, and part of the enemy's 12.7mm Browning heavy machine gun ammunition exploded. Despite the heavy damage to the aircraft, it did not crash, and Füleky slipped in front of the wingman, 2nd Lieutenant Robert W. Bean, who shot down the Hungarian pilot's aircraft. Bean, mistaking the type, reported a victory over an 'Me-309', the pilot of which bailed out of the aircraft. The combat claim form gave the time as 11:15, and the day's summary report for the group gives 12:15; one of these times is, therefore, obviously a typing error. The unusual aircraft type reported (only four Me 309s were ever made, and none was deployed in combat) was probably inspired by the aircraft insignia, which was very different from that of the Germans, which was also reported. The Hungarian Messerschmitts were described by the Americans as 'experienced and very aggressive attackers'. The reported location of the victory differed significantly from where the air combat actually took place (the goal of the mission was a free hunt between Zagreb and Szombathely, and Bean provided a location of Zagreb in his report – a good example of the highly inaccurate way in which the American pilots filled their combat claim forms), but it certainly referred to the same event as the source details on both sides match exactly; nor was there any other air combat on that day and in that area. This was Bean's only confirmed kill during the war.

According to the Hungarian casualty report, Füleky bailed out of his aircraft at 11:50 in the area of Somlószőlős. His Bf 109 G-14/U4 aircraft had arrived with the squadron in November

243 *HM HIM HL*, documents of 101 Fighter Wing, box nr. 110, Wing Order Nr. 1945/62; Horváth, *Bostonok a magyar égen és földben*, pp. 109–110.

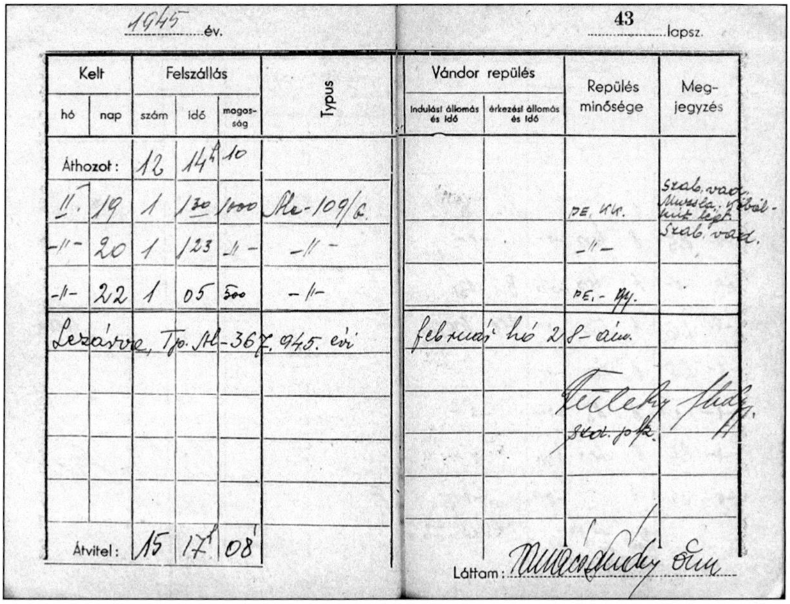

The energetic autograph of *főhadnagy* Béla Füleky in the logbook of *őrmester* Sándor Tanács during the monthly closing of February 1945. (From the collection of the Tanács family)

(it was the W-128), and was manufactured in Wiener Neustadt. Upon landing on the hard snow, the pilot suffered extensive bruising to his left foot, both arms, his hands and around his eyes; he received the second clasp for his *Tűzkereszt* as a result of these injuries. He did not need to go to hospital and was able to remain with the squadron.

Importantly, a Mustang of 317th Fighter Squadron has also crashed soon after the air combat in Croatian territory because of engine stoppage. The crash of the aircraft was reported to the combat post of the Hungarian fighter wing, and the kill was claimed by Füleky and by his wingman, *szakaszvezető* László Lehoczky as well, who told the author he felt he had achieved hits on the nose and engine of the Mustang during his head-on attack (the American report only mentions damage to the wings, which was achieved by Füleky). The Mustang was nevertheless never officially confirmed either to Lehoczky or to Füleky. According to an eyewitness in the American casualty report, this Mustang was lost due to mechanical problems; there is no mention of damage from air combat, although this cannot be fully excluded; thus the pilot of the Mustang that had been seriously damaged by Füleky probably reached the area controlled by the Allies and thus avoided being taken prisoner. There was another P-51 which emergency landed in the Island of Vis (flown by 1st Lieutenant R.L. Fort), so it must be either the crashed or the emergency landed Mustang, which was damaged by Füleky.[244]

244 NARA 325th FG Combat Claim Forms, MACR 11275, Air Force Historical Research Agency 325th FG Narrative Mission Report Nr. 179, 19 January 1945; *HM HIM HL*, HM 35970/8. nyv. o.-1945; the interview of László Lehoczky (1922–2008) by the author, 6 February 2000. George Daniel Aiken, who baled out from his P-51 over Croatia on 19 January 1945 passed away in 1981, therefore the author was not able to ask him about the real cause of his crash.

On 20 January 1945, *főhadnagy* Füleky was leading a flight of his squadron when they destroyed three Il-2s from a Soviet formation; he shot down one of them in person. His opponent was probably the aircraft of 672nd SAP flown by *mladshiy leytenant* P.A. Kuzmin (serial number 9505), which belly-landed two kilometers southwest of Ráckeve. Three days later, Füleky achieved his last confirmed aerial victory against a Yak-9. These two victories were confirmed in Wing Order Nr. 1945/62.[245]

Following the Soviet Vienna offensive that began on 16 March 1945, the Hungarian air force units were soon forced to retreat to Austria. Mainly in April, the Hungarian fighter wing was deployed to fly intensive strafing missions against the Soviet forces that were speedily thrusting forward. During his eight strafing runs completed at this time, Füleky personally destroyed five trucks, one anti-aircraft gun position and four railway freight cars, and also effectively attacked two marching columns (after he was appointed squadron commander, he always took care to have the highest number of sorties and strafing runs). He carried out a very effective strafing run with his flight on 19 March 1945 between 17:00 and 17:20 in the area of Csákvár and Vértesacsa, during which they destroyed eight vehicles and set a light tank on fire.[246]

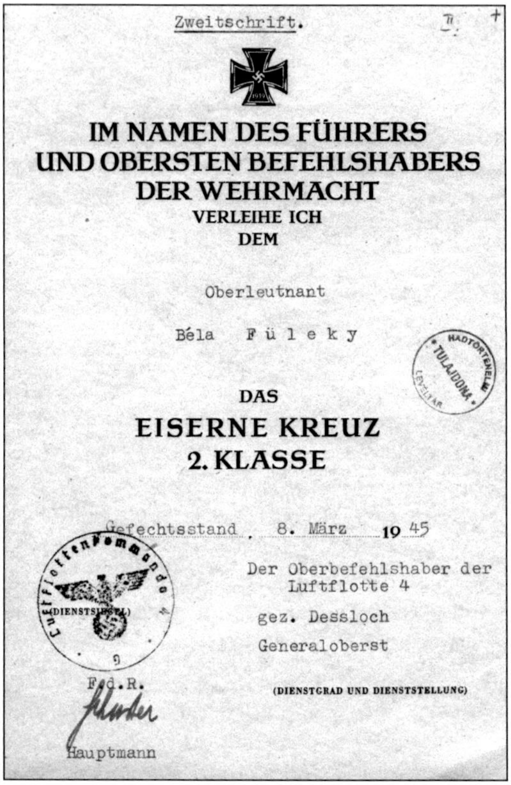
Zweitschrift.

IM NAMEN DES FÜHRERS
UND OBERSTEN BEFEHLSHABERS
DER WEHRMACHT
VERLEIHE ICH
DEM

Oberleutnant

Béla Füleky

DAS
EISERNE KREUZ
2. KLASSE

Gefechtsstand, 8. März 1945

Der Oberbefehlshaber der Luftflotte 4
gez. Dessloch
Generaloberst
(DIENSTGRAD UND DIENSTSTELLUNG)

F.d.R.
Hauptmann

The awarding certificate of the German Iron Cross 2nd Class belonging to *főhadnagy* Béla Füleky (*HM HIM* Military Archives)

Főhadnagy Füleky took off with his flight on 3 April 1945 at 16:50 for another strafing run from the airfield of Tulln, during which they were also tasked with completing a reconnaissance of the enemy forces. During the mission, flying at low altitudes, they strafed the Soviet vehicles and marching infantry moving along the Sopron–Wiener Neustadt road and along other roads west of the Leitha Mountains. The aircraft of *főhadnagy* Füleky was hit by an anti-aircraft gun during the mission, and he had to crash-land at 16:56 with his burning aircraft on own territory, northeast of Langmannersdorf. The courier aircraft that was sent for him brought him back that

245 *HM HIM HL*, documents of 101 Fighter Wing, box nr. 110, Wing Order Nr. 1945/62; Gábor Horváth on documents of TsAMO.

246 *HM HIM HL*, documents of 101 Fighter Wing, box nr. 113, recommendation of Béla Füleky for decoration, 24 April 1945; box nr. 113, combat mission log of 101 Fighter Wing, 19 March 1945.

evening, unharmed. During the mission, his flight destroyed eight to 10 trucks and also blew up an ammunition carrier vehicle.[247]

The forced strafing at low altitude continued next day, with heavy losses: 101/II Fighter Group lost three of its successful fighter pilots in that day. The young *szakaszvezető* Pál Fülöp, from the first formation deployed from the squadron, fell victim to anti-aircraft fire during the morning. The second victim was *hadnagy* Kálmán Nánási, who was killed during the second mission, in the afternoon. The third casualty was *főhadnagy* Füleky. His last mission began at 17:56 on 4 April 1945; he took off from Tulln with his wingman for a strafing run in the area of Malacky. This was the last (fourth) mission of 101/II Group that took place on that day. During the strafing run, Füleky's element knocked out a truck, two horse-drawn vehicles and a light anti-aircraft battery; his wingman, however – who was, according to recollections, a young *hadnagy* – lost sight of his commander and returned alone. The fact that his wingman lost sight of him might be ascribable to the fact that reckless Füleky – despite having been shot down by anti-aircraft artillery the day before – flew right into the heaviest anti-aircraft fire, and his wingman simply did not dare follow him. What is certain is that his wingman last saw *főhadnagy* Füleky at 18:30, five kilometers south of Malacky, flying at a low altitude in an area where anti-aircraft artillery fire was extremely heavy. According to civilian eyewitnesses from the area, on 4 April (the day Malacky was occupied by the Soviets), the Soviet anti-aircraft artillery shot down a Messerschmitt flying at a low altitude; its pilot died. This was almost certainly Füleky, as there were no known German losses from the area on that day. It is therefore most probable that the squadron commander crashed in the same area where his wingman last saw him alive.[248]

ZÁSZLÓS ANDRÁS HUSZÁR

Number of aerial victories: 5 (+1)
Successes against ground targets: n.d.a.
Number of flown combat sorties: 77 (16 against Americans)[249]
Number of hours flown in the air force: 399 hours 53 minutes
Nickname: *Pufi*
Identification number: n.d.a.

247 *HM HIM HL*, documents of 101 Fighter Wing, box nr. 113, combat mission log of 101 Fighter Wing, 3 April 1945.

248 *HM HIM HL*, documents of 101 Fighter Wing, box nr. 113, combat mission log of 101 Fighter Wing, 4 April 1945. The author wishes to express his gratitude for the help of Slovakian researcher Milan Benček.

249 This data was taken from the logbook of András Huszár and compared with (and double-checked against) the squadron logs and his *Repülési napló motoros sportrepülők számára*. The original *Logbook* and *Repülési napló motoros sportrepülők számára* are owned by the author. At the end of the war, on 18 April 1945, a summary of 101 Fighter Wing credits András Huszár with 79 sorties, but this summary contains a number of errors compared with the logbooks of other pilots. Note the abovementioned document: *HM HIM HL*, documents of 101 Fighter Wing, box nr. 113, high command of the Royal Hungarian 101 Honvéd Fighter Wing, summary of the missions of I and II class aviators of the wing staff of 101 Fighter Wing over enemy territory.

Decorations

- *Kormányzói dicsérő elismerés Magyar Koronás Bronz Érdemérme hadiszalagon a kardokkal* (1 November 1944)
- *Tűzkereszt I fokozata a kardokkal és koszorúval*
- German Iron Cross 2nd Class (8 March 1945)
- Silver *Frontflugspange* (20 April 1945)

Victories

Number	Date	Aircraft	Location
1	16 June 1944	P-38	Balaton S
2	30 June 1944 at 10:03	B-24	Nemesvita
3	7 July 1944	B-17	Megyercs (Cerová, Slovakia)
–	27 July 1944	American aircraft	
4	11 January 1945 at 10:50	Yak-9	Zámoly area
5	11 March 1945 at 11:28	Il-2	Adony SW

Aircraft flown

Bf 109 G-6: V.808 (the beginning of summer 1944), V.842 (26 July 1944), Bf 109 G-6/U4: W-021 (11 October 1944), W-101 (4 January 1945), Bf 109 G-14/U4: W-139 (15 January 1945), W-106 (4 February 1945), Bf 109 G-10/U4: 'Blue 10' (25 March 1945), 'White 14' (14 April 1945)

András Huszár was born on 12 July 1919 in Budapest. He had one sibling, a younger sister; their father was a medical records clerk. Huszár graduated from high school in the 2nd District of Budapest in 1937 (*Érseki Katolikus Gimnázium*, now *Budapesti Egyetemi Katolikus Gimnázium*). After graduation, he completed a one-year specialist trading course in 1937–38. From 1939, he attended university and read law; he completed only one year of the course before starting to work as a bank clerk.[250]

Aviation was a childhood dream for Huszár. His sports aviator career began in June 1937 at the Farkashegy near Budaörs, the cradle of Hungarian glider flying. In the same year he achieved the A badge, then the B badge in 1938 and the C badge in 1939. He completed the requirements for the Silver Badge (D badge) on 11 June 1940, following which he became the 29th Hungarian glider pilot to receive the Silver Badge (it was the 1754th international, *ISTUS* badge). He completed a flight with a duration of 5 hours and 30 minutes on 3 June 1940; he achieved a flight distance of 170 km on 11 June 1940; and he completed a flight gain of 1,293 meters the same day.[251]

250 András Huszár does not have a personal document folder in the Central Record Office of the *HM HIM*. General biographical data is taken from documents preserved by the family and provided to the author for research.

251 András Huszár's *Repülési napló motor nélküli sportrepülők számára* (Flight log for sport aviators of non-powered aircraft) (original owned by the author); Mitter (ed.), *A magyar vitorlázórepülés képes története*, p. 230; *Magyar Szárnyak*, 15 March 1942, p. 28.

András Huszár takes off on 5 December 1937 with a Zögling (registration number A-0103) at the Szélmérő hill. (From the author's collection)

András Huszár before the start at his successful C Badge flight at Szekrényes hill, with the Hol's der Teufel, individually named *Taifun*, registration number B-0104. (From the author's collection)

From July 1937 to January 1944, he flew with 18 glider aircraft types and spent 63 hours and five minutes in the air altogether with gliders. During his sports aviation career, he never damaged any aircraft. He successfully completed the hillside glider instructor course in June 1940, organized by the *Magyar Aero Szövetség* (the Hungarian Aero League).[252] Because he was the first of the Puma pilots to acquire his silver level glider badge (D), and because he had also completed an instructor course, he is considered the most successful sports aviation pilot among the airmen of 101 'Puma' Fighter Wing.

Huszár completed his primary flight training in the summer of 1941 at Ferihegy, given by the *Műegyetemi Sportrepülő Egyesület* (*MSE*, Polytechnic University's Sports Aviation Group) of *HMNRA*. After only 27 takeoffs, he was able to fly solo with a Bücker. At the *MSE*, from 20 May and 1 November 1941, following 234 takeoffs, he spent 54 hours and 47 minutes in the air, double of the usual training time for a newcomer, and this was probably due to his past experience as a sport aviator (in other words, the instructors provided more opportunities for him to fly than they did for his training group members).[253]

Huszár graduated as reserve *zászlós* on 6 December 1943 (second in the class among those of the same rank), in the same class as István Kálmán, László Dániel and Mihály Karátsonyi. After the graduation, he was assigned to Mátyásföld with 5/I Fighter Group. In March 1944, he retrained to Bf 109s at Börgönd and was transferred to the newly created 101/3 Fighter Squadron.

He flew his first combat sortie on 30 May 1944. During his third combat sortie, on 16 June, he reported his first aerial victory over a Lightning in heavy air combat with the American fighters in the Balaton area. This victory was certainly confirmed, although no order survives in which it is included. According to the author, Air Force Command Order Nr. 1944/9, issued on 18 July 1944, included confirmations for aerial victories achieved on 16 June 1944; the later Air Force Confidential Order Nr. 1944/63 does not contain all the kills scored on that day.

252 András Huszár's *Repülési napló motor nélküli sportrepülők számára.*
253 András Huszár's *Repülési napló motoros sportrepülők számára.*

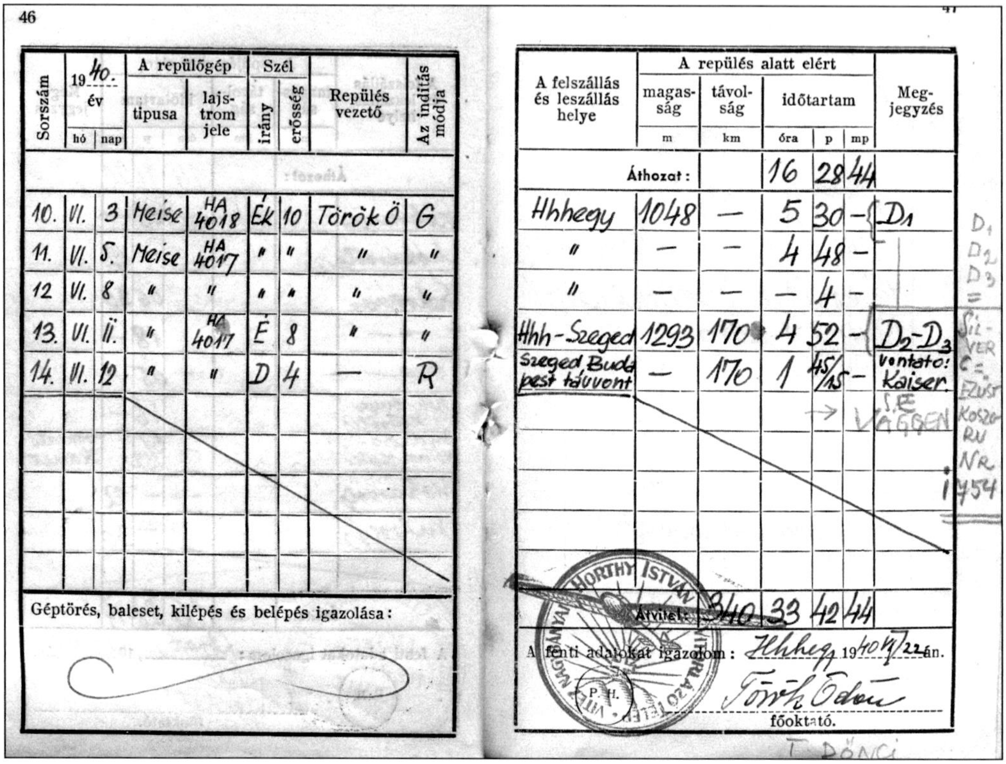

Registry entries of András Huszár of his D (silver) Badge performance flights from June 1940 in the *Repülési napló motor nélküli sportrepülők számára* (Flight log for sport aviators of non-powered aircraft). (From the author's collection)

Among the surviving documents, this victory was included in the squadron log, the individual documents of the pilot and in a decoration recommendation issued in mid-December 1944.[254]

Huszár took off on his seventh combat sortie on 30 June 1944, during which the Hungarian fighters engaged a Liberator formation that was returning after an aborted mission in cloudy weather. During the air combat, he managed to shoot down an enemy aircraft. His element leader, *hadnagy* László Molnár, recounted the mission and the kill in a letter to his parents written the next day:

> Yesterday we went on a mission again, my 115th combat sortie. Although the weather was extremely cloudy, the danger of ice was apparent and visibility was very low, the Americans flew several successive waves. Between Győr and Komárom, we took up a German destroyer formation that again came in many waves; we had to provide support and escort them throughout their attack. Because of the impaired visibility, ground control

254 *HM HIM HL*, documents of 101 Fighter Wing, box nr. 113, names list of personnel recommended for the German pilot badge.

had a very hard time trying to guide us. We were at the end of our fuel supply when we received directions to go south. The height: 8,500 meters! At the front were two destroyer formations; on their sides and above them were the German escorting fighters and our own aircraft. Our height was 9,000 meters. We were on our last 100 liters of fuel, as indicated by a small red light. Below us, a completely closed cloud base. After eight minutes of flight, we noticed an enemy bomber formation approximately 30km ahead of us. Unfortunately, we could not reach them because they fled into the clouds.

Three good sport aviator friends, now in primary flight training at the *HMNRA* (from right to left): Lajos Buday, András Huszár and János Nyemecz. Nyemecz later belonged to the same squadron as András Huszár at 101/3 Fighter Squadron. János Nyemecz was, like László Molnár, shot dead by the Mustangs of 31st FG while descending on parachute on 7 August 1944. (From the author's collection)

Our fuel was almost completely used up! On the right, a closed Liberator (four-engine) formation appeared out of the clouds. Attack! The 110s German Bf 110 destroyer aircraft dived on them in successive passes. I also gave the order to attack to my flight. The first 110s destroyers opened fire. The scene was beautiful: a Liberator at the back spun round and fell headlong into its white grave of clouds. Another fell like a burning torch; another exploded into a thousand pieces. The air was full of wing and fuselage parts, engines, aircraft skin pieces, small aircraft parts and columns of flame. Below us, parachutes began to open. The enemy bomber formation split apart and fled into the clouds one by one, but unfortunately I was not able to reach them. I pulled up at 700km and luckily noticed a tiny hole in the clouds – ground and water. With a sharp turn I dived through the hole and realized that directly below me was the airfield of Tapolca and Lake Balaton. My calculation was that an aircraft would fall out of the clouds and would lose track in this mad combat, flying blindly – and I was right! I noticed a four-engined over the Balaton flying from Keszthely to Tihany. We attacked. My wingman, *zászlós* Huszár, was close at my side; after him, Gyurka Debrődy, who experienced radio problems, and he closed up on me. He lost his wingman during the dive through the clouds. I dived on this monster head-on, from the side, from above. The defensive fire was extremely heavy; the tracer bullets were coming at my face, 10–12 cannons [sic – in reality, 12.7mm heavy machine guns] were firing. I waited calmly to shoot back, because all the hits from my wingman depended on me, given the fact he was flying so close. The aircraft got bigger by the second, and the enemy defensive fire was getting even stronger.

The muzzle fires flashed rapidly as though the aircraft was on fire. I measured the distance – 300 meters. Now! I opened fire from all of my weapons. My wingman was after me. The burning flame hit the cockpit and the port root of the wing directly. The inner port engine caught fire; the aircraft lurched and fell in a left descending spin. We flew past it by a matter of centimeters for a second rush forward, then we turned and rushed back. Gyurka Debrődy was just hitting it right in the nose; now it was our turn to attack from behind, from the side, from above. The starboard wing also caught fire; the aircraft was now speedily falling toward the ground. It was already shot down, but never mind! The crew was still firing at us from the burning aircraft. All right, then; we did the same. We made repeated passes to attack the aircraft. It was falling downward like a torch exactly toward the airfield at Tapolca. It was all right; we continued our attack, as there might be survivors in the aircraft. This was revenge for *főhadnagy* Bognár, who was shot down on his parachute by these murderers [on 16 June 1944]! We could not approach closer than 100 meters because the flames would consume us. Nobody had so far left the aircraft. Now a human body flew out of the torch and opened his parachute. It was too early! The fire caught him and he plunged down with a burning parachute. At that moment, south of the airfield and directly west of the railway line, there was a huge blast within a 50 meters radius. A towering black column of smoke and flames – it was gone! I took a look at my watch: 10:03. … Our fuel was down to one or two liters, so we landed at Tapolca. Many familiar faces all came to congratulate us; once had I promised them that when I was deployed, I shot a four-engined onto the corner of the airfield, and now I nearly did it! I was mistaken only by two kilometers. But never mind! We filled up our aircraft and took off again! This time, sadly, we met nobody up there. In Veszprém, we waggled our wings and landed to report the aerial victory. They asked to whom it should be registered. Gyurka Debrődy and I both said: 'To *zászlós* Huszár!' This way we did not get our 20th on paper, but it is not important at all. We shot down enough, but here are these young pilots, full of enthusiasm and the will to fight, and we have just lost the tenth of them in the person of Gyula Zsiros [a classmate of András Huszár, who was killed on the same day while crash-landing near Hajmáskér].[255]

András Huszár on his first solo flight of a powered aircraft with the Bü 131 (HA-LCS) on 28 May 1941. (From the author's collection)

The Liberator (B-24H, serial number 41-29291) that was shot down belonged to 460th BG's 760th Squadron, which was first attacked by the Bf 110 G-2 twin-engined destroyer aircraft of II./ZG 1. The aircraft, flown by 2nd Lieutenant Elder A. Erfeldt, crashed southeast of Nemesvita (the location is incorrectly stated as 'Nemesvitány' in Air Force Confidential Order Nr. 1944/63).[256] Seven of the 10-member crew of the heavy bomber were taken into captivity: two gunners had already lost their lives during the air combat due to hits to the fuselage of the aircraft, and

255 Letter of *hadnagy* László Molnár to his parents, 1 July 1944 (copy owned by the author).
256 NARA MACR 6394; *HM HIM HL*, documents of 101 Fighter Wing, box nr. 110, Air Force Confidential Order Nr. 1944/63. For the day's air combat, see Mohos, 'A 460. Bomber Group légi harca Magyarország felett 1944 június 30-án', pp. 33–39. The remains of one of the gunners who was remained inside the aircraft, Martin F. Troy, were uncovered in 2007 and were identified by the Joint Prisoner of War/MIA Accounting Command (JPAC), which is dedicated to finding the missing soldiers of the United States.

the radio operator bailed out but his parachute was engulfed in flames. The sight of the American soldier, who screamed and shouted uncontrollably until he crashed to the ground, was for many eyewitnesses (among them Hungarian airmen who had had to leave the Tapolca airport because of the air raid alert) one of the most horrifying personal experiences of the war.[257]

According to Huszár's logbook, he landed at Tapolca because of a fuel shortage after a flight of two hours and five minutes. The American survivors found in the vicinity were taken to the airfield, where Huszár exchanged words with 2nd Lieutenant Erfeldt. After that, he flew back to Veszprém.

His next successful combat sortie (his ninth) was flown on 7 July 1944, during which he reported shooting down a B-17. This was credited to him as a shared victory with György Debrődy, with a location of Megyercs (see Debrődy's entry for details). At the end of the mission, Huszár landed in Győr; he managed to get back to Veszprém on the same day. On 26 July 1944, *zászlós* Huszár took part in the air combat fought over Austrian territory; at the end of the mission, he again landed in Győr because of a fuel shortage with his aircraft the V.842 (serial number 95403).[258]

On 27 July 1944, *zászlós* Huszár took off on his 12th combat sortie. The mission took two hours and 20 minutes and was his longest flight; at the end of it, he belly-landed on Veszprém airfield. In the notes column of his logbook, beside the 'combat sortie – air combat' text, a note appears reading '1 L', which may refer to an individually registered, unreported and thus unconfirmed victory ('1 L' meaning either '1 shot down' (*Lelövés*) or '1 victory' (*Légi győzelem*)).[259]

Huszár's next significant sortie was flown on 11 October 1944 which was a strafing attack. On this occasion, the Soviet anti-aircraft artillery shot him down and he crash-landed on a territory controlled by his own forces, near Pálosszentkút – today Petőfiszállás – with the

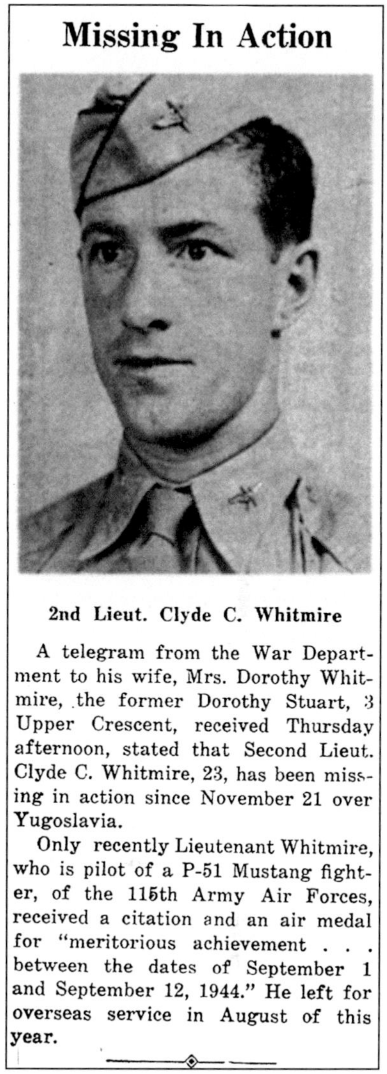

Missing In Action

2nd Lieut. Clyde C. Whitmire

A telegram from the War Department to his wife, Mrs. Dorothy Whitmire, the former Dorothy Stuart, 3 Upper Crescent, received Thursday afternoon, stated that Second Lieut. Clyde C. Whitmire, 23, has been missing in action since November 21 over Yugoslavia.

Only recently Lieutenant Whitmire, who is pilot of a P-51 Mustang fighter, of the 115th Army Air Forces, received a citation and an air medal for "meritorious achievement . . . between the dates of September 1 and September 12, 1944." He left for overseas service in August of this year.

Contemporary article about the disappearance of 2nd Lieutenant Clyde C. Whitmire (325th FG): On 12 October he has shot down the Storch in which András Huszár was travelling from Budapest to Veszprém, then on 21 November 1944 he was shot down by the German anti-aircraft artillery over Yugoslav territory, and was briefly missing. The Partisans helped him avoid capture by the Germans and he returned to Italy (East Rochester Department of Local History)

257 Based on the interview of an eyewitness, János Pocskai, who was serving at Tapolca Airfield, 2 October 1998.

258 *HM HIM HL*, box 1122 microfilm, logs of 101/3 Fighter Squadron, logbook of András Huszár (original owned by the author).

259 Logbook of András Huszár.

same Bf 109 G-6/U4 (W-021, WNr. 760381, serial number 95456) that had mostly been flown earlier by *hadnagy* Dániel; the aircraft suffered 40 percent damage. According to the squadron log, Huszár belly-landed near Kistelek, which is south of the location mentioned above, but Huszár's own notes are almost certainly more accurate than the squadron log. The most likely scenario is that the aircraft belly-landed south of Pálosszentkút and north of Kistelek. From here, he reached Ferihegy, and a Storch was sent for him the next day. During the return trip on 12 October, however, the Storch was attacked by an American Mustang and was shot down. In a very short time, therefore, Huszár had been shot down twice: once by enemy anti-aircraft artillery, and once by an enemy fighter aircraft.

The victory over the courier aircraft was reported by 2nd Lieutenant Clyde Carl Whitmire from325th FG's 319th Fighter Squadron, who reported shooting down a 'single-engine reconnaissance aircraft' at 14:45 'north of Budapest' (the direction in the report is almost certainly a typing error, because the air victory was achieved south of the capital). According to his report, the aircraft attacked by him was trying to evade combat by flying at a low altitude and maneuvering slowly with the intention of landing somewhere, while he fired approximately 200 rounds with 30 percent deflection; the aircraft then caught fire. According to the Hungarian police report, the Fi 156 was shot down near Szigetbecse at the weir-keeper's house; the two members of the crew were wounded. The documents of the fighter wing do not hold any notes on the injuries of the two airmen, and there is no sign of wound clasps being granted to either, which means the two airmen probably only suffered minor injuries or bruises.[260]

1st Lieutenant Henry L. Long, a pilot of 325th FG's 318th Fighter Squadron, also reported shooting down a Fi 156 over Hungary this day; this has previously been identified as the aircraft carrying Huszár, with a crash location of Csorna.[261] This identification, however, is incorrect, as the Fi 156 reported by Long (which blew up in the air due to the machine gun fire inflicted upon it) was a German aircraft that crashed near Tata, and the pilot and two passengers – among them, a *Major* – were killed (Fi 156 C-3, WNr. 110049). Long reported the kill with a location of Győr, which again shows the inaccuracy of American encounter reports and navigation during combat missions.[262]

Huszár's Storch was the only confirmed aerial victory of Clyde Whitmire (born on 25 June 1921), but his combat tour, which began in August 1944, was not without excitement. On 21 November 1944, during a strafing run, German anti-aircraft fire shot him down over Yugoslavia and he had to bail out. He avoided being taken prisoner with the help of local Partisans, and after six days he returned to his unit. After the war, he worked in the civilian field and died on 1 February 1981 in Missoula.[263]

From the second half of November 1944, Huszár flew as an element leader in the first flight led by the new squadron commander, *főhadnagy* Halasi. On 11 January 1945, Huszár took part in two missions. The first took place between 10:20 and 11:30 (his 41st combat sortie), and he reported shooting down a Yak-9 in the area of Zámoly. Although this air victory was mentioned

260 NARA 325th FG Combat Claim Forms; *HM HIM HL*, Personalia nr. 249, summary of events, 13 October 1944, pt. 12.

261 Pataky, Rozsos, and Sárhidai, *Légi háború Magyarország felett*, vol. 2, p. 199.

262 NARA 325th FG Combat Claim Forms.

263 East Rochester Department of Local History; letter of Tom Batey (a former comrade of Whitmire) to the author, 7 October 2014.

in the squadron log and the individual documents of the pilot, it was left out of later registries and confirming wing orders, probably because of an administrative error. The reason for this might be that Huszár's wingman, *őrvezető* Erdész, attested the kill via radio, but after the air combat he was separated from the formation and did not return, so he was unable to provide paper-based evidence. According to Soviet sources, there were no Yak-9 losses on that day in that area.[264]

András Huszár completed his 50th combat sortie on 12 February 1945. On 11 March 1945 (his 59th combat sortie), he joined the Dániel flight on a free hunt mission in the area of Székesfehérvár, where he shot down an Il-2 (witnessed by *hadnagy* Dániel). The aircraft probably belonged to 210th SAP (see the details at *hadnagy* Dániel). This kill was included in the wing's mission log as Huszár's fourth confirmed aerial victory. Probably the Lightning was the first, as it was also included in a recommendation for the German Iron Cross 2nd Class of December 1944, while the Yak is left out of the registry. This Il-2 was later confirmed in Wing Order Nr. 1945/62.

On 29 March 1945, *zászlós* Huszár flew a 20-minute reconnaissance mission (his 66th combat sortie) from the airfield at Grosspetersdorf to clarify the ground situation. He flew a Bücker Bü 131, and this was probably the only flight of this type classified as a combat mission in the Royal Hungarian Air Force. It was followed by two strafing runs on 4 and 5 April, this time with Bf 109.[265]

He flew his last three combat sorties – all three free hunt missions, two of which were combined with relocation – on 18 April 1945.

During his 77 combat sorties (16 against Americans), Huszár took part in 24 air engagements and flew at least eight strafing runs, during which he scored the five aerial victories detailed above. At each subsequent victory, I have detailed any issues regarding their registry, confirmation and documents that survive; there are no surviving documents of any of his successes against ground targets.

Huszár had intensive and successful combat service, and his achievements were not reflected by the single *Signum* he received. His first recommendation for a *Signum* was filed on 17 June 1944 (also showing that the Lightning shot down the previous day was practically taken as confirmed). He was recommended for his second *Signum* on 24 October 1944, but this was never received; nor was he recommended again on 24 April 1945, when the pilots of the wing were recommended *en masse* (also for the killed and missing ones). For the sake of comparison, one of his comrades in the squadron, *hadnagy* Gyula Pintér, flew 29 combat sorties between November 1944 and April 1945 and achieved three confirmed aerial victories; he received two *Magyar Koronás Érdemérem*, the second on 25 April 1945.

The reason why Huszár did not receive a further Hungarian military decoration on 25 April 1945 may have been an administrative error. There is no evidence that he had any conflicts with any of his superiors that might have resulted in his name being deleted from the list of decoration recipients. Nor was he sent back to Pocking sooner – which would also be a possible sign of conflict – as he was kept with the unit until the end, and he was flying missions throughout April, a clear sign that his skills were acknowledged; the author has spoken with one of his

264 *HM HIM HL*, box 1122 microfilm, logs of 101/3 Fighter Squadron, logbook of András Huszár. Erdész was lost and crash-landed beyond Soviet lines due to lack of fuel, where he was taken POW.
265 Logbook of András Huszár.

András Huszár used his knowledge of English from May 1945 as an interpreter at 101 Fighter Wing. This photograph of him – with a much taller American soldier – was taken at the end of the war. (From the author's collection)

former instructors, who also held the opinion that András Huszár was a highly skilled pilot. When the unit was taken into American captivity, Huszár was employed as interpreter, which was again a sign of trust in him, as he was not the only one in the wing to speak some English.[266]

While in American captivity, besides being the wing's interpreter, he was also a courier for the Hungarian Red Cross. He returned from American captivity relatively early, in September 1945. After this, for a short time in the autumn of 1945, he worked as an aviation instructor for the national sports aviation club (*Kinizsi Sportközpont*) of the *Független Kisgazda-, Földmunkás és Polgári Párt* (Independent Smallholders, Agrarian Workers and Civic Party); thereafter, he worked as a bank clerk.

Huszár emigrated to Sweden in 1947. Ostensibly, he was taking part in a half-year training course, but he did not return home. He could settle instantly in Sweden because he received a job in the banking sector. He retired as a director of the foreign currency branch of a Swedish bank.

In Sweden, he only flew in sports aircraft if one of his friends took him on a ride with a Klemm 35, but during his business trips, he flew as a passenger to all parts of the world. Once he especially requested to travel at a cheaper rate than business class, just to be able to try the Concorde. His wish was granted and he crossed the Atlantic ocean in this aircraft.

András Huszár died on 27 April 1995 in Stockholm. He was laid to rest in the Skogskyrkogården cemetery, which is a World Heritage site.

266 The author was only able to do this much for the rehabilitation of this sadly undervalued and forgotten pilot of the Second World War: he has deliberately included a longer bibliography for him based solely on primary sources. From a number of sources regarding this pilot that the author only acquired at a later date, it became apparent that Huszár's fifth aerial victory was validated by a number of official sources; however, he was sadly left out of the 2006 (first Hungarian) edition of the present work.

FŐHADNAGY TIBOR PAPP

Number of aerial victories: 5
Successes against ground targets: n.d.a.
Number of flown combat sorties: 62 (22 against Americans)
Number of hours flown in the air force: n.d.a.
Nickname: *Tibci*
Identification number: n.d.a.

Decorations

- *Újólagos Kormányzói dicsérő elismerés Magyar Koronás Ezüst Érdemérme hadiszalagon a kardokkal* (1 November 1944)
- *Kormányzói dicsérő elismerés Magyar Koronás Bronz Érdemérme hadiszalagon a kardokkal* (24 February 1944)
- *Tűzkereszt I fokozata a kardokkal és koszorúval*
- *Felvidéki Emlékérem*
- *Erdélyi Emlékérem*
- *Délvidéki Emlékérem*
- German Iron Cross 2nd Class (8 March 1945)
- Bulgarian Pilot Badge (summer of 1939)

Victories

Number	Date	Aircraft	Location
1	7 July 1943	La-5	Belgorod–Volchansk
2	3 August 1943 at 07:10	Il-2	Belgorod W
3	3 August 1943 at 17:00	La-5	Chuguyev S
4	3 April 1944	B-24	Kulcs
5	22 August 1944	B-24	

Aircraft flown
n.d.a.

Tibor Papp was born on 9 June 1916 in Slavonsi Brod, Croatia, where his father worked as a land surveyor engineer. He had two sisters and a younger and an older brother, who all worked as civilians; his younger brother completed industrial school and, during the war, worked at the *MWG* aircraft factory in Győr. Unlike his siblings, Papp went to a military high school and graduated in Sopron at the Royal Hungarian *II Rákóczi Ferenc Reáliskolai Nevelőintézet*. According to those who remember him, aviation was Papp's childhood dream.

He received his primary flight training in 1936 in Nyíregyháza; at the primary flight training, he was the first to fly solo in his class. According to one of his former classmates, Adolf János Péterdi, he was the best-skilled pilot in the whole class. The classmate of Pál Irányi, he graduated

The majority of the members of the air force officer class who graduated on 20 August 1939 as students at the *Repülőakadémia*, in the summer of 1938, in Nyíregyháza, in front of a Heinkel HD 22 trainer aircraft, the basic training aircraft of the Royal Hungarian Air Force until the war broke out. From left, the fifth in the standing row is Tibor Papp, the eight is Endre Németh and the ninth is Pál Irányi, the prospective aces of the class. (From the author's collection)

Table of *hadnagys* graduated on 20 August 1939 at 2nd Department of the Ludovika, among them the 14 air force officers on the right at the top. Of them, Pál Irányi is first in the upper left corner; beside him is Tibor Papp. Second from Papp is Endre Németh. These were the three future aces in the class. (From the author's collection)

At Vát, the fighter school, with a Fw 56 Stösser damaged in a landing accident. In the foreground, with his hands on his hip, stands *százados* István Fülöp; on the right is *hadnagy* Tibor Papp with flying helmet and goggles. (*HM HIM Hadtörténeti Múzeum* Photographic Archives 97.601/081)

Főhadnagy Tibor Papp as an instructor of the *Repülőakadémia* in 1943. (From the author's collection)

to *hadnagy* on 20 August 1939 in Budapest, as of 1 September 1939, with rank number 8 (altogether 79th).[267]

Papp attended the fighter combat training in Börgönd from September 1939 to March 1940 (he also completed an observer course in 1939). During the spring, he served as a fighter pilot in the same place for a few months. From 1 June 1940, he was deployed to Szombathely and Tapolca as an instructor pilot; during the short campaign against Yugoslavia in April 1941, he was deployed and reassigned to 1/I Fighter Group. Throughout April, he flew covering missions over the ground forces; for this, he received a commendation from the commander of the Honvéd Army Staff.

After the campaign against Yugoslavia, he returned to Szombathely, where he was promoted to *főhadnagy* on 1 April 1942. This balanced, calm and very patient officer was an excellent instructor.

From September 1942, he was the instructor at the *Repülőakadémia* at Kassa until 1 June 1943, when he was deployed to the Eastern Front to gain combat experience with two other fellow instructor officers, *százados* Antal Békássy and *százados* Miklós Scholtz. He arrived on the Eastern Front on 2 June 1943, where he received a short Bf 109 training course. After this, his first combat sortie with Messerschmitts was completed on 6 July 1943 with 1/1 Fighter Squadron, of which he became the deputy commander.

He scored his first aerial victory the next day, on 7 July 1943, during his second combat sortie, with *törzsőrmester* Dezső Szentgyörgyi as his wingman. They were flying over the advancing

267 *HM HIM KI*, document folder nr. 11 111; *Honvédségi Közlöny* (*Személyes ügyek)*, nr. 1939/6 (19 August 1939), p. 31; also based on the interview of János Adolf Péterdi, 8 March 1997.

German troops and met an La-5 pair, which they attacked, and one of the Soviet fighter aircraft was shot down by *főhadnagy* Papp. In July, he completed 14 combat sorties.[268]

The first day of the Soviet counteroffensive, 3 August 1943, was not only the busiest but also the most successful day for Papp: he flew seven combat sorties altogether and scored two confirmed aerial victories, both with wingman *törzsőrmester* Szentgyörgyi. The first aircraft was shot down in the morning, not long after 07:00, west of Belgorod; his victim was an Il-2. He and Szentgyörgyi found a Soviet ground-attack formation of 12 aircraft flying close to the ground, and Papp attacked and shot down the aircraft on the far left while Szentgyörgyi dealt with the one on the far right. Papp's second opponent was shot down late in the afternoon, south of Chuguev; it was another La-5. The field magazine of 5/I Fighter Group, *Üvölt a Puma*, contains an article about these two kills. The laconic *főhadnagy* Papp answered questions from the editors of the magazine: 'At 07:05, north of Belgorod, we noticed a number of Il-2s. We picked two, shot them down with Szentgyörgyi, and then came home. But now I am in a hurry, as I again have a mission to complete.' After the editors asked him again at noon about the details of the victory, *főhadnagy* Papp said only this: 'I cannot tell you more. I shot him and he crashed.' He explained his second kill of the day late in the afternoon in the same laconic manner at 17:47: 'With *törzsőrmester* Szentgyörgyi, we came from the sun and attacked two unsuspecting La-5 Soviet fighters. By the time they noticed us, they were already down. Both of us shot down an aircraft.'[269]

Papp probably did not go on any more missions after the end of August, and returned home from the front in the autumn. On the Eastern Front in 1943, *főhadnagy* Papp flew 36 combat sorties altogether and achieved three confirmed aerial victories. After he returned from the Eastern Front, he was deployed to Szolnok with the rest of the pilots of 1/1 Fighter Squadron.

His first mission against the Americans was flown from Szolnok on 3 April 1944, during which he reported shooting down a B-24 at Kulcs near the Danube. This aerial victory was deleted almost a year later in Wing Order Nr. 1945/27, but it was sent again to the air force command to confirm it after it was deleted and many sources later added it to his individual successes.

He went from Szolnok to Veszprém with his squadron in May 1944 as the deputy commander of the new 101/2 Squadron. He scored his second kill against a four-engined on 22 August 1944 (the list of four-engined air victories credits him with one kill against four-engines; another document credits him with two, and he is registered as having five victories. He himself counted both four-engines as part of his successes).

Papp was credited in a recommendation on 17 December 1944 as having flown 62 (22 American, 40 front-line) combat sorties. A recommendation of 19 February 1945 spoke of 55 (36 on the Eastern Front in 1943, 15 American and four new Soviet). There are clear discrepancies, as shown by the fact that seven combat sorties against Americans were noted down by one of the sources and not by the other. Unfortunately, Papp's logbook was lost after his death, so we cannot use it to reconstruct the exact number of his combat sorties.[270]

268 Excerpts from the logs of 1/1 Fighter Squadron.
269 *Üvölt a Puma*, 3 August 1943, pp. 1–2.
270 *HM HIM HL*, documents of 101 Fighter Wing, box nr. 113, names of those recommended for the German pilot badge; summary of the missions executed by 101/2 Squadron against Americans and Soviets.

On 19 September 1944, Papp became commander of 101/2 Fighter Squadron, replacing *százados* Ujszászy, who left the unit. In November, the new 101/6 (combat training) Fighter Squadron was formed within the second group of the fighter wing, and Papp (an experienced instructor) was assigned commander of the new squadron. He flew his last combat sortie on 4 November 1944. Although there were plans to convert 101/6 Squadron into another combat squadron, as a result of which combat training would be removed from the direct tasks of the wing, this did not happen until the end of the war. Therefore, the combat training *'Kölyök'* squadron did not fly on combat missions. *Főhadnagy* Papp finished the war as the commander of this squadron; he went into captivity in May 1945 with the rest of the wing.

Főhadnagy Tibor Papp, *hadnagy* Lajos Tóth and *százados* Gyula Horváth in Veszprém, during the summer of 1944. *Százados* Gyula Horváth (1910–1984) was at first the commander of 5/2 Fighter Squadron on the Eastern Front, then the deputy commander of 101/I Fighter Group for home defense, who completed more than 80 combat sorties during the war. (From the author's collection)

He returned to Hungary in September 1945. From 26 October to 10 February 1946, he was commander of 6/II truck column at Székesfehérvár, before being discharged from the military. In 1946, he attended a tram driving course in Budapest; with the help of his older brother, who was in the profession, he found a job as a tram driver until the summer of 1948, when he was accepted into the *Maszovlet*. However, he was discharged in 1950 because of his military past, and was not allowed to fly again. Following this, he found a job in the hotel industry. In the military supervision file investigating his role in the Hungarian Revolution of 1956, the following committee opinion and suggestions can be found: 'Based on fresh and earlier opinions, as a highly decorated former officer of the Horthy era, he is not trustworthy for the

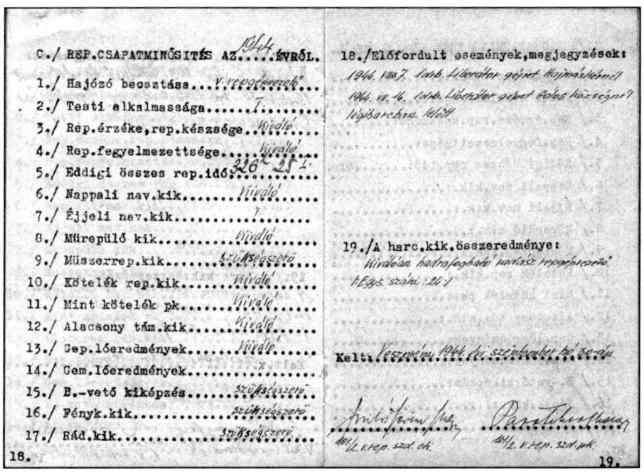

C./ REP.CSAPATMINŐSITÉS AZ 1944. ÉVRŐL.

1./ Hajózó beosztása...
2./ Testi alkalmassága...
3./ Rep.érzéke,rep.készsége... Kiváló
4./ Rep.fegyelmezettsége... Kiváló
5./ Eddigi összes rep.idő... 326h 25'
6./ Nappali nav.kik... Kiváló
7./ Éjjeli nav.kik...
8./ Műrepülő kik... Kiváló
9./ Műszerrep.kik... szükségszerű
10./ Kötelék rep.kik... Kiváló
11./ Mint kötelék pk... Kiváló
12./ Alacsony tám.kik... Kiváló
13./ Gep.lőeredmények... Kiváló
14./ Gem.lőeredmények...
15./ B.-vető kiképzés... szükségszerű
16./ Fényk.kik... szükségszerű
17./ Rád.kik... szükségszerű

18./Előfordult események,megjegyzések:

19./A harc.kik.összeredménye:

Kelt: Veszprém 1944. évi szeptember hó 30-án

18.

19.

Gellért Barsi's *Repülő Csapatminősítés* (Aviation Unit Qualification) from 1944. Both his Liberator kills were shared victories with aces (the one at Hajmáskér was shared with Heppes, and the other at Gálos with Szentgyörgyi). At the bottom of the document the autograph of his squadron commander, Tibor Papp, can be seen. At the end of October 1944, Barsi was reassigned from 101/2 Squadron to 101/5 Squadron. (From the collection of the Barsi family)

people's army. According to his origins and based upon his rank and role in the past, he is a class-alien and enemy [sic]. We suggest demotion.'[271]

Papp was forced to endure the last stages of humiliation when he was stripped of his officer rank and demoted to private in 1958. There are no surviving observation files and documents in the *Állambiztonsági Szolgálatok Történeti Levéltára* in connection with him; his name is only mentioned in trial documents.

Tibor Papp died on 13 November 1991 in Budapest. His ashes were laid to rest in the *Új Köztemető* in Rákoskeresztúr. Unfortunately, his rank has not been restored to this day.

SZAKASZVEZETŐ ERNŐ KISS

Number of aerial victories: 5
Successes against ground targets: n.d.a.
Number of flown combat sorties: about 160
Number of hours flown in the air force: n.d.a.
Nicknames: *Balbó*, *Sheriff*
Identification number: 1219-22-0058

Decorations

- *Magyar Nagy Ezüst Vitézségi Érem* (28 January 1944)
- *Magyar Kis Ezüst Vitézségi Érem* (30 December 1944).
- *Magyar Kis Ezüst Vitézségi Érem*, for the second time (25 April 1945)
- *Magyar Bronz Vitézségi Érem* (29 April 1944)
- *Tűzkereszt I fokozata a kardokkal és koszorúval* (with one wound clasp?)
- German Iron Cross 2nd Class (1945)
- Gold *Frontflugspange* (1945)

Victories

Number	Date	Aircraft	Location
1	5 (8?) January 1944	Il-2	Sosovo–Vahnovka E 1km
2	5 (8?) January 1944	La-5	Sosovo–Vahnovka E 4km
3	15 August 1944	La-5	Opatov E 5km
4	1944	Soviet aircraft	
5	16 March 1945 (December 1944/January 1945)	Yak-9	Bicske N 10km

Aircraft flown

Bf 109 G-6: V-388 (16 September 1944)

271 *HM HIM KI*, document folder nr. 11111.

Ernő Kiss was born on 5 June 1922 in Nagykörű, Jász-Nagykun-Szolnok County, to a farming family of five children. They moved to Budapest in 1926, where his father became a policeman.[272] Ernő Kiss's original occupation was as a tradesman assistant in Budapest. He was keenly interested in aviation from early childhood, and began his aviator career in glider planes on the Hármashatárhegy.

He answered the call of the *HMNRA* and, as a member of the 1941 primary training (enlisted) class, he received his primary flight training at Marosvásárhely in the summer of 1941, in the same group as Mátyás Lőrincz.

After completing the *Regvi* in Szombathely over the winter of 1941–42, he served in Börgönd from April 1942 to September 1943 with the combat training group, where he also received reconnaissance combat training. In the autumn of 1943, he retrained to Messerschmitt Bf 109s from the Germantraining detachment stationed there.

He was deployed to the Eastern Front on 7 November 1943 as part of the independent 5/2 Fighter Squadron, and he remained on the front with his unit until the end of the war (later the independent 102, then 102/1 Squadron, in the end renumbered 101/7 Squadron).

He scored his first two kills on 5 January (or least possible 8 January) 1944 as the wingman of *hadnagy* László Molnár, while flying over enemy territory east of Sosovo–Vahnovka (the surviving documents refer to the location as 'Sugovachnovka'). They attacked a Soviet formation consisting of approximately 40 aircraft and dispersed them. They reported shooting down six; two were attributed to Kiss. First he shot down an Il-2, then an La-5 by attacking it head-on. The witness in both cases was *hadnagy* Molnár. For these successes, Kiss received the *Magyar Nagy Ezüst Vitézségi Érem*. (Details of the mission can be read in the biography of his element leader, László Molnár.)

The enlisted class trainees of the *HMNRA* at Marosvásárhely in 1941. Of those on the bench, the third from the right is Ernő Kiss. (From the collection of the Kiss family)

Unfortunately there are uncertainties connected with Kiss's victories, and for one of them we have no data or details.

His next known aerial victory was achieved on 15 August in 1944; this time, he shot down an La-5 fighter five kilometers east of Opatov. The witness was *hadnagy* Lajos Galánfy.[273] According to his former squadron commander, then his group commander *őrnagy* József Kovács,

272 *MNL Jász-Nagykun-Szolnok Megye Levéltára* (National Archives, Jász-Nagykun-Szolnok County Archives), XXXIII/1 state birth registry of the village of Nagykörű for 1922, counterpart, acc. nr. 8; *HM HIM KI*, document folder nr. 48584.

273 *HM HIM HL*, documents of 101 Fighter Wing, box nr. 113, 101/III Fighter Group, record of victories, Wels, 30 May 1945.

Enlisted class pilot students with their instructors at the *Regvi* in Szombathely in December 1941. In the middle of the standing row, the instructors can be seen, among them in the centre *hadapród őrmester* Kálmán Nánási. Apart from Nánási, three of the students became aces during the war: in the standing row, third from left, is Ernő Kiss; in the kneeling row, second from left, is Lajos Krascsenics; and in the sitting row, fifth from right, is Pál László Szikora. The majority of those marked with a cross lost their lives either on the battlefield or due to accidents, although not all of them. (From the author's collection)

szakaszvezető Kiss had flown 138 combat sorties and had achieved five confirmed aerial victories prior to 29 January 1945.[274]

Kiss's last confirmed kill was scored on 16 March 1945, 10km north of Bicske, where he shot down a Yak-9. This is mentioned in the fragmentary documents of 101/III Fighter Group, witnessed by *hadnagy* János Kovács.[275]

In this case, the date is certainly an error, as the intact and complete mission logs and combat reports of 101 Fighter Wing do not refer to any victories on 16 March (nor was there any Soviet fighter loss on that day of that type of aircraft). Based on this, if the location was correct, then this victory must have been scored either in December 1944 or January 1945, when there was intense fighting in the area. According to the

Enlisted pupils at the *Regvi* in Szombathely in the spring of 1942, in front of an Arado Ar 96 training aircraft. Two of the airmen in the picture later became aces: Mátyás Lőrincz is second from the right, kneeling on the wing bare-chested; the first man standing on the left in front of the engine is Ernő Kiss. (From the author's collection)

274 *HM HIM HL*, documents of 101 Fighter Wing, box nr. 112, Royal Hungarian 102 Honvéd Fighter Group, summary of decorated officers and enlisted.

275 *HM HIM HL*, documents of 101 Fighter Wing, box nr. 113, 101/III Fighter Group, record of victories, Wels, 30 May 1945.

author, the reason for the error was that the clerk filling out the document erroneously wrote the same date twice on two different wrong lines. The line beneath the one in question contains the victory of *főhadnagy* László Szénássy on 16 March 1945, which date was confirmed both by the squadron log and the combat report. In the author's opinion, the secretary wrote the same date by accident for Kiss and did not realize his error. Unfortunately, as the document has no other copies and the date is only mentioned this once, we cannot correct it based on the documents that survive today.[276]

As the registry clearly stated this as an aerial victory, and as no victory was confirmed for Kiss in the Wing Orders issued at the end of the war, this kill must therefore have been confirmed in a lost Air Force Order, probably Nr. 1945/2 or Nr. 1945/3 (and which certainly would have noted the correct date for the victory). A summary report from February 1945 exists from 101/III Group, and the mission logs and combat reports of the wing also exist from 20 February until the end of the war; none of these source reports any further kills for Kiss. The author thus deems this incorrectly dated victory as the last of the five aerial victories mentioned in the summary created on 29 January 1945 by the group commander, because there is no data to suggest that Kiss scored any further air victories after 29 January 1945; he therefore had five confirmed victories. This is further strengthened by a document from 21 February 1945, which mentions that Kiss had five victories. A later document credits him with a different number of air victories, but fewer rather than more, and so was probably due to a typing error. A personal achievement report created on 1 March 1945 credits Kiss with 143 combat sorties – three completed in February – and four air victories. Although the above-mentioned summary of aerial victories (which contains the mistaken date of 16 March) also lists four kills for him, it does not exclude the possibility that there may have been a fifth, because

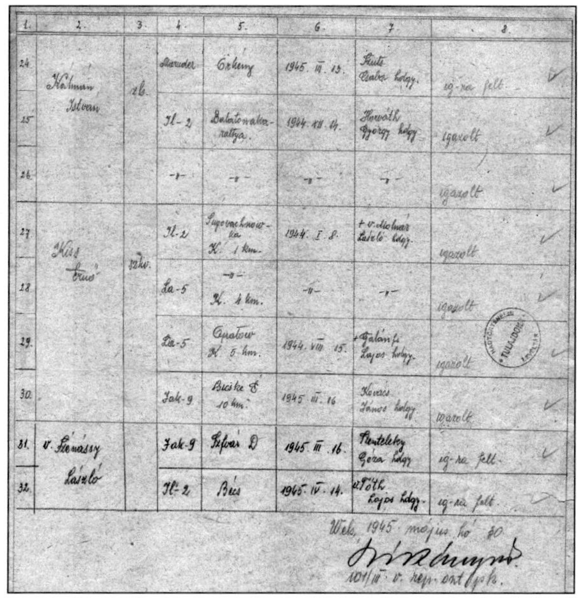

The remains of the victory registry of Ernő Kiss. For the fourth victory, the written date clearly matches the date in the line below – that is, the date of the victory of *főhadnagy* László Szénássy on 16 March 1945, but this must be the clerk's error (the date of the first two kills, I.8. is also an error, and in reality it has to be I.5.) From this example, it can clearly be seen that we need to be careful with the few primary sources that survive, because these may also contain errors. (*HM HIM* Military Archives)

276 *HM HIM HL*, documents of 101 Fighter Wing, box nr. 113, 101/III Fighter Group, record of victories, Wels, 30 May 1945.

other pilots also had victories left out of their summaries that were otherwise recorded in official documents.[277]

During the war, Kiss was also shot down at least twice. On the first occasion, he belly-landed; on the other, during a strafing run, he was hit by anti-aircraft artillery and bailed out over no man's land before being picked up by a Hungarian patrol. The latter event probably occurred at the end of 1944.[278]

Kiss went into captivity with his wing in May 1945. While a prisoner of war, he worked as a chef, and organized the workers. He planned not to return to Hungary, and in 1947 he set off for the United States with the American unit he was working for. In Reims, France, however, he left the vehicle column at the request of an American officer, who asked him to buy some drinks. He asked a local policeman for directions; the policeman found his accent suspicious, and he was arrested as a fleeing Nazi, as he had left his documents in the car. By the time he was released, the column was nowhere to be seen and he had to return to Hungary in the summer of 1947.[279]

At home, his whole life was haunted by his past. He was often unemployed, as he found it hard to find a job because of his military past. After his return, he worked as a day-labourer, then as a railway builder. In 1948, he applied to be part of the air force following its reorganization; he was accepted in the following year and served as an instructor pilot from May 1949 in Kecskemét. From August of the same year, he was employed in Szolnok at the *Kilián György Repülő Hajózó Tiszti Iskola* (György Kilián Flight Technical College). Following 1 May 1950, he was commissioned and promoted to *alhadnagy*. He was promoted *hadnagy* out of turn on 15 October of the same year. His aviation career, however, did not last long in the new armed forces, and he was forced to leave military aviation on 31 May 1951.

His service qualification file issued in 1949 contains the following description of him:

> He is excellently trained, and has much experience in instructing and flying fighter aircraft. ... He is disciplined, soldierly, of good countenance, hard-working and always implementing his orders. He is sometimes a bit childish and influenced by his younger comrades. In an appropriate environment he is serious. He is very comradely. With his subordinates, he enjoys good comradeship; he likes to instruct them. He offers a good example to his subordinates and can lead them very well. He has been in service for a long time, and despite having a wife, a family and serious financial problems, his service has never faltered. He is moderately trained in politics, but he is continuously self-educating himself. He is clearly knowledgeable about everyday political questions. He is strengthening the people's democracy with his work. He is a true believer in people's democracy. He is very good at taking in the overall picture.[280]

277 *HM HIM HL*, documents of 101 Fighter Wing, box nr. 112, message with the list of names of 101/III Fighter Group who achieved outstanding results, and names of decorated pilots (21 February 1945); high command of 101/III Fighter Group, personal score report (1 March 1945); box nr. 113 101/III Fighter Group, summary of victories, Wels, 30 May 1945.

278 Based on a fragmentary interview preserved by the family; it was not possible to uncover which newspaper contained the article.

279 Based on a fragmentary interview that was preserved by the family; it was not possible to uncover which newspaper contained the article.

280 *HM HIM KI*, document folder nr. 48584.

He also loved to fly, but could no longer do so after 'officially' being stripped of opportunities.

Kiss was a dispatcher at the *Mátravidéki Fémművek* (Mátra Iron Works) in Sirok during the revolution of 1956, where he became a *nemzetőr* (armed home guardsman during the Hungarian Revolution), then a deputy chairman of the local worker's committee. He did not keep his opinions secret: 'During the counter-revolution, he made a number of statements that are particularly serious. Mainly about the Soviet troops, and about their role in Hungary. He took critical notes also about the *ÁVH*'[281] – this was reported by one of his 'well-wishers' to the officers at the People's Army who were investigating his actions during the revolution. Although he avoided serious reprimand, he was stripped of his rank of reserve *hadnagy* in 1958 and demoted to private. After the revolution, he worked in the building industry, and in his older years he was a cow inseminator at the *téesz*. No data survives in the *Állambiztonsági Szolgálatok Történeti Levéltára* regarding his possible observation by the Ministry of Interior, although any investigation into the details of his life is complicated by his extremely common family name.

Ernő Kiss died on 14 May 1990 in Törökszentmiklós, where he is buried. On 15 February 1991, at his widow's request, his rank of reserve *hadnagy* was restored.[282]

281 *HM HIM KI*, document folder nr. 48584.
282 *HM HIM KI*, document folder nr. 48584.

Reconnaissance Aces

FŐHADNAGY VITÉZ ENDRE NÉMETH

Number of aerial victories: 8
Successes against ground targets: n.d.a.
Number of flown combat sorties: about 70
Number of hours flown in the air force: n.d.a.
Nicknames: *Bandi*, *Spahi*
Identification number: n.d.a.

Decorations

- *Magyar Érdemrend lovagkeresztje hadiszalagon a kardokkal* (18 March 1943)
- *Újólagos Kormányzói dicsérő elismerés Magyar Koronás Ezüst Érdemérme hadiszalagon a kardokkal* (1 October 1942)
- *Kormányzói dicsérő elismerés Magyar Koronás Bronz Érdemérme hadiszalagon a kardokkal* (15 September 1941)
- *Tűzkereszt I fokozata a kardokkal és koszorúval*
- *Felvidéki Emlékérem*
- *Erdélyi Emlékérem*
- *Délvidéki Emlékérem*
- German Iron Cross 1st Class (? October 1942)
- German Iron Cross 2nd Class (August 1942)
- Bulgarian Pilot Badge (summer 1939)

Victories

Number	Date	Aircraft	Location
1	2 July 1942	LaGG-3	Voronezh W
2	2 July 1942	LaGG-3	Voronezh W
3	2 July 1942	LaGG-3	Voronezh W
4	5 August 1942	Soviet fighter	Povorino
5	5 August 1942	Soviet fighter	Povorino
6	5 August 1942	Soviet fighter	Povorino
7	13 August 1942	Soviet fighter	
8	13 August 1942	Soviet fighter	

Aircraft flown

He 70 K: F.410 (12 April 1941), He 111 P: F.703 (2 July 1942), F.706 (5 August 1942), F.705 (13 August 1942), Ju 88 D: F.911 (22 April 1943)

Endre Németh as a student at the Academy in 1939, shortly before his graduation. (From the author's collection)

Endre Németh was born on 20 February 1918 in Nagykároly (today Carei, Romania), the older son of a family of two children. As his hometown was given to Romania following the Treaty of Trianon, the family moved across the new borders. In 1940, his father, Dr Endre Németh (1891–1976), after pursuing a number of important, mostly hydrographical-related occupations, became a university professor and head of the *Budapesti Műszaki Egyetem, Vízépítéstani Tanszék* (Department of Hydraulic Engineering at the Budapest University of Technology).[1] The younger Endre Németh was a *cőger* who graduated in Pécs from the Royal Hungarian *Zrínyi Miklós Reáliskolai Nevelőintézet.* He then went on to attend the 2nd Department of the Ludovika in 1936.

Németh graduated as *hadnagy* on 20 August 1939 in Budapest, as of 1 September 1939, with rank number 9 (altogether 84th); he was in the same class as Pál Irányi and Tibor Papp.[2] As there was then a serious lack of officers in the long-range reconnaissance units, he was assigned to 1 Independent Long-Range Reconnaissance Group, 1/2 Squadron, equipped with Heinkel He 70 Ks, although he very much wanted to be a fighter pilot. Of the 14 *hadnagy* officers graduated on 20 August 1939, eight were assigned to the long-range reconnaissance-group because of the lack of officers: two became bombers and only four became fighters. This was extraordinary in terms of the distribution between service positions, and the final decision

Part of the service personnel of 1/2 Long-Range Reconnaissance Squadron in the summer of 1940, in the background their Heinkel He 70 K aircraft. In the sitting row, the second from the right is *hadnagy* Endre Németh; the fifth is *százados* János Vesztényi (1907–1977), the commander of the squadron. (From the author's collection)

1 *Budapesti Műszaki és Gazdaságtudományi Egyetem Levéltára* (Archives of the Budapest University of Technology and Economics), 30.*fond*, personal document folder nr. 201.152.

2 *Honvédségi Közlöny* (*Személyes ügyek)*, nr, 1939/6 (19 August 1939), p. 31.

Endre Németh's crew on 12 April 1941, after they belly-landed with their He 70 F.410 near Dunaföldvár due to lack of fuel. (From the author's collection)

A game of cards on the Eastern Front in the breaks between long-range reconnaissance missions, in the summer of 1942. On the far left is *főhadnagy* Endre Németh, in the middle facing the camera is reserve *százados* László Újvári (1893–1951), a fighter ace of the First World War, who was commander of the courier flight of the long-range reconnaissance unit. (From the author's collection)

very much hurt those who were deployed to the long-range reconnaissance unit 'by force'.[3]

Németh's situation was worsened because the commanders of 1/2 Long-Range Reconnaissance Squadron, *százados* Pál Szabados and then *százados* János Vesztényi, assigned the freshly deployed officers to thorough observer training because the lack of observers was most acute. The observer position in the Royal Hungarian Air Force was an officer position exclusively, while many enlisted airmen and non-commissioned officers were pilots, so Németh was compelled to fly as an observer for a long time. His first flights over enemy territory were flown in August 1940 over Transylvania during the period of Hungarian–Romanian tension before the Second Vienna Award. Although the Romanian fighters tried to intercept them a number of times, these flights were not yet counted as combat missions.

Németh's first real combat missions took place during the campaign against Yugoslavia in April 1941. Two members of his permanent crew were then *zászlós* Gyula Torbágyi (pilot) and *tizedes* Róbert Kiss (wireless operator).

One combat mission during the campaign against Yugoslavia needs to be detailed. In the morning of 12 April 1941, during their first combat flight over Yugoslavia after taking off from Budaörs, they spent so much time in Yugoslavian airspace that they used up all their fuel. On their return leg, north of Dunaföldvár and east of the Danube, they had to belly-land on the floodplain between the floodbank and the river with their He 70 (F.410, WNr. 2230).[4]

Németh received a commendation from the commander of the Army Staff for his missions flown during the Yugoslavian campaign.

At the time of the beginning of combat activities against the Soviet Union, Németh was again deployed with his whole crew until 1 July 1941, when the engine of his He 70 was hit by anti-aircraft artillery over Striy and he was forced to crash-land in the Carpathians on the way

3 Based on the correspondence of Adolf János Péterdi, who was also assigned to the long-range reconnaissance unit.

4 Gyula Torbágyi, 'Meleg pillanatok', *Magyar Szárnyak Évkönyv*, 1990, p. 134.

back near Kőrösmező (today Yasinia, Ukraine). The aircraft was completely destroyed. Of the crew, *hadnagy* Németh suffered bruises on his legs and a sprained left ankle, *zászlós* Torbágyi bumped his head on the instrument panel and knocked out six of his teeth. *Tizedes* Kiss remained unharmed. Németh did not fly any further missions over the rest of the year; neither did the long-range reconnaissance group itself, after the first period of July. Neither unit was deployed to the fronts that were moving further and further from the borders of the country. After they lost another He 70 on 4 July 1941, they flew their last reconnaissance missions of the year with their two available He 111s.[5]

At the beginning of 1942, a decision was made to send the Hungarian 2nd Army to the Eastern Front, in support of which the long-range reconnaissance units were also deployed to the front. The deployed crews included Németh, who was promoted to *főhadnagy* on 1 April 1942.

The air crews of the long-range reconnaissance group, the 1/1 Long-Range Reconnaissance Squadron led by *százados* János Hollós, took off from Budaörs on 12 June 1942 to the Eastern Front. They arrived to their first combat airfield on 15 June, to Amasovka south of Kursk. On 20 June, they started to fly missions with their He 111s. After the large summer offensive of the Germans and their allies, '*Operation Blau*', launched on 28 June, the activity of the Hungarian long-range reconnaissance units and their Soviet counterparts intensified.

Főhadnagy Németh achieved his first aerial victory on 2 July 1942 in the morning. The long-range reconnaissance crew of the He 111 P F.703 (*százados* Antal Kelemen, pilot; *főhadnagy* Németh, observer; *őrmester* Géza Koczka, wireless operator; *őrmester* Nándor Halmai, mechanic; and *őrmester* Ádám Hajdufi, photographer) were tasked with photographing the area around Voronezh and the region ahead of the Hungarian troops advancing forward, to check the effects of an earlier bombing raid. Over Voronezh, the Hungarian aircraft was greeted by heavy anti-aircraft fire. On the return journey, five Soviet LaGG-3 fighter attacked them. During the 18 minutes of air combat, first the wireless operator, then the photographer and finally the mechanic-gunner also reported shooting down one enemy aircraft each.

This success was followed by another during a mission on 5 August. The crew of the He 111 F.706 (*őrmester* Lajos Cseh, pilot; *főhadnagy* Németh, observer; *őrmester* Géza Koczka, wireless operator; *szakaszvezető* Imre Lőrincz, mechanic; and *őrmester* Ádám Hajdufi, photographer) was engaged in combat with eight enemy aircraft for 35 minutes, during which they reportedly shooting down three enemy aircraft. The Hungarian aircraft was also hit a number of times – a contemporary source states 60 hits – but, fortunately, all members of the crew were unharmed.[6]

Németh was engaged in his heaviest air combat on 13 August 1942. At dawn, his He 111 (F.705) took off along the railway lines linking Balasov–Povorino–Talovaya–Svoboda to reconnoiter railway and road traffic. The crew was *főhadnagy* Németh, observer; *őrmester* Lajos Cseh, pilot; *őrmester* Géza Koczka, wireless operator; *szakaszvezető* Imre Lőrincz, mechanic; and *őrmester* János Deme, photographer. They also needed to observe the enemy airfields. The Soviet fighters proceeded to attack the Hungarian long-range reconnaissance aircraft near the most difficult target to approach – the heavily defended Povorino. The attackers came in waves: a first wave of three, then a second wave of three and lastly a wave of two aircraft

5 HM-HIM Military Archives, HM 641542/22.o.-1941; Torbágyi, 'Meleg pillanatok', pp. 134–136.
6 HM-HIM Military Archives, documents of the Hungarian 2nd Army, box 6, log appendix nr. 340; 'Hadijelentések, csaták és új fordulatok', p. 19.

The damaged vertical stabilizer of the He 111 F.706 long-range reconnaissance aircraft after the air combat on 23 July 1942 on the frontline airfield of Amasovka. In the white shirt *főhadnagy* Gyula Bánhidy (1917–1995), the observer of the aircraft for that mission and a classmate of Endre Németh. The F.706 was the most successful long-range reconnaissance aircraft of the Royal Hungarian Air Force, with five aerial victories: 2 July 1942, one victory, 23 July 1942, one victory, 5 August 1942, three victories. (From the author's collection)

Endre Németh and the crew after the air combat with the He 111 P F.703 on 12 July 1942. From left to right: *főhadnagy* Endre Németh, *őrmester* Ádám Hajdufi, *százados* Antal Kelemen, *őrmester* Nándor Halmai, *őrmester* Géza Koczka. On the vertical stabilizer of the Heinkel a hit from a Soviet 20mm cannon is clearly visible. (From the author's collection)

The He 111 P F.706 of 1 Long-Range Reconnaissance Group with five air victory markings, in the late summer of 1942. (From the author's collection)

(altogether eight). The air combat lasted 28 minutes and the crew of the Hungarian He 111 reported two kills, but their aircraft was also badly damaged. The attackers have not so far been identified; in the author's opinion, the experienced pilots of 487th IAP with their Yak-1b aircraft also took part in the battle. The Hungarian long-range reconnaissance aircraft was hit by thirteen 20mm cannon rounds and more than 200 machine gun bullets, but luckily only *őrmester* Deme was injured lightly on his right cheek from a splinter. During the heavy air combat, both engines of the Heinkel were hit, but the excellent pilot, *őrmester* Cseh, reached the airfield at Ilovskoye by gliding, and crash-landed the aircraft. It was damaged beyond repair; after all usable parts and instruments were removed from it, the aircraft was therefore transported back to Germany. The clerks at the Royal Hungarian Air Force registered the aircraft as late as 1 March 1943 as being 'in Germany for repair',[7] although the wreck was probably melted down in the autumn of 1942. Unfortunately, we do not have surviving Air Force Orders from 1942 to tell us about confirmed victories, but the 12 victories of the long-range reconnaissance unit achieved during that year were contained in other summary documents of the Hungarian 2nd Army (undetailed).

The Hungarian long-range reconnaissance unit received a number of Dornier Do 215s from the Germans over the summer of 1942, and in the autumn the first Ju 88s also arrived. Although the first arriving Ju 88s consisted of the old version D-2 subtype, which had no armored glass protecting the machine guns firing backward and upward, making them vulnerable (and sealing the fate of many aircraft and crew in 1943), these aircraft were nevertheless a step forward compared to the slow and windy He 111s.

After the beginning of the Soviet counteroffensive against the Hungarian 2nd Army on 12 January 1943, the Hungarian long-range reconnaissance units started to fly on new types of missions: instead of the photographic reconnaissance flown at high altitudes, they flew at low altitudes close to the ground on forced reconnaissance missions by visual observation while firing at every single target that presented itself. During one of these missions – on 20 February 1943, flying with He 111 F.703 – they were hit three times, one of which damaged the water cooler of the port engine, but Lajos Cseh again managed to bring the aircraft back to the airfield.[8]

In the spring of 1943, *főhadnagy* Németh at last received his retraining to Ju 88, so his wish was granted and on his last 20 missions or so he was able to fly as a pilot.

The notes of his new squadron commander, *százados* Adorján Mersich, preserve some of the details of his missions. For example, *főhadnagy* Németh and his crew were sent to photograph the usual 'hotspots' (railways and airfields in the Chuguyev–Kupiansk–Valuki–Kastornoye area) on 22 April 1943 in the Ju 88 F.911. Németh's observer on these last missions was the excellent *főhadnagy* Gábor Visnyei, who was later killed in air combat on 5 October 1943.[9]

Főhadnagy Németh flew his last mission on the Eastern Front on 26 April 1943. Between June 1942 and that date, he had flown 65 combat sorties altogether over the Soviet Union. After this, he briefly trained two young pilots to Ju 88 who had arrived for replacement, then

7 HM-HIM Military Archives, documents of the Hungarian 2nd Army, box 17, 1/1 Long-Range Reconnaissance Squadron reports on aircraft stock, 1 March 1943.

8 HM-HIM Military Archives, documents of the Hungarian 2nd Army, box 17, war diary of 1/1 Long-Range Reconnaissance Squadron, January–February 1943.

9 Notes of *százados* Adorján Mersich from 1943 (copies owned by the author).

One of the defense machine guns on one of the He 111s of 1 Long-Range Reconnaissance Group under maintenance, during the summer of 1942. This 7.92mm MG 17 type, belt-fed pedal-activated machine gun was built in the tailcone of the He 111 in a fixed position. The machine gun was used to repel the enemy fighters who positioned themselves into the dead space of the aircraft behind the stabilizers. (From the author's collection)

(on 7 May 1943) he finally returned home from the front. During his long-range reconnaissance missions in 1942–43, *főhadnagy* Németh and his crew were engaged in air combat 10 times, during which they scored eight aerial victories. They carried out their tasks under heavy anti-aircraft artillery fire more than 50 times, and they were badly damaged on three occasions (in one of these cases, returning with only one operating engine).[10]

After his return, Németh was an instructor pilot for the long-range reconnaissance-home group. In 1944, with his experienced long-range reconnaissance pilot comrade, *főhadnagy* Adolf Péterdi, he worked on the testing of the Hungarian-manufactured long-range reconnaissance variant, the Me 210 Da. Németh

Főhadnagy Endre Németh with his impressive collection of decorations in the summer of 1943. (From the collection of Endre Németh)

10 Gyula Kádár, 'Harctéri beszélgetés Németh Endre repülőfőhadnaggyal, aki megkapta a Magyar Érdemrend Lovagkeresztjét', *Magyar Szárnyak*, 1 July 1944, p. 13.

brought the Fw 189 A–2/U–3 (with dual controls) back from Germany, which was purchased for mapping.

After the disbandment of the long-range reconnaissance-group in the autumn of 1944, as Németh aspired to attend the Technical University, he was patronized by combat engineering *hadiműszaki törzskari alezredes* Lóránd Dóczy, the former commander of the also disbanded *RKI.* Németh was thus not transferred to a fighting unit again before the end of the war. After the war, he emigrated to Canada, where he rebuilt his life through hard physical labor as an employee of a Hungarian farm owner. He had a number of interesting and arduous jobs during his life; at the end, he retired as the director of one of the Ford factory agencies in Vancouver. Endre Németh died on 2 August 2007 in Vancouver, where he was laid to rest.

ZÁSZLÓS VITÉZ LAJOS CSEH

Number of aerial victories: 5
Successes against ground targets: n.d.a.
Number of flown combat sorties: 75+
Number of hours flown in the air force: 2,000+
Nickname: –
Identification number: 2092-12-0009

Decorations

- *Magyar Koronás Bronz Érdemérem hadiszalagon a kardokkal* (10 April 1945)
- *Magyar Nagy Ezüst Vitézségi Érem* (26 January 1943)
- *Magyar Kis Ezüst Vitézségi Érem* (11 November 1942)
- *Magyar Bronz Érdemérem hadiszalagon* (27 February 1942)
- *Magyar Bronz Vitézségi Érem* (24 November 1941)
- *Tűzkereszt I fokozata a kardokkal és koszorúval*
- *Felvidéki Emlékérem*
- *Erdélyi Emlékérem*
- *Délvidéki Emlékérem*
- German Iron Cross 1st Class (14 October 1942)
- German Iron Cross 2nd Class (23 January 1942)

Victories

Number	Date	Aircraft	Location
1	5 August 1942	Soviet fighter	Povorino
2	5 August 1942	Soviet fighter	Povorino
3	5 August 1942	Soviet fighter	Povorino
4	13 August 1942	Soviet fighter	
5	13 August 1942	Soviet fighter	

Aircraft flown

He 46 E–2/Un: F.301 (spring and summer of 1941), He 111 P: F.706 (5 August 1942), F.705 (13 August 1942)

Lajos Cseh was born on 30 January 1912 in the small village of Benk in Szabolcs County. His father, Károly Cseh, was a *néptanító* (village teacher).[11] At the time, his family was living in nearby Beregdéda (today Dijda, Ukraine), Bereg County, but this area was given to Czechoslovakia as a result of the Treaty of Trianon, so they moved beyond the new borders to Tiszamogyorós. Cseh began his studies on 1 September 1925 at the *Jutasi Honvéd Altisztképző és Nevelőintézet* (non-commissioned officer training school at Jutas); he completed them on 28 July 1929 with good grades and graduated as *tizedes*. His pilot training (primary, basic and advanced level) was completed between 1 August 1929 and 31 July 1930 in Szombathely. In the period after his training, he served for shorter periods in Szombathely, in Budapest Mátyásföld, in Pécs and in Miskolc as an instructor, reconnaissance and night bomber pilot, but he was also listed in the *Malért* (Hungarian airlines, the predecessor of *MASZOVLET*) as a commercial pilot. His first surviving flight statistics are from 1934, when he also completed a number of night flights. In Szombathely, he experienced the only damage to his aircraft we know of during his peacetime career when, on 26 February 1936, he emergency landed with a Heinkel HD 22 as a result of a fuel pipe breakage. During the landing, the undercarriage of the aircraft was damaged to an extent of approximately 10 percent.[12]

Őrmester Lajos Cseh (in light colored clothes) in September 1940 in Nagyvárad. (From the author's collection)

Cseh was promoted to *őrmester* on 1 January 1937. The experienced pilot was deployed to Budapest-Mátyásföld in 1939, to I Short-Range Reconnaissance Squadron, which was equipped with Heinkel He 46s.

He experienced his baptism of fire as a short-range reconnaissance pilot during the campaign against Yugoslavia. At that time, the commander of I Short-Range Reconnaissance Squadron at Mátyásföld was *százados* László Bibity-Horváth. During the campaign, Cseh flew one mission from the squadron's home base, Mátyásföld, with his observer, *hadnagy* József Molnár. The

11 Beregdéda is mistakenly listed as the birthplace of Lajos Cseh in the official military registers. In the state birth registry of Mezőladány, his birthplace is unambiguously registered as Benk. The address of his parents was in Beregdéda at that time, so this was probably mistaken for his birthplace in the military records. For this, see *MNL Szabolcs-Szatmár-Bereg Megye Levéltára* (National Archives, Szabolcs-Szatmár-Bereg County Archives) XXXIII/1, State birth registry of the village of Mezőladány for 1912, counterpart, note acc. nr. note 9; *HM HIM KI*, document folder nr. 12295.

12 MNL Csongrád Megye Hódmezővásárhelyi Levéltára (*National Archives, Csongrád County Archives, Hódmezővásárhely*), XIV/3, documents of László Bibithy-Horváth, box nr. 2, evaluation report of Lajos Cseh.

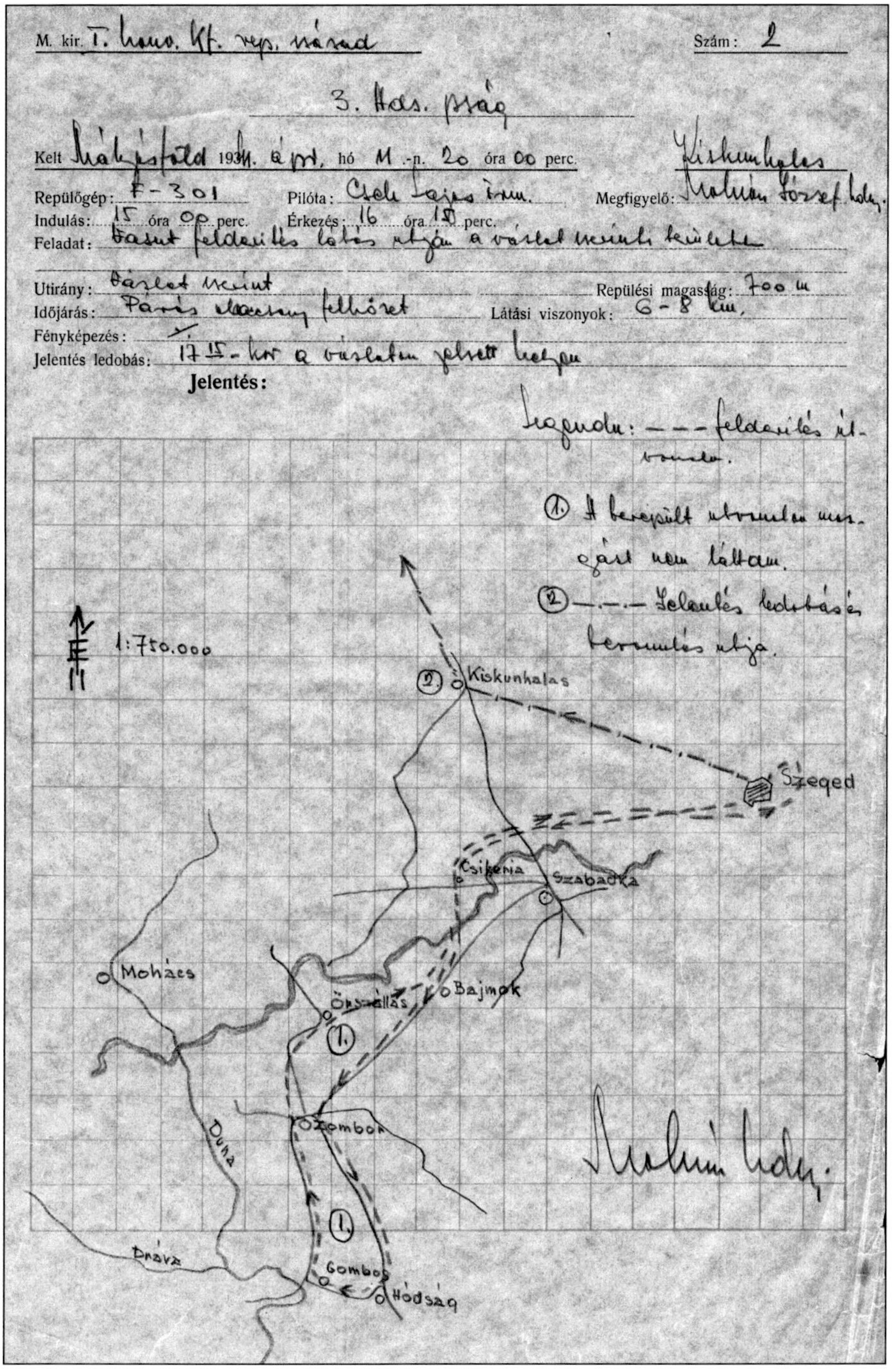
M. kir.
Szám: 2
Kelt 194 hó -n. 20 óra 00 perc.
Kiskunhalas
Repülőgép: F-301
Pilóta: Cseh Lajos
Megfigyelő: Molnár József
Indulás: 15 óra 00 perc. Érkezés: 16 óra 15 perc.
Feladat:
Utirány:
Repülési magasság: 700 m
Időjárás:
Látási viszonyok: 6-8 km
Fényképezés:
Jelentés ledobás:
Jelentés:

The report submitted about the combat mission carried out by *őrmester* Lajos Cseh and his observer, *hadnagy* József Molnár, on 11 April 1941 over Yugoslavia (*MNL Csongrád Megyei Levéltár Hódmezővásárhelyi Levéltára*)

mission was flown on 11 April 1941 in the afternoon, the day the squadron began their combat operations. The crew executed visual reconnaissance with the F.301 aircraft between 14:50 and 15:50 in the area between Csikéria and Őrszállás (now Станишић, Serbia), at the border fortress line and to the south of it, closely observing the roads and the railway, but in both directions they did not see any columns or troops in motion. The aircraft landed in Szeged for refueling because of the large distances they had covered. They also landed on their way back to Budaörs, where they were forced to remain by the unfavorable weather conditions. They only returned to Mátyásföld the next day. The reconnaissance report had been properly dispatched on 11 April at 17:15 at the drop-off point on the western outskirts of Kiskunhalas appointed by the Hungarian 3rd Army. Because of the large distances to the combat areas, the squadron moved to Szeged on 13 April to be closer to the front (Szeged airfield was very crowded by this time, as two squadrons of 1/II Fighter Group also moved here from Mátyásföld). Cseh's 11 April mission, as detailed above, was the second of 12 combat missions flown by I Short-Range Reconnaissance Squadron during the campaign against Yugoslavia, but it was Cseh's only one. According to his excellent grade qualification document issued during the period directly following the campaign against Yugoslavia, Cseh had amassed 1,401 hours and 53 minutes of flight time by 10 May 1941.[13] He also took part with his squadron in the campaign against the Soviet Union: their unit was deployed to Ukraine on 13 July 1941, from where they returned to home on 6 October, having completed 77 individual combat sorties without losing any aircraft or any crew member. *Őrmester* Cseh and his permanent observer, *hadnagy* József Molnár, took part in seven missions, of which six were visual reconnaissance and the seventh a night bomber mission. The missions are detailed below:

1. 19 July 1941, from Jezierzany airfield: reconnaissance with F.307, with observer *hadnagy* Molnár (the 9th combat mission of his squadron)
2. 24 July 1941, from Bar airfield: reconnaissance with F.301, with observer *hadnagy* Molnár (the 21st combat mission of his squadron)
3. 31 July 1941, from Annopol: reconnaissance with F.301, with observer *hadnagy* Molnár (the 35th combat mission of his squadron). The successful completion of this mission failed twice because of engine problems and they were forced to return
4. 1 August 1941, from Annopol: reconnaissance with F.308, with observer *hadnagy* Molnár (the 37th combat mission of his squadron)
5. 4 August 1941, from Annopol: reconnaissance with F.301, with observer *hadnagy* Molnár (the 46th combat mission of his squadron)
6. 13 August 1941, from Pervomajsk: night bombing with F.301, with observer *hadnagy* Molnár (the 66th combat mission of his squadron). Their sortie failed because the observer accidentally dropped their bombs earlier and their bomb bay was empty by the time the target was being attacked
7. 13 August 1941, from Pervomajsk: reconnaissance with F.301, with observer *hadnagy* Molnár (the 68th combat mission of his squadron)[14]

13 *MNL Csongrád Megye Hódmezővásárhelyi Levéltára*, evaluation report of Lajos Cseh.

14 *MNL Csongrád Megye Hódmezővásárhelyi Levéltára* (National Archives, Csongrád County Archives, Hódmezővásárhely), XIV/3 documents of László Bibithy-Horváth, box nr. 2, based on the mission reports of I. Short-Range Reconnaissance-Squadron.

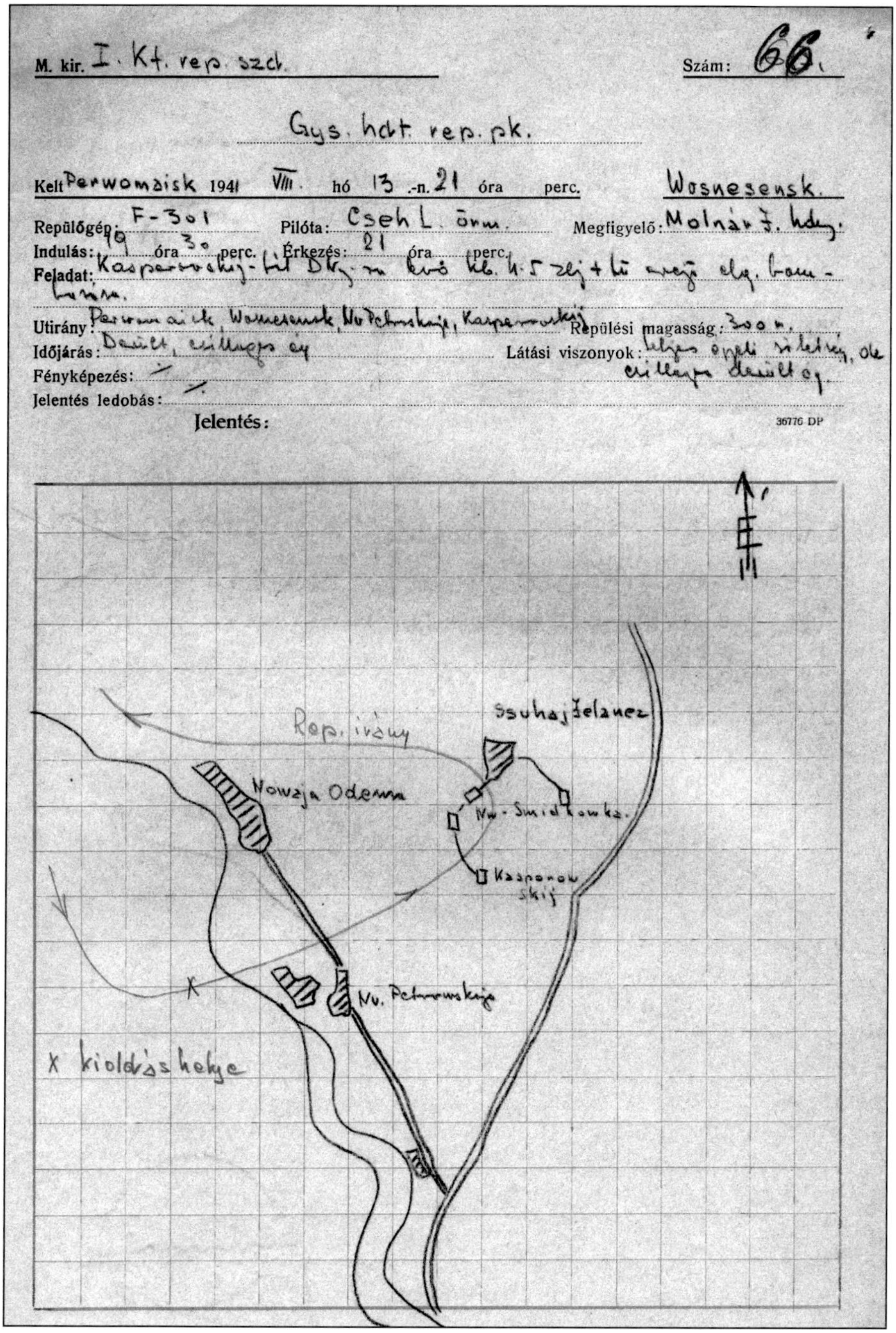

M. kir. I. Kf. rep. szd. Szám: 66.

Gys. hdt. rep. pk.

Kelt Perwomaisk 1941 VIII. hó 13.-n. 21 óra perc. Wosnesensk.

Repülőgép: F-301 Pilóta: Cseh L. őrm. Megfigyelő: Molnár J. hdgy.

Indulás: 19 óra 30 perc. Érkezés: 21 óra perc.

Feladat:

Utirány: Repülési magasság: 300 m.

Időjárás: Látási viszonyok:

Fényképezés: –

Jelentés ledobás: –

Jelentés:

36776 DP

The most interesting combat sortie of *őrmester* Lajos Cseh and his observer, *hadnagy* Molnár József, was a night bombing mission over the Soviet Union on 13 August 1941. As the observer accidentally released the bombs earlier, they flew over the target area with empty bomb bay (the releasing point is marked with an x). (*MNL Csongrád Megyei Levéltár Hódmezővásárhelyi Levéltára*)

Őrmester Cseh has received his first Hungarian and German military decorations for these missions: a *Magyar Bronz Vitézségi Érem* and the German Iron Cross 2nd Class.

Törzsőrmester Lajos Cseh – second from the left – with his crew in front of a yet-unpainted Ju 88 D-2 bearing German markings, in the spring of 1943. (From the collection of the Cseh family)

As a result of the reorganization of the air force after 1 November 1941, I Short-Range Reconnaissance-Squadron was disbanded, and Cseh was reassigned from Mátyásföld to Budaörs to 1 Long-Range Reconnaissance Group, where he quickly mastered the heavy twin-engined aircraft. Besides his military service, he managed to continue his education and graduated from high school on 23 December 1941 in Budapest, at the *Szent István Felsőkereskedelmi Fiúiskola* (Szent István Boy's Merchant School).[15]

In June 1942, Cseh was also ordered to the Eastern Front on the strength of the long-range reconnaissance group. He particularly excelled in the air combats fought on 5 and 13 August, during which he and his crew achieved five confirmed aerial victories (the details of which can be read in the biography of Endre Németh).

He was promoted to *törzsőrmester* in the autumn of 1942.

Cseh continued to fly combat missions until the spring of 1943. After his 65th long-range reconnaissance mission in April of that year, he was briefly reassigned to the command of the Hungarian Air Brigade as a Heinkel He 111 courier pilot, and returned home a few months later. After returning from the Eastern Front, Cseh was reassigned to Budaörs as an instructor for the long-range reconnaissance-reserve group.

An infamous typing error appeared in the press in the spring of 1943 regarding Cseh. The experienced pilot had received the *Magyar Nagy Ezüst Vitézségi Érem*, and the contemporary aviation magazine, the *Magyar Szárnyak*, claimed he had received this decoration posthumously.[16] Nevertheless, the superstition holding that those believed to be dead when they are still alive will live long lives proved correct in the case of Lajos Cseh.

After completing the chief non-commissioned officer course, he was promoted to *zászlóshelyettes* on 15 March 1944 as of 1 January, with rank number 5, along with two of his long-range reconnaissance pilot comrades, János Dörflinger and Sándor Székely.[17] Dezső Szentgyörgyi from the fighters were also promoted at the same time.

In 1944, Cseh admitted into the *Vitézi Rend* based on his own merits. When the long-range reconnaissance-reserve group was disbanded on 15 September 1944, Lajos Cseh was reassigned

15 Based on his matriculation certificate nr. 1941/42/6 (copy owned by the author). The majority of the bibliographical data is provided by his family, based on documents preserved by them.

16 'Katonai hírek', *Magyar Szárnyak*, 1 March 1943, p. 22.

17 *HM HIM KI*, document folder nr. 12295.

Mixed German-Hungarian night fighter group photo from the end of the war. Lajos Cseh is second from the right in the upper, sitting row. (From the collection of the Cseh family)

Graduation of *zászlóshelyettes* pilots in front of the Ludovika Academy on 15 March 1944. In the back row, the first from the right is Lajos Cseh, and the second is Dezső Szentgyörgyi. (From the author's collection)

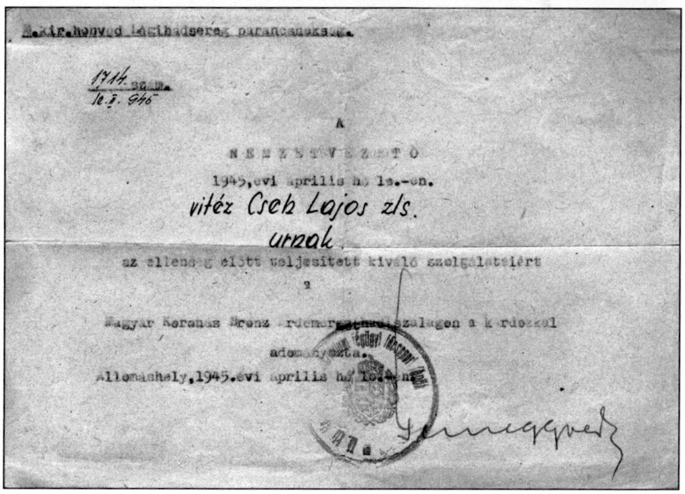

M.kir.honvéd légihadsereg parancsnokság.

1714. szám.
le.I. 945

A

NEMZETVEZETŐ

1945.évi április hó 1...-én.

vitéz Cseh Lajos zls.

urnak

az ellenség előtt teljesitett kiváló szolgálataiért

a

Magyar Koronás Bronz Érdemérem ... szalagon a kardokkal

adományozta.

Állomáshely,1945.évi április hó 1...-án.

The document of the last military decoration of *zászlós* Lajos Cseh. Although the charter is only a small piece of paper, it features the characteristic autograph of the last commander of the Royal Hungarian Air Force, *vezérezredes* Kálmán Ternegg, although it does not conform to the regulation, as it is written in pencil. (From the collection of the Cseh family)

to the night fighters as a person over the personnel strength, but he was not sent to combat again. In the meantime, on 1 November 1944, the officers' rank group of senior non-commissioned officers (and thus the rank of *zászlóshelyettes*) was abolished; Cseh officially became an officer with the rank of *zászlós*.

Among the pilots featured in this work, the excellent and modest Cseh flew for the highest number of hours in the Royal Hungarian Air Force.

At the end of the war, Cseh retreated west via Várpalota, Lesvár and Wiener Neustadt, then went into American captivity on German territory at Wittibreut, near the Austrian border. He did not return to Hungary, but settled in Germany with his German wife. They resided there until 1951, when they moved to Brazil with the help of the IRO. He found work in Belo Horizonte, then moved back to Germany in 1961. The former Hungarian pilot worked in the textile industry, where he earned a leading position through his skill and diligence. He died on 26 May 2002 in Wuppertal and is laid to rest there.

Bomber Ace

FŐHADNAGY LÁSZLÓ PAJTÁS (RÓTH)

Number of aerial victories: 5
Successes against ground targets: n.d.a.
Number of flown combat sorties: 100+
Number of hours flown in the air force: n.d.a.
Nickname: *Laci*
Identification number: 3330-20-0152

Decorations

- *Magyar Érdemrend lovagkeresztje hadiszalagon a kardokkal* (20 September 1943)
- *Újólagos Kormányzói dicsérő elismerés Magyar Koronás Ezüst Érdemérme hadiszalagon a kardokkal* (18 March 1943)
- *Kormányzói dicsérő elismerés Magyar Koronás Bronz Érdemérme hadiszalagon a kardokkal* (2 December 1941)
- *Tűzkereszt I fokozata a kardokkal és koszorúval*, with one wound clasp
- *Erdélyi Emlékérem*
- *Délvidéki Emlékérem*
- German Iron Cross 1st Class (summer 1943)
- German Iron Cross 2nd Class (1942)
- Bulgarian Observer Badge (summer 1939)

Victories

Number	Date	Aircraft	Location
1	11 August 1941	I-16	Nikolayev
2	11 August 1941	I-16	Nikolayev
3	11 August 1941	I-16	Nikolayev
4	Summer 1943	Soviet fighter	
5	Summer 1943	Soviet fighter	

Aircraft flown

Ca.135bis/U: B511 (11 August 1941), B-542 (summer of 1942), B-560 (6 August 1942), Ju 88 A-4: B.135 (1 December 1943)

Two gunners of the Ca.135 B.511 pose proudly at the vertical stabilizer of their aircraft following their success on 11 August 1941. The victory markings have already been painted on the vertical stabilizer; over the white lines, small red stars can be seen, with the names of the gunners: in the first two cases it was *szakaszvezető* Mester (sitting on the right), and in the third case *őrmester* Bánkuti (sitting on the left). The inscription on the side of the aircraft reads '*vitéz*'. (From the collection of the Bánkuti family)

Főhadnagy István Szakonyi (1911–1974) – already a *százados* – was the pilot of the Ca.135 on 11 August 1941 that achieved three aerial victories. According to the Hungarian regulations, the victories were credited to all of the crew members, and thus also to him. (From the author's collection)

László Róth was born on 2 February 1920 at Kassa; both of his parents were teachers. His family settled beyond the new, Trianon borders and they moved a number of times, the last in June 1937. He graduated with excellent results from *Gyulai Római Katolikus Gimnázium*, today *Karácsonyi János Római Katolikus Gimnázium*.[1] He immediately applied for the *Repülőakadémia* and graduated as *hadnagy* on 4 July 1940, a classmate of László Máthé, with rank number 2.[2] Róth now took his mother's family name (Pajtás), a name change that was officially verified on 10 July 1940 (his original family name was mistakenly entered in military documents as 'Rotth'). After the graduation, for some time he was employed as an instructor at the bomber training unit; he was then assigned to Debrecen, where the bombers were being rearmed to Caproni Ca.135s. He went to the front for the first time in the summer of 1941 as part of the mixed bomber squadron of the air force group supporting the Hungarian Ist Rapid Corps, where he served as the chief observer and completed four combat sorties between 28 July and 17 August 1941.

His most outstanding of these sorties was flown on 11 August against Nikolayev, during which *hadnagy* Pajtás was the observer of the Ca.135 B511. Other members of the crew included *főhadnagy* István Szakonyi as pilot, *őrmester* János Bánkuti as wireless operator and

1 József Németi (ed.), *A Gyulai Római Katolikus Gimnázium értesítője az 1936–37-es tanévről* (Gyula: Római Katolikus Gimnázium, 1937), p. 42.
2 *Honvédségi Közlöny* (*Személyes ügyek)*, nr. 1940/20 (4 July 1940), p. 154.

Hadnagy László Pajtás with the crew of his Caproni Ca 135bis/U bomber on the Eastern Front, in the summer of 1942. From left to right: *főhadnagy* Tihamér Ghyczy, *hadnagy* László Pajtás, *őrmesters* Tibor Benkő Tibor and János Lukács. (From the author's collection)

szakaszvezető János Mester as mechanic, as well as *vezérkari alezredes* Sándor András, who was also present as a member of a committee investigating the military performance and serviceability of the Caproni Ca.135bis/U aircraft on the Eastern Front. Pajtás's bomber's designated target was the railway station at Nikolayev, but during the approach of the target over the city, the aircraft's starboard engine was damaged in the heavy anti-aircraft fire and the Caproni lagged behind the formation. In this vulnerable situation, it was attacked by multiple Soviet fighters. Probably three different Soviet fighter units sent aircraft into the combat; of these, 9th IAP-ChF (9th Fighter Regiment of the Black Sea Fleet) lost two pilots killed while fighting the Hungarian fighters and bombers.[3]

Főhadnagy Szakonyi remembered the difficult moments:

> Suddenly, I hear a loud bang, and the inside of the aircraft fills with bitter, pungent smoke. We have been hit. For a moment, I notice the green Rata underneath us, which is trying to get away with a sharp turn out of our firing range. The red star shines brightly on its side. He was our attacker. I notice a hole on my glove just over my right wrist; a few drops of blood drip from it. When I take a look, I see there is a place as large as a cent where my skin has come off. I am unbelievably lucky as the bullet has only bruised me! … The party goes on in the meantime. First, my turret machine gun fires again; then my belly machine gun joins the fight again, firing short clicking bursts as if answering each other. It seems the situation is worsening at the rear; maybe my attacker is no longer alone. I am able to reach a low flying cloud to hide in, if only for a few seconds. … Thank God, there is no problem yet; we have managed to ward off all attacks. But how long can we keep them at bay in this uneven fight? At last, I reach the more intense rain clouds. It is in time. When we are in, one of my gunners, *szakaszvezető* Mester, runs forward and reports delightedly that they have managed to shoot down two Ratas. … This uneven combat has now been going on for more than 10 minutes; the poor bomber pilot has no other job than to fly his aircraft calmly, a living target for the enemy fighters. I am well aware that every Rata fighter wants to shoot me down. But their plan does not seem to be working this time. Now my observer, *hadnagy* L. Pajtás, waves at me from the nose of the aircraft and shows me a notebook with a large hole in the middle. It was shot through while he was holding it in his hand. He shows the

3 Becze, *'Kőr Ász'*, pp. 41–46.

The Ca.135 B-542, ready to take off for a combat sortie in the summer of 1942. The airmen were usually very superstitious, and they did not like to be photographed before going on a mission; they considered this a bad omen. (From the author's collection)

> number 10 with his fingers, indicating the number of bullet holes the observer position received from every direction. … The combat will soon be over; in front of me, there is a large, unified, greyish-black cloud base. If we can keep ourselves together until then, we will be saved. A few more bursts are shot; then, silence around me. We are in milky white fog, surrounding and protecting us. It is in time, because our ammunition is starting to get low. The crew is smiling; we are saved. Now, my radio operator and gunner, *őrmester* Bánkuti, comes forward and brags that he has also shot down a Rata. That is three in all. But it could be even more; we have just seen three falling down in smoke.[4]

Apart from the kills reported by the crew, the escorting Hungarian CR.42s also shot two Soviet fighters down from behind the Caproni, which was considered to be an easy target and thus acted as a magnet for Soviet fighters. The Hungarian bomber received more than 30 splinters and 7.62 machine gun hits from anti-aircraft fire and during the air combat, but fortunately, none of them hit the vital parts of the aircraft or the crew members.[5]

Pajtás was also very interested in theoretical questions, as shown by the two studies he published in the *Magyar Katonai Szemle* (Hungarian Military Review) during this period, both based on his personal experiences gained during 1941.[6] According to the diary of *őrnagy* Mocsáry, he was the most receptive officer regarding mathematical questions in 4 Bomber Group at Debrecen.[7] This interest in theory probably led to his being given another observer position in 1942 instead of being made a pilot, a decision he clearly did not like, as his comrades remembered. He shared the position of chief observer with *hadnagy* Dezső Tóth, the observer of *százados* András Inokai (the commander of 4/1 Bomber Squadron).

4 Lajos Raczkó and István Jánosy, *A légierők haditudósítói jelentik…* (Budapest: Stádium, 1943, 2nd edition), pp. 140–142.
5 István Szakonyi, 'Bombáztuk Nyikolajevet', *Magyar Szárnyak*, 15 March 1942, pp. 11–13.
6 *Hadnagy* László Pajtás, 'Fényképészfeladatok a háromszögmegoldó tárcsával,' *Magyar Katonai Szemle*, 1941:9, pp. 676–687; *hadnagy* László Pajtás, 'A bombázórepülők felderítő feladatai', *Magyar Katonai Szemle*, 1942:3, pp. 563–571.
7 Wartime diary of *őrnagy* István Mocsáry from 1942 (full copy owned by the author), note on 24 June 1942.

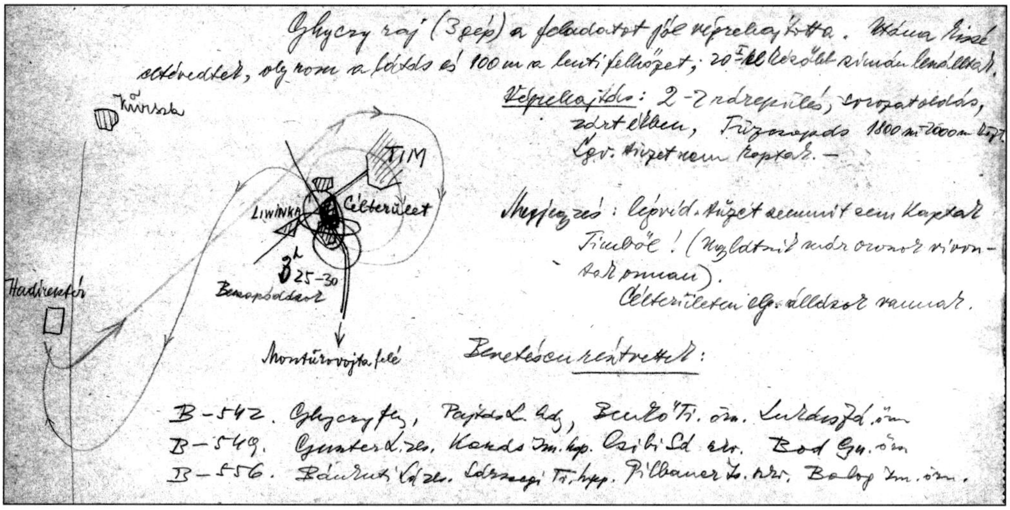

Diary entry of *őrnagy* István Mocsáry regarding the first combat sortie from 1942 of *hadnagy* László Pajtás on 1 July 1942. (From the collection of the Mocsáry family)

Pajtás himself flew with *hadnagy* Tihamér Ghyczy, the deputy commander of 4/1 Bomber Squadron in 1942. The further crew members of the aircraft B-542, were *őrmester* Tibor Benkő, wireless operator, and *őrmester* János Lukács János, mechanic. The 4 Bomber Group – consisting of the group staff and 4/1 Squadron – was deployed to the Eastern Front at the end of June 1942 to support the Hungarian 2nd Army. During their destination flight, they brought another mechanic, who was not a flying crewmember: *szakaszvezető* Károly Resetál.[8]

The mechanical problems haunting the Capronis are well demonstrated by the fact that the crew was unable to carry out their first combat sortie (on the morning of 30 June 1942) because the aircraft's undercarriages could not be retracted, and oil from the Caproni was dripping away; they were thus forced to return after a large circle. Their first completed combat sortie took place on 1 July 1942 at dawn, during which they attacked targets 6km southwest of Tim.[9]

Hadnagy László Pajtás flew approximately two dozen Ca.135 combat sorties between June and October 1942, and in September 1942 also worked as a liaison officer with the ground forces during the third Uriv–Storozhevoye bridgehead battle.

After returning from the front in November 1942, a decision was made to retrain the unit using modern Junkers Ju 88 bombers. Pajtas completed his type retraining in the spring of 1943 in Southern France, at Istres airfield north of Marseille. In Istres, Pajtás was retrained as a pilot for Ju 88s, so he was at last able to fly as a pilot on the front. In the meantime, he was promoted to *főhadnagy* on 1 May 1943.

After completing the retraining course, 4/1 Squadron was deployed to the airfield at Kharkhiv-Osnova. At the end of May 1943, Pajtas began to fly combat sorties with the new type, this time as a dive-bomber.

8 Wartime diary of *őrnagy* István Mocsáry from 1942, note on 22 June 1942.
9 Wartime diary of *őrnagy* István Mocsáry from 1942, note on 30 June and 1 July 1942.

The Junkers Ju 88 A-4 dive-bomber of László Pajtás on the airfield at Kharkhiv-Osnova in a box in the summer of 1943. The insignia of 4/1 '*Boszorkány*' Squadron a witch flying on a broom can clearly be seen on the nose of the aircraft. (From the author's collection)

Sometime during the summer of 1943, *főhadnagy* Pajtás committed a heroic deed (the details of which are unfortunately lost). As a result, he was recommended for the *Magyar Tiszti Arany Vitézségi Érem* by the Hungarian Air Brigade. Upon this recommendation, he received the *Magyar Érdemrend lovagkeresztje hadiszalagon a kardokkal* instead of the *Magyar Tiszti Arany Vitézségi Érem*. Sometime during the summer, he achieved another two aerial victories with his crew, possibly these victories may have been achieved during the same outstanding combat sortie.[10] Unfortunately, no details of his aerial victories of 1943 survive; only the bare facts are known.

Although the majority of the airmen of 4/1 Bomber Squadron were sent home from the front in August 1943, a few crews remained (Pajtás's among them). Along with the replacement 3 Bomber Group (in other words, 3/1 Squadron strengthened with the group commander's flight), they continued their intensive combat activity.

Főhadnagy Pajtás took off on his last combat sortie on 1 December 1943, from which he never returned. His Ju 88 A-4 (B.135, WNr. 300637) was hit by anti-aircraft artillery and crashed north of Korosten, at the village of Vaskovichi, along the Korosten–Ovruch railroad. The plane was destroyed and the whole crew – *főhadnagy* Pajtás, pilot; *zászlós* Antal Götz, observer (but also trained as a pilot); *tizedes* Zoltán Bartos, wireless operator; and *őrvezető* János Garai, mechanic – was killed.[11]

One of the eyewitnesses in the formation wrote in his diary about the death of Pajtás and his crew:

> This is a very sad day for us. On our first mission, we have lost one of our aircraft (*fhdgy.* Pajtás, *zls.* Götz and two other men), which was hit while diving down and exploded on impact on the ground. It is a very sad report: we have completed the mission, but one of our aircraft did not return. But we must not be sad – we need to rest in God's will.[12]

10 *HM HIM HL*, recommendations for decorations, group 180.a, acc. nr. 15.
11 *HM HIM HL*, HM 603379/22.o.-1944, Bundesarchiv-Militärarchiv RL 2 III/1196/96.
12 Wartime diary of *főhadnagy* Kornél Majoros, 1943 (original owned by the author).

According to a contemporary note, the crew members – excluding Pajtás – were buried in Zhitomir, but this must be false. As the above diary entry notes, the aircraft crashed in the target area, that is, an area in Soviet hands, so his own forces were not able to bury Pajtás. This would not have been possible even if the Ju 88 had crashed on own territory, as there would not be much to bury from an aircraft's crew that had crashed to the ground with great speed, loaded with bombs and fuel, exploding on impact. This is why László Pajtás never had a registered grave.

Ground-Attack Ace

SZAKASZVEZETŐ JÁNOS RÓZA

Number of aerial victories: 5 (+3)
Successes against ground targets: 5+ armored fighting vehicles, 10+ motor vehicles + ? (very successful)
Number of flown combat sorties: over 180
Number of hours flown in the air force: 800[1]
Nickname: *Jani*
Identification number: 1368-22-0069

Decorations

- *Magyar Nagy Ezüst Vitézségi Érem* (20 January 1945)
- *Magyar Kis Ezüst Vitézségi Érem* (22 February 1944)
- *Magyar Bronz Vitézségi Érem* (18 January 1943)
- *Tűzkereszt I fokozata a kardokkal és koszorúval*
- German Iron Cross 1st Class (summer 1944)
- German Iron Cross 2nd Class (November 1943)
- Gold *Frontflugspange* (1945)

Victories

Number	Date	Aircraft	Location
1	14 December 1944	La-5	
2	14 December 1944	La-5	
3	22 January 1945	Yak-9	Ráckeresztúr
–	4 February 1945	Yak-3?	
4	7-10 April 1945	Soviet fighter	
5	7-10 April 1945	Soviet fighter	
–	1945	Soviet aircraft	
–	1945	Soviet aircraft	

1 A contemporary document, found by the author contains this flight hours number, but accoring to the author's estimate, it must be approximately 200 hours less.

Enlisted trainees of the *HMNRA* receiving primary flight training on the airfield at Debrecen-Nyulas in the summer of 1941. In the middle, in white, is Dr Károly Stepper, their chief instructor. János Róza kneels besides Stepper on the left, and on the far right stands Lajos Krascsenics. Behind the group, the Klemm Kl 31 type four-seated courier aircraft of the *HMNRA* can be seen (registration HA-NAB). (From the author's collection)

János Róza is sitting on the neck of his fellow student and friend, Gyula Szilaj Varga, pushing a wooden pipe in his mouth on the Nyulas airfield in the summer of 1941. Gyula Szilaj Varga (1922–2005) served in short-range reconnaissance, fast bomber and target tug units in the war. (From the author's collection)

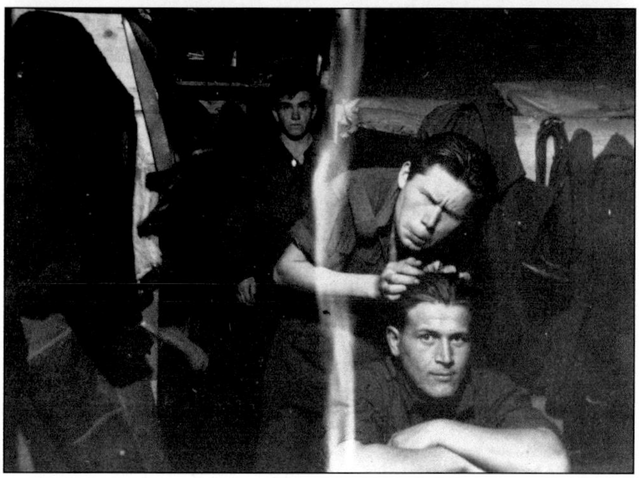

János Csizmadia, Sándor Loós and János Róza in 1942 in a barrack in Veszprém are making fun for the photographer (Loós is searching for fleas in Róza's hair, like monkeys do). From the enlisted, primary flight training class of 1941, 12 airmen were sent to dive-bomber combat training, and eight of them did not survive the war. These three pilots were among the four survivors. (From the author's collection)

Aircraft flown
Ju 87 D-5: B-705 (summer 1944), Fw 190 F-8: W-530 (beginning of 1945)

János Róza was born on 28 October 1922 in the village of Mohora in Nógrád County, the elder son of a farming family of two children. His family soon moved to Budapest in the hope of a better life; he was brought up there and attended elementary school in the capital. After completing four years of state civic school (*polgári iskola*), he acquired a car mechanic assistant certificate in 1940, at the workshop of the Erdős brothers.

Answering the call of the *HMNRA,* he applied for the primary flight training, which he completed at the *HMNRA* Debrecen-Nyulas group in the summer of 1941, in the same group as Lajos Krascsenics.[2] He was sent to the *Regvi* in Szombathely during the autumn, and then – as he had been put forward for bomber combat training – he took the bomber course in Veszprém, where he retrained to Ju 86s, Ca.135s and Ju 87s.

Róza became a member of the first Hungarian dive-bomber squadron established at Kolozsvár, which received the unit number 2/2 in the spring of 1943, under command of *százados* Jenő Korosy – without aircraft, for the time being. The unit deployed to the Eastern Front in June 1943, where they received further training in the area of Kiev; the Germans mainly trained them in close formation flight tactics, because the concentrated fire from the gunners was the most effective protection against the Soviet fighters, who were becoming more numerous and more dangerous adversaries.

The squadron finished its training flights at the end of July and was deployed to Gomel with their new Ju 87 D-3s to support the Hungarian occupational forces. Their first missions were flown against the partisans on 1 August 1943. As of 10 August, the Hungarian squadron relocated to Poltava, where they were subordinated to the German II./St.G. 77 (led by *Hauptmann* Helmut Leicht) as the group's fourth squadron. After the lost battle of Kursk, the squadron mainly supported the combat activity around Kharkhiv. The squadron was in constant retreat and fought intensive combat operations; it had already completed over 1,000 combat sorties by 8 October. This very intensive period lasted until the end of that month, when the squadron was called back for replenishment as a result of their severe losses. Róza luckily survived all the missions of this tour of duty without ever being shot down. The lost pilots, however, mainly also came from the 1941 enlisted class, and were Róza's friends and classmates (including Miklós Arany, who died in July during a training flight; Gábor C. Veress, who was killed in September; and Lajos Dévényi and András Felvégi, who were killed in October during combat).[3]

The squadron's reinforcements were sent to the Eastern Front, but the squadron was withdrawn to Kolozsvár, and only returned to the front in the summer of 1944. This time, the Hungarian Ju 87 squadron was under the name 102 Dive-Bomber Squadron, commanded from the autumn onwards by *százados* Győző Lévay, who had been deputy commander to *százados* Korosy during the summer of 1943. The unit was deployed to the combat area in June with their new Ju 87 D-5s and began to fly combat sorties on 30 June, again subordinated to SG 77. Their

2 Csaba Becze, 'Haderőn kívüli repülőgép-vezetői kiképzés a *HMNRA* debreceni kiképzőkereténél 1941 aug. 1–okt. 21', *Magyar Szárnyak Évkönyv*, 2004, pp. 183–186.

3 For the Ju 87 Squadron, see Győző Lévay, 'A zuhanóbombázók (Zubók) rövid története,' *Magyar Szárnyak Évkönyv*, 1985, pp. 23–36; József Tarlós, *Légcsavarszélben. Egy volt hadirepülő visszaemlékezései* (Székesfehérvár: privately published, 1999), p. 194.

tour of duty for this year was shorter, and lasted until the beginning of August (Róza's wireless operator was at this time Kálmán Marosvölgyi).

Unfortunately, no data survives regarding any outstanding or extraordinary deeds or successful missions connected with Róza, because most of the related documents have been lost. We can, however, still quote an example of how brave and dauntless he was. In the morning of 9 July 1944, during a strafing run, a Soviet 37mm anti-aircraft gun shot down the aircraft of *százados* Lévay, who crash-landed with his smoking Ju 87 beyond the first lines, after he jettisoned his main landing gear struts. Seeing this, Róza instantly turned back to land near the aircraft and save his comrades. However, *százados* Lévay had landed in an extremely swampy area, where such an attempt was impossible to carry out – it would lead to the instant overturn of the aircraft. The commander therefore convinced his pilot to abort the attempt by gesticulating wildly. Without diminishing Róza's merits, it should be noted that such rescue attempts were much easier to do with Ju 87 then with Bf 109. We know a number of successful rescue attempts on the German side with this type, but only one successful attempt took place with a Bf 109 – the rescue of *hadnagy* Debrődy by Kenyeres.[4]

The squadron handed over its aircraft in August 1944 and returned home by train, first to Sárospatak, then to Börgönd. Here, they slowly retrained to Focke-Wulf Fw 190 from the second half of September. Even during the training, it was obvious that the new type was a perfect one for *szakaszvezető* János Róza.

The squadron received their new aircraft at the beginning of November, and (under the name of 102/1 Fighter-Bomber Squadron) flew its first mission with Fw 190 F-8s on 16 November. It was still fighting as late as 10 April 1945; they were later renamed a ground-attack squadron, and the documents also refer to it as such. On paper, a new ground attack wing was formed. However, only the first group's first two squadrons ever saw combat.[5]

Szakaszvezető János Róza on 14 December 1943, after he had successfully served his first tour of duty on the frontline. (From the author's collection)

Szakaszvezető János Róza in the summer of 1944 in front of his Ju 87 D-5. (From the collection of the Róza family)

4 Győző Lévay, 'Így is lehet vitát nyerni', *Magyar Szárnyak Évkönyv*, 1995, pp. 195–197.

5 For the detailed combat activity of the ground-attack aircraft (fighter-bombers) flying with the Fw 190s, see Csaba Becze, 'A 102 vadászbombázó osztály története I', *Magyar Szárnyak Évkönyv,* 2000, pp. 54–60; Becze, 'A 102 vadászbombázó osztály története II 1945', pp. 32–39.

Focke-Wulf Fw 190 F-8 ground-attack aircraft of 102/1 Fighter-Bomber Squadron at the airfield at Kemenesszentpéter at the beginning of January 1945. (From the collection of Sándor Banai)

MÉDAILLE COMMÉMORATIVE
DE LA CAMPAGNE D'INDOCHINE

ATTESTATION

Le Lieutenant Tavier Commandant la Compagnie des Bateaux Blindés du GENIE 71/4

Atteste que le : Caporal Roza Janos Mle : 78.154

a droit au port de la Médaille Commémorative de la campagne d'Indochine créée par le décret N° 53.722 du 1-8-53 (J. O. R. F. du 12-8-53).

Le Commandant de Compagnie

A S. P. 52.269 le 20 janvier 1954.

The certificate of János Róza on the reception of the Commemorative Medal of the Indochina Campaign (*Médaille Commémorative de la Campagne d'Indochine*). This commemorative medal did not come with the usual charter, but with a certificate issued by the commander stating that the given soldier had take part in the campaign. (From the collection of the Róza family)

Unfortunately, the full documentation for the 102, then 1/I, Ground-Attack Group is lost, but the fragmentary supplementary documentation that remains states that, in addition to their significant successes against ground targets, they shot down approximately one and a half dozen Soviet and two American aircraft during the last months of the war. Only one aerial victory confirmation has survived in an Air Force Order for the ground-attack squadrons, recording the success of *főhadnagy* Kázár on 22 December, in Air Force Order Nr. 1945/10.

Although the author has usually only taken official records and data into account, this has been impossible in this case because of the loss of the official documents. It would, however, be highly unfair to leave Róza out of this work; he was one of the most successful combat pilots of the Royal Hungarian Air Force. As one of his squadron comrades, Sándor Horváth, remembered, Róza shot down eight Soviet aircraft altogether by the end of the war. Of these, unfortunately, the exact details are known only for one, including a specific location. In the early afternoon of 22 January 1945, as confirmed by a note in the diary of *hadnagy* István Majoros (a pilot from the sister squadron who was killed on 14 March 1945), *szakaszvezető* Róza shot down a Yak-9 in air combat with Soviet fighters over Ráckeresztúr. We also have a war correspondent's report for this victory. In the case of Róza's other victories, the author was only able to collect approximate details, including dates and types.

According to the author, Róza flew around 110–120 Ju 87 and approximately 50–70 Fw 190 combat sorties, a total of slightly over 180. Besides his commander, Győző Lévay, he was the only pilot who served throughout the Ju 87 combat tours of 1943 and 1944 and the Fw 190 combat sorties of the winter of 1944/45 and the spring of 1945, and survived them all. The high number of his combat sorties definitely means significant successes; one can therefore safely assume that this young dive-bomber and ground-attack pilot was one of the most successful individual pilots of the Royal Hungarian Air Force during the Second World War.

Róza was taken POW in Austria by the Americans in May 1945. He soon returned to Budapest, where he and his girlfriend were employed for some time distributing foreign aid from UNRRA (United Nations Relief and Rehabilitation Administration. In October 1948, he emigrated to France via Austria, and on 28 October he joined the French Foreign Legion.

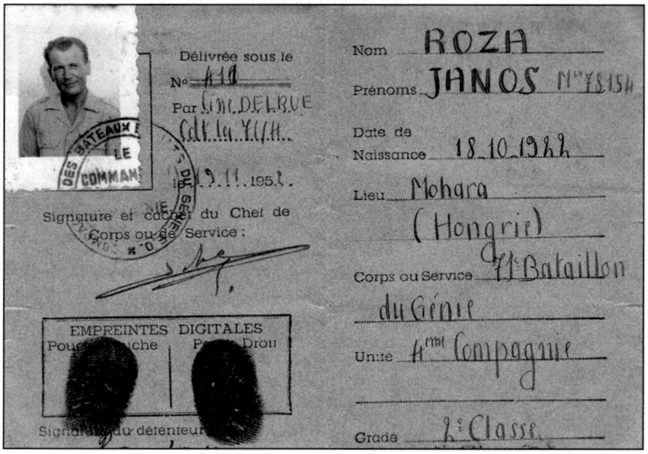
Délivrée sous le
Signature et cachet du Chef de Corps ou de Service :
EMPREINTES DIGITALES
Signature du détenteur
Nom ROZA
Prénoms JANOS
Date de Naissance 18.10.1922
Lieu Mohara (Hongrie)
Corps ou Service 71e Bataillon du Génie
Unité 4ème Compagnie
Grade 2e Classe

The identification card of János Róza in the French Foreign Legion. (From the collection of the Róza family)

During his five years of service, he spent three and a half years in French Indochina (from 18 December 1951 to 6 June 1955) with the Foreign Legion's 71st Pioneer Battalion's 4th Company, partly serving on armored riverboats. He was promoted twice: to *légionnaire de 1re classe* (1st class legionnaire) as of 1 May 1953, then to *caporal* (corporal) as of 1 October 1953. He received two commemorative medals for the Indochina Campaign (the *Médaille Coloniale* and the *Médaille Commémorative de la Campagne d'Indochine*). On 29 November 1957, two years after his discharge from the French Foreign Legion on 28 October 1955, he was naturalised and received French citizenship. Following his discharge, he settled in Algeria, where in July 1962 a civil war broke out following independence. He returned to France and worked as a businessman; as he had acquired a civilian pilot license, he was also able to fly. After his retirement, he resettled in Argentina.

János Róza died on 7 August 1991 in Pedro Luró (Buenos Aires province), and is laid to rest there.[6]

6 János Róza does not have a personal document folder in the Central Record Office of the HM-HIM; the correct biographical details were provided by his family, based on documents preserved by them.

Flying Under a Foreign Insignia: Ace in the *Luftwaffe*

A number of excellent pilots who served in the Second World War were of Hungarian origin, and the majority of them served in the *Luftwaffe*. Although this chapter has been compiled to introduce a pilot who was a Hungarian national, received his full training in Hungary and spent a significant time in the Royal Hungarian Air Force, later serving in the *Luftwaffe* and becoming an ace, he was not the only pilot with a Hungarian name in the various foreign air forces.

In addition, therefore, the author will also mention one pilot each of Hungarian origin from the German and from the American Air Forces, who also became aces.

Josef Fözö was born in Vienna on 7 November 1912. The family remained in Austria after the dissolution of the Austro-Hungarian Monarchy; even before the *Anschluss,* he had entered the Austrian Air Force and was automatically reassigned to the *Luftwaffe*. He flew his first combat sorties in the Spanish Civil War and achieved his first three aerial victories there, the first being over an I-16 on 18 September 1938. From 1939, he served in the JG 51 as *Staffelkapitän* (squadron commander), and from February 1941 he led I./JG 51 as *Gruppenkommandeur* (group commander) and achieved 24 more victories. On 2 July 1941, he was awarded the German Knight's Cross of the Iron Cross. He suffered major injuries in two air accidents and did not fly combat sorties again. He was a training unit commander and held the rank of *Major* at the end of the war. He died in Vienna on 4 March 1979.[1]

Donald Harlow Bochkay was born on 19 September 1916 in Ashtabula, Ohio, to an immigrant Hungarian family. He entered the USAF in 1940, started his training in 1941 and completed it in 1943. By the end of January 1944, he had collected 618 hours and 35 minutes of flight time (of this amount, 226 hours and 25 minutes were training time). As an outstanding pilot of 357th FG – the 'Yoxford Boys', stationed in England – he achieved altogether 13.83 confirmed victories between 5 March 1944 and 18 April 1945 while flying with different Mustang subtypes.[2] His last two aerial victories were scored over Me 262s. He ended the war as a Major and the commander of 363rd Fighter Squadron. After the war, he was discharged from active service, but flew again in the National Guards from 1956 and was promoted to Lieutenant Colonel on 15 April 1956. Donald Bochkay died on 9 January 1981 in Las Vegas.[3]

1 For Fözö, see Josef Fözö, *Freie Jagd von Madrid bis Moskau. Ein Fliegerleben mit Mölders* (Berlin: Verlag Wehrfront Alfred Becker, 1943), p. 294; Obermaier, *Die Ritterkreuzträger der Luftwaffe 1939–45*.

2 This strange number of victories is due to the fact that he also had a 'half' and a 'tierce' victory.

3 Olynyk, *Stars and Bars*, pp. 150–151.

ZÁSZLÓS BÉLA LIPCSEY (GERMAN *OBERLEUTNANT*)

Number of aerial victories: 7
Successes against ground targets: –
Number of flown combat sorties: n.d.a.
Number of hours flown in the air force: n.d.a.
Nickname: –
Identification number: 2900-19-0391

Decorations

- *Felvidéki Emlékérem*
- *Erdélyi Emlékérem* (?)
- German Iron Cross 1st Class (summer 1944)
- German Iron Cross 2nd Class (spring 1944)
- German Silver? *Frontflugspange* (1944)
- German Black Grade Wound Badge (1944)
- German Pilot Badge (1944)

Victories

Number	Date	Aircraft	Location
1	19 March 1944 at 14:05	B-24	Maribor SW
2	23 April 1944 at 14:10	P-38	Győr SW 43km
3	24 April 1944 at 13:55	B-17	Petershausen D (HSS München N)
4	12 May 1944 at 13:00	P-51	Gelnhausen S 20–25km
5	12 May 1944 at 13:03	P-51	Düdelsheim NW 12km (Gelnhausen)
6	16 June 1944 at 20:55	P-47 (Spitfire?)	Caen N
7	28 June 1944 at 20:20	P-47 (Spitfire?)	Tilly-sur-Seulles

Aircraft flown

Bf 109 G-6: WNr. 441141 (12 May 1944); no data is available on the markings of the aircraft

Béla Lipcsey was born on 11 September 1919 in Sátoraljaújhely, to a family of five children. His father, Tivadar Lipcsey, was a teacher.[4] Béla Lipcsey graduated in his hometown in June 1937 from the local Piarist high school. His admiration and devotion to aviation led him to apply to the Minister of Defense when he was in 8th grade to serve as a volunteer in the air force after graduation by reducing the required age to join (the required minimum age was 21).

His request was granted, thanks to his many supporting certificates and a thorough check of his physical abilities, and he entered the *Regvi* at Nyíregyháza on 5 October 1937 as a reserve officer candidate. He received his flight training there, which was completed on 26 September

4 *MNL Borsod-Abaúj-Zemplén Megye Levéltára* (National Archives, Borsod-Abaúj-Zemplén County Archives), XIV/3. documents of László Bibithy-Horváth, box nr. 2, XXXIII/1 state birth registry of the town of Sátoraljaújhely from 1919, counterpart, acc. nr. note 391.

1938 – the crowned golden eagle, the badge of Hungarian pilots, was presented to him on this date.[5] Two days later, the following was added to his aviation qualification document: 'He is very skilled and has a great sense for aviation. He needs to be monitored, however, because his self-confidence is greater than his knowledge or talents. His takeoffs and landings are carried out well, he is skillful in aerobatics and he has completed his training in less time than usual. He is a very good pilot.'[6]

Zászlós Béla Lipcsey, an excellent fighter pilot who was undeservedly forgotten, in Budapest in the autumn of 1939 (*HM HIM* Photographic Archives 97.196/005)

The young *hadapród őrmester* was sent to Kecskemét as of 1 October 1938 as part of 1/6 Fighter Squadron. From here, he was ordered to Börgönd to take the fighter training course, which he attended from 21 October 1938 to 14 March 1939 with excellent grades. Because of the military operations in *Kárpátalja* in March, he only completed his gunnery training between 17 April and 2 June 1939.

Meanwhile, his squadron relocated to Mátyásföld from Kecskemét in the middle of December 1939. As of 1 October 1939, Lipcsey was reassigned to 1/1 Fighter Squadron and promoted to *zászlós*. He also served in 1/4 Fighter Squadron from 1 October 1939 to 10 January 1940.

Főhadnagy László Tomor wrote as part of *zászlós* Lipcsey's aviation qualification for the period from 2 July 1939 to 10 December 1939:

> He has an excellent talent for aviation. He is energetic, skilled, brave, fine-handed in both aerobatics and air combat. He has an outstanding talent for formation flight, and he is capable of great achievements in this field. Excellent in gunnery. His fighting spirit is high, he loves aviation very much. An excellent fighter pilot.[7]

At 1/1 '*Ricsi*' (former '*Íjász*') Fighter Squadron, stationed in Mátyásföld, and led by *százados* Aladár Negró (from December 1940 Szobránczy), Lipcsey also served as the deputy engineering officer under Pál Irányi. The squadron relocated to the airfield of Kolozsvár-Szamosfalva after the Second Vienna Award in September 1940, where they remained permanently (the relocation was officially dated 31 October). They were renumbered there to 2/3 Squadron (the squadron's name, '*Ricsi*', remained, after the enormous Great Dane of Aladár Szobránczy). Here in Kolozsvár, at the beginning of 1941, an event forced Lipcsey to quit the Royal Hungarian Air Force. According to a surviving abstract of a penalty record, he abandoned his position on two

5 *HM HIM KI*, document folder nr. 52881.
6 *HM HIM KI*, document folder nr. 52881.
7 *HM HIM KI*, document folder nr. 52881.

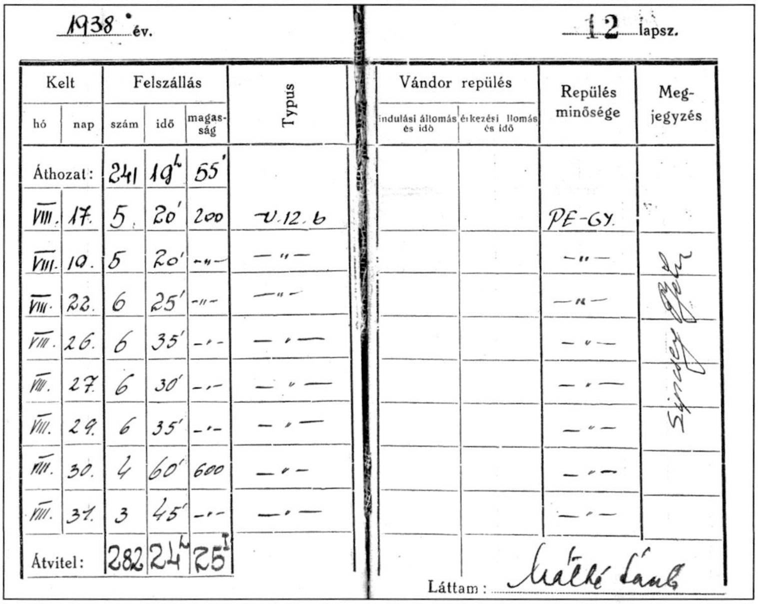

1938. év | 12. lapsz.

Kelt		Felszállás			Typus	Vándor repülés		Repülés minősége	Megjegyzés
hó	nap	szám	idő	magasság		indulási állomás és idő	érkezési állomás és idő		
Áthozat:		241	19h	55'					
VIII.	17.	5	20'	200	V.12.b			PE-GY.	
VIII.	19.	5	20'	-"-	-"-			-"-	Lipcsey Béla
VIII.	22.	6	25'	-"-	-"-			-"-	
VIII.	26.	6	35'	-"-	-"-			-"-	
VIII.	27.	6	30'	-"-	-"-			-"-	
VIII.	29.	6	35'	-"-	-"-			-"-	
VIII.	30.	4	60'	600	-"-			-"-	
VIII.	31.	3	45'	-"-	-"-			-"-	
Átvitel:		282	24h	25'					

Láttam: Máthé László

Logbook of László Máthé from August 1938; the flight supervisor is Béla Lipcsey. (From the collection of László Máthé)

occasions at the beginning of 1941 – not with the intention to desert, but without the consent of his superiors. Because of this, he was under remand from 31 March to 22 June 1941, and this caused his discharge from the air force.[8] However, a former squadron comrade of him and someone who knew him well told a completely different story to the author.

As Béla Lipcsey is long dead and has no close living relatives who could confirm or refute this story, the author provides this account based on memories.

According to the memories of his comrade, when they were relocating to Szamosfalva, some of the Romanian fuel left there was distributed among those who had a personal car. In 2/3 Squadron, this applied to two people: Lipcsey and the squadron commander. Lipcsey's fiancée was from Székesfehérvár and, because of the large distances involved in visiting her, he used up his amount of fuel quite quickly; Negró, in contrast, who only drove his car around Kolozsvár, had almost all the remaining fuel. Negró's home was open to his comrades, and his big Great Dane, Ricsi, knew them all and let them enter at any time of the day. According to the storyteller, Lipcsey saw that Negró had almost all his fuel left in the basement. Perhaps he thought Negró did not even need it, so he started to carry it off during the night. When Negró noticed his fuel was missing, he beat his dog, who did not let Lipcsey go the next night but caught him, thus revealing who was carrying off the fuel. Following this, his squadron commander offered Lipcsey two choices: either he requested his discharge or he would face a court-martial. Lipcsey chose the first option, and according to the memories of his comrade everything was done very silently and quickly. The whole process lasted just two days, and Lipcsey left Kolozsvár discreetly for Budapest (the longer remand was not mentioned in this reminiscence).[9]

8 *HM HIM KI*, document folder nr. 52881.

9 This former comrade– who had already passed away – considering the delicate nature of the issue, requested that his name not be mentioned.

The Italian Edmondo Lenzi between *zászlós* Albert Seres (on the left) and *zászlós* Béla Lipcsey (on the right) on the airfield at Mátyásföld in 1939. Lenzi arrived from Torino as an engineer together with the Fiat CR.42s to 1/3 Fighter Squadron, and helped with the instalment of the new aircraft. Albert Seres was the most successful pilot of the squadron during the campaign against the Soviet Union in 1941, with four confirmed aerial victories. Of these, the first was credited to him as a shared victory with *szakaszvezető* Lajos Göcsei (*HM HIM* Photographic Archives 97.196/100)

Béla Lipcsey officially resigned from his *zászlós* rank as of 1 May 1941. Following this, he was placed in the reserve of 2 Supplementary Fighter Squadron as a private. As of 2 July 1942, he was completely removed from the Air Force and was reassigned into the 2/III Infantry Battalion.[10]

Béla Lipcsey was a kind, funny, and extremely popular pilot, and everybody loved him in his squadron. They were very sorry to see him leave, especially his squadron commander, Aladár Szobránczy, for whom – even despite what had happened with the fuel, according to his comrade – he was a favorite, not only because he was charming, but also because, as shown by his earlier qualifications, he was an excellent pilot and a very talented airman.

At his discharge, Lipcsey had no military decorations. The *Felvidéki Emlékérem* was given to him on 6 December 1939. He was entitled to wear the *Erdélyi Emlékérem* also, but by the time these were awarded to the pilots, Lipcsey had already been discharged, and therefore it is not certain that he actually received his medal (the documents regarding the award of his medal were not found among his surviving personal files).[11]

The grudge he held because of his discharge – even if it had been his own fault – probably remained with him for the rest of his life. However, he later made his name again in a spectacularly unique way. Unfortunately, the author has not been able to find any information about what he was doing in Hungary during the 1941–43 period, but he probably did not turn away from sports aviation entirely. However, in 1944, he was a military pilot again in the *Luftwaffe*, which

10 *HM HIM KI*, document folder nr. 52881.
11 *HM HIM KI*, document folder nr. 52881.

he joined voluntarily, serving under the name of Adalbert von Lipcsey, initially as *Oberfeldwebel*. In his German personal files, his first registered unit was the *Luftgau-Kommando XVII* (Vienna Air District Command). Maybe he was an interpreter for its commander, the *Kommandeur der Luftgautruppen XVII*, or (more plausibly) this refers to *Flieger-Ersatz-Bataillon XVII* stationed at Vienna-Seyring, where he was stationed for a few months waiting for his permanent unit to serve (this reserve air battalion was mostly responsible for replenishing the personnel of the district's air units).[12]

The unit to which he was assigned in the end was I./JG 27, which made itself famous in North Africa and which was stationed on the airfield of Fels am Wagram since August 1943. The 'Star of Africa', Hans-Joachim Marseille, who had one of the most outstanding individual air records in the war, had earlier flown with the third squadron of this group.[13] The unit was deployed in combat from the second half of February 1944 and fought against both 8th AAF operating from British territory and 15th AAF operating from Southern Italy.[14]

Lipcsey was assigned to the second squadron, and his commander was *Hauptmann* Josef Jansen. His first combat sortie in the I./JG 27 was probably flown at the end of February 1944, during the 'Big Week', the American offensive aimed at the German aircraft production and defeating the *Luftwaffe's* fighter arm.

Lipcsey achieved his first confirmed aerial victory on 19 March 1944 in the early afternoon, when he shot down one of the Liberator heavy bombers of 454th Bombardment Group over Slovenia, southwest of Maribor, at an altitude of 6,000 meters. This was the first American four-engined heavy bomber destroyed by a Hungarian pilot. His second victory was achieved in Hungarian airspace on 23 April 1944. The German group was attacking a Liberator formation escorted by Lightnings southwest of Győr. In the air combat, fought with the escort fighters, his squadron lost two killed, while Lipcsey reported shooting down a P-38. The 306th Fighter Wing did not report any total Lightning-losses over enemy territory that day, so the aircraft was probably just damaged. Indeed a number of the Lightnings of 1st FG were damaged during the air combat.[15]

His third victory was scored the next day, on 24 April, when he shot down a B-17 of 8 AAF north of Munich. This kill is somewhat controversial in German sources: officially it was confirmed as a full value kill, but in the unit history it is listed as a Herausschuss (HSS).[16]

Lipcsey was reassigned on 12 May from 2./JG 27 to 1./JG 27, the commander of which (until he was wounded on 28 May) was *Hauptmann* Josef Jansen, who had also been reassigned to this squadron in April.[17]

12 Bundesarchiv-Militärarchiv, personal document folder of Adalbert von Lipcsey.
13 For Hans-Joachim Marseille (Berlin, 30 December 1919–Sidi Abdel Rahman, 30 September 1942), see Obermaier, *Die Ritterkreuzträger der Luftwaffe 1939–45*, p. 20.
14 Bundesarchiv-Militärarchiv, personal document folder of Adalbert von Lipcsey; Jochen Prien, Peter Rodeike, and Gerhard Stemmer, *Messerschmitt Bf 109 im Einsatz bei Stab und I./Jagdgeschwader 27* (Eutin: Struve Druck, 1998), p. 606.
15 Prien, Rodeike, and Stemmer, *Messerschmitt Bf 109 im Einsatz bei Stab und I./Jagdgeschwader 27*, pp. 397–398; John D. Mullins, *An Escort of P-38s. The 1st Fighter Group in World War II* (St. Paul, MN: Phalanx, 1995), p. 111.
16 Prien, Rodeike, and Stemmer, *Messerschmitt Bf 109 im Einsatz bei Stab und I./Jagdgeschwader 27*, pp. 389–390, 397–399.
17 Prien, Rodeike, and Stemmer, *Messerschmitt Bf 109 im Einsatz bei Stab und I./Jagdgeschwader 27*, p. 404.

On 12 May 1944, the Americans launched another large-scale air raid against the Third Reich, which resulted in heavy air battles. The I./JG 27 was thrown into combat north of Frankfurt and met a B-17 formation soon after 12:30 east of Eschborn. They reported shooting down three B-17s, another two shot out of formation and also a final destruction,[18] before the 'Mustang-cloud' could arrive. This was Lipcsey's time; in short succession, he shot down two American fighters. His victims were probably from the aircraft of 357th Fighter Group belonging to Captain John B. Carder (P-51B, serial number 42-106777), who had seven air victories and who bailed out near Bischoffen, east of Herborn, and was captured; and 2nd Lieutenant Roger A. Hilsted (P-51B, serial number 43-6634), who was killed. On their part, 357th FG reported shooting down 14 German fighters on this day.[19]

After Lipcsey fought his own personal war with the Mustangs, he crash-landed his Messerschmitt (Bf 109 G-6, WNr. 441141) at Altenburg because the aircraft had been badly damaged by the American fighters. (The I./JG 27 suffered 10 total losses on 12 May, and five other Messerschmitts were also damaged to various degrees; the wounded pilots included the group commander, *Major* Ludwig Franzisket.)[20] The Hungarian pilot was also wounded, and although some sources indicate he was seriously wounded, it could not have been true, because he was flying again in June. Lipcsey returned to his squadron after a short stay in hospital, probably at the beginning of June. Meanwhile, he was promoted to *Leutnant* as of 1 June.[21]

On 6 June, the Allied forces landed in Normandy. Different units of the *Reichsverteidigung* were immediately alerted, and their relocation to French territories immediately began. The I./JG 27 relocated to France on 7 June, to the airfield of Vertus, south of Reims, from whence they went on a mission for the first time on 10 June. Their task was mainly to protect their own troops and fight against the Allied fighter-bombers, which were deployed in huge numbers.[22]

During June, Béla Lipcsey reported shooting down two P-47s during two twilight missions. The first took place on 16 June at 20:55 north of Caen, at an altitude of 1,200–1,400 meters. This aircraft might have been a P-47D of 9th AAF, probably from 405th FG. Its pilot, 2nd Lieutenant Schallehn, avoided being captured and reached the Allied lines; albeit this aircraft was hit perhaps by anti-aircraft artillery,[23] although he more probably shot down a British Spitfire and reported the type erroneously (another pilot in his unit noted that he was engaged in combat with Spitfires, and the German group reported three victories, two over 'P-47Ds' and one over a Spitfire, while they each lost a missing and a woulded pilot). The 443 Squadron

18 The final destruction (*endgültige Vernichtung*) on the German side meant shooting down a damaged four-engined aircraft – which, in many cases, had previously been shot out of the formation – and a smaller number of points were allocated for such a victory. On the Hungarian side, this category did not exist.

19 NARA MACR 4700 and 4701. For 357 Fighter Group, see Merle C. Olmsted, *To War with the Yoxford Boys: The Complete Story of the 357th Fighter Group* (Hamilton, MT: Eagle Editions, 2004). For John B. Carder, see also Olynyk, *Stars and Bars,* pp. 179–80.

20 For Ludwig Franzisket (Düsseldorf, 26 June 1917–Münster, 23 November 1988), see Obermaier, *Die Ritterkreuzträger der Luftwaffe 1939–45*, p. 113.

21 Prien, Rodeike, and Stemmer, *Messerschmitt Bf 109 im Einsatz bei Stab und I./Jagdgeschwader 27*, pp. 403–404.

22 Prien, Rodeike, and Stemmer, *Messerschmitt Bf 109 im Einsatz bei Stab und I./Jagdgeschwader 27*, pp. 446–448.

23 John C. McManus, *The Americans at Normandy* (New York, NY: Forge Books, 2004), pp. 152–153.

of the 2nd TAF[24] lost four Spitfire Mk. IXs, and 274 Squadron of the ADGB[25] lost one further Spitfire around this time in this area (partly while in combat with the Fw 190s of I./JG 1). The 28-year-old commander of the unit, Squadron Leader James Dickie Hall was among the three killed pilots from the Canadian 443 Fighter Squadron.[26]

Lipcsey's last confirmed aerial victory was achieved on 28 June, again in the evening, at 20:20 over Tilly-sur-Seulles at an altitude of 1,200 meters. According to the author's research, on this day, at this time and in this area there were no American P-47 losses, so this kill was either an overclaim or actually a Spitfire: one of the aircraft of 411 Squadron of the 2nd TAF was damaged around this time in the area. In the invasion area German fighters often overclaimed massively, and in many cases the sources and documents are so chaotic from this period that it is nearly impossible to follow what could have happened exactly. Besides, pilots who had never met Spitfire and P-47 fighters before frequently confused the two types because of their similar elliptic wing structure, and this makes it even more difficult to pinpoint what happened.[27]

Lipcsey's squadron suffered heavy losses in men and aircraft during this month. The appointed commander of the unit, *Leutnant* Horst Grimm, was among the four pilots killed on 12 June, and the same combat activity with heavy losses continued in July. On 2 July, Spitfires shot down Lipcsey's wingman, *Unteroffizier* Günther Wiegmann (the skilled young pilot scored four victories before his death).[28] But in the middle of July Lipcsey was reassigned as a fighter instructor to the *Jagdgruppe West* (commander: *Hauptmann* Herbert Wehnelt). Lipcsey was assigned to the second squadron stationed in Pomerania at the airfield of Stargard-Klützow, so he did not take part in further combat. As of 1 October, he was promoted to *Oberleutnant*, and from the middle of October he was reassigned from 2./JGr West to 14.(Erg.)/JG 1. His task as an instructor was unchanged, and he lived to see the end of the war near Holzkirchen, Bavaria. He soon disappeared from the prisoner of war camp, leaving behind him his German comrades, who soon received a postcard from him postmarked Brazil, but they never heard from Lipcsey again.[29]

His German comrades remembered loving and honoring him as a great pilot and comrade. The surviving documents of I./JG 27 mention him as one of the most outstanding and successful pilots of the given period (the spring and early summer of 1944).[30] The unit history written by Hans Ring and Werner Girbig in the 1970s credits Lipcsey with eight air victories, of which three were against four-engined bombers.[31] The author has not found any traces of a possible

24 The 2nd TAF (Tactical Air Force) was created for the tactical air support of the British ground forces and their allies in the summer of 1943 and remained operational under the same name until 1959.

25 Air Defense of Great Britain (ADGB): the command of the Royal Air Force responsible for the air defense of the British Isles, operational between 1925–36 and 1943–44.

26 Prien, Rodeike, and Stemmer, *Messerschmitt Bf 109 im Einsatz bei Stab und I./Jagdgeschwader 27*, pp. 454–5, 575; Christopher Shores and Thomas Chris, *2nd Tactical Air Force Volume One Spartan to Normandy June 1943 to June 1944* (Hersham: Classic Publications, 2004), pp. 164–165.

27 Prien, Rodeike, and Stemmer, *Messerschmitt Bf 109 im Einsatz bei Stab und I./Jagdgeschwader 27*, pp. 458, 575; Shores and Chris, *2nd Tactical Air Force Volume One*, pp. 183–184.

28 Prien, Rodeike, and Stemmer, *Messerschmitt Bf 109 im Einsatz bei Stab und I./Jagdgeschwader 27*, p. 459.

29 Letter of Sighart Dinkel (Traditionsverband JG 27) to the author, 7 April 2005.

30 Bundesarchiv-Militärarchiv RL 10/538; letter of Sighart Dinkel (Traditionsverband JG 27) to the author, 7 April 2005.

31 Hans Ring, and Werner Girbig, *Jagdgeschwader 27* (Stuttgart: Motorbuch Verlag, 1972), 2nd edition, p. 309.

eighth victory, and considers, therefore, that this data may have been a typing error. Lipcsey always stressed his Hungarian nationality while in the *Luftwaffe* and demanded that his German comrades call him Béla, not Adalbert, the German version of his name.

Béla Lipcsey emigrated to Brazil via France in the autumn of 1945, and from there he went to Argentina in 1946. He then moved back to Brazil and settled in São Bernardo do Campo which is a suburb of São Paulo and began working as an engineer (which he had given as his profession on the emigration documents in 1945). No documentation on him is kept by the archives of the *Budapesti Műszaki és Gazdaságtudományi Egyetem* (Budapest Technical University) to show that Lipcsey had ever been a student of the university before 1945; probably he stated this profession in his documents to gain a visa more easily. His family emigrated from Hungary and also settled in Brazil; they ran a small sewing workshop in Porto Alegre. The last official mention of Béla Lipcsey can be found at the end of October 1961 from Brazil: an eviction statement.[32] Lipcsey neither demanded from Hungary nor from Germany that his military service time should be included for his pension after his retirement. According to Hungarian emigrants to Brazil, Lipcsey died at the end of the 1980s in São Bernardo do Campo, and was also buried there.[33]

32 *Diário Oficial do Estado de São Paulo*, 31 October 1961, p. 42.

33 The author has long sought traces of Lipcsey and his family in Brazil; he has also been looking for any people who might have known them personally. Sadly, Lipcsey had no children; his widow died in 2008, and (according to the knowledge of the author) even his siblings had no children. This, combined with the lack of help from the local officials, has considerably hampered research. At last, the Cvitko family was able to help with a few details, for which the author would like to express his gratitude.

The Others

This section lists the fighter pilots (in alphabetical order and not according to the number of their air victories) who are erroneously listed in some publications as having five air victories, or who claimed five air victories in their own personal registry, and for whom at least two air victories were confirmed by either Air Force Orders or by witnesses. Apart from these airmen, the author knows of a number of pilots who personally registered five or more air victories, but the surviving documents have confirmed only one. The only exception here is József Nagy, because there were two pilots of that name in 101 Fighter Wing, both with one confirmed air victory, and this has caused much confusion. The fact they shared the exact same name and rank has not made it easy to clear these problems up, but the most important data on both can be found here, and in their detailed biography in the reference literature. I also mentioned in these short biographies the communist retributions after 1945 at the affected pilots.

SZÁZADOS GYÖRGY BÁNLAKY

Born: Budapest, 17 March 1913
Died: Gyirmót, 6 November 1944 (killed in action)

Victories

Number	Date	Aircraft	Location
1	16 December 1942	Il-2	Pavlovsk S
2	16 December 1942	Il-2	Pavlovsk S
3	2 November 1944	Il-2	Cegléd SE 15km

Hadnagy György Bánlaky graduated on 15 January 1939 with rank number 10 (in the same class as József Bejczy) and was assigned to Börgönd as part of 1 Fighter Wing. From here he was reassigned to 1/I Fighter Group in Szolnok in 1941. After the reorganization of the air force on 1 November 1941 (on which date he received his rank of *főhadnagy*), the Szolnok group became 1 Fighter Training Group. He remained on the strength of this unit until the summer of 1942. At that time he was deployed to the Eastern Front as deputy commander of 1/1 Squadron; he served there until the late spring of 1943. From Szolnok he was reassigned to Börgönd (as of 1 October 1943) as part of the fighter combat training department of the combat training group (*harckiképző-osztály vadászrepülő harckiképző részlege*). After the German occupation of Hungary on 19 March

1944, he was transferred with this department from Börgönd to Pápa at the end of March 1944, where he remained until the end of the summer. He was subsequently reassigned to Szolnok, where he took command of the newly formed 101/4 Fighter Squadron.[1]

During 1942 and 1943, as a member of 1/1 Fighter Squadron, Bánlaky flew 81 combat sorties on the Eastern Front; he flew four more combat sorties as commander of 101/4 Fighter Squadron in October and November 1944. A number of sources wrongly credit Bánlaky with seven air victories;[2] in reality, he achieved three confirmed victories, and there is no data regarding additional aerial victory claims by him.

Százados György Bánlaky was killed at noon on 6 November 1944 (12:00 exactly as per the casualty report, 12:15 according to the local police report) near Gyirmót, most probably because of hypoxia caused by the malfunctioning of his aircraft's oxygen system. There were no enemy hits, either on the aircraft or on the pilot's body.[3]

György Bánlaky as a young *hadnagy* in Szolnok. Bánlaky was one of the best Hungarian fighter leaders. (From the author's collection)

HADNAGY LAJOS BENKŐ

Born: Veszprém, 21 August 1920
Died: Veszprém, 20 July 1975

Victories

Number	Date	Aircraft	Location
1	24 May 1944	B-24	Over Austrian territory
–	26 June 1944	'1/2' P-38	Pápa N 18km (in personal notes)
2	2 July 1944	B-24	Pettendpuszta
3	7 July 1944	B-24	Felsőörs NW
–	16 July 1944	B-17	Mosonszentjános (deleted in Wing Order Nr. 1945/27)

1 *HM HIM KI*, document folder nr. 3452 (which only contains his registry file); István Csóka, 'Az 1942-es évfolyam rövid története (folytatás)', *Magyar Szárnyak Évkönyv*, 1992, pp. 213–214; also based on the data provided by István Csóka, 4 February 1998, and his recollections (a copy of the latter is owned by the author).

2 Gyula Sárhidai, 'Repülő ászok', in *Magyarország a második világháborúban: Lexikon A–Zs* (Budapest: Petit Real, 1996), p. 371; also see many of his published works.

3 *HM HIM HL*, HM 1945 8 nyv. oszt. 35346; *MNL Győr-Moson-Sopron Megye Győri Levéltára* (National Archives, Győr-Moson-Sopron County Archives) IV. B. 454/a, documents and administrative files of the vicecomes of Győr-Moson-Pozsony t. u. a. (temporarily unified for administrative reasons, k. e. e., '*közigazgatásilag egyelőre egyesített*') counties, box 388, report of the chief constable of the processus of Sokoróalja, 9 November 1944.

Hadnagy Lajos Benkő at the tail of his aircraft, early summer of 1944. *Hadnagy* Benkő was among the successful pilots against the Americans during 1944. (From the collection of the Benkő family)

Lajos Benkő graduated as *hadnagy* on 20 August 1943, as of 1 September 1943, with rank number 41.[4] Between 12 April 1944 and 22 February 1945, as a pilot in the *RKI* and then in 101/1 Fighter Squadron, *hadnagy* Benkő flew 44 combat sorties (27 against Americans). He was engaged in 14 air combats and scored three confirmed aerial victories; one additional was later deleted, and another shared victory was registered personally by him. Contemporary media credited him with six kills, but the author has not found any references to a sixth claim.[5] He was shot down twice during the war. On 7 August 1944, a Mustang shot him down over Vágvölgy and he bailed out of his Bf 109. Two days later, his own anti-aircraft artillery shot him down by error at Iszkaszentgyörgy; he again needed to bail out and was seriously wounded. After returning to his unit, from December 1944 to early March 1945 he was again sent to combat until he was grounded because of the Irányi issue.

Importantly, in 1956 Benkő's workplace was the *Magyar Ásványolaj és Földgáz Kísérleti Intézet* (Hungarian Oil and Gas Research Institute), where he was part of the *munkástanács* (workers' committee) and the commander of the factory's armed guard. After the fall of the Hungarian Revolution of 1956 he was therefore interned for a short time. In 1958, his rank was stripped and he was demoted to private. In 1991, he received a posthumous Commemorative Medal for his actions in 1956.

Upon the request and petition of the author, the Minister of Defense of Hungary restored the rank of Lajos Benkő as *hadnagy* in Order Nr. 1705/114-123/2017, as of 23 October 2017.[6]

4 *Honvédségi Közlöny (Személyes ügyek)*, nr.1943/48 (1 December 1943), after correction, p. 1710.

5 For example, see Lajos Kutasi Kovács, 'Levél egy begyulladt barátomhoz', *Összetartás*, 14 September 1944, p. 8.

6 For the life and military career of Lajos Benkő, see Becze, 'Benkő Lajos', pp. 13–31.

SZAKASZVEZETŐ LÁSZLÓ BOLDIZSÁR

Born: Foktő, 7 June 1922
Died: Kalocsa, 29 June 1984

Victories

Number	Date	Aircraft	Location
–	2 July 1944	P-38	Deleted in Wing Order Nr. 1945/27
1	30 July 1944	B-24	Nádasdladány
2	30 July 1944	B-24	Nádasdladány
–	5 November 1944	B-17	Deleted in Wing Order Nr. 1945/31
3	16 November 1944	La-5	Jászfelsőszentgyörgy

László Boldizsár received primary flight training in 1941. As a pilot of 101/3 Fighter Squadron, he flew approximately 60 combat sorties during 1944 and 1945, 15 against the Americans. A number of sources credit him with five air victories, but in 1945 two of his claims were deleted. He was the fourth pilot accompanying László Molnár on 30 July 1944 when three aces reported shooting out two Liberators from their formation. Boldizsár belly-landed twice: on 3 January 1945 at Vöröstó, and on 21 February 1945 at Bana.[7]

Szakaszvezető László Boldizsár was the pilot of 101/3 Fighter Squadron in 1944–45. '*Boldi*' flew a lot as wingman for the aces of the squadron. (From the collection of the Boldizsár family)

7 *HM HIM HL*, box 1122, microfilm, logs of 101/3 Fighter Squadron.

HADNAGY PÁL FORRÓ (GYERGYÁK)

Born: Nagykanizsa, 28 April 1920
Died: Fonyód, 13 November 1981

Victories

Number	Date	Aircraft	Location
1	14 June 1944	P-38	Pusztavám, Lippa well
–	14 June 1944	B-17	According to his own notes, not claimed/ unconfirmed
2	2 July 1944	B-24	Budapest SW?
–	2 July 1944	P-38	Deleted in Wing Order Nr. 1945/27
3	21 January 1945	Il-2	Pusztaszabolcs
–	14 March 1945 at 14:00	P-51	Ozora S (no witnesses; unconfirmed)
–	20 March 1945 at 11:51	Yak-9	Csór N 6-8km (no witnesses; unconfirmed)

The second from the left in the first row – between András Huszár and László Dániel – Pál Forró, a student of the *Repülőakadémia* in Veszprém in 1943. *Hadnagy* Forró was a successful pilot of 101/2 Fighter Squadron in 1944–45. (From the author's collection)

Pál Forró's original family name was Gyergyák, but he and his father Hungarianized this to Forró at the end of October 1943, directly before his graduation.[8] Pál Forró graduated on 6 December as *hadnagy*, as of 1 September 1943, with rank number 72.[9] *Hadnagy* Forró is credited in many sources with five aerial victories (according to his own register, he scored five or six victories over 68 combat sorties). In reality, *hadnagy* Forró had three confirmed kills, among these a four-engined, which is listed on the victory list against four-engines, but has not been traced in any surviving Air Force Orders – most probably it referred to a Liberator he shot down on 2 July. His first victory on 14 June 1944 was confirmed as a shared kill with *hadnagy* László Dániel. On 14 March 1945, he also reported a victory over a Mustang – his fourth aerial victory, according to the mission log of the wing, although he had no eyewitness to confirm it (this victory was not confirmed in a Wing Order at the end of the war). He was first shot down in a *Héja* on 13 April 1944, and bailed out near Ócsa. In the summer of 1944, with 101 Fighter Group, the Americans shot down his aircraft three times: on 14 June 1944 he belly-landed north of Várpalota; two days later, he crash landed his aircraft in Veszprém; and on 2 July 1944, he bailed out at Enying, when he was wounded.[10]

Pál Forró later served in the military aviation, which was reorganized after 1945. He was the fifth level defendant in the trial known as 'Barna Horváth and companions'; as a result, he was sentenced to 15 years in prison and demoted to private. He served his sentence from 3 March 1951 to 16 August 1956. Pál Forró was acquitted in 1958 when the case was renegotiated; he was rehabilitated, and in 1962 his former rank of *százados* was restored (he achieved this rank in 1950).[11]

SZAKASZVEZETŐ PÁL FÜLÖP

Born: Hajmáskér, 6 March 1924
Died: Himberg S 15km, 4 April 1945 (killed in action)

Victories

Number	Date	Aircraft	Location
1	20 January 1945 at 15:25	La-5	Seregélyes S (Seregélyes–Sárosd– Sárkeresztúr)
2	22 January 1945 at 11:00	Il-2	Szigetszentmiklós W 2km
–	22 January 1945	Il-2	
–	22 January 1945	La-5	
3	19 February 1945	La-5	Salka W

Pál Fülöp received his primary flight training in 1942. From the end of 1944, he served at the 101/5 Fighter Squadron; throughout 24 combat sorties he scored three confirmed aerial

8 *MNL Zala Megye Levéltára* (National Archives, Zala County Archives), XIV/3, documents of László Bibithy-Horváth, box nr. 2, XXXIII/1, state birth registry of the town of Nagykanizsa for 1920, counterpart, acc. nr. note 327, 213/1943 sz. UB.

9 *Honvédségi Közlöny* (*Személyes ügyek*), nr. 1943/48 (1 December 1943), p. 1708.

10 Based on the manuscript recollections of Pál Forró (copy owned by the author).

11 *HM HIM KI*, document folder nr. 20627.

victories, which were included in Wing Order Nr. 1945/62. However, according to his comrades, on 22 January 1945 he shot down not one, but three Soviet aircraft. If these further two kills had been incorporated in official documents, then the talented Fülöp would have been the youngest ace of the Royal Hungarian Air Force at the age of 20.[12] As it stands, however, the most efficient pilot in his class was not Fülöp but *szakaszvezető* László Kérges, who survived the war and achieved four confirmed aerial victories over 31 combat sorties (included in Wing Orders Nr. 1945/62 and 1945/67). The only reason Kérges is not featured here in his own right is that no data survives of him having one more claimed but unconfirmed victory.

Szakaszvezető Pál Fülöp was killed when his aircraft was shot down by anti-aircraft fire on 4 April 1945 at 08:20, 15km south of Himberg.[13]

Pál Fülöp as *őrvezető* in April 1943. The young pilot, who flew a comparatively small number of hours, nevertheless fought successfully at the beginning of 1945. (From the author's collection)

SZAKASZVEZETŐ JÓZSEF NAGY

Born: Tatabánya, 8 June 1922
Died: Tatabánya, 25 March 1983

Victories

Number	Date	Aircraft	Location
1	24 May 1944	B-24	Over Austrian territory
–	2 July 1944	B-24	Deleted in Wing Order Nr. 1945/27
–	22 August 1944	B-24	Lenti SE (according to his own notes)
–	5 November 1944	B-24	Deleted in Wing Order Nr. 1945/31

Szakaszvezető József Nagy ('Juju') received his primary flight training in 1941. He served in 2/1, then 101/1 Fighter Squadron (the latter unit originated from the former one). From his first sortie on 31 January 1944 until April 1945, he flew more than 60 combat sorties, 29 of them against Americans. Many sources credit him with five kills, as well as his own recollections. Official sources confirm one aerial victory for him. Certain deletions of victories in 1945 hit him hard because two of his Liberator kills (claimed and registered) were also deleted. He was shot down by the Americans twice: on 26 June 1944 near Vanyola, and a crash-landed on 2 July 1944 near Magyaralmás.

12 Pál Fülöp does not have a personal document folder in the Central Record Office of the HM HIM. A further two victories achieved by him are mentioned in the recollections of his former classmate, István Csóka (copies owned by the author).

13 *HM HIM HL*, documents of 101 Fighter Wing, box nr. 113, combat mission log of 101 Fighter Wing, 4 April 1945.

There was another pilot in 101 Fighter Wing with the same name. This second József Nagy was two years younger than 'Juju' and received his primary flight training in 1942. He served from the autumn of 1944 in 101/5 Fighter Squadron (yet another József Nagy served as a mechanic for the wing). The second József Nagy was born on 23 February 1924 in Budapest, and his identification number was 3008-24-1062. He flew 24 combat sorties, during which he achieved one confirmed and one unconfirmed aerial victory before being killed in air combat on 14 April 1945. His confirmed kill is often attributed to 'Juju', but this is an error.[14]

Szakaszvezető József Nagy, the prospective pilot of 101/1 Fighter Squadron, as *tizedes* with his brother, *honvéd* Sándor Nagy in 1942. Sándor Nagy (1920–1943), serving in 3/II Infantry Battalion, went missing while retreating from the Don area on 4 February 1943, and was considered killed in action. (From the collection of the Nagy family)

Victories

Number	Date	Aircraft	Location
-	3 January 1945	Yak-9	Without witnesses; not confirmed
1	22 January 1945	La-5	Sóstó

HADNAGY GYULA PINTÉR

Born: Adony, 11 January 1924
Died: Budapest, 13 February 2013

Victories

Number	Date	Aircraft	Location
1	16 November 1944	La-5	Jászberény SE
–	20 November 1944		Misleading entry; not a kill
2	9 March 1945 at 13:20	Boston	Igal
–	11 March 1945 at 11:30	Il-2	Székesfehérvár S/SE (impact not observed, without witnesses)
3	16 March 1945 at 15:04	Il-2	Pátka S
–	20 March 1945		Misleading entry; not a kill

14 Of the lives and military careers in detail of the two József Nagys, see Csaba B. Stenge, '"Juju" – egy tatabányai vadászpilóta a második világháborúban', in Éva Ravasz (ed.), *Férfiportrék a XX. századból* (Tatabánya: Tatabánya Megyei Jogú Város Levéltára, 2011), pp. 83–106.

Gyula Pintér graduated on 20 August 1944 as *hadnagy* as of 1 September 1944, with rank number 16.[15] He was one of the most talented pilots of his class; from November 1944 to the end of the war, despite his serious accident on 19 November 1944 (due to mechanical problems) and his lengthy recuperation, he flew 29 combat sorties and achieved three confirmed aerial victories (all confirmed in Wing Order Nr. 1945/62) as a pilot in 101/3 Fighter Squadron. Apart from these victories, he claimed an Il-2 on 11 March 1945, and two more notes in his logbook marked with a star on 21 November 1944 and 20 March 1945 may indicate a victory; however, he did not score any kills on these days.[16]

Hadnagy Gyula Pintér was one of the most talented of the young pilots who graduated on 20 August 1944. (From the author's collection)

ZÁSZLÓS BÉLA SŰRŰ

Born: Görgeteg, 15 April 1921
Died: Keszthely, 26 August 2004

Victories

Number	Date	Aircraft	Location
–	(Possibly 13 or 16) November 1944	Il-2	Szolnok SW (no witnesses; not confirmed)
1	14 January 1945	La-5	Ercsi
–	14 January 1945?	Boston	Shared kill with *százados* Pottyondy, confirmed to Pottyondy
–	March 1945	Il-2	Vasvár (impact not observed, without witnesses)
–	March 1945	Il-2	Vasvár (impact not observed, without witnesses)
2	16 April 1945	P-51	Raffelding S (no witnesses in the air, confirmed by ground witnesses)

Zászlós Béla Sűrű graduated as reserve *zászlós* on 20 August 1944.[17] He served in 102/2, then in 101/8 Fighter Squadron from November 1944 to the end of the war, and flew 46 combat sorties. He was wounded three times in 1945 (16 January: a fracture of his right shinbone; 10 March and 16 April: light fragment wounds). According to his own recollections, he achieved six victories during the war. Of these, the La-5 on 14 January was confirmed in Wing Order Nr. 1945/75; his

15 *Honvédségi Közlöny (Személyes ügyek)*, nr. 1944/35 (19 August 1944), p. 745.
16 For his life and military career in detail, see Csaba B. Stenge, '*In memoriam* Pintér Gyula', *Magyar Repüléstörténeti Társaság Évkönyve*, 2013, pp. 20–26.
17 *Honvédségi Közlöny (Személyes ügyek)*, nr.1944/35 (19 August 1944), p. 751.

last registered kill was confirmed by ground eyewitnesses, but was not confirmed in a wing order by the end of the war. The Mustang that he attacked on 16 April 1945 south of Raffelding, which was hit in its wing then crashed, was one of the last P-51s lost in air combat over Europe during the Second World War.

Sűrű was the 10th level defendant in the trial known as 'Barna Horváth and companions'; he was sentenced to five years in prison and demoted to private. He was in prison from 26 April 1951 to 25 September 1955. Sűrű was acquitted in 1958 when the case was renegotiated and rehabilitated, but his rank was not restored. His rank of *zászlós* was only reinstated on 13 December 1993 by Ministry of Defense Order Nr. HM 88/1993. At the same time, he was promoted to *alezredes*.[18]

Zászlós Béla Sűrű was also graduated on 20 August 1944: he was older than the average pilots in his class, and was also more dauntless: he was wounded three times at the beginning of 1945. (From the collection of the Sűrű family)

FŐTÖRZSŐRMESTER VITÉZ SÁNDOR SZOBRÁNCI (SZOJÁK)

Born: Krassóvermes (today Vermeş, Romania), 2 October 1908
Died: Melbourne, 23 September 1983

Victories

Number	Date	Aircraft	Location
1	24 March 1939	Avia B.534	Lúčky
2	24 March 1939	Avia B.534	Senné
3	27 August 1941	'I-17' (MiG-3/LaGG-3)	Ulyanovka
4	27 August 1941	'I-17' (MiG-3/LaGG-3)	Ulyanovka
–	27 August 1941	'I-17' (MiG-3/LaGG-3)	Ulyanovka

18 *HM HIM KI*, document folder nr. 550/119; logbook of Béla Sűrű (full copy owned by the author); also based on Béla Sűrű's interview, 16 April 2004.

Sándor Szoják graduated from the *Kinizsi Pál Honvéd Altisztképző és Nevelőintézet* at Jutas (the non-commissioned officer training school). On 24 March 1939, as a member of 1/1 *'Íjász'* Fighter Squadron, he shot down two Slovakian Avia aircraft on two combat sorties (one in the morning and one in the afternoon). He subsequently changed his name from Szoják to Szobránci in 1940 before his admission into the *Vitézi Rend.* In 1941, during the campaign against the Soviet Union, as a pilot of 1/3 Fighter Squadron, he flew 37 combat sorties and achieved a further two confirmed kills. Both successes were reported on 27 August 1941 in the morning against modern monoplanes reported as I-17s, which might have been an early series of LaGG-3s or MiG-3s. During this mission, he also hit a further Soviet aircraft; according to the Germans, the Hungarians may have destroyed one more aircraft during the air combat. If true, then Szobránci was the first Hungarian pilot in the Second World War to achieve five aerial victories.[19]

Főtörzsőrmester Sándor Szobránci with two German instructors in front of a German Messerschmitt Bf 109 E in Székesfehérvár. On the left of the Hungarian pilot stands Rudolf Rothenfelder, a pilot of 9./JG 2 during the Battle of Britain. Szobránci was the only non-commissioned officer in the Royal Hungarian Air Force who received the *Magyar Arany Vitézségi Érem*. (From the author's collection)

HADNAGY VITÉZ TIBOR TOBAK

Born: Budapest, 24 November 1921
Died: Budapest, 8 January 2001

Victories

Number	Date	Aircraft	Location
–	16 November 1944	La-5	Confirmed to Gyula Pintér
1	22 December 1944	Yak-9	Iszkaszentgyörgy
2	22 December 1944	Il-2	Csór
3	16 March 1945 at 15:08	Il-2	Pátka S
4	21 March 1945 at 07:45	Yak-9	Várpalota S

19 For his life and military career, see Stenge, *Baptism of Fire*, p. 116.

Hadnagy Tibor Tobak, still a student at the *Repülőakadémia*, shortly before his graduation. In 101/3 Fighter Squadron, Tobak achieved four confirmed kills and was wounded twice in air combat. (From the collection of Tibor Tobak)

Hadnagy Tobak graduated on 20 August 1943, as of 1 September, with rank number 31;[20] he served from the end of July 1944 until the end of the war in the 101/3 Fighter Squadron. During this time, he flew 43 combat sorties from 7 August 1944 to 16 April 1945. He was wounded twice in air combat. On 22 December 1944, in the airspace of Csór, a Yak-9 wounded him on his left wrist and left leg; and on 16 April 1945, he was shot down by a Mustang over Raffelding and badly burnt; he bailed out of his aircraft. Many sources credit *hadnagy* Tobak with five aerial victories,[21] but in reality he had four confirmed aerial victories – one was confirmed by Air Force Order Nr. 1945/13, and three by Wing Order Nr. 1945/62. The fifth claim was deleted and credited to *hadnagy* Pintér, who attacked the same La-5 as Tobak on 16 November 1944 and carried out the first successful pass.

After 1945, Tobak also served in the reorganized Hungarian Air Force. However, he became the 8th level defendant in the trial known as 'Barna Horváth and companions', as a result of which he was sentenced to 10 years in prison and demoted to private. He served his prison term from 2 April 1951 to 19 July 1956. Tobak was acquitted in 1958 when the case was renegotiated and rehabilitated, but his rank was restored only after the democratic transformation in 1989. His rank was rehabilitated in three steps. At first he was only promoted to *százados*, then to *alezredes* following Ministry of Defense Order HM 177/1990; Ministry of Defense Order Nr. 25/1993 promoted him to *ezredes* on 31 March 1993.[22]

20 *Honvédségi Közlöny* (*Személyes ügyek)*, nr.1943/48 (1 December 1943), following correction, p. 1709.
21 See for example Sárhidai, 'Repülő ászok', p. 372.
22 *HM HIM KI*, document folder nr. 52721. For more details of Tibor Tobak, see Tobak, *Pumák földönégen*, p. 285.

Bibliography

UNPUBLISHED SOURCES

HM HIM Military Archives, Budapest

Documents of Departments 8, 10 and 22 of the Royal Hungarian Ministry of Defence (I/31 M. kir. Honvédelmi Minisztérium), 1939–1945

Documents of Department 1 of the Chief of Staff of the Royal Hungarian Honvéd Army (I/89 M. kir. Honvéd Vezérkar főnöke [Vkf.]), 1938–1945

Surviving documents of 101 Fighter Wing (combat mission logs, combat reports, regimental orders, air forces orders, registries and documents concerning decorations) (II/1565)

Logs of 101/3 Fighter Squadron (on microfilm)

Daily reports of the Hungarian 2nd Army and surviving documents of its aviation detachment (II/1453)

Documents of the Military Academy (*Ludovika Akadémia*) (V/6)

Documents of proceedings of the Military Courts of Justice in Budapest (XI/22)

Personal document folders (AKVI: officers' birth certificates and personal document folders in the Record Office of the Archives)

Recommendations for decoration (separate collection)

Bequest of *alezredes* Jenő Andreánszky: incident reports of the central command of investigation of the Royal Hungarian *csendőrség* (police force), 1944 (VII. *Personalia* Nr. 249)

Diary of *tizedes* József Tóth (VII. *Tanulmánygyűjtemény*, *Tgy* [Collection of papers] Nr. 3181)

Bundesarchiv-Militärarchiv (Freiburg, Germany)

German and Hungarian aircraft losses (RL 2 III)

Successes of the German anti-aircraft artillery in Hungary (RL 5)

Fighter aircraft victory reports (RL 10)

Surviving documents of the I./JG 27 (RL 10/538)

Centralni Arhiv Ministarstva Oboroni Rossijskij Federaciji (Podolsk, Russia)

Documents of 567 Ground-Attack Regiment (fond 58 opis 818883, delo 1798)

National Archives and Records Administration (Washington DC, United States)

Missing Air Crew Reports (RG 92 M1380)

Victory reports of 325 FG (RG 18 Entry 7 Box 3350)

Air Force Historical Research Agency (Montgomery, AL, United States)
Documents related to the action of the 325. FG in January 1945 (RG 18)

Állambiztonsági Szolgálatok Történeti Levéltára (Historical Archives of the Hungarian State Security)
Operatív és hálózati nyilvántartások (operative and network registries) (2.2)
Beszervezési dossziék (recruitment files) (3.1.1)

***Budapesti Műszaki és Gazdaságtudományi Egyetem Levéltára* (Budapest University of Technology and Economics Archives)**
Personal document folder Nr. 201.152 (30 fond)
Student registries

***Budapest Főváros Levéltára* (Budapest City Archives)**
State birth certificates of Rákospalota, 1920, counterpart (XXXIII/1)

***Magyar Nemzeti Levéltár* (Hungarian National Archives)**
State birth and death certificate counterparts (XXXIII/1)
Documents and administrative files of the *vicecomes* (IV)
MNL Veszprém Megyei Levéltára (National Archives, Veszprém County Archives), matriculation register of the Piarist High School in Veszprém (VIII/52/5)
MNL Csongrád Megyei Levéltár Hódmezővásárhelyi Levéltára (National Archives, Csongrád County Archive, Hódmezővásárhely), documents of László Bibithy-Horváth (XIV/3)
MNL Győr-Moson-Sopron Megyei Levéltár Győri Levéltára (National Archives, Győr-Moson-Sopron County Archives, Győr), documents of the Hungarian Wagon and Machine Factory (*Magyar Wagon és Gépgyár, MWG, Győr*) XI/15)

High school record offices
Record office of the *Táncsics Mihály Gimnázium* at Kaposvár (Táncsics Mihály High School), matriculation register
Record office of the *Eötvös József Gimnázium és Kollégium* at Tata (József Eötvös High School), matriculation register
Record office of the *Piarista Általános Iskola, Gimnázium és Kollégium* in Kecskemét (Piarist Elementary School, High School and Boarding School), matriculation register
Record office of the *Gróf Széchenyi István Katolikus Gimnázium* at Jászapáti (Gróf István Széchenyi Catholic High School), matriculation register

Manuscripts
Excerpts from the war diary of 102/1 Fighter Squadron, 14–16 September 1944 (copy owned by the author)
Excerpts from the war diary of 1/1 Fighter Squadron prepared by *százados* Ujszászy, 1942–43 (owned by the author)
Recollections of Delore Athmann, manuscript (copy owned by the author)
Evaluation report of *hadnagy* Gellért Barsi (copy owned by the author)
Recollections of *zászlós* Géza Bartos (copy owned by the author)

Logbook of *hadnagy* Lajos Benkő (full copy owned by the author)
Diary and notes of *hadnagy* Lajos Benkő (copies owned by the author)
Mission summary of 1st Lieutenant Louis Benne (copy owned by the author)
Original notes of *tisztjelölt őrmester* Lajos Buday (copies owned by the author)
Recollections of *szakaszvezető* István Csóka (copy owned by the author)
Logbook of *hadnagy* László Dániel (original owned by the author)
László Dániel, *Így kezdődött...* (manuscript, copy owned by the author)
Logbook of *százados* György Debrődy (partial copy owned by the author)
Evaluation report of *százados* György Debrődy (copy owned by the author)
Recollections of György Debrődy, February 1976 (copy owned by the author).
Flugbuch (Flight book) of Heinz Ewald (partial copy owned by the author)
Recollections of *szakaszvezető* Károly Faludi (copy owned by the author)
Recollections of *hadnagy* Pál Forró (copy owned by the author)
Repülési napló motoros sportrepülők számára (flight log for sport aviators of powered aircraft) of Pál Gótzy (partial copy owned by the author)
Logbook of *alezredes* Aladár Heppes (partial copy owned by the author)
Recollections of Aladár Heppes (copy owned by the author)
Repülési napló motor nélküli sportrepülők számára (flight log for sport aviators of non-powered aircraft) of András Huszár (original owned by the author)
Repülési napló motoros sportrepülők számára (flight log for sport aviators of powered aircraft) of *zászlós* András Huszár (original owned by the author)
Logbook of *zászlós* András Huszár (original owned by the author)
A fragment of a letter of *hadnagy* Miklós Kenyeres from 1943 (copy owned by the author)
Logbook of *zászlós* István Kálmán (partial copy owned by the author)
Interview with István Kálmán on 28 September 1991 (copy on tape owned by the author)
Recollections of Anatoly Leonidovich Kozhevnikov, in manuscript, of his 158th mission (copy owned by the author)
Logbook of *zászlós* Ottó Lukács (full copy owned by the author)
War diary of *főhadnagy* Kornél Majoros from 1943 (original owned by the author)
Diary of *hadnagy* István Majoros (full copy owned by the author)
Logbook of *főhadnagy* László Máthé (full copy owned by the author)
Diary and notes of *százados* Adorján Mersich (copies owned by the author)
War diary of *őrnagy* István Mocsáry from 1942 (full copy owned by the author)
Letters of *hadnagy* László Molnár from 1944 (copies owned by the author)
Logbook of *zászlós* Tibor Murányi (full copy owned by the author)
Repülési napló motoros sportrepülők számára (flight log for sport aviators of powered aircraft) of *zászlós* Tibor Murányi (full copy owned by the author)
Repülési napló motoros sportrepülők számára (flight log for sport aviators of powered aircraft) of *szakaszvezető* József Nagy (original owned by the author)
Recollections of *szakaszvezető* József Nagy (copy owned by the author)
War diary of *alezredes* János Németh from 1942 (copy owned by the author)
War diary of *őrmester* Ferenc Nyakas from 1943 (copy owned by the author)
Diary of *hadnagy* Gyula Pintér (copy owned by the author)
Logbook of *hadnagy* Gyula Pintér (original owned by the author)
Letter of *százados* Miklós Scholtz from 1961 (copy owned by the author)

Recollections of James C. Smyth (copy owned by the author)
Diary of *tizedes* Géza Stahl (partial copy owned by the author)
Logbook of *zászlós* Béla Sűrű (full copy owned by the author)
Dezső Szentgyörgyi's flight service logs and flight logs after 1945 (full copies owned by the author)
Diary of *vezérőrnagy* Aladár Szirmay (original owned by the author)
Diary of *tizedes* Sándor Tábori (copy owned by the author)
Logbook of *szakaszvezető* Sándor Tanács (full copy owned by the author)
Logbook of *hadnagy* Lajos Vargha (full copy owned by the author)

PUBLISHED SOURCES

17-aja vozdushnaya armija v bojah ot Stalingrada do Venü (Moscow: Vojenizdat, 1977).
Aders, Gebhard, and Held, Werner, *Jagdgeschwader 51 "Mölders"* (Stuttgart: Motorbuch Verlag, 1985).
'A KPM és a Malév tájékoztatója a koppenhágai légi katasztrófáról', *Népszabadság*, 31 August 1971.
'A lelkiismeret súlyával fel lehet-e szállni?', *Top Gun*, 1992/4.
'A Magyar Aero Szövetség Közleményei: üzemi jelentések [1940] július–augusztus hóról', *Magyar Szárnyak*, 1 October 1940.
'A megtett út hossza: 5 000 000 km', *Ország-Világ*, 3 December 1969.
Amos, Robert F., Koller, Rudolph C., Lloyd, Alwyn T., and Martin, Earl W., *Defenders of Liberty 2nd Bombardment Group/Wing* (Paducah, KY: Turner, 1996).
'A Pumák egy napja', *Magyar Szárnyak*, 15 August 1944.
'A Pumák egy napja. II. rész', *Magyar Szárnyak*, 1 September 1944.
Barbas, Bernd, *Die Geschichte der II. Gruppe des Jagdgeschwaders 52* (Überlingen: Traditionsgemeinschaft JG 52, 2004).
Becze, Csaba, '2 pilotes juifs dans les forces de l'Axe', *Aero Journal*, 2008:4.
Becze, Csaba, 'A 102. vadászbombázó osztály története I', *Magyar Szárnyak Évkönyv*, 2000.
Becze, Csaba, 'A 102. vadászbombázó osztály története II. 1945', *Magyar Szárnyak Évkönyv*, 2001.
Becze, Csaba, 'A magyar királyi 1. honvéd éjjeli vadász repülőszázad', *Magyar Repüléstörténeti Társaság Konferencia Közleményei*, 1999.
Becze, Csaba, *'A pokol tornácán…' A magyar királyi 2. honvéd hadsereg hídfőcsatái a Donnál (1942. július–szeptember)* (Budapest: Paktum, 2006).
Becze, Csaba, *Az Arany sas nyomában. Gyula Szilaj Varga és a magyar gyorsbombázók a II. világháborúban* (Nagykovácsi: Puedlo, 2008).
Becze, Csaba, 'Benkő Lajos – egy veszprémi vadászpilóta a a második világháborúban', *Veszprémi Szemle*, 2010:1–2.
Becze, Csaba, 'Haderőn kívüli repülőgép-vezetői kiképzés a HMNRA debreceni kiképzőkereténél 1941. aug. 1–okt. 21', *Magyar Szárnyak Évkönyv*, 2004.
Becze, Csaba, *'Kőr Ász' – Egy vadászrepülő század története 1936–1941* (Nagykovácsi: Puedlo, 2007).
Becze, Csaba, 'Vadászpilóta "komiszban"', *Magyar Szárnyak Évkönyv*, 1999.

Bikhov, Mihail, *Sovetskie Asy 1941–1945. Pobedy Stalinskich sokolov* (Moscow: Eksmo, 2008).
Blake, Steve, 'Ambush over Hungary. A "Puma" pilot's revenge', *Fighter Pilots in Aerial Combat*, Fall, 1984.
Bob, Hans-Ekkehard, *Betrayed Ideals. Memoirs of a Luftwaffe Fighter Ace* (Bristol: Cerberus, 2004).
Bognár, István, *A győzelmes repülés titkai* (Budapest: Jövő nyomda, 1942).
Budapesti Közlöny, 10 February 1911.
Bulletin of the Dunántúli Református Egyházkerület Pápai Főiskolája (Pápa College of the Reformed Church in Dunántúl), 1936–40.
Bulletin of the Szent István Reálgimnázium (Szent István high school of the Cistercian Order), 1932–42.
Bús, János, and Szabó, Péter, *Béke poraikra…*, vols. 1–3 (Budapest: Varietas, 1999–2001).
Crawford, George, *Three Crawford Brothers: The WW II Memoirs of Three Pilots* (Bloomington, IN: AuthorHouse, 2008).
Csóka, István, 'Az 1942-es évfolyam rövid története (folytatás)', *Magyar Szárnyak Évkönyv,* 1992.
Csonka, Pál, 'Kezdő szárnypróbálgatások', *Magyar Szárnyak Évkönyv,* 1989.
Czirók, Zoltán, 'Az első légi háború Magyarország felett – 1919', *Hadtörténelmi Közlemények,* 2011:2.
Davtjan, S.M., *Pjataja vozdusnaja* (Moscow: Vojenizdat, 1990).
'Debrődy civilben (1946–1984)', *Magyar Szárnyak Évkönyv,* 1984.
Diário Oficial do Estado de Sao Paulo, 31 October 1961.
Domonkos, János, 'Egy Messerschmitt szerelő hadi- és „egyéb" tapasztalatai', *Magyar Szárnyak Évkönyv,* 1982.
Düttmann, Peter, *Wir kämpften in einsamen Höhen* (Leipzig: Traditionsgemeinschaft JG 52, 2002).
'Eltemették a koppenhágai légi szerencsétlenség áldozatait', *Népszabadság,* 14 September 1971.
Endrői, György, 'Velem történt 1944–45-ben', *Magyar Szárnyak Évkönyv,* 1996.
Evangélikusok Lapja, 25 November 1923.
'Évfolyamtörténetek – Az 1942. június 18-án felavatott évfolyam', *Magyar Szárnyak Évkönyv,* 1995.
Ewald, Heinz, *Esau – Heinz Ewald als Jagdflieger im erfolgreichsten Jagdgeschwader 1943–1945* (Coburg: Eigenverlag, 1980).
Farkas, György, *Horthy István repülő főhadnagy tragikus halála* (Budapest: Auktor, 1992).
Farkas, Jenő (ed.), *A m. kir. vitéz nagybányai Horthy István Honvéd Repülő Akadémia 1944. augusztus 20-án felavatott évfolyamának Emlékkönyve* (Gödöllő: privately published, 1994).
Farkas, Jenő, *A m. kir. vitéz nagybányai Horthy István Honvéd Repülő Akadémiai évfolyamom története.* Szombathely-Veszprém, 1943. 09. 15.–1944. 08. 20 (Gödöllő: privately published, 2010).
Földes, Pál, *Két ugrás az ismeretlenbe* (Budapest: Zrínyi Kiadó, 1975).
Forgon, Mihály, *Gömör-Kishont vármegye nemes családai* (Somorja: Méry Ratio, 2001).
Fözö, Josef, *Freie Jagd von Madrid bis Moskau. Ein Fliegerleben mit Mölders* (Berlin: Verlag Wehrfront Alfred Becker, 1943).
Francis, Charles E., *The Tuskegee Airmen: The Men Who Changed A Nation* (Boston, MA: Branden Publishing, 1997).

Freeman, Roger A., *Mighty Eighth: A History of the US Eighth Air Force* (Garden City: Doubleday, 1970).
Gaál, Gyula, 'A Pumák első nyara', *Magyar Szárnyak Évkönyv*, 1990.
Gaál, Gyula, 'Egy önálló vadászszázad életéből', *Magyar Szárnyak Évkönyv*, 1991.
Gaál, Gyula, 'Hadszíntér a felhők felett', *Magyar Szárnyak Évkönyv*, 1984.
Gaál, Gyula, 'Légi győzelmek: tízen felül', *Magyar Szárnyak Évkönyv*, 1998.
Gaál, Gyula, 'Légi győzelmek: tíz és kettő között', *Magyar Szárnyak Évkönyv*, 1999.
Gaál, Gyula, 'Légi győzelmek: egy és kettő', *Magyar Szárnyak Évkönyv*, 2000.
Gaál, Gyula, 'Légi győzelmek: a többiek', *Magyar Szárnyak Évkönyv*, 2001.
Gaál, Gyula, 'Szabadvadászat', *Magyar Szárnyak Évkönyv*, 1992.
Genersich, Tivadar, 'Vadászrepülő feladatok', *Magyar Katonai Szemle*, 1943:9.
Geroi Sovietskovo soyuza, vol. 1 (Moscow: Vojenizdat, 1987).
Goebel, Robert J., *Mustang Ace. Memoirs of a P-51 Fighter Pilot* (Pacifica, CA: Pacifica Military History, 1991).
Gorbach, Vitaliy, *Nad Ognyennoi dugoi. Sovietskaya aviatsiya v Kurskoy bitve* (Moscow: Eksmo, 2007).
Guttman, Jon, 'P–38s vs. Pumas: Dogfight over Hungary', *Aviation History*, March 2001.
Gyulai, Jankovits Ferenc, 'Repülő bajtársak', *Magyar Szárnyak*, 15 April 1944.
'Hadijelentések, csaták és új fordulatok', *Magyar Futár*, 11 November 1942.
Hatch, Herbert, *'Stub': An Ace and his Angel. Memoirs of a World War II Fighter Pilot* (Paducah, KY: Turner, 2000).
Hefty, Frigyes, 'Visszavágás', *Magyar Szárnyak*, 1 December 1944.
'Hivatalos tájékoztató a koppenhágai légi szerencsétlenségről', *Népszabadság*, 5 September 1971.
Honvédségi Közlöny (Személyes ügyek), 1939–44.
Honvédségi Rendeletek (Személyes ügyek), 1944–45.
Horváth, Gábor, *Bostonok a magyar égen és földben (1944–1945)* (Szolnok: privately published, 2013).
Illésfalvi, Péter, Kovács, Vilmos, and Maruzs, Roland, *'Vitézségért': A Magyar Tiszti Arany Vitézségi Éremmel kitüntetettek a második világháborúban* (Szeged: HK Hermanos Kiadó, 2011).
Irányi, *hadnagy* Pál, 'Kiválasztás a repülőfegyvernemhez lélektani alapon', *Magyar Katonai Szemle*, 1941:10.
Jánkfalvi, Zoltán, *Gépmadarak a szabolcsi égen 1865–1947*, vol. 1 (Budapest: T.M. Repüléstechnika, 2005).
Járomy, Árpád, *Csatarepülők* (Budapest: Stádium, 1943).
Kádár, Gyula, 'A magyar vadászrepülők harca a szovjet túlerő ellen', *Magyar Szárnyak*, 15 July 1943.
Kádár, Gyula, 'Harctéri beszélgetés Németh Endre repülőfőhadnaggyal, aki megkapta a Magyar Érdemrend Lovagkeresztjét', *Magyar Szárnyak*, 1 July 1944.
Kádár, Gyula, *Sasok harca* (Budapest: Magyar Repülő Sajtóvállalat, 1943).
Karátsonyi, Mihály, 'Lőttem... lőttünk... lőttek...', *Magyar Szárnyak Évkönyv*, 1981.
Karsai, Elek (ed.), *'Fegyvertelen álltak az aknamezőkön...': Dokumentumok a munkaszolgálat történetéhez Magyarországon*, vol. 1 (Budapest: MIOK, 1962).
Kaššák, Peter, and Hrodegh, Marián, *Konečná Zastávka: Slovensko!* (Martin: Klub Priateľov Vojenskej História Slovenska, 2007).

'Katonai hírek', *Magyar Szárnyak*, 1 March 1943.

Kelemen, Antal, *A szétzilált szivárvány* (Budapest: privately published, 1992).

Kempelen, Béla, *Magyar nemes családok*, vols. 1–11 (Budapest: Grill Károly Könyvkiadóvállalata, 1911–32).

Kossuth-díjasok és Állami díjasok almanachja 1948–1985 (Budapest: Akadémiai Kiadó, 1988).

'Két levél a frontról...' *Magyar Szárnyak*, 15 February 1944.

'Kétszázötven magyar légigyőzelem. Helyszíni szemle a "Pumáknál" – a legeredményesebb Magyar vadászrepülők névsora', *Egyedül vagyunk*, December 1944.

Krascsenics, Lajos, *Egy magyar királyi vadászrepülő visszaemlékezései* (Budapest: Tipo Kolor, 1990).

Krascsenics, Lajos, *Repülő hétköznapok, avagy a reptéren mindig történik valami – Egy repülőiskola életéből 1949* (Győr: privately published, 1999).

Kucera, Dennis C., *In a now forgotten Sky. The 31st Fighter Group in WW2* (Stratford, CT: Flying Machines Press, 1997).

Kutasi Kovács, Lajos, 'Levél egy begyulladt barátomhoz', *Összetartás*, 14 September 1944.

László, István, 'Két bevetésen 27 légigyőzelem'. *Magyar Szárnyak*, 1 July 1944.

Lévay, Győző, 'Így is lehet vitát nyerni', *Magyar Szárnyak Évkönyv*, 1995.

Lipfert, Helmut, *Das Tagebuch des Hauptmann Lipfert* (Stuttgart: Motorbuch Verlag, 1973).

Lorant, Jean-Yves, and Goyat, Richard, *Jagdgeschwader 300: A Chronicle of a Fighter Geschwader in the Battle for Germany, Volume 1: June 1943 – September 1944* (Hamilton, MT: Eagle Editions, 2005).

Loving, George, *Woodbine Red Leader* (New York, NY: Ballantine, 2003).

McManus, John C., *The Americans at Normandy* (New York, NY: Forge Books, 2004).

Magó, Károly, 'Pilótasírok', in Zsolt Tóth (ed.), *Hőseink nyomában. Tanulmánykötet a hadisírok kutatásáról* (Budapest: Zrínyi Kiadó, 2013).

Magyar Repülés, 10 October 1949.

Magyarország a második világháborúban: Lexikon A–Zs (Budapest: Petit Real, 1996).

Mitter, Imre (ed.), *A magyar vitorlázórepülés képes története 1929–1999* (Budapest: 3,14 L Kft., 1999).

Mohos, Nándor, 'A 460. Bomber Group légi harca Magyarország felett 1944. június 30-án', *Magyar Repüléstörténeti Társaság Konferencia Közleményei*, 1996.

Movero Esztergomi Sportrepülő Egyesület Közlönye, 1936:1.

Mullins, John D., *An Escort of P–38s. The 1st Fighter Group in World War II* (St Paul, MN: Phalanx, 1995).

Nagy, Béla, 'Egy magyar vadászrepülő leküzdi a balszerencsét', *Egyedül vagyunk*, 25 February 1944.

Nagy, Béla, 'Szomolnoki Imre Pánczél m. kir. repülőhadnagy', *Magyar Szárnyak*, 15 November 1943.

Nagy, Sándor, 'A győztes vadászok. Sanyi első légi győzelme', *Magyar Szárnyak*, 15 April 1944.

Nagymarosy, Tibor, Guthy, Zoltán, and Homér, Imre, 'Tovább zuhannak a "Boszorkányok"', *Magyar Szárnyak Évkönyv*, 1987.

'Német haditudósítók írják', *Magyar Szárnyak*, 15 October 1944.

Németi, József (ed.), *A Gyulai Római Katolikus Gimnázium értesítője az 1936–37-es tanévről* (Gyula: Római Katolikus Gimnázium, 1937).

Nemzetvédelmi Tudósító, 21 February 1945.

Obermaier, Ernst, *Die Ritterkreuzträger der Luftwaffe 1939–45: Band 1, Jagdflieger* (Mainz: Verlag Dieter Hoffmann, 2. überarbeitete Auflage, 1989).
Olmsted, Merle C., *To War with the Yoxford Boys: The Complete Story of the 357th Fighter Group* (Hamilton, MT: Eagle Editions, 2004).
Olynyk, Frank, *Stars and Bars. A Tribute to the American Fighter Ace 1920–1973* (London: Grub Street, 1995).
Ormay, József, 'Debrődy György emlékezete', *Magyar Szárnyak Évkönyv,* 1984.
'Őszinte beszéd a rádióban a Magyar vadászrepülők Budapest feletti harcairól', *Egyedül vagyunk,* 5 May 1944.
Pajtás, *hadnagy* László, 'Fényképészfeladatok a háromszögmegoldó tárcsával', *Magyar Katonai Szemle,* 1941:9.
Pajtás, *hadnagy* László, 'A bombázórepülők felderítő feladatai', *Magyar Katonai Szemle,* 1942:3.
Pataky, Iván, Rozsos, László, and Sárhidai, Gyula, *Légi háború Magyarország felett,* vol. 2 (Budapest: Zrínyi Kiadó, 1990).
Péterdi, János A. (ed.), *Távolfelderítőink* (Budapest: privately published, 1998).
Platthy, Árpád, 'Repülő sportolók', *Magyar Szárnyak Évkönyv,* 1981.
Pottyondy, Béla, csáfordi és potyondi, *A Pottyondy család monografiája* (Szombathely: Martineum Nyomda, 1937).
Prien, Jochen, *Geschichte des Jagdgeschwaders 53, Teil 3* (Eutin: Struve Druck, 1991).
Prien, Jochen, and Rodeike, Peter, *Messerschmitt Bf 109 F, G, K Series* (Atglen: Schiffer, 1995).
Prien, Jochen, and Rodeike, Peter, *Messerschmitt Bf 109 im Einsatz bei Stab und I./Jagdgeschwader 27* (Eutin: Struve Druck, 1999).
'Puma vadászrepülők pusztítják az orosz erőket Siófok és Kaposvár között', *Lármafa,* December 1944.
Punka, György, *A Messzer. Bf 109-ek a magyar Királyi Honvéd Légierőben* (Budapest: OMIKK, 1995).
Raczkó, Lajos, and Jánosy, István, *A légierők haditudósítói jelentik…*, 2nd ed. (Budapest: Stádium, 1943).
Rajninec, Juraj, *Slovenské letectvo 1939–1944,* vol. 1 (Bratislava: Ministerstvo Obrany, 1997).
Reschke, Willi, *Jagdgeschwader 301/302 'Wilde Sau'* (Stuttgart: Motorbuch Verlag, 1999).
Ring, Hans, and Girbig, Werner, *Jagdgeschwader 27* (Stuttgart: Motorbuch Verlag, 2. Auflage, 1972).
Rosch, Barry C., *Luftwaffe Codes, Markings and Units 1939–1945* (Atglen: Schiffer, 1995).
Rust, Kenn C., *Fifteenth Air Force Story* (Temple City, CA: Historical Aviation Album, 1976).
Sallay, Gergely, 'Magyar hadikitüntetések posztumusz adományozása a második világháború idején', in Roland Maruzs (ed.), *Vitéz és önfeláldozó magatartásért. Hősi halált halt és posztumusz kitüntetett katonáink adattára 1939–1945* (Nagykovácsi: Puedlo, 2009).
Sárhidai, Gyula, 'Repülő ászok', in *Magyarország a második világháborúban: Lexikon A–Zs* (Budapest: Petit Real, 1996).
Sarkady, Sándor Jr., *Az Ász és a Polihisztor* (Feketeerdő: Mosonvármegye Könyvkiadó, 2016).
Schabes, Alois, *Der Markt Leobersdorf. Von der ältesten Zeit bis zur Gegenwart* (Leobensdorf: Marktgemeinde Leobensdorf, 1976).
Shores, Christopher, and Thomas, Chris, *2nd Tactical Air Force Volume One Spartan to Normandy June 1943 to June 1944* (Hersham: Classic Publications, 2004).
Soproni Hírlap, 1944–45.

Speer, Frank E. *Debden Warbirds. The 4th Fighter Group in World War II* (Atglen, PA: Schiffer, 1999).

Stenge, Csaba B., '70 éve történt: Az első magyar Messerschmitt pilóta', *Katonaújság*, 2012:5.

Stenge, Csaba B., 'A legidősebb még élő magyar vadászrepülő ász volt: in memoriam Mátyás János', *Katonaújság*, 2011:1.

Stenge, Csaba B., *Baptism of fire. The First Combat Experiences of the Royal Hungarian Air Force and Slovak Air Force, March 1939* (Solihull: Helion, 2013).

Stenge, Csaba B., 'Egy kecskeméti repülő ász, Szeverényi Kálmán életútja', *Hadtudományi Szemle*, 2013:4.

Stenge, Csaba B., 'Horthy Miklós vadászpilótájából Sztálin-díjas író: Nagy Sándor élettörténete', *Katonaújság*, 2013:6.

Stenge, Csaba B., 'Egy igazi repülő sportember – Hennyey Imre,' *Katonaújság*, 2012:4.

Stenge, Csaba B., 'In memoriam Gersy Tamás', *Magyar Repüléstörténeti Társaság Évkönyve*, 2013.

Stenge, Csaba B., 'In memoriam Michna György', *Magyar Repüléstörténeti Társaság Évkönyve*, 2012.

Stenge, Csaba B., 'In memoriam Pintér Gyula', *Magyar Repüléstörténeti Társaság Évkönyve*, 2013.

Stenge, Csaba B., '"Juju" – egy tatabányai vadászpilóta a második világháborúban', in Éva Ravasz (ed.), *Férfiportrék a XX. századból* (Tatabánya: Tatabánya Megyei Jogú Város Levéltára, 2011).

Stenge, Csaba B., 'Majoros Kornél repülő főhadnagy emlékezete', *Katonaújság*, 2012/6.

Stenge, Csaba B., 'Vitéz nemes belényesi Heppes Miklós repülő alezredes', *Magyar Repüléstörténeti Társaság Évkönyve*, 2012.

Stenge, Csaba B., '„Lázadás" a 101. vadászrepülő-ezrednél 1945-ben' in László Anka, Gábor Hollósi, Eszter Zsófia Tóth, Gábor Ujváry (eds.), *Historia est lux veritatis. Szakály Sándor köszöntése 60. születésnapján* (Budapest, Veritas Történetkutató Intézet, 2016, 2nd vol.).

Stenge, Csaba B., 'Egy kis "Puma" történelem: Repülő hagyományok, csapatszellem a magyar királyi honvéd légierőkben', *Seregszemle*, 2016:2.

Stenge, Csaba B., 'Kivonat a 102. vadászrepülő-század hadinaplójából, 1944. szeptember 14-16.' *Hadtörténelmi Közlemények*, 2017:1.

Stirling, György, 'Magyar vadászok között', *Magyar Szárnyak*, 1 July 1944.

Susa, Éva, and Molnos, Mária, 'Jeltelen eltemetések (1945–1962) kutatása', in *Trezor 3. Az átmenet évkönyve, 2003* (Budapest: Állambiztonsági Szolgálatok Történeti Levéltára [Historical Archives of the Hungarian State Security], 2004).

Szabó, Miklós M., *A magyar királyi honvéd légierő 1938–1945* (Budapest: Zrínyi Kiadó, 1999).

Szakonyi, István, 'Bombáztuk Nyikolajevet', *Magyar Szárnyak*, 15 March 1942.

Számvéber, Norbert, *Páncélos-hadviselés a budapesti csatában 1944. október 29.–1945. február 13* (Nagykovácsi: Puedlo, 2011).

Szenteleky, Géza, 'Emlékeim a 102/2. századnál eltöltött időmről', *Magyar Szárnyak Évkönyv*, 1992.

Szentgyörgyi, Kálmán, *Pilóták egy családban*. Szekszárd, Babits Kiadó, 2000.

Szobránczy, Aladár, 'A vadászrepülőgép kérdése', *Magyar Katonai Szemle*, 1941:4.

Tálosi, Zoltán, *Háborús évek 1941–1945. Légiesemények és harcok Tolna megyében* (Szekszárd: privately published, 2002).

Tarlós, József, *Légcsavarszélben. Egy volt hadirepülő visszaemlékezései* (Székesfehérvár: privately published, 1999).
Tillmaan, Barrett, *Above and Beyond. The Aviation Medals of Honor* (Washington DC: Smithsonian, 2002).
Official commissioned officer lists, 1938–44.
Tobak, Tibor, *Pumák földön-égen* (Budapest: Háttér Kiadó, 1989).
Toliver, Raymond F., and Constable, Trevor J., *Fighter Aces of the USA* (Fallbrook, CA: Aero Publishers, 1979).
Tomor, László, *Harcok az orosz égen* (Budapest: Stádium, 1942).
Torbágyi, Gyula, 'Meleg pillanatok', *Magyar Szárnyak Évkönyv,* 1990.
Tóth, Lajos, 'Kobrát fogtam…' *Magyar Szárnyak,* 1 April 1944.
Üvölt a Puma, 1943.
Veress, D. Csaba, *A Balatoni csata* (Budapest: Zrínyi Kiadó, 1976).
Veress, D. Csaba, 'Veszprém Megye és a Szövetséges Hatalmak stratégiai légitámadásai a második világháborúban', *A Veszprém Megyei Múzeumok Közleményei*, 1980:15.
Zhirohov, Mikhail Aleksandrovich, *Istrebiteli na vzlet!* (Moscow: Veche, 2013).

INTERNET SOURCES

Website of Dr János Szentváry-Lukács about decorations: http://rendjel.myhunet.com/hu/.
German victories, 1939–44, compiled by Tony Wood based on microfilms in the Bundesarchiv-Militärarchiv: https://web.archive.org/web/20130928070316/http://lesbutler.co.uk/claims/tonywood.htm.